strangers & pilgrims

Now faith is the substance of things hoped for, the evidence of things not seen.... By faith Abraham, when he was called to go out into a place which he should after receive as an inheritance, obeyed; and he went out, not knowing whither he went. By faith he sojourned in the land of promise, as in a strange country, dwelling in tabernacles with Isaac and Jacob, the heirs with him of the same promise: For he looked for a city which hath foundations, whose builder and maker is God. Through faith also Sara herself received strength to conceive seed, and was delivered of a child when she was past age, because she judged him faithful who had promised....

These all died in faith, not having received the promises, but having seen them afar off, and were persuaded of them, and embraced them, and confessed that they were strangers and pilgrims on the earth.—Hebrews 11:1–13

Gender & American Culture

THE UNIVERSITY OF NORTH CAROLINA PRESS / CHAPEL HILL AND LONDON

Female

Preaching

in America,

strangers & pilgrims

1740–1845

Catherine A. Brekus

© 1998 The University of North Carolina Press

All rights reserved

Designed by Shelley Gruendler

Set in Monotype Garamond

by Keystone Typesetting, Inc.

Manufactured in the United States of America

Publication of this work was aided by a grant included in the 1996 Frank S. and Elizabeth D. Brewer Prize of the American Society of Church History.

The paper in this book meets the guidelines for permanence and durability of the Committee on Production Guidelines for Book Longevity of the Council on Library Resources.

Library of Congress Cataloging-in-Publication Data

Brekus, Catherine A.

Strangers and pilgrims : female preaching in America, 1740–1845 / by Catherine A. Brekus.

p. cm. — (Gender and American culture)

Papers presented at several seminars and conferences.

Includes bibliographical references and index.

ISBN 0-8078-2441-0 (cloth: alk. paper)

ISBN 0-8078-4745-3 (pbk.: alk. paper)

1. Preaching—United States—History—18th century. 2. Preaching—United States—History—19th century. 3. Sermons, American—Women authors—History and criticism. 4. Women in Christianity—United States—History—18th century. 5. United States—Church history—18th century. 6. Women in Christianity—United States—History—19th century. 7. United States—Church history—19th century. I. Title. II. Series: Gender & American culture.

BV4208.U6B74   1999

251'.0082'0973—dc21   98-11394

CIP

09 08 07 06 05   6 5 4 3 2

For Erik

Contents

Illustrations

strangers & pilgrims

 # Introduction

Recovering the History

of Female Preaching

in America

On a cold Sunday morning in January of 1827, "all the taste and fashion" of Washington, D.C., streamed toward the Capitol to witness one of the most remarkable events ever to take place in the Hall of Representatives: Harriet Livermore, a devout evangelical, had convinced the Speaker of the House to allow her to preach to Congress. According to the *National Intelligencer*, a Washington newspaper, the news caused such a sensation that "it was almost impossible to gain admission." Huge crowds of people gathered outside of the building, excitedly trying to push their way up the steps and into the Hall. They all wanted to see the famous woman who described herself as a "stranger and a pilgrim," a woman who had sacrificed her former life of privilege to wander across the country leading revivals and "saving" sinners.[1]

More than a thousand people were waiting in the Hall of Representatives when Livermore entered the room at eleven o'clock. Straining to catch a glimpse of her as she walked through the crowd, they saw a striking, thirty-nine-year-old woman with large, piercing eyes who was dressed in a very simple gown and bonnet. According to the rumors that many had heard, she was a "great preacher" who could make audiences shout for joy or fall to their knees in prayer, but as she ascended into the Speaker's chair, which was draped

Daguerreotype of the Capitol, Washington, D.C., east front elevation. Courtesy of the Library of Congress.

dramatically in red silk, she looked surprisingly frail and "delicate." As she sang a hymn, and then cast down her eyes during a brief prayer of supplication, she hardly looked like the "bold," "eccentric," "crazy," and "wild" evangelist of their expectations.[2]

When Livermore announced the text of her sermon, however, her voice was so resonant that she could be heard in every corner of the crowded room. Standing underneath a small, gold statue of an eagle, the symbol of the republic, she opened her Bible to a particularly fitting verse from Samuel: "He that ruleth over men must be just, ruling in the fear of God." Preaching without notes for more than an hour and a half, she admonished, instructed, and beseeched her listeners until many of them began to weep. "It savored more of inspiration than anything I ever witnessed," one woman marveled. "And to enjoy the frame of mind which I think she does, I would relinquish the world. Call this rhapsody if you will; but would to God you had heard her!" More negatively, President John Quincy Adams, who sat on the steps leading up to her feet because he could not find a free chair, slighted Livermore as a religious fanatic. "There is a permanency in this woman's monomania which seems

Harriet Livermore. Engraved by J. B. Longacre from a painting by Waldo and Jewett (1827). Courtesy of the National Portrait Gallery.

accountable only from the impulse of vanity and love of fame," he wrote later. Echoing his words, many middle-class clergymen scorned her as a disorderly woman who had sacrificed her "feminine" modesty for public glory.[3]

Harriet Livermore was only one of more than one hundred evangelical women who preached in eighteenth- and early-nineteenth-century America. Between 1740, when the revivals of the First Great Awakening began in New England, and 1845, when a second wave of revivals ended with the collapse of the Millerite movement, several generations of women struggled to invent an enduring tradition of female religious leadership. Like Livermore, many of these women were belittled as eccentric or crazy, but they repeatedly insisted that God had called them to preach the gospel as his "laborers in the harvest."[4] Outspoken, visionary, and sometimes contentious, they defended women's right to preach long before the twentieth-century battles over female ordination.

Livermore and other female preachers have been virtually forgotten by modern-day historians. Despite the remarkable number of books and articles published about women and religion during the past twenty-five years, there has been no social or cultural history of female preaching in early America.

Historians have studied women's religious leadership in missions, Sunday schools, charities, and radical sects such as the Shakers and Spiritualists, but most have assumed that large numbers of women did not become ministers until after the Civil War.[5] As a result, few people today know the stories of Margaret Meuse Clay, who barely escaped a public whipping in the mid-1760s for "unlicensed preaching"; or "Old Elizabeth," a former slave who courageously traveled to the South to preach against slavery in the early nineteenth century; or even Harriet Livermore, who not only preached to Congress, but published sixteen books over the course of her long career.

As if they knew they would one day be forgotten, these women often described themselves as "strangers in a strange land" or "strangers and pilgrims on the earth." Comparing themselves to the biblical heroes and heroines who had lived by faith, they wondered if they would always be exiles who "sojourned in the land of promise, as in a strange country." When Harriet Livermore pored over the Epistle to the Hebrews, she understood that she might always be a pilgrim, a wanderer, a seeker in search of something that ultimately could be found only in the city of God. Even though she believed that God had given women as well as men the right to preach the gospel, she also knew that even Abraham and Sarah, God's chosen, had never "received the promises" on earth. If people scorned her as a religious enthusiast instead of recognizing her genuine call to preach, then she would have to wait patiently for God to reveal his will. True faith, the faith of the prophets and apostles, meant trusting in "things hoped for" and "things not seen."

This book is about Harriet Livermore and all of the other female evangelists, both white and black, who tried to forge a tradition of female religious leadership in early America. It is about women's refusal to heed the words of Paul, "Let your women keep silence in the churches," despite clerical opposition, public ridicule, and their own fears of appearing radical or deviant. It is about the possibilities and limitations of religious populism during a century of dramatic economic, political, and social change. It is about women's theological creativity in defending their right to preach. Most of all, it is about the importance of remembering a group of forgotten "pilgrims" who force us to question many of our assumptions about the history of women and the history of religion in America.

For the past several years, I have studied the lives of these female preachers in what can only be called a pilgrimage of my own. It started in graduate school, when a favorite professor suggested that I read a rare religious memoir he had recently found in the library. Having already spent far too many hours scrutinizing seemingly identical conversion narratives, I wondered whether his enthusiasm was entirely warranted, but despite my skepticism, I went to the library and checked out a small, worn volume with a decidedly antiquated title: *Vicissitudes Illustrated, in the Experience of Nancy Towle, in Europe and America.* Slowly turning the crumbling pages, which were yellowed with age, I learned that Nancy Towle had been a popular female preacher who had spoken to thousands of evangelicals in churches, schoolhouses, and open fields during the 1820s and 1830s. Describing herself as "a solitary wanderer through the earth," a pilgrim who had been called to preach the gospel to "a world lying in darkness," she flaunted middle-class codes of domesticity by speaking publicly in front of "promiscuous" audiences—that is, audiences including both men and women.[6] Even more surprising, she had not been alone. As she had traveled across America by horseback or on foot, she had shared pulpits with several other women, including the celebrated Harriet Livermore.

That first, unexpected introduction to the history of female preaching seized my imagination in a way that is difficult to explain. In part, I was stunned that I had never heard of these women despite my interest in women's history. Thanks to the groundbreaking work of several historians of black women, I knew the names of Jarena Lee, Sojourner Truth, Zilpha Elaw, Rebecca Jackson, and Julia Foote, but I had never realized they had been part of a larger evangelical culture—both black and white—that sanctioned women's religious leadership.[7] Even though I had read many studies of eighteenth- and nineteenth-century revivalism, I had never stumbled across more than a few isolated references to female evangelists.

The more I studied these women's lives, the more enthralled I became. Their stories seemed almost too dramatic to have been true. Huge crowds of curious spectators had gathered at camp meetings to hear them preach. Angry clergymen had locked them out of meetinghouses, while sympathetic clergymen had written them letters of recommendation. Conservative critics had accused them of being jezebels or prostitutes. Fervent converts had swooned at their feet. Strangers had threatened to tar and feather them.

These women simply did not sound like the eighteenth- and nineteenth-century women whom I thought I knew: the colonial women who had prided themselves on being "goodwives," or the genteel women who had founded benevolence or temperance organizations, or the slave women who had toiled in southern fields. Nor did they conform to my image of nineteenth-century evangelicals, whom I pictured as middle-class merchants and professionals who had eagerly embraced the capitalist ethic of the market revolution.[8] In contrast to famous clergymen such as Asahel Nettleton and Charles Finney, most female preachers belonged to the lower or lower-middling class, and they expressed deep ambivalence about the growing individualism and consumerism of American culture. Even Harriet Livermore, the privileged daughter of an affluent New England family, worried that Christians had begun to worship mammon more than God. Why had I never read the story of her preaching to Congress? Why had she and so many other female preachers been forgotten?

How and why these women have disappeared from the historical record is a central concern of this book. At first, I assumed that female preachers had been forgotten because they had been radicals on the fringes of American culture. Like most historians, I began my research with an implicit script. The book that I would write (or so I thought) would examine a group of early female radicals—feminist crusaders before their time—who had fought for their full religious, political, and legal equality to men. Because they were the first group of women to speak publicly in America, preaching to large audiences long before the controversies caused by female platform speakers, I assumed they had been closely linked to early women's rights activists such as Sarah Grimké and Fanny Wright.

As is so often the case in historical research, however, I soon discovered that the evidence I found in the archives told me a far more complicated story, and perhaps a far more interesting one as well. To be sure, female preachers were often accused of being radical, and they were forceful, courageous women who passionately defended women's right to preach. Harriet Livermore, for example, published her first book, *Scriptural Evidence in Favor of Female Testimony in Meetings for the Worship of God*, in order to "exhibit the truth, that woman was designed to be a helpmeet for man, not a slave." God had created woman to be "'a help meet'—an equal—a partner—a companion—an assistant," she wrote angrily, not "a servant, to sit at the feet of man, and do him homage."[9] Over the course of her long career, she never wavered in her commitment to female evangelism.

Yet Livermore and other female preachers were firmly rooted in their own place and time, and their revolutionary vindication of women's right to preach was always secondary to their faith in biblical revelation. These women were "biblical" rather than secular feminists, and they based their claims to female equality on the grounds of scriptural revelation, not natural rights. Even though they brought hundreds of new converts into evangelical churches, they never asked for permission to baptize them or give them the Lord's Supper. Nor did they broach the forbidden topic of female ordination. Instead of demanding the full power of priesthood, they resigned themselves to serving as men's helpmates or assistants. "The scriptures are silent respecting the ordination of females," Livermore wrote. "I conclude it belongs only to the male sex."[10] Although she did not die until 1868, twenty years after the first women's rights convention at Seneca Falls, she never demanded women's full political and legal equality to men.

It soon became clear why Harriet Livermore and other female preachers had been forgotten. Despite their popularity in the early nineteenth century, almost no one had wanted to preserve their memory. Revolutionary in their defense of female preaching, yet orthodox in their theology, female preachers had been too conservative to be remembered by women's rights activists, but too radical to be remembered by evangelicals. On one hand, they were ignored by early feminists who wished they had been more aggressive in demanding political change, and on the other, they were deliberately forgotten by evangelicals who wished they had never been "suffered to teach." Their lives, no matter how fascinating, said things about early American culture that few people wanted to commemorate. Few wanted to pass down these women's stories to future generations as part of a usable past.

Yet it is precisely because these women were neither entirely radical nor entirely traditional that they offer such a revealing glimpse of early American history. Even though female preachers were exceptional women, most were relatively poor and uneducated, and they shared many of the same values as the countless numbers of anonymous women who sat in the church pews every Sunday. Because they did not join the women's rights movement, but still defended women's essential worth and dignity, they were far more representative of nineteenth-century women than freethinking radicals such as Elizabeth Cady Stanton. Like many other women of their time, they were active participants in the public sphere, but they never challenged the political structures that enforced their inequality in the family, church, and state. To study their lives is to understand both the possibilities and the limitations of biblical feminism.

Female preachers were virtually written out of their churches' histories in the mid-nineteenth century—a silence that has been perpetuated ever since.

During the eighteenth century, many dissenting New Light, Separate, and Baptist churches had allowed women to speak during worship services, but as the new nation was born, they traded their early egalitarianism for greater political power and influence. Later, during the early decades of the nineteenth century, the Christian Connection, the Freewill Baptists, the Methodists, the African Methodists, and the Millerites allowed more than one hundred women to preach, but as they grew from small, marginal sects into thriving, middle-class denominations, they began to rewrite their histories as if these women had never existed. By the 1830s and 1840s, few clergymen wanted to be reminded of the visionary, often uneducated women who had traveled across the country thundering out their condemnations of sin. As a result, when Elisabeth Anthony Dexter, an early women's historian, combed through dozens of church histories, she found only "one or two scanty references" to female preachers. "I have wondered," she wrote, "whether some of the authors—all of them men—may have felt that a woman preacher was a monstrosity best forgotten."[11]

The invisibility of these women in denominational histories has made writing their history a difficult and daunting task. Where does one look for female preachers whom later generations of evangelicals wanted to forget? Sources are particularly scarce for eighteenth-century New Light, Separate, and Baptist women, who left very few letters or diaries. Besides a few conversion narratives, I have been forced to rely almost exclusively on the brief, often fragmentary descriptions of female evangelists that appear in church records and clergymen's tracts and memoirs. More material is available on Ann Lee and Jemima Wilkinson, the two best-known female religious leaders in Revolutionary America, but they too left few records of their own. Although Jemima Wilkinson's followers preserved a small number of her manuscripts, Ann Lee was illiterate, and all that we know about her comes from two very different groups of people: those who truly believed that she was the second incarnation of Christ, and those who utterly despised her as a religious fraud. Unfortunately, eighteenth-century women's *own* voices are difficult to hear.

In contrast, nineteenth-century female preachers left behind a rich legacy of personal memoirs and theological tracts. These women seem to have *wanted* to be remembered, and in response to the opposition against them, they used the press to defend their right to preach. Almost all of their manuscripts have disappeared, but as a group, they published more than seventy-five books and articles and contributed almost fifty letters to religious periodicals. In 1839, for example, Elleanor Knight published her *Narrative of the Christian Experience, Life and Adventures, Trials and Labours of Elleanor Knight*, and in 1841 Rebecca Miller wrote a scriptural defense of female evangelism.[12] Even though these women longed for "a better country—that is, a heavenly," they did not want their stories to be forgotten, and they hoped to inspire future generations of women to preach.

Large numbers of clergymen also published their memoirs, and before the backlash against female preaching, they recorded sharing pulpits with women, writing them letters of recommendation, and defending them against their critics. In all, I have examined more than 150 of these works from the eighteenth and nineteenth centuries, ranging from the Reverend Charles Burritt's memories of *Methodism in Ithaca* to Abraham Snethen's autobiography of his life as a "barefoot preacher." Taken together, these books make it possible to situate female preachers within the broader context of eighteenth- and nineteenth-century revivalism.

Religious periodicals are also important sources for reconstructing the history of female preaching. During the eighteenth century, ministers published accounts of revivals in *The Christian History*, and by the nineteenth century, there were hundreds of competing religious journals and newspapers. The approximately forty periodicals that I examined contain frequent letters from female preachers as well as descriptions of their meetings. They also reprint conference minutes listing the names of both ordained clergymen and "female laborers." More than any other source, they demonstrate the surprising acceptance of female preaching during the first decades of the nineteenth century.

Besides personal memoirs and religious periodicals, I also read more than twenty collections of manuscript records from Freewill Baptist, Christian Connection, and Methodist churches. Because these records tended to focus on the mundane concerns of church governance—choosing new ministers, raising money for charity, disciplining wayward members—they could be tedious to read, but no other source plunged me as fully into the world of early-nineteenth-century evangelicalism. Here I found a wealth of information about ordinary converts' attitudes toward education, social reform, technological progress, wealth, and lay religious leadership. I also found several references to female preachers buried in accounts of routine church business. For example, the records of a Freewill Baptist Quarterly Meeting held in New Durham, New Hampshire, in 1803 listed three women—Fanney Proctor, Hannah Lock and Eliza More—as "Publick Preachers and Exhorters."[13]

Finally, I looked at a wide variety of other books and manuscripts in order to reconstruct the vibrancy of eighteenth- and nineteenth-century evangelical culture. Local histories helped me to imagine the small, outlying towns and villages where women often preached; clergymen's diaries offered colorful descriptions of boisterous camp meetings and revivals; and denominational histories helped clarify questions of church doctrine. After reading several polemical tracts against female preaching and sermons on women's "natural" domesticity, I began to realize the intensity of the clerical debates over women's right to speak in public.

All of these records have helped me to piece together the story that I tell in this book, but much to my frustration, many offered me only the most fleeting glimpses of female preachers. For example, while reading the diary of William Smyth Babcock, a Freewill Baptist minister, I found a brief sketch of Nancy Mitchell, "a celebrated Preacher in this & the neighbouring towns; whose character for truth is very doubtful."[14] Intrigued by this tantalizing description, I searched for Mitchell's name in countless numbers of periodicals, church records, and clerical memoirs, but to my disappointment, I never found another mention of her. Who was she? Why did Babcock question her "character"? And why was she so "celebrated"? I will never know. Such have been the challenges of writing a history of "strangers and pilgrims" who never "received the promise" of historical fame.

Recovering the stories of these pioneering female preachers sheds new light on many of the most important debates about the history of women and the history of religion in America. In some ways, of course, their stories simply confirm what scholars have long known or suspected about eighteenth- and nineteenth-century American culture. For example, few religious historians will be surprised to learn that evangelicals offered women one of their few opportunities for public leadership, nor will many women's historians be shocked to learn that ordinary women often violated the "cult of domesticity." In that sense, this book builds on a wealth of critical scholarship published over the last twenty-five years.

Yet the history of female preaching also expands and challenges our understandings of the American past. As feminist historians have argued time and again, integrating women into history involves more than merely pasting them into previous grand narratives of political events. "The effort to conceptualize women's history as a collection of 'missing facts and views' to be incorporated into the empty spaces of traditional history is too limited, even fallacious," Gerda Lerner has written.[15] Since women's experiences often do not fit into the conventional categories for understanding American history, we must learn how to ask new questions and create new paradigms. In some cases, adding women to history simply bolsters our commonly accepted interpretations, but in others, it requires us to rethink our assumptions about the effects of cultural, political, economic, and religious change.

When seen through the eyes of women as well as men, the eighteenth-century revivals, collectively labeled the Great Awakening, look particularly significant, even extraordinary, but also surprisingly ephemeral. For the first time in American history, large numbers of evangelical women spoke publicly in their churches, and for a few brief years, they seemed to stand on the verge of a new era of female religious leadership. Within a decade, however, most evangelical churches in New England and the South tried to prevent women from testifying or witnessing, and during the American Revolution, they drew sharper lines between the "masculine" and the "feminine," the public and the private. Contrary to what I had originally expected, fewer women seem to have been allowed to preach during the Revolution—the celebrated era of the common man—than during the earlier revivals. Even though the Great Awakening decisively influenced the future shape of American culture, especially in breaking down colonial habits of deference and hierarchy, it ultimately did not change the gendered lines of authority within the churches.

Besides illuminating the short-lived radicalism of the Great Awakening, the stories of female preachers also offer a unique perspective on nineteenth-century revivalism. In many ways, the presence of large numbers of white and black women in the pulpit seems to offer evidence of the democratization of American Christianity. Intoxicated by the republican rhetoric of equality, the Methodists, African Methodists, Christian Connection, Freewill Baptists, and Millerites insisted that the distinctions of race, class, and sex were less important than whether or not one had been "saved." As historian Nathan Hatch has argued, the revivals of the Second Great Awakening (1790–1845) represented an "explosive conjunction of evangelical fervor and popular sovereignty," "an upsurge of democratic hope."[16] Populist and egalitarian, they helped transform America into a liberal, competitive, and market-driven society.

Yet at the same time that evangelicals welcomed the birth of a new democratic culture, they also expressed profound doubts about America's future as a redeemer nation. Throughout American history, many populist movements have been characterized as much by nostalgia for the past as by hope for the future, and nineteenth-century evangelicalism was no exception. However else these revivals can be interpreted, they also must be understood as a response to the anxieties created by rapid changes in American culture between 1790 and 1845. Politically, Americans experimented with a new republican form of government; religiously, they disestablished the colonial churches in favor of religious freedom; and economically, they fueled a market revolution that transformed the patterns of everyday life. Caught up in vast political and economic transformations that seemed beyond their control, evangelicals struggled to preserve traditional Christian virtues against the centrifugal forces of mobility and commercial expansion. Instead of celebrating the triumph of secular progress, they longed to recapture the primitive simplicity of the first Christian churches.

Female preachers were revolutionaries who defended women's right to proclaim the gospel, but they were also reactionaries at odds with an increasingly individualistic and materialistic society. Rejecting the American faith in progress and social reform, many claimed that the world was so filled with evil that God would soon destroy it in a fury of fire and blood. There would be no thousand-year reign of peace before the second coming of Christ, no heaven on earth, but only a conflagration of unimaginable horror. When Harriet Livermore preached before Congress in 1843, her fourth appearance in the Hall of Representatives, she implored her listeners to prepare for the impending terrors of Judgment Day. Towering above the crowd in the Speaker's chair, brandishing a Bible in her hand, she sternly warned them to "flee the wrath to come."[17]

Michael Kammen has described Americans as a "people of paradox," and the story of the Second Great Awakening is certainly paradoxical.[18] On one hand, the evangelicals who participated in the revivals celebrated freedom, individualism, and economic mobility, but on the other, they seem to have longed for greater order and communal responsibility. They were religious individualists who argued that every Christian could choose whether to be saved or damned, but they rejected the rugged individualism of the secular marketplace. They prided themselves on their egalitarianism, but they established coercive church structures to monitor religious behavior. They condemned the materialism that they associated with the market revolution, but they used new commercial techniques to publicize their traditional message of repentance. They were primitivists who were fascinated by the early Christian churches described in the New Testament, yet their attempts to recapture "oldtime" religion led them to create something newer than they had ever intended. Finally, they allowed women to preach, but they set firm limits on their religious authority. No matter how much they praised women such as Harriet Livermore, they always treated them as strangers and pilgrims, outsiders in an evangelical culture that reserved its greatest public honors for men alone.

Besides contributing to a greater understanding of eighteenth- and nineteenth-century revivalism, the stories of female preachers force us to look beyond the public/private dichotomy that has characterized so much of the scholarship on women and gender. Until very recently, the dominant paradigm of nineteenth-century women's history has been the concept of "separate spheres." Historians have argued that the lines between public and private, male and female, were sharper in the nineteenth century than at any other time in American history. The "female world of love and ritual" and the male world of politics and commerce were two distinct cultures, each with its own set of morals and values. Politically, women were excluded from officeholding and voting, and legally, they had no independent identities apart from their fathers and husbands. Even in religious tracts, popular novels, and advice books, women were told that they were essentially different from men. "By definition," one historian has written, "the domestic sphere was closed off, hermetically sealed from the poisonous air of the world outside."[19]

As several recent historians have noted, however, there was also a vast middle ground between the public and the private that was shared by men and women alike—an arena they have variously described as "civil society," "the social," or the "informal public." In the words of Linda Kerber, "We can no longer construe the history of women as the history of marginality."[20] In the seventeenth and eighteenth centuries, the sexes mingled in taverns, in the streets, and especially at communal occasions such as barn raisings. In the early nineteenth century, as American society grew increasingly complex, this informal public expanded to include antislavery and temperance organizations, orphanages, home missions, and a wide variety of other organizations that mediated between the family and the state. To be sure, most of these groups barred women from formal leadership positions, but they still brought women into partnership with men to work on behalf of the common good. Despite the rhetoric of separate spheres, women were active participants in shaping civil society. An ideology of domesticity may have shaped women's self-perceptions, but it did not determine their destinies.

The emergence of widespread female preaching in the early nineteenth century was closely connected to the expansion of civil society, especially because churches themselves became part of the informal public. In the seventeenth and eighteenth centuries, almost every colony had allowed an "established" church to collect taxes for its support, but after the American Revolution, when the separation of church and state led to the disestablishment of the colonial churches, Protestant denominations no longer enjoyed the privileges of formal state authority. As churches became simply one more kind of voluntary association competing for members, they no longer seemed as much like public institutions that should be governed by men alone. Because churches bridged the public and the private, the "masculine" world of government and the "feminine" world of the family, many evangelicals claimed that women as well as men had the right to organize home mission societies and distribute religious tracts. Taking this logic even further, several dissenting groups claimed that women also could vote on church business and serve as preachers.

In addition to church disestablishment and the corresponding expansion of civil society, the rise of female preaching was also related to changing perceptions of gender. "Gender," as I use the term here, refers to the cultural meanings that men and women have ascribed to sexual difference over time. As many historians have illustrated, the meanings of "masculinity" and "femininity" have not been stable or fixed throughout history, but changeable and contested. In the eighteenth century, for example, most Americans understood gender according to a "one-sex" model: there was only one sex, the male sex, and women were simply incomplete men. During the early nineteenth century, however, most Americans began to argue that women were not similar to men, but distinctively different in physiology, psychology, and intellect. Instead of one sex, there were *two* sexes with fundamentally different natures.[21]

Historians have debated whether this transformation represented a decline or a gain for women, but whatever the losses involved, the "two-sex" model of gender clearly helped to expand women's opportunities for religious leadership. Even though eighteenth-century evangelicals believed that the sexes were almost identical physically, they also imagined women as inferior, weaker versions of men: they were particularly emotional, passionate, and deceitful. As a result, most argued that women could preach only if they had transcended the limitations of their gender. Influenced by the words of Paul, "There is neither male nor female: for ye are all one in Christ Jesus," they claimed that women who had been genuinely called would virtually lose their "feminine" identities—and hence their "feminine" weakness—in union with Christ. In some ways, of course, this could be a deeply empowering message for women, but in its most extreme form, it also had the potential to reinforce negative stereotypes of womanhood: only women who had freed themselves from the taint of femininity could claim the authority of the pulpit.

In contrast, in an ideological shift of stunning proportions, many nineteenth-century evangelicals affirmed that women had a right to preach as *women*. They described women not only as "instruments" of God who had transcended their gender, but as "Mothers in Israel" and "Sisters in Christ" who had been divinely inspired to preach the gospel. Influenced by a new ideology of republican motherhood, they celebrated women's natural virtue and morality in the family of God. Despite their "weakness," virtuous women as well as men had the right to labor in God's harvest.

My purpose here is not to suggest that the two-sex model of gender was inherently better for women, since it certainly carried its own disadvantages.[22] Indeed, this stereotypical vision of femininity was invoked to restrict as well as to enlarge women's participation in the public sphere. Since conservative critics claimed that women were too delicate and modest to allow men to stare at them in public, especially in the "masculine" space of the pulpit, they were shocked by women such as Harriet Livermore. Belittling them as fallen women, they compared them to shameless actresses and prostitutes. Despite these accusations, however, many women used the language of female difference to justify their participation in civil society.

Partly because of the antagonism they faced, and partly because of the changing definitions of womanhood between 1740 and 1845, female preachers failed to create a lasting, coherent tradition of female evangelism. From Bathsheba Kingsley in the 1740s, to Jemima Wilkinson in the 1770s, to Harriet Livermore in the 1820s, there were large numbers of women who spoke publicly in their churches, but they had to repeatedly reinvent their identities as "laborers in the harvest." Much to my surprise, none of the early-nineteenth-century women that I studied seemed to know about their eighteenth-century foremothers, nor did later generations of twentieth-century feminist ministers ever mention the names of women such as Harriet Livermore. Cut off from their collective past, women struggled to defend their right to preach without ever realizing that others had fought the same battles before them. As a result, the story I tell in this book is one not of upward progress, but of unexpected disjunctions, failures, new beginnings, and reinventions—proof that history is never as orderly as we would like it to be. Female preaching has not been a continuous tradition in American history, but a disconnected and broken one.

A few comments about the scope of this book. First, this is not a history of *all* the women who preached in the eighteenth and nineteenth centuries. Early in my research, I decided not to focus on Quaker as well as evangelical female preachers because of the significant differences separating them. With the exception of Chapter 2, which tells the stories of Jemima Wilkinson and Ann Lee, the two most controversial female religious leaders in Revolutionary America, this book concentrates almost exclusively on the *evangelical* female preachers who helped shape the revivals of the First and Second Great Awakenings. While these women were deeply influenced by the examples of Quaker women ministers, they shied away from the Quakers' social and political radicalism, particularly their involvement in the women's rights movement. Evangelical women had their own distinctive understanding of theology: they believed in the necessity of being born again, the binding authority of the Bible, and the existence of Jesus as a personal savior. No matter how much they admired the Quakers' defense of female preaching, they never identified themselves as part of a common religious heritage.

Just as this book is not about all nineteenth-century female preachers, neither is it about all the revivals of the Second Great Awakening. There was no monolithic "evangelicalism" in nineteenth-century America, and fault lines divided Protestants by region and class. In contrast to northern evangelicals, who allowed scores of white and black women into the pulpit, southern evangelicals refused to allow women to "teach." Similarly, lower-class evangelicals tended to be more tolerant of female preaching than those who were economically better off. Even though Protestants shared many beliefs, they quarreled over how to be true to their faith in their day-to-day lives.[23] Instead of linking evangelicals together, the controversial issue of female evangelism helped drive them apart.

Finally, a few words about my approach to studying American religious history. Throughout this book, I have placed female preaching within a broader context of social, intellectual, and economic change. For example, I argue that the Freewill Baptists, Methodists, African Methodists, Christian Connection, and Millerites allowed women to preach in order to symbolize their counter-cultural identity, including their opposition to the market revolution. Yet I do not believe that eighteenth- or nineteenth-century revivals were simply the byproduct of larger social or economic forces, or that religious *belief* had no independent force of its own. Indeed, female preachers understood their faith as something that transcended the struggles of history—as an encounter with the mysterious, the marvelous, the divine. They genuinely believed that God had inspired them to preach. If there is one thing I have learned from studying their lives, it is that religion is an irreducible part of human experience that shapes as well as reflects culture.

Because I prize the storytelling dimension of history, I have tried to combine argument and analysis with close attention to plot. Although I hope to contribute to scholarly conversations about revivalism, gender roles, and women and religion, I have also tried to write a book that people outside of the academy, especially women ministers, can read as a window on their past. Perhaps some of my readers will not be interested in the historical arguments that frame this book: the short-lived radicalism of eighteenth-century revivalism; the populist conservatism of nineteenth-century revivalism; and the rise of female preaching in response to church disestablishment and the two-sex model of gender. Nevertheless, I hope they will be interested in the overarching plot: women's repeated attempts to forge an enduring tradition of female ministry.

In the pages that follow, I trace the history of female preaching both chronologically and thematically. Part 1, "There Is Neither Male nor Female," is a chronological survey of female evangelism from the 1740s to the era of the American Revolution. Part 2, "Sisters in Christ, Mothers in Israel," focuses on the rise of female preaching in the early decades of the nineteenth century. Organized thematically, it examines women's conversions, their calls to preach, their evangelical theology, their style in the pulpit, their defense of female preaching, and their use of promotional techniques. Part 3, "Let Your Women Keep Silence," examines the growing restrictions on female evangelism during the late 1830s and 1840s and its brief resurgence among the Millerites, a sect that predicted the apocalyptic destruction of the world. An epilogue examines the reinvention of female preaching yet again during the later nineteenth century.

In order to recover the stories of several generations of strangers and pilgrims, and to show both the continuities and disjunctions in the history of female preaching, I begin each chapter by briefly examining the life of a particular woman, from Bathsheba Kingsley in the 1740s to Olive Maria Rice one hundred years later. Each chapter also begins with a passage from the King James Version of the Bible, the book that shaped these women's identities the most deeply. Female preachers saw the Bible as the literal word of God, and by studying the lives of the strangers and pilgrims who had gone before them, they hoped to find the key to understanding their past, their present, and especially their future.

Partly because she was one of the first female preachers whom I discovered, and partly because her life was so richly dramatic, I began the Introduction by telling the story of Harriet Livermore. On one hand, she may not seem like a fitting symbol of eighteenth- and nineteenth-century female preachers as a group. Unlike most of these women, who were uneducated (or self-educated) and relatively poor, she was both socially and economically privileged. Her grandfather, Samuel Livermore, was a delegate to the Continental Congress and later a United States congressman and senator, and her father, Edward St. Loe Livermore, was elected to three terms in Congress and served as a justice on the New Hampshire Supreme Court. In all likelihood, these family connections made it possible for her to preach to Congress. Despite disagreements over whether she was a monomaniac or an "instrument" of God, she was permitted to preach in the Hall of Representatives four different times, always to large crowds. No other woman except Dorothy Ripley, a famous missionary from England, was ever given the same honor.[24]

Yet despite Livermore's unique access to the halls of power, she seems to have felt most at home among the lower-class "enthusiasts" who founded new sects in the wake of the American Revolution. Disowned or ignored by most of her family, she willingly embraced a life of poverty and hardship in order to fulfill her mission to "preach the gospel to every creature." Even though she ministered to congressmen and bankers, she worshiped most frequently with poor farmers, mill girls, and factory workers who felt besieged by the rapid social and economic changes that were reshaping early national and antebellum America.

Livermore resembled other female preachers in more poignant ways as well. Like scores of other evangelical women, she became quite popular in the early nineteenth century, but after the backlash against female preaching during the 1830s and 1840s, she was scorned by the clergymen who had once supported her. Penniless and alone, she clung to her faith—"the substance of things hoped for, the evidence of things not seen"—but she was eventually forgotten by the American public, even by the women who followed her into the pulpit. In 1868, at the age of eighty, she died in an almshouse in Philadelphia, and in accordance with her wishes, she was buried in an unmarked grave.

A stranger and a pilgrim, Harriet Livermore spent her life trying to create a lasting tradition of female preaching, but despite her hopes, she never received the promises. In many ways, her story is the story of every woman in this book. Recovering her history, and the histories of all the other female evangelists in the eighteenth and nineteenth centuries, reminds us that the struggle over women's religious leadership stretches deep into the American past.

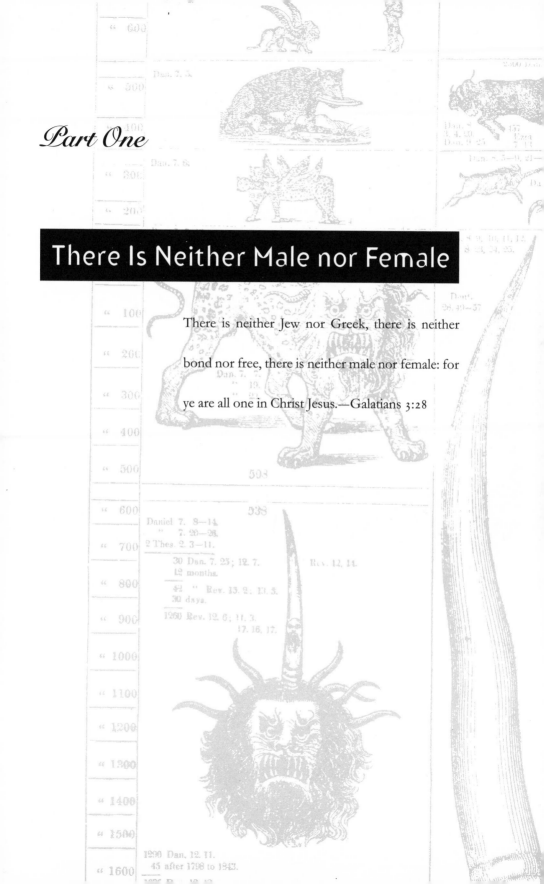

Part One

There Is Neither Male nor Female

There is neither Jew nor Greek, there is neither

bond nor free, there is neither male nor female: for

ye are all one in Christ Jesus.—Galatians 3:28

1

Caught Up in God

Female Evangelism in the Eighteenth-Century Revivals

I will come to visions and revelations of the Lord. I knew a man in Christ above fourteen years ago, (whether in the body, I cannot tell; or whether out of the body, I cannot tell: God knoweth;) such an one caught up to the third heaven. And I knew such a man, (whether in the body, or out of the body, I cannot tell: God knoweth;) How that he was caught up into paradise, and heard unspeakable words, which it is not lawful for a man to utter. Of such an one will I glory.—2 Corinthians 12:1–5

In October of 1741 in Westfield, Massachusetts, during the height of the revivals known as the Great Awakening, a visionary woman named Bathsheba Kingsley stood before her church as a humble penitent. In a public confession, she admitted that the charges her congregation had brought against her were true: she was guilty of "stealing a Horse [and] riding away on the Sabbath with[ou]t her husbands Consent." To justify herself, she explained that she had been obeying the will of God. After receiving "immediate revelations from heaven," she had stolen her husband's horse—or snatched one from a neighbor—so she could travel from town to town proclaiming the gospel.[1]

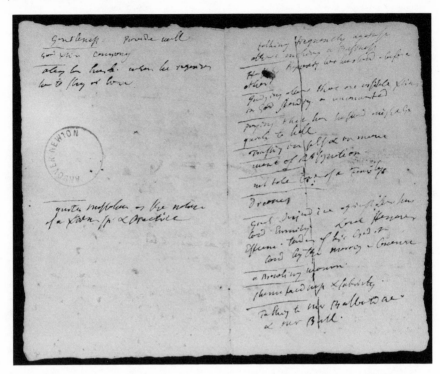

In 1743 Jonathan Edwards jotted down these notes before drafting his "Advice to Mr. and Mrs. Kingsley." He described Bathsheba Kingsley as a "brawling Woman." Courtesy of the Andover Newton Theological School, Franklin Trask Library.

Two years later, it was plain that Kingsley's repentance—and her humility—had been short-lived. In February of 1743, she faced congregational discipline once again, this time in the form of an ecclesiastical council that met at her house. Her pastor, John Ballentine, called together several neighboring clergymen, including Jonathan Edwards, the renowned revivalist, to discuss her extravagant religious behavior and offer her spiritual guidance. For two days, the ministers listened in shock and bewilderment as she made extraordinary claims to a special relationship with God. Testifying that he had spoken to her through dreams and "impressions," she proudly described herself as "a proper person to be improved for some great thing in the church of God; and that in the exercise of some parts of the work of ministry." For at least two years, according to Jonathan Edwards, she had wandered "from house to house, and very frequently to other towns, under a notion of doing Christ's work and delivering his messages." "Caught up" in God, she claimed that she was no longer an ordinary goodwife (as Puritan wives were called), but a divinely inspired prophet.

Confident that she had been saved, Kingsley made it her mission to show "sinners" their moral failings. As the church council complained, she not only "talk[ed] against others" wherever she went, but singled out individuals by name for their "vileness and wickedness." Even more galling, she assailed her ministers with "messages" predicting imminent judgments against them. Overturning the traditional roles in the clerical-lay relationship, she demanded that her ministers listen to her in silence—instead of vice versa—while she instructed them how to be better Christians. *She*, not they, had been inspired by God, and she expected them to defer to her greater spiritual authority. To use eighteenth-century terminology, Kingsley was an "enthusiast" who claimed to have received direct revelations from God.

Because of her caustic tongue, her heavenly "revelations," and her disdain for the clergy, Kingsley posed a threat to male authority in both the church and the family. It would be misleading to argue that Kingsley was subjected to church discipline solely because she was a woman, since her behavior would have shocked church authorities even if she had been a man. Nevertheless, the surviving documents suggest that her pretensions to clerical authority were particularly offensive because of her sex. In the words of the church council, she had "almost wholly cast off that modesty, shamefacedness, and sobriety and meekness, diligence and submission, that becomes a Christian woman in her place." Indeed, Kingsley had "gone quite *out* of her place": she was a "brawling woman" who had never learned how to subordinate herself to her husband, the clergy, or God. Instead of obeying her husband, who tried to control her with "hard words and blows," she prayed that he "might go quick to hell."

After two days of heated conversations with Kingsley and her husband, the council offered them warnings and advice. Surprisingly, they decided not to excommunicate her, and in some ways, they treated her with remarkable lenience. Fearful of stifling the fervor of the revivals, they refused to "quench the spirit" by forbidding her to testify to her faith. Instead of defending her husband, who complained bitterly about her "ill treatment" of him, they chastised him for resorting to violence to control her. Although they acknowledged his right to inflict punishment if "the extremity of the case" required it, they advised him to treat her with greater "patience and gentleness." Besides allowing her to invite fellow Christians to their house, he should encourage her to visit "Christian neighbors and brethren for mutual edification." Even though she failed to conform to the ideal of a virtuous goodwife—and in fact, she seemed to revel in her role as the village scold—she might still possess a spark of true grace.

On the other hand, however, the council also demanded that Kingsley put an end to her career as an itinerant evangelist. Since church and state were closely linked in Puritan New England, ministers worried that women who tried to "rule" in their churches might refuse to accept their subordinate status in the political order as well. Drawing sharp lines between the informal public of the neighborhood and the formal public of the established churches, they encouraged Kingsley to share her faith with other Christians, but not to speak with the authority of an ordained minister. If she stayed within her station, she could "prudently and humbly . . . counsel, exhort, and intreat others," but she did not have the right to wander from village to village as a public evangelist. In her role as a goodwife, she should "keep chiefly at home."

Bathsheba Kingsley was only one of many women who stretched the boundaries of traditional "feminine" religious behavior to their breaking point during the revivals of the eighteenth century. Although historians have long recognized and debated the significance of these revivals, which they have labeled the Great Awakening, they have generally ignored the question of women's participation in them. Scholars who have been sensitive to the re-vivals' social and political implications have missed the most momentous development of all: the unprecedented appearance of women's voices in the churches. In local communities throughout New England and the Middle Colonies, women not only cried out and testified during church services, but spoke as "exhorters" counseling others on how to live a full Christian life.[2] In the South, where the revivals were even more radical, Separate Baptist women demanded the right not only to exhort, but to serve as deaconesses and el-dresses. Like Bathsheba Kingsley, they claimed to have been so utterly "caught up" in God that they had virtually transcended the limitations of their gender.

For the first time in American history, large numbers of evangelical women tried to forge a lasting tradition of female ministry. Ultimately they failed, but for a few brief years during the 1740s and 1750s, it almost seemed possible to imagine a church where women as well as men would be free to speak in public—a church where there would be "neither male nor female."

"It Is Required She Should Ask Her Husband at Home": Women and Religion in Seventeenth-Century America

The revivals marked a decisive break with an earlier tradition of female piety. In the seventeenth and early eighteenth centuries, most women confined their religious activities to praying, reading the Bible (if they were literate), attending church, and overseeing the catechism of their children. Certainly women, like men, held strong religious opinions, but they tended to voice them in familial settings. For example, William Byrd, a southern planter, overheard an argument between his wife and his sister-in-law, who could not agree about the Bible's infallibility.[3]

Defining the boundaries of public and private is uniquely difficult in the case of colonial America. Unlike later generations of Americans who equated "public" with male and "private" with female, colonists did not understand these words in strictly gendered terms. As historian Mary Beth Norton has noted, the word "private" could mean secret or not public, but its definition was so ambiguous that it could be interpreted in many different ways. The word "public" could refer to the formal institutions of church and state, but also to the whole community of men, women, servants, and even slaves. Reflecting common English views, colonists believed that the family was inextricably linked to the state: it was not a retreat from the pressures of the world, but a little commonwealth that served as the model for the hierarchical ordering of society as a whole. According to popular understandings of gender, women were subordinate to men and could not participate in the formal public of colonial politics, but because of the close relationship between family and state, they could still wield significant influence in the informal public of community life.[4]

Before the rise of the ideology of separate spheres in the nineteenth century, no clear, simple lines separated women's world from men's. In a subsistence economy, men and women worked together at home, and they relied on each other to produce the goods they needed for daily survival. Although few families were completely self-sufficient, they had to depend on their own labor for much of their food, clothing, and shelter. Husbands and wives were partners in domestic manufacturing: men sowed barley, oats, wheat, and rye that women kneaded into bread or brewed into beer; men planted flax that women spun into clothing. Most commonly, women worked as housekeepers and mothers, but because of the demands of agricultural production, they could also be "deputy husbands" who temporarily took over their spouses' responsibilities.[5] Any role was appropriate for a goodwife as long as it furthered the good of her family and was acceptable to her husband.

Nevertheless, women were absolutely excluded from holding positions of institutional power in the formal public of the church and the state. In contrast to modern American churches, which have no legal connections to the government, many colonial churches were established by law, and they worked hand-in-hand with the state to enforce religious conformity. In New England, for example, as historian Harry Stout has explained, the government "existed primarily for religious reasons and represented, in effect, the coercive arm of the churches." With the power to collect state taxes for their support, the Anglican churches in the South, the Puritans in New England, and the Dutch Reformed in New York all prided themselves on being the guardians of public order. Like colonial governments, which were built upon hierarchy and exclusion, they encouraged women to take an active role in community life, but they forbade them to "rule."[6]

Despite significant theological differences, the Anglicans, the Puritans, the Presbyterians, and the Dutch Reformed were united in their attitude toward female speech: they all demanded that women must obey Paul's command to "keep silence in the churches." As mothers, women could instruct their children in Christianity, but because God had created them to be subordinate to men, they could not sit in authority as deacons or ministers. According to the Reverend John Cotton, women could speak in church when they were singing hymns or answering questions during disciplinary proceedings, but at any other time they violated biblical law. Armed with references from 2 Timothy 2:13–14, he declared that a woman was not permitted to speak "by way of teaching, whether in expounding or applying Scripture. For this the Apostle accounteth an act of authority which is unlawful for a woman to usurp over the man." A woman was not even allowed to ask her minister questions inside the walls of the church. Echoing the words of Paul, Cotton insisted that "she should ask her husband at home."[7]

Only a few radical sects outside of the formal public allowed women to testify or witness in public. In New England, a few scattered followers of Samuel Gorton gave women liberty to speak, but their numbers were too small to make a dent in the Puritan orthodoxy. Similarly, there is fragmentary evidence that the Separate churches of Plymouth permitted lay men and women to "prophesy" during public meetings, but the experiment, if it actually occurred, was short-lived. Even though sectarian groups dissented from Puritan doctrine, most seem to have shared the gender anxieties of the larger culture. Since they had no formal connection to the state, they did not necessarily view women's public speech as a threat to political as well as religious stability, but they still argued that women should "govern their tongues." Even the iconoclast Roger Williams, who founded Rhode Island as a monument to religious tolerance, described female preaching as "a business all sober and modest Humanity abhor to think of."[8]

Before the revivals of the Great Awakening, only the Religious Society of Friends—more popularly known as the Quakers—allowed large numbers of women to serve as religious leaders. Like the Puritans, the Quakers yearned for a more primitive, pure church, but they were markedly more radical in their theology. Organized in England during the tumultuous years of the Puritan Revolution, an era when the world seemed to be turned upside down, they experimented with new forms of religious worship that broke down the distinctions between laity and clergy.[9] Rather than creating a separate class of ministers who were set apart by special training and ordination, the Quakers abolished the concept of clergymen altogether. According to their leader, George Fox, there was no need for an ordained ministry because all men and women possessed an inner light that allowed them to communicate directly with God. Intensely individualistic, they located religious authority in each person's direct revelation from Christ.

Following this doctrine, George Fox and other early Quakers gave women unprecedented freedom to speak in religious assemblies. Both Fox and Margaret Fell, revered as the "Nursing Mother of Quakerism," published tracts arguing that women as well as men could be chosen to speak as vessels of the Holy Spirit.[10] Although most Quaker meetings were held in total silence without ritual or ceremony, converts who felt inspired were encouraged—even required—to stand and share God's word with the entire assembly. Whether male or female, these Quakers were recognized as "Public Friends" who had been specially chosen by God to spread the faith. Since they did not deliver prepared sermons on biblical texts, they were not "preachers" in the Anglican or Puritan sense of the word, but according to their fellow Quakers, their speech was even more authoritative. As "witnesses" who had been directly inspired by God, their spontaneous sermons carried much more weight than the formal discourses delivered by ordained clergymen.

Because of their belief in ongoing revelation, Quakers of both sexes faced persecution, but women posed a double threat to Puritan orthodoxy. In the Puritans' orderly view of the world, every individual knew his or her place: children were subordinate to their parents, wives to their husbands, husbands to their ministers and rulers, and rulers to God. By witnessing in public, Quaker women defied the patriarchal authority of the family as well as the religious authority of the church. To use Puritan language, they refused to "bridle" their tongues, shocking their listeners by their diatribes against church and state. "God will not be mocked," Mary Dyer warned the General Court in 1660. "The Lord will overthrow both your law and you, by his righteous Judgments and Plagues poured justly upon you."[11] Such angry, combative speech not only slandered the Puritans' piety, but openly subverted their model of womanly submission. In response, the General Court tried to force Dyer to leave the colony, but their attempts at coercion were futile: she clung tenaciously to her conviction that she was fulfilling the will of God. In 1660 she was martyred for her beliefs, scorning Puritan pretensions to godliness all the way to the gallows.

The Puritans' darkest fears about the dangers of uncontrolled female speech seemed to be confirmed by the Quakers' "lewd" custom of "going naked as a sign." Modeling themselves on the prophet Isaiah, they stripped off their clothes in public, sometimes even in the aisles of churches, as a protest against their treatment by Puritan authorities. Such behavior seemed to offer concrete evidence that female preaching would inevitably lead to sexual as well as religious disorder. As John Cotton explained, a woman who was allowed to speak or testify in the church "might soon prove a seducer." Tellingly, his choice of words explicitly linked "unbridled" female speech to heresy and promiscuity, sins that had to be swiftly punished if the holy commonwealth were to survive. Indeed, after Deborah Wilson appeared naked in the public square in Salem, she was forced to walk half-clothed through the streets pulling a garbage cart, a constable lashing her from behind.[12]

Such stories have led many historians to the conclusion that the Puritans were deeply and irredeemably misogynistic.[13] Puritans did view women as intellectually and physically inferior to men, and like societies throughout premodern Europe, they tried to control every facet of their behavior, not least of all their speech. Yet the Puritans' attitudes toward women were considerably more ambivalent than the word "misogyny" allows. Besides ordering goodwives to keep silence in the churches and hanging "witches" in the public square, they also defended the spiritual equality of the sexes. Even though ministers forbade women to speak in the formal public of the church, they encouraged them to engage in godly conversation within their communities and households. For example, the Reverend James Hillhouse praised his mother for being such an "expert" on the Bible that "she was capable on many occasions very seasonably and suitably to apply it, and that with great facility and aptness, to the various Subjects of Discourse, that offered themselves."[14] As long as she limited her "preaching" to her friends and family, she was praised as a virtuous goodwife.

In the early years of settlement, the Puritans' careful rules of "right conversation" sometimes broke down under pressure from the women who sat in the pews. Unwittingly, the Puritans inspired a small group of intelligent, articulate women to question the restrictions on their speech. A few socially prominent women vexed their clergymen by taking Puritanism's egalitarian rhetoric to an extreme. Instead of "governing" their tongues, they competed with their clergymen for the spiritual leadership of their congregations. Even though they did not identify themselves as preachers, their claims to religious authority made them more radical than women in almost any other denomination. If there were any female religious leaders among the Anglicans, Presbyterians, or Dutch Reformed, their names have disappeared from the historical record.

Without a doubt, the most celebrated female evangelist in the seventeenth century was Anne Hutchinson, the "American Jezebel" who was prosecuted for sedition in Massachusetts Bay. She was "a woman of a haughty and fierce carriage, of a nimble wit and active spirit," Governor John Winthrop complained, and she had a dangerously "voluble tongue." Although Hutchinson never described herself as a minister, she took on a clerical role by holding large religious meetings at her home—meetings that the General Court warned were "not tolerable nor comely in the sight of God nor fitting for your sex." During her trial, Hutchinson insisted that she had merely repeated the substance of the previous Sunday's sermons, but her accusers knew better: "Shee would comment upon the Doctrines," John Winthrop wrote, "and expound dark places of scripture." Perhaps Hutchinson would have escaped the wrath of the clergy if she had upheld Puritan orthodoxy, but she accused her ministers of preaching a covenant of works rather than a covenant of grace, a serious charge in a culture that prized its Calvinist heritage. Upsetting the Puritans' precarious balance between faith and works, she and her followers proclaimed that good deeds meant absolutely nothing in God's scheme of salvation. Most alarming of all, she claimed to be absolutely certain of God's will because she had directly communicated with him during a moment of "immediate revelation." Like the great patriarch Abraham, she had heard the "voice of his Spirit" instructing her what to believe. Horrified by her "desperate enthusiasm," the clergy offered a simple prescription: she needed to be "reduced." To rid themselves of her "infection," they excommunicated her from the church and exiled her to the wilderness of Rhode Island, "the Sinke into which all the Rest of the Colonyes empty their Hereticks."[15]

Several other outspoken women also faced church discipline in the years following Hutchinson's trial. Like Hutchinson, who was the wife of one of the leading merchants in Massachusetts Bay, they were all wealthy, high-ranking women who did not hesitate to match wits with college-educated clergymen. Perhaps they thought their social prominence within their communities would protect them from prosecution, but eventually they discovered that their sex was even more important than their rank.[16] In 1643, when Lady Deborah Moody, a wealthy and respected widow, questioned the validity of infant baptism, she was excommunicated from her church in Salem, Massachusetts. Even though Moody was not as theologically radical as Hutchinson, her beliefs threatened to overturn one of the fundamental tenets of the Congregational orthodoxy: the right of the "elect" to claim the covenant for their children. Under her influence, Anne Eaton, the wife of the governor of New Haven, also opposed infant baptism, and after mobilizing a small group of religious dissidents, she was excommunicated from her church in 1644.[17]

Another female religious leader, Sarah Keayne, was admonished by the First Church of Boston for "Irregular prophesying in mixt Assemblies and for Refusing ordinarily to heare in the Churches of Christ." The daughter of Thomas Dudley, the governor of the Massachusetts Bay Colony, and the sister of Anne Bradstreet, the famous poet, Keayne became a religious radical after visiting London with her husband in 1646. "She is growne a great preacher," her cousin complained. Unfortunately, however, little else is known about her. What did she say during her religious meetings, and how did she justify her right to speak? How many people were sympathetic to her beliefs? Only one further piece of evidence about her survives. After receiving a divorce in 1646, she was excommunicated because of her "scandalous uncleane behavior" with a man from Taunton. In her case, as in others, clergymen linked "irregular" female speech to sexual "lewdness."[18]

The stories of Eaton, Keayne, Hutchinson, and Moody reveal the limitations of women's religious authority in the century before the Awakening. Only elite women dared to challenge the authority of the clergy, and even then, they never identified themselves as preachers or exhorters who had the right to speak from the pulpit. Instead, they held informal meetings in their homes or shared their beliefs during the daily rounds of their domestic chores. Yet even these seemingly limited challenges to men's control of the church were suppressed. Outside of the tolerant culture of Quaker Pennsylvania, women who held mixed meetings, who led others in questioning doctrine, or who presumed to "teach" were admonished or excommunicated. Indeed, in the wake of Hutchinson's trial, the Puritans drew even sharper divisions between the clergy and the laity, the pulpit and the pew. In 1637 a synod recommended that men as well as women be prohibited from asking questions after lectures or sermons, and in 1648 the Cambridge Platform limited the laity's right to participate in discipline cases. By the middle of the seventeenth century, the laity enjoyed considerably less power than they had in the early years of settlement, and according to historian Mary Maples Dunn, women were disciplined out of proportion to their numbers.[19] In the new Israel that the Puritans carved out of the wilderness, public religious speech was explicitly gendered as male. Women who refused to govern their tongues could expect to suffer the same fate as the "voluble" Anne Hutchinson: they were "reduced."

During the 1740s, in the most turbulent years of the revivals, all this would change. Women began to make public professions of faith in New Light and Separate churches; they openly challenged their ministers' interpretations of Scripture; and a few gained recognition as exhorters or spiritual leaders within their communities. For the "brawling" Bathsheba Kingsley and her spiritual sisters, the revivals marked a dramatic transformation. Instead of keeping silence in the churches, large numbers of ordinary women claimed the right to pray and exhort in public.

The World Turned Upside Down: Religious Enthusiasm in New England and the Middle Colonies, 1739–1750

Defining the "Great Awakening" is difficult. There were Dutch Reformed and Presbyterian revivals in the Middle Colonies as early as the 1720s, Puritan revivals in New England during the 1740s, and Baptist revivals in the South during the 1760s. In turn, these revivals were part of a much larger transatlantic awakening that encompassed England and Scotland as well as America. Given the chronological and geographical breadth of the revivals, it is misleading to group them together under one term as loose as "the Great Awakening."[20] Yet despite the involvement of groups as theologically diverse as Moravians, Methodists, and Calvinists, the revivals were all marked by charismatic preaching, emotional outbursts, public conversions, and heated debates among the standing clergy. Whether Dutch Reformed or Calvinist, ministers preached a "heart-centered" religion that transcended denominational boundaries.

The most revolutionary phase of the revivals occurred in New England and the Middle Colonies during the 1740s.[21] In the remarkable years between 1740 and 1750, both the clergy and laity experimented with new religious ideas that threatened to overturn all the traditional relationships of authority. Wives rebuked husbands for their lack of piety; children evangelized their parents; the clergy undermined one another by quarreling openly in public and in the press; lay men became exhorters; and even women refused to keep silence in the churches any longer. Like the tumultuous decade of the 1640s in England, for a brief moment it seemed as if the world had been turned upside down. In the words of the Reverend Ezra Stiles, it seemed as if "multitudes were seriously, soberly and solemnly out of their wits."[22]

It is difficult to sort out what economic, political, social, or religious forces ultimately caused the revivals. Historians have offered a variety of conflicting interpretations that only underline the revivals' regional and denominational complexity. Nevertheless, it is clear that they began amidst widespread fears of religious decline and cultural breakdown. Epidemics of diphtheria and scarlet fever, shortages of land and hard currency, racial tensions in the cities, and fears of war with France were all interpreted through a religious lens. In New England, especially in Connecticut and Massachusetts, ministers told their congregations that God was angry with them for losing the vital piety of their Puritan forefathers. Even though ministers continued to bring converts into the churches during periodic "seasons of grace," they bewailed the encroachments of religious pluralism and toleration. In the wake of the 1689 Act of Toleration, they could no longer count on the state to enforce conformity by punishing dissenters. If measured by rates of church membership, religious "declension" was more perceived than real, but clergymen devoted many of their public pronouncements, such as fast day, election, and artillery sermons, to lamenting the fading glory of the city on a hill. The only remedy was revival. As Gilbert Tennent thundered from his pulpit, "Awake, Awake Sinners, stand up and look where you are hastning, least *you drink of the hand of the Lord, the Dregs of the Cup of his Fury.*"[23]

In part, clergymen such as Tennent seem to have been concerned about the growing commercialization of the colonial economy. Although seventeenth-century farmers had never been completely self-sufficient, they had traded goods and services in local rather than intercolonial or international markets. By the middle decades of the eighteenth century, however, trading networks had become much less personal and considerably more complicated. Merchants in the port cities of Philadelphia, New York, and Boston shipped goods not only to other American colonies, but to Europe and the West Indies. Gripped by a speculative spirit that threatened to shatter colonial habits of deference and hierarchy, a new class of upstart merchants grew wealthy by exchanging furs, fish, flour, and lumber for a variety of goods manufactured in England.

Eighteenth-century men and women responded to these dramatic social and economic changes with a mixture of hope and anxiety. On one hand, the expansion of the economy promised to offset the crisis of land availability by offering young men new opportunities for employment. In New England, land had become so scarce that many had to wait until their thirties or even forties before they could expect to inherit farms. On the other hand, the growth of the market also strained the fabric of community relations by creating conflict and competition among farmers, petty traders, and merchants.[24] Few were more ambivalent than clergymen, who alternately decried and exploited the growing commercialism of the economy. Ironically, George Whitefield condemned "the Polite, the Rich, the Busy Self-righteous Pharisees of this Generation" for neglecting faith in favor of "Merchandize," but he also publicized his conservative message by using distinctly commercial techniques, including newspaper advertising, discount pricing of his books, and serial publication.[25]

As Whitefield's example suggests, the revivals represented both an accommodation to and a protest against the expansion of market capitalism. Although historians have debated over whether the revivals appealed more to one social class than another, no clear pattern has emerged.[26] Goodwives, farmers, merchants, and the strolling poor all flocked to the churches, and they were all affected differently by the expansion of markets and the increased availability of goods. They shared only one thing: they were all uneasy at the prospect of sudden change. As they struggled to make sense of the dramatic transformations that were reshaping their lives, they instinctively sought answers in the churches.

The transformation of the mid-eighteenth-century economy was only one of a multitude of factors that contributed to the emergence of the revivals. Above all, they were a *religious* phenomenon with distinctively religious roots. Revivalism has always been an intrinsic part of the Protestant impulse toward reform and renewal, and in the 1730s and 1740s, a rising generation of young, energetic ministers tried to rekindle "vital piety" by experimenting with more popular and emotional styles of preaching. Theologically, they shifted their focus away from the head and rational understanding to the heart and sensation. This theology was not new: Solomon Stoddard, known as the "Pope" of Connecticut Valley, had brought hundreds of new converts into his Northampton church at the turn of the century by combining standard Puritan preaching with appeals to the emotions. By the 1740s, however, heart-centered preaching had wrought a revolution in evangelical churches. Even though clergymen such as Jonathan Edwards, Theodorus Frelinghuysen, and Gilbert Tennent argued over doctrinal issues, they all preached an intensely spiritual, "experimental" theology that stressed the work of the Holy Spirit in the heart.[27] Contrary to what their opponents claimed, most New Light clergymen (those who were sympathetic to the revivals) did not denigrate logic or rationality, but they clearly believed that preaching had to move the emotions as well as the understanding. Jonathan Edwards, certainly no foe to clerical education, explained that "Our people don't so much need to have their heads stored, as to have their hearts touched." Edwards did not want ministers to move their listeners' *passions* (a negative term for him), but their *affections*, which he defined as involving not only the heart, but the understanding as well.[28]

This new emphasis on experiential piety turned churches upside down by giving virtually unprecedented authority to the laity. Even though most New Light ministers believed that clergymen should be classically educated, they also insisted that no amount of studying could substitute for the actual experience of the new birth. In an incendiary sermon that was published in both Philadelphia and Boston, Gilbert Tennent attacked "unconverted" clergymen as "dead dogs that can't bark." He asked, "Is a blind Man fit to be a Guide in a very dangerous Way? Is a dead Man fit to bring others to Life?" In his opinion, a minister who had not yet tasted the sweetness of God's grace was so spiritually dead that he could not possibly lead others to salvation.[29] Although Tennent never meant to imply that an inward experience of grace was the *only* qualification for ministry, he lost control over how his congregations and the reading public interpreted his words. Despite his opposition to lay exhorting, he unwittingly inspired a multitude of uneducated men and women to claim the authority of ministry. By emphasizing religious experience over education, he helped to break down the boundaries separating laity from clergy.

Those boundaries were physical as well as metaphorical. Before the revivals, most ministers stood at a distance from their congregations by preaching from the pulpit or at least from the very front of the church. In contrast, the most radical New Light clergymen transformed the meetinghouse into a more egalitarian space by stepping out of the pulpit and into the pews. In a symbolic recognition of the laity's religious authority, they descended from their elevated place of dignity in order to mix with the ordinary converts who usually (quite literally) looked up to them. Andrew Croswell, a celebrated itinerant, supposedly liked to leap out of the pulpit and go "skipping like a ram from pew to pew, and from seat to seat, even from the upper gallery to the floor of the house." Daniel Rogers, another itinerant, broke down the hierarchy of the church space by going from pew to pew "like a mad man," crying "Come to Christ, with out intermission."[30] In this chaotic, egalitarian atmosphere, it was hard to tell the shepherd from the flock.

The "boundlessness" of the revivals brought converts together in communities of faith that temporarily transcended the divisions of class, race, or sex. Even though most New Light clergymen did not intentionally set out to undermine the traditional values of hierarchy and deference, during the revivals they erased virtually all social distinctions except two: the saved and the damned. Once men and women entered the doors of the church, they left behind the badges of wealth and social status to become simply *Christians*. Middle-class merchants, poor farmers, free blacks, slaves, and Native Americans all mixed in the church pews. According to the Reverend Joseph Park of Westerly, Rhode Island, almost one hundred Indians attended his church "very constantly," and elsewhere in the colonies, New Lights "wounded" large numbers of slaves with their hellfire preaching. Although clergymen had always ministered to converts from different social stations, rarely had they so openly celebrated the wisdom of the "weak." When George Whitefield visited Boston, he was more impressed with a "poor," illiterate girl who had "got a saving knowledge of Christ" than he was with all of the students he met at Harvard. He confided to his diary: "The Lord chooses the foolish things of this world to confound the wise."[31]

Even differences of gender faded in the excitement of the revivals. For generations, more women than men had joined evangelical churches in New England and the Middle Colonies, perhaps because church membership was the only public distinction open to them.[32] During the New England revivals, however, almost 50 percent of new converts were male, a remarkable reversal of earlier patterns of feminization. As the Reverend Peter Thacher explained, "In the *ordinary* Excitations of Grace before this Time, there were more *Females* added than *Males*, as I suppose has been usual in other Churches; but in this *extraordinary* Season, the Grace of GOD has surprizingly seized and subdued the hardiest *Men*, and more *Males* have been added here than of the tenderer Sex."[33] Although ministers took women's presence for granted, the sight of men in the pews signaled that something "extraordinary" was taking place. Indeed, the revivals attracted particular attention as a "great and general reformation," a "great awakening," because "hardy" men as well as women had been "subdued" by God.

Men as well as women responded eagerly to the emotional, "experimental" preaching of New Light clergymen. In the topsy-turvy world of the revivals, they embraced a style of heart-centered piety that was implicitly gendered as female. Drawing on the passionate and erotic language of the Song of Solomon, they imagined themselves as "brides of Christ" ardently longing for union with their spiritual "husband." In one of his most popular sermons, *The Marriage of Cana*, George Whitefield implored his listeners, "Come then, my Brethren, come to the Marriage.—Do not play the Harlot any longer.—Let this be the Day of your Espousals with *Jesus Christ*—he only is your lawful husband."[34] Of course, there was nothing inherently feminine about this marital language; throughout Christian history, men as well as women have described themselves as "virgins" and Christ as a loving "bridegroom." Nevertheless, men who described themselves as brides implicitly subverted their status as men. After Joseph Bean experienced conversion in 1741, he solemnly wrote out a "marige Covanant" promising his wifely obedience to Christ. He swore to take Christ "for my head husband for biter [better] for worse for richer for poorer for all tims and Conditions to love honour and obay the[e] before all others." For men as well as women, the soul was imagined as female:

to be a convert was to be a wife. Like many other evangelicals, Isaac Backus referred to his soul as "she."[35]

Despite differences in their social roles, men and women were linked together during the revivals by the shared experience of conversion. Often their conversion narratives sound so similar that they can be difficult to tell apart. In part, these similarities reflect the intercolonial and even international scope of the revivals. Through listening to religious celebrities like George Whitefield and reading religious newspapers and books, New Lights in many different towns, cities, and countries learned a common language of conversion. Yet the similarities between men's and women's narratives also reflect genuine parallels in their personal religious experiences. For both men and women, conversion was a metaphorical "new birth" that combined self-abasement with exaltation. According to Nathan Cole, he felt as if he had been "shrinked into nothing," a loss of self that sent him into raptures of joy: "Now I perfectly felt truth; now my heart talked with God; now everything praised God; the trees the stone, the walls of the house and every thing I could set my eyes on, they all praised God."[36] He truly felt as if he had been born again.

No matter how much the revivals blurred the distinctions of gender, however, they did not completely erase them. Despite striking similarities, men's and women's conversion narratives also differed in subtle yet important ways. First, female converts tended to describe themselves in particularly passive and submissive language. For example, in the surviving narratives from John Cleaveland's New Light congregation in Chebacco, Massachusetts, women tended to use the passive voice more frequently than men. Female converts such as Sarah Butler, Elizabeth Marshall, Ester Willi[a]ms, and Sarah Eveleth all described how they were "bro't to see" their sinfulness, while men such as Nathan Burnham and Abraham Choate described what they "saw." Although the choice of this more active voice may seem minor, it affected the whole tone of men's accounts. In contrast to Mercy Holmes, who testified that "I was bro't to see yt [that] I was nothing and could do nothing and lay at the mere mercy of God," Abraham Choate implied that the decision to be saved was his own: "I saw the Importance of an Interest in Christ, and found that I could accept of him as my Prophet Priest and King to rule in me and over me." Even though both Holmes and Choate claimed to be helpless, Choate's syntax suggested that he pictured himself as an active agent of God's grace rather than as a passive recipient.[37]

As reflected in the narratives, women also seem to have had a greater sense of original sin than men. Both sexes lamented their failure to live up to God's commandments, but while men tended to reproach themselves for specific immoral actions, women bewailed their inherent corruption. In contrast to male converts such as John Lendal and Jeremiah Kinsman, who confessed they were "void" of "Morality" or had "backslidden" by neglecting their "Duty," women described themselves in vivid, disturbing language as "polluted," "leprous," or "infectious." Although *all* women did not use this language, and individual men sometimes described themselves as "Univarsally Corrupted," women used these images more frequently than men. Quoting from Isaiah 1:6, one woman lamented, "I am unclean from the Crown of my Head, to the Soles of my feet. I am full of Wounds, Bruises, and putrifying Sores."[38] Deborah Prince, daughter of the clergyman Thomas Prince, wondered whether she would ever be "pure": *"By Nature I am half a Devil and half a Beast; I know that in me, that is in my Flesh, dwells no good Thing."* And Susanna Anthony, a young convert from Newport, Rhode Island, described herself as "so defiled, that I pollute all I touch!" She was "a polluted, infectious leper" who was "poor, vile, worthless."[39] Like the men in their churches, these women were Calvinists who believed in their inherent sinfulness, but they persistently identified their bodies, not their hearts, as the source of their corruption.

At first glance, this gendered language of pollution and defilement seems surprising. Why did so many more women than men portray themselves as physically unclean? Unlike later generations of Americans, who emphasized the inherent differences between men's and women's bodies, most people in the eighteenth century believed the sexes were more alike than different. According to medical treatises, women's sexual organs were identical to men's except they were turned inside out: the vagina was an interior penis, the ovaries were testes, and the uterus was a scrotum. Anatomically, men and women were simply two representations of a single model of sexuality.[40]

Yet despite this belief in the essential complementarity of the sexes, colonial Americans did not believe that men and women were physically or intellectually equal. Since they saw men's bodies as the norm, they believed that women were inferior, underdeveloped versions of men. On one hand, they imagined women and men as almost identical physically, but on the other, women were *lesser* men who were governed by different bodily fluids that influenced their characters. In contrast to men, whose "humors" were dry and warm, women were dominated by cold, wet humors that made them more deceitful, erratic, and passionate than men. By extension, they were also more licentious. Indeed, before the exaltation of women's sexual passivity and purity in the nineteenth century, women's "archetypal sin was their inability to control their lusts."[41] By nature, women were less pure than men, and they had a greater proclivity toward sexual "uncleanness."

Although Puritan clergymen began to challenge these images of female sinfulness as early as the seventeenth century, they proved remarkably persistent. On one hand, ministers praised women for their "*Zeal*, Faith, Purity, Charity, [and] Patience," and as growing numbers of women swelled the pews, they began to argue that women were inherently more pious than men. In 1736, when Jonathan Edwards penned his famous account of the revivals in his Northampton congregation, *A Faithful Narrative of the Surprising Work of God*, he filled it with descriptions of godly women, including the "frivolous girl" whose sudden conversion was "the greatest occasion of awakening to others, of anything that ever came to pass in the town." On the other hand, however, Edwards also remained suspicious of women's "passions." As one historian has explained, "He publicly elevated examples of female piety while consistently expressing abhorrence of female physical seductiveness and sexual desire." Although he helped lay the groundwork for a more positive conception of female virtue, Edwards never completely overcame his assumptions about women's sinfulness and inferiority.[42]

Although these two cultural images of women as naturally pious and naturally passionate may seem contradictory, they were actually closely intertwined. Because evangelicals believed that women were weaker and less rational then men, they assumed they would be as likely to be overpowered by Satan as by Christ. Indeed, they imagined the soul as "feminine" because it was inherently weak and in need of protection. When Bathsheba Kingsley claimed to have communicated with God through visions and dreams, the church council offered a far different interpretation of her "enthusiasm": she had been easily deluded by Satan because of her "weak, vapory habit of body." Without the advantages of "masculine" strength and rationality, women were both archetypal saints and archetypal sinners.[43]

Influenced by these images of "feminine" weakness and pollution, women tended to describe their battles with Satan in particularly vivid and immediate language. Even though both male and female converts mentioned being tempted by Satan, women imagined him in personal rather than abstract terms as a malevolent "lion" or a beast who had viciously "assaulted" and "attacked" them.[44] In contrast to men, who rarely claimed that Satan had physically possessed them, women's sense of pollution could be so overwhelming that they wondered whether Satan had literally invaded their bodies. As Susanna Anthony recounted in horrifying detail:

> I seemed as one really possessed of the devil. For, when at secret prayer, I should be so surprised, hurried and distracted, as to start right up, and run about, not knowing what I did, or why I did it. . . . I should be filled with such horror, that I could rest in no one posture; but rolling from place to place; wringing my hands; expostulating with God to take me out of the world . . . I was ready to wish I never had been. . . . I seemed as though I should have twisted every bone out of its place: And have often since wondered that I never disjointed a bone, when, through the violence of my distress, I wrung my hands, twisted every joint, and strained every nerve; biting my flesh; gnashing my teeth; throwing myself on the floor.[45]

Satan had attacked her not only from outside of herself, but from *within* herself. The evil that Anthony so desperately wanted to escape was contained within her own flesh.

Women's greater emphasis on their weakness and their bodily corruption set them apart from men, but for a few brief years in the Awakening, these differences were ultimately less significant than the similarities. For both men and women, conversion represented a transcendence of self, a stripping away of personality, that ideally did away with the distinctions of sex as well as class and race. Even though women were supposedly weaker than men, the gendered self became meaningless at the moment of union with Christ. Indeed, men and women commonly described conversion as being caught up by a force that freed them from the burden of individual identity. To use twentieth-century language, the goal of conversion was not self-realization, but self-abnegation: the eclipse of the self in blinding unity with God. For example, the Reverend Timothy Allen exulted that he had spent three weeks in such spiritual ecstasy that he felt "even swallowed up in God." Similarly, Sarah Gill, the daughter of the New Light clergyman Thomas Prince, longed to be "absorbed in the ocean of immensity," to have "no Will of my own," to be "swallowed up in him who is the brightness of the father's glory."[46]

This language may sound repressive to some twentieth-century ears, but being caught up in God was a deeply empowering experience for many eighteenth-century converts, especially for women who felt weak and polluted. During an intense, ecstatic religious experience that lasted for more than a week, Sarah Edwards, wife of the famed theologian Jonathan Edwards, felt so "overwhelmed," "melted," "overcome," and "engrossed" by God that she was liberated from all of her former fears and anxieties. In her words, "I seemed to be lifted above earth and hell, out of the reach of everything here below, so that I could look on all the rage and enmity of men or devils, with a kind of holy indifference, and an undisturbed tranquillity." This "indifference" brought her so close to God that it was as if she had left behind the confines of her physical body. Often she fainted or felt so weak that she could not stand up without assistance; at other times, she jumped up as she felt pulled toward heaven. "Melted and overcome," she lost all sense of self:

> God and Christ were so present to me, and so near me, that I seemed removed from myself. The spiritual beauty of the Father and the Saviour, seemed to engross my whole mind; and it was the instinctive feeling of my heart, "Thou art; and there is none beside thee." I never felt such an entire emptiness of self-love, or any regard to any private, selfish interest of my own. It seemed to me, that I had entirely done with myself. . . . The glory of God seemed to be all, and in all, and to swallow up every wish and desire of my heart.[47]

Her sense of peace and calm came from feeling that she was no longer an individual, but a part of God. Conversion had stripped away her personal identity and her self-reliance, but it had also made her feel more secure and more confident than ever before. Paradoxically, she gained greater personal religious authority even as her mind, her social status, and her *sex* were eclipsed in mystical communion with God. She was no longer an ordinary woman beset by fears and temptations, but a holy vessel of Christ.

Historians have argued over whether the revivals fostered "individualism" or "communalism" (words that are frustratingly imprecise), but for converts such as Edwards, they represented a volatile mix of both. In many ways, revivalists were conservatives who wanted to subordinate individual selfishness to the greater good of God's new Israel, but their emphasis on religious affections also contained the seeds of a particular kind of individualism. Converts wanted to submerge "every wish and desire" in the ocean of God, but after being "born again," they put more trust in their own heartfelt piety than in the teachings of educated clergymen. What New Lights most wanted was a return to an old way of life, yet ironically, they ultimately helped to create a more individualistic and pluralistic society. By valuing individual religious experience over the distinctions of education, wealth, age, race, or sex, they inadvertently dismantled the social hierarchy that had once underpinned their communities of faith. In the words of historian Martin Marty, "The Great Awakening might be seen as a conservative revolution, but a revolution it was."[48]

What made the Great Awakening *great* was its brief but dramatic challenge to the gendered divisions of male and female, clergy and laity, speech and silence. As the expansion of the economy chipped away at old models of deference, and as ministers celebrated the piety of the poor and the weak, women turned the world upside down by questioning the received wisdom about their place in the church. Should women keep silence in the churches? In the fervor of the revivals, many New Lights thought not.

"Swallowed Up by God": Female Witnessing and Exhorting

For both women and lay men, the revivals had the revolutionary effect of breaking down the restrictions on their religious speech. Since heartfelt experience was the most important qualification for ministry, anyone who had experienced the new birth could be an evangelist for Christ. When Sarah Edwards felt as if she had been swallowed up by God, she found that she "could not forbear expressing aloud, to those near me, my exultation of soul."[49] Paradoxically, her loss of self had helped her overcome her doubts about the authority of her religious voice.

Determining the true extent of female witnessing and exhorting during the revivals is difficult. Sources are not only fragmentary, but contradictory. As New Lights and Old Lights debated heatedly about whether or not the Awakening was a work of God, the significance of women's participation became a contested issue. ("Old Lights," in eighteenth-century usage, were ministers who opposed the revivals.) According to the most outspoken Old Light, Boston's young and combative Charles Chauncy, the revivals were nothing more than the product of women's overheated "passions." In his *Seasonable Thoughts on the State of Religion in New England*, Chauncy complained that the people who fainted, screamed, or cried out were "*Children, Women*, and *young-erly* Persons . . . 'tis among *Children, young People* and *Women*, whose Passions are soft and tender, and more easily thrown into a Commotion, that these Things *chiefly* prevail."[50] Comparing the revivalists to the seventeenth-century Antinomians, especially the despised Anne Hutchinson, Chauncy claimed that they deliberately aimed their sermons at women because they were "weaker to resist" and "more flexible, tender, and ready to yield."[51] Ludicrously, he even compared New Lights to the zealous French Prophets, an early-eighteenth-century British sect that espoused truly radical beliefs: besides defending female preaching, they claimed to have the power to heal the sick and raise the dead. By linking the French Prophets to the more conservative New Lights, Chauncy hoped to discredit the revivals as yet another example of frenzied enthusiasm.[52]

While critics of the revivals implied that only "weak" women were affected, clerical supporters of the revivals tended to go to the opposite extreme, ignoring or denigrating their participation in an effort to give the revivals greater legitimacy. Even Jonathan Edwards, the most prominent spokesman for the Awakening, implied that women were so "silly" that they easily lost control of their passions. In *Some Thoughts on the Present Revival*, he justified crying out during church services by including an example of a "man of solid understanding" who had cried out, not just "a silly woman or child." Similarly, Joshua Hempstead, a New London farmer, took pains to point out that among the sixty who had been "wounded" by James Davenport's preaching, there were "many strong men as well as others."[53]

Because ministers have left such conflicting accounts, historians must interpret the sources with caution in order to avoid misrepresenting the extent of women's public evangelism. Contrary to what Charles Chauncy wanted his readers to believe, women had not abandoned their domestic duties to exhort on every village street, and there were certainly no French Prophets in eighteenth-century New England. Nevertheless, large numbers of evangelical women made their voices heard in the churches by crying out, testifying about their own personal religious experiences, or fervently exhorting their friends and neighbors to repent and seek salvation.

Most commonly, women spoke publicly when they shared their conversion stories with their congregations. Many New Light churches, following the example of seventeenth-century Puritans, required both male and female converts to make public declarations of their faith before being admitted into full fellowship. Since women rarely spoke in public, this experience could be intimidating, but many found the courage to tell their own stories rather than asking ministers to read their words aloud. For example, Esther White of Raynham, Massachusetts, stepped forward to give "a clear and Satesfying account of her experiences," while Susannah Backus (the wife of the famous Baptist itinerant, Isaac Backus) enjoyed such "Blessed Clearness" during her profession that "it Seemed to affect the whole Church."[54] Although women's conversion accounts, like men's, were often formulaic, their symbolic importance cannot be overestimated. Unlike men, who frequently spoke in courthouses, town meetings, or militia musters, women's only opportunity for formal self-expression lay in the churches.

During the revivals, conversion became a public event as well as a private encounter between a sinner and God. Instead of confining their piety to the privacy of their "closets," converts flaunted it in the churches and streets. As Solomon Prentice explained, people could experience the new birth anywhere: "at Home in their own Houses, in their Fields, in their Beds; by Night and by Day; in other private Houses, and about their common Secular Busines; alone and with private company, as well as in the publick Meeting Place; at Prayer, when singing, and when Speaking." Conversion often had a theatrical quality: it was a dramatic spectacle that others could actually see and hear. Jonathan Parsons, a Connecticut clergyman, urged his congregation to show greater restraint after several emotional converts interrupted one of his sermons: "Several stout men fell as though a cannon had been discharged, and a ball had made its way through their hearts. Some young women were thrown into hysteric fits."[55]

At the height of the revivals, clergymen often complained that lay people in the throes of the new birth interrupted church services by crying out in joy or distress. In a predominantly oral culture that regarded speech as powerful, persuasive, and even potentially dangerous, converts were expected to listen silently while their ministers explained the Word, but revival meetings were so emotional that all semblance of "Order and Method" often disappeared.[56] According to the Reverend Solomon Prentice, "the Crying out" could be so "very great and peircing that the Preachers could at Some times be Scarce heard." One of his sermons was interrupted by a woman who "was in Such wracking Horrer, and Distress about her Soul, which she tho't was dropping into Hell, that She Cryed out at that rate She might be heard far off . . . Several beheld with wonder and amaizement." Similarly, one of Ebenezer Parkman's female congregants "cry'd out with loud crys and Lamentations and fervent Beseechings to all about her." These examples could be multiplied tenfold. In ministers' journals and letters one can find references to women who "wept most of the Service Time," "burst forth with great agony of soul," and "cried out in great distress." Other women "broke forth in Sermon Time Blessing and praising of God," "spake much Publickly," "broke out in a way of praising God," or related their religious experiences with a "boasting air."[57]

In some cases, women's emotional outbursts seem to have undermined their clergymen's authority. For example, the Reverend David Hall complained that a "troublesome woman" had rudely interrupted his sermon by singing hymns and falling into noisy "panting fits." Even though he tried to ignore her, she was so disruptive that his congregation turned their attention away from the pulpit to the pew. Whether they were shocked or amused, they quickly looked away from him—the voice of biblical learning and education—to her, an ordinary woman in ecstatic communion with the Holy Spirit. By singing and "panting" during his sermon, she juxtaposed her direct, heartfelt experience to his clerical and intellectual authority.[58] Without ever saying a word, she managed to deflect attention away from Hall onto herself.

Yet it is difficult to know whether this woman *intended* to be troublesome. Since so many female converts expressed themselves by crying out inarticulately, they made it possible for their audiences to project a variety of meanings onto their behavior. Indeed, some women may have actually heightened their ministers' religious authority by shrieking or fainting to the floor. Even though Old Light clergymen complained bitterly about women's disorderly behavior, many New Lights were thrilled by such visible proof of the power of their sermons. According to Jonathan Edwards, for example, true converts could not always control their overwhelming feelings of terror and ecstasy: weeping and swooning were natural reactions to the power of the Holy Spirit.[59] If women clapped, sang, fainted, or even panted during his sermons, he assumed they were overcome by religious ecstasy.

Time and again, women used their bodies to act out the emotions that they could not—or would not—put into words. Instead of clearly expressing their feelings of joy, anger, or doubt, they jumped into the air or fell to the ground in agonies of "hysterick fits." Sarah Sparhawk, a convert from Massachusetts, lost control over her body so completely that she seemed "unbounded, and like one deprived of her reason." Other women moaned or sobbed uncontrollably as they sat in the pews.[60]

On an unconscious level, women's unintelligible fits and cries may have symbolized their ambivalence over speaking publicly. Even though many female converts seem to have wanted to testify to their faith, they feared appearing too "masculine" or bold. After her conversion, Abigail Hutchinson decided to go from house to house urging sinners to repent, but she was quickly "restrained" by her brother, who warned her of "the unsuitableness of such a method."[61] Reminded of her "feminine" subordination, Hutchinson realized that she would never be allowed to preach as a traveling evangelist. As a woman, she had to learn how to govern her tongue.

Only the most radical female exhorters dared to openly subvert the conventions governing women's speech. As defined in the eighteenth century, an "exhorter" was an informal evangelist who publicly admonished or encouraged others to repent. Unlike ordained clergymen, exhorters had no institutional authority: they did not have the right to deliver formal sermons explaining biblical texts, and they usually spoke from the pew rather than the pulpit. Nevertheless, male and female exhorters claimed to have been divinely inspired, and according to contemporary accounts, they often spoke in front of large crowds of fervent converts. As a sign that God chose the "weak things of the world to confound the mighty," they caused a sensation in evangelical churches.

Lay exhorting was part of a larger New Light challenge to the authority of the established clergy. Even though the most prominent leaders of the revivals were ordained ministers who had been trained at Harvard or Yale, they were joined by large numbers of uneducated farmers and artisans who spoke in local churches. Perhaps Charles Chauncy was exaggerating when he complained that "Swarms" of "*raw, illiterate, weak and conceited young Men, or Lads*" were traveling across the countryside as itinerant exhorters, but no matter how overblown his rhetoric, it was grounded at least partially in fact. According to the most radical New Lights, religious authority came only from the experience of conversion, not education, and lay people could speak whenever they felt divinely inspired.[62]

The Strict Congregationalists, or Separates, as they became popularly known, explicitly sanctioned lay exhorting for a few brief years during the 1740s and 1750s. Between 1744 and 1754, more than one hundred new Separate churches were formed by converts who dissented from the Congregationalist orthodoxy.[63] Besides demanding changes in church doctrine and polity, the Separates complained that Old Light pastors had "persecuted" them by refusing to allow them to testify and exhort during meetings. Using evocative language, they urged Christians to "improve their gifts" by sharing their religious stories with others. All believers, no matter what their sex, race, age, or rank, had been given the "spirit of prophecy . . . in a greater or lesser measure."[64]

Proclaiming their commitment to "gospel freedom," the Separates allowed women as well as men to pray aloud during meetings. Because of the scarcity of historical evidence, it is impossible to know how many women spoke in Separate churches, but according to clerical memoirs, religious periodicals, and church records, scores or even hundreds of women may have witnessed to their faith every Sunday. Setting themselves apart from almost every other church in eighteenth-century America, the Separates avowed that women had a "just *Right* . . . to speak openly in the Church."[65] Instead of sitting quietly in the pews, women stood up to share their stories of religious pilgrimage with neighbors and friends.

As religious dissenters, the Separates may have allowed women to exhort as a sign of their opposition to the Congregational establishment. Historically, sectarian religious movements have tended to be particularly tolerant of female preaching, and the Separates clearly prided themselves on their stance as outsiders who rejected dominant religious values. Indeed, when critics complained that their support of female exhorting made them seem different from other denominations, the Separates responded that they *were* different: they had been chosen by God to be the leaders of the revival. At the beginning of Christian history, God had singled out Mary, a woman, to be the first witness of the resurrection, and in the 1740s, he had chosen "some Women, and despised Brethren, to be the first Witnesses of the Reviving of a glorious and wonderful work of God."[66] Only the Separates, not the Congregationalists, allowed women to exhort, and they alone were the true heirs of the primitive Christian church.

Ebenezer Frothingham, a leading Separate minister, defended female exhorting in his religious manifesto, *Articles of Faith and Practice, with the Covenant, That is Confessed by the Separate Churches of Christ*. Poring over the Bible, he compared Paul's injunction to keep silence with other passages describing female prophetesses and evangelists. For example, he closely examined a passage from Luke describing a woman who "lifted up her voice" during one of the speeches of Jesus. After the woman cried out, "Blessed is the Womb that bare thee," Christ responded, "Yea, Rather blessed are they which hear the Word of God and keep it." Although this exchange was brief, Frothingham interpreted it as an irrefutable defense of women's right to speak in "public assembly." Indeed, even though this woman had interrupted Jesus in mid-sentence, he did not accuse her of being "disorderly": "Doth Christ, who is the great Head of the Church, say, Woman, be silent, and not disturb the public Worship of God, by speaking with such a loud Voice, whilst I am a Preaching; you are disorderly; you have broken the Commandments of God, and the civil Law: Constable, Take her out of the Assembly, and let her be fined, or cast into Prison, 'til she is more regular, and learns not to disturb the Public Worship? Was this Christ's reply to the Woman? Surely, No! but the contrary."[67] If Jesus himself had allowed women to exhort, then certainly Paul's words had been misunderstood.

Despite their defense of female evangelism, however, the Separates never suggested that women were the true equals of men. Fragmentary evidence suggests that they may have allowed two young women to attend the Shepherd's Tent, an alternative college that prepared men for the ministry, but they never allowed women to serve as settled pastors, and they certainly never considered ordaining them. Even though Ebenezer Frothingham believed in women's "gospel liberty," he never questioned the justice of their subordination to men in the patriarchal family: "What a beautiful, good, and ravishing sight it would be, to see a family well ordered and governed," he exulted. "The man in his place, in right government from love to God, and his dear family.—The woman in dutiful subjection to her husband."[68] Despite women's freedom to exhort, they still had to submit to the authority of their husbands and fathers.

Like the Separates, the Baptists were also religious dissenters, and they too may have condoned female exhorting. Even though the Philadelphia Baptist Association warned that women "ought not to open the floodgate of speech in an imperious, tumultuous, masterly manner," at least one Baptist church in Connecticut allowed their female members to testify in public. There is also scattered evidence that Baptist women voted in church meetings, participated in disciplinary decisions, and chose new ministers.[69] Although the Baptists were not as anti-intellectual or as visionary as the Separates (with whom they eventually united), they still argued that women as well as men had the liberty to improve their gifts. Their only stipulation was that converts respect the boundaries of Christian order. After Isaac Backus, who tended to be sympathetic to lay evangelism, was interrupted in mid-sermon by three "Sisters" who "were much overcome, and Spake much Publickly," he warned them "with tenderness . . . of Snares that I feared they were in danger of."[70]

Since both the Separates and the Baptists stood outside of the formal public of the state, they may have been less hesitant than the established churches to experiment with gender norms. Far removed from the centers of political power, they were dissenters who occupied a middle ground between church and state, and they may have thought it was possible to defend women's *gospel* liberty without raising questions about their *political* liberty as well. Severing the connection between religion and politics, they saw no reason why women should not be allowed to speak during religious meetings. If churches were simply an extension of the informal public of neighborhood gatherings and social visits, then there was no reason to fear that female exhorters might go out of their place.

In contrast, established churches were still closely linked to the government, and befitting their status, they required women to "learn in silence with all subjection." After the 1689 Act of Toleration, which guaranteed freedom of worship to all Protestant sects, they could no longer rely on the state to punish heretics, but they still had the right to collect taxes from religious dissenters (including Baptists, Separates, and Quakers), and they still prided themselves on being the protectors of public order. Despite welcoming large numbers of women into the church, they denied that women had the right to "govern" men as exhorters or preachers. Dismissing the claims of converts such as Bathsheba Kingsley, they insisted that only ordained ministers could serve as "public teachers." As Jonathan Edwards explained, "The common people in exhorting one another ought not to clothe themselves with the like authority . . . which is proper for ministers." As the subordinate sex, women in particular needed to beware of trespassing beyond their station.[71]

Yet even though Edwards and other moderate New Lights warned converts not to exceed the bounds of proper "Christian conversation," their words often went unheeded. According to contemporary accounts, "many women" prayed aloud or exhorted "for an Hour together" or "laid aside their female Modesty, and set up to be Teachers in the Church." After attending a revival meeting, Charles Chauncy complained he had seen several boastful *"young Women"* walking through the meetinghouse and exhorting sinners to repent. And Nathan Bowen, a Massachusetts lawyer, grumbled that he had even seen women striding into the pulpit, where they harangued their "betters" in front of "large assemblys."[72]

There were two different kinds of female exhorters during the revivals. Despite the complaints of ministers such as Chauncy, most New Light and

Separate women seem to have exhorted only occasionally, perhaps only a few times during their lives, and they waited to speak until after the sermon. In Separate churches, for example, many ministers invited converts to testify to their faith after formal services were over. In contrast, a smaller group of women made a virtual career out of exhorting sinners to repent, and they saw themselves as religious *leaders* who spoke with as much authority as their clergymen. Besides Bathsheba Kingsley, the "brawling woman" who traveled from town to town on horseback, at least twelve other women identified themselves as public evangelists.[73] Speaking in houses and at neighborhood gatherings as well as in churches, they became well known for their diatribes against the temptations of sin. A few of the most daring even ventured into the pulpit—a symbolically masculine space—rather than speaking from the pews.

Unfortunately, there is very little evidence of how these women justified their right to speak. Without their own letters or memoirs, we must rely on the accounts left by clergymen and curious spectators, who often ridiculed them as enthusiasts. Yet it is possible that a few may have followed the example of Ebenezer Frothingham, who meticulously combed the Bible in search of references to women speaking or prophesying. Since female exhorters were evangelicals who believed every word of Scripture was literally true, they must have been heartened by the stories of biblical heroines such as Deborah, Anna, or Phebe. Later, during the revivals of the Second Great Awakening, many evangelical female preachers would borrow biblical language to defend themselves as "Mothers in Israel" or "Sisters in Christ."

According to surviving evidence, however, most eighteenth-century female evangelists argued that they could exhort *despite* their sex, not because of it. Rather than likening themselves to the holy women of the Bible, they implied that they had transcended the limitations of their gender. Influenced, perhaps unconsciously, by persistent images of female inferiority and corruption, they seem to have seen their bodies as obstacles to their religious authority. Before they could speak God's words, they had to become more pure, more virtuous, more holy—and less "feminine." Like Sarah Edwards, who had been swallowed up in a moment of mystical communion with God, female exhorters claimed to have virtually lost their individual identities in union with Christ: they no longer knew whether they were "in the body, or out of the body." Caught up in ecstasy, it was as if they had become "neither male nor female."

The drawbacks to this model of female religious leadership are obvious. Although Susan Juster has suggested that eighteenth-century Baptists (whom she portrays as representative of evangelicals in general) embraced a "feminine" faith, many women seem to have tried to deny their gender in order to assert their religious authority.[74] Unfortunately, these women never articulated their understanding of sexual difference because they took it for granted: they did not need to explain what it meant to be female or male because they assumed other people in their culture shared their presumptions. Nevertheless, it is clear that female exhorters saw their "femininity" as a burden rather than a blessing—after all, Eve had been cursed in the Garden of Eden—and they longed to obliterate their sex in union with the divine. In order to speak as God's prophets, they believed they had to lose their identities as women.

It is sadly ironic that a biblical text that has been so inspirational to contemporary feminist theologians—"There is neither male nor female: for ye are all one in Christ Jesus"—could be interpreted in such a repressive way. On the surface, these words seem immensely liberating, suggesting that God does not make distinctions on account of sex. Indeed, many theologians have seen this verse as evidence of the "radical sexual equality" inherent in Christ's gospel. Yet when read in the context of Paul's other comments on womanhood—"the head of the woman is the man," the "man . . . is the image and glory of God; but the woman is the glory of the man"—his denial of gender can also be construed more darkly. According to one critic, for example, this verse can be interpreted as "a negative view of sexuality and of women as females" because it denies women's innate dignity and worth as *women*.[75] (Of course, one could argue that it also denied *men's* inherent worth, but since Paul elevated men as models of humanity in other scriptural passages, few have made this argument.) Clearly, Paul's words can be interpreted in multiple ways—and it is possible that biblical scholars will never reach a consensus on his intended meaning.

Whatever Paul's intentions, however, female exhorters read his words through the lens of their own cultural assumptions. On the negative side, they saw their "femininity" as a defect, and they longed to be so caught up in God that they would lose their sexual inferiority. Raised to view themselves as lesser, underdeveloped versions of men, they found it difficult to believe their bodies had been created in the image of God. More positively, however, they also interpreted Paul's words as a justification of their essential equality in Christ. According to women who had been born again, they had become entirely "new creatures" whose weak, "feminine" bodies meant nothing in the larger scheme of salvation. Saved by their faith, they were no longer ordinary

women, but *Christians* who could do things they never thought possible. Whatever the liabilities of their sex, nothing mattered more than their devotion
to God.

In their greatest claim to power, many female exhorters portrayed themselves as prophets who had communicated with God through dreams, visions,
or voices.[76] Throughout history, people who have been excluded from the
formal structures of church governance—including the enslaved, the poor, the
uneducated, and the female—have been particularly likely to claim the authority of visionary experience, and New Light and Separate women were no
exception. Unlike ordained clergymen, who prided themselves on their di-
plomas from Harvard or Yale, visionary women asserted that *God* had educated them: he had told them where to travel, what to say, and even who would
be saved. When Charles Chauncy met two female visionaries in New Haven in
1742, he was shocked by their audacious claim that God had given them "a
special Commission, or endow'd [them] with some *special Authority*." In contrast
to Chauncy, these women had not read the tomes of Augustine or Calvin, but
supposedly they had studied a far more authoritative "book": "They had been
to Heven, [and] had seen the Book of Life, [and] the Names of many Persons
of their Acquaintance wrote in it."[77]

Recapitulating the central paradox of conversion, these two women both
asserted and denied their religious authority. On one hand, they asserted their
right to speak publicly in religious meetings, but on the other, they denied
having any agency of their own. Caught up in God, they were so overwhelmed
by religious "Extasie" that they fainted in the street. As they lay together "as
though in a Sleep, or uttering extatic Expressions of Joy," they testified to their
power in powerlessness. At the same time as they denied having any control
over their words and actions, they invoked a higher authority by revealing
that *Christ himself* had "bid" them where to hold meetings and what to say.[78]
Like the visionary Bathsheba Kingsley, who claimed to have been guided by
dreams, impulses, and impressions, they insisted that they spoke God's words,
not their own.

From a modern-day perspective, these women seem to have blunted the
effects of their public and vocal self-assertion by stressing their passivity. Yet in
the view of radical New Lights, they were true Christians who had placed their
entire dependence on God. Rather than preaching a gospel of free will, Calvinists rejected the notion that people could do anything to achieve their own
salvation: converts were helpless to sway the will of an all-powerful and in-

comprehensible Father. Even ordained ministers protested that they were nothing more than God's "instruments." Despite his education, the Reverend Samuel Buell denigrated himself as "the most Vile Poluted Lump of Clay, that Could Bee found to open Blind eyes."[79] Like the two women whom Chauncy had met, he insisted that his words and actions had been entirely determined by God.

In practice, women's "passivity" transformed them into influential spiritual leaders who wielded genuine power within their congregations. Perhaps no single individual better illustrates this than Mary Reed, a visionary woman from New Hampshire. Her pastor, Nathaniel Gilman, was so impressed by her prophetic utterances that he read them aloud to his church each Sunday as she sat with quiet importance in the pews. Certain that she had been inspired by God, he followed her instructions to the letter, even allowing her to decide what passages of Scripture he should explicate in his sermons. (On one occasion, she informed him that she had been "bidden" to instruct him to preach from Revelation.) Gilman also visited her for personal spiritual guidance, reversing the usual practice of congregants seeking advice from their ministers. After hearing rumors that she had fallen into a trance, he hurried to her house to ask her "whether I ought to mind what men said of Me?" Speaking as a prophet, Reed answered, "No, No, Mind what the Spirit of Christ says— Take Him for your Guide, and his Word for your Rule." At other times, Reed subtly reminded Gilman of her power over him by keeping her revelations a secret. On one occasion when he came to her house to ask about her most recent vision, she refused to speak to him or even see him. Through a messenger, she announced that she "incline[d] not at present to declare what she saw."[80]

Although it would be fascinating to know how Reed and other women sounded as they delivered their informal "sermons," the evidence is thin. Did women try to copy the formal style of their ministers, or did they speak in the same homely language that they used in everyday life? Only a few clues survive, but they suggest that women's *manner* of speaking made them appear particularly deviant. Not only did they defy the Pauline injunction by speaking publicly in the churches, but they were loud, contentious, and usually disruptive. When a minister on Cape Cod called a church meeting to discourage lay exhorting, his angry wife and another man began speaking "in so clamorous a manner that sundry bretherin tried to withdraw from the noise, but they followed them out of doors, with such a noise that (it being a clear evening) they were heard a mile or two and some were alarmed that murder was committed." This noisy, angry woman made a parody of the quiet goodwife celebrated in so many clergymen's sermons, perhaps even those preached by her own husband. Despite her later attempts to justify her behavior, she was sternly admonished by her church for her unseemly "clamour."[81]

Joshua Hempstead, a New London farmer, included a description of a particularly contentious female exhorter in his diary in 1742. After traveling one evening to a New Light meeting that was supposed to be led by the Reverend Timothy Allen, he found several men and two or three women all praying aloud at the same time. Overwhelmed by the cacophony of competing voices, he complained that "No one could understand Either part." After a long delay, the Reverend Joseph Fish finally arrived in Allen's place and tried to restore order, but when he ascended into the pulpit, one of the women tried to drown out his voice with her own. According to Hempstead, Fish and the woman spent several minutes trying to outshout each other, but finally, "she grew Silent & Mr. fish had all the work to himself." Angry and embarrassed, Fish eventually managed to regain control of the congregation, but his authority had been badly compromised by a woman who believed that *her* voice was the one that should be heard.[82]

As these examples illustrate, many female exhorters were openly contemptuous of clerical authority. With little of the Christian humility that their culture prized, they interrupted their ministers' sermons or harshly accused them of being unconverted. According to Jonathan Edwards, for example, Bathsheba Kingsley took it upon herself to "reprove and warn her own ministers."[83] Even though none of these women ever seem to have imagined the possibility of female ordination, they clearly believed in their own authority to interpret God's word. Indeed, some seem to have believed in their *superiority* to their ministers. Unlike the female converts who fell into fits or cried out inarticulately, they made it absolutely clear that they had no intention of listening "in silence with all subjection."

According to spectators, female exhorters were not only belligerent, but vulgar in their speech and behavior. Of course, many of the people who wrote descriptions of these women were critical of the revivals' disorder, and they may have exaggerated women's crudity. Nevertheless, they identified an important trend. Unlike seventeenth-century female religious leaders such as Anne Hutchinson, Deborah Moody, Sarah Keayne, and Anne Eaton, who were all well educated and relatively affluent, many of the women who exhorted during the revivals belonged to a lower social and economic rank. Although there is no evidence that Native American or slave women ever spoke during meetings, it is clear that female religious leadership was no longer the exclusive calling of the learned or the affluent. Since New Lights emphasized the importance of religious affections as much as clerical training, even poor white women claimed to have the authority to speak publicly. One man who attended a meeting held by Andrew Croswell, one of the most radical revivalists, was disgusted by the sight of a "big-bellied Woman from an hindseat" who "straddled into the pulpit." Her physical appearance, her gestures, her behavior, and her speech all contributed to his hostility. Not only was she "big bellied," but her speaking style was outlandishly crude: during her long, thirty minute speech, she "extend[ed] her arms every Way, and not a Muscle of her Body but in Action." Yet even though her performance was far removed from the model of refined dignity set by Anne Hutchinson, she seems to have had a raw, charismatic power. When she finished speaking, her listeners were so agitated that they followed her in a "singing Procession" around Plymouth, and each person "delivered the yell he was particularly inspired with, join'd with all the mad Gestures and Actions that *Franticks* show."[84]

Such extravagant behavior alienated all but the most radical New Light clergymen. For every Separate or Baptist minister who assured women they had the right to speak, a multitude of others warned them to "learn in silence with all subjection." Repeating the words of the apostle Paul, Charles Chauncy complained that allowing women to speak in "assemblies for religious worship" was "a plain breach of that *commandment of the* LORD, wherin it is said, *Let your* WOMEN *keep silence in the churches*; for it *is not permitted to them to speak—It is a shame: for* WOMEN *to speak in the church*."[85] Ironically, Chauncy was a theological liberal, but in contrast to Ebenezer Frothingham, the Separate minister who defended women's gospel freedom, he found little ambiguity in Paul's commandment: *any* form of women's public evangelism, whether exhorting or preaching, was a sin against God.

Although New Light ministers such as Jonathan Edwards and Gilbert Tennent rarely agreed with Chauncy, the most vituperative critic of the revivals, they began to move in more conservative directions as growing numbers of converts insisted on improving their gifts. In the early years of the revivals, New Lights had hoped to unify a culture that seemed to be fraying at the seams, but by the mid-1750s, they realized that the zeal they had helped inspire was too volatile to keep contained. Instead of fostering community, the revivals had splintered century-old congregations, turned Old Light and New Light clergymen against one another, and paved the way for a more individualistic, pluralistic society. Disillusioned, the same ministers who had once rejoiced at the outpouring of God's grace now tried to put a stop to the visions, outcries, and fits that smacked of excessive enthusiasm. Even the radical James Davenport, who had once consigned the books of some of the greatest Puritan divines to a public bonfire, apologized for his earlier "Errors."[86]

Despite continuing recriminations from both sides, New Lights and Old Lights were increasingly united by their shared anxieties about disorderly evangelical women. Like Chauncy and other opponents of the revivals, they labeled female exhorters as "troublesome," "brawling," "imperious," "ridiculous," and "clamorous," but rarely as pious. When a "cunning" woman in North Haven, Connecticut, claimed to have been divinely inspired to speak, her minister showed little tolerance for her pretensions to ministerial authority: she was disciplined for "contending and wanting to govern."[87]

Why did these ministers react so strongly to the sight (and sound) of women speaking in public? In part, they seem to have regarded female exhorting as a troubling sign of men's declining authority within the family. In the seventeenth century, the family had been a "little monarchy" in which the father reigned virtually supreme: he disciplined his children and servants, educated them, oversaw their choice of marriage partners, and controlled the family's property. Even his wife, his "yoke fellow" and partner, was expected to submit to his government. In theory, although rarely in practice, women, children, or servants who challenged paternal power through sexual misconduct or disobedience could be punished by the courts. Yet by the middle of the eighteenth century, land shortages and the expansion of the market had combined to weaken men's authority over the family. Fathers could no longer guarantee that they would be able to provide land for their sons, and they lost control of children who moved away from home in search of greater economic opportunities. Although they still tried to maintain their control over whom their children would marry, they had little success. By the 1740s and 1750s, the premarital pregnancy rate had risen as high as 40 percent.[88]

To men who were already deeply worried about the changes in the traditional family, female exhorting stood as a vivid symbol of the breakdown of their authority as husbands and fathers. After the Bathsheba Kingsley case, Jonathan Edwards worried that women might feel compelled to "go forth and halloo and scream in the streets, or to leave the families they belong to, and go from house to house." Old Lights put the case more baldly. According to Robert Ross, female exhorters who dared to "instruct and govern Men" threatened to reduce them to an effeminate state of "*tame Subjection*" and "abject Submission." Convinced of their husbands' "weakness" and their own "Superiority," they had expressly broken God's commands against speaking in public. Some were merely "misguided," while others were "under the immediate powerful Influence of an evil Spirit," but all wanted to "usurp" their husbands' authority so they could be "Queens for Life."[89]

Other ministers expressed fears that female exhorting would lead to sexual as well as religious disorder. Like the Puritans who had complained of Quaker women's "lewdness," they explicitly linked women's public speech to sexual deviance. After a Philadelphia woman led an angry crowd of "Negroes, and other Servants" out of the meetinghouse where their pastor was preaching, the *American Weekly Mercury* hinted that she might be a prostitute: she "support[ed] a Character as Modesty forbids to mention."[90] Even though female evangelists claimed to have been swallowed up by God, many people still saw them as common women with common "feminine" vices—deceitfulness, pride, and wantonness.

Beginning in the mid-1750s, even the Separates and the Baptists began to bar women from praying aloud or exhorting publicly. Only a few short years after Ebenezer Frothingham's defense of female evangelism, the Separate Church in Canterbury, Connecticut, disciplined Benjamin Kent for asserting that "a woman hath Equal Right with the man in all publick improvement in ye Ch[urc]h," a conclusion he had reached by reading the Bible allegorically rather than literally. According to Kent, the Pauline command that the woman should not usurp authority over the man really meant that the *church* should not usurp authority over *Christ*. Perhaps his reasoning would have been more persuasive a decade earlier, but in 1754 an ecclesiastical council expressed outrage at his "horable way of perverting the scriptures." By the 1760s and 1770s, women had lost the institutional support of the only evangelical churches who had allowed them to speak publicly. In 1760, when Lois Adams, a Separate from Canterbury, dared to "authoritivey teach and admonish the houle Church," she was found "Gilty" of "usurp[ing] authority over the Ch[urc]h."[91]

Only a few iconoclastic Separates continued to allow women to improve their gifts, and then only in the face of stiff opposition. A Separate church on Long Island, for example, allowed Sarah Wright Townsend, a schoolteacher, to speak nearly every Sunday for at least fifteen years, but a conservative faction in the congregation began to question her religious authority during the 1770s. Led by Peter Underhill, who was Townsend's son-in-law as well as her pastor, they held a meeting in 1773 in order to propose uniting with the "Regular" Baptists, a decision that would have resulted in greater restrictions on lay preaching. Whatever the personal issues at stake (and one cannot help speculating about strained family relationships), Underhill and Townsend clearly disagreed over women's right to speak publicly. Since Townsend was not merely an exhorter, but a *preacher* who delivered formal sermons explaining biblical texts, she must have seemed particularly radical. Nevertheless, Underhill failed to convince most of her supporters to abandon her, and they angrily followed her out of the meeting, screaming, *"Babylon! Babylon! Babylon! . . .* with such tremendous force of lungs, that the cry was heard at a distance of two miles." Mary Cooper, Townsend's sister, remembered that "the out cry was very greate. Some exorteing, some talking, some cryin[g], others falling on the ground and all so loud as to be heard some miles."[92] Although there is no record of whether Townsend continued to preach after 1773, she seems to have prevailed. Her church did not unite with the Baptists until 1789, nine years after her death.

Townsend's church was exceptional in the closing decades of the eighteenth century. Most Separate churches either reunited with the Congregational churches or became Baptist after the upheaval of the revivals, and the few that survived faced a difficult choice. Should they change with the times and abandon their earlier dissent? Or should they preserve their historic identity as religious outsiders at all costs? With membership shrinking, most clergymen chose power over purity, repudiating their past in order to seek greater respectability in the religious mainstream. In 1781, when the remaining Separate churches met to draw up new denominational guidelines, they renounced many of their past positions, including the once-treasured belief that all members had a right to improve their gifts publicly. Although female exhorting had always been linked to the exhorting of lay men, even men were now required to listen to their ministers in respectful silence. As the Separates explained in the clear, blunt language they had always favored, "That every Brother hath a Right to set up to be a Publick Teacher, or Exhorter in the Church, we deny."[93]

Like the Separates, the Baptists traded their early radicalism for greater legitimacy and power. As one "very fashionable" Baptist clergyman explained, "We wish to make our denomination respectable as well as the rest." For decades, Baptists had been persecuted by New England governments who had forced them to pay taxes to support the Congregational establishment, but as they matured from a weak, loosely organized movement into an institutional church, they began to seek greater power in both local and national politics. They were remarkably frank about their political ambitions: in 1767 the Warren Association of Baptist Churches announced that it wanted to become more "important in the eye of the civil powers." Hoping to forge closer links to the formal public of the state, they eventually rose to national prominence as advocates of religious freedom, but only at the cost of betraying their earlier ethic of sexual egalitarianism. By the end of the eighteenth century, as historian Susan Juster has explained, Baptists no longer allowed women to vote in church meetings, choose new ministers, or exhort publicly.[94] For Baptist women, as for their Separate and New Light sisters, denominational respectability had come at a very high price.

Women and Revivalism in the South, 1754–1776

In New England and the Middle Colonies, the most radical phase of the revivals had ended by the early 1750s. Even though awakenings continued in many congregations throughout the 1760s, the spirit of experimentation and innovation would not be rekindled on such a large scale again until the nineteenth century.

In the South, by contrast, the revivals did not even begin until the late 1740s. Presbyterians led an awakening in Virginia under the preaching of Samuel Davies, while both Separate Baptists and Methodists gained new converts during the 1760s and 1770s. The number of New Light churches grew rapidly. In 1769 there were only seven Separate Baptist churches in Virginia, but by 1774, that number had increased to fifty-four.[95]

The Separate Baptists were dissenters who traced their roots to the Separate movement of New England. Shubal Stearns, a Separate preacher from Connecticut, formed the first Separate Baptist church in North Carolina after settling there in 1754. With the help of his brother-in-law, the exhorter Daniel Marshall, Stearns led a revival that soon spread to Virginia, South Carolina, and Kentucky. In his own congregation, the Sandy Creek Separate Baptist Church, the number of members quickly swelled from 16 to 606. Throughout North Carolina, 1,452 people had joined Separate churches by 1780. In Virginia, the number was even higher, reaching 4,800.[96]

The southern revivals shared many similarities with the Great Awakening in the North. Many converts indulged in emotional and "enthusiastic" behavior, such as the "young lady" who "began to weep and tremble" until "the effect spread through the whole house, with solemn groans and lamentations." While some claimed to have seen divine visions, others attracted attention by "crying out under the ministry" or "falling down as in fits."[97] As in New England and the Middle Colonies, conservative clergymen lamented that the world had been turned upside down.

The Separate Baptist women of the South were as vocal and contentious as their counterparts in New England. By "weeping and crying in a most extraordinary manner," or falling into "ecstasies of joy," they transformed themselves into models of piety for others to emulate. Caught up in God, they no longer hesitated to compete with their ministers for the leadership of their churches. As the Reverend John Taylor lamented, Hannah Cave Graves was a pious and intelligent woman, but "her blunt dealings with preachers at times, seemed as if she ran some hazzard of violating a saying of God himself, 'touch not mine anointed, and do my prophets no harm.'" On one occasion, she reportedly railed at a minister for being a "hireling" who "fled when the wolf came, and seemed not to care for the sheep."[98] Even though Graves could not be a minister because of her sex, she still viewed herself as the spiritual guardian of her church.

Like the Separate churches of New England, the Separate Baptist churches of the South allowed women to speak publicly. Besides the countless numbers of women who improved their gifts at the end of church services, a few particularly charismatic women became known as religious leaders. Perhaps the most celebrated was Martha Stearns Marshall, the sister of Shubal Stearns and wife of Daniel Marshall. As a native of Connecticut, she may have first learned to exhort in the Separate churches of New England, although little is known about her youth. According to the Reverend Robert Semple, the first Baptist historian, Marshall was "a lady of good sense, singular piety, and surprising elocution" who frequently "melted a whole concourse into tears by her prayers and exhortations." Careful to shield her from criticism, Semple also assured his readers that she never "usurped authority over the other sex" by speaking.[99]

Margaret Meuse Clay of Virginia also gained a reputation as an unusually gifted speaker. Like Marshall, Clay enjoyed the support and encouragement of her family, who appear to have been deeply committed to the Baptist cause.

Because she was so renowned for her piety, ministers often suggested she lead public prayers. According to her descendants, her exhorting caused so much controversy that she was ordered to appear in court on the charge of unlicensed preaching. With eleven other Baptists, all male, Clay was sentenced to a public whipping, but an anonymous man stepped forward to pay her fine at the last minute, sparing her both pain and humiliation.[100]

Although most female exhorters seem to have been white, a few black women may have spoken in religious meetings as well. Under the preaching of clergymen such as George Whitefield, who prided themselves on their ministry to the poor and oppressed, large numbers of slaves and free blacks began to convert to Christianity. Unfortunately, there are very few eighteenth-century accounts of black women exhorting or testifying on their plantations, and it is possible that ministers may have been reluctant to give them the same gospel liberty as white women. Nevertheless, later generations of slaves passed down stories about their grandmothers and great-grandmothers praying aloud or witnessing during church services. "My grandmother was a powerful Christian woman, and she did love to sing and shout," one woman testified. "Grandma would git to shouting so loud she would make so much fuss nobody in the church could hear the preacher."[101] Perhaps large numbers of slave women did not exhort until the nineteenth century, but there are tantalizing clues that they refused to keep silence even before the American Revolution.

Whatever restrictions the Separate Baptists may have imposed on black women, it is clear that they gave white women greater religious freedom than almost any other church in colonial America. Besides allowing white women to speak publicly, they created independent leadership positions for them—an experiment that made them more radical than the New England Separates. Modeling themselves on the early churches described in the Bible, they appointed women as both deaconesses and eldresses. When Morgan Edwards, a Baptist minister, traveled through Virginia, North Carolina, and South Carolina in 1771 and 1772, he found deaconesses in forty church branches, and eldresses in six. Deaconesses cared for "the sick, miserable, and distressed poor," while eldresses served as female "pastors" counseling women converts. According to Edwards, the office of eldress "consists in praying, and teaching at their [women's] separate assemblies; presiding there for maintenance of rules and government; consulting with the sisters about matters of the church which concern them, and representing their sense thereof to the elders; attending at the unction of sick sisters; and at the baptism of women, that all may be done orderly."[102] Although eldresses and deaconesses could not speak publicly, they were recognized as spiritual leaders by their congregations, and like male elders and deacons, they were set apart in a special church ceremony.

The Separate Baptists were the only Christians in the South who permitted women to exhort. As dissenters from the Anglican establishment, they were part of the informal rather than formal public, and like their counterparts in the North, they argued that women should be as free to raise their voices in churches as they were in social gatherings. Of course, they never argued that women should "rule," and they never questioned whether women were naturally inferior to men. However, because they did not view their churches as microcosms of the state, they did not fear that female exhorting would undermine political order.

Beyond the issue of institutional identity, the Separate Baptists' support for female exhorting also grew out of the unique culture of southern evangelicalism. At the same time as the hierarchy of New England culture was eroding under the pressures of secularization and voluntarism, the South was becoming even more patriarchal. Although slavery also existed in the North, it was especially entrenched in the South, where its influence permeated every facet of life, including the government, the economy, the family, and the church. A small group of wealthy, slaveholding planters dominated both colonial assemblies and church vestries, and in the interest of preserving Christian order, they demanded that blacks accept their subordination to whites, women to their fathers and husbands, and farmers to the gentry. Although there were many conflicts bubbling underneath the surface of southern society, planters had virtually succeeded in creating the world of mutual obligation that many nostalgic clergymen in the North claimed to want: it was a communal, well-ordered society in which everyone knew his or her place.[103]

Rejecting this traditional world of deference and hierarchy, the Separate Baptists of the South longed for a more egalitarian community. In many ways they were far more radical than New Lights in the North, whose challenges to established authority were often more inadvertent than deliberate. The Separate Baptists' areas of strength lay in the backcountry, where lower-class whites and black slaves embraced the revivals as the means for both religious fulfillment and social protest. Much more than northern New Lights, who had appealed to people of all social classes, they tended to attract the poor and dispossessed. Even the preachers, according to the Reverend Robert Semple, were "without learning, without patronage, generally very poor, very plain in their dress, unrefined in their manners, and awkward in their address." Countercultural and egalitarian, the Separate Baptists implicitly set themselves apart from the Anglican gentry (who were notorious for "convivial excess") by their simple dress, strict sobriety, and emotional worship services. Besides resurrecting older customs that Anglicans found scandalous, such as foot washing, laying on of hands, and the kiss of charity, they took the bold step of allowing women, slaves, and lay men to exhort.[104]

More "respectable" ministers objected to all of these innovations, particularly the practice of allowing women and slaves to speak publicly. Drawing on stereotypes of "feminine" licentiousness, they accused female exhorters of sexual as well as religious deviance. According to Charles Woodmason, an Anglican itinerant, one female Baptist who claimed to have received "extraordinary Illuminations, Visions, and Communications" was actually a promiscuous woman who had lost control of her passions. "It was very true that she was visited in the Night, and that the Apparation did jump down upon her Bed . . . and that it came to her all on Fire. Yes! But it was in the Fire of Lust," he wrote. The "Angel," he mocked, was actually an ignorant Baptist preacher, her illicit lover.[105]

Because of the Separates' support of female exhorting, even the Baptists declined to "hold fellowship" with them. In a slave-based culture where hierarchy and deference were all-important, they feared that any tolerance of "insubordination," even in the informal public of dissenting churches, might undermine political order. In 1765 the Philadelphia Association resolved that the Bible "excludes all women whomsoever from all degrees of teaching, ruling, governing, dictating, and leading in the Church of God," and in 1785 the Kehukee Baptist Association in North Carolina voted that women could not speak in the church in discipline cases "unless called upon, or where it respects their own communion." One Baptist minister even refused to assist Shubal Stearns in the ordination of Daniel Marshall because the Separates were "a disorderly set, suffering women to pray in public."[106]

Harassed and persecuted by both the Anglican establishment and their fellow Baptists, the Separates eventually followed the example of their northern counterparts by renouncing their support for female exhorting. The revivals subsided during the American Revolution, and in 1787, after the creation of the new republic, the Separates merged with the Baptists, forsaking their old customs for greater respectability and acceptance.[107] Vesting the authority of the church in men alone, they not only did away with the positions of deaconesses and eldresses, but forbade women to exhort or preach in public.

In a pattern that would appear over and over again in American history, evangelical women lost their public voice as a struggling, marginal sect matured into a prosperous denomination with all of the trappings of respectability, including a well-educated male clergy. Sects, as sociologists have defined them, tend to be small and countercultural, and they often place more value on lay inspiration than clerical education. In contrast, denominations are larger and more tightly organized, and they demand a learned clergy. As the Baptists grew more popular, they traded their sectarian roots for denominational power. Their ministers had become "much more correct in their manner of preaching," the Reverend Robert Semple commented. "A great many odd tones, disgusting whoops and awkward gestures, were disused: In their manner also, they had more of sound sense and strong reasoning. Their zeal was less mixed with enthusiasm, and their piety became more rational." The Reverend David Benedict made an even more telling observation. "In former times," Benedict commented, the Baptists had "decidedly approved of females taking a part in social religious meetings." By 1813, however, the year that he published his *General History of the Baptist Denomination*, Baptists had long been "as decidedly opposed to anything of the kind, as any of the pedobaptist churches." In conclusion, he observed, "This restraint on the freedom of females, right or wrong, is evidently on the increase."[108]

Benedict's words proved to be prophetic. In the nineteenth century, even the most radical southern evangelicals would never be as tolerant of female preaching or exhorting as their peers in the North. Women's subordination in the churches was important not only in itself, but as a symbol of the hierarchical ordering of southern culture as a whole. If white women were given the liberty to speak publicly, rejecting their subordinate position on the grounds that they were obeying God, then slave men and women might be tempted to do the same. By the end of the eighteenth century, the revolutionary experiment of the Separate Baptists had ended, and throughout the South, as in the North, women were once again instructed to keep silence in the churches.

Unfortunately, none of the women who had exhorted during the revivals, not even the flamboyant Bathsheba Kingsley, would be remembered by future generations of evangelicals. Since none of them published memoirs or defenses of female exhorting, they left behind little historical evidence of their existence. Clergymen briefly mentioned these women in their revival accounts, but usually only to condemn them, not memorialize them. Even the Separates eventually tried to forget the visionaries whom they had once defended. Even though female exhorters had hoped to forge a new tradition of women's ministry, they did not bring about any lasting change within their churches. Perhaps their stories continued to circulate in oral form, but by the end of the eighteenth century, they had virtually disappeared from the written records of history. As a result, future generations of evangelical women, bereft of their past, would have to invent new justifications for women's religious leadership.

Bathsheba Kingsley never lived to hear the news of the revivals in the South or the stories of women such as Margaret Meuse Clay and Martha Stearns Marshall. Nor did she live long enough to witness the growing restrictions on lay evangelism in the late eighteenth century. She died in 1748, only five years after Jonathan Edwards and the ecclesiastical council had met to discuss her visionary revelations. Little is known about her life during her last years, but it is clear that she did not take the council's advice to "keep chiefly at home." Despite clerical warnings, she continued to ride from town to town as a traveling evangelist, and when she refused to repent, her church barred her from receiving the Lord's Supper. Like many of the other women who cried out, prayed aloud, and exhorted during the revivals, she believed she had been so caught up by God that she had overcome the limitations of her "femininity." For a few brief years during the eighteenth century, she and other evangelical women claimed to have transcended their gender in union with the divine.[109] Heartfelt religious experience, not "masculinity" or a college education, was the most important qualification for ministry.

This vision of a more egalitarian church was increasingly contested during the upheavals of the American Revolution. The revivals of the Great Awakening had temporarily subverted the restrictions on women's religious speech, but by the mid-1750s in the North and the 1770s in the South, few evangelical women could find ministers who were willing to let them improve their gifts. Nevertheless, women continued to demand a public religious voice in the late eighteenth century and beyond. As we will see, the few women who dared to preach in Revolutionary America took Bathsheba Kingsley's language of self-transcendence to an extreme, but they were linked to her by a deeper affinity. Long after the revivals had ended, they continued to cherish her dream of a world where there would be "neither male nor female" in the sight of God.

2

Women in the Wilderness

Female Religious Leadership in the Age of Revolution

And there appeared a great wonder in heaven; a woman clothed with the sun, and the moon under her feet, and upon her head a crown of twelve stars: And she being with child cried, travailing in birth, and pained to be delivered.... And she brought forth a man child, who was to rule all nations with a rod of iron: and her child was caught up unto God, and to his throne. And the woman fled into the wilderness, where she hath a place prepared of God, that they should feed her there a thousand two hundred and three score days.—Revelation 12:1–6

In 1776, as America stood on the brink of revolution, only a few radical sects still preserved a vision of women's public evangelism. In Revolutionary America, only the Quakers, Shakers, Universal Friends, and a few Come-Outers on the New England frontier allowed women to witness or exhort, and with the exception of the Quakers, they were as ambivalent about women's public speech as the New Lights and Separates had been. In the new American republic, the home of "life, liberty, and the pursuit of happiness," would women as well as men have the right to preach the gospel?

Two charismatic women in Revolutionary America, Ann Lee and Jemima Wilkinson, struggled to answer this question while traveling across the Northeast to herald the near approach of the kingdom of God. In 1776, as Thomas Jefferson put the finishing touches on the Declaration of Independence, Ann

Philip Dawes, *A Society of Patriotic Ladies* (1775). Dawes, a British cartoonist, took a dim view of American women's political activism. After the women of Edenton, North Carolina, drafted a petition to boycott tea, he depicted them as homely, "masculine" women who neglected their children. A forgotten child sits under the table, licked by a dog who urinates on the floor. The most attractive woman in the cartoon, who wears a low-cut dress, does not appear to be thinking for herself, but takes directions from the man at her elbow. Courtesy of the Library of Congress.

Lee and a small group of followers arrived in Niskeyuna, New York, near Albany, with the dream of founding a new millennial church. In the same year, Jemima Wilkinson, a farmer's daughter from Rhode Island, woke up from an illness to proclaim her "resurrection" as the "Publick Universal Friend." There is no evidence that the two women ever met, but in the 1770s and 1780s, each claimed to be the apocalyptic woman in the wilderness who had been sent by God to prepare for the millennium. As the American republic was born, they wrestled with the limitations of female religious authority while trying to solve the "problem" of their sex. Like all of the other women who felt called to preach during the Age of Revolution, they soon discovered that religious leadership, like citizenship, was still the privilege of men.

Women's Unfinished Revolution

The men and women who lived through the American Revolution witnessed one of the single greatest moments of transformation in American history. In comparison to the brutal revolutions that convulsed France in 1789 or Russia in 1905 and 1917, the American Revolution may seem more like a political battle over constitutional authority, a skirmish over taxation without representation, than a true social or cultural revolution. Despite the Stamp Act riots, the mobs of Sons of Liberty, and the ravages of war, the American Revolution was remarkably orderly, civilized, even intellectual. In the witty words of historian Gordon S. Wood, men such as George Washington, Thomas Jefferson, and John Adams are poor candidates for wild-eyed revolutionaries: "They seem too stuffy, too solemn, too cautious, too much the gentlemen. We cannot quite conceive of revolutionaries in powdered hair and knee breeches." Yet even though there was no bloody Reign of Terror, no peasant uprising, no redistribution of wealth, the American Revolution was a *radical* revolution—perhaps "as radical and as revolutionary as any in history."[1] The colonial world of aristocratic privilege and social hierarchy was forever shattered by its collision with republican ideology. Seemingly overnight, America had become a nation that celebrated the inalienable rights and responsibilities of ordinary people, a democracy in which all property-owning men—whether farmers, artisans, merchants, or common laborers—were free and equal in the eyes of the law. "We hold these truths to be self-evident," declared Thomas Jefferson, "that all men are created equal; that they are endowed by their Creator with certain unalienable rights; that among these, are life, liberty, and the pursuit of happiness."

Yet there was also a harsher truth that Jefferson left unspoken but which was also self-evident. In Revolutionary America, only white men were created equal. White women, slaves, and Native Americans were all excluded from the privileges of citizenship in the new republic. Building on a long tradition of western thought, the Founding Fathers echoed such worthies as Plato, Aristotle, Hobbes, and Locke by relegating women to the world of domesticity and sentiment, a world of private rather than public speech.[2] Faced with the task of creating one nation out of thirteen separate colonies, they tried to unify all white men in a single American identity by defining citizenship against the subordinate position of women and slaves. "What then is the American, this new man?" asked Crèvecouer in 1782. At least one answer was embedded in the very phrasing of his question. The new American was a man, and as one historian has noted, "His reason, independence, bravery, moderation, productivity, and fiscal responsibility were demarcated against the other, the irrational, extravagant, passionate, seductive, dependent woman." Despite the egalitarian rhetoric of the Revolution, gender, like race, was central to the construction of the American republic. A true republic, John Adams wrote, would be an exemplar of "all great, manly, and warlike virtues."[3]

In the long term, the Revolution inspired women to demand a voice in the political as well as domestic life of the republic—a demand that still echoes in the corridors of government today—but in its immediate effects, it was far more revolutionary for white men than for women. Later feminist reformers would borrow the language of the Declaration of Independence to declare women's full equality to men, but in the late eighteenth century, only a few radical voices questioned the hierarchy of sex. When Abigail Adams threatened her husband John that women "are determined to foment a Rebelion, and will not hold ourselves bound by any Laws in which we have no voice, or Representation," she was speaking at least partly in jest. There was no female "rebellion" during the Revolutionary War, no organized movement for women's rights. Despite a few small gains, including the liberalization of divorce laws, women were still as legally, economically, and politically subordinate as they had been before. Even coverture persisted: any money that a woman earned, or any land that she inherited, automatically became her husband's property. Even though coverture undermined republican ideals by denying women the right to act as free individuals, the Founding Fathers could not imagine a country where they would share equal power with their sisters and mothers.[4]

This does not mean that women were not active participants in the political debates that took place in Revolutionary America. On the contrary, they invested their traditional household duties with political significance by refusing to buy British goods, especially tea and clothing. Symbolizing their devotion to the patriot cause, women wore homespun dresses and signed petitions promising to boycott tea. Most radically, they also surged into the streets to demonstrate against increased taxes or to tar and feather Loyalist politicians. Even though they could not vote in elections, they believed their support was crucial to the creation of a new republic.[5]

Nevertheless, gender loomed as an even greater "problem" for women during the American Revolution than it had before the war. Even though Americans had rebelled against the king, their metaphorical father, they still insisted that women must submit to male authority. At the same time as republican leaders invited the sons of loyalists to proclaim their filial independence and join the patriot cause, they ordered women to remain faithful to fathers and husbands no matter how traitorous their political sympathies. In the words of historian Linda Kerber, "Even for republican idealogues, it remained unnatural for daughters to reject familial direction, unnatural for women to reject their husbands." Unlike men, women were rarely recognized as individuals who were free to make their own moral decisions or form their own political opinions. First and foremost, they owed their allegiance to their husbands and fathers, not to the republic.[6]

Influenced by the political theories of John Locke and other Enlightenment philosophers, Revolutionary Americans increasingly imagined the public as a male realm that was completely separate from the private world of women and the family. In the seventeenth and early eighteenth centuries, the family had been perceived as a little commonwealth that was inextricably linked to the state, but by the 1760s and 1770s (and perhaps even earlier), it no longer held the same political significance. According to Locke, the power of the government did not flow from the hierarchical ordering of the family, but from the mutual consent of property-owning men. By the middle of the nineteenth century, this contractual model of the state would be used to challenge men's exclusive claim to citizenship, but its immediate effect was more ambiguous. Under the earlier conception of power, women had wielded authority in the informal public of community life because of their influence within the family, but under the Lockean system, the arenas of public and private became even more rigid, and more distinct. Because they had no right to own property or make contracts, women were absolutely excluded from the public sphere.[7]

This political transformation was connected to underlying changes in the organization of the family. In the colonial period, men and women had worked side by side in semisubsistent households, but in the late eighteenth century, their spheres became increasingly differentiated: men were expected to make their living in the competitive world of the marketplace while women took care of their children in the sheltered environment of the home. In reality, of course, many lower-class white women went to work for wages, and poor white and slave women toiled in the fields with their husbands and brothers. Nevertheless, the new middle-class emphasis on women's natural domesticity had a profound effect on cultural perceptions of both womanhood and manhood. Private women could have no place in the world of public men.[8]

The American Revolution could have been even more revolutionary if it had shattered the dichotomy between public and private, male and female, but those divisions persisted into the nineteenth century and beyond. Instead of leveling the hierarchy of sex, the Revolutionary cry that "all men are equated equal" only made women more acutely aware of their secondary status to men. Under the monarchical government of colonial America, both men and women had occupied a subordinate position in relationship to the king, but in the new republic, only white men had the potential to be full citizens. White women and other "subordinates," such as slaves and children, were perceived as too irrational to be trusted in the public world of politics.[9]

The women who lived through the 1770s and 1780s were poised between two competing ideologies of femininity. The passionate, disorderly, licentious woman of the seventeenth-century imagination had not yet been replaced by the passionless, virtuous, pure woman of the nineteenth. It is difficult to put a precise date on such a sweeping ideological transformation, but in the 1770s, many republicans still equated femininity with corruption and luxury. Echoing the language of his seventeenth-century forebears, Thomas Jefferson argued that women had to be excluded from the body politic because they would cause a "depravation of morals" if they were allowed to "mix promiscuously in the public meetings of men." "Virtu," the "male" quality of public spirit, had not yet become "virtue," the "female" quality of morality. Although middle-class women politicized their traditional domestic activities by boycotting

British goods and sewing homespun clothes, and working-class women staged riotous demonstrations in the streets, they were still struggling to carve out a meaningful role for themselves in the new republic. By the turn of the century, women had forged a new and powerful identity to justify their participation in civic culture, but during the 1770s and 1780s, the "republican mother," watchful guardian of public virtue and private morality, was still being born.[10]

The Limitations of Women's Religious Leadership in Revolutionary America

The restrictions on women's public roles in Revolutionary America extended beyond the halls of the Constitutional Convention and into the pulpits and pews of Protestant churches. As in the colonial period, churches gave women one of their few opportunities for public self-expression, but those opportunities were much narrower than they had been during the revivals of the Awakening. Instead of allowing women to make public professions of faith or exhort in public, most churches urged them to exert their influence through more private means: praying with their husbands, reading pious books to their children, and conversing about religion with other women. Behind such advice lurked the implicit threat of official church discipline or even excommunication. In 1812 Polly Hatheway was excommunicated by the Congregational Church in Berkeley, Massachusetts, for "taking part in a public religious meeting, praying, exhorting, &c." Instead of being allowed to improve her gifts, she was denounced as a "jezebel."[11]

Despite lingering memories of the outspoken visionaries who had exhorted during the revivals of the 1740s, very few women in established churches ever dared to speak publicly. Although these women were never as submissive as their clergymen instructed them to be, they were still reluctant, perhaps even afraid, to demand the power of platform or pulpit. Even Sarah Osborn, the leader of an extraordinary religious revival in Newport, Rhode Island, never dared to call herself a preacher even though she seems to have been more popular than any minister in the town. Osborn had hosted a women's prayer group in Newport for over twenty years, but in 1766, hundreds of white men, white women, children, and slaves began flocking to her house every night for prayer meetings and religious conversation. At the height of the revival, as many as 350 people crowded through her doors every week.[12] Since Osborn was an educated, respected member of the Congregational Church, her ministers generally approved of her meetings, especially those for women, girls, and young boys, but they were suspicious of her evangelism to adult men. Did she overstep the boundaries of female propriety by "teaching" them? Had she become a female preacher?

In letters to the Reverend Joseph Fish, her closest spiritual advisor, Osborn insisted that she had not become an "instructor" to men. When she met with white men, she rarely spoke unless they "condescend[ed] to direct part of the conversation to me," and in her meetings with black men, she simply talked, sang, or read to them. Since she could not read the Bible to slaves without also teaching them how to interpret it, Osborn knew that her missions came perilously close to preaching. Yet she repeatedly denied that she had any pretensions to clerical authority, and in case the strategy of denial did not work, she tried to drown Fish's objections in a flood of rationalizations: the slaves had only come to her because no one else would teach them; they were merely "children" ("tho for Stature men and women") who had sought guidance from her as a spiritual mother; they had been so changed by the gospel that they were no longer "unwilling to serve and saucy," but "diligent and condescending."[13] Osborn marshaled every possible argument to her defense except the one that she knew would most alarm her ministers. Whether out of true conviction or subterfuge, she never claimed the right to preach or teach in public.

As Osborn's example illustrates, it was difficult, though not impossible, for women in established churches to rise to positions of unofficial leadership. Those who were shrewd, intelligent, and yet still "womanly" could find ways to make their voices heard, but only through subtle manipulation. For example, when Osborn and the members of her female prayer group decided that Samuel Hopkins should be ordained as their new minister, they relied on their "feminine" powers of persuasion to overcome male opposition. Barred from voting in church elections, they wheedled, cajoled, and finally shed tears in order to convince male members to support their beloved Hopkins. Despite their efforts, the church council narrowly rejected him on the first vote, but they changed their minds after listening, or trying to listen, to his farewell sermon: his words were barely audible over the anguished sobs of his female supporters.[14] Even though these women had no political power in their church, they had learned how to convert their "feminine" weakness into a source of strength. Their tears, not their votes, brought Hopkins to Newport.

Of all the sects and denominations in Revolutionary America, only the Quakers fully recognized women's right to speak in public.[15] By 1800, almost half of the Quaker ministers in the Philadelphia Yearly Meeting were female.[16] Besides the countless numbers of women who witnessed during local meetings, there were also dozens who traveled as itinerant ministers in both America and abroad. Between 1700 and 1800, at least forty-two American women crossed the ocean to visit Quaker meetings in Britain, often leaving their families for months or even years at a time. (Charity Cook, a Public Friend from North Carolina, once left her husband and children for more than five years while she traveled through America, Great Britain, and Germany.)[17] Of course, many Quaker women still faced subtle (and not so subtle) forms of prejudice, and they often had to struggle to be recognized as the true equals of Quaker men.[18] Nevertheless, in comparison to women in other denominations, they enjoyed unprecedented sexual equality.

By the late eighteenth century, the Quakers had matured from a radical sect into a prosperous, middle-class, and politically powerful denomination. Gone were the radical practices that had so offended the New England Puritans: going naked as a sign or wearing nothing but sackcloth and ashes, quaking in the ecstasy of the spirit, disrupting church services by screeching in the aisles. In a startling reversal of their early history, the Quakers had grown as worldly as the churches they had once denounced. By the early 1700s in Philadelphia, a new Quaker aristocracy of merchants and politicians had won control of the government while growing rich from trading grain and flour to the West Indies. After Pennsylvania declared war against the Delaware Indians in 1756, most Quakers chose to renounce officeholding rather than compromise their peace testimony, but even after the "reformation" of 1756–58, they remained a sober, industrious people little given to the extremes of religious radicalism. The sons and grandsons of the downtrodden, lower-class farmers who had barely eked out a living in northwestern England became legendary for their business acumen in America. In 1769 Quakers were only one-seventh of the Philadelphia population, but they made up more than half of the people who paid taxes of more than one hundred pounds.[19]

Affluence brought respectability, and eighteenth-century Quaker female ministers were far less contentious and disorderly than their foremothers had been. Many were from prominent Quaker families, and even those who were poor sometimes married merchant husbands. (In contrast, later evangelical female preachers tended to be downwardly rather than upwardly mobile.) Admittedly, they were sometimes eccentric: Charity Cook attracted stares and whispers when she sauntered through the streets of London smoking a pipe. They could also be cutting in their rebukes to sinners. Patience Brayton, despite her mild demeanor (and her name), angrily reprimanded a man for preventing his wife from attending Quaker meeting.[20] But the female Friends of the Revolutionary era were middle-class reformers, not martyrs, and they witnessed in meetinghouses rather than screaming in the streets. Even as they provided a model of female religious leadership for other, more radical women to emulate, they embraced an inward, contemplative spirituality that set them apart from the zealous Come-Outers in the New England backcountry.[21]

The most militant religious radicals in Revolutionary America did not live in Quaker Philadelphia, but on the frontiers of northern New England, where small, charismatic sects competed with one another for converts.[22] Although membership in Protestant mainline churches declined during the Revolutionary era, perhaps because of the distractions of war and nation-building, radical evangelicalism flourished in the impoverished and isolated towns of northern New England.[23] In the 1750s and 1760s, many of the poorest Separates had moved to the frontier to avoid paying taxes to the Congregational establishment, and in the crucible of war, they mixed their visionary folk religion with the republican faith in individual equality. As struggling farmers, lumberers, and fishermen, they dreamed of a new, democratic republic in which they would finally win economic security and respect for their labor, a dream that was sorely tested by the crises of the 1780s and 1790s: the collapse of the Confederation, Shays's Rebellion, the Whiskey Rebellion, rampant inflation. Others were pacifists who opposed the Revolution, but they still imbibed its egalitarian, antiauthoritarian spirit: they demanded a *spiritual* revolution that would do away with creeds, clergies, and hierarchies.[24]

For many of these sects, the Revolution loomed as an ominous portent of a far greater cataclysm. To evangelicals who were well versed in the frightening, apocalyptic prophecies of the book of Revelation, the victory over the British and the creation of the republic seemed far too momentous to belong to merely human history. These men and women lived each day in the dizzying expectation that they were approaching the last days before the day of judgment, the last minutes or hours before the second coming of Christ. As one man later explained, "I entertained an opinion, that the millennium was near at hand, and that I should live to see it."[25] Although many mainline churches were also suffused by millennial expectations, radical sectarians were *pre*millennialists rather than *post*millennialists: they envisioned a violent, fiery apocalypse instead of a thousand-year reign of peace before Christ's return. Only a faithful remnant would be spared the wrathful vengeance of God's sword.

Certain that they were living in the last days, Revolutionary sects such as the Irelandites and the Merry Dancers placed their faith in the guidance of the Holy Spirit rather than the law of the state, a faith that took them perilously close to antinomianism. To their critics, who took a dim view of their zeal, they desired nothing less than the destruction of all authority itself. In Sanford, Maine, the so-called Merry Dancers scandalized their neighbors by boisterously disrupting Congregational worship, "drinking to excess," and shrieking "Woe! Woe! Woe!" at the top of their lungs, a practice they called "hooting the devil." And in nearby Gorham, a group of Come-Outers accused their minister of "preaching the doctrine of the devil instead of Christ" before driving him out of the church by brandishing axes and clubs. With no established minister to lead them, they began holding ecstatic meetings that featured "Exhortations of the most exciting nature, singing, dancing, and whirling." Even more shocking, other sectarians experimented with celibacy and free love (also known as spiritual wifery) or claimed to be perfect and immortal. For example, Shadrach Ireland, a pipefitter from Charlestown, Massachusetts, promised that those who attained true spiritual perfection would never die.[26]

New England women played a prominent role in many of these millennial, perfectionist sects. For example, among Gorham's Come-Outers, worship services were so unstructured and emotional that every convert, whether male or female, was encouraged to bear witness to the spirit. The leaders of the sect were lay men, but because they believed that the end of the world was imminent and Christ would soon return to earth, they suspended the normal restrictions on female testimony. In fulfillment of Joel's promise that "your sons and daughters shall prophesy," women as well as men thundered out their "exhortations," and according to an early historian, many "fell into trances" where they "held communion with God."[27]

As had been true during the revivals of the Great Awakening, female exhorting in Revolutionary America was linked to religious dissent. The only churches who allowed women to speak publicly were small, socially marginal sects who were not officially connected to the state. In contrast to the established churches, who saw themselves as virtually a branch of the government, sects such as the Come-Outers and the Merry Dancers stood between the "masculine" sphere of the government and the "feminine" enclave of the family, and they encouraged women as well as men to help build more godly communities. Despite their belief in women's legal and political subordination to men, they saw no reason why the "weaker sex" could not make their voices heard in the informal public of the church.

Nevertheless, these sects never encouraged women to serve as preachers or leaders. Barred from the rights of republican citizenship, few women dared to demand pulpits of their own. Sarah Prentice, the wife of Solomon Prentice, a New Light minister, scandalized her family by becoming a devoted follower of Shadrach Ireland, but even though she used her considerable influence to convert her friends to his gospel of immortality and perfectionism, she rarely preached in public—this despite her reputation as "a genius who knew most of the Bible by heart" who could "preach as good a sermon as any man."[28] Even though she was supposedly as charismatic as Ireland, who achieved no small fame during his days at his Square House, she was largely invisible in the public life of the sect.

In Revolutionary America, only Ann Lee and Jemima Wilkinson emerged as true religious leaders who achieved more than local renown. By the time Lee died in 1784, she had laid the foundation for a new religious movement, and under the subsequent leadership of Joseph Meacham and Lucy Wright, the Shakers created the most enduring utopian experiment in American history. By the 1840s, there were as many as 6,000 Shakers in eighteen separate villages from Ohio to Maine. Similarly, Jemima Wilkinson, the leader of the Universal Friends, preached to overflowing crowds in Pennsylvania and Rhode Island before founding her own religious community, "New Jerusalem," in the wilds of Yates County, New York, in 1790. According to the federal census, at its founding the community numbered an impressive 260 members.[29]

Both of these women gave voice to a tradition of female radicalism that had been suppressed by other sects, especially by the Separates, Quakers, and Baptists. Most of Ann Lee's converts, as Ezra Stiles noted, came "fr[om] the Rh[ode] Isl[an]d & Narraganset Baptists called there New Lights & Separates." Similarly, Wilkinson attracted radical Quakers who believed that the reformation of 1756–58 had not gone far enough. At least one of her female converts, Mehitable Smith, protested that the Quakers had unduly restricted her freedom to speak, perhaps by refusing to give her a "minute" (a license) recommending her as a Public Friend. Denouncing such "Bigottry" as intolerable, Wilkinson and her followers complained that the Quakers had lost their spiritual light in their haste to create formal institutional structures.[30] Instead of the quietism of Quaker merchants and farmers, they longed to recapture the visionary enthusiasm of the seventeenth-century martyrs.

Ann Lee and Jemima Wilkinson were the two most revolutionary female preachers in the Age of Revolution. Unlike Sarah Osborn and other mainline women, they founded their own sects instead of trying to convince the established churches to accept female evangelism. Unlike Sarah Prentice, they refused to lend their talents to the service of a charismatic male leader. And unlike Quaker women, they accepted no institutional checks on their authority at all, not even the relatively mild oversight of the monthly meeting. Independent, "manly" women, they seemed to stand dangerously beyond men's authority over the family or church, especially since both were celibate. Such self-reliance was praised as a virtue in men, but it seemed so unnatural in women that some of their listeners wondered whether they truly were women at all. Ann Lee was once forcibly stripped of her clothing by a group of men who thought she was a British spy, and Jemima Wilkinson confounded spectators who wondered whether her flowing, clerical gowns disguised a male or female body.

Yet even though Lee and Wilkinson rose to power as the leaders of their own sects, a privilege usually reserved for men, they were rarely as confident as they appeared on the surface. Like all of the other women in the late eighteenth century who struggled with the limitations of female religious authority, they still regarded their sex as a problem that had to be overcome. In the 1740s and 1750s, evangelical women such as Sarah Edwards had imagined being swallowed up by God, but Lee and Wilkinson took their denial of gender to an even greater extreme. Lee tried to suppress all vestiges of her "carnal" female body by adopting a strict code of celibacy, and Wilkinson claimed that her female self had died and been replaced with the gender-neutral Public Universal Friend. Both women succeeded in founding their own sects, but in the Age of Revolution, the illustrious age of freedom and equality, neither could imagine being a religious leader while still being a woman.

Jemima Wilkinson, the Public Universal Friend

In the fall of 1782, at the same time as female Come-Outers were filling frontier meetinghouses with their rustic exhortations, Jemima Wilkinson, a farmer's daughter from Rhode Island, arrived in the urban port of Philadelphia to the buzz of scandal. She "has occasioned much talk in this City," one woman noted in her diary.[31] It was Wilkinson's first trip to Philadelphia, but after almost six years of traveling as an itinerant preacher through Rhode Island and Connecticut, she had begun her climb to fame as one of the most notorious women in America. The rumors and questions were legion: Did she claim to be the second incarnation of Christ? Did she perform miracles? And did she really dress in men's clothing? The city's most prominent resident, Benjamin Franklin, was in London and Paris negotiating a peace treaty with the British, but scores of other Philadelphians devoted their attention to a more sensational event at home: the trustees of the Methodist Episcopal Church had decided that Wilkinson, the self-proclaimed Public Universal Friend, could preach from their pulpit.[32]

Crowds of curious spectators rushed to see and hear the infamous female preacher in person. At the Methodist meetinghouse, where she delivered a sermon on "the truths of the gospel of Jesus Christ," so many people pushed their way into the pews that many never even managed to catch a glimpse of her. The Marquis de Chastellux, visiting from France, later complained that "the crowd was so great, and, what is very uncommon in America, so turbulent, that it was impossible to get near the place of worship." Wilkinson knew that many in her audience hoped for entertainment rather than religious instruction, but with tears in her eyes, she chided them to repent and seek salvation. "Do not seek me, do not listen to me, unless you are touched by grace," she cried. "But if you are disposed to enter into the way of salvation, if my discourses have softened your hearts, if I can snatch a single one of you from the danger which he runs, I have not traveled too long a road in seeking it."[33]

In Philadelphia, like everywhere else she traveled, Wilkinson was greeted with a mixture of praise and derision. Although she added several new converts to her band of Universal Friends, including David Wagener, who became one of her most stalwart supporters, she also fended off insults about the immorality of female preaching. In a rare episode of violence, an "unruly company" assembled in front of the house where she was staying and attacked it with stones and brickbats. According to a Philadelphia magazine, she and her followers huddled inside with the doors and windows locked, "there being apprehension of personal insults from the liberties taken by the boys." Although Wilkinson escaped unharmed, and she never again faced the threat of mob violence, the commotion symbolized the animosity she often faced as a woman in the pulpit. Many of the men and women who heard her speak, even those who regarded her as deluded, conceded her "irreproachable" morals, but others denounced her as an "assuming, presumptuous woman" gone out of her place.[34]

In response to her enemies, Wilkinson proclaimed that God himself had inspired her to preach. As visionary women have done throughout Christian history, from the martyred female saints of medieval Europe to the radical Separates of the Great Awakening, she compensated for her exclusion from the "masculine" authority of ordination by claiming the "feminine" authority of divine revelation. In 1783, for example, she claimed to have seen a vision of "holy Angels" and "the Incarnate Son of God," and in 1789 she had a prophetic dream that God was preparing for the day of judgment. As she confided to Sarah Richards, she had seen a "learge pair of Scales let down to the earth, the cord held out of sight by an Invisible hand . . . To way [weigh] all the inhabitants of the Earth, all that the Lord calls into Judgment!"[35] Even though Wilkinson was a woman, and not even an educated woman at that, she insisted that she was not an *ordinary* woman: she was a prophet sent by God.

Wilkinson's most powerful defense of her right to preach, the defense that set her apart from all the other female visionaries in eighteenth-century America, was her extraordinary insistence that she had died and been resurrected as a spirit sent by God. Indeed, she claimed that in October of 1776, after a bout with typhus, Jemima Wilkinson had died and gone to heaven, but her body had been resurrected as the "tabernacle" for a perfect and sinless spirit: the Public Universal Friend. In her own words, as she recorded on a sheet that she tucked into her Bible, "On the fourth Day of the 10th. Month, on the Seventh Day of the weak, at night, a certain young-woman, known by the name of Jemima Wilkinson was seiz'd with this mortal disease. And on the 2d. Day of her illness, was render'd almost incapable of helping herself.—And the fever continuing to increase until fifth Day of the Weak about midnight, She appear'd to meet the Shock of Death." Emphasizing her new identity as the Public Universal Friend, she wrote about herself in the detached voice of the third person, explaining that Jemima, who was hovering between life and death, had soared to heaven and seen a vision of "too Archangels decending from the east, with golden crowns upon there heads, clothed in long white Robes, down to the feet; Bringing a sealed Pardon from the living god; and putting their trumpets to their mouth, proclaimed saying, Room, Room, Room, in the many Mansions of eternal glory for Thee and for everyone." Echoing the rich, figurative language of the book of Revelation, she rejoiced that Jemima had been forgiven for all of her sins.[36]

In heaven, the angels told Jemima that God was preparing to send his spirit to earth "for a second time." Her soul would remain with them, but her body would stay on earth as the temple of God's redemptive "Spirit of Life":

> And the Angels said, The time is at hand, when God will lift up his hand, a second time, to recover the remnant of his People, whos day is not yet over; and the Angels said, The Spirit of Life from God, had descended to the earth, to warn a lost and guilty, perishing dying World, to flee from the wrath that is to come; and to give an Invitation to the lost Sheep of the house of Israel to come home; and was waiting to assume the Body which God had prepared, for the Spirit to dwell in. For it is written, I will raise up a Tabernacle unto David, saith the Lord, which is fallen, and close up the breaches thereof.

At the end of this vision, Jemima "dropt the dying flesh and yielded up the Ghost," and "the Spirit took full possession of the body it now animates." Because her soul had gone to heaven, she was no longer a "she," but a genderless spirit sent by God. Although her female body had been left on earth as the "tabernacle" for the Public Universal Friend, she was no longer Jemima Wilkinson.[37]

In some ways, Wilkinson's remarkable account of her "death" and "resurrection" echoed common evangelical beliefs, but in an exaggerated and distorted form. New Lights commonly described conversion as being born again, but Wilkinson swore that she had *literally* died and been resurrected. New Lights celebrated Paul's promise, "There is neither Jew nor Greek, there is neither bond nor free, there is neither male nor female: for ye are all one in Christ Jesus," but Wilkinson proclaimed that she had *literally* transcended the distinctions of sex. Many other men and women yearned to rid themselves of the sinfulness and corruption of their bodies by being swallowed up in union with God, but Wilkinson insisted that she had been *literally* swallowed up: her identity as a woman had been completely obliterated by her contact with the divine.

Wilkinson was deeply influenced by the most radical and visionary strain of evangelicalism in Revolutionary America. Even though she had been raised as a Quaker, she began worshiping with a group of zealous New Lights in Cumberland, Rhode Island, several months before her "fatal" fever. Because she never wrote about her life before her "death," little is known about her experiences as an evangelical, but one fact is certain: she chose to join a church with a long reputation for religious extremism. During the revivals of the 1740s and 1750s, the Cumberland New Lights had scandalized their neighbors by preaching perfectionism, immortalism, and free love. (In 1749 two of the culprits, Molly Bennett and Solomon Finney, insisted that they were "man and wife in the sight of the Lord" even though Molly was already married to another man.) By the 1770s, the church had grown more moderate, but Wilkinson seems to have imbibed its earlier spirit. Admittedly, she preached celibacy rather than free love, and she never claimed to be physically as well as spiritually immortal. But like the earlier radicals of Cumberland, she testified that she was utterly perfect and without sin.[38]

Even Wilkinson's most arresting claim, that God had sent her to redeem the world, connected her to other religious radicals of her time. When she explained that God had sent his spirit to earth "*a second time*, to recover the remnant of his People," she insinuated that she might be not only a visionary or a prophet, but the second coming of Christ. Wilkinson never explicitly identified herself as Christ in either her public sermons or her private letters, and after she died, one of her female followers insisted that she had never portrayed herself in such grandiose terms. "She disclaimed all pretensions to miraculous gifts," this woman wrote. "That she pretended to be superhuman or immortal in any other sense than as all the redeemed of the Lord are, is also incorrect."[39] Rather than a savior, Wilkinson seems to have viewed herself as the biblical woman of Revelation who had been sent to prepare for the kingdom of God on earth. "She seemed to have an allusion that she was the woman spoke of in the revelations, that was now fled into the wilderness," Abner Brownell commented.[40]

Yet whatever Wilkinson may have said (or not said) about herself, her closest disciples had ideas of their own. As their letters and journals attest, they sometimes approached her with a deference that bordered on veneration. For example, Sarah Richards recorded a dream in which Wilkinson, standing amidst the sound of "hallelujahs," is virtually indistinguishable from Christ: she arrays her followers in martial order, announces "the time is Come the time is Come," and then leads them into a victorious battle over Satan. "Smoke of a purple color," the color of the royal Christ, comes out of her mouth, and at the dream's end, she sits majestically on an "eminence" above the city and smiles in celebration of her victory.[41] Perhaps Richards thought of

Wilkinson as a prophet rather than a savior, but clearly she expected her to play a messianic role in the creation of God's kingdom on earth.

If Wilkinson herself ever claimed to be Christ, she had plenty of competition. In the 1790s, for example, a man named Nat Smith made the startling announcement that he was God. According to Ezra Stiles, "Nat Smith proceeded to assume & declare himself to be the Most High God and wore a cap with the word GOD inscribed on its front. His Great Chair was a Holy Chair & none but himself must sit in it." In contrast, Smith's contemporary, the pipefitter Shadrach Ireland, never wore a cap with the word "God" sewn on it, and he never sat on a holy throne, but by claiming to be perfect and immortal, he too hinted that he might be Christ. Even after he proved his humanity by passing away during an illness, his followers refused to give up faith: they stored his body in a pit of lime in their basement and awaited his resurrection. "Don't bury me," he said before his death, "for the Time is very Short. God is Coming to take the Church."[42]

What separated Wilkinson from Ireland, Nat Smith, and other radical sectarians was not her spiritual perfectionism or even her identification with Christ, but her insistence that she had transcended her physical sex. From the moment that Wilkinson woke up from her vision in 1776, she claimed to be neither male nor female, and she adamantly refused to answer to any name except the Public Universal Friend. When people taunted her by calling her Jemima, she pretended not to hear them or berated them for their disbelief. According to an oft-repeated story, she once rebuked a man named Day for his impertinent questions about whether or not she had ever been named Jemima Wilkinson. "Day! Day!" she threatened. "Thy day will soon be turned into night unless thee mends thy ways." In obedience to her wishes, her followers always called her the Public Universal Friend, or more informally, "dear friend," "heavenly friend," or "best friend," and they scrupulously avoided using any gendered pronouns to describe her—a decision that often led to tortuous syntax. When Sarah Richards recorded her dream of Wilkinson defeating the devil, she used the convoluted, pronoun-free language that passed for standard English among the Universal Friends. She "saw the Friend lift up the Friends' Eyes toward heaven," and after the "Friend" vanquished the devil in a fiery battle, "the Friend I left seated on an Eminence, and on the Friend's Countenance a Smile." Even in the pages of his private diary, Abner Brownell never once referred to Wilkinson as "she," but only as the "Friend,"

Portrait of Jemima Wilkinson by John L. D. Mathies (1816). Courtesy of the Village of Penn Yan, New York.

or "P.U.F." for short.[43] Her followers, like Wilkinson herself, believed that she had transcended the category of sex.

Wilkinson's resurrection as the Public Universal Friend obliterated not only her sex, but her sexuality. Because she viewed her body as the temple of God's spirit, she vowed to keep it pure, and she enjoined celibacy as the surest path to salvation. As she warned her followers, "If ye sow to the flesh, ye must, of the flesh, reap corruption; but if ye are so wise as to sow to the Spirit, ye will of the Spirit, reap life everlasting." In contrast to Ann Lee, however, who threatened endless torment to those who gratified their lusts, Wilkinson never required her followers to be celibate, and despite the rumors spread by her enemies, she never forcibly separated husbands and wives. Several of her closest female followers, known as the "faithful sisterhood," imitated her life of chastity, but many other men and women chose to marry and have children without any fear of punishment. In 1776, shortly before her illness and resurrection, her own sister, Patience, had given birth to a child out of wedlock, and the scandal may have increased both her fear of sexuality and her sympathy toward those who could not control it. As historian Herbert Wisbey has conjectured, she may have agreed with the apostle Paul that "it is better to marry than to burn."[44]

Wilkinson emphasized her own bodily purity by dressing in clothes that disguised and veiled her female form. There were many different styles of dress in Revolutionary America, but in general, fashionable women fancied gowns with bustles, tightly fitted sleeves, and lowcut bodices that they sometimes covered with a kerchief, called a buffont, that exaggerated the bosom. (One historian has quipped that women looked like "pouter pigeons.") Although lower-class women could not afford to buy expensive or elaborate clothing, they tried their best to imitate the latest styles with cheaper fabrics and less vivid colors. Even Quaker women, who were renowned for plain dress, often wore fitted bodices, hoops, and cinched-in waists that accentuated their feminine curves. In contrast, Wilkinson wore long, loose gowns and cloaks that fastened at the neck and hid all but her hands, feet, and face from public view. Describing a gown that she wore at an appearance in Philadelphia, the Marquis de Barbe-Marbois commented, "It falls to the feet, without outlining her figure, and its sleeves reveal only the tips of her hands."[45] Although she looked like a minister wearing clerical robes, she added her own distinctive touches: the robes could be purple or white as well as black, and in imitation of a popular style among men, she knotted a handkerchief at her neck.

Everyone who met Wilkinson commented on her peculiar and, to many eyes, distinctly "masculine" style of dress. To accentuate her identity as the genderless Universal Friend, Wilkinson may have intended her clothing to appear neither male or female, but according to contemporary witnesses, she usually dressed more like a man than a woman. She was reputed to be quite beautiful, with glossy, "jet-black" hair and a "fine complexion," but after seeing her preach in New Haven in 1787, one critic described her as a virtual cross-dresser. As he remembered, she had appeared in public sporting "a light cloth Cloke with a Cape like a Man's—Purple Gown, long sleeves to Wristbands—Mans shirt down to the Hands with neckband—purple handkerchief or Neckcloth tied around the neck like a man's—No Cap—Hair combed turned over & not long—wears a Watch—Man's Hat." Jacob Hiltzheimer, who had seen her preach in Philadelphia, put the case bluntly. "She looks more like a man than a woman," he pronounced. Even her hair, which she wore loose instead of pinned up, appeared strangely "masculine." Instead of powdering, curling, or covering it with a cap, as most women did, she combed it away from her forehead and let it fall around her neck. "Her head is dressed like that of a man and she has the look of one," one man scoffed.[46]

By cultivating a "masculine" appearance, Wilkinson imitated scores of other women, from medieval female saints to Revolutionary female soldiers, who dressed as men in order to gain greater social, political, economic, or religious authority. Historically, dress has always been connected to power: people declare their wealth, social class, race, and sex by what they wear, whether it be trousers and neckties or dresses and high heels. Because clothing draws visible boundaries between men and women, it has functioned as one of the primary means of representing sexual difference and perpetuating sexual inequality. It is not surprising, then, that women who have wanted to increase their status have appropriated the most visible signs of men's power: their pants, vests, shirts, and even clerical robes. For example, the legendary Joan of Arc charged into battle wearing men's armor, and other saints, including Thecla and Perpetua, donned men's clothing to symbolize their identification with the male Christ.[47] According to legend, Perpetua even had a vision in which she switched sexes: she saw herself with male genitals. Of course, many female cross-dressers (including Joan of Arc) never denied being biologically female, but others successfully masqueraded as men for months or even years. While some were lesbians, others simply wanted to improve their lot in life. In early modern Europe, a small but significant number of lower-class women staved off destitution by pretending to be men and working as soldiers or sailors.[48]

Although Jemima Wilkinson differed from these women by describing herself as *neither* male nor female, she was accused of trying to act like a man. Her critics caricatured her as a power-hungry, domineering shrew who had turned the world upside down by refusing to accept her subordinate female place. Not only had she rejected her "femininity" by refusing to marry or have children, but she had encouraged other women to do the same. In reality, there is very little evidence that Wilkinson ever directly challenged men's authority as husbands or fathers, and she certainly never forced married couples to separate. However, because she was celibate, she was charged with trying to destroy men's rule over the family. According to David Hudson, who published a derogatory (and factually inaccurate) book about her in 1821, she had belittled marriage as "an invention of wicked men, for the purpose of enslaving the female part of creation." She supposedly preached that disobedience, not submission, was women's religious duty.[49]

All of these criticisms of Wilkinson boiled down to one recurring refrain: she was a manly woman who had emasculated her male followers. After meeting two of Wilkinson's male disciples in Philadelphia, the Marquis de Chastellux described them as "tall, handsome young men" whose looks were marred by "an effeminate dejected air." According to the exaggerated and sometimes ludicrous stories told by her enemies, Wilkinson stripped men of their manhood by forcing them to obey her every whim. She greedily took away their possessions, appropriating their latest purchases with the words, "The Lord hath the need of the one-half," or "The Lord hath need of the whole." She punished them for acts of disobedience by making them wear cow or sheep bells around their necks, treating them no better than animals. (When Amos Ganzey broke his shoulder after climbing up a tree to peep in the women's bedroom, she reportedly sentenced him to wear a sheep bell for three weeks.) She ordered them to "do her homage on their bended knees." And in yet another affront to their manhood, she commanded them to do her chores while she sat in idle luxury. In the bitter words of William Savery, a Quaker who met her in 1794, she was an "artful and designing woman" who had duped her "credulous" followers, even the men, into becoming her "hewers of wood and drawers of water."[50]

Although all of these stories and rumors plagued Wilkinson throughout her career, she was probably not the imperious queen portrayed by her enemies. She often sounded commanding in the letters that she wrote to her followers, but never unkind. For example, she urged Ruth Pritchard to "Obey" her instructions, "that the[e] may be remembered by the Universal Friend," but she also wrote a tender letter to James Parker assuring him that she thought of him often. "I have not forgotten thee," she wrote. "I have been many times seemingly present with thee in the silent watches of the night when deep sleep falleth upon man[.] in slumbring upon the bed I am sencible of thy hardships and tryals." In turn, her followers wrote her affectionate letters expressing their love or imploring her to visit them soon. One woman even described herself as "sick for want of seeing the friend."[51]

The image of Wilkinson as a manly despot probably said less about her actual character than it did about Revolutionary anxieties about women's proper place. If there were any who wondered what would happen if women were given the rights of citizenship, Wilkinson's "government" of her community served as a potent warning. How would women behave if they were given the power to rule over men? Like Wilkinson, they would lose their "feminine" virtues to virtually become men, but without men's capacity for rational reflection. Not only would they become proud, acquisitive, and domineering, but they would abandon their husbands and children for the lure of public recognition.

Despite these fears of a world turned upside down, however, most people regarded Wilkinson as the victim of "temporary Insanity or Lunacy" rather than as a serious religious leader. Wilkinson exposed the underlying fears about women's role in the new republic, but because she failed to mount a significant challenge to the hierarchy of sex, she could be dismissed as a harmless eccentric. Indeed, whether intentionally or not, Wilkinson's decision to dress in masculine clothing actually *reinforced* as well as subverted male authority. On one hand, she ridiculed men by implying that their power lay in the trappings of dress rather than in their natural superiority. If she could convince people to allow her to preach simply by donning ministerial robes, then it seemed as if clothing, not character, "made the man." Through her choice of "masculine" dress, she revealed that the binary categories of male and female were not natural at all, but socially constructed. As Marjorie Garber has argued about transvestites, Wilkinson created a "category crisis": she was a "disruptive figure" who occupied "the space of anxiety about fixed and changing identities, commutable or absent 'selves.'" Yet ironically, even as Wilkinson exposed the artificiality of the boundaries between the sexes, she also reaffirmed the principle of male supremacy by dressing as a man and denying that she was a woman. How revolutionary could it be for a woman to preach if she repeatedly insisted that she was *not* a woman? As she stood in the pulpit, her "masculine" clothing bore witness to how utterly she had rejected her "feminine" self. Instead of defending female evangelism, she implicitly sanctioned the cultural and institutional structures that consigned her to a place of subordination and inferiority. In her eyes, a woman had to be *beyond* gender in order to preach the gospel. As one of her critics noted, "Her followers do not admit she is a woman, as a female Messiah appears an incongruity."[52]

This surprisingly conservative message explains why Wilkinson encountered so much less hostility than other female sectarians, especially Ann Lee. Ezra Stiles, the president of Yale University, even invited Wilkinson to his house to have tea with him and his two daughters. Of course, it is important to remember that Wilkinson was often mocked and slandered by those who came to hear her preach, and she finally moved to the wilderness of New York to escape her "revilers."[53] Nevertheless, her trials pale in comparison to the persecution that Ann Lee faced during her missionary tour of New England between 1781 and 1783. Not only was Lee accused of being a witch—a stigma that Wilkinson largely escaped—but she was repeatedly threatened, harassed, and even beaten by angry mobs.[54] (Needless to say, Ezra Stiles never invited "Mother Ann" to tea.) Because Lee never denied that she was a woman, she appeared far more dangerous than the odd and "masculine" Public Universal Friend.

Many historians have suggested that seventeenth- and eighteenth-century women who dressed as men made a rational decision to increase their economic or social status.[55] Wilkinson probably did not act out of such calculated motives, but even if it was not intentional, her "masculine" appearance increased her standing in the eyes of the world. In contrast to other women sectarians, who were ignored or belittled, Wilkinson was invited to preach in many respectable churches, including the Methodist, Quaker, and Presbyterian meetinghouses in Philadelphia. By 1790, the year that she moved to western New York, she had made as many as 260 converts, and many of them were both wealthy and socially prominent. One of her first and most distinguished followers was William Potter, the chief justice of the Court of Common Pleas for King's County, Rhode Island, who built a fourteen-room addition to his mansion in order to accommodate her and her followers. Her other converts included David Wagener, a prosperous farmer from a "good and reputable family" in Pennsylvania, and Thomas Hathaway, a wealthy shipbuilder and Tory from Massachusetts. According to one of her neighbors in western New York, her followers were a "very orderly, sober, industrious, and some of them a well educated and intelligent set of people; and many of them possessed of handsome properties."[56]

How did Wilkinson, the daughter of an average New England farmer, attract such respectable and even distinguished converts to her community of Friends? Why did she not create as much of an uproar as Ann Lee, the other "woman in the wilderness"? Besides her conservative attitude toward gender roles, the answer lies in her unexpected conformity to traditional Christian beliefs. Despite Wilkinson's claims to spiritual perfection and immediate revelation, she made few original contributions to Protestant doctrine. Most of her sermons, as one observer complained, were "composed of commonplaces about the Bible and the Fathers." Her revelations usually echoed the language of the Bible, sometimes to the letter, rather than proclaiming anything new. According to a man who visited her community in New York in 1812, "She used few expressions which could not be found in the sacred books." In the *Universal Friend's Advice*, a tract that she published in 1784, she exhorted her readers to "live peaceably," "do unto all men as you would be willing they should do unto you," and "shun . . . the company and conversation of the wicked *world*"— hardly a unique message among eighteenth-century Christians.[57]

Theologically, Wilkinson was influenced by both her Quaker upbringing and her brief association with the Cumberland New Lights. Like other radical evangelicals, she believed in both free will and the imminent return of Christ. In her early career, according to one of her followers, she intimated that the world might end in 1780, but later resigned herself to waiting until "the Lord's own time." Wilkinson also borrowed from the Quakers, especially in her rejection of sacraments, creeds, and an ordained clergy. Even her name, the Public Universal Friend, echoed the title that Quakers gave to their traveling ministers: Public Friends. Although Wilkinson never explicitly acknowledged her debt to Quaker theology, her intellectual "borrowings" sometimes crossed the line into theft. In 1799 she published a book under her own name, *Some Considerations, Propounded to the Several Sorts and Sects of Professors of This Age*, that was almost entirely plagiarized from the works of two seventeenth-century Quaker authors, Isaac Pennington and William Sewel. Besides the title, virtually nothing in the book represented her own original thought.[58]

Because Wilkinson always preached without notes, there are few records of what she actually said as she stood in the pulpit. As the inspired "mouthpiece" of God, she relied on the spontaneous guidance of the inner light rather than scripting her sermons in advance, a legacy of her Quaker heritage. Nevertheless, many of the spectators who flocked to her meetings published descriptions of her sermons, and Ruth Spence, one of her most devout followers, left a detailed record of the biblical texts that she preached on between 1793 and 1795.[59] It is difficult to draw definitive conclusions about her theology on the basis of these texts alone, but without a corpus of manuscript sermons, such fragments offer the only clue to her theological beliefs. In total, there are records of sixty-five biblical texts on which Wilkinson preached during the first twenty years of her career, a small but suggestive sample of the themes she addressed in the pulpit.

Of these sixty-five sermons, Wilkinson preached thirty-four, more than half, on texts from Matthew, John, and Isaiah. Many of her listeners commented on her extensive knowledge of the Bible, but according to the surviving records, she actually preached on a relatively small portion of it. For example, in the entire New Testament, she preached only from Luke, Matthew, John, Hebrews, and Romans. She never chose texts from Mark, James,

Acts, or Peter, and perhaps not surprisingly, she virtually ignored the words of Paul. (According to the records, she never preached on Galatians, Ephesians, Philippians, Colossians, Timothy, Thessalonians, or Corinthians.) Even though she seems to have modeled her life on his promise to the Galatians—"There is neither male nor female"—she hesitated to invoke the authority of the man who had commanded women to keep silence in the churches. Instead, she combed her three favorite books of the Bible—Matthew, Isaiah, and John—for illustrations of her most important themes: the near approach of the kingdom of God (Matthew), the persistent disbelief and apostasy of Christians (John), God's wrath against sinners (First Isaiah), and Christ's free offer of salvation (Deutero-Isaiah).[60]

Perhaps because of her own persecution as the Public Universal Friend, Wilkinson was particularly drawn to the many biblical stories of sinners who refused to obey God. From the Old Testament, she chose texts from both Ezekiel and Jeremiah lamenting the "deceit" and "wickedness" of the heart, and from the New Testament, she preached at least two sermons on Christ's prediction of the passion: "The Son of Man shall be betrayed into the hands of men."[61] Since Wilkinson believed that she had been called by God to save souls, she may have found personal as well as prophetic meaning in these passages. According to Abner Brownell, she often lamented her fate as a martyr who had been chosen "to be trodden under foot by the children of men, and to go through many sufferings and trials, and afflictions, and hardships."[62] It was a martyrdom that she willingly embraced, but not without moments of bitterness.

Beyond her criticism of her persecutors, Wilkinson's sharpest rebukes were aimed at those who chose "the vanity of riches—the sinfulness of pride and pomp of the world" over the gospel of Christ. Ironically, Wilkinson herself was not immune to the temptations of wealth, and thanks to the generosity of her followers, she enjoyed a much more opulent lifestyle than she ever had as a farmer's daughter. (Her father was comfortably well-off, but certainly not rich.) She dressed in robes made of expensive silks and linens, dined from fine china and silver, and rode in a handsome carriage emblazoned with a cross and her initials, "U.F." Such ostentatious display fueled rumors that she was selfish and greedy, but even as she reaped the fruits of the new consumer revolution that was reshaping the Anglo-American world, she was deeply ambivalent about its consequences. In 1790 she led her followers away from the luxuries of the city to the wilderness of western New York, but even there she found that she could not escape the worship of money. Tempted by skyrocketing property values, two of her followers, William Potter and James Parker, left the Friends to make a fortune cheating them out of the title to their new land. Angrily, Wilkinson responded by preaching as many as five sermons on Matthew's famous condemnation of greed. "No man can serve two masters," she threatened. "Ye cannot serve God and Mammon."[63]

Disillusioned by the "vanity" and "deceit" of the sinful world, Wilkinson always sounded the same call for action. In almost all of her sermons, she exhorted her listeners to "repent and forsake Evil" before it was too late to seek God's forgiveness. Because she truly believed that the fires of the apocalypse would soon consume the earth—"the day of the Lord cometh, cruel both with wrath and fierce anger, to lay the land desolate"—she spoke with an urgency that transfixed and even frightened her audiences.[64] Even though she often strung together biblical texts "without connexion," her scriptural language made her sound so "grave" and prophetic that many trembled at her words. Because she was a woman, some may have expected her to stress God's motherly compassion more than his wrath, but according to one of her followers, "She Preaches up Terror very alarming." Quoting from Luke, she warned: "He that knew his Lord's will and prepared not himself, neither did according to his will, shall be beaten with many Stripes."[65]

Although Wilkinson's sermons often sounded indistinguishable from those of more conservative clergymen, she made one significant—and startling— innovation. In a doctrine that she seems to have revealed to only her most devoted followers, she rejected the Christian belief in a physical resurrection, preaching that only souls, not bodies, would rise to heaven. Because of her negative feelings about the "carnal" body, she could not imagine a heaven in which male and female bodies would still exist. "Flesh and blood cannot enter the kingdom of Heaven," she testified. "The resurrection is spiritual, and consists in the separation of the soul from its earthly tenement."[66] Just as "Jemima Wilkinson" had died and gone to heaven in 1776, leaving behind her body as a "tabernacle" for the Public Universal Friend, Christians would lose the burden of their flesh, their sexuality, their *sex* in spiritual union with God. Following in the footsteps of "Jemima Wilkinson," they would leave their bodies on earth and ascend to heaven, where Paul had promised there would truly be neither male nor female.

This could have been a deeply liberating message, and on the surface, it was. Since Wilkinson believed that souls had no sex, she imitated the Quakers by permitting women as well as men to witness to the light within them. After opening her meetings with a spontaneous prayer or sermon, she sat quietly and waited until someone felt moved to speak. Under her approving gaze, many women stood up to make their voices heard. For example, Lucina Goodspeed, one of the celibate sisterhood, often testified during public meetings, and Mercy Aldrich reputedly prayed "with ability and pertinence."[67] Wilkinson even sent her most loyal disciple, Sarah Richards, on several preaching tours without her.

Yet even as Wilkinson freed women to testify and preach in public, she never justified their right to speak as *women*. Through her own example, she taught them that preaching was a male privilege that they could achieve only by renouncing their "femininity." Although a few of Wilkinson's followers were celebrated as "mothers" of the community, the most prominent, especially Sarah Richards, her closest companion and second-in-command, copied her "masculine" clothing and appearance. As one person complained in 1787, Richards "would be a comely person, were she to dress as becomes her sex. But as she imitates the person they call the friend, in her external appearance, and particularly in wearing her hair down like a man, she is by that means somewhat disfigured."[68] Perhaps Wilkinson never explicitly instructed her female followers to dress or act like her, but according to rumor, she invited them to act like men by giving them the names of male prophets. Instead of christening them as "Deborahs" or "Huldahs," she embraced a distinctly "male" model of religious leadership. Besides elevating Sarah Richards as the "Prophet Daniel," she reportedly identified another woman as the "Prophet Enoch" and a third as "John the Beloved."[69]

As these examples suggest, Wilkinson's denial of gender was actually only a denial of the *female* aspects of gender. She did not encourage her male followers to wear long, loose robes that disguised their bodies; nor did she call them by female names. Instead, she held men up as the standard against which she measured herself and her female disciples. Whether consciously or not, Wilkinson seems to have understood her gender according to what Thomas Laquer has called a "one-sex model": she believed that women's bodies were inferior and incomplete versions of men's. (In the nineteenth century, scientists and clergymen alike would posit a "two-sex" model of the difference of the sexes. Many still stressed women's weakness, but they also viewed men and women as virtually two separate species.) In some ways, of course, the one-sex model had the potential to elevate women as the equals of men, since it defined the differences between the sexes as ones of degree, not kind. But its hierarchical ordering of male over female also doomed women to striving for an unobtainable "masculine" ideal. Wilkinson symbolized this struggle more vividly than almost any woman of her generation. To preach, she believed that she had to transcend her gender, but since she viewed her womanhood as a deviation from the male norm, she thought that becoming a genderless spirit meant becoming more like a man. Unlike women's bodies, which were inferior and underdeveloped, men's bodies represented perfection.[70]

In some ways, Wilkinson resembled the New Light and Separate women of the Great Awakening who had longed to lose their gender in union with Christ, but she took their language of self-transcendence to an extreme. Even though female exhorters such as Bathsheba Kingsley and Martha Stearns Marshall had longed to be caught up in God, they had never denied their sexual identities as women. In contrast, Wilkinson justified her right to preach on the grounds that she was *not* a woman, but a spirit who was neither male nor female. Even though she echoed the arguments of earlier generations of women, she ultimately created a new model of female ministry that was far more radical in its denial of "femininity."

Wilkinson clung to her vision of a world without female gender until the end of her life, even though in the nineteenth century it eventually lost its appeal for her followers. From the time of her "resurrection" in 1776, she had never once expressed doubts about her mission, but by the time she passed away in 1819 at the age of sixty-seven, only a few devout disciples remained to spread her gospel. When she had moved to western New York in 1790, she had dreamed of finding "a peaceable habitation for me & my friends to dwell," but instead, she found nothing but disappointment.[71] As she grew older and the novelty of her prophetic claims wore off, many rejected her leadership and left the community to worship elsewhere. Some were disillusioned by continuing legal battles over land ownership, while others may have simply tired of her conventional sermons on sin and salvation.[72] Did any question her insistence that she was not a woman? The records are silent, but perhaps a few of the most radical wondered why a woman could not preach as a woman rather than as a spirit or a man.

For better or for worse, Wilkinson's model of "masculine" religious leadership offered women one of their few opportunities to preach in Revolutionary America. Although it is doubtful that Wilkinson ever would have made so many converts if she had not denied her sex, she unwittingly strengthened the prejudices against female preaching by insisting that she was not a woman. When she died in 1819, she was buried as the Public Universal Friend, not as Jemima Wilkinson. Could a true, flesh and blood woman be a preacher in the new American republic? Sadly, Wilkinson's answer was no.

Ann Lee, Mother of the Apocalypse

Only one other female religious leader in Revolutionary America became as notorious as the "artful and designing" Jemima Wilkinson. In 1776, at the same time as Wilkinson was beginning her itinerant career as the Public Universal Friend, Ann Lee, a visionary "prophetess" from England, moved to the wilderness of Niskeyuna, New York, with a small group of devoted followers. In England, she had been a member of a small band of "Shaking Quakers" who had prophesied the imminent return of Christ, and in America, she proclaimed that the millennium had begun in her new Shaker church. Traveling with her disciples across New York and Massachusetts, she converted hundreds to her gospel of celibacy and perfectionism—a gospel that brought her both verbal and physical abuse. As the head of the Shakers, not only was she vilified in the press as a "strange WOMAN," a "harlot," and an "old witch" who had created a "monstrous" religion, but she was attacked several times by angry mobs, including a group of men who dragged her "like a beast" up a flight of stairs. Even more than Jemima Wilkinson, "Mother Ann" discovered that female evangelists, no matter how hard they tried to resolve the "problem" of their gender, were not welcome in the new republic.[73]

The story of Mother Ann, as her disciples called her, is a story of truly biblical proportions. Born in 1736 in Manchester, England, to a poor blacksmith and his wife, she hardly seemed destined for a life of historical significance. By the time that she died in 1784, however, she had matured into one of the most charismatic, visionary leaders of her time, and many of her followers had begun to suspect that she was not simply a prophet, or the "mother of the elect," or the "woman in the wilderness," but the *messiah*. Such claims were rarely voiced openly, but in 1808, twenty-four years after her death, Shaker leaders finally announced publicly what many had suspected privately. Ann Lee, an illiterate factory worker from England, had actually been the second incarnation of the spirit of Christ, "the *first born of many sisters*, and the true *mother of all living* in the new creation."[74]

Yet just as biblical scholars have debated over the identity of the historical

Jesus, very little is known about the historical Ann Lee. Who was the real Mother Ann? How did she define her relationship to God? Did she believe that she was the Christ? And how did she justify her role as a female religious leader? Unfortunately, these questions are difficult to answer because of the lack of reliable sources. Unlike her contemporary Jemima Wilkinson, Lee was "very illiterate; so that she could neither read nor write," and she left no diaries, letters, or sermons.[75] Neither did her early followers, who disdained reading and writing as distractions from the work of the Holy Spirit. Standing on the threshold of a new age of revelation, they claimed that their sacred knowledge could not be confined to the pages of a book.

Unfortunately, the only contemporary accounts of Ann Lee and the early Shakers were written by apostates who were highly critical of the new movement. For example, Valentine Rathbun, a Separate Baptist minister who had united briefly with the Shakers for three months in 1780, published the earliest description of them, *An Account of the Matter, Form, and Manner of a New and Strange Religion, Taught and Propagated by a Number of Europeans*, in order to expose Lee and her followers as the agents of a satanic "prank." They were Europeans, not Americans, and their antinomian reliance on the spirit threatened the very existence of the fragile young republic. "I have heard some of them say, that all our authority, civil and military, is from hell, and would go there again," he warned. In subsequent years, other disgruntled former Shakers such as Amos Taylor, Daniel Rathbun, Reuben Rathbun, Benjamin West, and Thomas Brown also published incriminating exposés of the Shakers' enthusiasm. Besides labeling them as un-American, they accused them of breaking up families in the name of celibacy, burning books, drinking to excess, running naked through the woods, and leaping, groaning, laughing, trembling, and dancing during worship.[76]

Because they were written by apostates, all of these accounts pose problems of accuracy and credibility, but they are still indispensable for understanding the early movement. Even though the most outrageous stories (and there were many) that were told about Lee and her followers may have been concocted out of spite, others were substantiated by several different witnesses or by the later Shakers themselves. For example, Valentine Rathbun's claims that Shakers burned "books of divinity" and "stripped naked in the woods" were echoed by several contemporary witnesses, and his description of the Shakers' faith in free will, celibacy, and public confession conformed closely to later statements of official doctrine. Even the most lurid accounts of Shaker extremism, such as Daniel Rathbun's portrait of Ann Lee reeling in drunken intoxication, may contain at least a few grains of truth. Like Rathbun, Isaac Backus accused the Shakers of "delight[ing] themselves" with "spirituous liquor," and Jeremy Belknap claimed that a group of New Hampshire Shakers began their meetings "by handing round a bottle of rum." Even one of Lee's most faithful followers once railed at her for behaving like a "drunken squaw."[77] Even though sensational accounts such as Daniel Rathbun's must be read critically because of their underlying hostility, they should not be dismissed as nothing more than anti-Shaker propaganda. If used carefully, they can provide a valuable glimpse of the Shakers' radicalism during their formative years in America.

The Shakers did not publish their own version of their history until 1816, thirty-two years after Ann Lee died. In order to preserve Lee's memory and instruct new converts in the faith, Shaker leaders interviewed "old Believers" about their recollections of James Whittaker, William Lee, and especially Mother Ann. Could they remember words that she had said? Miracles that she had witnessed? Prophecies that she had revealed? Eventually these stories were collected and published as the *Testimonies of the Life, Character, Revelations, and Doctrines of Our Ever Blessed Mother Ann Lee*, a thick chronicle of Lee's personal religious experiences, her missionary tour of New England, and her relationship with her followers.[78]

Like the accounts left by Shaker apostates (and for that matter, like all historical evidence), the *Testimonies* must be used critically and measured against other sources. First, because many of the elderly believers who told their stories were asked to describe events that had happened decades earlier, they often had to be prodded to remember crucial details. As the Shaker editors admitted, "It is worthy of particular notice, that many of [the stories], and those too, the most important, have been brought to remembrance by a special gift of God, and having been, as it were, entirely forgotten, for many years." Even though Mother Ann's sayings had probably circulated in oral form for years before being preserved in print, the words that the "eye and ear witnesses" attributed to her were almost certainly not the exact words that she spoke.[79]

Even apart from the problems created by the distortions of memory, it is unclear how much Shaker leaders may have edited the *Testimonies* to conform to their official view of Ann Lee. The book is full of accounts of miracles and providences that reveal as much (or more) about the Shakers in 1816 than in the 1770s and 1780s. Frankly admitting that the *Testimonies* was designed "to prove, to all faithful Believers, that Christ did verily make his second Appearance in *Ann Lee*," Shaker leaders were anything but subtle in their portrait of her as a modern Jesus. "Well might her sufferings and trials be compared with those of the Lord Jesus, when he was in the wilderness, tempted of the Devil," they wrote in a typical passage.[80] Rather than striving for historical accuracy, they presented Mother Ann as a redemptive figure who stood outside the bounds of human history.

Yet despite these obvious biases, the *Testimonies* is more than simply a Shaker apologetic. Even though Shaker leaders tried to mold believers' statements into their own interpretive framework, they ended up publishing a book that is riddled with inconsistencies and contradictions. It portrays Lee as an elder, a seer who could predict the future, a faith healer who could cure the sick, and a judge whose withering look could cause fits of terror, but only rarely as the second incarnation of the spirit of Christ. It shows her as a comforting mother, but also more negatively as a contentious scold whose "words were like flames of fire and her voice like peals of thunder." It is difficult to understand why Shaker leaders allowed such unflattering stories to be printed, but by the time the book was finished, they had realized how dangerous it could be if it fell into the wrong hands. Publishing only twenty copies, they instructed the elders in every community to guard it carefully from skeptics or outsiders. Three years later, in 1819, they desperately attempted to hide it from scrutiny by recalling all of the copies from the eastern societies. Seth Wells sent a letter to Benjamin Youngs, the leader of the community at South Union, Kentucky, ordering him to "commit it to the flames" rather than "expose it to your people."[81] In the eyes of the Shaker leaders, the Ann Lee of the *Testimonies* was too contradictory, too fractious, and perhaps too *real* to fit the image of a female Christ.

Because of the limitations of the sources, the historical Ann Lee will always be elusive. However, by carefully comparing the accounts of apostates with the *Testimonies* of 1816, we can draw at least a few conclusions about her theology, her relationship to her followers, and most important, her self-perceptions. The Ann Lee who emerges from these documents was neither a witch nor a saint (although she was called both), but a radical visionary who faced the same paradoxes of religious liberty as other female sectarians in the new republic.

On one issue in particular, the records are lamentably silent. What did Lee think of Jemima Wilkinson, the Public Universal Friend? Although there is no record that the two women ever met, it is difficult to imagine that they were unaware of each other's existence, especially since they were so often linked together in the public mind. For example, in his account of the Shaker "delusion," Valentine Rathbun warned his readers that Satan had sent "one woman from the state of New York and another from the state of Rhode Island (Jemima Wilkinson) who vie with each other, and are as dangerous to the heedless passenger as Scylla and Charbydes are to the unskillful mariner." Since Lee could not read, she may not have realized that Rathbun, her former disciple, had compared her to the Friend, but perhaps some of her more literate followers read his account aloud to her. Only one fact is certain: whether or not Lee knew anything about Wilkinson, Wilkinson knew about Lee. Her papers contain a brief letter from an admirer, identified only as "M.T.," who took pains to reassure her that she, not the inferior Mother Ann, was the true messenger of Christ. In 1799, long after Lee had died, Wilkinson even sent a missionary to the Shakers to try to convince them to join her society, a trip that apparently met with no success.[82]

Whether or not Wilkinson and Lee directly influenced each other, the parallels between them are striking. Both were perfectionists who began their American careers in 1776, and both founded their own religious communities in western New York. Theologically, both were inspired by the Quaker belief in an immanent rather than a transcendent God; both were millennialists who claimed to be the apocalyptic woman in the wilderness; and both rejected Calvinism in favor of free will.

Yet even as Lee seemed to echo many of Wilkinson's central beliefs, she took them to a radical extreme. For example, Lee not only recommended celibacy, as Wilkinson did, but made it an essential requirement for salvation. In 1762, while still living in England, she had married Abraham Standerin, a blacksmith like her father, but by 1770, she had renounced sexuality as inherently sinful. According to her later Shaker followers, those eight years of married life were filled with physical and mental anguish—anguish that she never seems to have entirely overcome. In 1766 she gave birth to a daughter, Elizabeth, who died soon after, and according to Shaker tradition, she gave birth to three other children who died in infancy as well.[83] Although it is difficult to imagine the depth of her grief during those difficult years, its effects on her religious faith must have been profound. Struggling to make sense of her suffering, she may have finally concluded that sexuality itself was to blame. In 1770 she had a revelation of "the root and foundation of human depravity; and of the very transgression of the first man and woman, in the garden of Eden," which eventually led to the dissolution of her marriage. (Her husband followed her to America in 1774 but did not join the community at Niskeyuna.) Unlike Wilkinson, who allowed her followers to marry and have children, Lee preached that Christians had to forsake the lusts of the flesh in order to be saved. "They tell the man to abstain from his wife, and the woman from her husband," Valentine Rathbun complained. "If the wife doth not agree to it, the husband must put her away; and if the husband will not agree to it, the wife must leave her husband."[84]

Theologically, Lee was much more radical than Wilkinson, who appeared almost staid in comparison. Although both women claimed to communicate directly with God, Lee was illiterate, and she put her faith in the immediate witness of the spirit rather than the authority of the Word. In contrast to Wilkinson, who devoted her sermons to examining scriptural texts, she dismissed the Bible as obsolete. "The Scriptures were good in their day," she reportedly said. "But nothing to us in this new dispensation."[85] Bibles, creeds, and written documents of any kind were far less important than the direct, personal witness of the Holy Spirit.

If Wilkinson or any of her followers had ever stumbled into a Shaker meeting in the early 1780s, they certainly would have been shocked by what they saw. Rather than delivering formal sermons on sin, grace, and repentance, Lee led her followers in singing, dancing, trembling, and whirling in communion with the Holy Spirit. Unfortunately, there are no records of what she said during her visionary trances, but words seem to have been far less important than symbolic action. As Valentine Rathbun recounted:

> In the best part of their worship, every one acts for himself, and almost every one different from the other; one will stand with his arms extended, acting over odd postures, which they call signs; another will be dancing, and sometimes hopping on one leg about the floor . . . some trembling extremely; others acting as though all their nerves were convuls'd; others swinging their arms, with all vigor, as though they were turning a wheel, &c. Then all break off, and have a spell of smoaking, and sometimes great fits of laughter.[86]

According to apostates, the Shakers' "enthusiastic" behavior grew even more radical in the two years before Lee died in 1784, when they experimented with new—and sometimes bizarre—forms of worship: they danced "stark naked together" (to symbolize their religious purity), burned books and furniture, performed faith healings, drank to excess, and exorcised demons.[87]

Besides these differences in theology and worship style, Lee and Wilkinson were also separated by subtle barriers of social rank and station, barriers that were no less sturdy for being invisible. According to Shaker tradition, Lee had worked as a velvet cutter and fur trimmer when she had lived in England, and in America she rarely (if ever) made converts among the privileged or well-educated. Unlike Wilkinson, she never spoke in established churches, lived in a mansion, wore gowns made out of silk or satin, or traveled across the country in a luxurious, monogrammed carriage. Instead, she preached her gospel to her own kind: struggling farmers, uneducated goodwives, and hired hands who were as poor as she was.

As all of these examples indicate, the theological and social differences dividing Lee and Wilkinson were ultimately as great as the parallels linking them. For all of Wilkinson's supposed radicalism, she was actually a reactionary who looked backward to the Quaker past for inspiration, while Lee was a true antinomian who disdained any appeals to tradition. Wilkinson promised her followers that the millennium would soon arrive, while Lee claimed that it had already commenced in the Shaker Church. Wilkinson preached a Christocentric faith that centered on the saving grace of Jesus, while Lee sought ecstatic communion with the Holy Spirit. Most important, while each hinted that she might be the woman in the wilderness who would help to bring about the end of history, each interpreted this figure according to her own distinctive needs. For Wilkinson, this woman was important not as a *woman*, but as a spirit sent by God, and she utterly ignored the biblical verses describing her painful "travail." In contrast, Lee saw the woman in the wilderness as a figure of maternal suffering—suffering that she knew from the scars of personal experience—and she used her as the model for her own identity as the mother of God's millennial church.

What most set Lee apart from Jemima Wilkinson, and what made her particularly radical in the eyes of the American public, was this "feminine" rather than "masculine" identity as the head of the new Shaker sect. However much she struggled with the restrictions on female religious leadership, she never dressed in men's clothing or refused to answer to her female name. Even though her followers debated over whether she was a prophet, the "woman clothed with the sun," or even a female Christ, they never speculated that she, like Wilkinson, might have transcended her gender to become a sexless spirit. When Valentine Rathbun joined the sect in 1780, he heard almost every conceivable interpretation of her calling, but always in distinctly female terms: she was the "woman clothed with the sun," the "mother of all the elect," "the queen of heaven, Christ's wife," and even the mother of Christ ("Christ through her is born the second time"). Some even proclaimed what the later Shakers would accept as gospel truth: she had "the fullness of the god head, bodily dwelling in her."[88]

It is important to note that Lee, like Wilkinson, never publicly identified herself as the second incarnation of Christ. Despite her later exaltation as a female messiah, there is little evidence that she herself ever made this claim. Even in the 1816 *Testimonies*, with its explicit goal of proving that "Christ did verily make his second Appearance in *Ann Lee*," very few believers ever remembered her making such an extraordinary assertion. There were only two exceptions: Eunice Goodrich described Lee scolding her male followers for doubting that she was Christ, and John Farrington testified that Lee had asked him, "Is not this Christ?" In contrast, most of the other Shakers remembered a more mysterious, enigmatic Ann Lee who intimated that she was a prophet, an elder, or the biblical woman in the wilderness. Unlike Nat Smith, the perfectionist who had brazenly stitched the word "GOD" onto his cap, Lee was much more ambiguous about her religious identity. While Hannah Cogswell and Elizabeth Hill remembered her saying that she was an "Elder" (or the "first Elder") in the new millennial church, others compared her to Moses. According to Rhoda Hammond, Lee had testified that "she spoke with God, face to face, as Moses did, and saw the glory of God, and had seen wonderful visions."[89]

According to the accounts left by apostates, most of the earliest Shakers believed that the second coming of Christ had taken place in their church as a whole, not in Ann Lee or any other single individual. When Amos Taylor became a convert in 1780 or 1781, he was taught that "Christ will never make any publick appearance as of a single person, but only in his saints." Similarly, Anna Matthewson, a devout Shaker whose recollections were included in the *Testimonies* of 1816, remembered Lee asserting that "the second appearance of Christ is in his Church."[90] Although Lee clearly saw herself as the mother of the new faith, she may never have claimed to be a female Christ who had the power to save the world from sin.

Rather than portraying herself as a female messiah or denying her womanhood, Lee tried to solve the "problem" of her gender by investing the experiences of pregnancy, birth, and motherhood with universal religious significance. Unlike Jemima Wilkinson, Lee tried to transform her "femininity" into her main source of religious authority. In response to her critics, who argued that she could not be a religious leader because she was a woman, Lee hinted at the reverse: it was *because* she was a woman that God had called her to "labor" for the salvation of souls. Indeed, Lee described her relationship to God and her followers in a distinctly "feminine" vocabulary. Rather than a gender-neutral "friend," she was the "bride" of Christ and the "mother" of the Shaker church.

If the testimonies of her followers can be trusted, Lee often described herself as Christ's lover or his bride. Like the converts during the Awakening who had promised to take Christ as a spiritual husband, Lee exulted that "Christ was her Lover." Despite her physical celibacy, she used erotic language to describe her spiritual union with Christ: they were passionate "lovers" who took long walks together "hand in hand." As she reportedly told Sarah Kendall, "I have been walking in fine vallies with Christ, as with a lover."[91]

Besides Christ's bride or wife, Lee also identified herself as the "mother of the elect," another image underlining her unique role as a female religious leader. She was "Mother Ann," or more simply, "the Mother," and her disciples lauded her as "a Mother indeed, in every good word and work." Instead of slighting the maternal work of cooking meals, washing clothes, and sweeping floors, she mixed religious instruction with traditional household chores. After she died, many of her followers (especially the women) fondly remembered her dispensing wisdom as she threaded a needle or pushed a broom. Like the virtuous woman of Proverbs, who "layeth her hands to the spindle, and her hands hold the distaff," Lee took pride in her reputation as a frugal housewife. On the occasions when she scolded her followers, it was often for "sloth." "Be neat and industrious," she instructed Zeruah Clark. "Keep your family's clothes clean and decent; see that your house is kept clean, and your victuals prepared in good order."[92] No Puritan goodwife could have been more exacting.

In her day-to-day care of her Shaker "children," Lee combined tenderness with discipline. She took converts by the hand, embraced them when they were discouraged, wept over their sins, and spoke comfortingly to them. After the only time that she ever reproved Jemima Blanchard, she "put out her arms and embraced her saying, 'Come, come, you shall be the least bantling Mother's got.'" (In eighteenth-century usage, a "bantling" was a young child.) She also listened patiently as her followers confessed their sins to her, a role that further heightened her maternal authority. As historian Stephen Marini has noted, she often claimed to know their most "secret sins"—"the kind of knowledge that a mother has of her small child." Although most of her followers were mature adults, many with children of their own, they looked up to her with the adoration that the very young bestow on their parents. In their eagerness to please their "Mother," they paid close attention to her erratic moods and tried to obey her every order. As Jemima Blanchard remembered, "Her smile was sunshine, and her frown was perfect darkness."[93]

By rooting her religious authority in her work as a mother, Lee drew on an ideology of "republican motherhood" that was just beginning to emerge during the 1770s and 1780s. In the aftermath of the Revolutionary War, women who were excluded from the "male" world of citizenship and officeholding began to create an alternative political role for themselves, a role that built on their traditional authority as wives and mothers. In the words of historian Linda Kerber, women "began to invent an ideology of citizenship that merged the domestic ideology of the preindustrial woman with the new public ideology of individual responsibility and civic virtue."[94] As mothers, women were still confined to the private world of the family, but they also had an important political and public responsibility: raising virtuous citizens for the new republic. By the early years of the nineteenth century, middle-class women would fashion this ideology into a compelling justification for their involvement in a multitude of public reform movements, including temperance and antislavery.

Yet if Lee hoped to placate the American public by styling herself as a republican mother, she failed to realize how *un*motherly she appeared to her critics. For one thing, many worried that her enforcement of celibacy would undermine or even destroy the existence of the traditional family. "Wives disown all natural affections to their husbands and children," wrote an alarmed Benjamin West. "Thus women become monsters, and men worse than infidels in this new and strange religion." Second, her moral opposition to the Revolutionary War made her immediately suspect on political grounds. What was this "mother," only recently a British citizen, teaching her impressionable children to believe? Many Americans feared that she might be a British spy, and in 1780 she and several of her followers were imprisoned for several months in Albany, New York, on suspicion of treason.[95]

Most important, Lee's understanding of motherhood harked back to an older, disciplinarian model that was increasingly criticized by those who praised mothers for their tenderness rather than their reproofs. Like earlier eighteenth-century parents, especially those with an evangelical bent, she believed in breaking the wills of her sinful "children" in order to bring them to salvation. Even though she was kind and loving to those who submitted to her rules, she could often be cruel to those who crossed her. Many of her punishments seemed expressly designed to cause shame: she singled out sinners for public humiliation rather than simply reproving them in private. For example, after she saw the young Lucy Bishop cutting her nails on the Sabbath, she ordered her to "Walk on your knees to Elder James, and ask him to teach you to pray." Lucy obeyed, and with "Mother" towering above her, she dutifully repeated every word that was required of her: "Pray God, make me a good child—Pray God, make me obedient to my parents—Pray God, purify and purge my soul from sin." Other followers sat meekly as Lee publicly berated them for being "lustful" sinners or "filthy whores."[96]

As a spiritual mother, Lee was certainly not the mild-mannered saint of later nineteenth-century Shaker hagiography. Instead, she was a formidable matriarch who was virtually obsessed with saving her children from the stain of sin. Her relationships with almost all of her followers were marked by a mixture of love and punishment, compassion and anger, that often left them feeling vulnerable and confused. Hannah Knapp remembered Lee condemning her as a "haughty creature" at their first meeting, but after she confessed her sins, Lee "took her into her arms and said, 'God forgive you child!'" Yet even though some converts were troubled by Lee's outbursts of rage, most seem to have had such a deep awareness of personal sin that they thought they deserved whatever punishments she inflicted. Sarah Robbins often smarted under the lash of "Mother's" sharp tongue, but she accepted her lot on the grounds that tenderness and love "would have made no impression on her."[97]

In keeping with her reputation for "great sharpness and severity," Lee may have been physically as well as verbally abusive. Daniel Rathbun claimed that she so frequently whipped and struck her followers that he was terrified of disobeying her. "Certainly she was a striker, both of me and many others," he wrote bitterly. He even accused her of battering her own beloved brother

William until "his face was in a gore of blood."[98] Since no other witness substantiated Rathbun's stories, they may have represented nothing more than a cruel attack on Lee's religious integrity. Yet given Lee's volatile temperament, perhaps they should not be completely discounted. Although more loyal Shakers never once mentioned Lee physically harming anyone, they admitted that she had once threatened a hostile crowd to "take care, lest some of you get your noses wrung." Even more telling, they also suggested that Lee may have been a victim of domestic violence during her earlier life in England. According to two of her female followers, Lee had an abusive brother who once tied her up and tried to throw her out of a window and, on another occasion, savagely beat her in the face with a staff.[99] Although Lee claimed that God had divinely intervened to protect her from harm in both of these instances, the scars may have been deeper than she acknowledged. The evidence is slim, but it is possible that she bequeathed a legacy of familial abuse to her own Shaker "children."

The motherhood that seems to have given Lee the greatest satisfaction was not the physical motherhood of nurturing and disciplining her earthly Shaker children, which could often be trying, but the *spiritual* motherhood of laboring for the salvation of the church. She rooted her claims to religious authority in her spiritual "travail" for each and every one of her followers. Since she had reportedly given birth to four infants in England, all of whom had died, she knew the pain of labor from personal experience, and she drew on the evocative language of pregnancy and childbirth in order to describe her conversion of sinners. Implicitly comparing herself to the biblical woman in the wilderness, who "being with child cried, travailing in birth, and pained to be delivered," she claimed to have given birth to the church of the apocalypse.

The Shakers believed that Mother Ann labored for the entire world, even for those who had already died and descended into hell. As the "mother of all living," she endured the perpetual agonies of childbirth in order to bring others to new life. "Sometimes for whole nights together, her cries, screeches, and groans were such as to fill every soul around her with fear and trembling," her Shaker followers testified. During visionary trances, she "bore for souls" by visiting and preaching the gospel to the dead, and then, like a nursing mother, she nourished them with the milk of the Shaker gospel. According to Lee, some refused to confess their sins to her, but others came like hungry infants who were eager to be nursed. As she explained to Samuel Fitch, "When the gospel was offered to them, they were so hungry for it, that they would come, with their mouths wide open, to receive it."[100]

Lee universalized the female experiences of pregnancy, birth, and lactation by encouraging men as well as women to labor in the "world of spirits." Even though she alone had been chosen as the "First Mother" of the church, *all* Shakers, male as well as female, could share her experience of travail by giving new life to those who had died in their sins. Because her maternity was spiritual rather than biological, it transcended the physical boundaries of sex. Like Lee, men such as Israel Chauncy and Philip Matthewson became spiritual "mothers" by enduring the birth pangs of "bearing" for souls. Matthewson suffered such "great distress of body and soul" while laboring for his dead father that he "appeared like a person under the pangs of death." Chauncy also labored for the salvation of the dead, and Lee exhorted him to "never give out, till the last soul is gathered in."[101]

On the surface, Lee's richly "feminine" descriptions of herself as the bride of Christ and the mother of the elect elevated women's ordinary experiences of marriage and childbirth to cosmic significance. Instead of trying to justify her religious leadership by denying her biological womanhood, Lee transformed it into the foundation of her spiritual authority. Not only did she reject the common wisdom that women's experiences of pregnancy and childbirth made them weaker than men, but she insisted that those experiences linked them to the divine. Because she drew on female rather than male symbols to describe her relationship to God, one historian has even hailed her as the founder of a "gynocentric" religion.[102] Unlike Jemima Wilkinson, Lee clearly believed that "feminine" qualities, especially maternal nurture, were valuable and should be preserved. Whether male or female, those who wanted to share in her redemptive power had to strive for spiritual maternity.

Yet even as Lee seemed to revel in the erotic language of marriage and motherhood, she ultimately based her religious authority on the rejection rather than the acceptance of the body. Her seeming celebration of the "feminine" masked a deep hostility toward female sexuality. From the moment that God had shown her Adam and Eve's sin of lechery in the Garden of Eden, she had suppressed her sexuality in order to live a completely celibate life, and she ultimately created a religion in which there was no room for the realities of biological rather than spiritual motherhood. *Real* motherhood and marriage were signs of lechery, not godliness, and women who failed to crucify their

"lusts" were "whores" who would suffer eternal punishment in hell. Ultimately, then, her resemblance to Jemima Wilkinson was much deeper than it
seemed. Even though she never denied that she was a flesh and blood woman,
a woman who had once been a wife and a mother, she still believed she had to
transcend her body in order to proclaim the gospel.

Even more than Wilkinson, Lee believed that she had to triumph over the
"filth" of the flesh in order to achieve true communion with God. Like the
evangelical female exhorters of the 1740s and 1750s who had lamented that
they were infectious, leprous, or unclean, Lee longed to lose the "pollution" of
her sinful body by being swallowed up by God. Of all the deadly sins, lust was
what she most feared and despised. "Leave your husband alone," she ordered
Hannah Goodrich. "Fastening your lust upon him!" And with blunt crudity,
she declared to a woman who had come to visit her: "You are a filthy whore."[103]

It was Lee's attitude toward celibacy, not the fact of her celibacy itself, that
ultimately weakened her message of female spiritual equality. Historically,
women have often chosen celibacy as a positive means of controlling their
fertility and establishing their independence from men. For example, since
Catholic sisters have considered themselves as married to Jesus, they have
declined physical motherhood in order to fully devote themselves to other
meaningful forms of work, such as praying for sinners and tending the sick.
But for Lee, celibacy was less a positive choice than a negative rejection of the
female body and all of its "lusts." Ironically, her later followers portrayed her as
the second coming of Christ made flesh, but she herself viewed that flesh as an
obstacle to her union with God.[104] Paradoxically, she believed that she had to
suppress the biological fact of her sex in order to serve as the mother of the
Shaker church, hardly a radical message in Revolutionary America.

If reports of her Shaker followers can be trusted, Lee was virtually obsessed
with rooting out lust. Although Wilkinson had also urged her followers to be
celibate, she had never disowned those who chose to marry. In contrast, Lee
threatened her followers with gruesome sexual punishments if they did not
forswear the sins of the flesh. According to Mehetabel Farrington, a devoted
Shaker, Lee warned: "The more people give way to the gratification of their
lusts, in this world, the stronger their passions will grow, and the more their
lusts will rise in hell; and their torments and plagues will rise in proportion;
they will be bound and tormented in the same parts where they have taken
their carnal pleasure. . . . They are bound in the prisons of hell, and their
torments appear like melted lead, poured through them in the same parts

where they have taken their carnal pleasure." Given these threats of sexual torture, perhaps there may have been some truth to the bizarre stories that Shakers stripped sinners naked, seized them by their sexual organs, and chastised them for their lust, or to the even more fantastic accusation, made by Daniel Rathbun, that Lee had "pound[ed] and [beat] the private parts of both men and women in her discipline."[105] Could such stories have been true? Without further evidence, it is impossible to know, but they certainly speak to at least one larger truth. Mother Ann insisted that her followers mortify their lusts, and she promised "lewd" sinners that they would burn in hell rather than rejoice in her millennial church.

Lee's hostility toward the body may have had many psychological causes, most of which we can only imagine. Perhaps her tragic experiences in childbirth convinced her that sexuality was the root of all suffering. In addition, it is difficult not to see her celibacy as an unconscious solution, at least in part, to the prohibitions against women's religious leadership. By denying her sexuality, though not her sex, Lee tried to set herself apart from the ordinary breed of "carnal" women who had been ordered to keep silence in the churches. Because she had transcended the sexual corruption of her body, she was no longer a woman, but a perfect vessel of the Holy Spirit. Hence the traditional rules against female preaching simply did not apply to her.

Even so, Lee remained deeply ambivalent about her role as a female religious leader. Although she claimed to have seen God face to face, and she tried to conquer her physical "corruption" through the discipline of celibacy, she still seems to have found it difficult to reconcile her religious calling with the cultural and biblical sanctions against female evangelism. According to her followers, she mixed her belief in the spiritual equality of the sexes with more traditional views about women's subordination to men on earth. For example, even as she tried to destroy the institution of marriage, she reportedly told Lucy Markham to "be obedient to your husband. . . . as the Church is to Christ: for the husband is the head of the wife, even as Christ is the head of the Church." Another follower, Jethro Turner, claimed that she used a similar language of submission when Joseph Meacham, visiting her for the first time, demanded to know the source of her religious authority. Quoting Paul's words, "Let your women keep silence in the churches," he asked: "You not only speak, but seem to be an elder in your church. How do you reconcile this with the apostle's doctrine?" Lee reportedly answered: "As the order of nature requires a man and a woman to produce offspring; so, when they both stand in their proper order, the man is the first, and the woman is the second in the government of the family. He is the father and she is the mother; and all the children, both male and female, must be subject to their parents; and the woman, being second, must be subject to her husband, who is the first; but when the man is gone, the right of government belongs to the woman: so is the family of Christ." In short, Lee agreed that women were naturally subordinate to men in the order of creation, but they had the right to take on "masculine" responsibilities when their husbands were absent. As Christ's "deputy husband," not his equal, she could substitute for him until his triumphant return.[106]

Perhaps this story from the 1816 *Testimonies* is apocryphal, especially since it was told at a time when many male Shakers were ambivalent about "petticoat government," but Lee asserted her deference to men through her actions as well as her words.[107] In contrast to Jemima Wilkinson, who braved the ridicule of strangers by speaking in public, Lee preferred to let the men do the "teaching." According to her followers, she was a "woman of few words" who preached infrequently. During her missionary tour of New England, she sometimes sat quietly in the audience while her brother William and James Whittaker held public meetings.[108] Despite her considerable religious authority, she preferred to share her beliefs by telling stories as she went about her daily round of chores—stories that mirror all of the contradictions and complexities of her life as the mother of the Shaker church.

Could women preach in the new republic? Lee answered yes, but not without reservation. In her new millennial church, women who wanted to gain recognition as religious leaders had to renounce or spiritualize the bodily experiences that physically defined them as women: pregnancy, childbirth, and nursing. These experiences still had value, but only if they were raised to a spiritual plane that was far removed from the realities of women's everyday lives in late-eighteenth-century America.

Ann Lee and Jemima Wilkinson stand as poignant symbols of the continuing limitations on women's religious liberty in Revolutionary America. Indeed, their examples suggest that female evangelists were even more confined by the boundaries of gender during the much-vaunted Age of Revolution than they had been during the earlier revivals of the Great Awakening. Even though Bathsheba Kingsley, the "brawling woman" who had exhorted in the 1740s, had wanted to be swallowed up by God in order to transcend the limitations of her gender, she had never tried to deny that she was physically female. In contrast, Wilkinson and Lee took the words of Paul literally—"There is neither male nor female"—and they tried to erase any bodily signs of their sexuality. Filled with ambivalence about their "carnal," "feminine" bodies, they took the evangelical language of transcendence to a self-denying extreme.

The stories of Wilkinson and Lee remind us that history is not always a record of either linear progress or decline: it is more complicated, more surprising, and often more chaotic than our narratives typically allow. Although the American Revolution *was* revolutionary for women, its effects would not be felt until the turn of the nineteenth century, when a sweeping ideological transformation changed ideas about women's sphere. Even then, its legacy would be deeply ambivalent. The ideology of republican motherhood, still developing in the 1780s and 1790s, did not usher in a golden age for women, but it gave them a new language of female virtue to challenge the constraints on their public speech. The few women who preached in Revolutionary America were truly women in the wilderness, but their "travail" eventually gave birth to a new generation of female preachers, a generation that was far less hesitant to demand a public role in the church.

Part Two

I commend unto you Phebe our sister, which is a servant of the church which is at Cenchrea: That ye receive her in the Lord, as becometh saints, and that ye assist her in whatsoever business she hath need of you: for she hath been a succourer of many, and of myself also.—Romans 16:1–2

The inhabitants of the villages ceased, they ceased in Israel, until that I Deborah arose, that I arose a mother in Israel.—Judges 5:7

3

Female Laborers in the Harvest

Female Preaching in the Early Nineteenth Century

And Jesus went about all the cities and villages, teaching in their synagogues, and preaching the gospel of the kingdom, and healing every sickness and every disease among the people. But when he saw the multitudes, he was moved with compassion on them, because they fainted, and were scattered abroad, as sheep having no shepherd. Then saith he unto his disciples, The harvest truly is plenteous, but the labourers are few; Pray ye therefore the Lord of the harvest, that he will send forth labourers into his harvest.
—Matthew 9:35–38

And I intreat thee also, true yokefellow, help those women which laboured with me in the gospel.—Philippians 4:3

In September of 1795 at the Yearly Meeting of Freewill Baptists in Edgecomb, Maine, Sally Parsons delivered a "most Marvelous & soul ravishing Relation" of her "travail thro[ugh] & deliverance from Great Tryals." Like many of the other people in attendance that day, Parsons had experienced both the joys of conversion and the "tryals" of trying to overcome sin, but she had also borne crosses that were distinctly her own. Disowned by her father because of her belief in free will, she was alone and

Many of the new sects that flourished in the new republic worshiped in small, rural churches. This Methodist church in Unity, New Hampshire (1823), was originally a Quaker meetinghouse. Reprinted from Hobart Pillsbury, *New Hampshire: Resources, Attractions, and Its People, a History* (New York: Lewis Historical Publishing Co., 1927).

virtually friendless, and she had come to the Yearly Meeting hoping to find a new family in her community of faith. Because she had been a loyal member of a Freewill Baptist church for two years, she hoped that clergymen would embrace her as a "sister in Christ," but as she herself knew, her story seemed too remarkable to be true. Even though she was young, uneducated, poor, and forsaken by her family, she insisted that God had called her to "labor" in his harvest as a preacher. As she stood in front of the Yearly Meeting on that autumn day, searching for the right words to reveal her call, she feared that she might be disowned yet again, but this time by her church.[1]

Instead of denouncing Parsons as an enthusiast, however, the Freewill Baptists praised her as a devout evangelical who had been genuinely inspired by God. Comparing her to Phebe, Priscilla, and all the other women who had labored with Paul in the early Christian church, they marveled at her "soul ravishing" description of her call to preach the gospel. Setting themselves apart from almost all the other churches in the early republic, they welcomed her as a spiritual sister who had been "chosen out of the world" to convert sinners.

Although there is no record that the Freewill Baptists ever officially licensed

Sally Parsons as a female preacher, she had begun speaking in churches throughout New Hampshire and Maine by 1796. Befriended by Benjamin Randel, the founder of the sect, she often traveled with him into the back-country as he founded new churches. (Randel became like a father to her, and she eventually married his son.) In July of 1796, the secretary of the Freewill Baptist church in Pittsfield, New Hampshire, scrawled in the record book: "Br[other] Randel and Sister Salley Persons ... brought us good News that the Lord was about to revive his work which Caused us great Joy." Preaching in churches, private homes, and even barns or fields, she continued to hold "blesed meetings" throughout the 1790s.[2]

Sally Parsons was only one of more than a hundred women who preached between 1790 and 1845 in new, dissenting sects that challenged the Calvinist orthodoxy. As Jemima Wilkinson ministered to her few remaining converts in New Jerusalem, and as the Shakers continued to ponder the meaning of Ann Lee's life and death, scores of other uneducated, visionary women began crisscrossing the American countryside as itinerant preachers. In the midst of a second Great Awakening, the Freewill Baptists, Christian Connection, Methodists, and African Methodists allowed women into the pulpit in numbers that earlier eighteenth-century evangelicals and sectarians never could have imagined. Although visionary women such as Bathsheba Kingsley had exhorted during the revivals of the 1740s and 1760s, they had never gained more than limited institutional acceptance. During the 1770s and 1780s, Ann Lee, Jemima Wilkinson, and a few female Come-Outers on the frontier had become preachers, but they had viewed their sex (and their sexuality) as a problem that had to be overcome. And even though the Quakers, progressive as always, continued to recognize women as Public Friends, they were still an exceptional minority in a culture largely shaped by evangelical Protestants.

It was not until the first decades of the nineteenth century that female preaching finally gained acceptance beyond the Quakers, Universal Friends, and Shakers. In evangelical churches across the country, women began to invent a new model of female ministry that was based as much on their "femininity" as on their transcendence of it. Like all of the visionary women who had gone before them, nineteenth-century female preachers clung to Paul's promise that there was neither male nor female, but they also portrayed themselves as *women* who had been called to minister to the family of God as "Sisters in Christ" and "Mothers in Israel." Instead of dressing in "masculine" clothing, advocating celibacy, or denying that they were female, they proudly compared themselves to biblical heroines and prophetesses such as Phebe, Huldah, and Deborah. When Sally Parsons and other women rode from town to town visiting churches, they explained that they, like Phebe, had been chosen as servants of the church, female laborers in the harvest.

As the result of sweeping political, religious, and ideological changes, there was a dramatic transformation in attitudes toward female religious leadership in the early republic. On the broadest level, the rise of female preaching was connected to the expansion of the informal public and the creation of a new ideology of "feminine" virtue. As Americans organized reform and benevolence organizations, tract societies, and a multitude of other voluntary associations that mediated between the family and the state—and as churches themselves became part of this informal public after disestablishment—women gained greater opportunities to participate in the public sphere. At the same time, many Americans began to perceive women, not men, as the more praiseworthy sex, and despite lingering images of feminine corruption, they urged them to help nurture an ethic of religious and civic virtue.

Besides these two broad transformations, a multitude of other factors contributed to the rise of female preaching in the early nineteenth century. Like earlier Separates, Baptists, Shakers, and Public Friends, the nineteenth-century evangelicals who allowed women to preach were dissenters, and they deliberately tried to create churches that stood apart from the secular world. By allowing women such as Sally Parsons to preach, they vividly symbolized their opposition to the dominant values of their culture. Not only did they argue that God could choose anyone, even the poor or female, to speak as his divine instruments, but they also claimed the millennium was near at hand. Because of their genuine belief that they were living in the last days before Armageddon, they encouraged all Christians, whether male or female, to put aside propriety in order to "save souls." Finally, on the most practical level, they eagerly welcomed anyone who had a talent for preaching because they desperately needed new laborers in the harvest. By locating ultimate religious authority in individual, heartfelt experience, they made it possible for both uneducated men and uneducated women to proclaim their religious beliefs to the world.

Revivalism and Voluntarism

America in the early 1800s was no longer a provincial backwater of England, but a rising national power. After the Revolutionary War, Americans proudly proclaimed that they were the only truly republican nation on earth—a nation that was divinely destined for political, economic, and military greatness. Not only had they defeated the British, the most powerful empire in the western world, on the bloodstained battlefields of Saratoga and Yorktown, but they had triumphed over the differences of party and section to form a single nation of "united states." Economically, America was blessed with an abundance of natural resources that promised wealth and prosperity, and geographically, its frontiers seemed to know no bounds. As the population nearly doubled from 5.3 million to 9.6 million between 1800 and 1820, and then almost doubled again to 17 million by 1840, thousands of pioneers began to make the trek west in search of open land and economic opportunity. "We have monopolized the best of time and space," Bronson Alcott exulted in 1834, "and stand on a vantage ground to which no people have ever ascended before."[3]

Yet mixed with this giddy optimism about America's future were deeper seeds of doubt and anxiety. Despite the celebration of America's glorious destiny, there were some who feared that the republic was too fragile to survive. George Washington and the other framers of the Constitution had been deeply suspicious of political parties, but by the 1790s, Federalists and Republicans were arguing bitterly about America's future. Should power be centralized in the federal government or in individual states? Should America be a commercial nation or an agricultural one? Sectional divisions split the republic as well, with northern and southern states squabbling over issues as diverse as slavery and commerce. At the Hartford Convention of 1814, the New England states briefly toyed with the idea of seceding from the union to found their own republic. Meanwhile the southern states, intent on preserving the "peculiar institution" of slavery, only reluctantly agreed to abide by the Missouri Compromise of 1819.

These political crises were compounded by the economic dislocations caused by the "market revolution." As early as the seventeenth century, farmers had bartered goods and services in their own local markets, but an ethic of mutual responsibility had prevented the emergence of a truly individualistic, capitalist economy. In Puritan New England, for example, magistrates had fixed prices and wages to prevent the wealthy from exploiting the poor.[4] By the 1740s, however, urban merchants in the North had begun to sell small consumer goods in the backcountry, and in the wake of the American Revolution, these commercial networks expanded and diversified. Textile and paper mills began to dot the New England countryside, and thanks to new turnpikes, canals, bridges, and eventually railroads, both merchants and farmers could sell their wares in a national rather than merely local market. Even people living in rural areas were drawn into the web of commercial relations: enterprising manufacturers sent the raw materials for making hats, shoes, and clothing to farming families in the countryside. For many Americans, the emergence of a market economy heralded a bright future: prosperity, a dazzling variety of new consumer goods, and upward mobility. But others lamented that an "anxious spirit of gain" had undermined the traditional values of communal responsibility and economic self-sufficiency.[5]

To add to this political and economic turmoil, religious leaders were deeply troubled by the spread of Deism and skepticism. Even though Deism never became a popular alternative to evangelicalism, many of the most influential men in Revolutionary America, including Thomas Jefferson and Benjamin Franklin, were openly sympathetic to the claims of "rational" religion—a dangerous heresy in the eyes of most established clergymen. After the publication of Thomas Paine's *Age of Reason*, Jedidiah Morse worried that America might lose its identity as a Christian nation: "The Christian religion, and its divine and blessed author, are not only disbelieved, rejected, and contemned, but even abhorred."[6] According to Morse, Americans were no longer linked together by a common Protestant faith in biblical revelation.

It was in this climate of upheaval, with its heady mixture of fear and optimism, hope and anxiety, that a new wave of evangelical revivals once again turned the world upside down. Sporadic revivals began as early as the 1770s and 1780s among radical sects in the New England backcountry, and by the early years of the nineteenth century, the impressive rates of church growth convinced ministers that God had sent another "great awakening" to America. Although the Methodists, with their young and zealous circuit riders, gained the most converts, the revivals touched all denominations, both Calvinist and Arminian. For example, the First Congregational Church of New Haven, one of the earliest and most orthodox Puritan churches in America, admitted only 90 new members in the sixteen years from 1789 to 1805, but it added 202 new converts in the four years between 1806 and 1810.[7]

Historians have argued over both the causes and the meanings of these emotional, evangelical revivals. Indeed, to sort through the literature on the Second Great Awakening is to confront a bewildering variety of conflicting interpretations. Some claim that the revivals came from the top down; others argue from the bottom up. Some suggest that middle-class merchants and entrepreneurs fostered revivals in order to control lower-class workers; others argue that poor laborers used evangelicalism to challenge industrialization. Some claim that the revivals represented the triumph of a liberal, capitalist order; others insist that they arose as a protest against the market revolution. Some have interpreted the revivals as a conservative response to widespread feelings of rootlessness and anxiety; others have seen them as a democratic and populist revolt against the established churches, and indeed, against all traditional authority.[8] And the list could go on.

In part, scholars have disagreed because they have lumped together so many different revivals under the label "the Second Great Awakening." If, as historian Jon Butler has argued, the concept of a coherent, eighteenth-century "Great Awakening" should be dismissed as an interpretive fiction, then referring to a nineteenth-century "Second Great Awakening" seems equally suspect. Even though the revivals were urban and rural, northern and southern, Congregational and Methodist, Baptist and Presbyterian, historians have often treated them as if they were interchangeable. In reality, however, the revivals were as diverse as the denominations that led them, and they mirrored all of the contradictions of early-nineteenth-century American society: its commitment to democracy and its fear of social disorder, its celebration of individualism and its longing for community, its faith in the future and its nostalgia for the past. At the same time as Charles Finney exulted that sinners could achieve spiritual perfection, William Miller predicted the apocalyptic destruction of the earth.

Yet this does not mean that the revivals were not linked together by any common themes at all. Despite denominational differences, evangelicals as distinct as Finney and Miller shared a commitment to emotional, heart-centered preaching, and theologically, they softened or abandoned Calvinism in order to focus more on human agency and free will. Unlike later liberals (such as Horace Bushnell), who believed that children could be gradually nurtured in the principles of Christian faith, they affirmed that people could be "saved" *only* if they went through a dramatic, life-changing experience of spiritual rebirth. In addition, all evangelicals saw Jesus as a personal, individual Savior, and all put their faith in the truth of Scripture.

Besides these theological affinities, all evangelical Protestants had to adjust to the separation of church and state after the American Revolution. Instead of simply revitalizing older forms of piety, the early-nineteenth-century revivals represented a fundamental restructuring of American religion around the principles of freedom and competition. In 1791 the Bill of Rights guaranteed that freedom of worship would be one of the principal tenets of the new republic, and in the following years, individual states began disestablishing the colonial churches. Instead of collecting state taxes, churches such as the Congregationalists and Episcopalians had to compete with new dissenting sects, especially the upstart Methodists and Baptists, for both membership and money. In the new republic, churchgoing would be voluntary, not required, and the churches that wanted to survive had to search actively for new converts. Religious authority had now shifted from the state to voluntary institutional bodies.[9]

After Congress declared that it would "make no law respecting an establishment of religion," all American churches, no matter what their status during the colonial period, eventually lost their connection to the state. Without the power to collect government taxes, they were no longer any different from all the other institutions competing for members in the vast informal public of American society. Rather than the state-supported guardians of public order, they were merely voluntary associations who brought together like-minded believers, and like all of the other independent associations in the nineteenth century, they could recruit new members only through persuasion, not coercion. Even though evangelical ministers continued to exert an enormous influence on American culture, they were helpless to enforce theological conformity in a new, pluralistic religious marketplace.

As churches ceased to be political, public institutions in the same sense as they had been in colonial America, clergymen began to give women greater opportunities for involvement and leadership. Following in the footsteps of eighteenth-century Separates, Baptists, Shakers, and Public Universal Friends, who had never been formally connected to the state, many evangelicals no longer feared that female religious activism would necessarily lead to political disorder. If churches were part of an expanding informal public that stood between the family and the government, then women as well as men could take an active role in church affairs without appearing too "masculine" or commanding. In virtually every Protestant denomination, women worked side by side with men to build a more Christian society. Even though they could not be ordained, they raised money for the poor, founded reform and benevolence organizations, distributed religious tracts from door to door, and even went on foreign missions to convert the "heathen."

Countless numbers of women as well as men joined voluntary associations during the early nineteenth century. When Alexis de Tocqueville visited the United States in 1831, he was amazed by the sheer number and variety of public associations that he found, whether "religious, moral, serious, futile, general or restricted, enormous or diminutive." "Americans of all ages, all conditions, and all dispositions constantly form associations," he wrote.[10] As he explained, democracy could thrive only as long as independent citizens were willing to come together to work on behalf of the common good. Just as men formed fraternal organizations, women devoted their talents to temperance societies, Sunday school unions, religious newspapers, and antiprostitution crusades. Far from sitting at home in isolated comfort, middle-class women were visible participants in civil society.

Yet even though clergymen praised women for their religious and civic activism, most still refused to let them preach. Not only did Congregational, Dutch Reformed, and Episcopalian ministers fight against the disestablishment of the churches, but they also tried to restrict the public authority of the pulpit to educated men alone. In Connecticut, for example, established ministers clung to their status as part of the formal public until 1818, when the state legislature finally cut its ties to the Congregational Church. Proud of its long Puritan heritage, the Massachusetts legislature did not vote to separate church and state until the late date of 1833. Although ministers such as Lyman Beecher eventually realized that disestablishment was "the best thing" to ever happen to the churches, they still chafed at the thought of "illiterate men" and "bold women" supplanting them as the guardians of American morality.[11] Even though they were no longer supported by the state, they still prided themselves on their public prestige and authority.

Generally speaking, the churches that were established by law, or only recently disestablished, tended to be the most opposed to female preaching. In other words, the most wealthy, powerful, and "respectable" churches were the least likely to allow women to speak publicly. For example, even though New England Congregationalists welcomed the revivals as a sign of God's grace, they also feared that "vulgar" female preachers would do more harm than good.[12] In 1817, at the same time as Freewill Baptist women such as Hannah Lock and Clarissa Danforth were claiming the pulpit as their own, the Reverend Matthew Perrine warned his female congregants to set their sights on more humble forms of religious service. "Women have a work to do in the house of God," he assured his listeners, but that work did not include "teaching" or "governing" men: women could counsel their children, visit orphans and widows, and instruct other women and children in the faith, but they could not "perform the office of public teachers, or . . . exercise rule, or . . . dictate in matters of faith and discipline."[13] Even though women could evangelize sinners informally, they could not usurp men's exclusive right to the pulpit.

Female preaching was especially contested by the Episcopalian churches in the slaveholding South. As many historians have noted, the South was the most socially conservative region in the United States, and its distinctive identity continued to grow stronger in the decades leading up to the Civil War. Southern culture was based on the hierarchy of white over black, male over female, free over slave—a hierarchy that many clergymen insisted had been divinely ordained. Despite their belief in the spiritual equality of all souls before God, Episcopalians also defended the natural subordination of women and slaves to white men. They urged white plantation mistresses to teach their children—and their slaves—to be good Christians, but not to pray or preach in public.

Even though clergymen from many different denominations worked together during the revivals because they wanted to ensure America's identity as a Christian nation, they often quarreled over issues of church doctrine and leadership. Indeed, even though many Protestant ministers seem to have hoped that the revivals would bolster their traditional authority in the wake of disestablishment, they soon realized that they would never recapture the power of their Puritan forefathers.[14] Even more than the first Great Awakening, the revivals of the Second Great Awakening splintered American churches into competing sects that battled over the interpretation of the Bible. As staid reformers such as Lyman Beecher vied with backwoods enthusiasts such as Lorenzo Dow, they wrangled over theology, church-state relations, and, last but not least, female preaching. Despite their shared belief that women could play an important role in promoting Christianity, they could not agree on whether women should keep silence in the churches.

The Rise of Female Exhorting

In stark contrast to the Congregationalists, Dutch Reformed, Episcopalians, and "Old School" Presbyterians, many of the dissenting sects that flourished in the new republic encouraged both women and lay men to pray aloud, testify, and exhort. Instead of viewing churches as part of the state, they saw them as voluntary societies that mediated between the family and the government.

Like eighteenth-century Separates and Baptists, they never suggested that women were *politically* equal to men, but they still argued that women could speak in the informal public of the church.

As part of their opposition to the religious establishment, sects as diverse as the Disciples of Christ, Cumberland Presbyterians, Methodists, O'Kellyites, and Freewill Baptists—to name just a few—allowed women to share their experiences of salvation with their brothers and sisters in Christ. Indeed, it is difficult to read any narrative of the revivals written by a member of one of these sects without stumbling across a reference to women's public religious speech. "There was a Number of Very weighty and Powerfull testimonies borne by many both Males and females," wrote the clerk of the Freewill Baptist Quarterly Meeting in 1803. "A number of brethren and sisters arose, and in faithful, affectionate and impressive exhortations, addressed the congregation," another clergyman reported in 1826. Although most of these sisters and brethren were never identified by name, sometimes they were so "gifted" or "remarkable for usefulness in prayer" that they were singled out for individual praise. According to a Methodist clergyman, Sally Schulyer's "gift in prayer, at all times, surpassed all I ever heard, of man or woman."[15]

Praying aloud was the most common form of women's religious expression, and also the least controversial. In their public prayers, which were often described as "fervent" and emotional, women called upon God to change their hearts, to forgive their sins, to show them compassion, or to give them strength to endure their tribulations. Besides praying for themselves and their family members, especially their husbands and children, they implored God to have mercy on all the nameless sinners who longed to be born again.[16] "Witnessing" or "testifying" (the terms were used interchangeably) was also deeply personal and emotional, but it tended to be more declaratory than invocative: women shared the intimate stories of their own religious trials and triumphs rather than imploring God for help. For example, after Margaret Huffman was disinherited by her father because of her religious beliefs, she assured her church that her *real* father had not abandoned her. "Brethren and sisters, you know my history, and think me poor. I am not poor," she insisted. "My Father is rich; heaven, and earth, and the cattle upon a thousand hills, are his, and I am his heir."[17] Witnessing was almost always an act of giving thanks, of praising God for his compassion in the face of suffering and adversity.

Although exhorting incorporated elements of witnessing and praying aloud, it tended to be more commanding and less personal. To be sure, exhorters often spoke about their own religious struggles, but their goal was more universal than simply testifying to their own saving experiences of grace. Above all, exhorters spoke words of warning: they sternly admonished hard-hearted sinners to seek salvation before it was too late. In Kentucky, one female exhorter warned her listeners that the damned "had no rest, day or night; there is a dreadful sound in their ears, and finally they should be punished with *everlasting destruction*."[18] Weaving scriptural references into her comments, she alluded to biblical prophecies without delivering a formal sermon.

Because many female exhorters were reputed to be riveting, even thrilling speakers, clergymen sometimes relied on them to help lead religious services. For example, when James Erwin lost his voice while preaching, he asked Alma Wright and Jane Smith to take control of the meeting. In a classic example of the role reversal that took place during the revivals, Erwin sat silently while his two female assistants entreated his audience to repent and seek salvation. "How they prayed!" he marveled. "For an hour or more these women took the kingdom by storm, and God answered prayer by converting several of the penitents." In other religious meetings, female exhorters spoke with so much emotion that listeners would "weep bitterly."[19]

However, even though evangelical women occasionally testified or exhorted during formal services, they spoke most frequently during social meetings for worship that were closed to the general public. For example, the Methodists organized praying bands, class meetings, and love feasts that brought believers together in settings that were less structured than Sunday services. While bands tended to be quite small and usually were segregated by sex, class meetings were larger, and in the early years of the movement, men and women sometimes met together. (This was especially true in towns where the Methodist community was small and there were not enough people to create more than one or two classes.) In these small, intimate gatherings, men and women shared their personal stories, witnessing to their faith in God. Similarly, in quarterly love feasts, which were often quite large, converts were expected to reveal their innermost religious feelings to their brothers and sisters in Christ. Such public scrutiny could be intimidating, but according to Methodist circuit riders, as many as one hundred or two hundred people could step forward during a single love feast to share their testimonies.[20]

In the South as well as the North, evangelical women who belonged to new, dissenting churches often refused to keep silence when they felt inspired to speak. Ministers' journals and church records are filled with examples of women's "irresistible" and "powerful" words of prayer and exhortation. "Old Sister Hampton" spoke during Methodist love feasts "in the strong language of feeling"; Hannah Swayze gained renown for "the eloquence and power of her public prayers"; and Nancy Mulkey, the daughter of an O'Kellyite minister, "would pour forth an exhortation lasting from five to fifteen minutes, which neither father nor brother could *equal*, and which brought tears from every feeling eye."[21] In addition, many southern planter women "preached" to the slaves on their plantations by reading the Bible to them or holding prayer meetings. "Miss Mag she uster come in eb'ry house and hol' prayer meetin'," one former slave remembered. "She go to one house on Sunday and another house de nex' Sunday 'till she go all roun' de quarters. And she could pray, too, lemme tell you. Sometime she git so happy she git to shoutin'."[22] Taken together, these bits and pieces of descriptions suggest that a profound transformation was taking place in southern churches: white women were speaking in public on a scale never before imagined.

Like their white mistresses, many southern slave women also gained renown as charismatic speakers. During Sunday services and secret meetings in "the fields and thickets," African American women prayed aloud, shared their stories of salvation, and shouted out their praises to God. "My mother could send up the most powerful prayer of anybody on the plantation," one former slave testified. Another remembered that "Aunt Sylvia," a slave in Mississippi, led religious services in her quarters every week. "She was a good thinker," he explained. "Looked as if she knowed everything just from her mother wit. She was the only preacher we knowed anything about." Despite the fact that they were enslaved and illiterate, these women insisted that they spoke as instruments of God whose words were divinely inspired. As one female visionary explained, God had made the same promise to her that he had once made to the prophet Jeremiah: "Open your mouth, and I will speak through you."[23] According to her, she spoke with as much authority as a divinely inspired prophet.

In the late 1790s in Georgia, a female slave identified only as Clarinda caused a sensation because of her attempts to convert people on the street. The mother of more than twenty children, Clarinda was illiterate, crippled, and according to a clergyman, "remarkably dissolute and profane," but after her conversion, she began exhorting sinners to repent and seek salvation. Deeply impressed by her piety, white evangelicals elevated her as a pillar of the Baptist church: she was "liberally supported" by many Christian families, including a woman who helped her to buy a small house; she learned how to read; and miraculously, she was freed by her master. In what must have seemed like a literal fulfillment of Christ's promise that the last would be first, she had been transformed from an illiterate slave into a paragon of piety. Despite the fact that she was black and female, the town's "first ladies" treated her "with respect and kindness . . . as a distinguished monument of sovereign mercy, and one of the greatest prodigies in the christian world."[24] Evangelicalism, as many historians have noted, had the radical potential to suspend the distinctions of race and sex.

Yet even though southern evangelicals allowed both white and black women to speak publicly during religious meetings—no small gesture—they drew a sharp line between praying aloud, witnessing, or exhorting, which they perceived as spontaneous and informal, and preaching, which was much more authoritative. Hannah Miller, a Mississippi Methodist (and the sister-in-law of the infamous itinerant Lorenzo Dow), reportedly "attracted the attention of the people as much as any preacher in the territory where she was known," but clergymen never suggested that she should actually *become* a preacher. Nor did anyone ever propose that black women should be licensed to spread the gospel in the slave quarters. Despite welcoming lower-class white men and male slaves into the sacred space of the pulpit, they never extended the same privilege to white or black women. The celebrated Harry Hosier, popularly known as "Black Harry," preached with Bishop Francis Asbury and other Methodist leaders in the years following the Revolution, but no black or white woman was ever invited to do the same. Surprisingly, southern evangelicals viewed sex, not race, as the most important determinant of religious leadership. Preaching was a privilege reserved for men, and even a male slave had a greater right to speak in public than a white woman.[25] "My sisters, be content to stay at home and guide the house," counseled Samuel Rogers, an itinerant for the Disciples of Christ. "This is the noblest work in the world; and a mission a thousand times nobler than any known by those who are continually croaking about woman's rights." In 1839, after "Sister" Roberts, a Primitive Baptist, "seized the pulpit" and delivered a sermon in her South Carolina church, she was excommunicated.[26]

At first glance, the conservatism of these southern sects is puzzling. Historians have typically treated them as the equivalents of the northern Freewill

Baptists and Christians, and with good reason: they all spoke on the same themes of sin, repentance, and salvation; they all favored highly emotional revival meetings; and they all insisted that ordinary people could read the Bible for themselves.[27] In addition, they all set themselves apart from the old established churches by encouraging women to pray aloud and exhort. Yet even though the O'Kellyites, Methodists, Baptists, Stonites, and Cumberland Presbyterians were "plain folk" who protested against the southern culture of honor, especially the immorality of slaveholding, they were never as radical as their northern counterparts.[28] Southern and northern Methodists were linked together in a single national church (and would be until the eve of the Civil War), but they often argued over whether Sisters in Christ and Mothers in Israel should be allowed into the "public pulpit."

The schism between southern and northern evangelicals on the question of female preaching points to the importance of region in understanding American religious history, especially in the years before the Civil War. Even though the sects who took root in the new, expanding informal public tended to give women greater freedom than the established churches, they were shaped by their own distinctive cultural environments in ways that they themselves would have been loathe to admit. The Stonites, O'Kellyites, Baptists, Cumberland Presbyterians, and Methodists were deeply ambivalent about the patriarchy of southern culture, but they still feared that too much religious liberty might lead to social disorder. Although they seemed to turn the world upside down with their anticlericalism, their attacks on the brutality of slavery, and their emotional camp meetings, they always spoke with a distinctively southern accent when it came to the issue of women's religious leadership. Even more than northern evangelicals, who also had a conservative streak, they mixed their commitment to gospel liberty with traditional beliefs about women's subordination to men.

It would not be until the decades after the Civil War that significant numbers of southern as well as northern women would be allowed to preach in evangelical churches. Perhaps there were many who longed to labor in the harvest, but if so, they were forced to content themselves with praying aloud, witnessing, or exhorting. Even though few southern white women actually lived up to the ideal of the genteel, modest, and refined southern lady, and few black women conformed to the stereotype of the submissive mammy, there was little tolerance for religious "disorder" in a society built on slavery.[29]

Female Preaching and Evangelical Sectarianism in the North: The Methodists,
African Methodists, Freewill Baptists, and Christian Connection

Only a few northern churches dared to take the momentous step of allowing
women to preach as well as exhort. Although female preachers, like exhorters,
often implored God for mercy, related their personal religious experiences,
and warned sinners to repent, they spoke with far greater authority than any of
their sisters who raised their voices from the pews. Not only did they stand
apart from the rest of the congregation at the front of the church, often in an
elevated pulpit, but they delivered formal sermons explaining the meaning of
biblical texts. Rather than mere witnesses to God's goodness, preachers were
authoritative *teachers* who were experts on God's sacred word.[30]

Priding themselves on their anti-intellectualism and visionary enthusiasm,
the Freewill Baptists, Christian Connection, northern Methodists, and African
Methodists welcomed scores of women into the pulpit. As sects rather than denominations, they were small, voluntary associations that prized personal religious experience and lay authority over formal creeds or an educated clergy.[31]
Drawing most, though not all, of their membership from the lower classes,
they self-consciously set themselves apart from the "worldliness" of established churches. Even though they were less powerful, less respectable, and less
wealthy than the Congregationalists or Presbyterians, they grew rapidly in the
first decades of the nineteenth century. By 1830, the Freewill Baptists counted
21,000 members; the Christians, 50,000; the African Methodists, over 10,000;
and the Methodists (both northern and southern), a remarkable 500,000.[32]

The Methodists were the most successful of the competing religious groups
that flourished in the aftermath of church disestablishment. Founded in England by John Wesley, they became enormously popular among ordinary
Americans after the Revolution because of their emotional, enthusiastic style
of worship and their theology of free will.[33] Instead of echoing the Calvinist
doctrines of predestination and election, they preached a religion that conformed more closely to the values of republican culture: they insisted that men
and woman were free to choose their own spiritual destinies. Gloating that he
"tore old Calvin up" in his sermons, Benjamin Abbott became one of the most
popular Methodist itinerants in the early nineteenth century.[34] Like other
Methodists, Abbott assured his congregations that they could conscientiously
choose whether to be saved or damned: self-made sinners had the power to
become self-made saints.

The Methodists boasted a tradition of female ministry that stretched back to John Wesley himself, who had allowed women to preach in England as early as the 1760s. Initially, Wesley had opposed female preaching, but true to his faith in the priesthood of all believers, he eventually decided that some women, such as the pious Mary Bosanquet Fletcher, had an "extraordinary call" from God that they could not disobey. Although Wesley never suggested that women should be officially licensed or ordained, he warmly supported their "labors" in spreading the Methodist gospel across the British countryside. By the 1840s, over two hundred women had served as preachers for Methodist sects in Great Britain such as the Bible Christians and the Primitive Methodists.[35]

In America, most Methodists were less tolerant of female preaching than Wesley had been, and they laid even greater emphasis on how extraordinary it was to find women who genuinely had been called. Shaped by the conservatism of their culture, southern Methodists refused to allow women into the pulpit, no matter how pious they were, and even northern and midwestern Methodists never passed any official resolutions recognizing women's right to preach. Of the more than one hundred female preachers whose names I have found, only nine belonged to the Methodist Episcopal Church.[36] In addition, three more female preachers were affiliated with the United Brethren, who resembled the Methodists in worship but did not formally unite with them until this century.

Yet because Methodist female preachers managed to find individual ministers to support them, they became successful and well-known evangelists in America. Ministers allowed women into the pulpit as early as 1792, when Sarah Riker "preachd with freedom" in the Wesley Chapel in New York City. (Given Wesley's much-heralded support for female preaching, the location must have seemed symbolic to both Riker and her listeners.) In theory, Methodist clergymen were supposed to submit to the wishes of their bishops, but in practice, they were often as influenced by local customs as by official doctrine. Heedless of ecclesiastical discipline, one daring minister in Ohio even tried to entice Ellen Stewart into his church by promising to give her "license to preach." By the 1820s, Elice Miller Smith, a Methodist from New England, had risen to become "more universally admired, than any other *female* [preacher] of America."[37]

The African Methodist Episcopal Church, organized in 1816 under the leadership of Bishop Richard Allen, was equally ambivalent about female preaching.[38] Although there were many local churches that welcomed women into the pulpit, I have found only two women whose bishops gave them explicit permission to preach: Jarena Lee, who traveled as an itinerant, and Rachel Evans, a local preacher who was married to an African Methodist clergyman. Perhaps Evans and her husband preached together, but according to Bishop William Paul Quinn, she was a far better speaker than her husband or any of his male colleagues. "She had not a superior in the Western Reserve," he testified.[39] In contrast, at least seven other black female preachers—Zilpha Elaw, Elizabeth (whose last name is unknown), Juliann Jane Tilmann, Sojourner Truth, Julia Foote, Julia Pell, and Rebecca Jackson—were never formally recognized by the African Methodist hierarchy, but they still gained renown as charismatic religious leaders.[40] Fragmentary evidence suggests that there may have been many other black women preachers as well—perhaps dozens—but unfortunately their names are difficult to find in historical records. In her memoir, Jarena Lee mentioned meeting several "sister speakers" as she traveled across the country, but she never identified them by name. Perhaps some of these women belonged to one of the other, smaller groups of black Methodists, such as the African Union Methodist church in Delaware or the African Methodist Episcopal Zion church in New York.[41]

Several Methodist splinter groups, all located outside of the South, lent greater institutional support to female preachers. Founded in the 1820s, 1830s, and 1840s in response to the Methodists' episcopal form of government and their growing authoritarianism, the Reformed Methodists, the Methodist Protestants, and the Wesleyan Methodists allowed both lay men and women to testify in public. Since all of these sects were much smaller than the Methodist Episcopal Church (the Reformed Methodists numbered only three thousand members in 1848), the numbers of women who preached for them were correspondingly small: I have found the names of only two female preachers who belonged to the Reformed Methodists, one who belonged to the Methodist Protestants, and one who belonged to the Wesleyans.[42] But what these sects lacked in numbers, they made up for in visibility. Determined to create a more American and republican church, they attacked the Methodist Episcopal Church as a dangerous "*Despotism*" that had granted full "Legislative, Judicial, and Executive powers" to a single body of bishops. As a further symbol of their egalitarian ethic, they invited popular female preachers such as Hannah Reeves and Ellen Stewart to speak at their Quarterly Meetings and General Conferences.[43]

The Freewill Baptists, organized in 1780, and the Christian Connection, organized in 1803, allowed greater numbers of women to preach. Their founders, Benjamin Randel and Elias Smith, both traced their heritage back to the Separates of New England, and they objected to the Baptists' growing formalism during the upheavals of the American Revolution. A "plain, devotional people," in Smith's opinion, had "gone into Babylon" by trading their spiritual fervor for wealth, political power, elegant meetinghouses, and "foppish" ministers.[44] Like the most radical eighteenth-century New Lights, Smith and Randel claimed that the first Christian churches had been led not by educated clergymen, but by ordinary farmers, sailors, and laborers—humble men whose only qualification had been their call from God.

In this spirit of gospel liberty, the Freewill Baptists and Christians welcomed women as well as uneducated men into the pulpit. Between 1790 and 1845, at least twenty-seven Freewill Baptist and twenty-three Christian Connection women crisscrossed the country preaching the gospel. Like Sally Parsons, the poor, young itinerant who helped Benjamin Randel found new churches in the New England backcountry, none of these women were ordained, and technically, they were not even licensed: the title "licentiate" referred only to men who were awaiting ordination. Nevertheless, clerical leaders wrote women letters of recommendation giving them official permission to preach. In 1826, for example, Susan Humes received a letter from the Quarterly Meeting of the Freewill Baptists in Burrillville, Rhode Island, endorsing her as a "public laborer." Whenever she wanted to preach in a Freewill Baptist church, she simply produced this letter as proof of her credentials.[45]

The Freewill Baptists and Christians allowed women to perform virtually all of the same duties as their male colleagues. Besides consoling the sick and the troubled, women visited converts in their homes, preached at Sunday services and camp meetings, and even presided over funerals. In 1833 Wealthy Monroe preached the funeral sermon for Esther Ames, a request that Ames had made shortly before her death. Other women were honored by being invited to preach at Quarterly and Yearly Meetings—the official conferences that ordained new ministers, heard reports from local churches, and resolved disciplinary or doctrinal problems. In 1817 Judith Prescott regaled the New Durham Quarterly Meeting of Freewill Baptists with a "good account of the work of God" in the towns where she had been preaching.[46]

In addition to allowing women to exhort and preach, these sects allowed them to vote, a momentous innovation in the context of Revolutionary debates about citizenship. According to local church records from the 1790s and early 1800s, many Freewill Baptists and Christians (though not Methodists) extended political rights to lay women as well as men: women could choose new ministers and deacons, make decisions in disciplinary cases, serve as messengers to Quarterly or Yearly Meetings, and vote on all aspects of church business. For example, the Freewill Baptist Church in Pittsfield, New Hampshire, permitted all full members, whether male or female, to vote at its Monthly Meetings.[47] As early as 1797, Sally Parsons voiced her opinion on a church disciplinary case, warning her male colleagues of "the danger of a persecuting spirit."[48] In their own small way, these sects gave women a taste of the political liberty that they lacked in the new republic.

Despite this symbolic gesture, however, these sects never claimed that women should be allowed to vote in state as well as church elections. Separated from the formal public of the government, they did not equate women's religious rights with political rights, and they had far less at stake than established churches in allowing women to participate in church business. Even though they allowed women to play a crucial role in selecting new ministers, they never questioned women's political subordination to men in the state.

Even though these sects emphasized their democratic values, they never extended the same religious authority to women as to men. None, even the most avowedly egalitarian, ever demanded fundamental, structural change in the power relations between the sexes. Whether Methodist or Reformed Methodist, Freewill Baptist or Christian, they forbade women to perform baptisms or administer the Lord's Supper, and they never even considered ordaining them, an idea that was far too radical to be taken seriously. As one Christian Connection clergyman explained, women could preach, but they could not "rule": "The man is to rule and be the head in the affairs both of church and state, as well as in his family. . . . [but] if a woman has a gift, she has as good a right to improve that gift as a man."[49] Although women's "gifts" enabled them to save sinners, they remained strangers and pilgrims in churches governed by men alone.

Despite encouraging women to pray aloud, witness, or exhort, the Freewill Baptists, Christians, and Methodists remained ambivalent about allowing them to preach. Indeed, their careful distinction between preaching and ruling seemed calculated to remind women of their natural subordination to men. Since they had no intention of challenging the unequal relationship between the sexes in the family or state, they were horrified by female rebels such as

Fanny Wright, the scandalous reformer who championed women's rights. Despite their praise of women such as Sally Parsons, who convinced the Freewill Baptist Quarterly Meeting to accept her as a female laborer in 1795, they were still not as egalitarian as the Quakers, who abolished a male clerical hierarchy because of their literal belief in the priesthood of all believers.

Yet we must also recognize that in the early nineteenth century, these sects appeared radical indeed. By the simple act of allowing women to speak in public, they opened up a world of possibilities that seemed to have closed during the era of the Revolution. By allowing women to vote, to exhort, and to preach, they implicitly promised to further the work that the Revolution had only begun—the work of extending religious liberty to women as well as to men. In the midst of political, economic, and religious turmoil, they launched one of the most daring experiments of their time. After a Congregational minister attacked female preaching as "unlawful and inexpedient," a Christian Connection clergyman retorted, "The prophet Joel foretold that in the gospel day females as well as males, should prophesy." Even though he never suggested that women had the right to be ordained, he still insisted that they, like the earliest Christian believers, could tell the story of their "salvation by the cross." He wrote: "It is lawful for pious females to *preach* the gospel—to preach it in the pulpit or out of it—in the dedicated sanctuary or the social chamber,—preach it in the city or the country, before saints, sinners, or devils."[50] Like hundreds of other clergymen in the early nineteenth century, he insisted that all Christians, whether male or female, had the right to publicly proclaim their faith in Christ.

Visionary Enthusiasm in the World Turned Upside Down

Given the long historical association between female preaching and religious disorder, it was remarkable that the Methodists, African Methodists, Christians, and Freewill Baptists allowed women into the pulpit. Besides being subtly influenced by changing ideas about the relationship between church and state, these groups were also shaped by the concrete realities of the revivals. Profound ideological change rarely occurs in a social vacuum, and the rise of female preaching was closely linked to such issues as the shortage of male ministers, the feminization of church membership, and the spontaneity and turbulence of camp and prayer meetings. On a more abstract level, it was also connected to the theological conviction that all Christians, regardless of age, sex, education, or class, could interpret the Bible for themselves and receive immediate revelations from God. Repeating the history of the eighteenth-century revivals, female preaching appeared at a time of religious disorder and theological ferment—an era when once again, the world seemed to be turned upside down.

Demographically, the sheer number of women sitting in the church pews subtly affected clerical attitudes toward female preaching. Because women increasingly dominated church membership lists in the years after the American Revolution, one historian has christened the nineteenth-century revivals as a "women's awakening." In 1798, for example, the Freewill Baptist leadership refused to allow a church in Brookfield, New Hampshire, to form its own Monthly Meeting because almost all of its members were women. "There is so few mail members it Dont look as if you Could be able to keep up proper order," they explained. Similarly, between 1800 and 1860, women made up a full 60 percent of the new members admitted to all the churches in Cortland County, New York.[51] Although clergymen feared that such large numbers of female converts might make the church peripheral to the larger culture, they also began to give women greater opportunities to testify and preach. On one hand, they did not want women to "rule" over men, but on the other, they had always encouraged them to meet in single-sex groups for prayer and spiritual reflection. There seemed to be no reason to prevent women from speaking publicly to other women.

These sects also allowed women to preach because of the shortage of ordained male ministers. In their formative years, the Methodists, African Methodists, Freewill Baptists, and Christians simply did not have enough ordained clergy to keep pace with their spectacular growth. In 1795, for example, when Sally Parsons told the Yearly Meeting of Freewill Baptists that she had been called to preach, they were desperate to find new laborers in the harvest. Even by 1810, after intensive recruiting efforts, there were still only sixty-four Freewill Baptist ministers to lead one hundred congregations.[52] Out of necessity, then, these sects turned to women as well as lay men to help lead meetings and organize new churches. As one Christian elder later remembered, his disapproval evident, "It was too much a fashion with the order of people with whom I had connected myself, to make preachers of almost all who opened their mouths in public." Even as late as 1838, when the Christians had become a popular and thriving denomination, the *Christian Journal* ran an article entitled "Laborers Wanted" encouraging lay people to appoint their own religious meetings "when ministerial help is not conveniently obtained."[53]

Because of the scarcity of laborers, particularly in remote areas of the country, women often held informal religious services for their friends and neighbors. During the 1770s, two Methodist "praying women" in the backwoods of Georgia began holding meetings that eventually attracted the "whole neighborhood." Although these women were too humble to presume to preach, they read chapters of the Bible aloud, sang hymns, and urged their listeners to shoulder the "cross" of Christian faith. At their first public meeting, one "offered up a most fervent and deeply impressive prayer to God," while the other told "the plain, simple story of her conversion." Moved by the power of their words, several fell "as if smitten with lightning to the floor," while "others fled from the house in the greatest consternation." The two women continued holding religious meetings until the Reverend Bennett Maxey, a Methodist itinerant, heard about their success and arrived to take control.[54] In a fitting irony, Maxey's name has survived in the historical record, but the women's names have not.

Emboldened by the absence of ordained clergymen, a few women asserted their call to preach as well as witness and exhort. When Abigail Roberts, a Christian, traveled to Milford, New Jersey, in 1833, there was not a single Christian Connection minister in the town, and as the sole representative of her church, she began holding meetings to explain her beliefs. Perhaps her male colleagues would have resented her boldness under different circumstances, but because they were anxious to find new laborers to minister to those who were "scattered abroad, as sheep having no shepherd," they gladly welcomed her help. "She was the first who carried the doctrine of the people known as the Christians . . . into the north and west of New Jersey," wrote David Millard. "For over one year she laboured alone, and may be said to have been the most efficient instrument of opening the way into most of the places where churches of our Connexion have since been planted in that state. Her labors have been abundantly blessed."[55] With few men available, Roberts helped to turn the Christians from a small, struggling sect into a successful denomination.

In addition to the shortage of clergymen and the growing numbers of female converts, female preaching was also linked to the emotionalism and turbulence of revival meetings. As ministers coaxed sinners to come to Christ, thundered out their condemnation of sin, wept openly, and raged at the power of the devil, their listeners responded in kind. Converts "shouted for joy," cried out, "Lord have mercy on me," "wept aloud," and even "fell to the floor as dead." Despite his support of the revivals, Francis Asbury, the first Methodist bishop in America, admitted that his congregations sometimes appeared more like "a drunken rabble" than "the worshippers of God." Levi Hathaway, a Christian Connection preacher, expressed horror at some of the "wild devotions" he witnessed while visiting a congregation in Connecticut: "Some would whine, bark, and howl, so near like a dog, that it would set a person's eyes and ears at variance, while others were screaming as if infernal demons were dragging them down to the regions of despair." After describing American camp meetings for his readers in France, Alexis de Tocqueville concluded: "Religious insanity is very common in the United States."[56] Even though the revivals of the first Great Awakening had caused an uproar in New England and the South during the 1740s and 1760s, they paled in comparison to the boisterous, chaotic revivals that transformed American religion in the decades after the Revolution.

Nineteenth-century evangelicals took the heart-centered preaching of earlier New Lights, Separates, and Come-Outers to an even greater extreme. Desperate to save souls, they experimented with new and sometimes controversial techniques of evangelism that were designed to provoke converts into expressing their feelings of religious ecstasy or terror. They held "protracted" meetings that stretched into the early hours of the morning; they invited men and women who were seeking salvation to identify themselves by stepping up to the altar for prayers; and they set aside "anxious benches" where sinners could sit and pray for Christ's mercy. Most important, they encouraged lay men, women, and even children to raise their voices whenever they felt divinely inspired. In the 1790s, for example, Benjamin Abbott allowed a woman to exhort even though she had interrupted one of his sermons. "I stopped preaching," he explained, "which I always judged was best, in similar instances, and let God send by whom he will send."[57]

Ministers also gathered thousands of converts together in emotional camp meetings that lasted for several days and nights. The spectacle was riveting. As clergymen towered above the crowds in lofty preaching stands, loudly warning sinners to repent, strangers knelt side by side on the ground begging for God's mercy. Throughout the day, trumpets blared whenever families were supposed to eat their meals, attend worship services, or pray privately, and at night, the

"Ein Methodisten Campmeeting." This wood engraving depicts an emotional Methodist camp meeting on "Church Hill" in Queen Anne's County, Maryland. A preacher urges people to repent, raising his arm for emphasis, as crowds of people kneel, pray, cook food, talk to friends, or simply watch in curiosity. Courtesy of the Billy Graham Center Museum.

grounds were illuminated by fires blazing on elevated platforms and candles flickering in the trees. "The nights were truly awful," remembered the Reverend James McGready. "The camp-ground was well illuminated, the people were differently exercised all over the ground—some exhorting, some shouting, some praying, and some crying for mercy, while others lay as dead on the ground. Some of the spiritually wounded fled to the woods, and their groans could be heard all through the surrounding groves, as the groans of dying men."[58] As less sympathetic ministers complained, Christian order seemed to have disappeared.

Because camp meetings were so dramatic and chaotic, men and women often lost their inhibitions after setting foot on the grounds. Indeed, some historians have suggested that camp meetings should be viewed as the precursors of twentieth-century rock concerts. At the most notorious camp meeting in American history, held in Cane Ridge, Kentucky, in 1801, stunned observers watched as converts fell "prostrate on the ground, and swoon[ed] away," "jerked" their bodies uncontrollably, rolled on the ground "like a wheel," ran with "amazing swiftness," danced with "not ungraceful motion," and most bizarre of all, growled, snapped their teeth, and barked like dogs. At other camp meetings, converts ran from tent to tent exhorting others to repent, fainted in religious ecstasy, and claimed to see visions of Christ. Even more shocking, crowds of rowdy spectators—labeled by Hiram Munger as "sons of Cain"—turned the periphery of the campgrounds into carnivals, disrupting solemn services with drunken brawls. (Munger and his friends took it upon themselves to imprison many of these "Cainites" in the preacher's stand.) As one clergyman lamented, the campground was "a place of fun and mischief for every abominable character in the land." When the Freewill Baptists announced they would hold a camp meeting in Gilmanton, New Hampshire, the selectmen of the town hastily passed a resolution forbidding "the sale of spirituous liquors in the street" and "other riotous proceedings."[59]

In the tumultuous atmosphere of these mass gatherings, anything seemed possible—even female preaching. Even though many women hesitated to speak in the formal space of a church, they were so carried away by the sights and sounds of the campgrounds—the sinners groaning, the fires blazing in the darkness, ministers weeping—that they lost their fears. As Rebecca Chaney Miller explained, she had struggled with "deep anxiety and sorrow" after feeling called to preach at the young age of only sixteen, but when she attended her first camp meeting, she finally overcame her "diffidence in public speaking." For months, she had feared that her parents and ministers would disown her if she revealed that she, like Phebe, had been called to labor in God's harvest, but as she stood on the campgrounds, she no longer cared about the scorn of the world. "Here my peace became as the river," she wrote later, "and my consolation like the waves of the sea. The cause of the Lord prospered, sinners obtained pardon of their past sins, converts crowded the gates of Zion, and I derived indescribable pleasure in persuading my fellow beings to become reconciled to God." It was the beginning of a fourteen-year preaching career that spanned her marriage, the birth of three children, and extensive travels throughout Ohio, Pennsylvania, and Virginia. When she died in 1844 at the age of forty, she was memorialized in the Christian press as a devoted female laborer who had enthralled "thousands" with her "flow of eloquence."[60]

Christian Connection ministers welcomed Rebecca Miller as an evangelist because of their conviction that she genuinely had been inspired by God. Even though she was young and female, she was a surprisingly charismatic preacher, and when she made sinners cry out for mercy or swoon to the ground, they saw the Holy Spirit at work. In contrast to more "respectable" clergymen, they insisted that no amount of education or biblical study could prepare preachers for the pulpit: only those who had been born again could proclaim the word. In the words of Rebecca Miller, "sisters" had the right to "speak for Jesus, whenever the spirit calls."[61]

All of these sects valued heartfelt religious experience more than theological education. Like the eighteenth-century Separates, they argued that religious authority came from conversion, the mystical moment of connection to God, rather than from the rigors of academic study. When a man asked a Freewill Baptist minister from Maine whether he believed that a "liberal education" at a college should be required before ordination, he replied: "A College, the *Government* and *regulation* of which being of *men*, (although I respect many such institutions,) is no place to obtain a *liberal* education: the definition of the word *liberal*, is free. It generally costs those who obtain an education at College, *money*, and often at an *extravagant price*. The *liberal* education, which I have obtained, is *free*, without money, & without price; 'For I neither received it of man, neither was I taught it, but by the *revelation* of *Jesus* Christ.' "[62] This minister claimed to respect many colleges, but clearly not enough to attend one himself. Since God had already inspired and educated him, he did not need to waste his money on a college education.

Other ministers were so anti-intellectual that they disdained the very idea of attending a college. Although Benjamin Putnam, a Freewill Baptist, thought that he would become a more eloquent preacher if he were better-educated, his colleagues assured him that the opposite was true. "When I consulted others," he disclosed, "they endeavored to convince me, that extensive literary acquirements would rather embarrass and lessen my influence, than increase it."[63] If he were going to preach to ordinary farmhands, sailors, and housewives, he needed to speak their own language, not the polished language of "literature." In the world of the Freewill Baptists, education could be more embarrassing than commendable.

These sects' hostility to formal education reflected their humble origins. In their early years, the Freewill Baptists, Methodists, African Methodists, and Christians were all led by lower-class, uneducated men who were suspicious of the "pomp" and "vanity" of better-off ministers. Many black preachers had been born as slaves, and although many white preachers had attended common schools as children, most had put aside their studies as soon as they were old enough to work. For example, Elias Smith, the founder of the Christian Connection, stopped attending school at the age of thirteen, and by fifteen he had read only four books: the Bible, Isaac Watts's collection of psalms and hymns, the primer, and Dilworth's spelling book. Although Smith eventually learned to quote the Bible from memory and explain difficult scriptural passages, his expertise came from long nights of solitary study next to the dim light of his fireplace. At a time when ministers in more reputable denominations had been trained in Greek and Latin, Smith and other ministers had never set foot within the gated walls of Harvard or Yale. Instead, they had been "called like the ancient prophets, and apostles, from the handles of the plow, the fishing boat, sail-making, and other useful avocations."[64]

In order to justify their lack of education, these ministers claimed that ordinary people could read and interpret the Bible for themselves. Stripping the Bible of its mystery, they promised that anyone with common sense could understand it. After Abraham Snethen, an illiterate farmer from Kentucky, taught himself how to read, he prided himself on being as much of a biblical expert as the most learned clergyman. "When I could read and quote for myself," he exulted, "I had but little difficulty in interpreting for myself."[65] Setting out as a poor but devout "barefoot preacher," Snethen carried this populist message to converts across Kentucky, assuring them that they too could decipher the meaning of the Bible on their own.

This individualistic, commonsense approach to the Bible led many evangelicals to question the rigid proscriptions against female preaching. When they read the Bible with new eyes, questioning the way it had traditionally been interpreted, they found many scriptural examples of women speaking and prophesying in the early church. Instead of keeping silence, biblical heroines such as Priscilla, Phebe, the four daughters of Philip, and Mary Magdalene had spread the gospel of Christ's resurrection as witnesses and evangelists. Their lives seemed to fulfill the prediction that the prophet Joel had made in the Old Testament: "I will pour out my spirit upon all flesh; and your sons and your daughters shall prophesy." Invoking these words, Rebecca Miller asked: "If God has declared, in the most positive terms, that under the new dispensation, his daughters shall prophesy, who dares to say they shall not? Let such reflect that it is a fearful thing to be found fighting against God."[66]

Most important, the Freewill Baptists, Christians, and Methodists argued that God could communicate directly with his chosen through impressions, dreams, visions, or voices. Like the most radical eighteenth-century New Lights and Separates, they blended their faith in the literal truth of the Bible with popular beliefs in supernatural wonders. Despite the supposed triumph of the Age of Reason, many men and women continued to believe that the world around them was a magical place populated with spirits, witches, and wizards. While Abraham Snethen confessed that he had once believed in "witches, ghosts, signs, lucky and unlucky days," Mary Coy Bradley, a Methodist exhorter from Nova Scotia, decided whether to accept a marriage proposal by casting lots. When "nine times running were for it," she decided it was God's will.[67] Instead of imagining a God who had left the world to run according to its own natural laws, these men and women put their faith in a God who was always present with them—an omnipotent creator who continually revealed himself in both ordinary and extraordinary ways. God inspired people not only through subtle impressions or dreams, but through direct, supernatural contact. During his conversion experience, for example, Benjamin Abbott claimed to see "the Lord Jesus Christ standing by me, with his arms extended wide, saying to me, '*I died for you.*' "[68]

Female preaching took root in this theological climate of divine inspiration and anti-intellectualism. Since clergymen freely admitted that some of their most "eloquent" colleagues had "never seen the inside of a college, and did not know the first principle of english grammar," they could hardly argue that women's lack of education made them unfit for the pulpit.[69] Like men, most women had been too poor to attend school for more than a few months, and they claimed to have been educated by voices, visions, and dreams. Elizabeth, an African Methodist who had been born as a slave, agonized over her call to preach because she had never gone to school and "could read but little," but at the moment of her greatest discouragement, when she "wept bitterly" at the thought of the sufferings she had been called to endure, she heard the voice of God reassuring her. "Weep not," she heard. "Some will laugh at thee, some will scoff at thee, and the dogs will bark at thee, but while thou doest my will, I will be with thee to the ends of the earth."[70] Since God himself had inspired her, she did not need education, wealth, or a white skin to justify her right to preach.

Populist and anti-intellectual, the Freewill Baptists, Christians, Methodists, and African Methodists created a religious culture in which even the most humble convert—the poor, the unlearned, the slave, or the female—felt qualified to preach the gospel. First intuitively, and then more deliberately and self-consciously, they shaped a culture in which inspiration was more important than education, emotional revivals more important than genteel worship services, and the call to preach more important than the hierarchy of sex. Influenced by the shortage of ordained ministers, the growing numbers of female converts, the turbulence of revival meetings, and popular beliefs in immediate revelation, they allowed hundreds of women to pray aloud, testify, exhort, and even preach in public, overturning cultural expectations of female silence.

Female Virtue in the Family of God

The similarities between these evangelical sects and the eighteenth-century Separates, Shakers, and Public Friends are striking. Like the Separates, they disdained education in favor of immediate inspiration. Like Jemima Wilkinson and the Public Friends, they thought that all converts should be able to use their gifts in public. And like the Shakers, they often expressed themselves through symbolic action, swooning or crying out in ecstatic communion with the Holy Spirit.

Yet the Freewill Baptists, Christians, and Methodists also differed from these earlier groups in significant ways. The Separates had allowed women to exhort, but not to preach on biblical texts, and they always remained suspicious of female "disorderliness." The Shakers and Public Friends had opened up religious leadership positions to women, but only if they tried to transcend their gender by dressing in "masculine" clothing or promising to be celibate. In contrast, the Freewill Baptists, Christians, and Methodists allowed much larger numbers of women into the pulpit with far fewer restrictions. Unlike Bathsheba Kingsley, the eighteenth-century visionary exhorter who had stolen her husband's horse to ride from town to town, Sally Parsons was *given* a horse by Freewill Baptist leaders so that she could travel more quickly across the rugged terrain of northern New England.[71]

Why were these sects more tolerant than their precursors? What had changed between the eighteenth and nineteenth centuries? In part, the answer lies in one of the most important ideological transformations in American history, a transformation that shaped perceptions of women throughout the nineteenth and even twentieth centuries. Unlike the Puritan clergymen of New England, or the Separates of the first Great Awakening, or the Founding Fathers of the American Revolution, nineteenth-century ministers believed that women were as virtuous, if not *more* virtuous, than men. In the wake of the American Revolution, "virtu," the "masculine" quality of courage and public spirit, had become "virtue," the "feminine" quality of morality and benevolence, and understandings of gender and sexuality would never again be the same.[72]

Historians still have not fully explained why there was such a remarkable shift in attitudes toward women in the late eighteenth and early nineteenth centuries. How did the sinful, lustful Eve become the pure and passionless Mary? How did the colonial goodwife, who was supposedly weak and easily led astray, become the republican mother, who was morally superior to her husband? Earlier generations of Americans, especially clergymen, had certainly praised individual women (such as Mary Rowlandson) for their virtue, but they had still regarded men as the more admirable sex. Child-rearing manuals were addressed to fathers, not mothers, because women were perceived as too weak and indulgent to instill proper discipline in their children. Of course, this prescriptive literature did not necessarily mirror real behavior, and women seem to have exercised considerable moral authority in their roles as wives and mothers.[73] Nevertheless, men rather than women were expected to be the spiritual leaders of the household, and images of "feminine" sinfulness powerfully shaped popular attitudes throughout the colonial period. Even though prominent male thinkers such as Benjamin Franklin praised women for their industry and economy, they also criticized them for their vanity, pride, and sensuality. Thomas Jefferson longed for the companionship of a "lovely woman," but he also copied the misogynist verse of Thomas Otway into the pages of his commonplace book. "I'd leave the World for him that hates a Woman," he quoted. "Woman the Fountain of all human Frailty! . . . Destructive, damnable, deceitful Woman!"[74]

In contrast, nineteenth-century Americans read sermons and tracts with titles such as *On Female Excellence*, *The Character of a Virtuous and Good Woman*, *The Excellency of the Female Character Vindicated*, and *The Excellence and Influence of the Female Character*—all of which praised women's natural piety and their natural goodness. "Their feelings are more exquisite than those of men," one author wrote, "and their sentiments greater and more refined."[75] On one hand, earlier ideas about female corruption never entirely disappeared: the evil female witch remained (and still remains) a stock figure in the popular imagination. Demonic and angelic images of womanhood continued to coexist, reminding "Marys" that they could still be "Eves" if they strayed. On the other hand, however, a new paradigm of female virtue decisively transformed cultural understandings of womanhood. By the end of his life, even the irascible Franklin had begun to celebrate women's inherent goodness, waxing sentimental as he praised their "Softness, Sensibility, and acute Discernment."[76] Although women were still perceived as the weaker sex, that weakness was now configured as softness rather than as deceitfulness. Significantly, sinful women were now described as "fallen" women, a term which implied that their natural state was far more elevated.

This sweeping ideological transformation was connected to larger ideological, religious, political, and economic changes in the early republic. Ideologically, it emerged out of currents of thought that preceded the American Revolution and were transatlantic in scope. As early as the seventeenth century, Puritan ministers such as Thomas Shepard and Solomon Stoddard had argued that conversion was a matter of the heart as well as the head, and they portrayed "emotional" women as the spiritual (though not social) equals of "rational" men. By the 1740s, Jonathan Edwards had come to the conclusion that women's emotionalism made them especially receptive to religion, and during the revivals of the first Great Awakening, he often singled them out as models of Christian piety. Even though Edwards never entirely overcame his suspicions of "female seductiveness," he and other New Lights helped to lay the groundwork for a more positive conception of women's benevolence. Beginning in the mid-eighteenth century, Scottish moral philosophers and British sentimental novelists built on these ideas by describing morality as emotional, and hence "feminine," as well as rational and "masculine."[77]

This belief in female virtue took on new significance in the aftermath of the American Revolution as women struggled to define their ambiguous relationship to the new nation. "Left to invent their own political character," as historian Linda Kerber has noted, they gradually developed a new ideology to justify their participation in civic culture: the ideology of republican motherhood.[78] Even though women did not claim the right to exercise any political authority as autonomous individuals—such a notion was unthinkable to most women in Revolutionary America—they insisted they could shape the future of the republic by raising virtuous citizens. As mothers, wives, and sisters, they held the fate of the republic in their hands. "The solidity and stability of the liberties of your country rest with you," one orator pronounced solemnly in 1795.[79]

This new rhetoric was especially reassuring at a time when traditional family structures seemed to be threatened by the transformations of the market revolution. If women could preserve the "feminine" virtues of selflessness and domesticity against the incursions of materialism and self-interest, then the modern world would not be quite so frightening. At a time when everything appeared to be in flux, when politics, economics, and the home were being fundamentally redefined, the belief that women were more virtuous than men—a new construction in and of itself—served a profound psychological need. Ironically, *men*, not women, were now seen as corrupt: they were viewed as selfish, competitive, ruthless, and aggressive.

In contrast to the eighteenth century, when most people understood gender according to a one-sex model, nineteenth-century Americans developed a new, two-sex model that emphasized the differences instead of the similarities between the sexes. According to Horace Bushnell, for example, a renowned clergyman, women and men shared so little that they seemed to belong to two different species. Instead of viewing women as lesser versions of men— incomplete men whose sexual organs were turned inside out—clergymen and scientists portrayed the sexes as essentially different in both biology and temperament. Although they still stressed women's weakness, they also began to elevate women as morally superior to men. "Pious women are not only more numerous, but more pious, than pious men," concluded one clergyman.[80]

The darker underside of this seemingly positive language is immediately obvious to anyone who has studied the Victorian "cult of true womanhood." However much women may have been praised for their morality, their virtue was inextricably tied to their domesticity, and they still had few concrete political or legal rights. Indeed, Thomas Laquer has suggested that men stressed women's inherent differences in order to claim political participation as a masculine prerogative. The more that women seemed to differ from men, the easier it was to justify their exclusion from the government. Equally important, the ideology of domesticity was a middle-class construction that explicitly denigrated black and lower-class women who worked outside of their homes. Ideas about female corruption had not disappeared, but had simply been displaced onto women who did not fit the model of middle-class gentility. In the words of historian Christine Stansell, "As propertied women began their ascent to republican motherhood, laboring women became the receptacle for all the unsavory traits traditionally assigned their sex."[81]

In its earliest incarnation, however, this new ideology of female morality had not yet become the stultifying domesticity of later Victorian womanhood. Until at least the 1820s, and perhaps even the 1830s (such cultural shifts are difficult to date), women seemed to find the language of "separate spheres" and female virtue more liberating than confining. Indeed, this language would never have become so popular if women themselves had not viewed it as a distinct improvement over an older conception of female sensuality. Middle-class women rarely remained in their domestic sphere, and armed with the faith that they were more virtuous and pious than men, they organized charities, raised money for their churches, and founded reform organizations to combat male vice.[82] Even though lower-class and black women rarely participated in these reform and benevolence organizations, they too tried to claim the mantle of superior godliness. Despite the stereotypes of the abandoned working girl and the lascivious female slave, churchgoing women, no matter how poor, were praised by their ministers as the guardians and protectors of Christian virtue.

The Freewill Baptists, Methodists, and Christians were as involved in shaping this rhetoric of female morality as Protestants in other denominations. Ministers' journals and religious periodicals are filled with accounts of pious women who singlehandedly converted their sinful husbands, brothers, and fathers to a new faith in Christ. In these stories, virtuous women inevitably triumphed over hardhearted men, conquering their passions through gentleness and meekness rather than physical force. Many of these stories appear contrived, and by the 1840s, narratives of devout, long-suffering wives and repentant husbands had become standard fare in journals such as the Methodists' *Ladies Repository*. Yet undoubtedly, many women did lead their male family members into the church. John Bangs remembered that before he left his home to travel to Canada, his "pious sister" took him by the hand and begged him to seek salvation. With tears, she reminded him that "if you die in your sins, where God and Christ is you will never come." Years later, he claimed that those words had ultimately been responsible for both his conversion and his decision to become a preacher. She "wounded my heart," he wrote, "and had a thunderbolt literally struck me I could not have felt much worse."[83] Even though his sister was merely a "weak" woman, she had saved him from damnation.

Most important, these sects extended the ideology of female morality beyond the middle classes to the farmwives, domestic servants, and factory girls who crowded their pews. Pliny Brett, the president of the Reformed Methodist Church, assured his fellow ministers that Salome Lincoln, a mill worker and female preacher, was a "person of unexceptionable character; both moral and religious." Similarly, the *Christian Herald* published an obituary of Dinah Lane, a black woman who had been twice sold as a slave, describing her as an admirable and esteemed Christian. Reflecting the racial prejudices of their time, the editors of the *Herald* explicitly noted her "Ethiopian" race, but they also insisted that she would have a "white" soul in heaven. (Although this might sound like condescension, they meant their words to be taken as praise.) Although Dinah Lane had certainly not lived a life of sheltered domesticity, her clergymen thought she deserved to be as celebrated for her virtue as her middle-class sisters.[84]

The Freewill Baptists, Christians, and Methodists crowned pious women such as Dinah Lane as "Mothers in Israel" and "Sisters in Christ." Drawing on both biblical imagery and the language of republican motherhood, they rooted women's religious authority in their traditional domestic roles as mothers and sisters. While Sisters in Christ were young or middle-aged women who had helped to foster the faith of new believers, Mothers in Israel tended to be older women who had been long and faithful pillars of the church. The criteria for their sisterhood and motherhood was *spiritual* rather than biological: they had helped to spread the Christian faith through their nurture of the family of God. After Catherine Mummey died, the Methodist Protestant church eulogized her as a beloved "Mother in Israel" who had devoted her life to "strengthen[ing] the hands" of her fellow Christians. "Who that had the pleasure of knowing her, that was not a witness of her meekness, her gentleness, her patience, her fortitude, and her intense labour of Christian love?"[85] Mixing tenderness with strength, she had been a model of "feminine" devotion.

Without realizing it, these sects echoed the same language of spiritual motherhood that Ann Lee had used during the 1770s and 1780s. Like Lee, who had rooted her religious authority in her maternal labors to save souls, the Freewill Baptists, Christian Connection, and Methodists invested motherhood with transcendent significance beyond the bearing and rearing of children. Even though they never denigrated biological motherhood or demanded that female religious leaders be celibate, they still viewed women's maternal role as an important foundation of their spiritual authority. Indeed, whenever female preachers labored to convince sinners to repent, it was as if they were "giving birth" to future saints. Of course, men also identified themselves as "laborers," but in their case, the word suggested the work of planting and plowing fields. In contrast, the term "*female* laborers" conjured up images of the travail of childbirth. Like the Shakers, evangelicals defended women's ministry by drawing on popular images of female nurture.

Despite these parallels, however, nineteenth-century evangelicals ultimately invented a new model of ministry that set them apart from all the earlier sects who had allowed women to exhort or preach. Because the New Lights and Separates of the first Great Awakening had tried their best to forget zealots such as Bathsheba Kingsley, the "brawling woman" who had stolen her husband's horse to ride from town to town, later evangelicals did not seem to know that these women had ever existed. In contrast, they certainly knew about the notorious Jemima Wilkinson and Ann Lee, but they took pains to distinguish *true* Mothers in Israel and Sisters in Christ from such zealous fanatics. As the Shakers grew increasingly popular in the early nineteenth century (far more popular than during Ann Lee's life), clerical leaders rarely missed an opportunity to tell their congregations what a wicked, deluded woman Lee had been.[86] Partly by choice, then, and partly from ignorance, evangelicals never defended women's right to preach by citing the examples of earlier generations of American women. Instead, they mentioned famous British women such as Mary Fletcher, an early Methodist evangelist, or most commonly, they repeated the timeless stories of biblical prophetesses.

Instead of justifying women's right to preach on the grounds that they had transcended their gender—that they were neither male nor female—these sects both shaped and reflected a new ideology of female virtue by identifying female preachers as "mothers," "sisters," or "prophetic daughters." Like earlier evangelicals, they claimed that visionary women had been caught up in God, but they never suggested that women's authority was linked to the loss of their "femininity." On the contrary, they compared female preachers to biblical heroines such as Deborah, Mary Magdalene, and Anna. "The church needs the whole influence of her female piety," one Christian Connection minister explained. Men could not save the world from "darkness" by themselves, but only with the help of "pious females."[87]

Although some historians have accused nineteenth-century Protestants of disempowering or "domesticating" women by emphasizing their motherhood, these sects did exactly the opposite. By borrowing the title of "Mother in Israel" from the pages of the Old Testament, they implicitly expanded the definition of what made a woman virtuous. There are only two "Mothers in Israel" mentioned in the Bible, and both were powerful women who took on leadership roles outside of the patriarchal household. Deborah, one of the most renowned military leaders in the Old Testament, rescued the nation of Israel from its enemies, while the other "Mother in Israel," a "wise woman," persuaded one of David's generals not to destroy her city. "Sisters" appear more frequently in the Bible, but they too defied conventional definitions of womanhood. In his letter to the Romans, Paul described Phebe as "our sister" and instructed the church to "assist her in whatsoever business she hath need of you: for she hath been a succourer of many, and of myself also." Although the nature of Phebe's "business" was disputed by nineteenth-century evangelicals, a few of the most progressive suggested that she had been one of the first female evangelists.[88]

Inspired by the examples of biblical women such as Deborah and Phebe, the Freewill Baptists, Christians, and Methodists lauded women for their "masculine" acts of courage as well as their "feminine" nurture of their families. As every clergyman knew, Mothers in Israel could also be "bold soldiers" for Christ. For example, the African Methodists honored Priscilla Baltimore, a free woman in the slave state of Missouri, for defying white authorities by organizing a black church in her home. Repeatedly risking imprisonment, "Mother" Baltimore ferried the Reverend William Paul Quinn across the Mississippi River in the dead of night so that he could minister to her fledgling converts. According to later legend, she also once shielded him from a "cruel mob." Similarly, the Christian Connection celebrated "*Sister*" Abigail Roberts, a female preacher, for her "indefatigable industry" in helping to gather several new churches in New Jersey.[89]

These sects took the republican language of female virtue in far more revolutionary directions than clergymen in more established denominations. Even though other ministers also lauded women for their piety, especially their maternal influence, they still claimed that women would sully their purity if they ventured too far into the public sphere. "There *is* generally, and should be always, in the female character, a softness and delicacy of feeling which shrinks from the notoriety of a public performance," Lyman Beecher explained. "No well-educated female can put herself up, or be put up, to the point of public prayer, without the loss of some portion at least of that female delicacy, which is above all price." In contrast, the Freewill Baptists, Methodists, and Christians expressed bewilderment at the way other denominations separated women's public from their private speech. As Charles Harding, a Methodist itinerant, confided in his autobiography: "I have always wondered that churches would ignore, and deprive themselves of one of the strongest elements of usefulness, and power, by forbidding women to speak, just as though a woman, who is allowed to talk in the home circle, at the social gathering, in the store, on the street, in stage coach[es] on board the steam boat, or the carrs, and in fine almost every where else, must keep silent when a dozen souls are met, to talk of God, and worship their maker."[90] In his opinion, churches were no different from all the other "social gatherings" that women commonly attended.

All of these sects refused to relegate female virtue to the realm of the purely domestic. On one hand, they were public institutions that helped shape American culture, but on the other, they had no official connection to the state. Like all of the other voluntary associations that brought women into the public sphere, they encouraged women to use their talents to build America into the most Christian, moral society on earth. Bridging the gap between the private and the public, the "feminine" and the "masculine," they saw no reason why women should keep silence in the churches.

Searching for the right words to explain their position in American culture, these sects often chose to describe themselves as "families" linking believers together in closely knit communities. Even though brothers and sisters in Christ were not related by blood, they promised to help one another in times of need. In 1801, for example, the Freewill Baptist Church in Pittsfield, New Hampshire, agreed to provide "Sister" Eaton, a widow, with "such things as she needs for a living." If church members refused to accept their spiritual kinship in the "family of God," they were admonished or even excommunicated. For example, when Lewis Dillingham told "Sister" Robbins that "he did not want her to call him brother," his Freewill Baptist church sternly ordered him to "confess his sin."[91] Even though churches had become part of the informal public because of disestablishment, they insisted on their difference from all the other voluntary societies in the new republic. In their opinion, they brought people together in far more intimate, meaningful fellowship than any other kind of association.

If the church was simply a family writ large, and if women were naturally virtuous, then there was no reason to restrict them from praying, exhorting, and even preaching as the companions of men. Besides using their powerful moral influence to convert family members, Mothers in Israel and Sisters in Christ could also minister to the larger family of God. As pious members of a church family, although not as autonomous individuals, they could help their clerical fathers in the work of saving souls.

Islands of Holiness

By allowing "virtuous" women to preach, these sects separated themselves from virtually all the other Protestant churches in the early republic, a separation that they deliberately fostered. During an era of unprecedented mobility, commercial expansion, individualism, and political competition, the Methodists, African Methodists, Freewill Baptists, and Christian Connection longed to create "islands of holiness" to counter the values of what they saw as an increasingly materialistic and secular society. Like the apostle Paul, who had counseled the early Christians to live *in* the world, but not *of* it, they put their faith in Christ rather than in the "artificial surface-polish of society" or the "pride of respectability."[92] Through their distinctive rituals and practices, especially female preaching, they tried to draw firm boundaries between their pure, covenanted communities and the sinfulness of the secular world—a world so corrupt it seemed poised on the brink of destruction.

These sects self-consciously modeled themselves on the early Christian churches portrayed in the New Testament. Drawing on a popular strain of Christian primitivism, they hoped to restore Christianity to its primordial purity before the rise of competing sects and creeds. John Buzzell, a Freewill Baptist, longed for a time "when all these *names*, and party *rules*, and party *principles*, and party *doctrines*, will be done away; and I trust buried in everlasting oblivion." Restoring Christianity to its original "sweet union and order" would be difficult, but if converts were willing to renounce the secular world as thoroughly as the first Christians, they could create a new society built on the rule of the Bible alone. "I have chosen you out of the world," Jesus told his disciples, "therefore the world hateth you." Self-consciously echoing his words, Zilpha Elaw warned, "Love not the world, for the love of God is not in those who love the world."[93]

Like the early Christians had done, the Freewill Baptists, Christian Connection, Methodists, and African Methodists used religious rituals to draw boundaries between their sacred communities and secular society. First and foremost, new converts signaled their rejection of the world through baptism, a symbolic death and purification of the self that brought them into selfless unity with God. Harriet Livermore, struggling to find the right words to describe such a transcendent experience, explained that she had been "buried" in a "temporary grave" during her immersion in the water, but had been born again as she surfaced into the light.[94] Her old self had died, and with it, all of her former ties to the world.

In another important ritual, all of these sects commemorated Christ's death through the sacrament of the Lord's Supper. As Leigh Eric Schmidt has argued, revivalism was based not on the "preached Word" alone, but also on the "visible Gospel" of the Eucharist. Even though Communion was celebrated only infrequently, it was a powerful symbol of both the inclusiveness and exclusiveness of the Christian community. On one hand, reenacting the Lord's Supper brought all Christians together as a communion of saints without regard to the distinctions of sex, race, or class. All believers, no matter what their rank in the world, had been redeemed by the suffering and death of Christ on the cross. In Freewill Baptist and Christian Connection churches, all evangelicals, no matter what their denomination, were welcome at the Communion table. On the other hand, however, the celebration of the Lord's Supper could also establish firm boundaries between the people of God and the people of the world. In Methodist and African Methodist churches, only the saved were allowed to partake of the bread and the wine.[95]

Other rituals also separated Christians from the world. Through singing hymns, foot washing, and shouting out their praises to the Lord, the members of these sects identified themselves as the specially chosen of God. Instead of singing the same popular hymns as other Protestants, such as those by Isaac Watts, they wrote their own lyrics and melodies in order to express their deepest religious convictions. They also freely expressed their spiritual zeal through clapping, dancing, and "shouting." "We had a shout among God's people," Heman Bangs, a Methodist, recorded in his journal. Most controversially, the Freewill Baptists practiced foot washing, an intimate ritual that many other churches found messy and embarrassing. Like Christ had done on the night of his betrayal, converts humbled themselves by bathing one another's feet, symbolically identifying with Christ's self-sacrifice.[96]

Clothing served as yet another marker dividing believers from "worldlings." The Freewill Baptists, Methodists, African Methodists, and Christians all demanded that their members dress simply rather than imitating the more elaborate fashions of the marketplace. Like Jemima Wilkinson, who had dressed in flowing black robes to symbolize her genderless identity as the Public Universal Friend, these sects believed that clothing "made the man" (or woman). In contrast to fashionable people, who wore showy outfits adorned with ruffles and ribbons, evangelicals shunned "costly apparel, gaudy trimmings," and jewelry for more sober attire. Protesting against a culture that identified social status with consumption, they tended to dress as plainly as eighteenth-century Quakers. Mary Stevens Curry, a female preacher, warned women that they could not "grow in grace" unless they forsook frills and cinched waists for more modest gowns and caps. "Let your dress be that which becometh women professing godliness," she wrote.[97]

This concern with plain clothing was symbolic of a far greater quarrel with the values of the world. Most of the early Freewill Baptists, Christians, Methodists, and African Methodists belonged to the lower or lower-middling classes, and they were deeply ambivalent about the social and economic changes wrought by the market revolution. By preaching an ethic of Christian love over economic ambition, these sects tried to resist the incursions of capitalism. Although they were far less radical than the Shakers, who abolished private property in favor of communism, they still tried to shield their members from the worst excesses of the market. When the first Freewill Baptist church was founded in 1780, the "brothers" and "sisters" signed a covenant pledging that "they should not follow the customs of the world in trade, but do as they *would* be done by, and not as they *are* done by." Modeling themselves on the early Christians, they also agreed not to sue other believers and to "admonish the covetous." Above all, they swore to preserve the element of "protest" in Protestantism by renouncing all of the vanities and temptations of the world. Preaching an ethic of resistance rather than accommodation, they solemnly swore not to "conform to the world in its customs, fashions, and idle conversation; nor countenance them who do, but rather reprove them."[98]

Above all, these sects tried to separate themselves from American culture by challenging its understandings of gender and race. Although one of the most popular symbols of manhood in the 1830s was Davy Crockett, the aggressive, Indian-fighting frontiersman, evangelicals such as James Finley, a Methodist, aspired to the "feminine" qualities of meekness, self-sacrifice, and emotionalism. "I am nothing, and helpless as a child!" he exclaimed. Describing himself as "weak" and utterly dependent on God's grace, he claimed he was unable to accomplish anything through his own strength. Similarly, other men described themselves in female terms as "brides of Christ," and they were not ashamed to shed tears during their sermons.[99] Like men have done in marginal or oppressed groups throughout history, they identified with the "feminine" in order to emphasize their renunciation of the dominant culture.[100]

The Freewill Baptists, Christians, and Methodists were equally countercultural in their attitudes toward race and slavery. Early leaders of the Methodist movement, including John Wesley, Francis Asbury, and Thomas Coke, viewed slavery as a disturbing symbol of the market's tendency to reduce people to mere commodities, and they condemned it as unscriptural and un-Christian. Similarly, even though the Freewill Baptists and Christian Connection tried to avoid becoming involved in political disputes, they lamented that their country was "stained in human flesh and blood!"[101] None of these sects treated blacks as the true social equals of whites, and the creation of a separate African Methodist Episcopal Church in 1816 was partially a response to white racism. Nevertheless, white and black evangelicals managed to forge religious friendships across the barriers of race, and despite America's tragic history of slavery, they helped to lay the groundwork for a more racially inclusive Christianity. White preachers such as David Millard, a Christian, and Salome Lincoln, a Reformed Methodist, addressed large interracial crowds, and in turn, black preachers such as Jarena Lee and Richard Allen spoke to white audiences.[102]

Given the failure of the American Revolution to extend true equality to either women or blacks, the decision to allow them into the sacred space of the pulpit was radical indeed. The Freewill Baptists, Christians, and Methodists all ordained black men to the clergy, and although they never gave the same privilege to white or black women, they still praised them for their labors.[103] When Charles Bowles, a black Freewill Baptist, and Clarissa Danforth, perhaps the single best-known female preacher of her time, held a joint meeting in 1817, they challenged their audience's most deeply held assumptions about the inferiority of white women and African American men. Despite popular prejudices, Bowles and Danforth had been given permission to preach by the Freewill Baptist Yearly Meeting, who believed that neither race nor sex could disqualify a person from being called. As they walked into the church side by side, apprehensive about the reception they might meet, they vividly symbolized their belief in the equality of all souls before God. John Lewis, Bowles's biographer, admitted that "a colored man and a woman, preaching in the same house on the same day, was rather a novel spectacle," but "in the importance of their subject, color and sex were all forgotten."[104]

The sight of a white woman and a black man standing together in the pulpit was a visible reminder of how much the Freewill Baptists were opposed to the values of American culture. Although clergymen in many other denominations also objected to the ethic of consumption that was reshaping everyday life, and several even allowed black men to preach, they never appeared as countercultural as the Freewill Baptists, Christian Connection, Methodists, and African Methodists.[105] Indeed, these sects stood virtually alone in their defense of female preaching. Even more than their emotional religious rituals, their distinctive clothing, and their hostility toward the market, their support of women such as Clarissa Danforth drew clear boundaries between their hallowed communities and the secular world.

These sects renounced the world because they believed it was too sinful to be saved. Even though most Protestants pinned their hopes on the triumph, not the failure, of human progress in ushering in the kingdom of God, others were far more pessimistic.[106] Instead of celebrating America's glorious destiny, many Methodists, Freewill Baptists, and Christians predicted that there would be a bloody and violent apocalypse before Christ's thousand-year reign of peace. Unfortunately, it is impossible to know how many people believed that they were truly living at the end of human history, but there was constant speculation in the religious press, especially among the Freewill Baptists and Christians, about when the "universal conflict" would begin. For example, the Freewill Baptist Home Mission Society published a report exhorting sinners to prepare for "the near approach of that last and most dreadful conflict between the militant Church of Christ and the spiritual and embodied forces of the Prince of Darkness." "We live in the last time," they warned.[107]

Whenever there was a comet, an earthquake, a violent storm, or any other natural disaster, doomsayers interpreted it as a portent of a far greater cataclysm. Abraham Snethen, the "barefoot preacher," remembered that after an earthquake rocked Kentucky in 1811, and then a comet blazed a trail across the sky, "Everybody was expecting the final windup of all things earthly, supposing that the end of the world had really come." Huddled in small groups, all listened fearfully as the one literate woman among them read from the Bible. Quoting from Luke, she warned, "Great earthquakes shall be in divers places, and famines, and pestilences; and fearful sights and great signs shall there be from heaven."[108] The "signs of the times" were ominous indeed.

Millennial expectations reached fever pitch in the early 1840s when William Miller, a New England farmer, predicted that the world would end on October 22, 1844. At least twenty-two women preached for the Millerites between 1841 and 1845, traveling from town to town warning people to prepare for the end of the world. Because the Millerites drew many of their followers from the Methodists, Christians, and Freewill Baptists, it is not surprising that they continued to allow women to speak publicly, but they seem to have been particularly sympathetic to female preaching. Living in sacred rather than secular time, they imagined a world in which the normal rules of religious and social life no longer applied. Confident that they were living in the last days of human history, they urged every convert, whether male or female, to spread the saving gospel of Christ. Like John of Patmos, author of the mystical book of Revelation, they were certain they would soon witness the creation of a new heaven and a new earth.

Whenever Millerites, Freewill Baptists, Christians, African Methodists, or Methodists sat in a church or stood in a field to see a woman preach, they saw not only an individual woman, but a symbol of their identity as a chosen people. Just as the Shakers had viewed Ann Lee as the harbinger of God's true church, the sign that the end of the world was near, these sects invested female preaching with transcendent significance. Indeed, they did not allow women to preach in spite of their "femininity," but *because* of it. A female preacher was a religious outsider in a way that a male preacher could not be. She was a stranger and a pilgrim who had sacrificed everything—pride, money, family, and security—for the glory of God. She was a "mother" or a "sister" who would nurture the family of God. She was a divine "instrument" whose "feminine" weakness made God's power even more visible. "Jehovah delights to use *weak means*, to effect *great things*!" Nancy Towle explained.[109] Most of all, a female preacher was a living embodiment of Joel's promise that women as well as men would prophesy at the end of time. Her sex made it impossible to view her as just another laborer in the harvest. Instead, she was a herald of Christ's imminent return to earth.

The tragedy of all these sects was that they never achieved their dreams of millennial perfection. The Day of Jubilee did not come, no matter how much they prayed for it, and despite their quest for religious purity, they were always ambivalent about separating themselves from the culture in which they lived. Like the early Christians whom they so admired, they were torn between "loving and hating the world," between abhorring its "perversions" and longing for its "wholeness." Even though they wanted to preserve the purity of their sacred communities, they also believed they had been called to save sinners from damnation. Like the Methodist founders who had promised to "reform the Continent, and to spread scriptural Holiness," their mission always pulled them back into the world they supposedly despised. As Elleanor Knight explained, God had called her to "maintain the pure, unadulterated principles of the gospel, and also to proclaim them to the world."[110]

Despite their stance as religious outsiders, these sects were deeply shaped by the society in which they lived, particularly in their attitudes toward women. Even though they set themselves apart from middle-class denominations by sanctioning female preaching, they still found it impossible to imagine women's ordination. Nor did they ever challenge the basic inequality between the sexes by fighting for women's full legal, political, or economic equality to men. Although they allowed women into the pulpit in order to symbolize their identity as the chosen people of God, they were too well versed in biblical history not to know the sorrows of being strangers and pilgrims, strangers in a strange land. If their love of the world ever triumphed over their hatred of it, then women such as Sally Parsons, disowned by her father, would be disowned by their churches as well.

If Sally Parsons had been asked to explain why the Freewill Baptists accepted her as a female laborer after her appearance at the Yearly Meeting in 1795, she certainly would have given a much different answer than the one I have sketched out here. Even if she had noted the scarcity of male preachers, the increasing numbers of women in the pews, and the spontaneity of revival meetings, none of these factors would have been very important to her. Nor would she have mentioned the new conception of female virtue or the changing relationship between church and state. Perhaps she would have mentioned her ability to interpret the Scriptures for herself, or her belief that the millennium would soon arrive, or her determination to separate herself from the conventions of the corrupt world. Perhaps she would have also explained that the Freewill Baptists, like many other evangelical sects in the new republic, valued personal religious experience more than clerical education. First and foremost, however, she would have insisted that her story be understood as part of sacred rather than secular history. In her mind, there was only one possible explanation for her remarkable success as a preacher. Despite her poverty, her lack of education, and her "feminine" weakness, God had sent her forth as a laborer to bring in his harvest.

4

The Last Shall Be First

Conversion and the Call to Preach

So the last shall be first, and the first last: for many be called, but few chosen.—Matthew 20:16

Before I formed thee in the belly I knew thee; and before thou camest forth out of the womb I sanctified thee, and I ordained thee a prophet unto the nations. Then said I, Ah, Lord God! behold, I cannot speak: for I am a child. But the Lord said unto me, Say not, I am a child: for thou shalt go to all that I shall send thee, and whatsoever I command thee thou shalt speak. Be not afraid of their faces: for I am with thee to deliver thee, saith the Lord. Then the Lord put forth his hand, and touched my mouth. And the Lord said unto me, Behold, I have put my words in thy mouth.
—Jeremiah 1:5–9

In 1820, during a revival in the town of Cranston, Rhode Island, Elleanor Knight, a wife and mother who was pregnant with her second child, began attending a Baptist church in search of spiritual "consolation." Not only had her father recently died, but after two years of marriage, she realized that she had pledged her future to a man who was alcoholic, unable to hold a steady job, and violent. Although she never accused her husband, Harding, of physically abusing her—a topic she may have been too ashamed to write about even in her memoir—she admitted hiding from him in terror whenever he fell into a drunken rage. "Sometimes when he was in a state of intoxication," she wrote, "he would appear to be in a state of partial derangement, and I underwent much with fear for my personal safety." "Sorrowful and dejected," she decided that she would never find happiness within her marriage, but only in a closer relationship to God. "A Christian could look to Christ for consolation in the time of trouble," she explained, "but there is no source of consolation for a sinner." With a deep sense of her own sinfulness, she pored over her Bible, wept during her clergyman's sermons, and prayed for mercy until she finally felt as if God had "cleansed" her "sin-polluted soul." Despite her sorrows, she had been "born again," and for the first time since her marriage, she felt truly happy and peaceful.[1]

Unfortunately, however, Harding's "fits of rage" continued. Besides subjecting her to "harsh conversation" and "ill treatment," he became increasingly resentful of her spiritual authority within her church. Angered by how frequently she prayed aloud and witnessed, he commanded her not to "talk so much." Reluctantly, out of desperation to please him, she agreed. "Perhaps you are deceived," she told herself. "Please your husband, and keep still." But the more that Elleanor tried to obey Harding by "quenching the spirit," the more she felt alienated from God. "I began to die in my mind," she remembered later. "I felt like an animal or reptile out of their element. My distress increased daily, until my mind was in agony; I began to cry mightily to the Lord."[2] Pouring out her heart to God in prayer, she begged him for guidance. Should she submit to her husband's wishes, or should she follow her own conscience?

The answer, according to Elleanor, came to her one night in 1829 in a dream. Just as God had communicated to biblical prophets in dreams and visions, he had sent her a revelation as she slept. It began as a nightmarish image of her past life: a man "came to my father's to invite us to go to a feast," she wrote in her narrative, but she was the only one who agreed to go with him. (Was the man Harding, and had he invited her to a wedding feast?) Leaving her father behind, she followed the man into a frightening world where "evil spirits" tried to "kill" her. Yet just at the moment when it seemed like her life—and her dream—would end, the demonic man disappeared, and she found her way to "a beautiful place" where she was "perfectly happy," much as she had been during her conversion. Filled with joy, she longed to stay

A

NARRATIVE

OF THE

CHRISTIAN EXPERIENCE,

LIFE AND ADVENTURES,

TRIALS AND LABOURS

OF

ELLEANOR KNIGHT,

Written by Herself.

TO WHICH IS ADDED A FEW REMARKS AND VERSES.

"Prove all things—hold fast that which is good."

Read and then judge.

———

PROVIDENCE.
1839.

Title page of Elleanor Warner Knight, *A Narrative of the Christian Experience, Life and Adventures, Trials and Labours of Elleanor Knight, Written by Herself* (1839). Courtesy of the John Hay Library.

there in peace, but a guide eventually carried her to "a straight and narrow road" and told her that God wanted her to become a preacher. She cried out in disbelief, "I could not preach," but he repeated his words, telling her that she *must* preach. When she awoke from her dream, she realized that even though she wanted to please her husband by "holding her peace," she had to submit to the will of God.[3]

At first, Elleanor responded to her call to preach with elation, marveling that God had chosen such a helpless, suffering woman to be his prophetic "instrument." Yet after stopping to consider her own weakness and "insufficiency," she realized what a cross God had asked her to bear. Even if she found the courage to defy Harding, she wondered who would take care of her children when she felt called to hold meetings away from home. She also feared that her minister would disown her for demanding the right to labor in God's harvest. Overwhelmed by her fears, she finally protested, "Lord, I cannot go." Even though she continued to testify and exhort during church meetings, she did not dare to "expound the scriptures" as a female preacher.[4]

According to Elleanor, the price of her spiritual disobedience was painfully high. Like the prophet Jonah, who had been swallowed alive by a whale after fleeing from God's call, she was severely punished for quenching the spirit. First, in 1830 or 1831 (the dates are unclear), shortly after giving birth to her fourth child, she discovered that Harding was having an affair with another woman. Then, just when it seemed as if her life could not become any more wretched, her infant and her two-year-old son died. Never had she felt so forsaken. Overcome by despair, Elleanor turned to God for comfort, but it seemed as if he were no longer listening: ever since she had refused to obey her call to preach, her prayers had brought her only "darkness." Remembering the fate of Jonah, she concluded that all of her sufferings, even the deaths of her children, had been her own fault. "I mourned for my children," she lamented in her memoir, "but I thought in this providence I could see the Lord was taking away my excuses, for not being willing to labor in his vineyard." Her reasoning was disturbingly simple. An angry God would never have taken away her children if she had been a more obedient Christian.[5]

As if all these crosses were not enough to bear, she was afflicted with one more. Even though she had lost almost everything that was important to her, she still believed that she had one final refuge: the fellowship of her church. But after discovering her desire to become a preacher, her congregation condemned her as a woman who had been "deceived." When she stood up to speak during a conference meeting in 1832, raising her voice so that the entire church could hear her, a deacon sternly ordered her to "be still." No words could have hurt her more deeply. As she knelt down in her pew, her head bowed in shame, she felt as if God had taken away virtually everything that mattered to her—her husband, her children, her friends, and, in the final blow, her right to speak as a Mother in Israel. "[I] began to weep," she remembered later, "and wept while the meeting lasted, and wept after I got home, and continued to weep, until I had a violent pain in my head, vomiting from the stomach; my flesh was cold, and I verily began to think that this scene would terminate my sufferings." Like Jonah, the reluctant prophet who had denied God's call, she no longer wanted to live.[6]

Yet Elleanor *did* survive, and with little left to sacrifice, she resolved to leave Harding and become a more faithful Christian. In 1833, carrying "a few articles of clothing in a small band-box, and two dollars only," she traveled to Fall River hoping to find a Freewill Baptist congregation who would allow her to preach. She was alone—"a stranger among strangers"—but for the first time in her life, she felt no fear. "At this time I had some faith in God," she remembered later. As she had hoped, the Freewill Baptists welcomed her warmly, and she began holding meetings in a local church with their approval. Eventually she also traveled to congregations in Connecticut, Massachusetts, New Hampshire, and Vermont, preaching to Christians and Methodists as well as Freewill Baptists. In a story of biblical proportions, she had been "tried in the furnace of affliction," but she left behind the anguish of her former life to become a well-known preacher.[7]

The inspiring, heartbreaking account of Elleanor Knight's conversion and her call to preach was echoed by scores of other female preachers in the early nineteenth century. It was an archetypal Christian story: a story of the last made first. Like Knight, many other female preachers had endured poverty, the death of loved ones, or abuse, and they portrayed themselves as weak, suffering women who had been transformed by the grace of God. According to the stories they told, they were sinful and unworthy, but God had chosen them to be his prophets as surely as he had chosen Jeremiah and Deborah. They had heard Christ's voice calling to them in dreams, and they had seen his face during waking visions. When they had foolishly tried to quench the spirit, God had refused to let them deny his call. Even though they had resigned themselves to being last, God had forced them to be first.

The story of Elleanor Knight reminds us that the history of female preaching is more than the history of institutional and ideological change. It is also the history of scores of individual women who found the courage to take up the "cross" of public evangelism. No matter how much Knight may have been influenced by the shortage of ministers, the disestablishment of churches, or the new conception of female virtue, she would never have become a preacher if not for the inner strength and courage that she found in her faith. In her opinion, no one could understand the meaning of her life without appreciating the two key events that had transformed it: her spiritual rebirth during her conversion, and her call to preach by the Holy Spirit. As she repeatedly told the American public, her strength was not her own, but the Lord's.

Scripting Their Life Stories

We only know the story of Elleanor Knight's conversion and call to preach because she published her memoir in 1839. In *A Narrative of the Christian Experience, Life and Adventures, Trials and Labours of Elleanor Knight, Written by Herself*, Knight responded to the rumors circulating about her by trying to make "a fair statement of the facts to the world": she described her childhood, her conversion, her abusive marriage, her call to preach the gospel, and her journeys as an itinerant preacher throughout the states of New England. It is difficult to imagine how she could have found time to write in between visiting her children, traveling to churches to preach, and working long hours in factories to pay her expenses, but she desperately wanted people to understand why she had decided to become a preacher. Angered by the gossip that she was "a worthless character" who had cruelly deserted her husband, or even worse, that she was nothing more than a "common prostitute," she took up her pen to defend herself. "I have had to endure much persecution," she confessed. "I have had powerful enemies, they have tried to hurt me, and I think it is right for me to stand in the defensive enough to state the true circumstances of the case." In the pages that followed, she tried to defend herself against her critics by showing that all of her words and actions had been divinely inspired. "God has given me authority to labor . . . to advance the cause of Christ," she insisted.[8]

Knight was only one of more than twenty female evangelists whose stories were told in print during the first decades of the nineteenth century. Besides Knight, nine other female preachers and five exhorters also published their memoirs during their lives, and three other women, Olive Maria Rice, Hannah Cogswell, and Rebecca Miller, wrote brief spiritual narratives that were printed in religious periodicals.[9] Elizabeth (whose last name is unknown) and Sojourner Truth were too uneducated to write their own narratives, but their stories were transcribed and published by sympathetic friends.[10] In addition, clergymen and family members published the biographies of four other female preachers shortly after they died. Even though these biographies tend to be less personally revealing than the first-person memoirs, they often contain fascinating excerpts from women's letters and journals.[11]

Unfortunately, very few of these women's private writings have survived. Martha Spence Heywood kept a diary that was preserved by her descendants, but it dates from her life after her preaching career had ended. More valuable are Rebecca Jackson's diary and a few letters written by Harriet Livermore, but other women's journals seem to have vanished without a trace. Salome Lincoln's husband reportedly gave her biographer, Almond Davis, a thirty-page journal, fifty of her personal letters, and another one hundred letters that had been written to her, but if they still exist, they are not owned by any major library or historical society.[12] In her memoir, Jarena Lee estimated that publishing her entire journal "would probably make a volume of two hundred pages," but historians have been unable to find her manuscripts.[13]

What this means is that virtually our only information about these women's private religious experiences comes from their published narratives. In other words, we only know what they wanted the reading public to know. Although their memoirs are valuable sources, they are stylized representations meant for public consumption, not transparent records of women's thoughts and actions. As one critic has noted, they should be read as apologies for their authors' "unconventional lives" rather than as unvarnished statements of the "truth."[14] Because female preachers were opposed by men and women who branded them as "masculine" or shameless, they used their memoirs to defend their right to preach the gospel. In a plea for sympathy, Elleanor Knight wrote on her title page: "Read and then judge."[15]

In order to win the acceptance of the reading public, these women modeled their narratives on popular religious books such as Philip Doddridge's *On the Rise and Progress of Religion in the Soul* and John Bunyan's *Pilgrim's Progress*. Both books were frequently republished in nineteenth-century America, and both charted the common stages in a Christian's journey from sin to salvation.[16] In addition, female preachers also self-consciously situated themselves within a tradition of women's spiritual autobiography. Although there were very few women's memoirs published in America before the 1740s, their numbers increased in the wake of the Great Awakening. Mary Clarke Lloyd's *Meditations on Divine Subjects*, Elizabeth Lawrence Bury's *An Account of the Life and Death of Mrs. Elizabeth Bury . . . Chiefly Collected out of Her Own Diary*, and Elizabeth White's *Experience of God's Gracious Dealing* all explored women's personal relationships to God and the joys and sorrows of trying to live a Christian life.[17] Elizabeth Singer Rowe (1674–1737), a British woman who wrote both religious poetry and prose, became such a popular author that her works were frequently reprinted throughout the eighteenth and nineteenth centuries. An excerpt from her *Devout Exercises of the Heart in Meditation and Soliloquy, Prayer and Praise*, first published in America in 1742, was reprinted in the pages of a Freewill Baptist journal as late as 1832.[18]

The most literate female preachers read as many of these books as possible in order to find models for their own stories of sin and salvation. When Harriet Livermore pored over the works of Jeanne Marie Guyon (1648–1717), a French mystic, she lamented that she would never be able to achieve such "angelick purity," but she adopted the same self-abasing tone when she wrote her own memoir. Unlike Guyon, who covered her skin with nettles and walked with pebbles in her shoes, Livermore never practiced any acts of bodily mortification except for fasting, but she still emphasized her passivity and humility. Echoing Guyon's words, she described herself as an "instrument" of God with no will of her own.[19] Other female preachers studied the memoirs of Mary Bosanquet Fletcher, one of the first female Methodist preachers in England during the 1760s, and Hester Rogers, a Methodist class leader who reportedly helped her minister husband convert more than two thousand people. Ellen Stewart remembered studying Rogers's narrative so closely that she could "repeat whole pages."[20]

Yet even though female preachers knew the stories of pious eighteenth-century converts such as Elizabeth Rowe, or British female preachers such as Mary Fletcher, none seemed to know anything about the female visionaries who had exhorted during the revivals of the first Great Awakening. As much as Elleanor Knight would have been encouraged to know that scores of other American women had once testified and exhorted in public, she thought that her generation was the first to demand women's right to speak publicly. Cut off from the stories of the strangers and pilgrims who had gone before her, she and other female preachers struggled to invent a tradition of female evangelism without realizing how deeply their lives reverberated with the past.

Female preachers never mentioned Quaker memoirs by name, but they may have found these books as they searched for stories of women in ministry. Since Quaker leaders often published the journals of Public Friends after they died, it is quite possible that evangelical female preachers read the narratives of women such as Patience Brayton, Elizabeth Ashbridge, or Jane Hoskens, all of which were published in the early 1800s.[21] Zilpha Elaw spent six years as a servant in a Quaker family, and after she felt called to preach for the African Methodists, she consulted several of her Quaker friends for advice. Harriet Livermore, the "pilgrim stranger," attended Quaker meetings for four months before deciding not to affiliate with any denomination at all. Other female preachers occasionally traveled and preached with Quaker women, and whether deliberately or not, they echoed common Quaker themes and images in their memoirs, describing themselves as "poor," "worthless worms" whose words and actions were entirely guided by God.[22]

Reading other women's spiritual memoirs helped female preachers to define who they were, but also who they were not. As much as they were inspired by the Quakers' model of female ministry, they disagreed with many of their theological positions, especially their rejection of baptism and the Lord's Supper, and they wanted to be sure not to be mistaken for them. Nor did they want to be confused with the notorious Ann Lee and Jemima Wilkinson, whom they regarded as wild enthusiasts. If they ever read the Shakers' *Testimonies of the Life, Character, Revelations, and Doctrines of Our Ever Blessed Mother Ann Lee*, or Jemima Wilkinson's *Universal Friend's Advice*, they never admitted it in print. With the exception of Maria Cook and Rebecca Jackson, who eventually became Shakers, they assured their readers that they viewed Mother Ann and the Public Universal Friend as deluded fanatics who never had been genuinely inspired by God. Ellen Stewart confessed that she had once resisted her call to preach out of fear of being led into the same "folly" as Wilkinson, but then she made it clear that nothing could have been more unlikely: "No thought was more awful to me than of being led into error of doctrine and fanaticism."[23]

Female preachers found more theologically acceptable models for their life stories in the narratives written by clergymen within their own sects. In the 1820s and 1830s, Methodists, Christians, African Methodists, and Freewill Baptists began to imitate the Congregationalists and Presbyterians by publishing the memoirs and journals of their most popular clergymen. Although female preachers seem to have been particularly attracted to *women's* narratives because they so desperately needed models of female religious leadership, they saw themselves as part of a larger evangelical community that transcended the boundaries of sex. By 1826, when Harriet Livermore became the first female preacher to publish her memoir, ministers such as John Colby, Levi Hathaway, and Billy Hibbard had already told their spiritual stories in print.[24]

The similarities between men's and women's memoirs are striking. Like men, women usually begin their narratives by telling the story of their childhoods in a brief paragraph or two, and then they follow a standard formula by recounting their conversions, their calls to preach, their travels, and their persecution by "worldlings." Male and female memoirs focus on the same themes of divine grace and prophetic inspiration, and because they are written in the same scriptural language, they sound almost identical in places. Although they differ in important ways as well, as I discuss in the pages that follow, women seem to have wanted to sound as much like male ministers as possible. Accused of being "deceived," they may have patterned their memoirs on male examples in order to sound more orthodox.[25]

Men's and women's narratives closely resemble one another in style as well as content. Fragmentary, rambling, and often shapeless, they tend to simply list the "facts" without explaining or interpreting them. These memoirs overflow with the details of dates, names, and places, but with a few notable exceptions, they contain comparatively little personal reflection. Even Elleanor Knight's book, which is crammed with stories from her marriage, contains long, tedious sections listing nothing but the places she visited. Similarly, a typical passage from Jarena Lee's *Religious Experience and Journal* reads more like a travel log than a compelling personal narrative:

> July 15th, 1838, I left for Westchester, preached two sermons. From there I went to Chichester, from that to the Valley, laboring as I passed along to lively congregations. On the 23d I left for Columbia, calling on Rev. S. S.—, he gave me three appointments. God revived his work in the hearts of his people, and while my pen moves my heart burns with love to God. Next I left for West-town and visited some aged friends, such as could not get to the church, and two remarkable ones in particular, which were regarded as pillars of the church. I was conducted on board the canal boat for Lewistown. I had a pleasant passage, arrived at 1 or 2 o'clock, A.M. and was kindly treated by them. Preached four sermons to a hard people.[26]

The rest of Lee's narrative continues in the same vein, and the concluding pages end abruptly with little sense of narrative closure. Indeed, her narrative does not end as much as it simply stops.

Why did these men and women publish narratives that were so monotonous in style? Perhaps some were simply poor writers who did not know how to make their lives sound interesting, but Jarena Lee certainly knew how to tell a riveting story, and many pages of her memoir pulse with life and color. Although she could be an eloquent writer when she wanted to be, she seems to have deliberately chosen to stifle her narrative voice in particular sections of her book. Like Elleanor Knight, she wanted her readers to believe that she was simply stating the facts, and for the sake of appearing objective, she mixed her accounts of supernatural visions with more mundane details about her life as an itinerant. It is also possible, as one critic has suggested, that her disconnected style may have reflected a deeper unwillingness to give narrative shape to her life: she could not give her story a conclusive ending because she herself did not know how it would turn out.[27] Unlike Ralph Waldo Emerson, who proclaimed that he was a "transparent eyeball" with vision as unmediated as God's, Lee believed she was too weak and sinful to write her own "ending." With Christian humility, she and other preachers, both male and female, insisted that God alone could "author" their stories.

To symbolize their complete reliance on God, these women modeled their spiritual narratives on the stories of biblical prophets such as Jonah, Deborah, Jeremiah, and Huldah. Like the men in their sects, they studied the Bible as the single most important archetype for their stories of sin and salvation, and they emphasized their typological resemblance to Old Testament prophets as much as their own individual distinctiveness. Comparing herself to Jonah, Jarena Lee confessed that she had "lingered like him, and had lingered to go to the bidding of the Lord, and warn those who are as deeply guilty as were the people of Ninevah."[28] By anchoring her narrative in scriptural precedent, she tried to weave her personal story into the fabric of sacred history, grafting her life onto the Bible. Jonah's story was as timeless as the Bible itself, and according to Lee, it was being recapitulated in her own life.

Female preachers quoted so extensively from the Bible that it is sometimes hard to tell which of their words are uniquely their own. As one scholar has noted, women tried to validate their call to preach by writing their stories *over* the Bible.[29] "I sometimes felt a longing desire, to go *'into all the world and preach the Gospel to every creature,'*" Nancy Towle wrote, quoting from Mark. When she described her anguish at the thought of the ridicule she would face as a female preacher, she echoed two verses from Psalms: "Sleep hence departed from my eyes, and slumber from my eyelids. My bread became like ashes, and my drink was mingled with my weeping." Like Jonah, she believed that preaching would cause her so much suffering that it would be better for her "to die, than to live," and like Jeremiah, she longed to flee from the world: "*'Oh! that I had in the wilderness a lodging place of way-faring men!'*" Only God's promise to Jeremiah brought her comfort: "*Refrain thy voice from weeping, and thine eyes from tears, for thy work shall be rewarded.*"[30] Towle filled her memoir with so many scriptural references that her language could sound stilted and artificial at times, but also powerfully prophetic. Indeed, by echoing the words of Jeremiah and

Jonah, she implied that she had virtually *become* these prophets: she felt the same impulse to preach the gospel, suffered the same gnawing doubts, received the same assurances from God, and most important of all, spoke the exact same words.

By borrowing her language from other women's memoirs, men's memoirs, and especially the Bible, Towle and other female preachers tried to convince the reading public that they genuinely had been inspired by God. Instead of "fair statements of the facts," their narratives were apologies and arguments for women's right to preach the gospel. As Elaine Lawless has argued about twentieth-century Pentecostal women, they "rescripted their narratives" in order to conform to convention: they carefully shaped their stories to fit the ideal of a true conversion experience or call to preach.[31] If they had not discussed their feelings of sinfulness before conversion, their joy at being born again, and their reluctance to obey God's call, their narratives would not have seemed genuinely Christian. In contrast to many modern-day Americans, who tend to equate authenticity with individual uniqueness, nineteenth-century evangelicals believed that a true Christian experience was a shared one. Because they believed that all Christians were essentially the same underneath the external differences of gender, race, or class, they expected converts to have similar—though not necessarily identical—experiences as they traveled from sin to salvation.

Yet even though female preachers portrayed themselves as representative Christians, they also wanted their readers to understand the individual experiences, problems, and quirks of temperament that had shaped their spiritual pilgrimages. Perhaps, as Elaine Lawless has argued about Pentecostal women, they were not completely free to author their own stories, and like men, they may have decided not to write about feelings that did not seem conventionally Christian. But this does not mean that they published "fictions" in the same sense as novels, or that they completely suppressed their own individual voices.[32] Even though Elleanor Knight built her story around the Christian framework of sin, repentance, and salvation, her narrative could never be mistaken for anyone else's. Indeed, Knight's story would never have sounded authentic if she had not focused on her own individual story as well as on universal Christian themes. Even though nineteenth-century evangelicals did not believe in scrutinizing the self for its own sake (unlike later Romantics such as Walt Whitman), they still thought that every person's life story should offer unique evidence of how God worked in the world.

Ultimately, then, these women published memoirs that wove together conventional Christian themes with the stories of their own unique struggles as female preachers. Their descriptions of their conversions and calls to preach are similar to men's, but not identical, and they crafted stories that speak volumes about how they wanted to be perceived by the American public. On the surface, they belittled themselves as "self-effacing, feminine apologists," but on a deeper level, they also likened themselves to divinely inspired biblical prophets.[33] Like Jeremiah, who resisted his call to preach because he was just a "child," they portrayed themselves as weak, unworthy women who had been miraculously "sanctified and ordained" by the grace of God. Even though the narratives that they scripted were not objective records of the facts, they still spoke to a deeper truth. These women believed that from the moment they had been born again, their weakness had been transformed into strength.

"Ye Must Be Born Again": The Experience of Conversion

Both male and female preachers began their narratives by describing how they had become "new creatures" in Christ. "Ye must be born again," Jesus reportedly told his disciples. "Except a man be born again, he cannot see the kingdom of God." In the first four paragraphs of her memoir, Jarena Lee briefly mentioned her place of birth, her parents' decision to hire her out as a servant when she was only seven, and her youthful sinfulness, but then she dispensed with her childhood to focus on the definitive moment of her life: her conversion. Although her first birth was not important, she recounted her second birth in Christ in meticulous detail, from her painful "conviction" of her "sinful nature" to her final submission to God. As Lee related in her narrative, she had suffered paralyzing feelings of hopelessness, but as she sat in church one Sunday listening to a sermon on the text "I perceive thy heart is not right in the sight of God," she finally surrendered to God. Searching for the right words to convey how utterly she had been transformed, she described feeling as if her old self had been stripped away as cleanly as a piece of clothing, leaving a new self in its place: "That instant, it appeared to me as if a garment, which had entirely enveloped my whole person, even to my fingers' ends, split at the crown of my head, and was stripped away from me, passing like a shadow from my sight." Leaping to her feet in "ecstasy," she interrupted her minister's sermon to tell the entire congregation that "God, for Christ's sake, had pardoned the sins of my soul."[34]

Almond Davis, Salome Lincoln's biographer, included this lithograph of her in his book, *The Female Preacher, or Memoir of Salome Lincoln*. Courtesy of the American Antiquarian Society.

Almost every preacher described his or her spiritual rebirth according to the same formula of conviction, repentance, and final justification in Christ.[35] Typically, most noted that a crisis had first "awakened" them to the fragility of their lives. For example, Mark Fernald began to strive for "a saving hope in God through Jesus Christ his Son" after surviving a near shipwreck on a sailing voyage, and Salome Lincoln experienced conversion soon after leaving home at the age of fourteen to work and board in a mill. Separated from her parents and living among strangers, she felt so "lost" and alone that she feared she might have "sinned away the day of grace." As she pored over the book of Deuteronomy, she shuddered at the thought of the punishments God would inflict upon her if she refused to "hearken" unto his voice: "The Lord shall smite you with a consumption, and with a fever, and with an inflammation, and with an extreme burning, and with the sword, and with blasting." Echoing one of these verses, she wrote: "I felt as if I were justly condemned, and despaired of the mercy of God. . . . it seemed to me as though the heavens were brass, and the earth was iron under my feet."[36] Like Fernald, she felt lonely, desperate, and too sinful to ever deserve salvation.

Unfortunately, very few preachers described the psychological contexts of their conversions in any depth, but according to scattered evidence in memoirs and religious periodicals, several experienced even greater anguish than Fernald or Lincoln. Even though many preachers led relatively ordinary lives before their conversions, a significant number had suffered the deaths of loved ones, debilitating illnesses, and even physical abuse. For example, at least five female preachers had been orphaned as children, and their lives seem to have been profoundly shaped by their feelings of loss. According to Zilpha Elaw, whose father died when she was only thirteen, she had often poured out her grief in long prayers to God. Longing for the guidance of a parent, she finally found comfort in the arms of Christ, who reassured her that he had "owned" her as his child. Despite the loss of her human father, she could depend on her heavenly father to protect her from harm.[37]

Several other men and women experienced conversion after losing a child. For example, Abigail Roberts and her husband were born again after two of their children died within months of each other, a tragedy that deeply shook their faith. Dolly Quinby, another female preacher, lost seven of her twelve children before they reached adulthood. It is hard to imagine the depth of anguish she must have felt as each child died—the despair, anger, and helplessness that must have consumed her as she watched over each deathbed. Why had God afflicted her with so much suffering? Overwhelmed by grief, she turned to the Bible for answers, and eventually she found peace in the life-changing experience of conversion. Like Abigail and Nathan Roberts, she never stopped mourning for her children, but she felt reassured by her belief in God's providence. If it was true that nothing in the world ever happened by accident, then even her sorrows had a larger meaning—a meaning that someday she would understand.[38]

Other men and women turned their thoughts to God during times of serious illness. For example, Clarissa Green, Clement Phinney, and Sabrina Lambson were all converted as they languished on their sickbeds expecting to die. As they confronted their mortality, they understood the precariousness of their lives in a way they never had before. Frightened by their vulnerability, they longed to be swallowed up by God—to lose their weakness in his strength. They prayed to be healed not only in their bodies, but in their souls.[39]

Finally, several other preachers experienced conversion as they struggled to cope with traumatic experiences of violence. Several male preachers had fought in the Revolution or the War of 1812, and they were haunted by the bloodshed they had seen on the battlefield. Writing to his wife after the battle of Plattsburgh, William Miller exclaimed, "My God! What a slaughter on all sides!"[40] After returning to his home in Vermont, he begged God to help him forget the horrors of what he had seen and heard.

Although most women had been spared the horrors of warfare, some had faced a more intimate form of violence—the violence of repeated domestic abuse. Besides Elleanor Knight, who hinted that her husband had beaten her, at least three other female preachers had been subjected to physical abuse. Both Sarah Hedges and Nancy Cram married "dissolute, licentious" men who battered them for several years before abandoning them, and Sojourner Truth, a former slave, was repeatedly whipped and beaten by her master. As historian Nell Irvin Painter argues, there are brief hints in her memoir that she may also have been sexually abused by her white mistress—a traumatic experience that seems to have caused her deep shame. In her memoir, she confessed that she had been subjected to something "so unaccountable, so unreasonable, and what is usually called so unnatural" that she could not divulge all the details to her readers.[41]

Whether psychologically or physically, these women and men felt weak before their conversions, and they longed to be strengthened by the power of God. Those who were sick wanted to be cured; those who were grieving wanted to be comforted; and those who had been abused or forsaken wanted to be loved. When they sobbed out their prayers for mercy, they gave voice to all of their suppressed feelings of worthlessness, despair, and rage. Psychologically, they seem to have turned their feelings of anger inward against themselves as well as outward against the corrupt world.[42] With numbing repetitiveness, they insisted that they were wretched sinners who did not deserve to be saved: they were weak, sinful, vile, ungodly, disobedient, and wicked. They were truly the last, and they thought they were too worthless ever to be first.

Women particularly emphasized the anguish they had experienced before being born again. According to Jarena Lee, she had been repeatedly tempted to drown or hang herself. "I was beset to hang myself by a cord," she confessed. Quoting from Jonah, she wrote: "I had come to the conclusion that I had better be dead than alive."[43] Filled with self-loathing, she longed to lose her identity in the oblivion of death—to submerge herself in nothingness. Convinced that she was too sinful to be saved, she wondered why she should continue to strive hopelessly for God's grace.

In general, women's descriptions of their sufferings tended to be more detailed and more intimate than men's. As historian Virginia Brereton has observed about nineteenth-century conversion accounts in general, women's narratives "reveal more struggle, more painful self-examination, more intensity, more agonizing about 'sins' that a later age would consider harmless," while men's accounts "appear to have been matter of fact; some even seem pro-forma." For example, Mark Fernald noted briefly that his "distress of mind was beyond description," but in contrast to Jarena Lee, who devoted several paragraphs of her narrative to her suicidal feelings, he wrote very little about his inward spiritual struggles.[44] Whatever his feelings may have been during the months before his conversion, he decided not to divulge them to his readers.

Whether or not women and men actually experienced conversion differently, a question that cannot be answered, it is clear that they chose to write about it in subtly distinctive ways. Despite their common beliefs, they scripted their conversion accounts according to different conventions. Even though there is no reason to doubt that Jarena Lee thought about committing suicide or that other women felt hopeless and worthless, they could have decided to leave these stories out of their narratives or, like men, tell them in far less detail. Conversely, men such as Mark Fernald could have put more emphasis on their distress, but they preferred to focus on the strength they gained from being born again.

The stories that these men and women chose to include in their memoirs reflected how they wanted their lives to be read. Like all authors, they had definite ideas about how they wanted their books to be interpreted, and they wrote with a particular audience in mind—an audience that seems to have encompassed more than their own sects. Whether they wanted to inspire, provoke, or justify, they used their narratives to influence public perceptions of them.

When men wrote only brief descriptions of their feelings of weakness, they may have hoped to defend themselves against charges that they were "feminine." By admitting their weakness at all, they deliberately set themselves apart from a culture that prized self-reliance as the consummate "masculine" virtue, and they self-consciously distanced themselves from popular images of aggressive manhood. Nevertheless, they could not help being influenced by the world they claimed to renounce, and they seem to have bristled at accusations that "real" men would never allow women to preach. In response to socially conservative clergymen who implied that any minister who allowed a woman into the pulpit had been emasculated, they denied allowing female preachers to "dictate." "The man is the head of the woman, as Christ is the head of man," one Christian Connection minister affirmed.[45]

Just as men tried to defend themselves against charges of effeminacy, female preachers took pains to deny that they were "masculine." Like men, they claimed to disdain the opinion of the world, but they were painfully aware that they did not meet middle-class expectations of "femininity." From reading popular magazines, tracts, and sentimental novels, they knew that "true" women—those who were pious, pure, and submissive—would never think of tainting their virtue by allowing strangers to stare at them in public. Nor would they ever consider leaving their homes and families to travel across the country as itinerants. As one minister assured his female congregants, "The *home* of a wife and mother has enough for her to do in the cause of God and religion." Determined to fulfill their responsibilities as Christian and republican mothers, many middle-class women agreed with him. After Catherine Williams saw a woman preach at a camp meeting in the early 1820s, she admitted that her sermon had been "good," but then quickly added a disclaimer: "The great effort of retaining such a masculine attitude entirely destroyed the effect."[46]

By describing themselves in their conversion narratives as distressed, frail women, female preachers implicitly defended themselves against critics who accused them of being "masculine." Responding to the charge that she was actually "a man dressed in female clothes," Jarena Lee chose to portray herself as a "true woman" who also happened to be black and a preacher. Indeed, the title page of her 1836 narrative, *The Life and Religious Experience of Mrs. Jarena Lee, A Coloured Lady*, proclaimed her status as a lady. Especially in the opening pages of her book, Lee described herself in conventionally "feminine" terms as weak, emotionally unstable, and sickly. Describing her despair after suppressing her call to preach, she wrote: "I fell into a state of general debility, and an ill state of health, so much so, that I could not sit up."[47] Despite her seeming strength, she wanted her readers to know she was also exceedingly vulnerable.

Yet even when nineteenth-century female preachers emphasized their weakness, they rarely sounded as self-abasing as their eighteenth-century foremothers. Even though Jarena Lee once described herself as "unclean," she never echoed earlier New Lights and Separates by denigrating herself as "wounded," "bruised," or full of "putrifying sores."[48] Unlike eighteenth-century female evangelists, she may not have been attracted to images of innate corruption because of her belief in free will. In addition, she may have understood her "femininity" in more positive terms because of new images of women's innate virtue. Even though she was influenced by lingering images of female pollution, she never claimed to have been so caught up in God that she had lost her gender. Unlike Jemima Wilkinson, she never claimed to be "neither male nor female."

Despite these differences, however, nineteenth-century female preachers were linked to their foremothers by their faith in the transforming power of Christ. Echoing all of the female visionaries who had come before them, they claimed to have triumphed over their feelings of sinfulness, weakness, and despair at the miraculous moment they had been born again. No longer despondent, they basked in sensations of contentment, "solemn stillness," or "sweet peace." In the words of Salome Lincoln, the young mill worker who had anguished over her wickedness, conversion had made her "clean." "It seemed as if the mountains rolled away, and I heard these words: 'be thou clean!'" she exulted. "My fears subsided. The throbbings of my bosom ceased; and a heavenly calm ensued."[49] Reborn in Christ, she had overcome all of the anguish of her former life.

Throughout their narratives, female preachers repeatedly undercut their descriptions of themselves as weak and sinful by hinting at their spiritual perfection. According to many Methodist and African Methodist women, for example, they had been not only born again, but "sanctified," or freed from the burden of committing intentional sins. Like many men in their sects, women such as Zilpha Elaw, Fanny Newell, Jarena Lee, E. J. Marden, and Julia Foote wanted their readers to know that they had been given a "second blessing": they had become so "completely identified with God in thought, word, and deed" that they had attained spiritual perfection. For example, Zilpha Elaw remembered feeling so "surrounded and engulphed" by God that it was as if she had been completely remade in his image. "My heart and soul were rendered completely spotless—as clean as a sheet of white paper," she wrote, "and I felt as pure as if I had never sinned in all my life."[50] Even though she had once been the worst of sinners, she had become the best of saints.

To borrow a turn of phrase from historian Virginia Brereton, Elaw scripted a narrative containing both a "surface plot" and a "submerged plot." According to the surface plot, she was a feeble woman who had never deserved to be touched by God's grace, but according to the submerged plot, she was a commanding prophet whose authority had come directly from God. Indeed, the story that Elaw scripted of her spiritual rebirth and sanctification was one of authority as well as submission. Like male preachers, she celebrated not only her loss of self in Christ, but her rebirth in his image. Paradoxically, her denial of self was also her greatest source of power. Conversion and sanctification entailed the extinction of the self, the absolute resignation of one's will to God, but also the exaltation of the self in blissful union with Christ. Once she had been reborn, she was no longer an ordinary black woman, but a Christian who was superior to all the women—and men—who had not yet been saved. As she told her readers, her conversion had truly turned the world upside down. "My strength is made perfect in weakness," she quoted from Corinthians.[51]

It was this theme of "feminine" weakness transformed into strength that made female preachers' conversion stories sound distinctive from men's. Like men, they claimed to have been empowered by the grace of God, but as "weak" females, they portrayed their journeys from sin to salvation as even more extraordinary. Not only had God saved them despite their sinfulness, their doubts, and their lowly station, but to fulfill Christ's promise that the last would be first, he had chosen them for an even greater distinction. Conversion had marked the beginning of their stories—their "birth"—but there was still much more to tell. Remarkably, God had not only changed them into new creatures, but had called them to preach the gospel.

The Moment of the Call

Both male and female preachers claimed that God had personally called them to labor in his harvest. As they revealed in their narratives, they did not understand why God had decided to choose them above the "learned, the wise [and] the experienced," but he *had* chosen them, and he had made his will unmistakably clear. Even though they were "weak and ignorant," and far less educated than clergymen in more established denominations, they had been called to preach by God himself, who had inspired them through the Holy Spirit.[52] Through no choice of their own, they had become sacred vessels of the divine.

Women's and men's descriptions of the call ranged from the mild claim that God had sent them inward impressions or impulses to the more extreme assertion that God had directly and personally communicated with them. Most typically, ministers such as Ransom Dunn and Abel Thornton (both Freewill Baptists) felt a "deep and settled conviction" that they must preach the gospel.[53] Other men and women reported being inspired by certain biblical passages that had particularly moved them. When Mary Coy Bradley opened her Bible and read God's words to Moses, "Come now therefore, and I will send thee unto Pharaoh, that thou mayest bring forth my people, the children of Israel, out of Egypt," she could not contain her "fear and amazement" because the words seemed to have been written just for her. Try as she might, she could not shake the impression that God had destined her to be a modern-day Moses leading sinners out of bondage.[54] Like other evangelicals, she did not read the Bible as a dead, lifeless text, but as "the word made flesh," a continuing and unmediated revelation from God.

Besides being inspired by the written word, both men and women claimed that God had personally instructed them to preach during a moment of immediate revelation. Yet just as men described their conversions as less tumultuous than women's, they also tended to downplay the more supernatural aspects of their calls to preach. Although David Millard, a Christian Connection minister, implied that he had heard an otherworldly voice, he also subtly distanced himself from that claim by writing ambiguously, "Something would *seem* to say, 'If you experience religion you will have to preach.'" Similarly, David Marks, a Freewill Baptist, remembered that when he was called, "I felt the first direct impulse *as if* from Heaven, '*Go thou and preach the gospel.*'" Even the intensely visionary James Horton, who described himself as living in a perpetual "heavenly ecstasy," usually stopped short of claiming that he had actually seen Christ or heard the voice of God. Describing a particularly powerful religious experience, he wrote, "It *appeared* to me that I could hear the angels around me singing the praises of God—heaven *seemed* to be open in all its immortal beauty before me."[55] Even though these men were more visionary than their Congregational or Episcopalian colleagues, their choice of language subtly undercut their claims to direct inspiration.

In contrast, female preachers insisted that they had personally encountered the divine through dreams, visions, or voices. Like the New Light and Separate women who had exhorted during the revivals of the 1740s and 1760s, they defended themselves against their critics by arguing that God had issued them an extraordinary call which could not be refused. For example, Nancy Towle claimed that she had never considered becoming a preacher until dreaming that she would "one day become religious, and bear testimony to the word of God's grace over the earth."[56] Like Jacob, who had dreamed of a ladder rising to heaven, or like Joel, who had promised that men and women would prophesy, dream dreams, and see visions in the last days, Towle argued that her dream had not been the offspring of her own imagination, but a miraculous communication from God.

If Towle sounded visionary at times, African American female preachers sounded even more so. Even though black female preachers published narratives that closely resembled those written by white women, they identified themselves even more closely with biblical prophets. Unlike white women such as Elleanor Knight, who had been called to preach during a dream, black female preachers insisted that they had seen heavenly visions or heard angelic voices while they were fully awake and conscious. According to Julia Foote, she had suddenly seen an angel hovering in front of her, who held a scroll in his hand imprinted with the words "Thee have I chosen to preach my Gospel without delay." Filled with fear, she cried out, "Lord, I cannot do it," but from that moment on, her life was no longer her own: she had literally seen her destiny spelled out in front of her.[57]

Foote's ecstatic experiences defy easy historical analysis because she claimed that they transcended history, occupying the realm of the sacred rather than the secular. In her opinion, her spiritual rebirth had less to do with the realities of her everyday life than with the mysterious workings of God. Yet without questioning or denigrating her religious sincerity, we can see other meanings in her experiences as well. Whether self-consciously or intuitively, Foote may have tried to compensate for her lack of formal religious authority by emphasizing her ecstatic communion with the Holy Spirit.[58] Doubly stigmatized because of her sex and her race, she had to defend her right to preach not only as a woman, but as an African American. At the same time as black ministers "sneered" at her for presuming to have been called, whites questioned whether a black person, especially a black woman, could ever speak for God. In response, Foote conceded that she seemed like an unlikely candidate for the ministry, especially since she "had always been opposed to the preaching of women," but the decision had not been her own. Just as God had revealed himself to Jeremiah and Jonah, he had revealed himself to her, and she had no choice but to obey his commands.[59]

Even more than white women, black female preachers insisted that their authority to preach had come directly from the Holy Spirit. They had been influenced not only by dreams, which were internal, but by visions and voices that had come from outside of themselves. When Zilpha Elaw claimed to have heard a voice proclaiming, "Thou must preach the gospel; and thou must travel far and wide," she hastened to add, "This did not occur in the night, when dozing slumbers and imaginative dreams are prevalent, but at mid-day, between the hours of twelve and two o'clock." By declaring that the voice she heard had not come from inside of her own head, but from "an invisible and heavenly personage sent by God," she tried to make it impossible for people to question her right to preach. Despite describing herself as "poor and weak," she also claimed to have been transformed into a prophet whose every word was divinely inspired. As she informed her readers, she did not write or speak with her own authority, but with the authority of God.[60]

Besides helping them defend their right to preach, black women's visions served more personal needs as well. Rebecca Jackson, an African Methodist who later became a Shaker eldress, probably never imagined that her private diary would be published, but like other black women, she filled it with descriptions of the audible voices, prophetic dreams, waking visions, and divine premonitions that had guided and educated her. Psychologically, these ecstatic experiences may have helped her cope with the hostility she often encountered as a preacher, especially the threat of physical violence. For example, on one occasion she was harassed by a group of Methodist ministers who fantasized about murdering her: "One said I ought to be stoned to death, one said tarred and feathered and burnt, one said I ought to be put in a hogshead, driven full of spikes, and rolled down a hill." Terrified of being physically attacked, she prayed to God to offer her concrete proof that he would protect her from harm.[61] In response, he sent her dreams, visions, and voices to reassure her that even in her moments of suffering, he would always be with her.

In one particularly brutal dream, "the dream of slaughter," Jackson saw herself being skinned alive by a male robber, helpless to do anything except pray. As the voice of God instructed her to remain perfectly still and unmoving, the man "took a lance and laid my nose open and then he cut my head on the right side, from the back to the front of my nose, and pulled the skin down over that side. Then he cut the left, did the same way, and pulled the skin down. The skin and blood covered me like a veil from my head to my lap. All my body was covered with blood. Then he took a long knife and cut my chest open in the form of the cross and took all my bowels out and laid them on the floor by my right side." With each act of torture, God watched silently, but he finally intervened when the robber prepared to cut out her heart. Awaking in terror, Jackson realized that God had sent her this dream in order to teach her two crucial lessons. First, she would have to suffer if she truly wanted to submit herself to his will. And second, she would only win his protection if she remained absolutely still and obedient to his every command.[62] No matter how much pain he might ask her to endure, he would never abandon her if she continued to put her trust in him alone.

Other African American women relied on dreams, visions, and voices to help them cope with the persistent racism they encountered in the pulpit. Even as they defended their essential humanity, they found it difficult not to internalize the damaging stereotypes of black inferiority. On one hand, Zilpha Elaw assured her readers that God had created blacks as the equals of whites. "The Almighty accounts not the black races of man either in the order of nature or spiritual capacity as inferior to the white," she wrote. "For He bestows his Holy Spirit on, and dwells in them as readily as in persons of whiter complexion." On the other hand, however, Elaw seems to have doubted whether she, like the bride of Solomon, could truly exhibit "comeliness with blackness." Despite condemning whites who treated their skin color as "a bauble of great value," she once saw a vision of herself in which her "complexion" had miraculously turned white.[63] Clearly, the psychic costs of defending herself as an African American, a woman, and a preacher were profound.

It is hard to imagine how women, especially black women, ever would have found the courage to preach if not for their belief in divine inspiration. Besides using scriptural examples to justify their decision to preach, they laid claim to an immediate encounter with the divine—a claim that others could question but ultimately never disprove. Even though Jarena Lee wondered why God would have chosen a "poor coloured woman" to preach, she triumphed over her fears because of her faith that she had "distinctly heard" God commanding her to "Go Preach the Gospel!" "I will put words in your mouth," God had promised, "and will turn your enemies to become your friends."[64] Her religious authority had come from the Almighty God himself, who had sent her visions, voices, and dreams to educate her in a way that no mere human, even the most learned, ever could.

All female preachers, whether white or black, described their calls to preach as immediate, irrefutable, and most of all, beyond their control. Even more than men, they declared that they never would have dared to speak publicly if not for the immediate revelation of the Holy Spirit. Defending themselves against their critics, they maintained that the decision to preach had been not their own, but God's. "No ambition of mine, but the special appointment of God, had put me into the ministry," Zilpha Elaw confided, "and, therefore, I had no option in the matter."[65] According to her, she was only a weak woman, but after actually seeing God and hearing heavenly voices, she could not deny that she had been called.

Quenching the Spirit

Throughout her narrative, Elaw portrayed herself as a helpless woman who would never have willingly chosen the rigorous life of a female preacher. Despite her revelations, she was so fearful of what people would think of her that she stubbornly refused to submit to God's commands. Disobeying Paul's command to the Thessalonians, "Quench not the spirit," she hesitated for a full two years before setting out as an itinerant. Torn between her desire to speak and her fear of persecution, she "became like a tormented demon."[66]

It was common for both male and female preachers to portray themselves as reluctant prophets who had resisted their calls to preach. Self-consciously echoing the words of the prophet Jeremiah, Joseph Badger remembered pleading to God, "I cannot speak, for I am a child." Similarly, Salome Lincoln, a Reformed Methodist from Massachusetts, explicitly compared herself to Jonah, who had "fled from the presence of the Lord, to get rid of duty." Fearful of the persecution she would face in her travels, she spent long hours weeping in her room, imploring God not to force her to make such an enormous sacrifice. "O, my soul shrunk from the work!" she exclaimed in a letter to a friend. In her most anguished moments, she claimed that she was almost willing to be "lost"—to be damned—rather than to accept the burden of God's call.[67]

Since the Freewill Baptists, Christians, and Methodists believed that it was natural for preachers to attempt to quench the spirit, Lincoln and Badger may have deliberately exaggerated their distress in order to conform to convention. According to Benjamin Putnam, a Freewill Baptist, "It was a prevailing sentiment among the people with whom I had become connected, that if a person be called to the work of the christian ministry, he will feel the greatest aversion to it, and that this is an evidence that his impressions are genuine." With a touch of embarrassment, Putnam admitted doubting whether his call was genuine because he "had so great *a desire for the office*."[68] Only those humble few who disparaged themselves as too ignorant, weak, or unworthy to serve God had truly been called. Paradoxically, then, Lincoln's description of herself sobbing in her room, overcome by fear, may have helped to convince many evangelicals that she genuinely had been chosen.

Yet even though Lincoln certainly knew that true prophets were supposed to suffer doubts, her expressions of anguish may have been more than simply rhetorical. As both men and women explained in their memoirs, they had good reasons to resist their calls to preach. First, many claimed to feel overwhelmed by their sacred obligation to lead sinners to salvation. "The work appeared so great, the calling so holy, and the responsibility so weighty, that I could not surmount all fears," Mark Fernald wrote. Because he believed that God would save only those who had been born again, he worried that his personal failures in the pulpit would have terrible consequences. If people were not "convicted" by his sermons, then it would be at least partially his fault if they were damned. Haunted by the fear that every sinner he failed to save would be eternally lost, doomed to face an eternity in hell, he begged God not to burden him with such a terrifying responsibility.[69]

Second, most of these preachers were uneducated, and despite their anti-intellectualism, they seem to have sincerely wondered how they could compete with college-educated clergymen. James Horton, a Methodist, jeered at "foppish" ministers who relied more on their sermon notes than on the inspiration of the spirit, but he also trembled with fear at the thought of speaking in front of a camp meeting filled with "doctors, lawyers, and merchants." How could such a "poor, weak creature"—a man who had barely attended school—make an impression on such a distinguished and wealthy group of men?[70]

Finally, all ministers, whether male or female, expressed fears about speaking in public. Even though there was a movement in post-Revolutionary America to cultivate a plainer and more democratic style of English, many preachers were not sure which words qualified as plain and which were unacceptably crude. Even though educators encouraged people to choose simple language to express their ideas, they also published grammars and dictionaries explaining the rules of correct speech—rules that could often seem obscure and confusing. Many lower-class, uneducated preachers wondered why the word "broken" was more grammatically correct than the word "breaked," or why "women" should not be spelled as "wimin." Fearful of displaying their ignorance in public, they hesitated for months or even years before delivering their first sermons. According to Heman Bangs, a Methodist, he had been so "bashful" about speaking in public that he had waited seven years to obey his call. Even speaking as a class leader sent him into fits of terror. "I could have willingly crept under the seats," he admitted, "or laid myself down to be

trodden upon." Too frightened to look at his audience, he confessed, "I generally spoke with my eyes shut, for I had not courage to open them."[71]

For women, the thought of speaking publicly was even more daunting. Besides Quaker women, there were very few female orators in early-nineteenth-
century America, and the few who dared to ascend the platform were condemned for stepping out of their "feminine" place. When Frances Wright, a
well-known author and reformer, delivered a series of lectures in Cincinnati in
1828, her listeners marveled at her "overwhelming eloquence," but they also
expressed shock at her brazen disregard for "decorum." Besides being offended by her freethinking support of women's rights, they were also shocked
by her willingness to let strangers stare at her in public. She had "leaped
over the boundary of female modesty," one newspaper wrote, and had virtually "ceased to be a woman." By speaking in public, she had become a "female monster."[72]

Despite their efforts to separate themselves from secular values, female
preachers frankly admitted their fears of being attacked as "monsters" or
viragos. Most of all, they worried that their friends and families would abandon them or, at the very least, be ashamed of them. According to Nancy
Caldwell, a Methodist, she sat through several church meetings in agonized
silence because she thought her husband would prefer to see her "dead" than
to expose her "ignorance" by witnessing in public. When Mary Coy Bradley,
also a Methodist, stood up to speak publicly for the first time, her anxiety so
overpowered her that she literally lost her voice. "I was struck speechless," she
wrote, "and all my strength left me. I was taken up and laid upon the bed."
Even though she eventually became an exhorter, she never dared to demand
the "masculine" authority of preaching. Rachel Baker, a Baptist who had been
raised as a Presbyterian, preached only in her sleep. Instead of standing in the
pulpit, she attracted large crowds who came to hear her "nocturnal perfor-
mances." When people questioned her motives, she insisted that she had no
control over her actions. Female preaching, in her words, was "wrong."[73]

According to the narrative of Ellen Stewart, a Methodist from Ohio, women
had to overcome "almost insurmountable" obstacles in order to find the
courage to preach. Even among the Methodists, who were relatively tolerant of
female evangelism, Stewart could find very few people who believed her claim
to divine inspiration. Tortured by self-doubts, she had almost steeled herself to
speak at a Methodist Quarterly Meeting in 1813, but then she was "nearly
electrified" by hearing a clergyman scoff at the idea of female preaching. As she

sat silently, he "spoke of some women on his circuit and remarked that they were very officious, and one or two had applied for license [to preach], and concluded in a contemptuous laugh, in which he was joined by the company." Frustrated and angry, she could not "join in the merriment," nor was she bold enough to confront him.[74] Instead, she tried to quench the spirit by choosing to get married rather than to preach, and as a result, she sank into a deep depression. It took her several years to find the courage to speak in local churches.

Perhaps Stewart would have been less timid if she had been supported by her husband, but as she complained, he was "very tenacious of the submission of wives." In a rare moment of compassion, he promised to help her fulfill her call, but as soon as he realized that she intended to travel away from home, he changed his mind. On one occasion, she planned to leave for a single night to attend a religious meeting, but he complained that it was "unreasonable" of her to leave him and their children alone. In a rare show of fortitude, Stewart stuck by her decision, but she felt so guilty that she spent the night imagining "a frowning husband, children wounded or drowning, or the house in flames." In 1836, after her husband died, she thought she would have greater freedom to travel and preach, but her children ridiculed her by calling her "'priest,' 'minister,' and so on, as an epithet of reproach." Dependent on them for financial as well as emotional support, Stewart suppressed her ambitions, but only at great psychological cost. "I felt like one enclosed within a stone wall," she lamented. "Like an imprisoned bird, I pined for liberty, and my spirit fluttered from side to side of its iron cage."[75]

If the opposition of her husband and children were not painful enough, Stewart also had to confront her own doubts about speaking in public--doubts that she never managed to overcome. In 1840, almost thirty years after she first had been called, she became so frightened on her way to a preaching appointment in Naples, New York, that she literally ran away from the church. In her words: "The Methodist ministers, and the Presbyterian minister of Naples, were to my apprehension what the giants and the sons of the Anakims were to the cowardly Jews who were sent to spy out the godly land; I dreaded to see the face of man, and hastened to make my escape; although I knew well it was temptation for the time being, I seemed to have no power to resist. I walked very fast, nay, almost ran, as if pursued by Satan, and I was glad when out of sight of the village." Even as a mature woman, Stewart had not conquered her anxiety that people would view her as "a strange enthusiastic creature" who was too "forward" and aggressive.[76]

Unlike Stewart, most female preachers eventually overcame their fears of public humiliation, but all quenched the spirit for months or even years. Nancy Towle debated for two years before finally becoming an itinerant; Jarena Lee waited eight years; and because she was illiterate and a slave, Elizabeth procrastinated for twenty-nine years. Of course, many men also agonized over whether to accept their calls to preach, but with the exception of the bashful Heman Bangs, few waited more than a few weeks or months to begin their careers in the pulpit.

Conventionally, both male and female preachers adopted a stance of Christian humility in their narratives, but women sounded particularly self-abasing. The difference was in degree rather than type: most men described their feelings of weakness in a few sentences or paragraphs, while women reasserted their frailty throughout their published writings. In contrast to Abel Thornton, who commented briefly on his "want of learning and inabilities," Elleanor Knight lamented the "small capacity" of her mind; Ellen Stewart despaired that she was too "ignorant and unlearned" to preach; Jarena Lee denigrated herself as a "weak female"; and Mary Coy Bradley belittled herself as "entirely incapable of performing any thing aright." In a particularly self-effacing narrative, Harriet Livermore emphasized her "imbecility" and even described her religious efforts as "infantine." She was "poor, and blind, and wretched," she confessed, and her life had been so "vain, unprofitable, [and] sinful" that she did not deserve God's mercy.[77] Despite her faith that God had called her, she could not understand why he had ever chosen such an "imbecile" to be his prophet.

As a woman, Livermore may have faced greater doubts than men about whether she had genuinely been called. She also had even more reason to express her doubts in print. In response to critics who scorned her as "a gazing stock," she depicted herself as a humble, virtuous woman who had only become a preacher in order to please God. Emphasizing her meekness, she swore that she never would have obeyed her call if God had not virtually forced her into the pulpit. For example, when she decided to take a job as a schoolteacher, he "sealed up" her mind so that she was incapable of teaching her students how to read a one-syllable word. Then, after only three days in the classroom, she developed a painful abscess on her shoulder that required surgery. As she revealed to her readers, her illness had been sent by God as fitting punishment for her "infidelity."[78]

Unanimously, female preachers testified that they had suffered either physical ailments or "severe mental suffering" because of their sinful attempts to quench the spirit.[79] Like Elleanor Knight, who believed God had taken away two of her children as a consequence of her spiritual disobedience, they portrayed themselves as the helpless victims of God's wrath. Instead of showing mercy on their "feminine" weakness, God had tormented them or their families with illnesses and other afflictions. After describing how she had almost died in 1819 from an internal inflammation, Zilpha Elaw admitted that her illness had actually been her own fault. "So sturdy had been my unbelief," she reflected, "that my merciful and indulgent God was thereby induced to adopt more severe and extraordinary means to bring me into subjection to his holy will."[80] Because she had refused to submit to God's commands, he had applied "the rod" to force her into the pulpit.

Time and again, these women insisted that they had not willingly *chosen* to become itinerants but had been coerced into preaching by the punishing hand of the Almighty God. Like the apostle Paul, who wrote in his first letter to the Corinthians, "Necessity is laid upon me; yea, woe is unto me, if I preach not the gospel," they claimed to have obeyed God's call out of necessity, not choice. As Harriet Livermore protested in her narrative, she had never wanted to become a female preacher—a "spectacle, a publick show, a kind of by-word among a multitude, a derision and scorn to thousands"—but the decision had not been her own.[81] Like her conversion and her call to preach, her decision to wander the world as a stranger and a pilgrim had been beyond her control. Even though she would have preferred the "honorable" life of a schoolteacher, the Holy Spirit had refused to be quenched.

Instruments of God

Instead of celebrating their own intelligence or strength, these women repeatedly denied having any control over where they would preach, what they would say, or how many people would be converted during their meetings. They claimed to be helpless "pens" in the hand of God, not creators of their own destinies, and therefore what they wrote, both figuratively and literally, was not truly their own. Like Jarena Lee, who described herself as "clay in the hands of the Potter," they exulted that they had become "instruments of God."[82]

Modeling themselves on Old Testament prophets, both male and female preachers asserted that all of their words and actions had been guided entirely by God. Just as Jeremiah had spoken God's words, not his own, they were "mouths for God" when they stood in the pulpit. Even though Jarena Lee admitted feeling apprehensive about preaching in front of the governor of Delaware in 1825, she found that she had no reason to be afraid. Echoing a verse from Psalms, she wrote: "It appeared to me as if I had nothing to do but open my mouth, and the Lord filled it."[83] Without even choosing a sermon text in advance, she simply waited to hear what words God would "pour" into her mind.

Female preachers not only denied having control over their words, but over their travels as well. As Harriet Livermore explained, she did not travel where *she* wanted to go, but where God led her. "My exertions in traveling and appointing meetings, owe their spring entirely to the supernatural agency of religion," she wrote in her narrative. In 1825, after trying to decide where to hold a meeting, she was struck by the name "Middleborough" and immediately packed her suitcase to travel there. Similarly, Elleanor Knight wandered wherever God's "spirit and his Providence seem to direct my way."[84] Despite her seeming independence, she was an instrument of God who never made a decision without divine guidance.

What did it mean to these women to be instruments of God? To many modern-day feminists, women's descriptions of themselves as instruments, mouthpieces, and vessels might seem stereotypically—and uncomfortably— "feminine." Even if women emphasized their weakness as part of a deliberate strategy for public acceptance, they ended up reinforcing negative images of frail womanhood. In striking contrast to literary figures such as Emerson or Thoreau, they contributed little to the American celebration of individualism and self-reliance. A woman who spoke as a mouthpiece was not an individual with a voice of her own, but a powerless object.[85]

From this perspective, women's emphasis on their victimization may be particularly troubling. Despite their obvious strength and courage, female preachers described themselves as weak, helpless victims whose sufferings almost overwhelmed them after their calls to preach. Even more than men, they described preaching as such an ordeal that it was a painful "crucifixion." With graphic language, Ellen Stewart explained that holding a public meeting was "the greatest sacrifice and crucifixion of self, of any I had yet made. Yes, reader, if you had been there, you might have heard the strokes of the hammer that nailed me to the Cross, and heard the cries of the victim." According to Stewart, preaching was a denial rather than an assertion of self, a "cross" to be born in suffering and anguish. A female preacher, in the opinion of Harriet Livermore, was "a spectacle and sufferer . . . a victim."[86]

Yet even though some modern-day readers, especially those of a secular bent, might wish that these women had never described themselves in such seemingly passive terms as victims or instruments, female preachers had a far different interpretation of their experiences as pens in God's hand. Just as Christ's sacrifice had been an act of strength as well as submission, they argued that preaching was a cross that both burdened and freed them. Even though Christ had been a victim, the lamb who had been sacrificially slaughtered, he was also the Savior, God in human form. By identifying so closely with him, as well as with biblical prophets such as Jeremiah and Deborah, they made the greatest possible assertion of their own authority and dignity. As Nancy Towle explained, she was not "merely *passive* in the building of the Lord Jesus," but "*a teacher of righteousness*."[87] By claiming to be God's instrument, she implied that every word she uttered was divinely inspired and therefore priceless. Even though she had not been chosen to preach because of any inherent talents or abilities of her own, she *had* been chosen, and in her eyes, her sermons were as authoritative as if Christ himself had delivered them.

In practice, "passive" women were capable of considerable courage and determination. Elleanor Knight had once feared appearing too "forward," but after leaving her alcoholic husband, she became an outspoken crusader for women's right to preach the gospel. Even though she continued to describe herself in conventionally "feminine" terms as weak or feeble, she also condemned men for treating their wives and sisters like "slaves." "There is no worse bondage than to bind the conscience," she wrote angrily. "There is no worse oppression than to press the word of the Lord within, and hinder those from speaking that long to speak, that their minds may be refreshed."[88] In the closing pages of her narrative, she urged her female readers not to quench the spirit because of their "fear of man." If they had read her book carefully, they knew that Christ could work the same miracle in their lives as he had in hers. If they were willing to obey him, he would fulfill the promise he had once made to his disciples. He would make the first last, and the last first.

5

Lift Up Thy Voice Like a Trumpet

Evangelical Cry aloud, spare not, lift up thy voice like a trumpet, and

shew my people their transgression, and the house of Jacob

Women their sins.—Isaiah 58:1

in the Oh that my head were waters, and mine eyes a fountain of

tears, that I might weep day and night for the slain of the

Pulpit daughter of my people! Oh that I had in the wilderness a

lodging place of wayfaring men; that I might leave my peo-

ple, and go from them! for they be all adulterers, an assem-

bly of treacherous men. . . . Shall I not visit them for these

things? saith the Lord: shall not my soul be avenged on such

a nation as this?—Jeremiah 9:1–2, 9

In the fall of 1828, Abigail Roberts arrived in the
town of Milford, New Jersey, and announced that she would hold a worship
meeting that evening. Within hours, the news had spread from neighbor to
neighbor, causing a sensation in the small community of farmers and merchants. One man later remembered that he had been hauling wood when he
heard rumors that "the woman, as she was then called—no one knowing her
name—was to preach." Like many other people in the town, he had never seen
an evangelical female preacher in person before, and as he finished his chores
for the day, he speculated excitedly about what "the woman" would say in her

sermon. According to the contradictory reports he had heard, she was either a devout Mother in Israel who had been called to nurture the family of God or, more negatively, a radical jezebel who wanted to corrupt the purity of Christianity. Only one fact seemed clear: she was a confident woman who paid little attention to her critics. When the trustees of the nondenominational chapel in Milford refused to open their church to her, she quickly made arrangements to speak in a nearby warehouse. Nothing could dissuade her from fulfilling her call to "lift up her voice like a trumpet" to show God's people their sins.[1]

That evening, an "overflowing crowd" assembled to hear Roberts preach. Impatient to see her, people pushed their way through the doors and then fidgeted in their seats, but when she and her husband finally entered the building, they fell silent. Straining to catch a glimpse of her in the glow of the oil lamps, they saw an attractive, thirty-seven-year-old woman dressed in a very simple gown and white bonnet, a Bible in her hand. With her husband at her side, she walked to the front of the room, where a table and chairs had been set up, and asked the congregation to join her in singing a hymn. Afterwards, climbing up on her chair so that the entire crowd could see and hear her, she delivered a riveting defense of women's right to preach the gospel. In a clear, loud voice, she argued that God had not only inspired her to preach, but also countless numbers of other women throughout Christian history. Citing the examples of women such as Huldah and Anna, she argued that the Bible itself was full of examples of female prophets and evangelists.

Roberts followed her brief remarks on female preaching with a sermon on a biblical text. Unfortunately, there is no record of exactly what she said that evening, but typically, she warned her listeners to repent and seek salvation. In a sermon delivered a few months earlier, for example, she had threatened the "wicked" that they would be cast into a fiery furnace unless they sought the grace of Christ. "So shall it be at the end of the world," she proclaimed. "The angels shall come forth, and sever the wicked from among the just, And shall cast them into the furnace of fire: there shall be wailing and gnashing of teeth." Even though she was a Mother in Israel who spoke to converts as if they were her children, she believed that she, like Isaiah and Jeremiah, had been called to warn her nation of God's impending vengeance.[2]

By 1828, Roberts had been preaching for almost fourteen years, and she had become accustomed to causing controversy wherever she traveled. According to her son Philetus, who published a biography of her after her death, she often met opposition from "narrow-minded sectaries" who "resorted to vile

Abigail Roberts.
From Philetus
Roberts, *Memoir of
Mrs. Abigail Roberts;
An Account of Her
Birth, Early Education,
Call to the Ministry.*

and low means to prejudice the public mind against her." One woman "was heard to say to her husband: 'If you will waylay and gag her, I will tar and feather her!'" Perhaps Philetus exaggerated her persecution, but several clergymen also complained about her treatment at the hands of "the haughty and high-minded." Because she was willing to speak publicly in front of "promiscuous" audiences of men and women, she was accused of subverting true Christianity.[3]

Despite her trials, however, Roberts became a popular Christian Connection preacher in New York and New Jersey. Such large throngs of curious spectators gathered to hear her sermons that she often held her meetings outdoors in fields or forests. "The idea of hearing a woman preach called together great multitudes," one minister explained. Even after her novelty wore off, people crowded into churches to hear her thunder out her condemnation of sin. As one admiring convert in Milford remembered, her words were so powerful that "silence reigned, every eye being fixed upon the speaker, astonished at hearing such preaching from a woman." So many converts came to her meetings that she eventually organized four new Christian Connection churches, including one in Milford.[4]

Once Abigail Roberts and other female preachers overcame their early doubts about whether it was proper for them to speak in public, they matured into charismatic, forceful religious leaders. On one hand, they seemed radical because of their emotional style and their impassioned defense of female preaching, but on the other, they delivered most of their sermons on the classic evangelical themes of sin, repentance, and grace. Revolutionary in their defense of female preaching, yet solidly evangelical in their theology, they caused a sensation in early-nineteenth-century Protestant churches.

"Cry Out and Shout"

Although they have largely disappeared from history books, evangelical female preachers were among the first women to speak publicly in America. To use the language of the time, they preached to "promiscuous" audiences composed of both men and women. Scholars have usually identified Maria Stewart, a black reformer from Boston, as the first American woman to lecture to a public audience, but as we have seen, female exhorters were speaking publicly as early as the 1740s.[5] By 1831, when Stewart delivered her first speech on "Religion and the Pure Principles of Morality," women such as Jarena Lee, Abigail Roberts, Sarah Hedges, and Ann Rexford had already been preaching for more than a decade. Inspired by their religious faith, they courageously challenged the traditional taboos against women speaking in public.

Because there were so few women in the early nineteenth century who dared to speak publicly, female preachers were faced with a dilemma: they did not know how they were supposed to dress, move, or sound when they appeared in the pulpit. Searching for models of female religious leadership, they turned to a group of women whom they genuinely seem to have admired: the Quakers. A few evangelical women had been raised as Quakers before being born again, including Abigail Roberts, and others sometimes held joint meetings with Quaker Friends. Despite the theological differences separating them, evangelical and Quaker women were linked together by their commitment to female ministry. Visually, they could be difficult to tell apart because both wore simple gowns and bonnets. Both Sojourner Truth and Zilpha Elaw reportedly wore such simple, neat clothing that they were thought to look like Quakers.[6]

Yet evangelical female preachers embraced a much different model of ministry than Quaker women. Theologically, the Quakers valued the purity of silence over the "carnality" of speaking: it was only in moments of silence that God's still, small voice could be heard within. Although outward religious speech was important, it had to come from the movings of the spirit, not the pride of the flesh. Hence all Quakers, whether male or female, hesitated to speak during meetings unless they were certain they genuinely had been called, and even then, they sometimes broke silence with only a few sentences or a single word.[7] In contrast, evangelical female preachers valued speech more than silence, and they delivered lengthy sermons explaining the meaning of biblical texts. Instead of witnessing to the light within them, they spoke as teachers who had been divinely inspired to interpret the Bible.

Although evangelical female preachers took every opportunity to see and hear other women in the pulpit, they were most influenced by clergymen from their own sects. As they searched for models of good preaching, they were particularly impressed by male itinerants such as Lorenzo Dow and David Marks—men who knew how to fill a camp meeting tent with the sound of sinners weeping and shouting out their prayers for mercy. The "awe-inspiring" Lorenzo Dow worked his audiences into a frenzy by telling humorous stories and even smashing chairs on the preacher's platform. Sometimes he took a gentle tone, reassuring his listeners that Jesus would save them, but at other times he graphically described the agonies of hell. According to a fellow clergyman, he was "uncouth in his person and appearance" and "entirely destitute of all natural eloquence," but he "understood common life, and especially vulgar life—its tastes, prejudices, and weaknesses; and he possessed a cunning knack of adapting his discourses to such audiences." Dow became so popular in the early nineteenth century that his congregations reportedly swelled to as many as five thousand people.[8]

As Dow's example illustrates, the early Freewill Baptists, Christians, and Methodists embraced a model of ministry that could hardly be called genteel. When a Freewill Baptist minister catalogued seven "wrong habits" he commonly witnessed in the pulpit, he included "speaking through the nose," "hemming, as though the speaking pipes were obstructed when they are not," inhaling with "a dismal sound like that of a person when dying, or when in the act of snoring," and making "strange writhings and contortions of the face, such as scowling with the eyebrows, twisting the mouths into all sorts of shapes." Unlike middle-class ministers, who cultivated a polished style, these men brought their rustic manners into the pulpit with them. Influenced by the Jacksonian celebration of the common man, they insisted that anyone could preach, even "uncouth" farmers who punctuated their words with groans and hallelujahs.[9]

Female preachers were no more refined in their speech or gestures than the men who spoke through the nose. Aiming their sermons at ordinary workers and farmwives, they cultivated a colloquial, even crude style that shocked middle-class sensibilities. Like eighteenth-century revivalists such as Jonathan Edwards, they perceived conversion as essentially a change in the affections rather than the intellect, but they took this heart-centered preaching to an even greater extreme. Instead of standing stiffly in the pulpit, they electrified their audiences by weeping, groaning, and clapping their hands in ecstasy. "Cry out and shout," Jarena Lee exulted, "for great is the Holy One of Israel in the midst of thee."[10]

Female preachers were renowned for their emotional, spontaneous style. Unlike middle-class clergymen, who wrote out their sermons beforehand and then read them aloud, ministers for the Freewill Baptists, Methodists, and African Methodists strode into the pulpit carrying nothing but the Bible. Claiming to be instruments of God, they spoke without notes or even "pre-meditation." In reality, many of these men and women preached on favorite texts over and over again, mastering the gestures and vocal inflections that provoked the greatest emotional response, but they wanted their audiences to think they were watching an unrehearsed drama rather than a set script.[11] And indeed, because they did not have prepared texts in front of them, anything might happen. Abigail Roberts might decide to rant at an immoral sinner sitting in the front row of the church, or Rachel Thompson might stop preaching in order to pray for a woman who had swooned helplessly to the ground. In their opinion, preserving order was much less important than following the immediate inspiration of the Holy Spirit.

Female preachers also sang hymns during their meetings, and some were as famous for their singing as for their preaching. After the governor of Massachusetts heard Harriet Livermore sing during one of her appearances in front of Congress, he described her as "without exception, the sweetest singer I [have] ever heard." When Livermore sang plaintive songs about sinners praying for mercy, she moved her audiences to tears, and when she encouraged them to join her in such rousing folk tunes as "Shout Old Satan's Kingdom Down," she made them jump to their feet in excitement. Since no revival meeting was complete without a round of exuberant singing, Livermore used hymns as well as sermons to kindle the fires of revival. Converts stamped their feet, joined hands, and shouted out lyrics at the tops of their voices. In part, religious songs were entertainment, but they were also an alternative form of prayer that touched on the themes of hope and despair, hardship and comfort, divine anger and divine grace.[12]

Despite the boisterousness of many of their meetings, female preachers set an intimate tone by describing themselves as mothers and sisters who had been called to preach to the family of God. Even though they often looked out at a sea of strange faces, they addressed their listeners as brothers, sisters, and especially children. Like Ann Lee, who had once identified herself as the mother of the Shaker church, they emphasized their maternal concern for their spiritual family. For example, Susan Humes, who was only twenty-three years old and unmarried, spoke to her listeners as if they were her children. When a group of converts "wept profusely" because she had decided to leave their town, she "rent herself from their embraces" and asked plaintively, "O children! What mean ye to weep and break my heart?"[13] Despite her youth, she was a Mother in Israel, and she mixed her stern demands for repentance with maternal words of affection.

Female preachers heightened the emotional drama of their meetings by filling their sermons with stories and examples drawn from their own lives. Instead of speaking on general, abstract themes, they captivated their audiences by describing their own personal doubts and struggles. For example, Elleanor Knight often preached on biblical texts describing God's compassion toward the suffering and his protection of the weak—themes which reflected the anguish she had endured in her troubled marriage. In 1836, when she assured her listeners, "God is our refuge," she spoke from her own personal experiences as the wife of an alcoholic, violent husband. Virtually everyone in the church knew the story of her broken marriage, and when she promised that God would grant them peace and safety, she forced them to reflect on their faith in a particularly personal way. In a sense, she herself was the text that she wanted them to read.[14] As her eyes welled up with tears, she used the story of her own life to prove Christ's love for the weak and oppressed.

Besides Knight, many other Mothers in Israel also shed tears for their "children" as they stood in the pulpit. For example, a man who had attended one of Nancy Cram's sermons remembered seeing "tears . . . coursing down her face." As Nancy Towle confessed, she could not keep herself from weeping aloud whenever she thought of how many sinners would die without Christ.[15] Overcome by emotion, she often stopped preaching in order to bow her head and wipe her eyes.

Despite these women's motherly tears and their emotional labors for sinners, however, they were often accused of being "masculine" woman who had violated the boundaries of their female sphere. On one level, those boundaries were metaphorical, but in more concrete terms, they were also spatial. When female preachers dared to speak from the dignified height of the pulpit, a space usually reserved for men alone, they quite literally stepped out of their place. The pulpit was not simply an elevated space at the front of the church, but a symbol of men's exclusive authority to interpret Scripture.

When Nancy Towle asked a minister for permission to preach in his church in Ithaca, New York, he reluctantly consented, but only if she promised to speak from "one of the front slips" instead of the pulpit. "After considerable negotiation," Towle supposedly agreed, but then she changed her mind at the last minute. Ignoring the minister's angry glares, she stood up, "marched" past him, and in her words, "stepped without hesitation into the pulpit:—which very much diverted, the whole assembly!" After delivering a sermon that lasted an hour and a half, she finally returned to her lowly place in the pews. "We never fully recovered from it," he complained later. If she had spoken from the floor, she could have maintained a semblance of womanly modesty, but by jostling her way into the pulpit, she symbolically announced her intention to speak with the authority of a man.[16]

Female preachers seemed to behave like men in other ways as well. First, many were so angered by clerical opposition that they were quick to respond to criticisms with belligerence. For example, after an elder disagreed with one of Harriet Livermore's sermons, she "called him a hypocrite, and told him I believed the devil was in him." On another occasion, she deliberately provoked a confrontation with a Universalist clergyman. "I recollected my sex . . . and the natural consequences of boldness in the cause of Christ," she wrote later. But "I knew I must declare open war with error."[17] Needless to say, she gained a reputation as a manly, combative woman who relished doing battle with her opponents. Because of her belief that she spoke as God's prophetic instrument, she never hesitated to proclaim her understanding of the truth, no matter how angry it might make her listeners.

Modeling themselves on Deborah, the biblical heroine who had led an army to victory, female preachers imagined Mothers in Israel as warriors as well as nurturers. Abigail Roberts was reputed to be "amiable" and "benevolent," but she mixed her maternal warmth with a decidedly caustic sense of humor. After a minister questioned her right to preach, suggesting that it would be more "feminine" for her to "go the heathen" as a missionary, she replied angrily, "Judging from what I witness, I am right in the midst of them!" With biting sarcasm, Nancy Towle described a preacher who told her to "stay at home" as "large in conceit, but little of stature." Instead of humbly submitting to his criticisms, she looked forward to the day when God would "raise up a host of *female warriors*" to avenge women's persecution.[18]

Besides their combative style, many female preachers seemed "masculine" because they had loud voices that carried over long distances. Eliza Barnes had a "strong voice," Sarah Hedges had a "heavy, masculine" voice, and Sojourner Truth had such a "powerful and sonorous voice" that several men questioned whether she was really a woman. "Your voice is not the voice of a woman, it is the voice of a man," a group of white men taunted, "and we believe you are a man."[19] Instead of trying to sound soft and delicate, these women spoke as loudly as possible in order to be heard by their audiences. They preached to large crowds not only in churches, but outside in fields as well, and they cared more about being heard than about sounding "feminine."

Female preachers also seemed "manly" because of their intelligence. Even though they were not well schooled, they were reportedly skilled at explaining difficult scriptural texts. As one Methodist clergyman remembered, Salome Lincoln "possessed an uncommon mind for one of her sex," and according to a Christian Connection preacher, Rebecca Miller was a "close and critical reasoner" who "was not excelled by any of her sex." Although both of these men meant their words to be understood as praise, they also implicitly conveyed a less positive message: female preachers were not like the rest of their sex.[20] Because they could quote long biblical verses from memory and clarify obscure passages, they did not seem like true women.

Finally, even though none of these women imitated Jemima Wilkinson by dressing in men's clothing, they wore such plain attire that they looked far more austere than almost any other group of women in the early nineteenth century. Unlike fashionable middle-class matrons, who wore elaborate, flounced skirts with tight waists, female preachers followed the example of the Quakers by choosing the simplest and most unadorned dresses they could find. Harriet Livermore's clothing was so drab that people commonly remarked that she appeared "singular, odd." Because of constant headaches, she

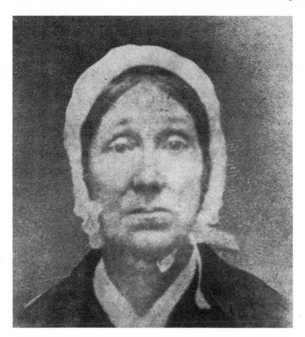

Sarah Righter Major. This picture is reprinted from Jesse O. Garst, *History of the Church of the Brethren of the Southern District of Ohio* (Dayton, Ohio: Otterbein Press, 1920).

also cropped her hair short, making herself appear even more peculiar. Other women hid their hair under simple caps or bonnets in order to obey Paul's injunction, "Every woman that prayeth or prophesieth with her head uncovered dishonoureth her head." Indeed, a rare picture of Sarah Major shows her wearing a white bonnet tied under her chin.[21] Major certainly does not appear "masculine" in this picture, but because she rejected curled hair, flounces, and jewelry as sinful displays of vanity, her critics did not think she looked particularly "feminine" either.

Female preachers may have dressed especially modestly because of accusations that they were lewd woman who scandalously allowed men to stare at them in public. On one hand, their critics belittled them as "masculine" women who were not the least bit attractive to men, but on the other, they charged them with inflaming male lust. Because "respectable" women did not put themselves on stage in the early nineteenth century, female preachers were often compared to actresses or prostitutes. In the angry words of Parsons Cooke, a Congregationalist minister, they were no better than "shameless" actresses who had invited men to gaze at their bodies in public. Despite their pretenses to piety, they had wantonly abandoned their "feminine delicacy," "trampling under foot the commands of God, and the decencies of [their] sex." Women who stood in front of male spectators and groaned or cried out were not Mothers in Israel, but jezebels leading men into sexual temptation.[22]

Even though female preachers denied being seductive jezebels, Cooke's overblown rhetoric held a small grain of truth: many nineteenth-century men seemed to have been attracted to the opportunity to stare at women in a public setting. Even though men rarely described the physical appearances of their male ministers, they emphasized women's physical attractiveness. For example, contemporaries described Ann Rexford as "young" and "rather beautiful to look upon" and Nancy Cram as "rather handsome." (In the early nineteenth century, the word "handsome" was used to describe both sexes.) John Greenleaf Whittier, the famous Quaker poet, remembered Harriet Livermore as both beautiful and "graceful": she was a "brilliant darkeyed woman" with a "Spanish looking face."[23] Despite her modest dresses and bonnets, she unwittingly prompted men to fantasize about her simply by speaking in public.

Disturbed by the sight of young, attractive women behaving like men, many critics spread rumors that female preachers were guilty of sexual promiscuity or even prostitution. Since at least one African Methodist woman, Julia Pell, had once been so poor that she had sold herself on the street, such rumors were not entirely unfounded. (After her conversion, Pell vowed that she would never cheapen herself that way again. In her words, "Hell clutched her, but hadn't energy enough to hold her.") However, there is no evidence that any other female preacher ever supported herself through prostitution, and the pervasive images of their "wantonness" reveal less about the realities of their lives than about their critics' overheated imaginations. Dorothy Ripley, a female preacher from England, was so renowned for her evangelism to slaves that she met with Thomas Jefferson, but because she was suspected of being a "lewd woman," one man tried "to take undue liberties" with her.[24] In nineteenth-century eyes, women who allowed men to stare at them in public were automatically suspected of sexual misconduct.

There were two vastly different images of female preachers in the early nineteenth century. According to their critics, female preachers were "masculine" and sexually aggressive, but according to their admirers, they were devout Sisters in Christ or Mothers in Israel who had been inspired by God. Standing at the crossroads of an older conception of female uncleanness and a new ideology of female passionlessness, these women were depicted as both seductive "Eves" and pious "Marys." During the tumultuous years of the early nineteenth century, when definitions of "masculinity" and "femininity" were being reshaped by religious, political, and economic change, female preachers epitomized the confusion over the proper boundaries of women's sphere. Because of their public visibility, they became the screen on which people projected their anxieties about the meaning of womanhood. While people who believed that women should play an active role in civil society often admired female preachers, those who held more restrictive ideas about motherhood and sisterhood found the same women alarmingly bold. As conservative clergymen complained, female preachers were fallen women who had sacrificed their virtue for the lure of public fame.

These contradictory images of female preachers were rooted in the politics of race and class as well as gender. Since several well-known female preachers, including Jarena Lee and Sojourner Truth, were African American, they caused particular controversy as they traveled across the country. If middle-class critics were disgusted by the behavior of white women such as Abigail Roberts, whose fiery calls for repentance made listeners cry out for mercy, then they were doubly shocked by the sight of poor, uneducated black women clapping their hands, yelling, and sobbing in the pulpit. According to popular stereotypes, black women were naturally licentious, and when preachers such as Jarena Lee "exposed" themselves by speaking publicly, they triggered fears of sexual as well as religious disorder.

Also, despite the fame of a few affluent women such as Harriet Livermore, most female preachers belonged to the lower or lower-middling classes, and wealthier, better-educated converts tended to look down on them as illiterate enthusiasts. Of course, the lines between social classes were not always rigid in the early nineteenth century, especially in newly settled regions of the country, and a few exceptional women managed to appeal to Christians across class boundaries. According to Zilpha Elaw, for example, she had been befriended by many of the "great folks" of Washington, D.C., including Lady Lee, who was related by marriage to Robert E. Lee, and Commodore John Rodgers, a former secretary of the navy. Nevertheless, the revivals of the Second Great Awakening deepened America's growing class divisions instead of diminishing them, and many middle-class evangelicals expressed disgust at the visionary, "ignorant" rabble who claimed to be born again. After leading a revival in Maine "among the lower class of people," Ephraim Stinchfield complained that it was "looked at something contemptibly by the higher Class & they began to speak in a reproachful Manner of the Subjects of this Work & consequently of the work." Shocked by the "singular exercises" of the converts, many of whom may have swooned, cried out, or seen visions, they refused to believe the revival was real.[25]

In the eyes of the "higher classes," the popularity of female preachers stood as a stark symbol of the excesses and enthusiasm of poor people's revivals. When "illiterate" women as well as men began competing with educated clergymen, many concluded that populist evangelicalism had gone much too far. After Catherine Williams attended a camp meeting in Smithfield, Rhode Island, in 1822, she complained that she had seen not only "uncouth" men preaching, but women as well. Strolling past one of the many tents dotting the campgrounds, she was appalled by the sight of two young women praying aloud in front of a crowd. After one woman "asked for the crumbs that fell from her master's table," the other slapped "her hands with great violence" and exclaimed, "Give us . . . not only crumbs, but loaves, Good God!" At the same meeting, she also heard "a very bold and uncouth looking young female, whose language was as coarse as her look and manner," haranguing people from the preacher's stand. When Williams and several other people began to laugh at her "singular expression," she responded defiantly: "She didn't care who laughed, she cared for nobody not a snap of her finger, (snapping her fingers in great style)."[26] All three of these women behaved as "boldly" as men, and their rustic appearance and bad grammar made it obvious that they would never conform to middle-class conceptions of true womanhood.

What most troubled Williams was that the rest of the crowd seemed to be thrilled by the sight of women in the pulpit. Even though these women appeared vulgar and unforgivably crude to her, other listeners responded "with inexpressible delight." Captivated by their earthy humor and colloquial style of speech, ordinary farmers, mill workers, and sailors fell down in "hysteric fits" or shouted "hallelujah."[27] As Williams lamented, the most popular preachers in a new democratic culture were not necessarily the most educated or polished, but the most zealous and "enthusiastic."

Combining maternal affection with angry condemnations of sin, and tearful appeals to sinners with acerbic humor, female preachers alternately fascinated and shocked their congregations. With their simple clothing, their folksy language, and their coarse gestures, they could hardly have been more different from influential, educated clergymen such as Lyman Beecher, but they were powerful preachers who held crowds of listeners spellbound. Despite their "crudity," they spoke with a democratic eloquence that appealed to thousands of evangelicals in search of a more populist and egalitarian style of worship.

Preaching Salvation

Although female preachers certainly attracted crowds of spectators because of their charismatic style, they also became popular because of their traditional message of repentance and conversion. Unfortunately, many historians have been so interested in examining women's social radicalism that they have ignored their theology, implicitly dismissing their beliefs as insignificant. The "real" importance of female preaching, they have suggested, lay in its symbolic challenge to class or gender hierarchies.[28] In the eyes of these women themselves, however, their *faith* was what defined them most clearly. If they ever had been asked to explain their appeal to lower-class evangelicals, they certainly would have discussed the substance as well as the style of their speech.

Reconstructing what male and female preachers said in the pulpit is a difficult task. Unlike Congregational or Presbyterian ministers, who wrote out their sermons or made detailed preaching notes, the Freewill Baptists, Christians, and Methodists spoke extemporaneously rather than scripting their sermons in advance. Claiming to be instruments of God, they denied choosing their sermon texts until they actually stood in front of their congregations.

Fortunately, however, even though female preachers left no written transcripts of their sermons, there are scattered references to the biblical texts on which they preached in denominational newspapers and religious memoirs. For example, in her *Narrative*, Elleanor Knight mentioned the texts of twenty-six sermons she delivered between 1835 and 1838, and a correspondent to the *Christian Herald* reported that Rachel Thompson preached on Hebrews 11:7, the account of Noah's decision to build the ark.[29] Although literally hundreds of descriptions of men's sermons have survived, the records for women are scarcer. Nevertheless, I have recovered the accounts of 190 sermons preached by twenty-one different women—a crucial index to the themes they commonly addressed in the pulpit.

Since female preachers from different sects competed with one another in an increasingly pluralistic religious marketplace, they often differed in the details of their theologies. Inspired by the belief that all Christians could read the Bible for themselves, they developed new and sometimes controversial doctrines. Like other Christian Connection preachers, for example, Abigail Roberts rejected the doctrine of the Trinity—the belief that God, the Holy Spirit, and Christ are three distinct persons linked together in a single mystical union—because she could not find a single reference to it in Scripture. Despite her belief that Christ was the Messiah who was "divine in nature," she insisted that there were "two persons . . . in heaven dwelling together," not one. If God "is the Father," one of her male colleagues explained, "he cannot be the son."[30]

Yet even though female preachers sometimes quarreled over particular doctrines, they hoped to break down sectarian barriers in order to re-create the primitive, universal church of the New Testament. Instead of focusing on their own unique convictions, they emphasized their unity with other lower-class Christians, especially those who set themselves apart from the values of American culture. Nancy Towle preached not only to Freewill Baptists, Christians, and Methodists, but also to Baptists, Lutherans, and Dutch Reformed. Describing herself as an independent "citizen of this world," she claimed to love true "Christians of every order" regardless of "party names, and human creeds." Even though she did not like the Methodists' hierarchical form of government or their practice of closed Communion, she greatly admired Elice Miller Smith, a popular Methodist preacher. She and Smith differed over several important issues, but they also shared a common desire to save souls.[31]

Just as they resembled one another, female preachers were also closely linked to the men in their sects. Shaped by the same evangelical culture, they shared a common belief in the importance of conversion, repentance, and good works, and they often examined the same biblical texts in their sermons. For example, both Salome Lincoln and Abel Thornton preached on a verse from John, "Behold the Lamb of God that taketh away the sin of the world." Assuring sinners of God's forgiveness, they repeatedly hammered away at the traditional themes of sin and repentance. Other male and female preachers celebrated God's goodness, urging their audiences to "Sing unto the Lord; for he hath done excellent things."[32]

Not surprisingly, both men and women preached the majority of their sermons on the single, all-important theme of conversion. Time and again, they admonished their listeners to repent *now* before it was too late. If sinners wanted to enter Christ's kingdom, if they wanted to save themselves from God's "unquenchable fire," then they had to be born again. "Repent ye, and believe the Gospel," Harriet Livermore proclaimed. "Except ye repent, ye shall all likewise perish." As large crowds of spectators thronged into buildings or stood outside in fields, she compared the joy of those who had been saved to the sufferings of the damned. Even though Christ had died for all, not everyone would taste the joys of heaven. The Lamb could wash them clean with his atoning blood, but only if they sincerely repented for their sins.[33]

Since both male and female preachers believed that conversion could not take place without an outward change in behavior as well as an inward change in the affections, they especially emphasized the importance of moral character. In a clear, methodical sermon, Salome Lincoln listed five connecting paths to holiness: "1. consideration, 2. prayer, 3. faith, 4. repentance, 5. living holy lives." Only those who obeyed God's commandments would taste the joys of salvation. If sinners wanted to be born again, they had to renounce all the temptations and wickedness of the secular world. "The tree must be good in order to bear good fruit," Mary Stevens Curry explained. "The Christian's fruit is the index of the heart."[34]

Perhaps some converts were heartened by this focus on good works, but others may have been distressed by the scope of their own moral accountability. Female preachers rejected the Calvinist doctrine that only the elect would be saved, but their celebration of free will did not necessarily mean that they preached a soft or indulgent creed. On one hand, they promised that individuals were free to choose their own spiritual destinies, a compelling message at a time when politicians were celebrating the powers of the common man. According to Elleanor Knight, for example, God would have mercy on all those who repented, even the "wicked and unrighteous."[35] On the other hand, however, Knight also warned people that it would be their own fault if they were shut out of heaven. Even though Jesus offered all sinners his free gift of salvation, the "pearl of great price," many were too proud to accept it, deliberately *choosing* to be damned.

The life of a Christian pilgrim, these women warned, was a strenuous one filled with anguish, temptation, and suffering. If sinners wanted to be born again, not only did they have to beg Jesus for mercy, but they had to do battle with Satan, the terrifying "deceiver" and "seducer" who wanted to drag them into everlasting torment in hell. At a time when Satan was losing his hold on the public imagination, lower-class evangelicals were too aware of the reality of human suffering to question their faith in his literal existence, and in contrast to many prosperous, middle-class Americans, they still imagined him in vivid, personal terms as "a cruel tempter, a malicious accuser, and a wretched liar." Struggling to understand how a loving God could permit the existence of slavery, black women in particular seemed to see Satan prowling in every dark corner. During a terrifying visionary experience, Jarena Lee saw him appear "in the form of a monstrous dog, and in a rage, as if in pursuit, his tongue protruding from his mouth to a great length, and his eyes looked like two balls of fire."[36] Like the vicious dogs who hunted fugitive slaves in the South, he lunged at her with open jaws.

No matter how horrifying this literal Satan was, however, female preachers claimed that he was only a pale reflection of the evil that lay deep within the human heart. Despite their belief in free will, these women never questioned the doctrine of original sin, and like Augustine, they believed that evil lay within as well as outside of the self. Remembering their anguish when they had quenched the spirit, they portrayed the devil as the absence of God, an estrangement and nothingness so terrifying that it defied human understanding. "A dreadful and chilling gloom instantaneously fluttered over, and covered my mind," Zilpha Elaw wrote in her memoir. "The Spirit of the Lord fled out of my sight, and left me in total darkness—such darkness as was truly felt; so awful a sensation I never felt before or since." Instead of imagining the devil in physical terms as a beast or a monster with horns and a tail, she shuddered at the darkness within her own soul. It was as if she herself had become a "demon."[37]

As Elaw reassured her congregations, however, she had been healed—just as they could be healed—by the soothing compassion of Jesus Christ. He was the "crucified redeemer," "the only foundation," and the "author of their salvation"; he was the "Divine Savior" who could cleanse their souls from the stain of sin. He was "gracious and merciful, slow to anger, long suffering, and abundant in loving kindness and tender mercies," and his love was "eternal," "impartial," and "unchangeable." Even if they could not always feel his presence, he bore their sorrows as his own. "Behold," quoted Jarena Lee from Isaiah, "the Lord's hand is not shortened, that it cannot save; neither his ear heavy, that it cannot hear."[38] Through his suffering and death on the cross, he had made it possible for even the most hardened sinners to be reborn as "new creatures."

Despite their fascination with Old Testament prophets, male and female preachers prided themselves on teaching "nothing but Christ." Of the twenty-six sermons that Elleanor Knight mentioned in her memoir, seventeen were drawn from the New Testament. Five others focused on the book of Isaiah, whose descriptions of a "man of sorrows, acquainted with grief" seemed to augur the crucifixion. Describing Jesus in strikingly intimate terms, evangelicals imagined him as a personal redeemer who had died to save each and every individual. When Christ "drank the bitter Cup" in Gethsemane, Harriet Livermore rejoiced, "my sins were in that Cup."[39] He had saved her *individually* as well as humanity more generally, selflessly atoning for her transgressions as he bled on the cross.

Both male and female preachers envisioned Christ as a friend or comforter, but in a subtle difference, women seem to have been particularly attracted to images of him as a loving bridegroom. Building on a long tradition of scriptural exegesis, they envisioned conversion as a mystical marriage, a spiritual union with God. For example, both Zilpha Elaw and Salome Lincoln preached on a verse from the parable of the foolish virgins: "And at midnight there was a cry made, Behold the Bridegroom cometh; go ye out to meet him!" Warning their listeners not to postpone conversion, they urged them to be ready to greet Christ as a spiritual husband. Although several male preachers, including Benjamin Abbott, used this language as well, women had been raised to imagine themselves as brides, and they welcomed the emphasis on Christ as a devoted suitor who would "ravish" them with his love.[40]

Much more than men, women filled their sermons with "feminine" imagery drawn from the Scriptures. Searching for biblical passages which included female as well as male symbols, they preached on texts personifying Israel, Jerusalem, or other nations as the "daughter of Zion" or the "daughter of my people." Just as Elleanor Knight spoke on Psalms 48:11, "Let Mount Zion rejoice, let the daughters of Judah be glad, because of thy judgements," Zilpha Elaw quoted from Zechariah 2:10, "Sing and rejoice, O daughter of Zion; for I come, and I will dwell in the midst of thee, saith the Lord."[41] Although these women probably selected these passages in order to illustrate God's mercy and goodness, they were particularly attracted to verses showing his love for his daughters as well as his sons. To compensate for the "masculine" language in the Bible, they included as much "feminine" imagery in their sermons as possible.

Because so many female preachers believed the end of the world was near, they were fascinated by the mysterious, evocative figure of the "woman clothed with the sun, and the moon under her feet, and upon her head a crown of twelve stars." Poring over the book of Revelation, they read that this woman would labor to give birth to the messiah, "a man child who was to rule all nations with a rod of iron," and then flee into the wilderness to escape the "great red dragon" who was pursuing her. Unlike men, who typically used this text to reflect on the "man child" who would redeem humanity, women such as Nancy Towle and Clarissa Danforth seem to have focused more on his mother. Echoing Jemima Wilkinson and Ann Lee before them, they envisioned the pivotal figure in the coming apocalypse as female, not male.[42] Because of their faith that God chose "the weak things of the world to confound the mighty," they believed women would help redeem the world.

Female preachers seem to have been especially intrigued by the biblical passages portraying God as nurturing or comforting, qualities that nineteenth-century Americans identified as "feminine." Strikingly, they spoke on the same biblical texts that recent feminists have used to challenge masculine definitions of God. In 1830, for example, Salome Lincoln preached on a passage from Deuteronomy that describes God as an eagle who "stirreth up her nest, fluttereth over her young, spreadeth abroad her wings, taketh them, beareth them on her wings." Emphasizing God's maternal qualities, she compared him to a protective mother hovering over his children with outstretched wings. Even though she always referred to God as "He," she clearly imagined him as possessing both "feminine" and "masculine" attributes.[43]

By imagining God as a mother as well as a father, female preachers reminded their listeners that women as well as men had been created in the divine image. Unlike eighteenth-century women such as Jemima Wilkinson, who had been taught to view themselves as lesser, inferior versions of men, nineteenth-century female preachers did not believe women had to transcend their gender in order to achieve spiritual perfection. There were two sexes, not one, and both mirrored aspects of God's nature. Women's "femininity" was not a defect that separated them from God, but a reflection of his motherly love and care. When Harriet Livermore imagined Judgment Day, she reassured the faithful that a loving Jesus would never hurt his children. Like a "mother" who would never "venture to frighten her baby," he would comfort the "wounded, sickly, diseased, poor, feeble, frightened sheep" in a "tender manner."[44]

Alongside this maternal language, however, female preachers also described God in more "masculine" terms as a punishing, angry father. (Just as nineteenth-century audiences saw compassion and mercy as female qualities, they regarded severity and discipline as male ones.) At the same time as Salome Lincoln portrayed God as an eagle "fluttering over her young," she also imagined him punishing the "wicked" with "snares, fire, and brimstone, and an horrible tempest." In 1832, after a cholera outbreak ravaged Canada, Nancy Towle delivered several sermons predicting America would be the next target of God's "wrath" and "vengeance." After traveling to Virginia, she boasted that she had delivered such a hellfire sermon that her audience had begun

Nancy Towle.
Courtesy of Virginia
Taylor.

shrieking with "loud cries." Her text was "Go ye after him through the city and smite; let not your eye spare neither have ye pity: Slay utterly, old and young, both maids and little children, and women."[45] Since Towle was imposing in appearance, with unusually large and piercing eyes, she must have cut a particularly forbidding figure as she described the agonies of the "slain." A righteous God, she warned, would punish Americans for straying from the purity of the primitive church.

Female preachers clearly did not embrace a "feminized" or sentimental faith, although some historians have argued that women "softened" evangelical theology in the nineteenth century. According to Ann Douglas, for example, mainline ministers increasingly depended on women's support after the disestablishment of the churches, and in order to make Calvinism more "feminine," they deliberately stripped it of its "toughness" and "sternness." Emphasizing devotion over doctrine, they sacrificed intellectual rigor for a cheap sentimentalism that poisoned American culture. Since nineteenth-century women were "oppressed" and "damaged," they created a religion that celebrated weakness and passivity instead of strength. Remaking God in their own image, they portrayed him as kind, loving, motherly, and, in Douglas's view, disturbingly effete.[46]

Whether or not this picture of nineteenth-century religion is accurate—and many critics have protested that it is not—it ignores women's continuing identification with the demanding, all-powerful God of the Old Testament. Besides assuming that the loss of Calvinism represented a decline (a claim that liberal theologians would dispute), Douglas also assumes that there was something inherently weak about "femininity." According to female preachers, however, they worshiped a "Mother" who was capable of infinite wrath as well as infinite tenderness. Despite their rejection of Calvinism, they clung to an older, traditional faith in an angry God who would wreak vengeance on those who persecuted the poor and the weak. Just as the God of the Old Testament had killed the enemies of his chosen people, the Israelites, he would avenge the wrongs committed against Christians. "Woe unto the wicked!" Abigail Roberts preached. "It shall be ill with him; for the reward of his hands shall be given him."[47] A just God would never allow evil to go unpunished.

Given these beliefs, female preachers had little in common with antebellum Christian pacifists who longed to put an end to the "bloodstained pages of history." Inspired by the triumph of republicanism, many radical Christian liberals, as Daniel Buchanan has called them, dreamed of creating a world that was completely free of coercion and violence. Whether temperance reformers, sentimental novelists, or abolitionists, they insisted that human beings were essentially good, not flawed by original sin, and they denied that warfare and brutality were intrinsic to the social order. With unbounded hope in the future, they predicted that ordinary people would bring about the millennium without divine intervention. There would be no apocalypse before Christ's return to earth, no terrifying cataclysm, because a new era of peace and justice had already begun.[48]

In contrast, many lower-class evangelicals were too convinced of the reality of original sin to share this optimistic faith in human progress. Instead of decrying violence, they believed that God sometimes used violent means to bring about social change. Because human beings were inherently (and stubbornly) sinful, God sometimes had to use force to compel them into obedience. When Jarena Lee reflected on the story of Nat Turner, the visionary slave who had led a bloody insurrection in Southampton, Virginia, she did not condemn him for murdering several white slave owners but wondered whether he had been genuinely inspired by God. "In 1831, a young man who professed to be righteous, says he saw in the sky men, marching like armies, whether it was with the naked eye, or a Vision by the eye of Faith, I cannot tell," she recorded. "But the wickedness of the people certainly calls for the lowering Judgments of God to be let loose upon the Nation and Slavery." Perhaps, Lee speculated, Turner had been an instrument of God. Insisting that the apocalypse was imminent, she threatened sinners—especially slaveholders—that God would soon burn them up like "chaff" in an "unquenchable fire."[49]

This violent God held little appeal for liberal, reform-minded Christians, but he clearly served the psychological needs of female preachers. Longing for the reassurance that God would punish their adversaries, they searched for evidence of his anger as well as his compassion. Even though they knew Jesus had commanded them to turn the other cheek, they also refused to believe he would ignore their sufferings. According to Jarena Lee, for example, it was no accident that one of her most bitter "enemies," a white indentured servant who had tried to have her imprisoned, was sold to another owner and separated from his family. "It is thus the Lord fights for Israel," she triumphed. Similarly, when a man disrupted one of Zilpha Elaw's sermons by groaning loudly and tittering, she stopped speaking in order to remind him of the frightening consequences of religious disobedience. Glaring into his eyes, she predicted that "he might be suddenly cut off from the land of the living, and required to give a woeful account of himself at the bar of God." When he died unexpectedly a few days later, she celebrated God's swift justice.[50] Whatever persecutions she might endure, a just God would always be on her side.

As these examples illustrate, female preachers were so certain of their own virtue that they often verged on self-righteousness. Anyone who hated them, they quoted from Luke, was guilty of despising the God who had sent them. Despite their insistence on their "feminine" humility, they swore that a vengeful God would punish anyone who dared to oppose them. As a result, they hardly appeared charitable or Christian in the eyes of their critics. Instead of turning the other cheek, they took distinct pleasure in imagining the horrible fate awaiting their enemies. Indeed, some of their sermons were almost voyeuristic in their graphic depictions of damnation. "FELLOW SINNER, of whatever rank or condition, I echo to you in friendship the voice of conscience,

'You are travelling down to HELL!' " Nancy Towle wrote in her memoir. "With every breath, with every beating pulse;—you are liable to plunge the *abyss*, of *everlasting woe!*" Even though Towle spoke to sinners in "friendship," her "love for precious souls" was sometimes tinged with aggression. In an ominous passage in her memoir, for example, she reported the sudden death of a man who had belittled her.[51]

Like the men in their sects, female preachers worshiped a God who was not only loving and compassionate, but also jealous and vindictive. God was both mother and father, comforter and warrior. Perhaps other nineteenth-century Christians, especially those of a more liberal bent, found these images contradictory, but female preachers saw God's mercy and his anger as simply two different manifestations of his love for his children. On one hand, he tenderly comforted his faithful during times of sorrow and distress, strengthening them with his grace. God would "swallow up death in victory," Rebecca Miller reassured her listeners, and "wipe away tears from all faces." Even when they walked through "the dark valley of the shadow of death," he would shelter them from harm.[52] On the other hand, however, God would also afflict anyone who tried to hurt his chosen people. Whenever his children were persecuted because of their faith, he responded with swift and dreadful justice. Moved by their sufferings, he proved himself capable of both boundless love and boundless wrath.

Whatever the flaws of this theology—its vindictiveness, its glorification of violence, its pessimism—female preachers were deeply strengthened by their belief that a just God would protect them from their enemies. As strangers and pilgrims, they knew what it meant to "suffer affliction with the people of God," but they clung to their faith that they would someday receive the promises. Even though their nation was filled with sin, they were sure that Christ would soon return to earth, and after destroying the wicked, he would comfort the oppressed.

Defending Women's Right to Preach

Like men, female preachers focused most of their sermons on the conventional themes of conversion and repentance, but they were also separated from their male colleagues by one crucial distinction. Besides combing the Bible in search of "feminine" as well as "masculine" imagery, they used the pulpit as a forum for defending female preaching. In a unique departure from tradition, they combined standard evangelical teachings with an emphasis on female spiritual equality, a potentially volatile mixture in a culture that excluded women from positions of religious leadership.

Like Abigail Roberts, who began her sermon in Milford by justifying her right to preach, many other women also explicitly defended female preaching in their sermons. When Sarah Hedges spoke at the Christian Connection General Conference in 1820, for example, she tried to prove from the Bible that "it is *right for women to preach*." Perhaps she, like other women, claimed to have been directly inspired by dreams, voices, or visions, but because of her faith in the literal truth of the Bible, she also searched for scriptural evidence of "female testimony." Weaving together a multitude of examples, she fascinated her listeners by listing all the biblical women who had been called to witness to their faith.[53]

Typically, women began their defenses of female preaching by examining the stories of Old Testament heroines such as Deborah, Miriam, Huldah, and Esther. Because all of these "public" women had been renowned for their strength and wisdom, they illustrated that God could call women as well as men to be judges, military leaders, and prophets. According to Rebecca Miller, for example, Deborah "was divinely authorized to declare the word of the Lord." Not surprisingly, few female preachers dared to mention Noadiah, a false prophet, but Nancy Towle cleverly managed to transform even her into an example of female virtue. In the days of Elijah, she reminded her audience, there had been "four hundred and fifty [men] that were false, to the little number 'one.' "[54]

Certain that they were standing on the verge of the millennium, female preachers were especially intrigued by Joel's promise that daughters as well as sons would prophesy in the latter days. Some claimed that this prophecy had been fulfilled on the day of Pentecost, when women as well as men had spoken in tongues under the influence of the Holy Spirit. But others believed that Joel's words held special meaning for their own time and place. Anticipating the later arguments of the Millerites, the millenarian sect that emerged in the early 1840s, they argued that female preaching was a symbol of the end times, a concrete sign of a new dispensation of history.[55] As the world teetered on the edge of apocalypse, Joel's prophetic daughters had been called to warn a sinful nation to repent.

Turning from the Old Testament to the New Testament, female preachers were forced to grapple with their least favorite passage from the Bible, a verse testimony of Sir Walter Scott: 'When he returned a trembling invalid from Italy, to die in his own native land, the sight of his sweet home so invigorated his spirits that some hope was cherished that he might recover. But he soon relapsed. He found that he must die. Addressing his son-in-law, he said, 'Bring me a book.' 'What book?' said Lockhart. 'Can you ask?' said the expiring genius, whose fascinating novels have charmed the world, but have no balm for death, 'Can you ask *what* book? There is but *one*.' No, there is but one that tells us how to live and how to die. MARY.

For the Christian Palladium.
Duty of Females.
BY REBECCA L. MILLER.

BR. MARSH—We find no difficulty in proving to most objectors to female public improvement, that it was right during the history of the Bible for females to prophecy, conduct, and engage in the public worship of God. But the grand difficulty is to get them to see that they were not disfranchised at the close of that dispensation, which virtually ceased at the death of Christ. For when we open the sacred pages of the Old Testament and prove that Miriam, and other women, publicly celebrated the passage of the Red sea—declaring the brilliant, glories, and praises of God—That Deborah was divinely authorized to declare the word of the Lord, and give orders for the defence and safety of the oppressed Israelites, (to say nothing of their coming to her for judgment,) and went up with them to the help of the Lord against the mighty, and mightily overthrew their enemies on every side.

That Huldah, being an approved prophetess of the Lord, was consulted by Josiah, the penitent King of Judah, to whom she sent so thrilling a message from the Lord that it caused all Judah and Jerusalem to tremble and turn to the Lord. And when we descend to the very dawn of the Christian dispensation, and exhibit the character and daily occupation of good old Anna, the prophetess, as publicly worshipping God in the temple; and in the same manner preaching Jesus to all that looked for redemption in Jerusalem, prophesying of his future glory, and vast achievements in human redemption ; and when we further trace those predictions to their fulfilment, and scan the effects produced by them, it forms a powerful argument in favor of the divine sanction in their administering the word of God.— The conviction is too powerful to be resist-

ed. And when they are assured that females have been authors of considerable of the scriptures, and that to reject them is to reject or oppose God, and deny the Bible, objections vanish like dew before the morning sun.

But, says the objector, there is a total prohibition of their public officiation in the new dispensation, made by the apostle Paul. Well, we will examine the apostle's testimony, so frequently quoted on the subject. And as soft words and hard arguments, well backed with scripture, are far the most potent in establishing truth, we shall forbear animadverting on those who err, not knowing the scriptures, nor yet consider the prerogative and power of God, and resort to the law and the testimony.

There are but two passages in the New Testament that objectors can select to found their quibbles upon. The first is in 1st Cor. xiv. 34, 35; 'Let your women keep silence in the churches, for it is not permitted unto them to speak ; but to be under obedience as also saith the law. And if they will learn any thing let them ask their husbands at home, for it is a shame for women (not a woman) to speak in the church.' The second is 1st Tim. ii. 11, 12 ; 'Let the women learn in silence with all subjection. But I suffer not a woman to teach nor usurp authority over the man, but to be in silence.' This we readily admit to be good and wholesome doctrine ; but where does the apostle consider it a shame for a woman to speak, teach, and usurp authority? Answer —In the church. Now what is a church? The practice of terming chapels churches is antiscriptural, and doubtless is one of the relicks of mystery Babylon. A poor church of Christ indeed, composed frequently of wood, one of the destructible materials of the false builder! A church is a compact or congregation of spiritual believers in Christ. Now the government of this body, under the great Head, devolves on men, and not on women. The voice of the church is that of the males, and not of the females. It is evident that Paul considered that women had no more to do with the arrangement of church business than they have in general with civil legislation ; besides there were some things in the Corinthian church that were of too indelicate a nature for women to discuss publicly. In the adjustment of such cases particularly Paul considered it a shame for women to take an active part; knowing that such cases were and would be of frequent occurrence, and that there must be a general rule adopted, from Paul's letter to the Corinthians: "Let your women keep silence in the churches." Because they believed that every word in the Bible had been literally dictated by God, they could not simply ignore these words, but they also refused to read them as transparent truth. Instead, they carefully weighed this text against other contradictory verses in the Bible. Pointing out the inconsistencies in Paul's epistles, Rebecca Miller noted that he seemed to be "at war with his own writings." In one letter, he forbade women to preach, but in another, he instructed them to cover their heads when they were "praying or prophesying" in public.[56]

Situating Paul within his own time and place, female preachers suggested he had objected to women "ruling," not preaching. In the early church, as they explained to their audiences, both male and female Christians had often interrupted their preachers in order to ask questions, but Paul had objected to this custom. He had been especially troubled by the disorderly women at Corinth, who badgered their minister with questions their husbands could have answered at home. As a result, he sternly ordered the women in Corinth—and only in Corinth—to keep silence, but he had never meant to prohibit *all* women from praying aloud, singing, witnessing, exhorting, and preaching. As long as women did not try to rob men of their rightful authority in the church, they could help them save souls.[57]

Quoting Paul's words to the Philippians, "Help those women which laboured with me in the gospel," many female preachers argued that Paul himself had sanctioned female evangelism. Combing the New Testament for references to women, they found that Phebe, Priscilla, the four daughters of Philip, Tryphena and Tryphosa, the sisters of Nereus, and the mother of Rufus had all "prophesied" or served as "helpers in Christ Jesus."[58] Fascinated by Phebe's life, Jarena Lee preached an entire sermon about her in 1834. According to Rebecca Miller, who published an article on the religious "duty of females," Phebe had the distinction of being the first recorded female preacher. Even though Paul had described her as a "servant of the church," she had not been simply a maid or housekeeper, but a female laborer. Quoting other passages in the Bible, she illustrated that the word "servant" was typically used in the Bible as a synonym for minister.[59]

Because their faith was so Christocentric, these women always capped their

Opposite: Rebecca Miller's article on the "Duty of Females" (1841). Courtesy of the American Antiquarian Society.

defenses of female preaching with their most important argument of all: Jesus had permitted "certain women" (such as Joanna, Susanna, and Mary the mother of James and Joseph) to travel with him "from city to city, and from village to village, with his twelve disciples." Not only had he chosen the woman of Samaria to be the first person to learn his true identity as the Messiah, but he had inspired her to testify he was the Christ. Most important, he had singled out Mary Magdalene, an obscure and uneducated woman, to be the first to see his empty tomb and proclaim his resurrection. (According to the Gospels of both Mark and John, the risen Christ appeared to Mary Magdalene before anyone else and told her to bring the good news to his disciples.) Inspired by this story, Jarena Lee exulted that Mary had "*first* preach[ed] the risen Savior." In a more sweeping claim, Nancy Towle argued that Christ had specially commissioned Mary to deliver "the most *important, Gospel message,* ever borne by mortals," a distinction that even "the Apostles themselves" could not boast.[60]

By insisting that the Bible itself sanctioned female preaching, these women tried to prove that their lives were not merely exceptions to the Pauline injunction, but evidence of a larger pattern in Christian history. Even though it would have been easier for them to insist that they were exceptional women who had been directly inspired by God, they wanted to make it clear that *all* women had the right to witness to their faith. Besides claiming that she had communicated with God through dreams and visions, Jarena Lee also took pains to mention the biblical women who had "preached Christ" in the early church. "Did not Mary, a woman, preach the gospel?" she asked in her memoir. "For she preached the resurrection of the crucified Son of God." Rebecca Miller stated her argument bluntly: "Female preaching, is nothing new under the sun."[61]

Excited by their revolutionary reading of Scripture, female preachers often spoke and wrote as if they were the first biblical feminists since Anna, Mary, and Phebe to defend women's religious equality to men. What they did not realize, however, was that they were part of a long tradition of feminist biblical criticism that stretched deep into Christian history. They did not know that many women in medieval and Renaissance Europe, including Hildegard of Bingen and Christine de Pizan, had once made almost the same arguments. Nor did they know the stories of the eighteenth-century New Light and Separate women who had treasured Paul's words to the Galatians, "There is neither Jew nor Greek, . . . bond nor free, . . . male nor female." Denied knowledge of women's collective history, they were forced to repeat the arguments of earlier generations of women instead of building on the past.[62]

Yet even though female preachers would have been immeasurably strengthened by knowing the stories of the women who had preceded them, they were intoxicated by their "discovery" of feminist biblical criticism. By focusing on biblical heroines and defending female preaching, they made their most significant theological contributions to nineteenth-century evangelicalism. Anticipating the arguments of contemporary feminist theologians, they transformed the Bible into a powerful defense of women's essential dignity and humanity.

The Limitations of Biblical Feminism

Nevertheless, female preachers were biblical rather than secular feminists, and despite their defense of women's spiritual equality, they rarely protested against women's political and economic subordination to men. They demanded women's right to preach, but not to vote—to testify, but not to control their own earnings. Deeply influenced by their literal reading of Scripture, few could imagine a world where Sisters in Christ and Mothers in Israel would have the same privileges and opportunities as ordained clergymen.

In some ways, of course, female preachers appeared dangerously radical. At a time when popular authors proclaimed that home was women's "appropriate sphere of action," they were virtually homeless because of their incessant travels. According to available evidence, the majority of women were single when they began preaching, and they did not have private homes of their own. Even though they described themselves as ladies, they implicitly challenged the ideology of separate spheres by roaming across the country as itinerants. Because Harriet Livermore spent so much time away from her family, she was often greeted with "a torrent of questions," such as "are your parents living? where do they live? how many brothers and sisters have you? do your friends like your traveling to preach? don't they oppose you? does your father assist you[?]"[63] Like many other female preachers, she appeared unnatural because she did not define herself in relationship to men. Even though she described herself in "feminine" imagery as a bride of Christ, a Mother in Israel, or a prophetic daughter, she caused controversy because she was not tied to a father-headed household.

In a move that was even more radical, at least five women openly defied their husbands or fathers by deciding to preach. Judith Mathers, Susan Humes, and Sally Parsons were all disinherited by their fathers after beginning their careers, but they chose to cut themselves off from their families rather than "quench the spirit." Zilpha Elaw blatantly ignored the orders of her husband, who commanded her to "decline the work altogether, and proceed no further." And Rebecca Jackson insisted that her relationships with her brother and husband were far less important than her duty to God. "I had started to go to the promised land and I wanted husband, brother, and all the world to go with me," she explained, "but my mind was made up to stop for none."[64] In some ways, these women were simply echoing what they heard from the pulpit every Sunday: converts should obey Christ before man. Yet even though all evangelical ministers, no matter how socially conservative, claimed that women had the right to resist men who tried to prevent them from going to church, few were sympathetic to female preachers. Virtuous women would never abandon their families in order to wander across the country alone.

Conservative critics were especially shocked by the small number of female preachers who chose to leave home rather than care for their young children. Although a few women took their sons and daughters with them on preaching tours, they usually left them with friends or relatives or hired them out as apprentices if they were planning to be away for more than a few days or weeks. After Jarena Lee, a widow, left her son when he was "very sickly," she denied suffering even a moment of guilt. "Not a thought of my little son came into my mind," she assured her readers. "It was hid from me, lest I should have been diverted from the work I had to do, to look after my son." As a Mother in Israel, Lee believed she had been called to nurture the entire family of God, not just her own family, but in the eyes of her critics, she had virtually abandoned her child. In every possible way, she failed to meet the middle-class ideal of domesticity. Not only did she lack a stable home, but she did not even choose the joys of motherhood over preaching the gospel.[65]

Yet even though female preachers rejected the confining ideology of separate spheres, they also held surprisingly traditional attitudes toward women and the family. Because they believed the Bible was the literal word of God, they rarely questioned the core assumptions of nineteenth-century evangelical culture, especially the belief that the man was the head of the woman. Even though they saw themselves as God's instruments, they never forgot their status as *women* who had been created in subjection to men. According to their reading of Scripture, they could help save men from sin, but not rule over them. They could labor in the informal public of the church, but not the formal public of the state.

Instead of criticizing women's subordination, female preachers assumed that the father-headed family had been divinely ordained. Unlike Lee, who was a widow, most were single when they began their careers, and they justified their right to preach on the grounds that they did not have husbands or children who depended on their care. According to most Freewill Baptists, Christians, African Methodists, and Methodists, the women who were the best suited for the rigors of itinerant life were those who were young and single. Without the responsibilities of caring for a family, they could travel wherever the Holy Spirit led them. According to Harriet Livermore, for example, she could preach because she was single, but married women were "not permitted to teach in public assemblies" because of their duties to their husbands.[66]

Although several female preachers eventually decided to marry—at least seventeen in all—few continued traveling unless their husbands agreed to accompany them. When Abigail Roberts held religious meetings, she almost always walked up the aisle and into the pulpit with her husband, Nathan, by her side. Perhaps she hoped he would protect her from unruly crowds, but by entering the church with him, she also hoped to silence her critics. She wanted people to know she had not usurped his authority by leaving home to preach.[67]

Since at least ten female preachers married clergymen, they defended their right to continue laboring on the grounds that they were simply helping their husbands. Instead of holding their own meetings, women such as Rebecca Chaney Miller, Sarah Righter Major, Mary Stevens Curry, and Almira Prescott Bullock spoke at the end of their husbands' sermons or substituted for them in the pulpit. All of these women had once been acclaimed preachers in their own right, but after their marriages, they deferred to their husbands as much as possible. Although Sarah Righter Major could reportedly "outpreach" most of the men in her sect, she always waited for her husband to speak first. Similarly, when the Methodist Protestant church offered Hannah Reeves her own circuit, she refused, choosing to travel with her husband, William, instead. As his helpmate, she chose to stay in her place by his side.[68]

Whether single or married, female preachers repeatedly denied having any desire to subvert male authority in either the home or the church. Even though they defended their right to speak publicly, they never claimed to be the political or legal equals of men. "I shall ever acknowledge the head of the woman to be the man," Sarah Righter Major proclaimed. Even Zilpha Elaw, who disobeyed her husband's orders to stop preaching, insisted that women had been created subordinate "by nature." Her own life had been exceptional because of her unfortunate marriage to an "unbeliever," but as a general rule, women had a religious duty to submit to "the paternal yoke or the government of a husband." "Woman is dependent on and subject to man," she wrote sternly. "Man is not created for the woman, but the woman for the man." "These principles lie at the foundation of the family and social systems," she warned, "and their violation is a very immoral and guilty act."[69] Like other female preachers, Elaw never suggested that women should be servile or obsequious, but because of her belief that men had been first in creation, she cautioned her female followers not to venture too far out of their station.

Perhaps these women exaggerated their conservatism in order to reassure their critics that they were not jezebels, but it would be a mistake to dismiss their words as mere rhetoric. As much as female preachers expanded definitions of womanhood, they also refused to challenge the fundamental sexual inequalities within their churches. Indeed, there is no evidence that any woman except for Laura Clemens, an evangelist for the United Brethren, ever asked to be ordained or set apart by the laying on of hands. (Not surprisingly, her request was refused by a ministerial conference in 1843.) Instead of demanding the same rights and privileges as male ministers, most women accepted their position as the subordinate sex. Despite her insistence that women were spiritually equal to men, Rebecca Miller admitted there was no "scriptural precedent" for them to perform baptisms. Even Deborah Peirce, who published an entire book defending women's right to spread "the good news of salvation," agreed that only men had the right to "rule and go forward."[70]

Only a small group of female preachers protested against women's political and economic subordination to men. Defending the social as well as spiritual equality of the sexes, Ellen Stewart, Nancy Towle, Laura Haviland, and Sojourner Truth all used their sermons to argue on behalf of women's rights. Neither Towle nor Stewart ever formally joined women's rights organizations, but both of them self-consciously echoed feminist language in their memoirs. Subtitling her book *Arguments in Favor of Women's Rights*, Ellen Stewart defended her right not only to preach, but to control her own earnings and vote in government elections.[71]

Nancy Towle, the daughter of a soldier who had fought in the Revolutionary War, was one of the most radical female preachers. Although Towle was not wealthy, she was relatively well educated, and besides imbibing her father's revolutionary zeal, she was influenced by such radical intellectuals as Mary Wollstonecraft. Allying herself with one of the most despised feminists of her time, a woman whom many condemned as "a vulgar, impudent hussey," she explicitly echoed Wollstonecraft's impassioned plea for female equality. After lamenting the exclusion of "female gifts" from the church, she wrote: "I wish to deliver up my life as a sacrifice . . . towards remedying those evils; and seal my testimony, as with my blood, in vindication of the rights of woman!"[72] First and foremost, Towle believed she had been called to save sinners, but in her view, the most flagrant sinners were men who taught women to see themselves as "subordinate beings." Swearing that she was willing to be martyred for the cause, she promised to "sacrifice" her life to win the crusade for female equality.

Although Towle never became a well-known feminist, both Sojourner Truth and Laura Haviland gained wide recognition as leaders of the women's rights movement. Haviland was a white Wesleyan Methodist who mixed her commitment to women's rights with a deep hatred of slavery. Besides preaching from the pulpit, she also founded an institute in Michigan to educate free blacks. When she published her memoir, a moving account of her work on the Underground Railroad, she included a picture of herself with the caption "Thine for the oppressed." Sojourner Truth, one of Haviland's friends in the antislavery movement, is much better remembered today as a pioneering black feminist than as an evangelical preacher. Speaking at conventions across the country, she captivated audiences with her "powerful form, her whole-souled, earnest gestures," and her "strong and truthful tones." A feminist who was also an abolitionist, she intuitively recognized the affinities between the subordination of women and the enslavement of Africans. For her, as Nell Painter has commented, these two issues were inextricably linked "in her one body."[73]

In contrast to Truth, however, most black female preachers were far more willing to challenge the inequalities between the races than the inequalities between the sexes. Even though Jarena Lee never joined the women's rights movement, she attended at least one meeting of the American Anti-Slavery Society, and she clearly identified herself as an abolitionist. "As we are all children of one parent, no one is justified in holding slaves," she protested. When she traveled to Maryland, a slave state, in 1836, she decided to preach on a famous passage from Isaiah: "The Spirit of the Lord God is upon me; because the Lord hath anointed me to preach good tidings unto the meek; he

Laura Smith Haviland. Frontispiece to her memoir, *A Woman's Life-Work: Labors and Experiences of Laura S. Haviland* (1889).

hath sent me to bind up the brokenhearted, to proclaim liberty to the captives, and the opening of the prison to them that are bound." Looking out at the crowds of slaves who had trudged long distances to hear her preach, she spoke on a potentially revolutionary theme: the liberty that rightfully belonged to black Christians.[74]

Even in their protests against slavery, however, female preachers combined a deep strain of conservatism with their seeming radicalism. At the same time as Zilpha Elaw denounced slavery as one of the deepest sins known to humankind, she also believed that true liberty could be found only in God. After meeting a slave preacher in Maryland who "seemed to manifest an undue anxiety for his freedom," she criticized him for his "impatience." "Certainly," she explained, "freedom is preferable to bondage," but true Christians knew that only *spiritual* freedom, not physical freedom, was eternal. Promising slaves everlasting bliss in heaven, she urged them to be "unconcerned" about their captivity on earth.[75] Even though she supported the American Anti-Slavery Society, she put her greatest faith in salvation through Jesus, not political action. With little faith in human progress, she feared that Americans were too innately sinful to ever willingly abolish slavery on their own. The Day of Jubilee would not come until the return of Christ.

Whether protesting against the wrongs of womanhood or the wrongs of slavery, most female preachers insisted that true change could come only from God. Even though they appeared radical to their critics, very few ever demanded sweeping political, legal, or economic reform. They longed for a world where people would recognize that slaves and women had been created in God's image, but they feared that sin would never be conquered without God's direct, violent intervention. From their reading of the book of Revelation, they were convinced that women would not be "clothed with the Sun" and "crowned with Apostolick glory" until Christ's second coming. According to their exegesis, God had ordained women's subordination because of Eve's disobedience, but he had also promised to elevate them to their rightful place at the end of human history.[76] Until then, women would have to humbly submit to men as the weaker sex.

A Blessed Sight

If nineteenth-century female preachers had ever demanded the authority of ordination or joined the women's rights movement, they certainly would have had a far more revolutionary effect on their churches. Clearly, however, they would never have gained such a wide following in nineteenth-century America if they had been more radical. Because of their essential conservatism, they gained the support of men and women alike, preaching to thousands of evangelicals across the country.

Despite the persistent opposition of middle-class critics, female preachers became immensely popular among lower-class Methodists, African Methodists, Freewill Baptists, and Christians in the early decades of the nineteenth century. According to almost every contemporary estimate, their meetings were packed with hundreds or even thousands of people. Perhaps these numbers were exaggerated, but even so, women seem to have spoken to unusually large audiences for the time. Nancy Towle claimed that she spoke to "more than three thousand" in Philadelphia in 1830; Ann Rexford and Sarah Hedges reportedly attracted audiences of between one and two thousand; and consistently "large congregations" assembled to hear Sally Thompson and Clarissa

Danforth. "Miss Parker," a nondenominational preacher who was loosely affiliated with the Methodists, reportedly spoke to crowds of a thousand people in Grasmere, New Hampshire, in 1841.[77]

Because it was so uncommon to see women addressing mixed audiences, female preachers attracted huge crowds of boisterous spectators. Although many of their listeners were motivated by genuine religious conviction, others simply wanted to see the spectacle of a woman speaking in public. In 1839, when Jarena Lee preached in Dayton, Ohio, her appearance "made quite an excitement" because "it was altogether a strange thing to hear a woman preach there." Exasperated, Lee worried that her listeners had ignored the content of her sermon. "The people were all eyes and prayed none," she complained. Eventually, however, she became accustomed to people staring at her. Because she was black, female, and a preacher, she created a commotion wherever she traveled.[78]

It is difficult to judge how many people genuinely respected female preachers, but their popularity seems to have been based on more than the novelty of seeing women in the pulpit. To be sure, their meetings were often crowded with curious bystanders, but because they tended to return to the same towns again and again, they eventually faded into the background of everyday life. Even though Salome Lincoln preached on Martha's Vineyard for seven months in 1831 and several more months during the spring of 1832, she continued to attract large audiences who praised her for both her charismatic style and her inspiring sermons on the new birth.

Female preachers seem to have made a particularly powerful impression on the women in their audiences. Many ordinary farmwives, mill workers, and domestic servants were amazed and gratified by the sight of women in the pulpit. Even if they had seen gifted women praying aloud in private devotional meetings, they had never imagined them speaking publicly in front of "promiscuous" audiences. For many, the experience marked a pivotal moment in their lives; for the first time, they began to question why they were required to keep silence in the churches. After Martha Spence attended a sermon given by Lucy Maria Hersey, a Millerite preacher, she wrote a glowing letter to *The Midnight Cry*, a popular religious journal, marveling over what a "blessed sight" it had been to see "a young female" in the preacher's stand. With obvious pride, she remarked that Hersey was "an able and very interesting Lecturer, as much so, I think, as any of our brethren in the field."[79] Inspired by Hersey's example, Spence later decided that she too had been called to labor in God's harvest.

Nineteenth-century women may have been particularly attracted to female preachers because they lacked satisfying relationships with their male pastors. Even though women comprised the majority of members in most churches, they were often neglected or ignored by their ministers. According to historian Karin Gedge, clergymen were never instructed how to "minister" to their female parishioners, and they tended to avoid intimate, face-to-face encounters because of their fear of scandal. In frustration, women turned to female relatives, friends, and even pious memoirs for religious direction. When they discovered female preachers, they finally found the guidance they needed. Lauretia Fassett, for example, spoke to individual women as she traveled from house to house, "reading the Bible to those within, and praying with them, as well as conversing with each one personally on the subject of their salvation." Often she simply sat quietly as women confided their religious doubts and questions to her.[80]

As they acknowledged in their memoirs, female preachers gained crucial psychological support and encouragement from their women followers. At the beginning of their careers, when they were still ambivalent about speaking in public, they often turned to other women for reassurance. When Ellen Stewart was agonizing over her call to preach, she revealed her feelings to "Sister" Mack, a friend and fellow member of her church. Mack was "my counsellor and my comforter in affliction," Stewart explained, and they were bound together "in the closest union." She never would have found the courage to preach without her help.

Offering more concrete forms of support, lay women opened their houses for meetings, arranged preaching appointments, and foiled would-be opponents. When a group of "brethren" locked Salome Lincoln out of a schoolhouse where she was supposed to preach, two "ladies" indignantly demanded the key. Other women accompanied female preachers into the pulpit, quietly standing or sitting behind them as they delivered their sermons. At a camp meeting in Waynesburg, Ohio, Ellen Stewart was escorted into the preacher's stand by her husband and "two or three other females."[81]

Because of their theological conservatism, female preachers also gained the support of many clergymen within their sects. Ministers for the Freewill Baptists, Christians, Methodists, and African Methodists wrote recommendations for women, invited them to speak, and collected money to help defray their expenses. Like Zilpha Elaw, who was "greatly encouraged" by her ministers, Jarena Lee eventually won the backing of the Reverend Richard Allen, the bishop of the African Methodist Church. Of course, all the men in these sects did not sanction female preaching, but even those who opposed it on principle sometimes made exceptions. Despite his "strong prejudice against female preachers," Lorenzo Johnson still judged that Salome Lincoln had "as great a CALL, as myself."[82] Even when it was grudging, men's support proved invaluable. Without their endorsements, female preachers might never have gained such widespread acceptance in the early nineteenth century.

Since several prominent ministers had been converted by female preachers, they tended to be particularly supportive of their labors. For example, Nancy Cram was responsible for the conversion of five male elders, including John Ross, John Hollister, and David Millard, and in gratitude, they praised her as an instrument of God. Remembering his first glimpse of her during a revival in 1814, Millard wrote: "I thought her prayer was the most able and powerful I had ever heard, and her exhortation was very affecting."[83] Because he had been converted by a woman, he became a lifelong supporter of female preaching.

Besides praising these women in person, clergymen helped make them visible to the American public by mentioning them in their memoirs and articles. Indeed, they left numerous testimonials praising women for leading revivals and saving sinners. Joseph Badger, for example, a prominent Christian Connection minister, wrote a letter to the *Christian Palladium* praising "Sister" Ann Rexford for her "able, faithful, and interesting labors." She "has endeared herself to thousands of our brethren," he wrote.[84] In addition to reporting when and where women were preaching, clergymen described both the style and content of their sermons. If not for their detailed records, much less would be known today about these extraordinary women.

Most important, many clergymen not only praised individual women, but defended women's divine right to preach the gospel. Surprisingly, many nineteenth-century men did not believe female preaching was either improper or unscriptural. In 1838, for example, P. R. Russell published an article in the *Christian Journal* ridiculing the idea of women's sphere. Appealing to his readers' common sense, he wrote: "It is . . . said—Woman's 'appropriate sphere' is the domestic circle. I answer—Man's 'appropriate sphere' is the field. At his creation, he was placed in the garden to till and dress it. What then? Shall he do nothing else but plough, plant, and gather into barns?"[85] In his opinion, it was ludicrous to confine women's religious influence to the privacy of the home. Like many other evangelicals, he insisted that women as well as men had a right to preach in the informal public of the church.

Despite their egalitarianism, however, it is important to recognize that these ministers did not sanction all female preachers. Although they were sympathetic to women who upheld their own theological beliefs, they condemned those who appeared more radical. After Christian Connection leaders discovered that Dolly Richards had begun performing baptisms and serving the Lord's Supper, they issued a public statement vowing that they had "no fellowship" with her. They also condemned Betsy Niles as a "fanatic" when she became the leader of her own religious sect.[86] Nevertheless, they gladly welcomed more conservative women into the fold, warmly praising them for their skill as public speakers.

When Abigail Roberts died in 1841, she was remembered as a powerful preacher who had converted countless numbers of people to her evangelical faith. In an obituary that appeared in a Christian Connection periodical, one clergyman wrote: "Many thousands have listened with breathless attention to the heavenly story, as it fell from her lips, and many hundreds will date their religious experience from the time they heard her preach."[87] Besides being a spellbinding storyteller who could make audiences cry out and shout, Roberts had been a devout evangelical who had devoted most of her sermons to the classic themes of repentance and conversion. As a biblical feminist, she had never demanded the right to be ordained, but by the sheer force of her example, she convinced many evangelicals that Mothers in Israel and Sisters in Christ could be independent, forceful, and courageous. Lifting up her voice like a trumpet, she had tried to save people from sin while laying the foundation for a new tradition of female preaching. Disturbed by the "progress" of the modern world, she had combined a revolutionary defense of women's public speech with a deeply traditional defense of evangelical Christianity.

6

God and Mammon

Female *Peddlers of* *the Word* — No man can serve two masters: for either he will hate the one, and love the other; or else he will hold to the one, and despise the other. Ye cannot serve God and mammon. Therefore I say unto you, Take no thought for your life, what ye shall eat, or what ye shall drink; nor yet for your body, what ye shall put on. Is not the life more than meat, and the body than raiment?—Matthew 6:24–25

In 1844, in the midst of a market revolution that was transforming both rural and urban America, Harriet Livermore decried the increasing commercialization of American culture. Addressing the American public in the pages of her book *The Counsel of God*, she complained that far too many people valued material wealth over Christianity. A man could not go to heaven "with golden weights upon his breast, and silver shackles about his feet," she argued. Claiming that speculating on stocks was "criminal," she pointed out that Christ himself had told his disciples, "It is easier for a camel to go through the eye of a needle, than for a rich man to enter into the kingdom of God."[1] Christians who had grown rich by exploiting the poor, who had chosen to worship mammon rather than God, were not truly Christians at all.

Livermore was a congressman's daughter who had been raised in a prosperous household, but after deciding to become a preacher, she deliberately chose the hardships of itinerant life over the world's comforts and luxuries. Although her education and refinement set her apart from other female preachers, she was linked to them by her devotion to "the Lord's outcasts,"

COMMUNICATION.—The Books mentioned by Miss Livermore at the Capitol on the last Sabbath, viz : A Wreath from Jessamine Lawn on Free Grace, and some others, can be had of Mr. John Woodsides, in the Six Buildings, Washington. Miss Livermore is on a journey to the Western Indians, with a view of aiding in their religious instruction. The sale of her Books will greatly aid her in this benevolent object. A friend of hers gives the Citizens of Washington this notice. Her Books, he is assured, are well worth reading, particularly adapted to the youth of both sexes.

The different Editors will confer a favor by giving insertion to the above.

This advertisement for Harriet Livermore's books appeared in *The Daily National Intelligencer* (May 30, 1832), a Washington newspaper, a few days after she preached in the Hall of Representatives in 1832. In order not to appear too presumptuous, Livermore asked a friend to run this advertisement for her. Courtesy of the American Antiquarian Society.

and like them, she often struggled to meet her expenses.[2] Leaving her family, who must have been horrified by her religious zeal, she became a literal stranger and a pilgrim with no home to call her own. Life was more than "meat," she quoted from Matthew, and the body "more than raiment." Unlike the self-made men who grew rich in a booming economy, her pilgrimage led her from affluence to poverty.

Despite Livermore's hostility to the consumer revolution, however, she depended on commercial strategies to "sell" her beliefs in the secular marketplace. Following in the footsteps of George Whitefield, the brilliant itinerant who had marketed his message of repentance during the first Great Awakening, she publicized her opposition to an increasingly materialistic, consumer-oriented society by mastering modern promotional techniques. Like hordes of itinerant peddlers, portraitists, and lecturers, she traveled from town to town in order to spread her beliefs to as many people as possible. Covering thousands of miles, she visited New Hampshire, Massachusetts, Rhode Island, Pennsylvania, and Virginia as well as the western territories of the United States. Remarkably, she also crossed the ocean to preach in Jerusalem on five separate occasions.

Besides her incessant travels, Livermore also relied on the press to publicize her evangelical faith. In 1824 the *Christian Herald* carried an advertisement for her first book, *Scriptural Evidence in Favor of Female Testimony in Meetings for the Worship of God*, praising its "able and luminous stile," and by 1845, she had filled the pages of fifteen volumes with her musings on female evangelism, the ten lost tribes of Israel, and the end of human history. Eager to appeal to a broad variety of readers, she published not only biblical commentaries, but poetry, a memoir, a novel, and even a children's story.[3]

Livermore was only one of many evangelical preachers who used commercial techniques to foster revivals in an increasingly market-oriented society. In order to compete with new merchants and entrepreneurs, the Methodists, African Methodists, Freewill Baptists, and Christians tried to "sell" their religion in almost every region of the country. Like itinerant peddlers, they traveled from place to place in order to reach as many people as possible, visiting both "burned-over" districts and outlying villages. In each town, they went from door to door visiting prospective converts in their homes. Through their skillful use of the press, they publicized where they were preaching. And in order to attract larger audiences and give themselves greater legitimacy, they relied on testimonials and endorsements.[4] Taken together, these techniques helped women promote their traditional, evangelical worldview and their defense of female preaching. By traveling and preaching across the country, they hoped to draw people away from the wagons of peddlers and entertainers and into the pews of the churches. In the battle to "win souls," they saw merchants and peddlers as their most threatening competition.

The Market Revolution

Beginning as early as the eighteenth century, a market revolution transformed the American economy. During the 1740s and 1750s, people in cities such as New York, Boston, and Philadelphia began importing a wide variety of British goods, and by the eve of the American Revolution, they were buying more British books, clothing, and, of course, tea than ever before. According to historian T. H. Breen, the American market for consumer goods rose 120 percent between 1750 and 1773. In cities, prosperous families bought luxury items, while in rural areas, people bought such basic amenities as tables and chairs. Even though rural families did not enjoy the same access to material goods as their urban counterparts, itinerant peddlers often penetrated even the most remote villages. As early as 1721 in Berwick, Maine, a Boston peddler sold Sarah Goodwin "Three quarters of a yard of muslin," and her father "a yard and halfe of Stuff for handcarchiefs."[5]

In the nineteenth century, as pioneers moved west and immigrants flooded into cities, these commercial networks expanded and diversified. Even though nineteenth-century rural America was not yet capitalist, yeoman farmers were increasingly dissatisfied with exchanging their goods and labor in local markets alone. They sought greater involvement in a national economic market as well. As historian Jonathan Prude has argued, industrialization affected not only artisans in large cities such as New York, Boston, and Philadelphia, but unskilled factory workers and farmers in small towns and rural villages. By 1850, more than half of the labor force worked for wages.[6]

Although it is clear that many entrepreneurs grew rich by taking advantage of the commercial boom, historians have disagreed about the effects of America's rapid economic expansion on ordinary workers. While some have lamented the loss of traditional patterns of self-sufficient farming, others have celebrated the birth of a modern, capitalist economy. On one hand, the average standard of living improved, and families owned a greater variety of material goods than ever before. Items that had been luxuries in the eighteenth century, such as forks, knives, and dinner plates, became commonplace after the Revolution. Technologically, new labor-saving devices meant higher rates of productivity. Most important, many hardworking Americans managed to achieve the dream of upward mobility, rising out of the lower classes to become successful merchants or master craftsmen. Indeed, many Christians, Freewill Baptists, Methodists, and African Methodists were so influenced by the Protestant work ethic that they eventually joined the ranks of the respectable sort whom they had once disparaged. Contrary to what some historians have implied, a market-oriented economy was not simply imposed on lowerclass families, but was *chosen* by them as well. Most Americans seem to have welcomed the chance to improve their lot in life, especially in order to ensure a better future for their children.[7]

On the other hand, however, it is clear that the market revolution caused anxiety and distress among small artisans and farmers who had to adapt to a new, cash-centered economy. Even though they marveled at the variety of goods and services available in an expanding marketplace, they were often bewildered by the invisible forces that determined supply and demand. In rural areas, farmers who had once grown crops for their own subsistence, or for exchange in the neighborhood, began to harvest grain to satisfy the demands of a national market. In cities, artisans worked fourteen-hour days, often in cramped, dirty conditions, as workshop masters demanded higher rates of production and efficiency. Although a few of these men managed to achieve financial security, others struggled to support their families in a boom and bust economy that veered wildly between inflationary speculation and recession. During the panic of 1819, an era of "hard times, hard feelings, hard money," agricultural prices collapsed and businesses failed as a result of the new, anti-inflationary policies of the Bank of the United States. "Go where you will," a New Jersey farmer reflected, and "your ears are continually saluted with the cry of *hard times! hard times!*"[8] In 1837, during one of the worst depressions in American history, lowered wages, food shortages, and mass unemployment took a devastating toll. In New York City alone, more than one-third of the workers lost their jobs. In the words of historian Jama Lazerow, early-nineteenth-century American culture was filled with contradictions: "Everywhere, hope mixed with fear, desire with disquiet, as prosperity and individual social mobility expanded alongside poverty, exploitation, dependency, frustration, insecurity, uncertainty."[9] Despite the image of America as a land of unlimited economic opportunity, the inequalities between rich and poor grew increasingly sharp throughout the century.

For women, the market revolution was especially disorienting. Unlike colonial goodwives, who had fed and clothed their families by churning butter, brewing beer, carding wool, and weaving clothing, nineteenth-century women no longer seemed to contribute crucial labor to the support of the household. Of course, many middle-class women continued to work long hours performing backbreaking chores, and there is no doubt that they played a central role in the family economy. Nevertheless, housewives did not receive wages for their work, and in a new cash market, their labor no longer seemed as valuable. Unlike men's work, it did not have a "price." Excluded from the national network of cash exchange, they were dependent on their husbands for support.[10]

In contrast to middle-class women, lower-class women often worked for wages, but their labor was hardly more valued. Unlike lower-class men, who could be farmers, tanners, carpenters, shoemakers, sailors, clerks, or blacksmiths—to name just a few popular occupations—women had fewer job choices, and they often received low wages. In the words of an angry female mill worker, "We never could understand why a man's services were, in fact, more valuable than woman's, when the labor was equally as well performed by the one as the other. Nor why every employment which was more lucrative, must also be masculine." Whether women worked inside their homes making palm-leaf hats or weaving cloth, or outside their homes as cooks, maids, or factory girls, most were paid only half as much as men for their labor. Rarely could they achieve the same economic self-sufficiency as their fathers and brothers. According to the criteria of the market, women's work was far less important than men's.[11]

The women and men who preached for the Freewill Baptists, Methodists, African Methodists, and Christian Connection knew the dislocations of the market revolution from personal experience. With a few prominent exceptions, including Harriet Livermore, most were from the lower or lower-middling classes, and they had been raised in families who had struggled to make ends meet. For example, Nancy Cram's parents, like thousands of other settlers, moved to northern New England in search of land and opportunity during the Revolutionary era; in 1773 they arrived in Weare, New Hampshire, with nothing but two steers, a four-year-old colt, and two pairs of saddlebags containing all their other possessions. They were reputed to be hardworking and "respectable," but they were also quite poor, and they spent their lives trying to scratch out a living from the rocky New England soil.[12]

Although female preachers rarely wrote about their childhoods, many seem to have been deeply influenced by early experiences of economic hardship. They seldom betrayed much emotion when they remembered growing up, but their tone of detachment may have masked memories that were too painful to share. At the beginning of her memoir, Jarena Lee summed up her childhood in a single sentence that was as powerful for what it left unsaid as for what it revealed. "At the age of seven years I was parted from my parents," she wrote, "and went to live as a servant maid, with a Mr. Sharp, at the distance of about sixty miles from the place of my birth." Leaving a multitude of questions unanswered, she said virtually nothing else in her memoir about her parents or her life as a servant. Was she angry at her mother and father for hiring her out as a maid? Did they have the time and money to make the sixty-mile trip to visit her? Was she mistreated by Mr. Sharp? One can only imagine how wrenching it must have been for her to have been sent away from home at such a young, vulnerable age. Like Ellen Stewart, who was also hired out as a maid, and Salome Lincoln, who worked long days in a factory when she was only fourteen, Lee knew what it meant to be poor, and she was forced to shoulder adult responsibilities at a far earlier age than children from better-off families.

Whatever hopes her parents may have cherished for her future, they needed her wages to help pay their expenses.[13]

Because many female preachers felt as if their families had lost as much as they had gained from the market revolution, they were deeply ambivalent about technological and economic "progress." On one hand, all of them had been raised to do "women's" work in the home—mending clothes, scrubbing laundry, canning fruit—and they certainly must have welcomed the invention of laborsaving devices such as washing and sewing machines. Even though most could not afford the tempting merchandise they saw in peddlers' wagons, they must have longed to buy the new tools that made housework easier and less time-consuming.[14]

Yet even though these women were not immune to the allure of the market, they also worried that Americans had lost their moral scruples in the race to acquire the most expensive consumer goods. At a time when thousands of people were captivated by the rags-to-riches stories of entrepreneurs such as John Jacob Astor, they lamented that self-interest, not communal responsibility, had become the guiding economic principle. "Gain" was not the same as "godliness," Jarena Lee preached. "For we brought nothing into this world, and it is certain we can carry nothing out." If Christians forgot that their ultimate responsibility was to God, not mammon, they would be guilty of the same idolatry as the Israelites who had worshiped the golden calf. Instead of viewing poverty as a punishment for idleness, a common view at the time, the Freewill Baptists insisted that it was actually a "blessing" in disguise: "Riches, it is well known, have been and still are, a curse to many; while poverty is a great blessing to others. The rich are seldom very pious, nor are they very benevolent, generally speaking." The rich might live in luxury on earth by "grinding the face of the poor," but in the world to come, they would be endlessly "tormented."[15]

In their sermons and books, female preachers repeatedly admonished their congregations to seek "the pearl of great price" rather than more material treasures. When they spoke to women, they warned them not to value "superfluous dress, trimmings, [and] ornaments." And in their comments to men, they urged them not to measure their worth by the money lining their pockets. In *The Counsel of God*, Harriet Livermore asked, "Can the hands that reach after gain, wield the sword of the Spirit, in defence of the Gospel?" Her answer was a resounding no.[16] True soldiers of Christ would never be tempted by the luxuries of the world.

Female preachers were especially troubled by what they perceived as a growing disregard for the poor and the dependent. If the church was truly the family of God, then Christians had a duty to care for their brothers and sisters in need. Decrying the competitive individualism of the marketplace, they urged people to subordinate their private ends to the public good. Mary Stevens Curry, a Christian Connection preacher, compared the "intemperate love for worldly riches" to a "contagious disease." Like many other evangelicals in the new republic, she worried that an "anxious spirit of gain" had replaced an earlier communal ethic of responsibility. "Set your affections on things above, and not on things of the earth," she commanded. "Envy not the rich, nor despise the poor."[17] Urging converts to live according to Christ's great commandment—"Thou shalt love thy neighbor as thyself"—she implored them not to exploit their fellow Christians for their own material gain.

Curry's nostalgia for a golden age—an age before factories, banks, labor disputes, and economic panics—was profound. Protesting against the unbridled pursuit of wealth, she longed for a bygone world of self-sufficient farms and independent laborers untouched by the corrosive forces of materialism and individualism. In her idealized vision of early America, a veritable peaceable kingdom, people had always cared for their families and neighbors and had always been satisfied with what little goods they owned. Instead of speculating on western lands, they had lived on the same farms for generation after generation, weaving past and present together in a seamless whole. Of course, if Curry could have magically transported herself back to the seventeenth or eighteenth centuries, she would have realized that even the Puritans had struggled to suppress the spirit of capitalism, but filled with nostalgia, she assumed that colonial America had been a more tranquil, serene world that had not yet been tainted by the frenzied spirit of monetary accumulation.

No matter how much Curry may have romanticized a primitive past, however, many other evangelicals shared her utopian vision. Indeed, whether or not capitalism had actually led to selfishness and an undue "love of the world," many Americans *believed* that it had, and in this case, perception was as important as reality. Perhaps, as Thomas Haskell has argued, the spirit of capitalism implicitly contributed to humanitarian reform, but for the lower-class evangelicals who participated in the revivals, it seemed far more menacing.[18] Like eighteenth-century New Lights and Separates, they perceived the growth of the market as a threat to an older, traditional way of life rooted in economic independence and generational stability.

With crusading zeal, female preachers took their critique of consumer America to the people who most wanted to hear it. Traveling to small towns and rural villages, they spoke to farmers, shoemakers, weavers, and other handicraft workers who worried about their ability to adapt to a changing economy. Since they often visited families from house to house, they may have sat in kitchens talking about religion as female "outworkers" made buttons or assembled the uppers of shoes to send to nearby factories. Perhaps they also visited men in the fields as they gathered crops to send to the market. Time and again, they reminded their listeners that they could be rich in God's blessings even if they were poor in material goods. "To be carnally minded is death," proclaimed Elleanor Knight. "To be spiritually minded is peace."[19]

Besides traveling to rural villages to speak to impoverished farmers and outworkers, female preachers also visited a string of mill towns across the Northeast. In 1826, for example, Susan Humes led a revival in Scituate, Rhode Island, a center of religious activity during the 1820s. Although there is no record of whether she held her meetings during the daytime or in the evenings, many other evangelicals intentionally disrupted factory discipline by preaching during working hours. After visiting Pawtucket, Rhode Island, a Freewill Baptist minister boasted: "The young people who labored in the factory, were so anxious to hear preaching, that they left their employment and attended meeting from morning till noon." During a revival in Fall River, Massachusetts, in 1836, a Christian Connection minister brought the town to a standstill when he baptized seventy-five converts in the Taunton River. Despite the threats of angry bosses, workers virtually shut down mills in order to listen to evangelical preachers thundering out their condemnation of greed. Acquiring a "*Fortune*" would not make men good or wise, the Freewill Baptists warned. "Base metal is base metal still, however it may be gilded over. It won't pass at last for more than its intrinsic worth."[20] Jesus had not been a rich tax collector, but a penniless carpenter who had supported himself by working with his hands.

Although female preachers seem to have been popular in mill towns, there is very little evidence of their attitudes toward the emerging labor movement. Since several of them helped to support themselves by working in factories, including Sarah Orne, Salome Lincoln, and Elleanor Knight, they may have been sympathetic to workers who complained of long hours and unsanitary working conditions. In 1829, after eight years of working as a weaver in a mill in Taunton, Massachusetts, Lincoln was so disillusioned by falling wages and production speed-ups that she led a walkout in protest. Unfortunately, however, it is unclear whether other female preachers took part in strikes or supported the movement for a ten-hour day.[21]

Whether or not these women identified themselves as labor activists, they seem to have had contradictory effects on the development of working-class consciousness. On one hand, they criticized employers who treated workers unjustly, but on the other, they also muted class antagonism by insisting that all evangelicals, whatever their economic status, were bound together in the family of God. As devout Christians, these women believed that the fundamental division in American culture was not between the rich and the poor, but between the saved and the damned. Instead of lumping all capitalists together in a single, oppressive class, they distinguished between those who had been born again and those who had not. The remedy for the materialism of American life was not class struggle or unionization, but conversion.[22]

Instead of demanding sweeping economic reform, female preachers offered sympathy and encouragement to people who feared they would be unable to meet the exacting demands of a new market-oriented economy. When Elleanor Knight preached in the factory town of Fall River, she comforted her listeners, many of whom may have been worn down by working fourteen-hour days in the mill, by imagining how richly they would be rewarded in heaven. "I reckon that the sufferings of this present time are not worthy to be compared with the glory which shall be revealed in us," she assured them. At the same time as she condemned employers for their greed, she blunted her critique by preaching an otherworldly message of consolation. Comforting the hopeless and the hard-pressed with promises of redemption, she devoted her energies to fighting the worst excesses of the market revolution, especially its exaltation of financial success, rather than its underlying roots. Despite their sufferings, Christian workers could look forward to eternal bliss in heaven. If Christians were "oppressed," Mary Stevens Curry advised, they should "bear it, knowing that all things work together for good to those that love God."[23] It was hardly a message calculated to inspire class warfare.

Unlike radical communitarians such as Robert Dale Owen or John Humphrey Noyes, these women never challenged the basic structures of capitalism by trying to create an alternative economic order. Just as they never demanded revolutionary changes in the relationship between the sexes, they never called for the abolition of private property or the redistribution of wealth. Nor did they ever follow the example of the Shakers by proposing that Christians should live communally. Despite their diatribes against the worship of wealth, they never claimed that money in itself was evil. As long as Christians remembered that their first responsibility was to God, not mammon, they were entitled to reap the rewards of their labors.

Because Christianity has often been invoked to discourage as well as incite class conflict, many historians have argued that antebellum revivalism made workers "singularly timid." According to scholars such as Paul Johnson and Bruce Laurie, evangelicalism was inherently conservative and oppressive, and middle-class manufacturers and businessmen deliberately fostered revivals in order to impose discipline on recalcitrant workers. In their view, the Second Great Awakening did not come from the bottom up, but only from the top down, and when lower-class laborers joined churches, they were brainwashed into "pious docility." Rather than being empowered by the new emphasis on free will and self-determination, they were oppressed by an individualistic theology that made them solely responsible for their own well-being. When employers claimed that men and women were free to make their own moral choices, they absolved themselves of responsibility for the poverty and suffering they saw in their midst. Just as workers could blame only themselves if they had not been born again, they could blame only themselves if they lacked food, shelter, or clothing.[24]

This neo-Marxist interpretation of the revivals as "the opium of the people" has been echoed by many historians, but it reduces a complex, fascinating history of accommodation and resistance to a crude story of social control. Perhaps a few clergymen hoped that the revivals would consolidate their power, but female preachers certainly did not use religion to suppress dissent, and like many other lower-class evangelicals, they transformed the Bible into a scathing indictment of class inequality. As historian Jama Lazerow has illustrated, the labor movement was deeply influenced by evangelicalism, and many preachers—especially Methodists, Freewill Baptists, Baptists, Universalists, and Christians—spoke at labor gatherings and volunteered their churches for union meetings. Promising that a righteous God would protect the poor and oppressed, they demanded that employers raise wages and shorten working hours to a ten-hour day. "If you refuse the entreaties of suffering humanity," one clergyman warned the manufacturers in Fall River, "you may be suddenly summoned before God. . . . Various are the ways in which God may disappoint you, if you trample his laws." For many ministers, the labor movement was inseparable from Christianity: it was a moral crusade against those who worshiped mammon more than God. Protestantism meant *protest*.[25]

Deeply ambivalent about the expansion of the market, female preachers were neither proto-Marxist revolutionaries nor "Christian capitalists." Standing between two extremes, they urged Christians to work hard in order to please God, but they also protested against the injustice of "wage slavery." They invited all evangelicals, whatever their social class, into their churches, but they warned the wealthy not to take advantage of the needy. They insisted that individuals could save themselves from sin, but they rejected the rugged individualism of the marketplace. Finally, they preached a gospel of free will, but they never argued that people could choose to be rich or poor as well as whether to be saved or damned. In other words, they never would have agreed with historians who claim that evangelical theology served the interests of middle-class shopkeepers and businessmen. According to these women's understanding of free will, it was not the freedom to blame the poor or the needy for their own misfortunes, but the freedom to imitate the life of Christ, who had taught his disciples to value all human beings as the children of God.

Female preachers saw themselves not as revolutionaries, but as defenders of a lost heritage of religious devotion and communal harmony that appeared to be crumbling before their eyes. In their backward-looking jeremiads, they blamed the market revolution for creating a culture so obsessed with getting and spending that it had begun to drift from its Christian moorings. However much they were attracted to the market's dazzling array of new products and its promise of upward mobility, they longed for a world that seemed to have been lost—a world of Christian harmony that may have never existed.

Pilgrims and Peddlers

In a history filled with ironies, perhaps the greatest one of all is that female preachers used commercial techniques to publicize their opposition to the consumer revolution. After the disestablishment of the churches, evangelicals realized that they could no longer coerce church membership, and they learned how to compete with one another and with other voluntary organizations—reform organizations, charities, and publishing associations—for membership and money. As early as the 1740s, revivalists such as George Whitefield had begun to "sell" their beliefs "alongside all the goods and services of this world," but after the Revolution, they realized they would have to master the language of the market in order to survive. The First Amendment, as R. Laurence Moore has noted, had the unintended effect of making religion into yet another commodity for sale.[26]

Like other evangelicals in the new republic, the Christian Connection, Freewill Baptists, Methodists, and African Methodists were eager to market their beliefs, and they seem to have been deeply influenced (probably unconsciously) by the success of itinerant peddlers and entertainers. In the early decades of the nineteenth century, thousands of "hawkers" traveled to small towns and villages in search of customers. Selling everything from razors, combs, spoons, spices, brooms, and needles to more substantial items such as pottery, chairs, and tinware, they served as a crucial link between urban merchants and rural consumers. Young and enterprising, they walked through densely wooded areas carrying their goods in trunks strapped to their backs or, if they were transporting larger items and could afford it, traveled in wagons. Admitting that their "sole object was to make money," they continuously reinvented themselves according to the demands of the market. One particularly ambitious peddler, James Guild, variously advertised himself as a tinkerer, schoolmaster, writing teacher, silhouettist, doctor, and portraitist. Determined to get rich, he also sold three-cent scissors for as much as twenty-five cents a pair.[27]

Peddlers were joined by a multitude of other itinerants in the early republic who crisscrossed the country selling their wares. In rural areas, people met traveling singing masters, lecturers, dance instructors, and artists. Outside of rural areas, particularly in the cities and along the East Coast, large crowds of spectators gathered to see acrobats, sleight-of-hand artists, jugglers, magicians, and even animal shows. While tramping through New York as a peddler, James Guild was startled to see a man leading a bison through the woods, taking the animal to exhibitions across the state. In the early decades of the nineteenth century, audiences were thrilled by the sight of lions, zebras, monkeys, tigers, porcupines, and even elephants that were put on display. In the words of historian Donald Scott, a "staggering number and variety of entertainers and performers, purveyors of this or that kind of lore or doctrine, agents or missionaries of one society or another," drifted across the country in the 1830s and 1840s.[28]

Because evangelical preachers had to vie with these itinerant "pests" for public attention, they deeply resented their popularity. Preachers wanted to convince people to repent and strive for salvation, but time and again they found that religion was only one of many goods offered for sale. Despite their dire warnings that "heathen entertainments" had "contaminated the hearts of hundreds of the youth of our land, [and] drawn them from the path of moral rectitude," they saw swarms of people across the country lining up for "theatrical exhibitions, caravans, circuses" and magic shows. Anxious to appeal to the masses, evangelicals held camp meetings that were as sensational as any drama in a theater, but even so, they found it difficult to compete with the entertainment offered by peddlers. Even a female preacher may have seemed tame in comparison to the sight of a fortune-teller, a magician, a lion, or an elephant.[29]

The competition between peddlers and preachers was particularly intense because they were marketing the same product: self-transformation. According to peddlers, people could utterly change their lives by buying fashionable clothing, learning how to sing or dance, or attending the most informative lectures. Geniuses of promotion, lecturers such as Ralph Waldo Emerson and Henry Ward Beecher guaranteed that their "useful knowledge" could help ordinary people improve their economic and social position in the world. Selling "culture" even more directly, portraitists promised instant status and prestige to those who were immortalized on canvas. All of these peddlers, whether singing masters, dance instructors, or lecturers, offered ordinary people the chance to change their lives by purchasing the right commodities.[30]

On the surface, the similarities between peddlers and preachers were striking. Just as peddlers insinuated that consumers could remake their identities by wearing the latest fashions or reading the most important books, preachers vowed that people could be reborn through religious faith. "If any man be in Christ, he is a new creature," Salome Lincoln promised. "Old things are passed away; behold, all things are become new." Just as portraitists pledged to immortalize people on canvas, preachers held out the promise of eternal life in heaven. And just as lecturers promised to increase their listener's social status, preachers suggested that religion would bring people greater respect in their communities. Pointing to the examples of sinners who had been "convicted" by friends or relatives, they argued that conversion could transform ordinary people into paragons of piety.[31] Religion, like the more material goods of the marketplace, could change even the lowliest outcasts into "new creatures."

Besides these similarities, preachers and peddlers also shared a common commercial language: they both measured their success by numbers. Like peddlers, who tallied up the amount of money they had earned each day, preachers carefully counted the number of souls they had saved. For example, when Henry Searls wrote a letter to a Christian Connection journal describing a revival in New York, he included a detailed account of how many people had been born again. "The church numbers now seventy eight members," he reported. "Nine were baptized and fifteen added to the church."[32] Keeping a careful balance sheet of his "wins" and "losses," he tried to determine how many saints he had added to God's kingdom.

Even more than men, female preachers had a passion for quantification: they carefully counted the numbers of converts who had swooned, cried out, or been born again during their meetings. Without the prestige of ordination, they may have tried to prove their worth by meticulously listing the number of miles they had traveled and souls they had saved. Perhaps hoping to sound impressive (and often succeeding), they filled their letters and memoirs with numerical evidence of their religious zeal. Jarena Lee revealed that she had journeyed 2,325 miles in 1827 and more than 2,700 miles between July of 1832 and October of 1833. She had preached 692 times in 1835 alone, averaging more than one sermon per day. With statistical precision, she also boasted that three people had "found peace" during one of her meetings outside of Baltimore, and two more the next day. Even though Lee was openly suspicious of the market revolution, she seems to have unwittingly internalized its scale of value. Instead of rejoicing that she had saved even one sinner, she equated quality with quantity. In the capitalist marketplace, as in the battle for souls, more was always better.[33]

Ironically, female preachers resembled the new breed of peddlers and entrepreneurs in more ways than they ever would have cared to admit. Despite their diatribes against American culture, they epitomized the qualities needed to succeed in a capitalist economy: they were energetic, hardworking, disciplined, and self-denying.[34] Not only did they work long hours, visiting "sinners" from early in the morning until late at night, but they did not hesitate to make sacrifices in order to fulfill their callings. Leaving their families for weeks or months at a time, they traveled thousands of miles to even the tiniest villages in America. If they had chosen to devote their lives to commerce rather than religion, their unremitting toil surely would have impressed even the shrewdest Yankee peddlers.

Yet female preachers and peddlers were separated by one significant difference that should not be forgotten—a difference that fundamentally shaped their attitudes toward their vocations. No matter how much they resembled one another on the surface, they stood on opposite sides of a chasm that could not be bridged. In contrast to many peddlers, female preachers did not measure their worth by how much money they had earned, but by how many souls they had saved. Only conversion, not consumption, offered a path to new life.

In order to protest against the materialism and rampant individualism that they associated with the market revolution, the Christians, Freewill Baptists, and Methodists appropriated its strategies. Setting out as pilgrims to "sell" their message of repentance, they rivaled even the most ambitious of peddlers in their grueling schedule of speaking and traveling. Mrs. Peavey, for example, a Christian Connection preacher, traversed an exhausting circuit throughout Maine, New Hampshire, Massachusetts, Rhode Island, Pennsylvania, and Ohio, and Nancy Towle's travels took her to a total of twelve states as well as Canada, England, and Ireland. Harriet Livermore tramped so many miles that she complained her feet were "badly festered." Even women who confined their itinerancy to one state or region of the country, such as Mary Stevens Curry, made long and frequent trips. Often she rode more than one hundred miles on horseback to lead religious meetings.[35]

Although itinerant preachers had been common in the eighteenth century, most notably during the revivals of the Great Awakening, their numbers exploded after the Revolution. By the early nineteenth century, the earlier debates over the legitimacy of itinerant preaching had largely subsided. In contrast to the controversies created by eighteenth-century "vagabonds" such as George Whitefield and James Davenport, who had been accused of subverting the hierarchy of the pastoral relationship, nineteenth-century itinerants were praised for creating new and stable churches on the frontier. Even the Congregationalists and Presbyterians recognized the advantages of an itinerant ministry. In 1801, in their joint "Plan of Union," they agreed to send missionaries to new western territories such as New York and Ohio. In theory, itinerants were not tied to individual congregations, but in practice, they helped to develop new churches by repeatedly visiting the same towns. For example, Hannah Cogswell, a Christian Connection preacher, spent at least three years preaching in the vicinity of New Durham, New Hampshire, during the 1830s. As members of the Ohio Central Christian Conference, Rebecca Miller and her husband, Frederick, were assigned to preach in Knox and

Licking Counties, and they returned to the same villages every few weeks or months.[36] By 1828, almost 2,500 Methodist clergymen alone had crisscrossed America preaching to new converts.[37]

Like peddlers, evangelical preachers traveled to regions of the country where they thought they could market themselves most effectively. Besides preaching in New England and the mid-Atlantic states, where new dissenting sects thrived, they traveled to new, sparsely settled territories such as Michigan and Wisconsin. Although Wealthy Monroe first began preaching in western New York in the early 1830s, she eventually decided to follow the trail of pioneers moving to Michigan. In 1841, recognizing the demand for new churches on the frontier, she and two other women, Abigail Stone and Elizabeth Stiles, became members of the Eastern Michigan Christian Conference.[38] All told, at least fourteen women preached in the Midwest and Northwest (defined as Ohio, Michigan, and Wisconsin) at some point in their careers; thirty-eight more preached in New England; thirty-six in the mid-Atlantic states; and four in Virginia.

As these numbers illustrate, very few women ever dared to venture into the Deep South. Although female preachers were a courageous group, most shied away from the prospect of confronting conservative southern clergymen. Through their religious networks, they knew that most ministers in the South, including the Methodists, firmly opposed women speaking in public. When Harriet Livermore and Nancy Towle traveled to Charleston, South Carolina, they were prohibited from holding public meetings there. Despite the cool reception, Towle confessed, "I love the people of the South. I love their free, and open manners."[39] Unfortunately, the admiration was not mutual. Although Towle lived with a family in Charleston for several months while she wrote her memoir, she, like Livermore, was permitted to preach only in front of small, private gatherings.

A few African American preachers also traveled to the South, although only to the border states of Virginia and Maryland. Ignoring the threats of white masters, at least three black women—Jarena Lee, Zilpha Elaw, and Elizabeth— claimed that God had specially called them to minister to slaves. Fortunately, none of them were harmed, but they could have been whipped, imprisoned, or even sold into slavery. In Virginia, for example, free blacks were not allowed to hold religious meetings in either the day or the evening, and if they broke the law, they could be punished with a public whipping of up to thirty-nine lashes. Even more frightening, most southern states allowed free blacks to be sold into slavery if they did not have legal certificates proving their status. As a result, when Zilpha Elaw preached in a small town in Virginia, she could not help fearing "the prospect of immediate arrest and consignment by sale to some slave owner." By traveling to the South, she quite literally risked her freedom.[40]

Most female preachers were not quite as courageous (or reckless) as Elaw. Instead of traveling to places where they knew they would be greeted with hostility, they visited towns where revival "enthusiasm" was the most intense. For example, at least fourteen women, including Susan Humes (a Freewill Baptist), and Maria Cook (a Universalist), preached in the area of western New York that historians have called the "burned-over district." As the birthplace of the Mormons, Millerites, Spiritualists, and Finneyites, the region gained a reputation as a spiritual hothouse where exotic new religious movements bloomed and flourished.[41] No other place in nineteenth-century America seemed as religiously creative or diverse or, in the opinion of East Coast clergymen, as strange and enthusiastic.

Following the trail of religious enthusiasm into other towns and states, many female preachers traveled to burned-over districts throughout the Northeast. For example, Sarah Hedges and Mary Stratton participated in intermittent local awakenings in eastern New York; Rachel Thompson and Sabrina Lambson made converts in Vermont; and Clarissa Danforth led a sixteen-month revival in Smithfield, Rhode Island.[42] From listening to the gossip of circuit riders and from reading the religious press, they knew the locations of the latest awakenings, and strategically, they roamed wherever they thought they could make new converts.

Generally speaking, most female preachers preferred to travel to small towns and villages where there were few settled clergymen to compete with them. Like peddlers, they did not relish the thought of walking or riding horseback across bumpy, rough terrain, but they thought the backcountry offered the best market for their "wares." Sally Thompson, Sarah Hedges, and Mrs. Peavey all preached in the tiny village of Cranberry Creek, New York, and Susan Humes traveled to Vienna, New York, a frontier town that was overrun with packs of wolves that were as "thick as black birds." Several other women, including Ann Rexford, Nancy Cram, and Abigail Roberts, preached in the famous New York resort of Ballston Spa, but they usually traveled there in the winter or spring, when the town was not flooded with thousands of vacationers. In these months, according to a contemporary observer, the town was a "dull place" with a small population. In 1823 Ballston counted only 1,909 permanent residents.[43]

Although female preachers seem to have been most popular in rural areas, many also traveled to major cities. Determined to make their voices heard in the urban Babylons that symbolized the growing materialism of American life, Sally Thompson delivered several sermons in the Christian chapel in New York City, and Salome Lincoln, Zilpha Elaw, Harriet Livermore, and Nancy Towle all spoke in Boston. Most important, African American female preachers frequently visited cities such as Baltimore and Philadelphia to hold meetings in independent black churches.[44]

After arriving in new towns, women presented letters of recommendation testifying to their character, a common technique used by peddlers. Like lecturers and singing masters, who often asked satisfied customers to endorse their products, female preachers hoped that testimonials would attract larger and more receptive audiences to their sermons. Besides carrying conference letters that approved them as "public laborers," they asked supportive male colleagues to write recommendations on their behalf. For example, Nancy Towle carried a letter from Robert Foster, the prominent editor of the *Christian Herald*, testifying to her "good, reputable, moral character."[45] Even though this letter did not guarantee that other clergymen would allow her to preach, it undoubtedly helped open church doors. By praising Towle's "labors," Foster lent her the prestige of his name and reputation.

Female preachers also relied on face-to-face encounters to market their religious beliefs. Besides lecturing from the distance of the pulpit, they offered private religious advice to the "anxious minded" who were seeking conversion. According to her son, Abigail Roberts often visited people at their homes, "conversing with such as desired her sympathy and counsel in relation to their spiritual state." More aggressively, Hannah Reeves knocked on strangers' doors whenever she first arrived in a new town, forcing unbelievers as well as Christians to listen to her warnings of damnation.[46] Demanding to know whether or not they had been born again, she refused to leave until they promised to pray for God's mercy. No peddler could have marketed her "product" more persistently or, in the opinion of her critics, more obnoxiously.

Despite their zeal at promoting their faith, few female preachers ever reaped financial rewards for their work. From studying the Bible, they knew that Jesus had ordered his disciples to "take nothing for their journey save a staff only; no scrip, no bread, no money in their purse," and they followed his instructions as closely as possible. Of course, they needed to earn enough money to pay their debts and care for their children, and they never refused to take financial donations from believers. Nevertheless, they hoped to live simply instead of worshiping "filthy lucre." When one of Zilpha Elaw's supporters in Maryland offered to buy her a house if she would settle there, she thanked him but declined. Setting herself apart from more powerful clergymen, she explained: "The love of mammon has no place in the hearts of his true ministers, who love the flock rather than the fleece."[47] Doing her "Master's work" was far more important than making money.

Unlike peddlers (or modern-day televangelists), few female preachers earned more than a pittance by "selling" themselves to the public. Before they began preaching, they had managed to support themselves as maids or seamstresses, but after setting out as itinerants, they lost the security of a steady income. Salome Lincoln once found herself more than one hundred miles away from home "without one cent of money," and Nancy Towle admitted that she did not have "a single farthing laid up in store." Sarah Riker, who preached as a Methodist in New York during the 1790s, was eventually forced to ask for poor relief.[48] As strangers and pilgrims, many female preachers were literally homeless.

Neither the Christians, African Methodists, Methodists, or Freewill Baptists paid women's preaching expenses. Since the Methodists and African Methodists did not officially sanction female preaching, they did not offer women even the meager salaries of male itinerants, and the Christians and the Freewill Baptists rejected the concept of a paid ministry altogether. Separating themselves from the established churches, who had collected state taxes, they argued that preachers should be supported entirely by voluntary contributions and their own labor. Like Benjamin Randel, the founder of the Freewill Baptists, who worked as a tailor when he was not traveling, many female preachers resorted to sewing or housecleaning in order to support themselves. Abigail Roberts stitched caps, bedding, and clothing between meetings, and Wealthy Monroe bought a new horse with the profits of her "needle." Elleanor Knight also relied on her sewing skills to earn extra money, knitting a pair of socks to pay for stage fare. On at least one occasion, she worked as a washerwoman as well.[49]

Besides their own labor, women also depended on the generosity of their audiences to help them pay their traveling costs. Aware of their financial difficulties, people sometimes collected contributions for them at the end of their meetings. Gratefully, Zilpha Elaw reported that "every congregation voluntarily made a collection for my aid; and every person at whose house I visited, gave me something for my journey." Because of her popularity, Maria Cook, a Universalist, reportedly earned more money than any of her male colleagues. Unfortunately, however, not all women were so lucky. After Elleanor Knight preached in Randolph, Vermont, in 1836, no one bothered to ask her if she needed money, and she was finally forced to ask some of her friends for help. With difficulty, they managed to scrape together nine shillings.[50]

Only a few exceptional women achieved true financial security, most through marriage. Clarissa Danforth, the single most popular female preacher during the late 1810s, wed a well-to-do merchant from Connecticut, and Ann Rexford married a successful lawyer. According to an elder who seemed dazed by her sudden wealth, Rexford traded her humble past for a future in a "mansion." Since both of these women were relatively well educated, they were able to make the transition from lower-class enthusiasts to respectable housewives, but not without sacrificing their preaching careers. Although Danforth was briefly coaxed out of retirement in 1834, Rexford never returned to the pulpit after her marriage.[51] Even though they remained devout evangelicals, they may have begun to question their assumptions about the sinfulness of the market revolution. No longer racked with anxiety about meeting their expenses, and surrounded by all the comforts of hearth and home, they may have found it more difficult to criticize the pursuit of material goods.

Of the small number of female preachers who managed to make the journey out of poverty, none was more remarkable than Isabella Van Wagenen, the charismatic evangelist who reinvented herself as Sojourner Truth. Born as a slave in New York, she seemed destined for obscurity, but she survived a life that should have defeated her. By the time she reached the age of forty, she had been beaten by her master, forcibly separated from her son, and exploited by a religious charlatan known as the "Prophet Matthias," who convinced her that he possessed the spirit of Christ, but because of her stubborn faith in God, she managed to find the strength to begin an entirely new life. On Pentecost in 1843, she "left everything behind" in order to become a traveling preacher—a stranger and a pilgrim with no home of her own. Refusing to "burden herself" with anything except for two shillings and a few pieces of clothing stuffed into a pillowcase, she also symbolically left behind her old name. As she explained later, the Lord told her to take the first name of Sojourner, "because I was to travel up an' down the land, showin' the people their sins, an' bein' a sign unto them," and the last name of Truth, "because I was to declare the truth to the people." As Sojourner Truth, not as the obscure and exploited Isabella, she became one of the most celebrated feminists and abolitionists of her time. Although she never grew wealthy, she marketed her persona so shrewdly that she eventually made enough money to buy her own house, her lifelong dream.[52]

It should come as no surprise that women such as Truth, Danforth, and Rexford should seize the chance to remake themselves as middle-class matrons. However romantic, adventurous, and prototypically American these lower-class preachers might seem to historians, their lives were filled with loneliness and hardship. No matter how strong their calls to preach, they could not help feeling "much worn down" by the rigorous demands of itinerant life. Separated from their loved ones and ridiculed by strangers, they could not always keep themselves from succumbing to despair. "What," asked Nancy Towle, "am I henceforth to be? A solitary wanderer through the earth, far, far, from every friend, and no more to a certain dwelling place, beneath the sun? . . . Am I able to endure?" There must have been countless days when she longed for the security of a home.[53]

Physically, moreover, traveling in the early nineteenth century was strenuous and exhausting. Trudging on foot or riding horseback through all kinds of weather—snowstorms, downpours, blistering heat—female preachers sometimes arrived at their meetings too hoarse and tired to speak. Since the market revolution was accompanied by a transportation revolution, women also traveled on stagecoaches, canal boats, turnpikes, and railroads, but tickets were relatively expensive, and even "modern" travel tended to be slow and grueling. It took twenty-eight hours to go from New York to Providence by steamboat, and forty-one hours (without an overnight stop) to get from New York to Boston by stagecoach via the Boston Post Road. When Jarena Lee took a canal boat from Albany to Binghamton, the journey took five days.[54]

Traveling presented other difficulties, too, especially for women who were alone. Although it was not unusual for women to take trips by themselves, and canal boats often had special "ladies' cabins," many women feared being robbed or, worse, sexually assaulted. After Ellen Stewart decided to hold a revival meeting in a neighboring town, she was too frightened to walk there by herself. "You are a woman, alone and unprotected," she thought. "You may meet mad dogs, or what is worse, mad men on the road." Perhaps her fears were exaggerated, but many women seem to have viewed canal boats, steamboats, and particularly stagecoaches (where people rubbed knees in uncomfortable intimacy) as places of sexual danger. With the exception of Harriet Livermore, who prided herself on traveling alone, almost all female preachers asked women friends to escort them on their journeys.[55]

For black women, traveling posed even greater anxieties. Even in the "free" North, African Americans were forced to ride in separate "nigger cars" on railroads or "nigger cabins" on steamboats, and despite their protests, they were often treated with contempt. After the captain of a steamboat refused to let Zilpha Elaw aboard, she commented angrily, "My complexion appeared to be the chief reason of his refusal." Even though she had a meeting in New York the next day, he left her stranded in Utica. Worse, when Sojourner Truth tried to board a streetcar in Washington, D.C., the conductor refused to wait for her, dragging her several yards through the streets.[56]

Finally, even beyond the difficulties of traveling from town to town, all female preachers, whether black or white, had to cope with the discomforts of lodging in cheap inns or strangers' houses. Sharing a room or even a bed with people they did not know, they rarely had any privacy, and often they were fed meals that made their stomachs turn. Reminiscing about his days as a Methodist itinerant, Robert Boyd complained of being "required to sleep in a dirty, ill-scented bed, and to eat dirty victuals." On one occasion, for example, a farmwife served him a pile of pancakes that some cats had begun to chew and a plate of butter that looked alarmingly like "Joseph's coat of *many colors*."[57] Of course, many female preachers also stayed with families who pampered them with clean sheets and hearty meals, but they never knew what to expect in new towns.

Itinerant life, as many preachers lamented, was filled with hardships and sufferings. Between traveling hundreds of miles, working at odd jobs to make extra money, and delivering several sermons each week, many women finally collapsed in exhaustion. After a convert asked Nancy Towle why preachers were "so often ill," she thought a better question was "how some of them could still be alive!" In her own experience, she had known many female preachers who had died young. Susan Humes was only twenty-three when she died; Salome Lincoln and Sabrina Lambson were thirty-four; Miriam Kent was twenty-seven; and Rebecca Miller was thirty.[58] Of thirty-four women whose ages at death I could positively determine, six died before the age of forty. Perhaps these women would have died young even if they had not become itinerants, but male preachers were also "worn out" by the rigors of incessant traveling and speaking. According to historian Nathan Hatch, 35 percent of the men who served as Methodist itinerants between 1780 and 1818 died between the ages of twenty-three and twenty-nine. Another 27 percent died between the ages of thirty and thirty-nine.[59] Clearly, itinerant life proved so physically taxing that many simply could not survive it.

Unfortunately, however, women who felt called to preach had little choice but to travel. Since women could not be ordained or set apart by the laying on of hands, they did not have the authority to serve as settled ministers or administer the sacraments of baptism and the Lord's Supper. Even Ann Rexford, who spent two years preaching in a chapel that had been built especially for her in Camptown, New Jersey, was forced to ask neighboring clergymen to substitute for her during important ceremonies. Because of her "natural" subordination to men, she could never hope to be a local pastor, but only a traveling evangelist.[60] Despite her popularity and her charisma, she remained a stranger and pilgrim in a church that forbade her to "rule."

In order to market their religious beliefs to the American public, female preachers made enormous financial and personal sacrifices. Hawking their wares in the open atmosphere of the marketplace, they traveled across the countryside promising their audiences that they could be reborn through Christ. In some ways, they were as successful as the peddlers whom they imitated: through their evangelistic zeal, they brought thousands of new converts into their churches. What they gained in spiritual satisfaction cannot be measured. In terms of material wealth, however, they surely lost more than they gained. Following the example of the first disciples of Christ, they embraced lives of poverty and self-denial, wandering from town to town with "no scrip, no bread, no money in their purse."

Female Preachers and the Publishing Industry

Besides traveling as itinerants, female preachers also depended on the publishing industry to help them spread their beliefs. During the first decades of the nineteenth century, technological advances made printing much less expensive and time-consuming, and American presses began publishing books and periodicals on an unprecedented scale. In 1800, for example, there were only 200 newspapers in the country, but by 1835, the number had swelled sixfold to 1,200.[61] These newspapers gave itinerants the ideal forum for communicating with the public. Like peddlers, who used local newspapers to advertise the new products in their wagons, lecturers and preachers relied on advertisements to announce where they would be speaking.

Flooding the public with scores of religious newspapers, memoirs, and articles, evangelicals fashioned the press into a powerful tool for broadcasting their faith. As one of the earliest groups in America to exploit the potential of mass media, they relied on the press to help them make new converts and gain public acceptance. In 1808 Elias Smith, one of the founders of the Christian Connection, published the first religious newspaper in the United States, the *Herald of Gospel Liberty*, and by 1818, he had attracted 1,400 subscribers and fifty agents. Building on this early success, Christians across the country created publishing associations to print periodicals, memoirs, pamphlets, and hymns. By 1845, the Christian Connection had published as many as seventeen separate periodicals. Some were small journals that did not survive for long, such as the *Gospel Palladium*, which folded after two volumes, but others survived for decades and helped to shape opinions within the evangelical community. Similarly, the Freewill Baptists published at least eight different journals, and the Methodists founded the Methodist Book Concern, an influential organization that financed the publication of both periodicals and pious memoirs.[62]

All of these sects published the memoirs of their most distinguished clergymen. Like Congregationalists, Presbyterians, and other "respectable" churches, they honored prominent ministers by printing their private letters and journals. Just as Jonathan Edwards had edited the diaries of David Brainerd in the eighteenth century, Methodists collected and published the private manuscripts of famous itinerants such as Francis Asbury. Although these books tended to be didactic, readers seemed to crave their unique mixture of personal confession and theological instruction. At least five editions of Asbury's journals were published between 1792 and 1852.

Unlike earlier evangelicals, however, the Methodists, African Methodists, Christians, and Freewill Baptists decided to publish the memoirs of young, popular ministers as well as posthumous tributes to past leaders. George Whitefield had published his personal journals during the 1740s, but shocked by his arrogance, few other ministers had followed his example. In contrast, nineteenth-century clergymen such as Elias Smith and Ephraim Stinchfield published their stories at the height of their careers, an unabashed strategy for self-promotion. David Marks, popularly known as the "boy preacher" because of his youth, did not hesitate to describe himself as a "powerful" speaker.[63]

By publicizing the dramatic stories of their conversions and calls to preach, these ministers turned themselves into celebrities. Amazingly, Lorenzo Dow printed over seventy editions of twenty different works between 1800 and 1835. By shrewdly marketing his writings to a public audience, he managed to transform himself from a common, backwoods preacher into one of the best-known religious personalities of his time. People swarmed to his meetings out of curiosity as well as genuine religious conviction, hoping to see the infamous "crazy Dow" in person. According to historian Jon Butler, "It was commonly said parents named more children after him than any other figure except Washington."[64]

Fascinated by the potential of mass communication, women as well as men relied on books and newspapers to make themselves visible to the American public. All told, twenty female preachers published their memoirs during their lifetimes, and because they were so determined to market their beliefs, all of them paid for the printing themselves. "I have paid a great deal of money, for printing my plain written works," Harriet Livermore admitted.[65] Before the rise of large publishing houses, it was common for authors to produce their own books, but the number of women who dared to publish themselves was relatively small. Few were as bold as female preachers, who openly trumpeted their success at leading revivals and saving sinners.

In part, these women were motivated by financial need. For example, Harriet Livermore helped to pay her traveling expenses by selling six hundred copies of *Scriptural Evidence in Favor of Female Testimony*, and Sojourner Truth used the profits of the first edition of her *Narrative* to pay off the mortgage on her house. Explaining that she "sold the shadow to support the substance," Truth also peddled small photographs of herself—*cartes-de-visite* and cabinet cards—in person and through the mail. Perhaps these women chafed at having to sell their books and pictures at "camp meetings, quarterly meetings, in the public streets," but they desperately needed the money. With no reliable source of income, they had to find a way to pay their bills while still remaining true to their callings.[66]

Besides these crucial financial considerations, female preachers also published their writings out of a larger sense of religious mission. At least fifteen women sent articles or letters to religious periodicals, and although they may have enjoyed seeing their names in print, they received no money for their contributions. Writing was hard work, especially for women who were not well educated, but by explaining their beliefs in the press, they hoped to minister to more sinners than they could ever meet face-to-face. Driven to save souls, they used every available means to preach the gospel.

In a newly mobile society where thousands of people heeded the cry to go west, these women hoped to build a community of saints that transcended geographical boundaries. In a culture intoxicated by the promise of open land and greater prosperity, family and church ties often seemed tenuous, but preachers tried to knit Christians together in a shared world of print. By publishing journals such as the *Christian Palladium*, which included "religious intelligence" from many different states, they created a truly national community of believers. After moving from New York to Pennsylvania, for example, Mary Stevens Curry felt cut off from her former "brothers and sisters," but she soon discovered that she could still "preach" to them through the pages of the *Palladium*, the Christian Connection's largest journal. Writing in 1839, she explained, "I think I do feel thankful for the use of my pen, that I can communicate my feelings to the saints scattered abroad with whom I have taken sweet council."[67] Wherever her pilgrimage took her, the press anchored her to a spiritual family that knew no bounds.

Theologically, female preachers used the press to express their opinions on such controversial issues as baptism, open Communion, and sanctification. Despite their anti-intellectualism, they were quite intelligent, and they seemed to relish arguing about theological doctrines with one another and with the leaders of their sects. For example, at a time when many Methodist and African Methodists questioned the popular belief in sanctification, both black and white female preachers used their writings to defend the possibility of attaining "spiritual perfection" in this life. Ignoring clerical opposition, Jarena Lee included a detailed account of her sanctification in both the 1836 and 1849 editions of her memoir. Other women tackled such weighty problems as the immortality of the soul or the Atonement.[68]

On a more mundane level, female preachers also used the press to publicize where their meetings would be held. Like platform speakers, who used newspaper advertisements and handbills to announce their lectures, they sent letters to religious periodicals listing their upcoming meetings. For example, in a small item published in the *Christian Palladium* in 1842, Sally Thompson informed readers that she and her husband were beginning a preaching tour that

Jarena Lee. Frontispiece to *Religious Experience and Journal of Mrs. Jarena Lee, Giving the Account of Her Call to Preach the Gospel* (1849). Courtesy of the American Antiquarian Society.

would take them to Maine. Similarly, in the *Christian Herald* in 1841, Elleanor Knight disclosed that she would be leading meetings in Rhode Island for several more months.[69] After reading these letters, both the devout and the curious knew where to go to hear a sermon by a female preacher. Given the size of women's meetings, which reportedly swelled into the hundreds or even thousands, their promotional tactics proved immensely successful.

In addition to books and articles, female preachers also relied on photographs to "sell" themselves to the public. In 1849, when Jarena Lee published a second edition of her memoir, she shrewdly decided to include a picture of herself next to the title page. Painfully aware of rumors that she was a jezebel, she purposefully did not include an image of herself shouting or weeping in the pulpit. Instead, she is shown sitting quietly at a desk with a pen in her hand and a Bible clearly in view in the foreground. Dressed in a very simple bonnet

Sojourner Truth. Unknown photographer (1864). Courtesy of the National Portrait Gallery.

and a shawl that covers most of her body, hiding it from view, she gazes slightly upward to heaven in quiet communion with God. Frozen in time for the American public, she does not look uneducated or uncouth, but scholarly, genteel, and utterly "feminine."[70] By carefully controlling both the content of her text and her visual representation, she tried to convince the evangelical public to respect her as a black "lady" who was also an instrument of God.

Because she was illiterate, Sojourner Truth was especially attracted to the new medium of photography. Although she collaborated with Olive Gilbert, a white reformer, on the *Narrative of Sojourner Truth*, a book she hoped would dispel many of the myths about her, she ultimately had little control over how her story was interpreted. For example, Gilbert described Truth as a powerful, charismatic preacher, but she also criticized her for not being a better mother. In her photographs, however, Truth had more control over her image, and like Lee, she chose to emphasize her middle-class gentility. Sitting up straight in a chair with her knitting on her lap and a book at her elbow, she gazes at the viewer with quiet dignity. Instead of allowing herself to be degraded as a "piteous slave mother," "an amusing naif," or an African "exotic," as Nell Painter has commented, she challenged people to look beyond the stereotypes of black womanhood.[71] She presented herself as an intelligent, refined woman who would be perfectly at home in a bourgeois parlor.

Yet even though these women repeatedly underscored their respectability, they ultimately hoped to "sell" an alternative model of womanhood to the one they found in pious memoirs and sentimental novels. Besides using their books, articles, and photographs to present themselves as ladies, they also tried to create a more expansive, flexible definition of women's sphere. In the vibrant world of revivalism that they showed their readers, pious women were far different from the swooning religious heroines of fiction: they were brave, independent, adventuresome, smart, capable, and confident. Indeed, in a striking omission that many readers must have noticed, they focused so single-mindedly on their public careers that they barely mentioned their domestic responsibilities. Although Sojourner Truth was photographed knitting, Nancy Towle discussed her household duties only once, when she complained about the drudgery of sewing and mending her own clothes.[72]

Female preachers' books shared little in common with the scores of women's narratives circulating in the first half of the nineteenth century, many of which were published as posthumous tributes to particularly devout women. Carefully edited by clergymen and middle-class matrons, these books praised women for leading charitable societies, visiting families as home missionaries, and teaching Sunday school, but they also emphasized the virtues of domesticity. For example, when Sarah Ingraham edited the journal of Margaret Prior, a member of the Moral Reform Society in New York City, she began by apologizing for Prior's public activism. "Lest the reader should suppose . . . that the beloved subject of this memoir was led by her interest for others to neglect the duties of *home*," she explained, "it may be proper to state, that the united testimony of her family, and of all who knew her, would prove the reverse of this." Even though Prior was reputed to have "preached the gospel" to as many as 350 families a month, Ingraham took pains to note that she was also a skillful housekeeper who ran her kitchen with "system and order."[73] Hoping to influence the way women would read Prior's story, Ingraham did not portray her as a "masculine" woman who had forsaken her family, but as a true woman who had combined public service with domesticity.

Prior's memoir, like hundreds of other female narratives that were published in the first half of the nineteenth century, was printed posthumously. After she died, her friends thought her story should become public, but while she was alive, they never would have suggested that she promote herself so audaciously. According to codes of middle-class domesticity, any woman who would willingly expose herself to a public audience was not truly a woman at all. Even though large numbers of women joined reform and benevolent organizations and worked for charities, advice books admonished them not to "mingle in any of the great public movements of the day." In 1831 Sarah Josepha Hale, the editor of the popular *Ladies Magazine*, warned her readers, "It is only in emergencies, in cases where duty demands the sacrifice of female sensitiveness, that a lady of sense and delicacy will come before the public, in a manner to make herself conspicuous." Tellingly, the Reverend Alfred Lee, an Episcopalian minister, decided to publish the memoirs of one of his parishioners, Susan Allibone, under the title *A Life Hid with Christ in God*.[74]

In contrast, even though female preachers knew that true women were supposed to "hide" themselves, they boldly published their narratives while they were still very much alive. On the surface, they conformed to convention by apologizing for being "too *assuming*,—and of aspiring too much, for *vain-glory*," and Harriet Livermore even described herself as a "victim" who had "martyred" herself by allowing people to peer into her private religious life. Despite these protests, however, female preachers had complete control over the information they conveyed to the public, and they simultaneously echoed and repudiated codes of middle-class "femininity."[75] No matter how much they may have envied women such as Susan Allibone, whose respectability went unquestioned, they did not want their lives to be "hidden with Christ in God."

In a decision that made them far more daring than most female novelists, female preachers published their books under their own names. "I send forth nothing anonymous," Harriet Livermore wrote. "I detest it." Even though she described herself as a "spectacle and sufferer," she appeared self-assured in comparison to middle-class, bestselling writers such as Susan Warner. As Mary Kelley has explained, nineteenth-century female authors grappled with "conflict, ambivalence, and guilt" because of their fears about trespassing beyond their sphere. They implicitly asserted themselves by telling their stories in print, but they vehemently denied any pretensions to being artists or "creators of culture." Insisting that they had become writers out of financial need, not self-fulfillment, they portrayed themselves as private women who had been unwittingly pulled onto a public stage. Many were so anxious to protect their privacy that they used aliases to conceal their true identities: Susan Warner published her books anonymously under the pen name "Elizabeth Wetherell," and Sara Payson Willis disguised herself as "Fanny Fern."[76] Unlike female preachers, they shuddered at the thought of strangers knowing their real names or the details of their personal lives.

What made female preachers so remarkable was how openly they marketed their new model of active, evangelical womanhood. Despite condemning people who yearned for "worldly honor" or "a vain show," they also frankly admitted their desire to make their lives public. By sharing their life stories, they hoped to convince their readers, especially their female readers, that there was nothing inherently unfeminine about women's religious leadership. More ambitiously, they also hoped to inspire future generations of women to preach the gospel. As Nancy Towle explained, she wrote her memoir "for the encouragement of my *own sex*, that may succeed me in the *Lord's vineyard*."[77] By publishing an account of both her triumphs and her "vicissitudes," she hoped to convince women that they could become not only missionaries, moral reformers, or Sunday school teachers, but also preachers.

Hoping to create an enduring tradition of female evangelism, female preachers tried to give younger women the knowledge and strength they would need to survive as strangers and pilgrims. Since so many female preachers had been tormented by feelings of despair and isolation early in their careers, they tried to reassure their "sisters" that they were not alone. Other women had experienced the same doubts and fears before them, and others had been inspired by the biblical stories of Deborah, Hannah, and Phebe. Ironically, nineteenth-century female preachers did not know that they themselves had been cut off from the stories of eighteenth-century female evangelists such as Bathsheba Kingsley, but intuitively they understood the power of collective memory. Because Ellen Stewart had once longed for a female mentor, she passed down her memoir to "my own sex, that they may be encouraged by my comforts and success."[78] Knowledge, she believed, was power.

Although Stewart and other female preachers were eventually forgotten, their stories buried in the flow of history, they had a powerful effect on many of the women in their sects. Indeed, many of the most successful itinerants of the 1820s, 1830s, and 1840s had been inspired by older Sisters in Christ or Mothers in Israel who had comforted them during times of despair. Abigail Roberts and Mary Stevens decided to preach after meeting Nancy Cram, and Nancy Towle was converted by Clarissa Danforth. Unfortunately for the young Harriet Livermore, she did not know a single female preacher, but after hearing stories of the courageous women who were traveling throughout western New York, she yearned to "sit at their feet." For the first time, she realized that she was part of a larger religious movement, a new evangelical community where women as well as men could preach the gospel. In later life, she encouraged Sarah Righter Major to become the first female preacher for the Church of the Brethren. For the rest of her life, she always described Major as her spiritual daughter.[79]

What Livermore wanted to sell to the public was nothing less than a new vision of female religious leadership, and she was willing to use both the press and the pulpit to make her voice heard. Despite her opposition to the values of the market revolution, she borrowed its techniques in order to publicize her evangelical theology and her defense of female preaching. Financially, she reaped few rewards, and like other female preachers, she knew what it meant to be poor. In 1843, according to John Quincy Adams, she was "so totally destitute" on Christmas Day that she had "only three borrowed potatoes and half an ounce of bread for nourishment." Her father had died in 1832, and most of her siblings seem to have ignored, if not disowned, her. Only her eldest brother, Samuel, tried to help her, but the annuity he left her in his will never reached her. Sadly, the woman who had once railed against consumer excess was finally forced to join the ranks of the peddlers whom she so detested, selling patent pills from door to door. By 1864, when she published her last book, *Thoughts on Important Subjects*—a rambling, circuitous, and sometimes incoherent vindication of biblical literalism and female evangelism— she was so lonely and heartbroken that she continually referred to herself as "poor Harriet."[80]

Despite her sorrows, however, Livermore took comfort from knowing that she had devoted her life to God, not mammon, and she was grateful to count women such as Sarah Righter Major as her spiritual children. With the help of many other preachers, both male and female, she forced an entire generation of evangelicals to question whether women should keep silence in the churches. Because of her success at marketing her beliefs to the American public, she helped to stimulate a national debate over female evangelism, a debate which centered on the very meaning of womanhood and domesticity.

Part Three

Let Your Women Keep Silence

Let your women keep silence in the churches: for it is not permitted unto them to speak; but they are commanded to be under obedience as also saith the law. And if they will learn any thing, let them ask their husbands at home: for it is a shame for women to speak in the church.—1 Corinthians 14:34–35

7

Suffer Not a Woman to Teach

The Battle over Female Preaching

Let the woman learn in silence with all subjection. But I suffer not a woman to teach, nor to usurp authority over the man, but to be in silence.—1 Timothy 2:11–12

In 1822 Sally Thompson traveled to Smithfield, Rhode Island, to preach at a Methodist camp meeting. Arriving at the campgrounds, she saw hundreds of people falling to their knees in prayer, crying aloud in anguish, and clapping their hands in joy. Countless numbers of curious spectators mingled with the devout, walking from tent to tent and marveling at the sights and sounds of "oldtime" religion. Some of the people in the crowd carried Bibles in their hands; others took furtive sips from bottles tucked inside their coats. Some listened intently as strolling preachers beseeched them to repent and be saved; others made fun of the preachers' shabby clothing and coarse language. But all turned their attention to the center of the campgrounds when they realized that Thompson, a woman, was climbing into the preacher's stand to deliver a sermon.

One of the people who listened to Thompson preach that afternoon was Catherine Williams, an educated, liberal woman who prided herself on her support of female evangelism.[1] Winding her way through the boisterous crowd, she managed to find a seat on a log in front of the preacher's stand, where she waited excitedly for Thompson to begin her sermon. Williams had heard Thompson preach on one occasion before, and she had been delighted by her "mild and pleasing manners" and her "plain good sense." When she saw

"Camp Meeting of the Methodists in North America" (1820). While a large crowd listens to a group of ministers, a man behind the preacher's stand swoons to the ground. Courtesy of the Billy Graham Center Museum.

her "favourite" again on the campgrounds, however, her "faith in woman's preaching began to waver." To her surprise and dismay, Thompson appeared disturbingly "masculine." Straining to be heard above the commotion, she raised her voice to such a pitch that "the blood looked as though it would burst through her face, the veins of her forehead and temples as well as those of her neck, 'swelled up like whip cords,' and her mouth, usually of sweet and placid expression, from her efforts to speak loud, was absolutely disfigured." She looked, according to Williams, like a woman who had gone "out of her place." Despite the eloquence of her sermon, her "contortions of countenance" had utterly "destroyed the effect."[2]

Fortunately for Thompson, not all of the people who heard her preach at the Smithfield camp meeting reacted so negatively. By 1822, she had been preaching for a little more than a year, and she had become a celebrated Methodist evangelist in Boston, where she lived with her husband. In contrast to middle-class critics like Williams, many Methodists argued that she had been genuinely called to save sinners from damnation. One particularly sympathetic clergyman, V. R. Osborn, urged her to continue preaching no matter how much persecution she might endure. "God has called you to exercise your talent publicly," he wrote. "And if you intend to reach heaven, you must continue to exercise it." Other Methodist ministers commended her as an "exemplary" Christian and offered to help pay her traveling expenses.

By 1830, however, Thompson had begun to lose the support of the Methodist hierarchy that had once defended her. Sometime during the late 1820s, she moved to a new home in Herkimer County in New York, and without the fellowship of her religious community in Boston, she met greater opposition than ever before. At first, "Brother" Hall, the most prominent local clergyman, allowed her to hold meetings, but unfortunately he changed his mind after "Brother" Grant, who was more conservative, was added to the circuit. Worried by their antagonism, Thompson tried to reassure them that she had no intention of undermining their authority, but to no avail. Even though she rarely traveled to a church without an invitation, or spoke until the presiding minister had opened the meeting, or stepped into the pulpit without first making an apology, her ministers thought she seemed too "masculine." At a Quarterly Meeting in 1830, they passed a resolution that "none of the brethren should convey [her] to or from a meeting; no collection or subscription should be taken up for [her]; that no meeting should be appointed for [her], and that they should not tell the people that [she] would be there."[3] Echoing the words of Catherine Williams, who had been horrified by Thompson's breach of "feminine" decorum, Methodist circuit riders insisted she had gone out of her place.

If Thompson had been less confident, she might have decided to give up her preaching career in order to avoid a confrontation with the clergy. As a crusading Mother in Israel, however, she continued to labor in the harvest, ignoring or ridiculing the men who warned her not to "teach." With absolute faith in her call, she implied that anyone who tried to prevent her from preaching was an instrument not of Jesus, but of Satan. As a result, she was ordered to appear in front of a committee of Methodist elders to face disciplinary action. The charges against her were serious: she was accused of evil speaking, immorality, and insubordination to the church.

In June of 1830, Brother Hall presided over Thompson's church trial in Cherry Valley, New York, in front of a crowd of as many as 250 or 300 people. After commanding Thompson to "be silent," depriving her of the right to testify in her own defense, he opened the trial by explaining that she had violated Methodist rules by holding meetings without clerical approval. Even worse, she had supposedly mocked any minister who dared to oppose her as a "snake in the grass," a "spy," or, in the choice words she reserved for Grant, an "enemy to the work of God."[4] Despite her claims to be a humble Christian, she had willfully fomented dissension within the Methodist Church.

In Thompson's account of her trial, which she published several years later in order to clarify the "facts," she expressed astonishment that she ever had been accused of insubordination. Even though she expected "worldly" people like Catherine Williams to condemn her, she thought that the Methodists, her spiritual family, genuinely understood her divine mission. By 1830, she had been a Methodist preacher for at least nine years, and despite grumblings from individual ministers, she had never been threatened with church discipline before. "It is extraordinary at this later period, to call my course in question," she protested. Despite admitting that she might have "spoken lightly" of ministers who questioned "female rights," she denied being guilty of evil speaking or immorality. Most important, she defended female preaching as an honest effort to "reform and convert the children of men." Citing the example of Mary Fletcher, one of the first Methodist preachers in England, she argued that Wesley himself had befriended many female "laborers."

Forbidden to testify at her own trial, Thompson relied on her supporters to speak on her behalf. Unanimously, they portrayed her as a sincere, faithful preacher who had "been the instrument of great good." One minister "spoke highly of her and praised her," and another noted that his congregation had "immediately increased after she commenced her labors." When a less tolerant man complained that she "moved in too large a sphere," two lay women retorted that she "behaved very well."[5] In total, almost two dozen witnesses testified at Thompson's trial, and although they often disagreed about details, few questioned her commitment to saving sinners. Despite Hall's accusations, the committee of elders pronounced her "not guilty."

Before Thompson could savor her victory, however, Hall announced that he would appeal her case to the Methodist Quarterly Meeting. Two months later, in August of 1830, she received a letter telling her that she had been excommunicated from her church on the grounds of insubordination. No matter how much individual clergymen might admire her, they could no longer allow her to preach to their congregations unless they wanted to risk discipline themselves. Siding with Hall and Grant, the Methodist hierarchy decided that female preaching was unacceptable under any circumstances.

Despite Thompson's popularity in the pulpit, she had become an outcast, a disorderly woman who no longer could be suffered to teach.

Thompson's trial was a harbinger of the sweeping backlash against female preaching that took place during the 1830s and 1840s. It began among socially conservative ministers and lay people, including women such as Catherine Williams, who were alarmed by the growing popularity of female evangelists, and it accelerated under the leadership of Methodists, African Methodists, Freewill Baptists, and Christians who wanted to build their small, counter-cultural churches into successful denominations. Recapitulating the history of the eighteenth-century Separates and Baptists, they traded their tradition of female evangelism for greater power and respectability. As early as 1830 among the Methodists, and later in the decade among the other denominations, clergymen began to deny that they had ever allowed women into the pulpit, rewriting their histories as if Thompson and other female preachers had never existed.

The 1830s and 1840s were difficult decades for female preachers. Besides being slandered as bold and shameless jezebels by mainline clergymen, they also began to lose the institutional support of the churches who had once defended them. Faced with growing restrictions on their religious speech, they struggled to preserve their identities as redemptive Mothers in Israel and Sisters in Christ. Like Sally Thompson, scores of other female preachers lamented that their Christian brothers and sisters had ordered them to learn in silence with all subjection.

Lost to Modesty and Prudence

Both male and female preachers among the Methodists, African Methodists, Freewill Baptists, and Christians faced opposition in the early nineteenth century. Because their belief in free will threatened the Calvinist orthodoxy, they were verbally and sometimes even physically abused. Clergymen were pushed and shoved, cursed as "Methodist dogs," spat upon, maligned as "heretics and infidels," and threatened with whippings. According to Elias Smith, one of the founders of the Christian Connection, angry mobs tried to force him to stop preaching by beating drums and making "hideous noises" outside of his church.[6] Because he and other Christian Connection preachers denied the doctrine of the Trinity, they seemed especially radical.

Yet no matter how much male preachers were persecuted for their beliefs, they rarely faced the same day in and day out harassment as women. Jabez King remembered encountering "the most opposition, of any place I was ever in," when he preached with Nancy Cram in Ballston, New York. Women, like men, were accused of preaching doctrines that would "destroy the soul," but they were also attacked simply because of their sex. When a group of hostile men confronted Ellen Stewart, they did not quarrel with her about her theology but quoted from "a book full of filthy, and obscene remarks about women."[7] George Keely, a Baptist, argued that any woman who dared to become a preacher, no matter how pious, was "lost to modesty and prudence." "If she were a relative of mine," he wrote in 1819, "I should request her to change her name and remove to a distance where her connections were not known."[8] There was simply no place for a female preacher in respectable society.

Not surprisingly, black female preachers faced even greater hostility than white women. Besides suffering verbal slurs on their character, they were threatened with actual physical violence. For example, Zilpha Elaw once preached in front of a group of angry white men who stood listening to her "with their hands full of stones." On another occasion, she was taunted by "an unusually stout and ferocious looking man" who circled the pulpit as if he intended to strike her.[9] Fortunately, none of these men ever harmed her, but she knew that she put herself at physical risk each time she appeared in public. As a black female preacher, she implicitly challenged the hierarchy of race as well as gender.

Female preachers were locked out of meetinghouses, booed by angry spectators, and ordered to "stay at home."[10] Often their sermons were interrupted by the sounds of jeers and catcalls. Most insulting, as we have seen in earlier chapters, they were forced to answer questions about their essential femininity and sexual morality. Even though they described themselves in domestic terms as Mothers in Israel or Sisters in Christ, they were accused of being either shrews or prostitutes. According to Jonathan Stearns, a Presbyterian, women could not speak publicly without sacrificing their womanly virtues. A "masculine woman," he warned, "is always despised." After Nancy Towle preached in Virginia, a Presbyterian minister wrote a letter to a newspaper implying that she was not a woman, but a man *"in the costume of a female."* No real woman would want to become a preacher.[11]

There was no collective, organized opposition to female preaching before the 1830s, but without a doubt, women's most vocal and influential critics were mainline clergymen who traced their heritage back to the established churches of colonial America. Most Congregationalists, Episcopalians, Presbyterians, and Dutch Reformed took the words of Paul literally—"Let your women keep silence in the churches"—and they absolutely forbade women to preach or even pray aloud in public.[12] According to E. F. Newell, a Methodist, Calvinist churches were "bitterly opposed" to women's public religious speech. When a Freewill Baptist woman made the mistake of interrupting a Congregationalist minister while he was preaching, her "tirade" was cut short by the "muscular Christianity of two or three of the congregation."[13] Despite her claim to divine inspiration, she was forcibly carried out of the church.

Why were mainline clergymen (not to mention their congregations) so opposed to female preaching? First, it is important to remember that they forbade *all* lay people, whether male or female, from speaking during meetings. In contrast to lower-class Methodists and Freewill Baptists, who likened themselves to Christ's humble disciples, they argued that ministers needed to be educated in order to interpret Scripture. Determined to maintain Christian order, they scoffed at visionaries who claimed to be guided by the Holy Spirit. The age of revelation had ended, and faith, as Paul had explained, needed to be nurtured by understanding.

Second, mainline clergymen, like other evangelicals, read the Bible as the literal word of God, and they genuinely believed that women did not have the right to "teach" men. This may be an obvious point, but it is worth emphasizing. Whatever else may have motivated them, these men believed they were defending the truth of the Bible. Even though they acknowledged that many biblical women had prophesied, they denied that Jesus had ever accepted women as his apostles. Citing a verse from Corinthians, they also pointed out that Paul, who had been inspired by Christ, had ordered women to "keep silence in the churches"—an injunction that seemed indisputably clear. As one Presbyterian minister explained, Paul's prohibition against female preaching was a "positive, explicit, and universal rule."[14] Despite women's objections, no other interpretation of his words was possible. Female preaching was a sin against God.

Rejecting this moralistic language, women suggested that ministers opposed them for more selfish reasons as well. According to Nancy Towle (who could be rather arrogant at times), many of the clergymen who refused to let her preach were motivated not by theological conviction, but by jealousy. At a time when Protestant denominations were openly competing for converts, a Presbyterian minister groused that a woman who "pretended" to preach the gospel "would draw together more people than those who preached it in truth and sincerity!" As Towle explained, "Many high-minded men, are aggravated to see a greater congregation, to hear a woman, than they could gain themselves." Annoyed by her popularity and frustrated by their inability to compete with her, they tried to discredit her on the grounds of her sex.[15]

Without more evidence, it is impossible to know whether mainline ministers were actually jealous of women such as Towle, or simply disdainful. Nevertheless, many do seem to have viewed female preaching as a symbol of their crumbling authority in the wake of church disestablishment. In 1832, when Massachusetts became the last state to sever the link between church and state, churches in America could no longer claim to be part of the formal public of government, but only the informal public of reform organizations, charities, and missions—a truncated public that carried far less power and prestige. Even though the Congregationalist, Presbyterian, and Dutch Reformed clergy accepted the principle of religious liberty, they lacked the political and intellectual authority that their colonial forefathers had taken for granted.[16] Cut off from state support, they may have resented having to compete in a new spiritual marketplace with "illiterate" farmers, sailors, and women. Indeed, if they were offended by the popularity of men like Abraham Snethen, who proudly described himself as the "barefoot preacher," they must have found it especially demeaning to compete with "jezebels" like Nancy Towle.

Ironically, however, these men may have inadvertently encouraged women to demand greater leadership roles in the church. After church disestablishment, mainline ministers felt pushed to the sidelines of American culture, and in the midst of a profound crisis of self-confidence, they increasingly relied on their female congregants—the majority of their church members—for legitimacy and respect. In countless sermons and tracts, they praised women for their piety and morality, not to mention their powerful influence over their children. "God made mothers before he made ministers," affirmed Theodore Cuyler, a Presbyterian. "There is a ministry that is older and deeper and more potent than ours. It is the ministry that presides over the crib and impresses the first gospel influence on the enfant soul."[17] Inspired by such glowing tributes to their authority, women could claim the awesome power to determine the character of the future generation, to save the world from sin.

Yet even though Cuyler and other ministers glorified the virtues of "femininity," they were determined to exclude women from positions of real institutional power. At the same time as they praised women for their moral influence, they tried to prevent them from becoming missionaries or Sunday school teachers. A few of the most conservative even objected to women's early benevolent and reform activities on the grounds that they were "ostentatious." According to the Reverend Walter Harris, women were inherently pious, but they could not be "public teachers of religion, nor take part in the active government of his church." Their role was far more subtle, but supposedly far more important: they could "strengthen the hands of the faithful ministers of the Gospel." Despite their "pulpit envy," women had to reconcile themselves to being men's helpmates, not preachers in their own right.[18]

Like many other Americans in the first decades of the nineteenth century, these ministers were troubled by the rapid pace of economic and social change, and they hoped that women could protect the "feminine" ethic of love against the "masculine" values of competitiveness and ambition. Ambivalent about the disruptions caused by economic growth, ministers urged women to create warm, nurturing homes in order to shelter their families from the harsh realities of an industrializing economy. By cultivating the virtues of domesticity, women could create a haven from the impersonal world of work, a retreat from the pressures of a capitalist market. "Women are the bonds of society," one minister explained in 1839. "The habits of men are too commercial and restrained, too bustling and noisy, too ambitious and repellent."[19] Only women had the power to knit together American culture by sustaining the values of hearth and home.

Certain that women belonged to a separate sphere, and worried about their own declining influence in American culture, mainline ministers stepped up their attacks against female evangelism during the 1830s. Between 1820 and 1830, growing numbers of women exhorted during love feasts and class meetings, and even more worrisome, a small but vocal army of Mothers in Israel and Sisters in Christ crisscrossed the country as itinerants. All told, at least five women began their preaching careers during the 1790s, six from 1800 to 1809, ten from 1810 to 1819, and twenty-nine more during the 1820s. If these women had been content to stay within their own local communities, they might have attracted little notice, but instead, they published scores of books and articles and traveled to countless numbers of churches across New England, the Mid-Atlantic, and the Midwest. With alarm, mainline ministers began to realize that their warnings to keep silence had done little to stem the tide of female preaching. By 1830, female preachers were more visible, more popular, and more aggressive than ever before.

Mainline ministers seem to have been especially troubled by the increasing acceptance of female evangelism within their own ranks. Experimenting with new forms of revivalism, a small number of Presbyterian and Congregationalist clergymen began to imitate lower-class evangelicals by allowing women to pray aloud, testify, and exhort. Charles Finney, the most influential, created a storm of controversy by encouraging women as well as men to testify in "promiscuous" prayer meetings. (His other innovations, all borrowed from the Methodists, included preaching in colloquial language, praying for converts by name, and inviting sinners to come forward to the "anxious" bench.) As Finney had hoped, his "new measures" helped kindle a widespread revival in Utica, New York, in 1825 and 1826, but even though he brought hundreds of middle-class merchants and shopkeepers (not to mention their wives) into the Presbyterian fold, his colleagues feared that he had opened a Pandora's box of female radicalism. "Whoever introduces the practise of females praying in promiscuous assemblies, will ere long find, to his sorrow, that he has made an inlet to other innovations," Asahel Nettleton predicted. Nevertheless, when eighteen ministers convened in 1827 in New Lebanon, New York, to debate Finney's new measures, they were unable to reach a consensus on whether women should be allowed to pray aloud in "social meetings" for "religious worship."[20] Conservative "Old School" and more liberal "New School" Presbyterians continued to argue about female evangelism in the decades leading up to the Civil War.

Despite continuing controversy after the New Lebanon Convention, however, growing numbers of Congregationalists and New School Presbyterians allowed women to testify and exhort during prayer meetings. As the Reverend Theodore Weld remembered, he often heard people debating about women's right to pray publicly, but he could not find "one in ten who *believed* it was unscriptural. They grieved and said perhaps, and that they didn't know, and they *were opposed* to it, and that it [was] not best; but yet the practice of female praying in promiscuous meetings grew every day." During the mid-1840s, Ellen Stewart was shocked to hear a Congregational minister in Ohio encourage the "sisters" as well as the "brethren" to speak during prayer meetings. "Speak loud, sisters," he prompted, "as loud as you do when you scold at your children. Take pattern by your Methodist sisters—you can hear them across the room."[21] Inspired by the success of the Methodists, this minister urged women not to keep silence if they felt inspired by the Holy Spirit.

Other ministers blatantly ignored denominational rules by inviting particularly popular female preachers, perhaps out of curiosity, to visit their congregations. In 1826, for example, the Presbytery of Philadelphia censured two different churches for allowing an itinerant female preacher into the pulpit. (The anonymous woman was probably Harriet Livermore, who spoke in several Philadelphia churches that year.) Ten years later, in 1836, the Presbytery of New York reprimanded a Pittsburgh church for the same offense.[22] As female preachers liked to boast, they spoke not only to Christians, Methodists, and Freewill Baptists, but to Congregationalists, Presbyterians, Episcopalians, Brethren, Lutherans, and Dutch Reformed.

To the eyes of mainline ministers, female preaching resembled a contagious disease: it spread from denomination to denomination instead of staying confined to a few countercultural sects. As early as 1811, Maria Cook, the daughter of a Presbyterian minister, preached at a Universalist meeting in Jericho, New York, to "multitudes." As one clergyman remembered, some of his colleagues were "a little fastidious about allowing a woman to preach, supposing that St. Paul forbade it," but under pressure from the laity, they finally consented: "And there was not a sermon delivered with more eloquence, with more correctness of diction, or pathos . . . as the one she delivered." Following in her footsteps, Sarah Barnes Dunn, another Universalist, became a well-known preacher and reformer in Maine.[23]

Like the Universalists, the United Brethren also allowed at least two women into the pulpit. In 1841 "Sister" Courtland claimed that she had been called to "public work," and although Brethren leaders could not decide whether she should be a preacher or exhorter, they accepted her call as genuine. After appointing a committee to discuss her case, they gave her their written consent to use "her gifts and callings in promoting the cause of Christ on earth."[24] Two years later, Laura Clemens, another female preacher, asked to be set apart as a minister by the laying on of hands. Not surprisingly, the Brethren refused, but there is no evidence that they forbade her to speak publicly or excommunicated her from the church. Much to the dismay of more socially conservative ministers, they believed that it was possible (although perhaps not desirable) to reconcile female preaching with the Bible.

Worst of all, even a few iconoclastic Presbyterians and Congregationalists questioned whether women should learn in silence with all subjection. Although the evidence is decidedly slim, there are a few clues that female preaching began to spread into the formerly established churches during the late 1820s and 1830s. As they lost their formal connection to the state, they became more tolerant of female evangelism. For example, when Nancy Towle visited Nova Scotia in 1827, she was shocked to meet a female preacher who was a "rigid Calvinist." In 1830 David Marks met a Presbyterian woman named Mrs. Gibbs who was suffered to speak not only in her church's private devotional meetings, but during Sunday worship as well. Perhaps because of clerical opposition, Gibbs later transferred her allegiance to the Freewill Baptists, but for at least a short time, she managed to convince her congregation to allow her into the pulpit. Surprisingly, the first American woman to be ordained was not a Methodist, Freewill Baptist, or Christian, but a Congregationalist who had studied with Charles Finney at Oberlin. In 1853 Antoinette Brown Blackwell was ordained by a local Congregational church in South Butler, New York.[25]

Besides fearing that female preaching had begun to gain acceptance within their own churches, mainline ministers also worried—with good reason—that it had paved the way for more radical kinds of women's activism. As early as the mid-1820s, platform speakers such as Frances Wright, Sarah and Angelina Grimké, and Abby Kelley began delivering public lectures on abolitionism and women's rights, and unlike female preachers, who tended to be theologically and socially conservative, they demanded sweeping political change. Rejecting the words of Paul to the Corinthians, "The man is the head of the woman," they demanded nothing less than the "perfect equality" of the sexes.[26]

By far the most controversial female lecturer was Fanny Wright, who went on a tour of American cities in 1828 that sparked widespread notice in the press. Speaking to packed audiences in Cincinnati, Philadelphia, New York, and Boston, she proposed a stunning variety of reforms: women's rights, the abolition of slavery, divorce, and birth control. No topic was too scandalous for her. Besides arguing that marriage was akin to slavery (because it unfairly deprived women of their independence), she argued that the best solution to America's race problem was miscegenation—the sexual mixing of whites with blacks. At the height of the Second Great Awakening, she also dared to question whether religion might be "*injurious* to virtue," describing institutional Christianity as "priestcraft." As a result, she was christened as the "Red Harlot of Infidelity."[27]

Other female platform speakers took pains to identify themselves as Christians, but they too criticized the clergy. Sarah Grimké, an Episcopalian who became a Quaker, claimed that ministers selfishly excluded women from the pulpit in order to preserve their own honor, money, and power. Rather than trying to protect female "purity," they had deliberately and systematically deprived women of their God-given rights. "From the days of Eve to the present time," she wrote angrily, "the aim of man has been to crush her. He has accomplished this work in various ways; sometimes by brute force, sometimes by making her subservient to his worst passions, sometimes by treating her as a doll." Using far more radical rhetoric than most female preachers, she railed against ministers who taught women to worship *men* rather than God.[28]

As "equalitarian" feminists who denied the principle of women's divinely ordained subordination, these women suffered even greater persecution than female preachers. Angelina Grimké learned to make herself heard above the sounds of mobs chanting and hissing. Abby Kelley, a white antislavery activist, dodged rotten eggs and tobacco spit. And when Fanny Wright spoke in New York City, hecklers broke a windowpane, threw stinkbombs, and set fire to a barrel of turpentine. Because she demanded the reorganization of American society around the equality of the sexes and races, a newspaper editor cursed her as "a bold blasphemer, and a voluptuous preacher of licentiousness."[29]

Nor did these women escape the wrath of the clergy, many of whom were staunchly committed to preserving male authority in the church and family. In 1840, after Abby Kelley asked for permission to speak in front of the Connecticut Anti-Slavery Society, the Reverend Henry Ludlow shouted, "I will not sit in a meeting where the sorcery of a woman's tongue is thrown around my heart. I will not submit to PETTICOAT GOVERNMENT. No woman shall ever lord it over me. I am *Major-Domo* in my own house." Unfortunately, no one found his words absurd (although they certainly sound that way to most modern readers), and the convention refused to allow Kelley or any other women to speak at their meeting.[30] According to most ministers, women were inferior to men by nature, and they had no authority to "rule." If women wanted to help reform society, they would have to learn how to rely on their "feminine" influence, not the power of the platform.

Because female platform speakers, like female preachers, refused to learn in silence with all subjection, the two groups of women were often linked together in the public mind. In many ways, they seemed remarkably similar: they criticized the clergy for barring women from the pulpit; they dressed in plain dresses and bonnets; they opposed the evils of slaveholding; and they spoke against the unbridled pursuit of wealth. Fanny Wright, like scores of evangelical female preachers, complained that economic competition reduced the "whole human race" to "idolaters of gold."[31] At a time when very few women spoke in public, it was deceptively easy to confuse radical female reformers with biblical feminists.

In the most important parallel, almost all of the women who spoke publicly in the early nineteenth century, whether preachers or platform speakers, justified themselves by using religious rhetoric. (The prominent exception, of course, was Fanny Wright.) For example, Sarah Grimké based her claim to equality on "the simple truths revealed in the Scriptures," and Abby Kelley claimed to have been "called." Maria Stewart, an African Methodist, described herself as an "instrument of God" who had been divinely inspired to encourage the "improvement" of her race. In 1833, echoing the words of scores of female preachers and exhorters, she asked: "What if I am a woman? Is not the God of ancient times the God of these modern days? Did he not raise up Deborah, to be a mother, and a judge in Israel? Did not Queen Esther save the lives of the Jews? And Mary Magdalene first declare the resurrection of Christ from the dead?"[32] Like Jarena Lee and Zilpha Elaw before her, she was forced to defend her right to speak as both a woman and a *black* woman, and she drew strength from her faith in God. Placing her life within the sacred narrative of Scripture, she portrayed herself as part of a long biblical tradition of pious female evangelists.

Despite these similarities between female preachers and platform speakers, however, there is no evidence that they saw themselves as part of a coherent movement. Socially, most female reformers came from wealthy, privileged backgrounds, and they had little in common with the poor, uneducated women who traveled into the backcountry as itinerant preachers. Indeed, it is hard to imagine a conversation between Sarah Grimké, the daughter of a southern planter, and Miriam Kent, a visionary "prophetess" from the woods of New Hampshire. Even Maria Stewart, who spent her childhood as a servant in a clergyman's family, never allied herself with lower-class female preachers.[33] Most female reformers demanded comprehensive changes in American politics, and they seem to have been frustrated and disappointed by the biblical feminists in their midst. Even though Sarah Grimké knew that the Methodists and the Christian Connection allowed women to preach, she explained that she, unlike them, believed in the absolute equality of the sexes.[34]

In return, most female preachers seem to have resented being confused with platform-speaking "radicals." Despite their sympathy for Angelina and Sarah Grimké, who shared their hatred of slavery, they did not want to be associated with women who denied their subordination to men. Nor did they want to be linked to Fanny Wright, who scandalized the American public by belittling religion as "the perverter of human virtue, the first link in the chain of evil."[35] Many must have shuddered to read Parsons Cooke's tract, *Female Preaching, Unlawful and Inexpedient*, which compared *all* female preachers, no matter how theologically conservative, to the notorious Wright. According to Cooke, Wright's "deepest condemnation" was not her "licentiousness" or her "infidelity," but her willingness to speak in front of men—a sin shared by every evangelical woman who ascended into the pulpit.[36]

Sadly, evangelical female preachers seem to have believed that the feminist reformers of the 1830s and 1840s hurt them more than they helped them. As one Christian Connection clergyman lamented, "Pious females have been in the weekly, daily habit of proclaiming the truths of religion in the Baptist, Methodist, Christian, and Quaker communities, but the public mind has not been shocked, no panic has been felt, no alarm sounded, until the Misses Grimkés ascended the pulpit or rostrum, to plead the cause of God's suffering poor."[37] Eventually, of course, Sarah and Angelina Grimké helped create a more sexually egalitarian culture, but during the 1830s and 1840s, they caused such a furor that *any* woman who spoke in public, even a theological conservative, seemed inherently dangerous. Ironically, the Grimkés had hoped to convince the American public to allow women into the pulpit, but instead, they inadvertently strengthened the prejudices against female preaching. They could never have foreseen how their battle for female equality would generate a conservative backlash against biblical as well as equalitarian feminists.

During the 1830s, in response to the exaggerated fears of female radicalism, ministers passed a flurry of resolutions forbidding women to pray aloud, lecture, or preach. As growing numbers of women laid claim to the pulpit and the platform, clergymen from a wide variety of denominations—Dutch Reformed, Presbyterian, Church of the Brethren, and Congregationalist— echoed Paul's words to the Corinthians, "Let your women keep silence in the churches." In 1831 the General Synod of the Dutch Reformed Church insisted that female preaching was "not only contrary to the word of God, but ruinous to the benign and permanent influence of pious females in the Church of

Christ." Reflecting their fear of religious "ruin," they also barred women from praying aloud or testifying in "promiscuous" meetings. A year later, in 1832, the General Assembly of the Presbyterians declared that "to teach and exhort, or to lead in prayer, in public and promiscuous assemblies, is clearly forbidden to women in the Holy Oracles."[38] After years of controversy over Finney's new measures, they voted that women could pray aloud in front of other women, but not in front of men.

In 1837, in a pastoral letter that was sent to churches across Massachusetts, the General Association of Congregational Ministers also condemned female preaching. Responding to the controversy caused by Angelina and Sarah Grimké, who had recently begun to deliver public lectures against slavery, they cautioned women to beware of the "dangers" threatening their character. "We appreciate the unostentatious prayers of woman in advancing the cause of religion," they wrote. "But when she assumes the place of man as a public reformer, she yields the power which God has given her for her protection, and her character becomes unnatural. If the vine, whose strength and beauty is to lean on the trellis-work, and half conceal its clusters, thinks to assume the independence and the overshadowing nature of the elm, it will not only cease to bear fruit, but fall in shame and dishonor into the dust." In a few short sentences, these men managed to touch upon virtually every negative stereotype of female preachers and reformers: they were "manly" ("independent" and "overshadowing"), sexually sterile (unable to "bear fruit"), and promiscuous ("fallen"). Over and over again, ministers argued that women who disobeyed Paul's injunction to keep silence were either "too stupid" or "too wicked" to obey God's word.[39]

Echoing these criticisms, conservative lay women also told women to stay within their "appropriate retirement." On one hand, they celebrated women's universal "sisterhood," claiming that all women were linked together by transcendent bonds of femininity, but on the other, they denounced female preachers as traitors to their sex. According to Harriet Livermore, she was "especially" persecuted by other women, who "branded" her with "the odious epithets, bold, immodest, or lunatick." Maria Cook, a Universalist, met many women who thought it was "very improper, and even indecent for a woman to preach, and especially to itinerate as she did." Even Abigail Roberts, a wife and mother of two, once overheard a woman plotting to tar and feather her. Apparently the "bonds of womanhood," no matter how resilient, could not be stretched to include jezebels.[40]

Many nineteenth-century women seem to have been concerned that female preachers were trying to undermine the "cult of domesticity." According to Catharine Beecher, the daughter of Lyman Beecher, a prominent Congregationalist minister, women needed to devote themselves to their families in order to save the new nation from chaos. Even though women were not naturally inferior to men (and in fact, they were *intellectually* equal), they should defer to their husbands and fathers for the greater good of society. Deeply disturbed by the tensions caused by slavery, rapid immigration, and the market revolution, Beecher envisioned a world in which sex—not race, class, or ethnicity—would serve as the primary social division. Ideally, sexual hierarchy would help reduce the inherent conflicts of a democratic society.[41]

Ironically, despite her emphasis on domesticity, Beecher resembled female preachers in more ways than she would have been willing to admit. She was a pious woman who believed that she had been called to serve God; she was deeply ambivalent about the dramatic changes reshaping American culture; and she marketed her beliefs to the public by publishing large numbers of books and articles. In another striking parallel, she argued that women as well as men had been chosen to play a redemptive role in history, particularly in bringing about the millennium. Even though Beecher did not believe in the imminent, apocalyptic destruction of the earth, she avowed that pious women—Joel's prophetic daughters—could save the world from sin.

Nevertheless, Beecher's vision of redemptive womanhood made no place for women's public activism, whether as preachers or reformers. Even though she wanted women to play a central role in national life, she expected them to rely on their private influence instead of subjecting themselves to "the ungoverned violence of mobs, and to sneers and ridicule in public places." Making an example of her own life, she published several books and founded the Hartford Female Seminary, but she still refused to lecture in front of men. Out of "feminine" modesty, she asked her brother to read her speeches for her. Like many other women of her time, she believed that public speaking was strictly a male prerogative.[42]

The battle over female preaching was a battle over women's proper place in nineteenth-century America. When conservative critics attacked female preachers for "exposing" themselves in public, they revealed their most deeply held assumptions about the limitations of women's sphere. If Mothers in Israel and Sisters in Christ truly wanted to redeem the world, then they did not belong in the pulpit, but in the home.

Let Your Women Keep Silence

If female preachers were stung by the criticisms of their middle-class opponents, they must have been far more troubled by the shifting tide of opinion within their own sects. During the early nineteenth century, most had been able to depend on the support of sympathetic ministers, but during the 1830s and 1840s, they were increasingly ignored and belittled by the men who had once defended them. As the Christians, Freewill Baptists, Methodists, and African Methodists became more successful, they tried to distance themselves from their earlier tradition of female preaching.

In their formative years, when these sects had been small and struggling, they had depended on both female and male preachers to lead revivals and organize new churches. Because of the shortage of ordained ministers, clerical leaders had warmly praised women such as "Sister" Wiard and Nancy Cram for laboring in God's harvest. Wiard gathered a new Freewill Baptist congregation in Cato, New York, and Cram founded two Christian churches in Ballston and Charleston, New York. Not to be outdone, Abigail Roberts founded at least four Christian churches over the course of her career.[43]

Ironically, however, these women were so effective at leading revivals and saving sinners that they helped build their sects into respectable, middle-class institutions that no longer welcomed their labors. As the Freewill Baptists, Christians, Methodists, and African Methodists grew from small, persecuted sects into flourishing denominations, they deliberately turned away from the experimentation which had marked their early histories. They insisted on an educated clergy, protested against disorderly meetings, and abandoned their earlier support for female preaching.[44] Echoing the words of Paul, they repeatedly warned women to "keep silence in the churches."

There were many factors that contributed to the internal backlash against female preaching during the 1830s and 1840s. First, even though clergymen for the Freewill Baptists, Christians, African Methodists, and Methodists allowed women into the pulpit, they shared the popular fear of female radicals. On one hand, they vigorously defended female preachers from the charge of "Fanny Wrightism," but on the other, they worried that women might overstep the boundaries of their proper authority. When Betsy Niles founded her own sect in the early 1820s, persuading at least two Christian Connection clergymen to become her followers, many ministers wondered whether all female preachers secretly longed to "rule."[45] Later in the decade, as female platform speakers called for a revolution between the sexes, ministers became increasingly suspicious of *any* demands for greater sexual equality, no matter how modest.

Second, the Freewill Baptists, Christians, African Methodists, and Methodists no longer needed women's labors as desperately as they had in the early nineteenth century. Even though the membership of all of these sects continued to grow at a faster rate than the number of clergy, numbers tell only part of the story.[46] For example, the Freewill Baptists suffered from a shortage of ministers throughout the 1830s and 1840s, but they became more efficient as they grew more successful, relying on the detailed reports of their Monthly and Yearly Meetings to decide where preachers were most needed. By assigning ministers to well-defined circuits, they guaranteed that every church in the denomination would be led by a licensed clergyman.

Finally, by the middle of the 1830s, the membership of all these sects had changed. Although the earliest Freewill Baptists and Christians had been poor farmers and artisans, their children and grandchildren were upwardly mobile, and they began to pride themselves on their gentility and refinement. In contrast to Ellen Stewart, who had grown up in a cabin with a dirt floor, her children enjoyed such middle-class niceties as tables and dinner plates. According to Charles Harding, a circuit rider, the earliest Methodists had been "farmers, mechanicks, or day laborers," but by midcentury, the pews were filled with "Methodist lawyers, Methodist Physicians, Methodist merchants," and scores of Methodist politicians.[47] In an ironic twist of history, these sects had become nearly as influential, educated, and affluent as the religious establishment they had once decried.

It is impossible to date exactly when these sects began to outgrow their lower-class roots. It seems to have happened first among the Methodists, who had begun to build large, ornate churches by the 1820s, and last among the Christians, who could still be found worshiping in barns during the 1830s. The transformation did not occur overnight, but came about gradually and almost imperceptibly over the course of more than forty years. Inspired by the Protestant work ethic, converts slowly began to move up the economic ladder, leaving behind their earlier poverty for greater financial security. With the encouragement of their churches, they saved their money, worked hard at their jobs, and tried to build a better future for their children. Year after year, decade after decade, they struggled to move into the same nebulous middle class whose values they had once scorned. Understandably, Ellen Stewart, who had

Wood engraving of St. Paul's Methodist Episcopal Church in New York City (1859). As the Methodists grew more successful, they built large, ornate churches that symbolized their new respectability. Courtesy of the Billy Graham Center Museum.

been hired out as a servant at the age of twelve, did not want her children to grow up in poverty. Dolly Quinby, one of the first Freewill Baptist female preachers, encouraged her son, Hosea, to better himself by attending college. Much to her pride, he became the first college-educated minister in the denomination, and in 1853 he was chosen to become the assistant moderator of the General Conference.[48]

By the middle of the 1840s, the Freewill Baptists, Christians, Methodists, and African Methodists had become far more affluent and powerful than their founders ever had imagined. The Freewill Baptists founded their first church in 1780 with only seven members, but by 1844, their membership had swelled to more than 60,000. In the same year, the Christians estimated their membership at 150,000. Even more dramatically, the Methodists grew into the largest religious denomination in America by 1844, numbering 1,068,525 members, 3,988 itinerant preachers, and 7,730 local preachers.[49] Instead of looking backward to their humble past—a past characterized by female preaching, visionary enthusiasm, and an uneducated ministry—church leaders concentrated on writing theological tracts and sending more ministers to college. No longer religious outsiders, they had built thriving, well-organized denominations with formal creeds and professional clergies.

As they grew more powerful, all of these denominations began to demand an educated ministry. In their early years, the Methodists, Freewill Baptists, and Christians had insisted that the only qualification for ministry was heartfelt religious experience: God called those whom he wanted to serve as his instruments. As Asa C. Morrison reminisced in 1835, "Time was when not a man in the [Christian] Connection would be found who would boldly advocate anything like educating our young men for the ministry. No! the very idea was generally contemned." But as Morrison lamented, the times had changed. In 1840 the Freewill Baptists organized their first Education Society, and by 1847, the Christians had founded three separate institutions to train men for the ministry. Between 1810 and 1819, only 2 percent of new Freewill Baptist ministers had been formally educated, but between 1840 and 1849, 30 percent had been specially trained for the ministry.[50]

This new emphasis on clerical education meant that many preachers, both male and female, were pushed to the sidelines of their denominations. When Brother Halman, a Methodist preacher in New Hampshire, asked the Quarterly Meeting to renew his local preaching license in 1845, they agreed, but only after determining that he had received "a good English education." In contrast to earlier generations of Methodists, who had prized "warm" inspiration more than "cold" book-learning, the Methodist leaders of the 1830s and 1840s believed that faith could be deepened by education. According to Daniel Alexander Payne, the bishop of the African Methodist Church, preachers should master "English Grammar, Geography, Arithmetic, Rollin's Ancient History, Modern History, Ecclesiastical History, [and] Natural and Revealed Theology." If men felt called to serve God, they needed to devote themselves to "diligent and indefatigable study" of the Bible.[51]

Although these new educational requirements must have troubled an older generation of visionary, uneducated clergymen, few seem to have been forced out of the ministry. Once a man had been ordained, or set apart by the laying on of hands, he could not be deprived of his right to preach, perform baptisms, or administer the Lord's Supper simply because of ignorance. (Halman had not yet been ordained when his preaching license was renewed; he was on probation during a trial period.) Even though an uneducated minister could be assigned to a less desirable circuit or scorned as an embarrassment to the denomination, he could not be stripped of his religious authority unless he had grossly violated the code of ministerial conduct.[52] If all else failed, "illiterate" men could try to salvage their reputations by agreeing to study the Bible at one of the many new seminaries.

In contrast, female preachers were shunned as enthusiasts and forced out of the pulpit because of the growing commitment to clerical education. Unlike men, they lacked institutional authority, and they had been allowed to preach only because individual clergymen accepted their claims to divine inspiration. By the 1830s and 1840s, however, most clerical leaders no longer believed that being called was sufficient preparation for the ministry, and they sternly warned their congregations not to put their faith in dreams, visions, or impressions that supposedly had been sent by God.[53] Instead of welcoming female preachers into the pulpit, they disdained them as an embarrassing reminder of their anti-intellectual, visionary past.

At the same time as the Methodists, Freewill Baptists, and Christians demanded a male, educated clergy, they also tried to distance themselves from the fervor of their early revival meetings. Because they wanted to attract more middle-class members, they urged converts to behave with greater restraint and decorum. In 1833 a Christian connection clergyman protested that "there are some among us, who seem inclined to testify their zeal in the service of God, by loud and frequent shouting, stamping of feet, clapping of hands, &c, to the great annoyance of those who wish to worship in a becoming manner." Significantly, he suggested that the men and women most guilty of "screeching" and "screaming" belonged to "the ignorant and lower classes."[54] Even though these "ignorant" men and women had been the ones who had built the earliest Christian Connection churches with their time and money, a new generation of educated ministers did not want to be reminded of their humble origins. In their desire to appear as respectable as their Congregational and Presbyterian colleagues, they discouraged the "disorderly" behavior that had once made them so popular among the "lower classes."

The effect of this new emphasis on order and decorum was to limit lay participation in religious meetings. Even though men and women continued to testify or exhort during services, ministers tried to prevent them from speaking too long or too fervently, urging them "not to ramble." By 1842, Abner Jones, one of the founders of the Christian Connection, expressed regret that he had ever encouraged lay people to speak during worship. "I do not believe that *every man, woman, and child* who are converted, have gifts to speak in public meetings," he asserted. Ironically, the *Christian Palladium* published an article condemning the same "disorderly" practices that the Christians themselves had once promoted: protracted meetings, lay exhorting, "groans and outcries," and "females speaking, and leading in prayer, in promiscuous assemblies."[55] Even though the Christian Connection reluctantly continued to allow women to pray aloud, testify, and exhort during revival and conference meetings, they became increasingly suspicious of female preaching. As a clergyman explained in 1841, women could "tell the story of Calvary, and invite sinners to Christ," but only as exhorters, not preachers. "The ministerial and pastoral office implies *authority*, and, as such, is given exclusively to men," he declared.[56]

As ministers set stricter limits on lay power, they forbade women not only to preach, but to vote on church business. In the early 1800s, many Freewill Baptist and Christian Connection churches had allowed women to vote, but during the 1830s and 1840s, they refused to give them an official voice on church discipline or the selection of new ministers. For example, in 1836 a Christian Connection journal published an article explaining that God had "vested the Government of his Church in the hands of the male members *alone*." Several years later, in 1844, the General Conference of Freewill Baptists reached the same conclusion: "We do not think it right for females to bear rule in the church; but they should be subject to the decision of the male members."[57] Instead of treating women as political equals in the priesthood of all believers, they insisted that they must defer to male authority.

In the midst of all these changes in institutional identity, the Freewill Baptists, Christians, African Methodists and Methodists also shifted their basic theological orientation to American society. Rather than a superficial attempt to fit into mainstream culture, their new attitudes toward church polity, education, and worship signaled a deep transformation in their underlying conception of human progress. No longer content to retreat into countercultural islands of holiness, they imitated middle-class churches (especially the Presbyterians and Congregationalists) by becoming more involved in reform and benevolence organizations. For example, in 1844 the members of a Freewill Baptist church in Northwood, New Hampshire, revised their church covenant to reflect their new commitment to social activism. In the future, all new converts would have to agree to "strive to promote as duty requires the benevolent enterprises of the day, such as the cause of *Temperance, Antislavery, Missions, Sabbath Schools, Education* and every other that may have the present and eternald well being of man kind for its object."[58] Instead of lamenting that secular society was too sinful to be saved, they resolved to make America a more perfect nation.

Theologically, all of these sects tempered their apocalyptic rhetoric as they grew more successful. The change was subtle, but profoundly significant: they still believed in the literal truth of the book of Revelation, but they began to place more emphasis on human agency in gradually bringing about the kingdom of God. Instead of imagining the world as an inherently evil place that had to be destroyed before Christ could return to earth, they wondered whether it might be ultimately perfectible. Inspired by the scale of the revivals, not to mention their own success at winning souls for Christ, they began to wonder whether humans could create a more just society without God's direct, cataclysmic intervention. Even though they still saw America as flawed and full of sin, they refused to see themselves as helpless pawns in the cosmic battle between God and the Antichrist.

From one perspective, this new faith in human progress represented a distinct improvement over an earlier mood of pessimism and despair. Instead of trying to flee from the corruption of the world, the Freewill Baptists, Christians, and Methodists resolved to do battle with evil, to conquer the world for Christ.[59] They founded charities to give money to the poor, orphanages to care for bereaved children, and temperance societies to help alcoholics and their families. They also encouraged missionaries to bring the good news of Christianity to "heathens" in other countries. Undoubtedly, many of them behaved condescendingly toward the people they wanted to help, especially toward foreign "savages," but there is no reason to question the sincerity of their motives. Like other evangelical Protestants in nineteenth-century America, they measured their faith by their works: they believed that true Christians should help the "sinners" in their midst, not ignore or condemn them.

From the standpoint of female preachers, however, this optimistic view of human history threatened to undercut one of their main sources of authority. Since the early 1790s, women had defended their right to preach on the grounds that they were Joel's prophetic daughters, harbingers of the apocalypse, but by the mid-1830s, most evangelicals no longer believed in the imminent destruction of the world. Stripped of its transcendent meaning, female preaching was no longer a miraculous sign of God's grace, but a sin against nature. According to clergymen, women could help to bring about the millennium, but only by fulfilling the domestic duties that God had assigned them in the order of creation.

Perhaps, as historian H. Richard Niebuhr once speculated, all successful American sects eventually mature into denominations. Building on the sociological theories of Max Weber and Ernst Troeltsch, Niebuhr drew a sharp distinction between sects, which begin as protest movements against the religious orthodoxy, and denominations, which are closely allied to "national, economic, and cultural interests." As "churches of the disinherited," sects set themselves apart from the larger culture, but historically, they tend to be short-lived. Within a generation, converts begin to create more formal institutions in order to pass on their beliefs to their children. As Niebuhr explained, "The sect must take on the character of an educational and disciplinary institution, with the purpose of bringing the new generation into conformity with the ideals and customs which have become traditional."[60] If the members of a sect want to perpetuate their vision, if they want to exert an enduring influence on future generations, then they must learn to compromise with their culture.

Most scholars, especially Niebuhr, have portrayed the evolution of sects into denominations as a decline, as an accommodation to middle-class conformity. Indeed, Niebuhr decried the growth of denominations as "the victory of the world over the church," a "moral failure" of tragic proportions. In contrast to sects, which value lay inspiration, denominations insist on strict theological conformity. In addition, they demand an educated clergy instead of celebrating the priesthood of all believers; they relax standards of discipline in order to be as inclusive as possible; and they capitulate to the secular social order instead of challenging it. In Niebuhr's opinion, denominations are less pure, less demanding, less countercultural, and less *Christian* than sects.[61]

In some ways, the stories of the Freewill Baptists, Christians, Methodists, and African Methodists fit Niebuhr's model of decline. All of these sects embraced mainstream values as they became more popular, choosing power over purity. By the 1830s, few Freewill Baptists believed that converts had to give up the seemingly harmless pleasures of jewelry, fashionable clothing, or curled hair, and few Christians argued that cardplaying or dancing should be grounds for excommunication. More seriously, growing numbers of Methodists, especially in the South, denied that slaveholding was sinful. In their desire to bring as many converts into the fold as possible, they sacrificed the doctrine that had made them the most countercultural and, in the eyes of slaves, the most Christian.[62] The boundaries between the world and the church had begun to disappear.

Understandably, many female preachers interpreted the changes in their churches as symptoms of decline. Indeed, instead of explaining the backlash against them in the neutral, sociological language of sects becoming denominations, they used a different vocabulary to describe what was happening to them—the vocabulary of sin. After Sally Thompson was excommunicated from the Methodist Church, she wrote angrily: "Men who are exalted without wisdom, or merit, to seats of authority, and thereby become great and mighty, are of all men the most to be dreaded." In a stinging reference to the two clergymen who had brought her to trial, "Brothers" Hall and Grant, she accused them of disobeying God in order "to support their honor and distinction."[63] According to Thompson, her critics had been motivated not by genuine religious conviction, but by a consuming desire for power. Instead of waging war against sin, they had followed the example of Esau, who had sold his birthright for a mess of pottage.

Despite Thompson's accusations, however, it would be a mistake to simply dismiss the Methodists, Freewill Baptists, or Christians as conformists who abandoned their quest for spiritual perfection as they grew more powerful. As much as they may have forsaken their early heritage, they were still torn between loving and hating the world, and no matter how much they muted their outsiderness, they continued to decry the spiritual corruption of secular society. "There remains an explosive element in Christianity which seems never to be completely bottled up," one sociologist has remarked.[64] On one hand, the Christian Connection placed far less value on plain dress than they had in their early years, but they still prided themselves on caring more about spiritual truths than worldly baubles. Similarly, the Freewill Baptists renounced their practice of footwashing, one of their most controversial rituals, but they still drew boundaries around their covenanted communities by forbidding converts to swear, drink excessively, or own slaves. They also continued to rail against the "heathen" who lured people away from the churches with "caravans, circuses, and feats of legerdemain."[65] Even the Methodists, who made a tragic concession to their southern members by abandoning their opposition to slavery, clung to the shreds of their early views on religious liberty: they encouraged large numbers of slave men, although not slave women, to preach the gospel.

Rather than celebrating their new education, prosperity, and refinement, many evangelicals openly worried that their desire for respectability might undermine their faith. Drawing the same connection between Protestantism and the spirit of capitalism that would later make Max Weber famous, they warned converts to beware of the spiritual dangers of wealth. In 1830 the editor of *The Morning Star*, a Freewill Baptist journal, reprinted a long extract from John Wesley on the decline of true faith: "I fear, wherever riches have increased, the essence of religion has decreased in the same proportion. Therefore I do not see how it is possible, in the nature of things, for any revival of true religion to continue long. For religion must necessarily produce both industry and frugality, and these cannot but produce riches. But as riches increase, so will pride, anger, and love of the world in all its branches. So, although the form of religion remains, the spirit is swiftly vanishing away." According to Wesley, there was only one solution to this "continual decay of pure religion." "If those who *gain* all they can, and *save* all they can, will likewise *give* all they can," Wesley explained, "then the more they gain the more they grow in grace, and the more treasure they will lay up in heaven."[66] Only charity could prevent Christians from becoming Pharisees.

As much as they welcomed their success during the 1830s and 1840s, the Christians, Freewill Baptists, Methodists, and African Methodists realized they were in danger of losing their religious distinctiveness. Even though they cherished their new influence, they also wondered how they would be able to perpetuate their spirit of dissent without separating themselves from American culture. How could they enjoy their hard-earned prosperity without worshiping mammon? How could they continue to live as if they were *in* the world, but not *of* it? How could they protect Christianity from the temptations of the modern world?

Their answer was deceptively simple. Unlike Wesley, who had argued that the affluent should give away as much of their wealth as possible, they offered a less radical solution to preserving Christian virtue. Despite urging all converts to reject the excesses of individualism and materialism, they increasingly depended on *women* to cradle the values of a Christian republic. Like many other evangelicals (not to mention Catholics and Jews), they urged women to devote their lives to easing the worst strains of economic, political, and social change. In a society suffering from the ills of ethnic conflict, racial hostility, and financial depression, women could anoint their families with the soothing balm of "feminine" compassion. As one Christian Connection writer explained, "It is hers to be the comfort and ornament of the domestic habitation, to render herself beloved and useful, and scatter here and there the flowers of life under the feet of those who surround her."[67] As "ornaments," not prophetesses or warriors, women could transform their homes into islands of holiness that would stand apart from the hostile, sinful world.

By emphasizing the redemptive power of womanhood, the Freewill Baptists, Methodists, and Christians tried to preserve one of the most important features of their early heritage, but in an attenuated form. They still claimed that women had the power to save the world from sin, but they began to define womanhood in far more narrow terms. A Mother in Israel or Sister in Christ was not a crusading evangelist who traveled from town to town preaching the gospel, but a Sunday school teacher, a temperance reformer, or an antislavery activist who deferred to the authority of her local pastor. She was not Deborah, the stern judge who had led her people to victory, but Mary, the sister of Martha, who had wiped Christ's feet with her hair. She was not a warrior or soldier, but a loving parent who nurtured her family by the warmth of her fireside. In short, she was a domestic, pious woman who—in the words of one Methodist—promoted her faith through the "eloquence which flows from subjection."[68]

This growing celebration of women's domesticity reflected larger currents of change in antebellum America. As John Higham has argued, the "boundlessness" of the Jacksonian era was eventually replaced by a trend toward greater order and consolidation. Rather than experimenting with new forms of politics and religion, Americans began to focus their energies on building stable, lasting institutions. As part of this conservative transformation, they also developed more restrictive ideas about men's and women's spheres. Instead of celebrating women's new involvement in civil society, they tried to draw firmer lines between the public and the private.[69]

Among the Methodists, the backlash against female preaching began as early as the late 1820s. Under the leadership of ministers such as the Reverend Nathan Bangs, the Methodists tried to eliminate the "disorders" in their churches. After being transferred to a station in New York City, Bangs dedicated himself to reforming the congregations under his charge, stamping out the "pride, presumption, and bigotry, impatience of scriptural restraint and moderation, clapping of the hands, screaming, and even jumping, which marred and disgraced the word of God." Bangs did not single out female preachers for criticism, perhaps because his own sister, Ellen Bangs Gatchell, was a renowned exhorter. Yet many other ministers attacked female preaching as unscriptural and immodest. Women such as "Sister" Mills, Sarah Riker, and Elice Miller Smith had all served as Methodist preachers in the early years of the church, but by 1829, the *Christian Guardian*, a Methodist journal, dismissed female preaching as an "eccentric effort."[70]

In response, many female preachers left the Methodists to join other denominations. For example, Sarah Hedges, who had preached for the Methodists for twelve years, eventually joined the Christians in search of greater freedom.[71] By 1830, the year of Sally Thompson's excommunication from her church in New York, not a single female preacher remained in the Methodist Episcopal Church. Instead, women such as Ellen Stewart and Salome Lincoln preached for the Reformed Methodists, a small sect formed in 1814, and Hannah Reeves served as an itinerant for the Methodist Protestants, a denomination that had grown to 60,000 members by 1830, only thirteen years after its founding.[72] Similarly, Laura Smith Haviland began preaching for the Wesleyan Methodists after the group was organized in 1843.[73] Women were attracted to these splinter groups because they were much more tolerant of female preaching. All three of these sects seceded from the Methodist Episcopal Church because they objected to its clerical hierarchy and growing social conservatism.

The African Methodists also sought greater respectability in the mid-1830s. Under the leadership of the Reverend Daniel Alexander Payne, they launched a full-scale assault against the beliefs and practices of the "ignorant masses." Like Nathan Bangs, Payne objected to the enthusiastic clapping, dancing, and shouting he witnessed in church meetings. He was particularly opposed to female preaching, arguing that women's most important role lay within the home. Because he believed that women should dedicate themselves to teaching their faith to their children, he wrote a book on child-rearing and also helped organize several Mother's Associations.[74]

As a result, the same black female preachers who had been praised as Mothers in Israel during the 1820s were discredited as jezebels during the 1830s and 1840s. In 1845, when Jarena Lee asked the African Methodist Book

Committee to help her publish an expanded version of her memoirs, they responded with open contempt. "The manuscript of Sister Jarena Lee has been written in such a manner as it is impossible to decipher much of the meaning contained in it," they wrote scornfully.[75] From a modern-day perspective, it is difficult to imagine what part of her narrative they could have found "indecipherable," but perhaps their true complaint was her impassioned *clarity*. Presumably, few African Methodist clergymen wanted to memorialize a woman who so perfectly symbolized the uneducated, visionary enthusiasm of their early history.

Troubled by the growing restrictions on women's speech, African Methodist women formed an organization to defend female preaching. In 1844, 1848, and 1852, they lobbied the General Conference in favor of licensing women, but they were defeated each time. According to Julia Foote, the clergymen at the 1844 conference were so "incensed" by the idea of allowing women to preach that they all "talked and screamed to the bishop, who could scarcely keep order." Frustrated by the pressures of defeat, these women eventually disbanded sometime during the mid-1850s. In the contemptuous words of Daniel Alexander Payne, "They held together for a brief period, and then fell to pieces like a rope of sand."[76] Despite their unwavering faith in women's right to preach, they were simply not powerful enough to fight the likes of Payne.

Besides being excluded from the pulpit, female preachers were also excluded from the pages of church record books and clerical memoirs. Indeed, many evangelicals seem to have been so embarrassed by their early support of female preachers that they deliberately tried to erase them from historical memory. For example, when David Marks published the first edition of his memoir in 1831, he mentioned meeting some of the most popular female preachers of his time, including Susan Humes, Clarissa Danforth, Almira Bullock, Dolly Quinby, and "Sister" Wiard.[77] Yet in 1846, when his wife, Marilla, published a posthumous edition of his memoir, she removed all the references—no matter how small—to the women her husband had once defended. Editing a passage where he had described Dolly Quinby as "a widow in Israel and a labourer in the gospel," she shortened his sentence to "a widow in Israel."[78] Similarly, even though David had viewed Susan Humes as "a very agreeable acquaintance" and had preached with her on several occasions, Marilla omitted entire paragraphs describing her.[79] She even left out his innocuous comment that he had visited Clarissa Danforth during his travels through Connecticut.[80] Because she wanted to protect her dead husband's reputation, she presented a new, sanitized version of his career—one in which female preachers simply did not exist. From reading the revised edition of his memoirs, one would never know that the Freewill Baptists had ever sanctioned female preaching.

Female preachers were repeatedly ignored in the denominational histories published in the late 1830s and 1840s. Ministers who had once worked side by side with these women now pretended they had never existed or, even worse, took credit for their successes. For example, when Jabez King published his memoir in 1845, he implied that he and Jonathan Thompson had been solely responsible for the creation of a new Christian Connection church in Charleston, New York, in 1813. According to David Millard, however, Nancy Cram had persuaded them to come to Charleston after leading a revival there in which "hundreds were hopefully converted." Cram had "astonished" the inhabitants of Charleston by her "gift of language," but because she did not have the authority to baptize her new converts, she had traveled all the way to a Christian Connection Yearly Meeting in Woodstock, Vermont, to ask ordained ministers for help. In 1818, in a letter to the *Christian Herald*, King remembered serving as a "fellow-laborer" with Cram, referring to her intimately as "sister Nancy." By 1845, however, long after she had died, he took full credit for the revival she had led, never mentioning her name even once.[81]

Levi Hathaway, a Christian Connection minister, had once praised Nancy Cram as one of Joel's prophetic daughters. In 1817 he wrote, "Her unwearied labours in the gospel of Christ will be held in long remembrance."[82] One wonders if he ever realized how mistaken he had been. As female preachers learned, people always rewrite their past in order to satisfy the needs of their present, choosing whose lives to celebrate and whose to forget. Historical memory is always partial, always fragile, and always contested. When the Christians of the 1840s reflected on their history, they chose to pay homage to Jabez King, a devoted clergyman, but to ignore Nancy Cram, a female enthusiast.

The few female preachers who *were* remembered were rarely portrayed in favorable terms. For example, Hannah Reeves was memorialized in 1877 in an article in the *Methodist Quarterly Review*, but the picture that emerged of her was deeply ambivalent. On one hand, she was praised for agreeing to serve as a "helpmeet" to her clergyman husband even though she was "superior to him in gifts" and could have demanded her own circuit. Yet Reeves was also described as a "masculine," "indomitable" woman who was willing to sacrifice her children's welfare to satisfy the demands of her career. Noting that she had given birth to three children, all of whom died in their youth, the author concluded: "They were born but to die thus prematurely; for the maternal profession—and it is such—precludes another set of duties alien to it."[83] According to this article, Reeves may have been a success as a preacher, but she was a failure as a mother. If she had been less selfish, less ambitious, and more "feminine," her children would have survived.

Instead of allowing women to preach, the Freewill Baptists, Christians, and Methodists tried to channel their religious zeal into other endeavors. For example, many ministers urged women to become Sunday school teachers or home missionaries. The Christians created a Female Sunday School Society in 1834, and the Freewill Baptists formed a Female Mission Society in 1847.[84] The Reverend George Ryerson, a Methodist, suggested that women could "preach" by sewing gloves and knitting mittens for the poor.[85] Other clergymen recommended that women dedicate themselves to teaching their faith to their children. Even though Mothers in Israel could not be ministers themselves, they could take vicarious satisfaction in raising godly men to labor in the harvest.

Of course, not all male ministers shared the new conservative bent of their denominations. A small but vocal minority lamented the passing of the old order, defending women's right to preach in spite of the quest for respectability. As late as 1843, for example, a Christian minister condemned the Congregational Church for "gagging" the "freeborn daughters of Zion." In the same year, another minister claimed that the Bible itself sanctioned female preaching: Anna, Mary, Phebe, and Phillip's four daughters had all been evangelists. Others continued to allow women into the pulpit, refusing to "quench the holy flame" by ordering women to keep silence.[86] A few brave Methodists even supported Sally Thompson, who had been excommunicated in 1830, because of their belief that she truly had been called. Flaunting the authority of their bishop, they invited her to visit their churches despite her radical reputation. Without their support, she would have found it far more difficult, if not impossible, to find places to preach.

Strangers in a Strange Land

Unfortunately, it is difficult to know how most female preachers responded to the growing controversy over whether they should be suffered to teach. Indeed, as the debates over female evangelism grew increasingly heated, women's own voices became harder and harder to hear. Because many religious journals stopped reprinting their letters or advertising their meetings, female preachers seemed virtually to disappear, almost as if they had never existed. For example, early records make it clear that Sarah Thornton, a Freewill Baptist, preached for at least eight years, but there is no evidence of what happened to her after 1833.[87] Perhaps she died young like so many other women, exhausted by her grueling travels, or perhaps she left the ministry to marry and have children. Or perhaps she continued to travel unheralded across New England, searching for ministers who still believed that women had a right to speak from the pulpit. We will never know. Like most of the other women who preached between 1790 and 1845, she was forgotten by the clerical leadership, leaving few traces of her memory in the historical record.

Despite these silences, however, it is still possible to tell the stories of a significant number of female preachers. First, it is clear that several women decided to give up their itinerant careers, perhaps because they were so troubled by the attacks against them. For example, Eliza Barnes, a Methodist, traveled across northern New England as a preacher for a few brief years in the 1820s, but she eventually decided to become a missionary to Native Americans in Canada instead. She was accompanied by another woman, who may have been Sally Waldren, a Christian who had once led a revival in Portsmouth, New Hampshire. Since neither woman published a narrative, it is impossible to know exactly why they chose missionary work over preaching, but it is likely that they welcomed the chance to appear more respectable. As missionaries, both women continued to preach informally, but instead of facing questions about their morality or femininity, they earned wide praise for their self-sacrificing devotion to the "heathen."[88]

At least three other female preachers left the ministry to devote themselves to marriage and motherhood. Ann Rexford, who had spent eleven years as a Christian Connection preacher, married a lawyer in 1832, and Salome Lincoln wed a Methodist clergyman in 1835. Unlike Rexford, who retired from her labors, Lincoln continued to preach occasionally, but she spent most of the few remaining years of her life caring for her husband and two young children. (Lincoln died of consumption in 1841 at the young age of thirty-four.) Similarly, Elice Miller, a Methodist who reportedly had once been "more universally admired, than any other *female* [preacher] of America," stopped itinerating after her marriage to William Smith, a Methodist clergyman in Virginia. Although she continued to serve as a class leader, she no longer preached from the pulpit—a loss of status that she may have found difficult. According to Nancy Towle, who seems to have taken a dim view of matrimony in general, "Since her confinement by marriage,—she had not that religious enjoyment, which she formerly had known."[89]

Overall, fewer women appear to have made the choice to become preachers during the 1830s than during the previous decade. According to the available records, twenty-nine women began their preaching careers during the 1820s, but only sixteen during the 1830s—the decade of the fiercest attacks against women speaking in public. Perhaps these numbers simply reflect women's growing invisibility in the historical records, but it would not be surprising if the decline was real. Even more than earlier female preachers, any woman who dared to become an evangelist during the 1830s knew that she soon would be mired in the ugly mudslinging over whether she should keep silence in the churches. Not surprisingly, devout women, no matter how strong their sense of call, may have hesitated to claim the pulpit as their own.

Instead of riding across the country as itinerants, many evangelical women found other ways to serve God. Some, like Deborah Millett Taylor, were so eager to save souls that they expressly chose to marry ministers. Taylor had always dreamed of becoming a minister's wife, and after her marriage to a Methodist itinerant, she became his devoted helpmate in prayer and class meetings. Even though she did not find the courage to deliver a formal sermon until 1859, she prayed aloud, testified, and exhorted by her husband's side for more than forty years. Similarly, Nancy Harding, the wife of Charles Harding, a Methodist circuit rider, became his virtual co-pastor, accompanying him on almost all of his journeys and visiting converts from house to house. In the words of her husband, she "had an excellent gift of prayer and exhortation, and was very useful, and much beloved by the people."[90]

Other would-be female preachers became Sunday school teachers, religious writers, and especially home and foreign missionaries. After Eleanor Macomber, a Baptist, sailed to Burma in 1836, she behaved as much like a preacher as a missionary: she held Sunday worship meetings, organized a church, and traveled deep into remote mountain villages preaching the gospel. (Because of the language barrier, she was aided by an interpreter.) Closer to home, more than five hundred women served as missionaries to the Indians between 1815 and 1865, and they too had much in common with female preachers. Indeed, one clergyman complained that Marcia Colton, a candidate for a missionary position, had once caused a "disturbance" in his parish by "insisting upon her right to address the brethren of the church and admonish them of their duty." A budding female preacher, she apparently decided to channel her ambitions into more "feminine" work, but she firmly believed that God had specially called her to be his instrument.[91]

Female preachers regarded their missionary sisters with a mixture of admiration and suspicion. They rejoiced to hear so many other evangelical women echo their language of call, but they also seem to have been frustrated by the false distinction between preaching and missionary work. Even though female missionaries delivered informal sermons in front of Indians, Hawaiians, or foreign "pagans," they (and their supporters) refused to call their work *preaching*. After Nancy Towle was insulted by a minister who condemned female evangelism, she complained bitterly about his hypocrisy. "I was much surprised at this manner of address," she explained, because "he had a daughter, gone on a foreign mission with her husband; with whom it appeared, he was well enough pleased!" As Towle knew all too well, female preachers were dismissed as "manly" women, but female missionaries were portrayed in glowing terms as models of "heroism and piety."[92] With disappointment, Towle realized that few missionary women would ever join her crusade; instead of fighting for the right to minister to other evangelicals, they fled to Indian reservations or sailed to the South Seas to save the "heathen."

By the end of the 1830s, it seemed to female preachers as if they had truly become strangers in a strange land. They had been ordered to keep silence by mainline clergymen who equated them with radicals like Fanny Wright; they had been rejected as enthusiasts by their own sects; and they had watched many of their evangelical sisters in Christ choose to become missionaries or Sunday School teachers instead of preachers. With sorrow, they wondered whether they would ever be accepted by Protestant churches. When Wealthy Monroe delivered a funeral sermon in 1833, four Methodist ministers refused to even sit in the same room with her. "They were careful to take their seats in a remote part of another room," a spectator commented sarcastically, "perhaps for fear of having their sanctuary defiled by the contaminating breath of a female preacher."[93] Like the biblical prophets whom she so admired, Monroe had become a stranger and a pilgrim, an exile who despaired of ever receiving the promises on earth.

Yet despite her moments of discouragement, Monroe refused to give up her call to preach. Instead of leaving the ministry for missionary work, Sunday school teaching, or marriage, she decided to go west, leading revivals on the vast expanse of the American frontier. After traveling far into the icy woods of Minnesota, she moved to Michigan, a sparsely settled state which had only recently been admitted to the union. With few ordained clergymen to compete with her, she faced far less antagonism than in New York. "The cause of God is on the rise in this western country," she wrote in 1841. "I shall do all I can to advance the cause of Christ." Even after her marriage to Robert Edmunds in 1842, she continued to hold meetings, preaching for at least another four years, if not longer.[94]

Besides Monroe, a surprisingly large number of other women continued to defend their right to preach as Sisters in Christ and Mothers in Israel. Even though the number of women who decided to become preachers appears to have declined during the 1830s, many who had begun their careers during earlier decades refused to yield to clerical pressure. In total, at least thirty-six women continued to labor as local or itinerant preachers during the 1830s. Betsey Stuart, Hannah Reeves, Hannah Cogswell, Harriet Livermore, Mary Stevens Curry, and Charlotte Hestes are only a few of the women who continued to travel across the country warning people to repent and be saved.

Like Wealthy Monroe, at least eleven of these women responded to the backlash against them by following the trail of pioneers moving west. In the great American tradition, they tried to remake their lives on the frontier, leaving behind the customs of the East for new opportunities in the "wilderness." Both Abigail Stone and Elizabeth Stiles settled in Michigan, and Martha Spaulding left her home in Rhode Island for lower Canada, where she may have founded as many as eight or nine new Freewill Baptist churches.[95] Several other women, including Molancy Wade Parker and Sarah Righter Major, moved to Ohio, a rapidly expanding state that was no longer part of the frontier, but which still felt far removed from the centers of national power. Instead of settling in large urban areas such as Cleveland or Cincinnati, they traveled to backcountry villages where there were comparatively few churches.

Other women responded to the increasing conservatism of their denominations by mixing their preaching with more traditional "feminine" work as reformers. Laura Smith Haviland, a Wesleyan Methodist, often delivered formal sermons from the pulpit, but she devoted most of her time to the Raisin Institute, an organization that she founded in Michigan to educate free blacks. Sarah Righter Major, a member of the Church of the Brethren, preached in Ohio jails and hospitals, and Elizabeth, an African Methodist who had once traveled south to preach to slaves, opened a school in Michigan for "colored orphans." By expanding their definition of ministry to include reform work, these women spared themselves much of the abuse that they had once faced as itinerant preachers.

At least twenty of the thirty-six women who preached during the 1830s belonged to the Christians and Freewill Baptists, who vested ultimate authority in individual congregations rather than in an episcopal hierarchy. In contrast to the Methodists, who imposed discipline from the top down, they governed from the bottom up. For example, even though both the Christians and Freewill Baptists organized Yearly Meetings to oversee local churches, they still preserved the principle of congregational autonomy. Although the Yearly Meeting could suggest that a particular person should be disciplined or could warn churches to beware of heretical ministers, it did not have the power of excommunication. As a result, female preachers learned how to maneuver within the system, avoiding clergymen who opposed them in favor of the few who remained sympathetic. Despite the antagonism of the most prominent clerical leaders, Anna Stone Anderson was licensed to preach by her Freewill Baptist church in 1839, and Hannah Peavey Cogswell was commended as a female laborer by a Christian Connection conference in New Hampshire in 1836.

Even more than earlier female preachers, these women had to fight to be recognized and accepted by their denominations. After Julia Foote, an African Methodist, began preaching in 1845, she suffered many "fiery trials," and following in the footsteps of Sally Thompson, she was excommunicated from her Boston congregation. "There was no justice meted out to women in those days," she complained later. "Even ministers of Christ did not feel that women had any rights which they were bound to respect." To comfort herself, she read the sixth chapter of Hebrews over and over again, poring over the verse in which Abraham—a stranger and a pilgrim—finally found glory in the city of God. "God is not unrighteous to forget your work and labour of love, which ye have shewed toward his name," she read.[96]

God would not forget—this much female preachers believed. But they were far less confident about whether they would be remembered by the clergymen who had once praised them as pious sisters and mothers. When Lydia Sexton attended a United Brethren conference to ask for a license to preach, she was incensed to hear a minister take credit for her work. Although she sat in front of him in plain view, he looked past her as if she were invisible. Boasting to his colleagues that he had "taken sixty members into the church," he blatantly

Lydia Sexton chose this stern picture of herself to include in her *Autobiography* (1882). Angered by clerical opposition to female preaching, she projects an image of fierce determination.

ignored her, even though she later claimed to have been responsible (as God's instrument) for converting every one of those new members. "No one without having the bitter experience that I had can imagine my feelings," she wrote angrily.[97] From ordeals such as these, she learned that no one would try to preserve her memory unless she told her own story in her own words.

Many other female preachers also tried to ensure their place in history by publishing their memoirs and narratives. Although women had always used the press to market their beliefs and publicize their meetings, the scale and pace of their publishing increased during the 1830s and 1840s. Instead of simply sending letters to denominational journals or writing brief scriptural defenses of female preaching, women such as Zilpha Elaw, Jarena Lee, Nancy Towle, and Elleanor Knight decided to share their entire life stories with the public. Even though Lee began preaching in 1819, she did not publish her memoir until 1836, a few years after the death of Bishop Richard Allen, her most loyal supporter. Increasingly ostracized by the most powerful men in her denomination, she decided to print the story of the "first female preacher in the African Methodist church" (as she described herself) at her own expense. Fearful that she would be forgotten, erased from historical memory, she left a public record of her words "for the satisfaction of such as may follow after me, when I am no more."[98] Her memoir can be read as a long, stubborn assertion of her influence, her popularity, her intelligence, her *existence*.

There is no doubt that female preachers wanted to be remembered, but even so, they were far too conservative to demand the kind of institutional change that would have guaranteed their place in history books. For instance, female preachers could have tried to foster a tradition of women's ministry by asking seminaries to open their doors to women as well as men, but no one ever proposed such a revolutionary experiment. In 1847 Antoinette Brown Blackwell convinced Charles Finney to admit her to Oberlin College (and today feminist historians remember the date), but more conservative women never demanded the right to a theological education. Because they believed in their natural subordination in the order of creation, few could imagine serving as pastors as well as preachers. "The man is not created for the woman, but the woman for the man," Zilpha Elaw quoted from the Bible.[99] Although women could preach if they had been divinely inspired by God, no amount of education could give them the authority to "rule" over men.

Nor did most female preachers organize collectively in order to protest against their exclusion from the pulpit. Besides the small number of African Methodist women who founded a women's group, there is no record that any other group of female preachers banded together to demand institutional change. Perhaps black women had been politicized by their involvement in the abolitionist movement, where they had begun to learn the effectiveness of political agitation. In contrast, even though white women continued to depend on one another, and on sympathetic laywomen, for support and encouragement, few believed in solving their problems through political action. Instead of demanding structural reform, they chose a more subtle weapon of resistance: their sheer persistence and stubbornness. By repeatedly refusing to learn in silence with all subjection, and by publishing their life stories, they tried to ensure that their churches would not forget them as strangers who had once wandered in a strange land.

Sally Thompson was one of the many female preachers who continued to defend her calling as a divinely inspired Mother in Israel. Despite her shame and anger after her excommunication, she decided to publish an account of her church trial in her own words. She wanted people to remember *her* version of events, not the accusations of the Methodist hierarchy. As the epigraph to her narrative, she chose a verse from Matthew: "Blessed are ye, when men shall revile you, and persecute you, and shall say all manner of evil against you falsely for my sake." By choosing these words, she tried to ensure that she would be remembered as a Christian martyr rather than as a "disorderly" woman who had been guilty of insubordination.

Although it is unclear exactly what happened to Thompson in the six years after her church trial in 1830, by 1836 she had joined a Christian Connection church in New York. Perhaps she thought that the Christians would give her more freedom as an evangelist, but to her disappointment, she eventually discovered that they were as enamored of respectability as the Methodists. Nevertheless, she remained a Christian Connection preacher for at least another eleven years, traveling far away from her critics to the small villages of western New York and the woods of Maine. Often she felt discouraged, but she comforted herself by praying for a better future—a future when women as well as men would be recognized as "the Anointed of God."[100]

In the early 1840s, as we will see in the next chapter, it seemed as if her prayers had been answered. After a sharp decline during the 1830s, the number of women choosing to become preachers began to rise again. Between 1840 and 1850, at least thirty-three women became local or traveling ministers, a substantial increase over the sixteen who had begun their careers during the previous decade. The majority of them, twenty-two in all, were followers of William Miller, a self-proclaimed prophet who predicted the imminent return of Christ in a blaze of glory. Like earlier generations of sectarians, the Millerites rejected the dominant faith in American progress, and they saw female preachers as heralds of the coming millennium. In the early 1840s, they made it possible for women such as Sally Thompson to imagine a world in which they still would be suffered to teach.

8

Your Sons and Daughters Shall Prophesy

Female

Preaching in

the Millerite

Movement

And it shall come to pass afterward, that I will pour out my Spirit upon all flesh; and your sons and your daughters shall prophesy, your old men shall dream dreams, your young men shall see visions: And also upon the servants and upon the handmaids in those days will I pour out my Spirit.—Joel 2:28–29

And at midnight there was a cry made, Behold, the bridegroom cometh; go ye out to meet him.—Matthew 25:6

On a summer night in June of 1842, Olive Maria Rice sat listening to a sermon by William Miller, a Baptist clergyman who had recently become famous for his apocalyptic predictions. As he quoted verse after verse from the books of Daniel and Revelation, she paged through her Bible in shock and exhilaration. Could his interpretation possibly be true? In a moment as climactic as her experience of conversion, she suddenly realized that all of the Bible's prophetic books pointed to the same extraordinary conclusion: God would destroy the world in 1843. Looking around the crowded church, Rice shuddered to think that all of the people assembled for worship that evening were truly living in the end times, the last months or days before the "midnight cry." Christ the Savior—the "Alpha and Omega, the beginning and the end"—would soon bring the cycle of history to a terrifying completion.[1]

Rice left that meeting with a new sense of divine calling. As a member of the

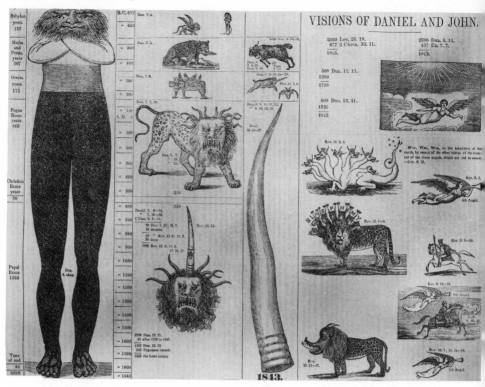

This Millerite chart was printed in *The Midnight Cry* 5, no. 2 (1843). Miller and his followers often carried prophetic charts with them on their travels. Besides clarifying their mathematical calculations, these charts portrayed graphic images of the apocalypse. Courtesy of the American Antiquarian Society.

Methodist Missionary Board, she had spent the previous two years preparing to become a foreign missionary, but after hearing Miller preach, she decided that God had called her to labor in a vineyard closer to home. After returning to her hometown in Vermont to warn her family and friends of Christ's return, she traveled throughout Connecticut and New York as an itinerant preacher. As she later explained, "I could not conscientiously return to my studies in North Wilbraham, Mass[achusetts], to prepare for future usefulness, when a few months at the longest must close not only my labors in this world, but those of all mankind." It made no sense for her to stay in school if souls needed saving immediately. "I feel assured, from the power of God's truth set home to my heart by his spirit, that all the missionary work I do must be done quickly," she confessed. "And probably God has made me the humble instrument of saving more souls, within a few weeks past, by sounding the midnight cry, than most missionaries in the east, at least, have had as the fruits of their labors in many years."[2] As Joel had promised, Christ had called his daughters as well as his sons to prophesy.

Inspired by one of the greatest outpourings of millennial fervor in American history, Rice became a well-known Millerite preacher during the early 1840s. Like earlier female preachers among the Methodists, African Methodists, Freewill Baptists, and Christians, she was often ordered to keep silence, but she insisted that her sex was less important than saving souls. In a letter to *The Midnight Cry* she declared, "While God works in such power, and converts so many souls where I labor, I cannot—dare not stop for the only reason that I am a sister."[3] She seemed radical because she spoke in front of "promiscuous" audiences, but she was also a reactionary who believed that the modern world was too corrupt to be saved. Filled with melancholy and pessimism about the future, she longed to escape from history into a millennium out of time.

The Millerites were the last evangelical sect in antebellum America to sanction female preaching. Between 1840 and 1845, at a time when other denominations were trying to force women out of the ministry, they allowed at least twenty-two women to serve as itinerant preachers. Like Rice, who had studied the Bible as part of her missionary training, most of these women were better educated than earlier female preachers, but they still described themselves as prophetic daughters, sisters, and mothers who had been called to "sound the midnight cry." "I am confident that it is the Lord that is doing these marvelous things," Rice testified. On the eve of the millennium, God had called her and other female preachers to warn sinners to prepare for Judgment Day.[4]

The Millerites represented both the culmination and the exhaustion of antebellum revivalism. Although some historians have portrayed the Millerites as cranks or eccentrics, they were part of a larger tradition of religious revivalism that stretched back to the upheavals of the first Great Awakening.[5] Like the Separates in the eighteenth century, the Shakers and the Public Friends in the Revolutionary era, and the Freewill Baptists, Christians, and Methodists in the early nineteenth century, they were dissenters who prized charismatic inspiration over clerical education. As part of their new measures, they held emotional camp meetings, encouraged lay people to speak during religious services, and permitted women to preach. Even though most Millerites belonged to a higher social class than earlier sectarians, they shared the same antipathy toward the "progress" of the modern world. For a few brief years during the 1840s, they rekindled the egalitarian spirit of the early revivals.

The Signs of the Times

The story of the Millerites begins with William Miller, a farmer-prophet who predicted the world would end in 1843. Born in Pittsfield, Massachusetts, in 1782, Miller moved to the frontier town of Low Hampton, New York, as a child. His father, a former Revolutionary soldier, and his mother, the daughter of a Baptist clergyman, were poor, hardworking farmers who followed the trail of pioneers moving west in search of better economic opportunities. Like other farmers' sons, Miller attended school only three months a year, but he was an "avid reader" who soon gained a reputation as a "prodigy for learning." Under the influence of his pious mother, who reared him on the Bible and Psalter, he became gravely concerned about "the welfare of [his] soul." He remembered later, "I spent much time in trying to invent some plan, whereby I might please God." In 1803, however, after marrying Lucy Smith and moving to Poultney, Vermont, he began reading the works of many of the most controversial authors of his time, including Ethan Allen, Voltaire, and Thomas Paine, and renounced his earlier Christian beliefs to become a Deist. "I believed in a God," he explained in his memoir, "but I could not, as I thought, believe the *Bible* was the *word of God.*" It was too full of "contradictions and inconsistencies," he complained, and even the most devout Christians admitted that it was "so dark and intricate that no man could understand it." Like other Deists, he could not believe that a rational God would reveal "the way of eternal life" in the Scriptures but then "clothe them in a mantle of mysticism."[6]

Miller remained a Deist until his experiences as a soldier during the War of 1812. Amazed by the American victory, he concluded that the defeat of the British, one of the greatest military powers in the world, had been "the work of a mightier power than man." In a letter to his wife, Lucy, he affirmed, "The Supreme Being must have watched over the interests of this country in an especial manner, and delivered us from the hands of our enemies." Following in the footsteps of his Puritan forebears, he regarded America as a redeemer nation, a city on a hill specially favored by God.

Yet even though Miller described the victory as "a day of great joy," he was also horrified by the suffering and death he had seen on the battlefield. "How grand, how noble, and yet how awful!" he exclaimed.[7] After the bloody battle of Plattsburgh, he no longer believed in the benevolent God of Deism, but in the Calvinist God of his Baptist childhood—a God who was loving and merciful, but also full of wrath.

After returning home to Vermont in 1815, Miller became a born-again Baptist who was determined to prove that the Deists had been mistaken: the Bible was not "dark and intricate," but logical and consistent. Influenced by the populist culture of evangelicalism, he insisted that every individual could be his or her own interpreter of the Bible. "Nothing revealed in the scripture can or will be hid from those who ask in faith," he declared. When he began his own studies, he decided to "read and try to understand for myself" instead of relying on biblical commentaries or the interpretations of learned clergymen. If every word in the Bible was literally true, as he believed, then even the most obscure and figurative passages could be deciphered with common sense.[8]

Miller's quest for the truth led him to the book of Revelation, the mystical book of the Bible that describes the destruction of the "beast" and the creation of "a new heaven and a new earth." After all the bloodshed of the battlefield, he found himself mesmerized by John's vivid, strange, and often frightening vision of the apocalypse. Trembling with fear, he read that at the end of the world, seven angels would sound seven trumpets of destruction: "The first angel sounded, and there followed hail and fire mingled with blood, and they were cast upon the earth: and the third part of trees was burnt up, and all green grass was burnt up. And the second angel sounded, and as it were a great mountain burning with fire was cast into the sea: and the third part of the sea became blood." In other passages, he read about a horde of locusts who "had hair as the hair of women, and their teeth were as the teeth of lions"; a "great red dragon" who had "seven heads and ten horns, and seven crowns upon his heads"; and the "great whore" of Babylon, who was "drunken with the blood of the saints, and with the blood of the martyrs of Jesus."[9] Miller was horrified by these images, but the more he studied them, the more he became convinced that the loosing of the "seven seals," the sufferings of the "seven plagues," and the final destruction of Babylon represented genuine historical events that were beginning to unfold in his own age.

As we have seen in earlier chapters, Miller's beliefs were hardly unique in the early nineteenth century, an era that was rife with millennial speculation. After the American Revolution, many Protestants predicted that the war had marked "the birthday of a new world," the beginning of a new and more glorious dispensation of history.[10] More pessimistically, others speculated that the millennium would bring "judgments" and "calamities" so awful that they surpassed the imagination. Writing in 1835, Harriet Livermore warned the American public that they would soon witness "a day of trouble—of alarm—

of tempest—of great heats—and of great frosts—of sore famines—wars—pestilences—noisome beasts—awful delusions! and horrid desolations!" In the South, a slave "prophetess" named Sinda predicted that the world would end in 1839.[11] Like Miller, these women understood the book of Revelation not as mere allegory or metaphor, but as an accurate (and terrifying) description of the end of the world.

What separated Miller from other evangelicals was not his belief in an imminent millennium, but his certainty that "the end of all things was clearly and emphatically predicted, both as to time and manner."[12] Unlike other millennialists, he was convinced that he knew the *exact date* when Christ would return to earth. Piecing together evidence from the prophetic books of the Bible, he came to an alarming conclusion: the world would end in 1843.

Miller based his calculations on the mystical prophecies contained in the book of Daniel. The pivotal text was Daniel 8:14, which predicted that the "sanctuary would be cleansed" in 2,300 days. Like other biblical critics of his time, Miller believed that the word "days" actually meant years. When he read in Daniel 9:25 that the 2,300 days began at "the going forth of the decree to build the wall of Jerusalem" in 457 B.C., he subtracted 457 from 2,300 to arrive at his notorious date: 1843.[13] His "prophetic arithmetic" was simple and easy to duplicate, and many of his contemporaries seem to have been impressed by his rational and scientific method.

Although Miller published a small book explaining his doctrines in 1836, his prophecies were not widely studied and debated until Joshua Himes joined the movement in 1839. A Christian Connection preacher and Garrisonian abolitionist, Himes was also a consummate salesman. Flooding the country with apocalyptic books, pamphlets, and newspapers, he turned William Miller into a national celebrity by the early 1840s.[14] Even though Miller was not known as a particularly charismatic preacher (he could never compete with the likes of Lorenzo Dow or Charles Finney), thousands of evangelicals squeezed into churches to hear him explain his apocalyptic prophecies.

By 1842 or 1843, according to one recent historian, there were at least 50,000 committed Millerites and perhaps as many as a million more who were "skeptically expectant." Because most of them continued to worship in their own evangelical churches instead of forming separate congregations, their precise numbers are difficult to estimate, but it is clear that tens of thousands subscribed to Millerite periodicals and attended Millerite camp meetings. Even evangelicals who never joined the movement feared that they might soon hear the midnight cry. For example, even though Charles Harding was a Methodist, he shared many of the Millerites' fundamental beliefs—"the second coming of Christ, the resurrection of the dead, a future judgment"—and worried that their predictions might come true. "I did not feel like opposing these men," he admitted in his memoir. "They might be right, how did I know?"[15] Despite his reluctance to identify himself as a Millerite, he tried to live each day as if it were the last before the apocalypse.

Theologically, the Millerites placed so little value on doctrinal conformity that they appealed to evangelicals from many different sects and denominations. Despite the fact that Miller was a Calvinist, many of his most devoted followers were Freewill Baptists and Methodists. Even though they disagreed with him and with one another about issues as diverse as infant baptism and free will, they were linked together by their common faith in "the personal, Premillennial Advent of Christ, and his personal, bodily reign on the earth with his Resurrected and glorified saints." Whatever else may have separated them, it is clear that they firmly believed in "Christ's speedy coming."[16]

What is more puzzling is why these men and women were willing to trust the predictions of an obscure New England farmer. Why did so many thousands of people believe that the world was poised on the brink of destruction? Who were the evangelicals who joined the movement, and why did they have so little faith in America's future? Historically, most apocalyptic movements have involved poor, marginalized people who have felt besieged by forces beyond their control. For example, the Ghost Dance religion of the Sioux appeared when their civilization was on the verge of collapse. Decimated by war and forced off their lands by white settlers, the Sioux predicted the imminent, cataclysmic return of an avenging messiah. Similarly, the Iroquois religion of Handsome Lake began in response to the ravages of disease, war, and alcoholism; the prophet Handsome Lake preached that the world would be destroyed in a fiery holocaust. From examples such as these, anthropologists have concluded that millenarian beliefs arise in response to cultural stress and anxiety. Apocalyptic movements typically appear in societies undergoing rapid decline or catastrophic change, representing a collective effort for reformation and revitalization.[17]

Yet the Millerites did not fit the common profile of apocalyptic millennialists. Unlike the Sioux or the Iroquois, the Millerites were not outcasts facing cultural collapse or devastation, nor were they poor, powerless, or marginalized. According to historian David Rowe, most were actually *above* average in wealth, and they tended to be ordinary Americans from all walks of life. As a contemporary observer noted, Millerite meetings were filled "with people of all sorts, including Judges, Doctors, Lawyers, 'common people.'" Geograph-ically, the movement was centered in the burned-over district of western New York, the hotbed of nineteenth-century revivalism, but Millerites could be found in both rural and urban areas. Indeed, what has most fascinated histo-rians about the Millerites is how much they resembled other nineteenth-century Americans. Religiously, they believed in the new birth and the author-ity of the Bible—doctrines widely shared by other evangelicals—and socially, they tended to be farmers and artisans who were neither very rich nor very poor. Contrary to what their critics argued, the Millerites were not outcasts or deviants who stood on the far fringes of American culture. As historian Edwin S. Gaustad has commented, their beliefs were simply an unusually extreme representation of "broad cultural and existential concerns."[18]

By the very fact of their "normalcy", the Millerites remind us that the Age of Jackson was a time of anxiety and apprehension as well as optimism. On one hand, many Americans in the 1830s and 1840s were thrilled by the spirit of expansion, diffusion, and universality that defined their age. "Men forget the limits of their powers," William Ellery Channing exulted. "They question the infinite, the unsearchable, with an audacious self-reliance."[19] From his stand-point, there was nothing that hardworking, idealistic Americans could not accomplish. They built canals, steamboats, and railroads that revolutionized transportation; they invented new laborsaving devices that led to mass pro-duction; they defeated "savage" Indians on the frontier; and they founded reform organizations in order to conquer the vices of intemperance, prostitu-tion, and slavery. As God's chosen people, a new Israel, they were engaged in creating the most technologically advanced, morally perfect society that ever had been seen on earth.

At the same time, however, many Americans were so dizzied by the pace of economic and social change that they yearned for greater stability. Econom-ically, the 1820s and 1830s were years of unparalleled prosperity, but the panic of 1837 ushered in one of the worst depressions in American history. The meteoric rise of the Millerites during the early 1840s coincided with the col-lapse of the national market; they reached the height of their popularity at the same time as the economy hit bottom.[20] Distressed by the seemingly random fluctuations of the market, many farmers and businessmen rejected the Amer-ican faith in hard work and progress for a far darker creed. Invoking the angry

God of the book of Revelation, they described themselves as helpless pawns in the final battle between Christ and Satan.

Besides their fears of economic collapse, many Protestants also felt threatened by the growing numbers of Roman Catholic immigrants flooding into American ports. In 1780 there were only 56 Catholic churches in America, but by 1820, that number had grown to 124. Decrying Catholics as un-American because of their obedience to Rome, an angry mob burned down a convent in Charlestown, Massachusetts, in 1834. Ten years later, thirteen people were killed during anti-Catholic riots in Philadelphia.[21] According to the Millerites, who vilified the pope as the Antichrist, Catholic immigration represented yet another sign that America was destined for imminent destruction. A vengeful God, they predicted, would destroy the Catholic "beast" in a fiery holocaust.

If the presence of large numbers of Roman Catholics on America's shores was not alarming enough, conservative Protestants were also frightened by the unusual number of natural disasters that occurred during these years. During the first three decades of the nineteenth century, epidemics of cerebrospinal meningitis ("spotted fever") and cholera killed thousands; floods destroyed farms and mills; and crop failures led to food shortages and even famine. The year 1816 was immortalized as the year without a summer because there were snows and frosts in northern New England throughout June, July, and August. According to sociologist Michael Barkun, temperatures were "among the lowest in the recorded meteorological history of the western world."[22] During the 1830s, spectacular meteor showers and comets further intensified the sense of impending doom. Despite the celebration of American progress, many found the signs of the times ominous indeed.

Most of all, many Protestants were troubled by the dramatic theological changes taking place within their own churches. Even though they tended to project their anxieties onto the Catholic "menace" or the capitalist market, they knew that their most dangerous enemy did not lie without, but within. In the early nineteenth century, Protestants were increasingly divided in their attitudes toward economic and social change. At the same time as liberal clergymen celebrated the rapid advances in technology and commerce, conservatives lamented the loss of the traditional world of communal responsibility. In contrast to liberals, who were so impressed by human abilities that they painted a rosy picture of Christ's appearance after a thousand-year reign of peace, conservatives protested that humans were too weak and sinful ever to bring about the millennium through their own actions. Thus, when a Methodist minister asserted that "*It is in accordance with the divine economy to save man by human instrumentality*," other clergymen in his denomination protested that only God had the power to bring about the millennium.[23] Rejecting the popular language of self-reliance and individualism, they insisted that Christians were frail instruments who were utterly dependent on God's grace. When the millennium arrived, as it surely would, it would be a demonstration of the infinite power of God—a conflagration of unimaginable horror.

What linked together the Millerites, then, was not only their belief in an imminent apocalypse, but their suspicion of the modern world. Even though they were not economically or socially disadvantaged, they protested against the dislocations of rapid change by fleeing from the "corruption" of secular society. The world "is polluted with the works of satan, sin, death, and the curse," Emily Clemons warned, "and is only kept in store, reserved unto fire, against the day of judgment and perdition of ungodly men."[24] In contrast to liberal clergymen, who imagined history as an upward spiral culminating in moral perfection, the Millerites rejected the secular faith in human progress. Seeking refuge in the safety of their churches, they tried to create countercultural islands of holiness to preserve traditional Christian values against the corrosive forces of individualism and materialism. Protestantism, in their opinion, was in danger of losing its historical identity as a movement of protest.

This message attracted thousands of Christians, Freewill Baptists, and Methodists who were dissatisfied with the increasing formalism of their denominations. Statistics are fragmentary, but in a random sample of 174 Millerite lecturers, historian Everett Dick discovered that 44 percent were Methodist, 27 percent were Baptist (including Freewill Baptist), 9 percent were Congregationalist, 8 percent were Christian, and 7 percent were Presbyterian. Similarly, in his study of Millerism in New York State, David Rowe found a "preponderance" of Christians and Baptists. These men and women hoped Millerite doctrines would help restore their churches to their "primitive simplicity," but in the face of widespread hostility—and even, in some cases, excommunication—they resolved to "come out of Babylon." Beginning in 1843, large numbers of Millerites began to form their own separate congregations. According to Charles Harding, a Methodist minister, they splintered his church into two warring factions. "At times it seemed we should break all in pieces," he remembered later. "To save the church from rupture, and loose none was no small task."[25]

The Millerites built a new sect that looked strikingly like the Freewill Baptists, Christians, and Methodists of the early 1800s. Like these earlier evangelicals, they emphasized the literal truth of the Bible, the ability of individuals to read the Scriptures for themselves, and the reality of wonders and providences. For example, instead of discouraging the popular faith in divine visions, a Millerite journal printed the account of a woman who had seen several angels, "winged and beautiful beings," as she lay in a trance.[26] Most important of all, the Millerites preached the imminence of a violent, cataclysmic apocalypse—an apocalypse that many evangelicals had been predicting for forty years.

Hoping to recapture the fervor of the early revivals, many Christian, Freewill Baptist, and Methodist clergymen left their congregations in the early 1840s to join the Millerites. Ministers such as Joseph Marsh, the prominent editor of the *Christian Palladium*, and Joshua Himes, a well-known antislavery activist, staked their reputations on their faith in the second advent. George Storrs, who had been a Methodist circuit rider for fifteen years, joined the Millerites as well.[27] Disturbed by the signs of the times, these men tried to rekindle the spirit of dissent and experimentation they feared their own churches had lost. Traveling across the country on horseback or on foot, they gravely warned people to prepare for the end of the world.

These ministers were joined by large numbers of lay women who were frustrated by the growing restrictions on their religious speech. Cordelia Thomas, a Methodist, explained that she had been so dissatisfied with her "humble" duties as an itinerant's wife that she had longed for a larger "sphere of usefulness." After reading the memoir of Mary Bosanquet Fletcher, one of the earliest Methodist female preachers in England, she dreamed of becoming a "Christian of no ordinary grade"—a "great" woman whose piety would inspire sinners to seek salvation. In the early 1840s, her aspirations finally led her to the Millerites, who encouraged her to do everything in her power to prepare for the kingdom of God. To the dismay of her husband and her family, she left the Methodist church to become a Millerite exhorter.[28]

Besides lay women such as Thomas, several female preachers also abandoned their sects in search of "oldtime" revival religion. Women such as Dolly Richards (a Christian), and Mary Seymour (a Freewill Baptist), decided to "come out of Babylon" in search of greater religious freedom.[29] Increasingly pushed to the sidelines of their own denominations, they sought—and found—a larger sphere of activity within the Millerite movement.

Prophetic Daughters

Like earlier generations of Methodists, Freewill Baptists, and Christians, the Millerites actively encouraged women's participation in the movement. They were anxious to attract male converts as well, but at a time when the majority of church members were female, they seemed to recognize they could not survive without a vital ministry to women. Besides participating in official conference meetings, women often prayed aloud, witnessed, and exhorted during church and camp meetings. For example, at a service in Patchogue, Long Island, in 1843, "many females gave testimonies to the blessings they received."[30]

The Millerites also tried to attract female converts by featuring women's personal religious accounts in their journals and newspapers. Like the Freewill Baptists, Christians, and Methodists, they reprinted correspondence from prominent female preachers, but in their own distinctive innovation, they also published large numbers of letters and articles written by ordinary women. Although women such as Sophronia Murray, E. S. Bryant, and I. N. Perkins were rank-and-file Millerites, their words were read by thousands of people across the country. Perkins, for example, offered "A Word of Exhortation" to the readers of *The Voice of Truth*.[31] Whether or not she ever spoke publicly in her own local congregation, she used the medium of print to exhort sinners to heed the midnight cry.

The Millerites even created a journal that was explicitly marketed to women. Entitled *The Advent Message to the Daughters of Zion*, it was designed to strengthen women's faith in Christ's "coming glory." The journal was edited by a popular female preacher named Clorinda S. Minor, who opened the first issue with "An Appeal to the Women of Our Beloved Country." Warning her female readers that Christ would "certainly come quickly," she urged them to "flee the fascinations of earth, and, like Mary, secure that better part, which shall survive the cleansing fires of the coming day." In subsequent issues, she tried to bring more women into the movement by explaining the logic of Miller's chronology, especially his use of the book of Daniel. All of the articles in the journal were written by women, and they ranged from scriptural exegesis to personal religious testimony. For example, Emily Clemons, a well-known preacher, contributed inspirational poems such as "The End of All Things is at Hand," "Be Not Afraid, Only Believe," and "The Coming Savior."[32]

Most important, the Millerites allowed at least twenty women to preach, or in their terminology, to "lecture." Like earlier female preachers, these women were never ordained or set apart by the laying on of hands, but they were widely recognized as important spiritual leaders within the movement. Even though they never made up more than 5 percent of the total number of Millerite preachers, they were prominently featured in the religious press.[33] In 1843 Olive Maria Rice was the subject of lengthy articles in both *The Midnight Cry* and *Signs of the Times*, and other periodicals reprinted letters from women such as Mary Bone Ongley, Martha Spence, and H. A. Parks.

Even more than the Freewill Baptists, Methodists, and Christians, the Millerites championed women's right to speak publicly. Although Millerite clergymen were quick to denounce female "fanatics" such as Elizabeth Stone and "Miss Thompson," who supposedly claimed they could perform miracles, they offered lavish praise to the more orthodox women in the movement.[34] J. D. Pickands described Emily Clemons as an "excellent sister" and Sarah J. Higgins as a "lovely sister" who was "intelligent and sensible." Similarly, Olive Maria Rice was commended for being a "devoted sister" who had led a "glorious revival" in Oxford, New York.[35] There were certainly ministers who regarded female preaching as unscriptural or improper, but in the early years of the movement, they rarely expressed their opinions in print. Published accounts of women's meetings were overwhelmingly favorable, and women were repeatedly singled out for special praise. In 1844 *The Midnight Cry* not only extolled Sarah Higgins for preaching with "great power" at a camp meeting, but reported that Lucy Maria Hersey had spoken to "crowded audiences" who "listened with profound attention, and not unfrequently in tears to her discourses."[36]

Like female preachers in other denominations, Millerite women became so popular that they often spoke to hundreds or even thousands of excited spectators. Olive Maria Rice estimated that she had lectured to crowds of "1000 to 1400 people," and Emily Clemons, Mary Seymour, and Lucy Maria Hersey reportedly preached to more than 4,000 at a camp meeting in Rochester, New York.[37] Although these numbers were almost certainly exaggerated, they still suggest that women attracted significant public attention. In the eyes of the Millerites, who believed that every event was invested with divine significance, these women's popularity was a concrete sign of God's blessing: if they had not been genuinely called to preach, they would never have inspired so many revivals.

Following in the footsteps of earlier evangelicals, the Millerites supported female preaching for both practical and ideological reasons. On the practical level, there were simply not enough clergymen to spread the message of the midnight cry. Even in western New York, where the movement was strongest, there was a scarcity of male ministers. "The field is emphatically large," *The Midnight Cry* reported, but "the laborers are few." In addition, many Millerites believed that saving souls was more important than preserving women's traditional roles or debating the merits of separate spheres. If God were truly preparing to destroy the world with earthquakes, hailstones, and coals of fire, then women as well as men had an obligation to warn sinners.[38]

Other Millerites permitted women to preach *because* of their gender rather than despite it. Even more than earlier evangelicals, they identified female preaching as a sign of the coming apocalypse. Because they were convinced that every word of prophecy would literally come true—angels would appear with trumpets, the dead would rise out of their graves, and Christ would descend out of the clouds to begin a thousand-year reign of peace—they carefully examined every event in their lives for parallels to Scripture. After Lauretia Fassett delivered her first sermon in Seneca Falls, New York, in 1844, her husband immediately remembered Joel's prophetic description of the end of the world: "And it shall come to pass afterward, that I will pour out my spirit upon all flesh; and your sons and your daughters shall prophesy." Even though both of the Fassetts had once viewed female preaching as "immodest and unbecoming," they changed their minds because of their belief in the coming millennium. Given Joel's prophecy, the sight of a woman standing in the pulpit had cosmic significance: she was a living symbol of the last days, a reminder that the end of the world had truly come.[39]

Besides describing themselves as Joel's prophetic daughters, Millerite women also defended their right to preach by citing the examples of Old and New Testament heroines such as Deborah, Priscilla, and Anna. Comparing herself to Mary Magdalene, Martha Spence claimed it was her duty "to go from place to place on *the run* till my Jesus comes."[40] Instead of trying to deny her gender, as Jemima Wilkinson and Ann Lee had done during the Revolutionary era, she defended her right to speak as a flesh and blood woman. Identifying herself as the heir of a biblical tradition of female ministry, she portrayed herself as a Mother in Israel who had been directly inspired by God.

Even the most radical and visionary women in the movement never defended their right to preach on the grounds that they were "neither male nor female." In 1844 Ann Matthewson imitated Jemima Wilkinson by claiming that she had died and gone to heaven, but despite her insistence that she had been literally resurrected, she never suggested that her "death" had obliterated her sex. Unlike Wilkinson, she neither dressed in men's clothing nor refused to answer to her female name.[41] Even though she described herself as a prophet, she never denied being a woman as well.

Like earlier nineteenth-century female preachers, Millerite women solved the "problem" of their gender by arguing that God had transformed their weakness into strength. "Surely God chooses the weak things of the world to confound the mighty," Olive Maria Rice exulted. Even though she was sinful and unworthy, God had chosen her to be his instrument, promising to guide all her words and actions. As she explained, "I have often felt those words applied, 'It is not you that speaketh but the spirit of your Father which speaketh in you.' " Similarly, E. J. Marden, an exhorter, claimed that she was often "astonished" to hear the words that God had put in her mouth. Instead of preparing her sermons in advance, she waited to see what "utterance the spirit gave."[42]

Yet no matter how much these women insisted that they were merely the mouthpieces of God, they were hardly passive in the building of the movement. Determined to spread the doctrine of the second advent, they walked, sailed, and rode thousands of miles across the country. Most frequently, women traveled to congregations in rural areas, but they also targeted cities such as New York, Philadelphia, and Boston. For example, in 1844 Sarah Higgins reportedly preached to "overflowing" crowds in New York City. Because these women honestly believed they had a divine mission to warn people of Christ's impending return, they devoted themselves to a strenuous schedule of both traveling and lecturing. When Lucy Maria Hersey visited Otsego County, New York, she sometimes preached more than twice a day, averaging nine sermons a week.[43]

Like female preachers in other denominations, Millerite women learned how to market their ideas to the public at the same time as they protested against the materialistic values of a new consumer culture. Following in the footsteps of the Freewill Baptists, Christians, and Methodists, the Millerites were promotional geniuses who excelled at public communication. One of their most brilliant strategies was the purchase of the "Great Tent," an enormous camp meeting tent which had a circumference of over 120 yards and a center pole that rose fifty-five feet into the air. Reputedly the largest tent in America, it could seat 4,000 people and accommodate up to 2,000 more in the aisles and around the perimeter. First pitched in 1842, it was eventually trans-

This engraving of the Millerites' "Great Tent" was published in *The Advent Herald* 8, no. 3 (August 21, 1844). Courtesy of the American Antiquarian Society.

ported to towns all across the country, including Lexington, Kentucky, where "Sister" Brewer and her husband used it for a mass camp meeting.[44] In the age of P. T. Barnum, Americans seemed to have a boundless appetite for spectacle and entertainment, and the tent turned out to be an inspired advertising ploy. Barnum himself, the master of humbug, later imitated the Millerites by buying an enormous tent for his "Greatest Show on Earth."[45] Whether or not Barnum ever attended a Millerite meeting, he knew expert salesmanship when he saw it. Many of his circus posters, with their pictures of ferocious-looking beasts, looked remarkably like the Millerites' prophetic charts.

The Millerites attracted crowds of spectators by carrying huge, colorful diagrams with them as they walked to their meetings. Although these charts depicted Miller's millennial chronology in graphic form, their main appeal seems to have been their bizarre and often disturbing images of the apocalypse. Based on the descriptions contained in the books of Daniel and Revelation, they typically pictured angels blowing trumpets, lions with wings, dragons with seven heads, men with horns, and grotesque beasts with bared teeth. The Millerites published three hundred of these charts, each one measuring three feet wide and six feet long, and preachers such as Olive Maria Rice carried them on their travels. Whenever they wanted to publicize a religious meeting, they simply displayed their chart in a public place and waited for the crowds to appear. Indeed, people were so fascinated by these mysterious symbols that entrepreneurs began using them in commercial advertising. In 1843 an advertisement featured an angel flying through the heavens with a scroll proclaiming, "The Time Has Come." The caption underneath the advertisement read, "When consumption may be classed with curable diseases. Wistar's Balsam of Wild Cherry."[46] Since the "gloomy" Millerites were deadly serious about their belief in the end times, they probably did not find it humorous that their charts were being used to hawk patent medicine.

Nevertheless, the Millerites themselves were deeply influenced by the strategies of the market revolution. Under the skillful leadership of Joshua Himes, they developed sophisticated methods of publicity and advertising that propelled them from a small sect into a mass movement. Even though earlier evangelicals had realized the potential of the press, the Millerites published tracts, memoirs, and newspapers on a scale never before imagined. Whenever they began an evangelistic campaign in a new city, they printed thousands of copies of their newspapers and peddled them from every street corner. In 1842, when they began preaching in New York City, they printed 10,000 copies of *The Midnight Cry* every day and gave away many of them for free. A year later, they flooded Philadelphia with 50,000 copies of the first volume of *The Trumpet of Alarm*.[47] Although most of their newspapers were published in major cities such as Boston, New York, Philadelphia, Cincinnati, and Toronto, they also sent bundles of their publications to post offices across the country. Even in Maine, far removed from the centers of Millerite propaganda, the Methodist E. F. Newell found "pamphlets, papers, charts, and questions everywhere." Remarkably, the Millerites produced approximately 4 million pieces of literature in only four years, averaging one book, tract, or newspaper for every five people in the United States.[48]

Female preachers contributed to this promotional onslaught by publishing both letters and articles in Millerite periodicals. For example, Mary Seymour used the press to explain her theological doctrines and advertise where she was preaching.[49] Similarly, H. A. Parks wrote several letters to *The Voice of Truth* describing the revivals she had led in cities and towns across the country, including New York, Canada, Vermont, and the western territories of Indiana, Michigan, and Wisconsin.[50] Others relied on the press to prove how invaluable they were to the success of the movement. Lacking the institutional authority of ordination, they tried to demonstrate their worth by listing the number of sinners they had converted. For example, in a letter to *The Midnight Cry*, Olive Maria Rice provided a precise account of the number of people she had "saved" during nine weeks of lecturing throughout New York: thirty in Oxford, ninety or one hundred in McDonough, one hundred in Smithville, and forty in Greene. Lest anyone question her authority, she insisted that her preaching had produced "glorious results."[51]

No woman was more successful at promoting her beliefs than Emily Clemons, a respected preacher, writer, and former principal of a women's high school in Rochester, New York. After joining the Millerites in 1844, Clemons quickly became one of the most visible and respected women in the movement. Not only was she reputed to be a charismatic speaker, but she was also a prolific author who contributed more than twenty-five articles to the Millerite press in only two years. Her essays ranged from personal meditations to biblical commentaries. Besides writing about the meaning of faith and "the hope of the gospel," she explored the meanings of difficult prophetic texts. Her genius was her ability to appeal to readers of all levels and tastes. Besides theological tracts, she also wrote simple, sentimental poems for women and children with titles such as "The Importunate Widow" and "Lay Me on My Little Bed."[52] She also coedited two different journals, *Hope Within the Veil* and *The Hope of Israel*, and after her marriage to Charles H. Pearson, she cofounded *The Bible Advocate* with him.[53]

Because of their aggressive use of the press, their popularity, and their claim to divine inspiration, women such as Clemons sound strikingly similar to earlier generations of female preachers. Yet it is important to recognize that they were separated by significant differences as well. Despite their desire to recapture the spirit of the early revivals, the Millerites were not identical to the sectarians of the 1810s and 1820s. Socially, they drew their membership from a higher economic class, and theologically, they placed almost as much emphasis on education as divine inspiration. Even though they did not require lecturers to be college-educated, they expected them to be able to interpret Miller's intricate prophetic charts. At a minimum, preachers were supposed to have mastered the books of Daniel and Revelation.

Reflecting the larger constituency of the movement, most Millerite female preachers seem to have been better educated than their predecessors, and they were also economically more secure. For example, Lucy Maria Hersey had once been a schoolteacher, and Emily Clemons had been the principal of the Ladies High School in Rochester, New York. One of the most popular female preachers, Clorinda Minor, was the wife of a wealthy Philadelphia merchant. Because these women tended to come from relatively privileged families, they spoke in a far more refined style than the "uncouth" women who had shocked middle-class audiences during the 1820s and 1830s. Lauretia Fassett, the daughter of a former senator from New York, had been raised in too genteel a household to feel comfortable yelling out her praises to God. Nor did she cry aloud or clap her hands to emphasize the force of her words. Despite her dedication to saving sinners, she did not want to be mistaken for "a poor-white-trash-preachin'-woman."[54]

Even more than earlier generations of female preachers, Millerite women took pains to reassure the American public that they were neither crude nor immodest. First, they tended to describe themselves as lecturers rather than preachers. Perhaps they were simply following the example set by lay men, who often used this terminology as well, but it is hard to imagine that Mary Seymour, who had once been allowed to preach by the Freewill Baptists, did not understand that the word "lecturing" did not carry the same air of religious authority as "preaching." Second, these women seem to have chosen to speak from the pew or from the floor at the front of the church rather than from the dignified height of the pulpit. Although the evidence is scarce (very few articles mention where women stood as they spoke), it is telling that Olive Maria Rice, a former Methodist, thought she needed to make excuses for speaking from the pulpit. In an apologetic letter to *The Midnight Cry*, she explained that her audiences were often so large that she had "been compelled to go into the desk in order to be heard in the galleries and back parts of the house."[55] Unlike Nancy Towle, who had once shocked a minister by elbowing her way past him into the pulpit, Rice expressed far more reluctance about encroaching on "masculine" territory.

Millerite female preachers also seemed particularly conservative in their attitudes toward the family. Earlier women had also defended the integrity of the traditional, father-headed family, but many of them, including Zilpha Elaw and Elleanor Knight, had disobeyed their husbands or fathers by deciding to preach. In contrast, Lucy Maria Hersey, who began her career when she was only nineteen, never lectured without her father in attendance. More important, at least nine of the twenty-two women who preached for the Millerites were married, and they often traveled in company with their husbands. For example, Mary Bone Ongley and her husband took turns lecturing to congregations in western New York, advertising themselves as a preaching team.[56]

Tentatively at first, and then with growing confidence, Millerite women began to invent a new justification for female preaching. Throughout the eighteenth and nineteenth centuries, as we have seen, evangelical women showed enormous theological creativity in defending their right to preach, developing new lines of argument to suit the tenor of their times. While female evangelists in colonial America had claimed to be neither male nor female, female preachers after the Revolution drew on a new ideology of female virtue to identify themselves as pious Mothers in Israel and Sisters in Christ. By the 1840s, however, women began to voice yet another argument. In contrast to earlier Freewill Baptists, Christians, and Methodists, the Millerites argued that *married* women, not single women, were best suited for careers in the pulpit. By claiming to speak as their husbands' helpmates, female preachers tried to counter accusations that they were promiscuous, shameless, or "masculine." Nothing could be more "feminine" than a woman helping her husband in his spiritual labors. By the late nineteenth century, growing numbers of women would preach as co-pastors with their husbands.

Despite obvious advantages to co-ministry for women, there were significant drawbacks as well. On the positive side, Millerite female preachers who were married to clergymen may have felt less lonely and vulnerable than women who traveled alone or with female companions. If they walked into meetings side by side with their husbands, they were less likely to be verbally or physically harassed by unruly spectators. More negatively, however, they were almost always treated as their husbands' assistants rather than as authoritative preachers in their own right. For example, even though several correspondents to *The Midnight Cry* and *The Advent Herald* praised Sidney Brewer and his wife for "*their* labors" at camp meetings, they never clearly identified her as a preacher. Because none of her admirers ever bothered to write down her full name, she is known to us today only as "Sister" Brewer.[57]

Yet if Brewer or other women resented their secondary status in their families or in the movement as a whole, they never said so publicly. Even though they were forbidden to vote for new ministers, be ordained, or administer the sacraments of baptism and the Lord's Supper, they never protested against the sexual inequalities that undergirded their churches. If the world was going to end in a few years, months, or days, then there was no reason for them to waste their energies on reform. Instead of demanding sexual equality on earth, they longed to escape from history into a millennium out of time.

Female preachers took an apolitical stance not only on the question of women's rights, but on abolition as well. Emily Clemons, like many other Millerites, was strongly opposed to slavery, but she never became actively involved in the antislavery movement because of her confidence that Christ would personally free the slaves on the Day of Jubilee. In her poem "A Voice from Slave Land," she wrote: "The Lord from Heaven *alone* can break, the bondsman's clanking chain, / And in his Holy Word we read that he will come again."[58] Unlike abolitionists, she could not imagine achieving sinless perfection on earth, but only in an otherworldly kingdom.

Like earlier female preachers, Millerite women also kept their distance from feminist lecturers such as Frances Wright. Ironically, two of the best-known feminists of the nineteenth century, Angelina Grimké and Sojourner Truth, were briefly attracted to the Millerites during the early 1840s, but both eventually regretted their millennial "enthusiasm," and there is no record of other Millerite women ever becoming involved in the women's rights movement.[59] Few biblical feminists wanted to be associated with women who supposedly sought to destroy the traditional family.

It is deeply ironic, then, that Millerite female preachers were accused of being radicals who had sacrificed their modesty for public fame. Even though they were better-educated, more prosperous, and generally more refined than earlier generations of women, they faced the same insults and slanders. Besides complaining that it was "very *immodest* for *ladies* to be studying and explaining the prophecies," their detractors questioned their sexual morality. Even those who were willing to tolerate husband and wife preaching teams were shocked by the thought of young, single women "exposing" themselves in public. In a letter to a Baptist newspaper, a man claimed that Olive Maria Rice, a supposed "angel," was actually a "fallen" woman. "There was a good many 'fellers' after her," he jeered, "and they said that Sam'l Noyes and Holmes flipped a cent to see which should go home with her the last night."[60] In his opinion, she was no better than a common prostitute.

Other critics asserted that Millerite women lost their softness and "femininity" by lecturing publicly. When Jane Marsh Parker, the daughter of a prominent Millerite leader, wrote a novel about her memories of the movement (aptly entitled *The Midnight Cry*), she described one of her female characters, an exhorter, as "a masculine woman." She also explicitly compared one of her main protagonists, "Letitia Barkenstone," to Jemima Wilkinson, the infamous Public Universal Friend. "They were not so very different," one of her characters proclaimed. In reality, no Millerite female preacher ever dressed in men's clothing or denied being female, but Marsh believed that any woman who stood in the pulpit had a secret longing to be a man.[61] Modeling the character of Barkenstone on the real-life Clorinda Minor, she described her as an educated, pious woman who had tragically sacrificed everything—her money, her family, and even her gender—on the altar of "fanaticism." Even though Parker portrayed Minor in a sympathetic light as a vulnerable woman who had been misled by religious zealots, she clearly doubted whether any female preacher could preserve her "feminine" delicacy under the glare of public exposure.

In the eyes of the American public, the Millerites seemed to have little respect for the distinctions of either "masculinity" or "femininity": they turned women into men and men into women. While Millerite women were seen as jezebels who presumed to "teach" men, Millerite men were considered effeminate "dupes" who shirked their financial responsibilities as breadwinners. At a time when most Americans equated work with masculinity, Millerite men seemed shockingly lazy: many were so certain of an impending apocalypse that they closed their businesses and stopped plowing their fields. According to an article in *The Advent Shield*, a group of Millerites in New Hampshire had stopped planting and harvesting their crops:

> Some of our brethren in the north of New Hampshire had been so impressed with the belief that the Lord would come before another winter, that they did not cultivate their fields. About the middle of July . . . others, who had sown and planted their fields, were so impressed with a sense of the Lord's immediate appearing, that they could not, consistently with their faith, harvest their crops. Some, on going into their fields to cut their grass, found themselves entirely unable to proceed, and, conforming to their sense of duty, left their crops standing in the field, to show their faith by their works.[62]

These farmers believed that it would be sinful to work if they honestly believed in Christ's imminent return, but their critics saw their "idleness and *profligacy*" as an affront to Victorian definitions of manhood. "Go to work you sanctimonious rascals," one man ordered.[63] Any man who did not labor on behalf of his family was not really a man at all.

Despite the ridicule of the American public, Millerite men and women clung fiercely to their belief in the second advent. Persecution only confirmed their sense of divine destiny: the bridegroom would soon sound his midnight cry. In 1843, following the chronology set by William Miller, they confidently declared that the millennium would begin within a few short months. (Because of the calendar change, they defined 1843 as the year between March 21, 1843, and March 21, 1844.) When 1843 drew to a close and their Savior still had not appeared, they refused to give up hope. Samuel Snow, one of Miller's followers, used the texts of Habakkuk 2:3 and Leviticus 25:9 to argue that there would be a "tarrying time" of seven months and ten days. Christ would certainly return to earth, the Millerites now claimed, on October 22, 1844.

The Great Disappointment

During the summer and fall of 1844, thousands of Millerites across the country turned their eyes heavenward in expectation of their Savior. They confessed their sins, took their children out of school, closed their businesses, and settled their debts. The United States Treasury reportedly received large sums of money from people who wanted to repay their creditors before Judgment Day. As each day passed, the excitement and anticipation grew stronger. In the words of Luther Boutelle, a Millerite lecturer from Massachusetts, "Such a oneness of faith was never before witnessed; certainly not in modern times. All that did speak spoke the same things. Solemn, yet joyful. Jesus coming! we to meet him! Meetings everywhere were being held. Confessions made, wrongs righted; sinners inquiring what they should do to be saved."[64] Certain that they would soon hear the midnight cry, Millerites all across the country joyfully prepared to meet Christ.

With soaring hopes, Millerite leaders returned home from their preaching tours, stopped their printing presses, and dismantled the Great Tent for the last time. On October 16, 1844, *The Advent Herald* notified its readers that no more issues would be published. "We shall make no provisions for issuing a paper for the week following," they announced. "And as we are shut up to this faith . . . we feel called upon to suspend our labors and await the result. Behold, the Bridegroom cometh; go ye out to meet him! is the cry that is being sounded in our ears; and may we all, with our lamps trimmed and burning, be prepared for His glorious appearing." The day had finally come when the saved would be "caught up together to meet the Lord in the air," while the damned would be "left to destruction."[65]

On October 21, the eve of Christ's expected return, congregations began gathering together to wait and pray. In Philadelphia, a group of Millerites took warning from the story of Lot's wife and resolved to flee the city without looking back. (When Lot's wife dared to take one last look at Sodom, she was turned into a pillar of salt.) Led by Clorinda Minor, George Storrs, and George Grigg, they camped in the countryside to await Christ's glorious appearance in the clouds.[66] On October 22, Millerites all across the country anxiously trained their eyes at the sky and waited for a sign. From morning to noon to night, they watched as each hour went by, expecting to see stars falling from the skies, or lightning shriveling up the land, or the dead coming out of their graves. In a small town near Rochester, New York, "a terrible storm" frightened many into believing "the end of the world had truly come," but when the thunderclouds passed, they found the earth had been spared. "We looked for the coming of the Lord until the clock tolled 12 at midnight," the farmer Hiram Edson remembered, and then, "We wept, and wept, till the day dawn[ed]."[67]

October 22 was immortalized in Adventist history as the day of the "Great Disappointment." At first, Millerites reacted with shock and disbelief, refusing to accept that their calculations had been wrong. "We are yet on the shores of mortality," one journal declared, "but He is at the door. He has given a few days more for the trial of our faith." As days turned to months, however, many Millerites began to lose faith. Besides trying to cope with their own self-doubts, they were mocked by people in the streets who asked, "Have you not gone up?" In a letter to Joshua Himes, Miller wrote bitterly, "Even little children in the streets are shouting continually to passers-by 'Have you got a ticket to go up?'" The disappointment was "a humiliating thing," Luther Boutelle admitted, and it made the "faithful and longing ones" "unspeakably sad."[68] In despair, many wished they had never listened to the predictions of William Miller, who now seemed like a false prophet.

The Great Disappointment eventually led to the collapse of the movement. The Millerites were linked together only by their belief in Christ's imminent return, and when prophecy failed, they split into competing factions. Small Adventist sects proliferated, each differing in their interpretation of the disappointment. Some stubbornly continued to set new dates, speculating that Christ would appear in 1845 or 1851. For example, writing in 1846, Sarah Higgins insisted that the millennium was imminent. "I do not see any way to evade the conclusion that this present year will bring deliverance to all the waiting people of God," she testified. Others claimed that Christ *had* returned on October 22, but only in a spiritual way. After welcoming his "brides" to the wedding feast, he had shut the door against sinners. This group of Adventists

Martha Spence Heywood. Disillusioned by the Great Disappointment, Spence traveled west to join the Mormons. Courtesy of the Utah Historical Society.

came to be known as "door-shutters" because of their belief that anyone who had not experienced conversion before the midnight cry would be consigned to damnation. According to contemporary accounts, they practiced foot washing and "holy kissing." Still another group organized around the issue of the Sabbath, claiming that keeping a seventh-day Sabbath was essential to salvation. Under the leadership of Ellen Harmon White and her husband, James White, they planted the seeds for what would eventually become a new denomination: the Seventh-Day Adventists. Finally, many former Millerites simply left their churches entirely or joined other sects. While Martha Spence found her true millennium with the Mormons, other former Millerites fled to the Shakers.[69]

The most moderate Adventists were alarmed by the splintering of the movement and the radicalism of the smaller sects. In 1845 *The Morning Watch* printed a "Warning to Adventists" cautioning their readers to beware of three "fanatics" named Dorinda Baker, Israel Damon, and John Moody, who supposedly taught "disgusting extravagances" such as "public feet-washings, embracings, [and] kissings."[70] Many Millerite leaders, including the influential

Joshua Himes, now feared that the "ultraists" were taking over the movement. In 1845 Himes convinced William Miller and other leaders to attend a conference in Albany, New York, to set new guidelines for worship and doctrine. During the early 1840s, the Millerites had prided themselves on their organizational fluidity, but in the aftermath of the Great Disappointment, they decided to create a formal creed and a formal clergy. Remarkably, they had matured from a sect to a denomination in the course of only one year.

The Albany Conference represented the beginning of the Adventist Christian Church, a new denomination with its own distinct beliefs and rituals. Ironically, the Millerites had protested the formalization of dissenting sects such as the Methodists and Freewill Baptists, but their own history followed the same path. "Order is heaven's first law," they proclaimed in 1845. "Nothing exists without form." Replacing the flexibility of their early churches with greater structure and discipline, they discouraged visionary enthusiasm, established a professional clergy, and forbade women to serve as evangelists. At the Albany Conference, they resolved that all ministerial candidates would be carefully screened and only *"brethren"* would be permitted to preach.[71] Following the pattern set by the Separates, Freewill Baptists, Methodists, and Christians before them, they sacrificed their tradition of female ministry for greater power and public acceptance. Even though Adventist journals continued to print news about women such as Sarah Higgins and "Sister" Plumb throughout the 1840s, many clergymen no longer welcomed their labors.

Yet no matter what their fellow ministers thought, many Millerite women were so committed to their mission to warn sinners that they refused to stop preaching. As long as they could find congregations willing to listen to them, they could not be forced out of the ministry. Unlike the Puritans, who had exiled Anne Hutchinson to the wilderness in the seventeenth century, nineteenth-century evangelicals did not have any formal connection to the state, and they had to rely on persuasion rather than coercion to attract new converts. Unless they could convince every single evangelical to reject female preaching—an impossible task in a free society—they would never be able to completely suppress women's religious leadership. In the wake of the Revolution, women had devoted their talents to nurturing civil society, and even though many showed little interest in voting or holding office, they still demanded that their voices be heard.

All told, at least eight Millerite female preachers continued traveling and lecturing after the Great Disappointment. Frustrated by the opposition of the

Adventist leadership, some moved to the frontier in search of greater opportunities. Traveling to states where there were relatively few ordained ministers to compete with them, Mary Seymour went to Michigan and H. A. Parks began a new career in Indiana and Wisconsin. Most dramatically, Clorinda Minor left the country altogether, traveling to Jerusalem in the hope that Christ would someday appear in the holy land. In 1851 she founded an agricultural colony in Artas, near Bethlehem, in order to fulfill a verse from Isaiah: "Instead of the thorn, shall come up the fig tree; and instead of the brier shall come up the myrtle tree, and it shall be to the lord for a name, for an everlasting sign, that shall not be cut off." When she died there in 1855, still waiting for Christ to appear in the clouds, she had not lost her faith that her Savior would "set His hand a second time, to recover Israel," and she was certain it would be soon.[72]

Inspired by these models of female religious leadership, Adventist women continued to enter the ministry during the late 1840s and 1850s. For example, both Mary Wellcome and Abigail Mussey first felt called to preach after the Great Disappointment, and despite their fears of clerical opposition, each eventually took up the cross of public evangelism. The best known Millerite female preacher, Ellen Gould Harmon White, the visionary founder of the Seventh-Day Adventists, did not begin her remarkable career until December of 1844, the date that she claimed to have received her first revelation from God. Despite the fact that she was only seventeen at the time, White began preaching to Millerite churches throughout New England, often addressing large crowds. In 1846 she married James White, a Millerite lecturer who encouraged her to publish her visions, and together they "traveled on foot, in second-class cars, or on steamboat decks" across the northern states in order to publicize their belief in the seventh-day Sabbath. Because of the responsibilities of raising four children, she rarely spoke publicly between the years of 1852 and 1863, but in later life she became a well-known lecturer on temperance and health reform. The sect that she founded still endures today, numbering over 2.5 million members.[73]

Although White, Mussey, and Wellcome managed to preserve the Millerite legacy of female evangelism, they moved in increasingly conservative directions during the 1850s and 1860s. In part, they were influenced by pressure from men and women within their own denomination. During the 1850s, for example, ministers such as Henry Grew and Z. G. Bliss urged women to fulfill their Christian responsibilities by staying at home and caring for their husbands and children. Dismissing Joel's prophecy as obsolete, Grew insisted that Paul had superseded it by ordering women to keep silence in the churches. "No prohibition or command is stated in plainer terms," he concluded.[74] After the Great Disappointment, female preaching no longer appeared to be a herald of the coming millennium, but a radical innovation that threatened the stability of the family. A true woman belonged not in the pulpit, but in the kitchen.

Besides responding to clerical opposition, Adventist female preachers were also deeply influenced by the emergence of an organized women's rights movement during the late 1840s. Even as early as the mid-1820s, many evangelical female preachers had condemned "infidel" female lecturers such as Frances Wright, but after the first women's rights convention in Seneca Falls, New York, in 1848, they took even greater pains to emphasize their conservatism. On the surface, they seemed to have much in common with Elizabeth Cady Stanton, Lucretia Mott, and the other women who gathered in 1848 in Seneca Falls, the same rural town where Lauretia Fassett had delivered her first sermon four years earlier. Indeed, Millerite women could easily have written parts of the "Declaration of Sentiments," the feminist manifesto which was modeled on the Declaration of Independence: "It is demonstrably the right and duty of woman, equally with man, to promote every righteous cause by every righteous means. And especially in regard to the great subjects of morals and religion, it is self-evidently her right to participate with her brother in teaching them, both in private and in public, by writing and by speaking, by any instrumentalities proper to be used, and in any assemblies proper to be held."[75] However, even though the Millerites agreed that women deserved to play a wider role in the Christian church, they were also separated from women's rights activists by seemingly insurmountable theological and cultural differences. Many feminist reformers claimed to be fighting for "God's cause," but as Hicksite Quakers, Christian Unionists, and Congregational Friends, their version of biblical feminism was theologically more liberal.[76] In order to justify equal property rights and women's suffrage, they were willing to appeal to the spirit as well as the letter of the Bible—a position that made them appear dangerously freethinking to conservative evangelicals.

Determined not to be mistaken for "hens that crow," as feminist leaders were belittled, the Adventist female preachers of the 1850s and 1860s tried to reassure clergymen that they were not radicals who questioned women's divine subordination to men, but pious Christians whose voices deserved to be heard. According to Beulah Matthewson, who published an article and a book defending female preaching, women could speak as men's helpmates, but they certainly could not be ordained. Even though they could pray aloud, sing, witness, exhort, or preach, they were forbidden to "assume the leadership," or rob men of their rightful authority in the home and the church. Like Olive Maria Rice, who had abandoned her training as a missionary to preach to thousands of Millerites during the early 1840s, Matthewson believed that women had a right to labor in the harvest, but they could not be men's true equals until Christ's miraculous return. Until history came to an end, they would have to humbly accept their subordination to men.[77]

Perhaps it is appropriate that the last chapter of this book should end with a question: What happened to Olive Maria Rice, the young Millerite preacher who believed that God had made her a humble instrument of saving souls? Like so many of the other evangelical women who preached in the early nineteenth century, Rice disappeared from the historical record after 1845. Although it is clear that she married a man named Patten in 1844, nothing else is known about her later life. Perhaps she stopped preaching after the collapse of the Millerite movement, or perhaps she continued to travel in company with her husband. Either way, she seems to have been deliberately forgotten by clergymen who regretted the egalitarianism of their formative years. Despite her popularity, her religious zeal, and her self-sacrificing labors, her name never appeared in the histories of Adventism that were written in the later nineteenth century. For her, as for many other strangers and pilgrims, the collapse of the Millerite movement had been truly a great disappointment.

Epilogue

Write the Vision

Write the vision, and make it plain upon tables, that he may

run that readeth it. For the vision is yet for an appointed

time, but at the end it shall speak, and not lie: though it tarry,

wait for it; because it will surely come, it will not tarry.

—Habakkuk 2:2–3

When Christ did not return to earth in 1844 as the Millerites had hoped, the most devout argued that there would be a "tarrying time" of a few more months or years. Even though it seemed as if their millennial dreams had come to nought, many refused to give up hope. "As to my faith, it is increasing every day," H. A. Parks testified in 1845. "The hour of our last and final meeting will soon arrive." Echoing her words, Lauretia Fassett wrote: "To doubt that the righteous will soon realize the promised glory, is impossible. I can as soon doubt my own existence."[1] The Great Disappointment was not the end of their pilgrimage, but only a new beginning.

Like Parks and Fassett, many other female preachers continued to hold meetings during the 1840s and 1850s, and they resigned themselves to waiting for both the return of Christ and true equality between the sexes. They believed that only God could elevate women to their rightful place in history, and yet inscrutably, God had decided that their time had not yet come. Even though he had called them to preach the gospel, he had also sent them into a sinful world to be oppressed and rejected. In despair, Harriet Livermore asked, "How long, O Lord, how long, ere woman shall be clothed with the

Sun, walk upon the moon, and be crowned with Apostolick glory?" Yet even though she struggled with doubts about whether she would ever live to see women treated as men's "equals" instead of as their "servants," she took comfort from reading the words of the Bible: God had promised to fulfill all of his prophecies in "due time."[2] Disappointed, but not defeated, she and other evangelical women continued to pray, to preach, and to wait for the coming of the kingdom.

The most literate female preachers also resolved to "write the vision" in letters, articles, and memoirs. The more opposition that they faced in the pulpit, the more they realized the importance of writing their life stories. They did not want to be forgotten by future generations, and most important, they insisted that *God* did not want them to be forgotten either. As Nancy Towle explained, "The *great*, and *marvelous things*, the Lord hath wrought for me . . . he will not suffer, to be buried in the dust." Despite the persecution she had endured, she was confident that God had chosen her to be a sign to the rest of the world—a sign that women as well as men could be called to preach the gospel. Her remarkable story of grace belonged not to her alone, but to the entire family of Christians. Most of all, it belonged to the community of women who would succeed her in "the Lord's vineyard." By publishing her memoir, Towle hoped to reach out to the sisters and mothers who would someday follow her into the pulpit, reassuring them that she too had once felt too weak and unworthy to preach. In her words, "When my voice, is lost in death; may my labours still exist; (even for the encouragement of multitudes, that come after me, to 'love and fear' the Lord) *till time shall be no more!*" Through the pages of her book, she hoped to "labor" to bring forth a new era of female evangelism—and ultimately, the kingdom of God.[3]

It is deeply ironic, then, if not tragic, that Towle and other female preachers were forgotten by those whom they most wanted to inspire. Despite their faith that they would be remembered, they were written out of their denominations' histories during the late 1830s and 1840s. Few evangelicals wanted to preserve the memory of the female visionaries who had once made the campgrounds ring with the sound of their impassioned hallelujahs. Clergymen such as Nathan Bangs embraced a different vision of the evangelical past and future, a vision that did not include disorderly women such as Towle.

Sadly, it was not only evangelical men who wanted to forget female preachers, but evangelical women as well, even some of the women who stepped into the pulpit for the first time during the 1840s and 1850s. Reflecting the changing membership of their churches as a whole, these women tended to be educated and middle-class, and they seemed to be embarrassed by the uncouth, contentious women who continued to roam across the American countryside. Instead of trying to follow in their footsteps, they disowned them as lower-class enthusiasts.

In 1840, at the same time as Towle and other women were struggling to be remembered, Phoebe Palmer began hosting the Tuesday Meeting for the Promotion of Holiness in her home, launching a public career that would span more than thirty years. As one of the most popular female preachers of her time, Palmer certainly must have heard stories about the women who had preceded her. (There is no record that she had heard any of them preach, but it is hard to imagine that she could have been unaware of the controversy they caused.) Nevertheless, she seems to have felt the same way about them as they had once felt about Jemima Wilkinson and Ann Lee: they were enthusiasts best forgotten. Separating herself from the "coarse," visionary women who preached to factory workers and sailors, she embraced a more domestic, middle-class model of ministry that endeared her to Methodist ministers such as Nathan Bangs. Even though she spoke to thousands of converts in meetings across the country, she refused to call her work "preaching." As she explained, "It is our aim, in addressing the people . . . to simplify the way of faith. . . . Preach we do not; that is, not in a *technical* sense."[4] Instead of building on the work of the women who had gone before her, she tried to forge a new and more genteel model of ministry.

Nor were female preachers remembered by the other group of women who might have been sympathetic to their plight as strangers and pilgrims: the liberal feminist reformers who lent their voices to the emerging women's rights movement. Although middle-class feminists such as Elizabeth Cady Stanton and Susan B. Anthony must have known that female preachers existed, they never mentioned them in their writings. Did they admire their willingness to speak publicly? Were they embarrassed by their lower-class vulgarity? Without any evidence, it is hard to imagine what they must have thought of their evangelical "sisters," but they must have been deeply frustrated by their biblical conservatism. Unlike Sojourner Truth, the crusading evangelist who became one of the most famous feminists and abolitionists of her time, most evangelical female preachers never demanded their political, legal, or economic equality to men. Even though they defended their right to preach, they insisted that women could not "rule."

As biblical feminists, female preachers stood outside of the two communities who might have tried to preserve their memory. Too radical to be accepted by evangelicals and too conservative to be accepted by women's rights activists, they were caught between two worlds. Remembered by neither, they disappeared into the silence of the past.

It is tempting to write the history of eighteenth- and nineteenth-century female preaching as a story of decline. For many scholars, the history of early American evangelicalism appears as a fall from grace, a capitulation to middle-class conformity. To Russell E. Richey, for example, the early Methodists seem to have lived in a kind of Eden, a utopian world that was shattered as they sacrificed their egalitarianism in favor of cultural acceptance.[5] Certainly many early female preachers would have agreed with his assessment. Despite the sacrifices that they made for their church and their immense popularity in the early nineteenth century, they were belittled, persecuted, and eventually forgotten by their "brothers" and "sisters" in Christ. As the Methodists, Freewill Baptists, Christians, and Millerites embraced an ideology of domesticity, they deprived women of their earlier liberty of speech, urging them to keep silence in the churches. Clearly, they lost a vibrant part of their heritage when women such as Nancy Towle and Jarena Lee were forced out of the ministry.

However, history is rarely a record of either absolute progress or absolute decline; it takes unexpected twists and turns, transforming our perceptions in surprising ways. Even as one chapter in the history of female preaching came to an end in the 1840s, another one was just beginning. Indeed, it should come as no surprise that later generations of women proved to be as creative and persistent as their foremothers had been. Throughout most of American history, female preaching has been characterized not by upward progress, but by discontinuity and reinvention. Nineteenth-century female preachers such as Harriet Livermore did not know that Separate women had exhorted during the revivals of the Great Awakening, nor did twentieth-century women know that Livermore had ever preached to Congress. Yet even though women were repeatedly denied knowledge of their collective past, they managed to reinvent a tradition of female preaching from generation to generation.

During the later nineteenth century and beyond, hundreds of women continued to demand the right to labor in the harvest. Like earlier women, they were often slandered as "masculine" or "shameless," but because they had so little knowledge of their heritage, they did not realize how deeply their lives reverberated with the past. During the 1870s and 1880s, for example, many women who belonged to the Evangelical Free Church and the Church of God became traveling evangelists, but they were never given the same authority as ordained ministers. In the early twentieth century, scores of Pentecostalist women became popular preachers—including Aimee Semple McPherson, Agnes Ozman, and Florence Louise Crawford—but they were eventually excluded from holding formal leadership positions. Many early fundamentalist women also became preachers, but by 1941, when John R. Rice published his infamous treatise against women's rights, *Bobbed Hair, Bossy Wives, and Women Preachers: Significant Questions for Honest Christian Women Settled by the Word of God*, they were no longer welcome in the pulpit.[6] Recapitulating the stories of Nancy Towle, Harriet Livermore, and all of the other strangers and pilgrims who had gone before them, these women were ignored and forgotten when their small sects grew into powerful denominations. As in the early nineteenth century, the battle over female preaching continued to be a battle over women's proper place in American culture.

Yet even though female preaching in America remained a broken and disconnected tradition, growing numbers of women struggled not to repeat the failures of the past. In the late nineteenth century, after the backlash against female itinerants, evangelical women began to seek new justifications for their right to preach. Echoing the language of the "cult of true womanhood," they argued that God had inspired them to preach because of their purity and domesticity. Like earlier female preachers, they described themselves as sisters or mothers who had been called to nurture the family of God, but they took this domestic language to a greater extreme. Instead of imagining themselves as Mothers in Israel who were also fierce warriors (in the tradition of Deborah), they emphasized their maternal tenderness. Anna Oliver, a Methodist, argued that she belonged in the pulpit because of her "natural qualifications" as a woman. "Pastoral work is adapted to women," she explained, "for it is motherly work. The mother has her little group, the pastor the flock. As a mother spreads her table with food suited to the individual needs of her family, so the pastor feeds the flock."[7] According to Oliver, who embraced a far more refined model of ministry than earlier generations of women, her authority to preach came from her "femininity."

Despite their domestic language, however, women such as Oliver were far more radical than the women who had gone before them, and far more determined to be remembered. Slowly and tentatively, and then with increasing confidence, they began to demand what earlier women had never dared to imagine: the right to be ordained.[8] Instead of accepting their subordination to men, they called for a fundamental transformation in the relationship between the sexes. By demanding complete political, legal, economic, and religious equality, they tried to guarantee that women would never again have to reinvent a tradition of female preaching. Instead of waiting for Christ to return in glory, they would begin the hard work of building his kingdom on earth.

As part of that work, later generations of nineteenth- and twentieth-century women ministers published hundreds of books, sermons, and biblical defenses of female preaching. Even though they differed from earlier generations of women in their political radicalism, they shared their faith in the power of historical memory. From reading the Bible, they knew that the past, the present, and the future were inextricably connected, and they believed that their lives pointed both backward and forward: backward to biblical heroines such as Deborah and Phebe, and forward to the prophetic daughters of the millennium. Women never stood alone, but always in company with those who had gone before them and those who had yet to be born. If they wrote the vision— and if people read their words—they would not only record history, but change it.

Bathsheba Kingsley, Jemima Wilkinson, Nancy Towle, and Anna Oliver were connected by bonds that they themselves could not see. Denied knowledge of their collective history, they unknowingly fought the same battles generation after generation, repeating one another's stories across the span of more than one hundred years.[9] Despite their struggles, however, all of them refused to give up hope in the future. By preserving their faith in a world that seemed to scorn them, by trusting in the goodness of God, they hoped to inspire future generations of evangelical women to claim the pulpit as their own. Over and over again, they wrote the same vision: Christ would not tarry; the kingdom would surely come; and those who had once wandered the world as strangers and pilgrims, who had chosen to "suffer affliction with the people of God," would receive the promises at last.

Appendix

Female Preachers and

Exhorters in America,

1740–1845

Name	Denomination	Year First Mentioned in Records
Anna Stone Anderson (1813–?)	Freewill Baptist	1839
Dorinda Baker	Millerite	1845
Rachel Baker (1795–?)	Baptist	1814
Eliza Barnes (1796–1887)	Methodist/became a missionary to Indians	1825
"Sister" L. Berry	Freewill Baptist	1829
Mary Coy Bradley (1771–?)	Methodist exhorter	1803
"Sister" Brewer	Millerite	1844
Almira Prescott Bullock (1800–?)	Freewill Baptist/founded a new sect, the Bullockites, with her husband, Jeremiah Bullock	1821
Nancy Caldwell (1781–?)	Methodist exhorter	1806
Clarinda (last name unknown)	Baptist	1790s
Margaret Meuse Clay (1735–1832)	Separate exhorter	
Laura P. Clemens	United Brethren	1843
Emily C. Clemons	Millerite	1844
Hannah Peavey Cogswell (?–1853)	Christian Connection	1836
Maria Cook (1779–1835)	Universalist/became a Shaker	1811
Mrs. Cook	African Methodist exhorter	1811

Name	*Denomination*	*Year First Mentioned in Records*
L. Courtland	United Brethren	1841
Nancy Gove Cram (1776–1816)	Freewill Baptist/preached for Christian Connection	1812
Clarissa Danforth (1792–?)/became Clarissa Richmond in 1822	Freewill Baptist	1817
Sally Barnes Dunn (1783–1858)	Universalist	
Mary Dyer (1780–?)	Freewill Baptist	1823
Zilpha Elaw (1790?–)	African Methodist	1827
Elizabeth (last name unknown) (1766–?)	African Methodist	1808
Rachel Evans	African Methodist	
Lauretia E. Fassett (1821–84)	Millerite	1844
Hannah Fogg	Freewill Baptist	1821
Julia A. J. Foote (1823–1900)	African Methodist	1845
Ellen Bangs Gatchell	Methodist exhorter	1810
Mrs. Gibbs	Presbyterian/transferred to Freewill Baptists	1830
Clarissa Green	Christian Connection	1836
Polly Hatheway	Congregational exhorter	1812
Laura Smith Haviland (1808–98)	Wesleyan Methodist	1844
Sarah Hedges (1791–1843)	Methodist/Christian Connection	1809
Lucy Maria Hersey (1823–?)/became Lucy Stoddard in 1845	Millerite	1844
Charlotte Hestes	Christian Connection	1837
Sarah J. Higgins	Millerite	1844
Doritha Hill	African Methodist exhorter	
Martha Howell	Baptist exhorter	1808
Hannah Hubbard	Freewill Baptist	1818
Susan Humes (1804?–27?)	Freewill Baptist	1822
Rebecca D. Hutchins	Methodist	1813
Rebecca Cox Jackson (1795–1871)	African Methodist/became a Shaker	1833
Miriam H. Kent (1794–1821)	Christian Connection	1820
Bathsheba Kingsley (?–1748)	New Light exhorter	1742
Elleanor Knight (1799–?)	Christian Connection	1833
Sabrina Lambson (1799–1833)	Christian Connection	1824
Ann Lee (1736–84)	Shaker	1776
Jarena Lee (1783–?)	African Methodist	1819
Abigail Leister	Methodist exhorter	1790s
Salome Lincoln (1807–41)	Freewill Baptist/transferred to Reformed Methodists	1827
Harriet Livermore (1788–1868)	nondenominational	1822
Hannah Lock	Freewill Baptist	1801

Name	Denomination	Year First Mentioned in Records
Rachel Macomber	Christian Connection exhorter	1830
E. J. Marden	Millerite exhorter	1842
Martha Stearns Marshall	Separate exhorter	
Judith Mathers (?–1827)	unknown	1827
Ann Matthewson	Millerite exhorter	1844
Beulah Matthewson	Millerite	1840s
Elice Miller/became Elice Miller Smith	Methodist	1826
Rebecca Chaney Miller (1814–44)	Christian Connection	1830
"Sister" Mills	Methodist	1790s
Clorinda S. Minor (1808–55)	Millerite	1842
Louisa Mitchell	Freewill Baptist	1827
Nancy Mitchell	unknown	1802
Wealthy Monroe/became Wealthy Edmunds in 1843	Christian Connection	1833
Eliza More	Freewill Baptist	1801
Nancy Mulkey	Christian Connection exhorter	1810
Fanny Newell (1793–1824)	Methodist exhorter	1809
Betsey Niles	leader of her own sect	1821
Mary Bone Ongley	Millerite	1844
Sarah Orne	Methodist	1839
Sarah J. Paine	Millerite	1840s
Miss Parker	Methodist/nondenominational	1846
"Miss" or "Mrs." Parker	Millerite	1845
H. A. Parks	Millerite	1843
Sally Parsons	Freewill Baptist	1797
Mrs. Peavey	Christian Connection	1835
Deborah Peirce	Christian Connection	1820
Julia Pell	African Methodist	1841
"Sister" Plumb	Millerite	1844
Judith J. Prescott	Freewill Baptist	1817
Fanney Procter	Freewill Baptist	1801
Dolly Atkins Quinby	Freewill Baptist	1821
Hannah Pearce Reeves (1800–68)	Methodist Protestant	1819
Ann Rexford/became Ann Brown in 1832	Christian Connection	1820
Olive Maria Rice/became Olive Maria Patten in 1844	Millerite	1842
Dolly Richards	Christian Connection/became a Millerite	1840
Lydia M. Richmond	Millerite	1840s
Polly Richmond	Freewill Baptist	1830

Name	Denomination	Year First Mentioned in Records
Sarah Righter (1808–84) / became Sarah Major in 1842	Church of the Brethren	1826
Sarah Riker	Methodist	1792
Abigail Hoag Roberts (1791–1841)	Christian Connection	1814
Mary (Molly) Savage / became Mary (Molly) Card in late 1790s	Freewill Baptist	1791
Lydia Sexton (1792–1843)	United Brethren	1843
Mary A. Seymour	Freewill Baptist / became a Millerite	1844
Nancy Shepard (?–1822)	Freewill Baptist	1817
Sinda (last name unknown)	millennialist slave preacher	1839
Martha N. Spaulding	Freewill Baptist	1822
Martha Spence (?–1873)	Millerite	1844
Mary Stevens / became Mary Curry in 1837	Christian Connection	1831
Ellen Brown Stewart (1792–?)	Reformed Methodist	1829
Elizabeth Osborne Stiles (?–1862)	Christian Connection	1840
Abigail Stone	Christian Connection	1845
Elizabeth Stone	Millerite	1842
Mary Stratton	Christian Connection	1822
Betsey Stuart	Freewill Baptist	1825
Sylvia (last name unknown)	slave preacher	
"Miss" Thompson	Millerite	1843
Rachel Hosmer Thompson (1805–?)	Christian Connection	1827
Sally Thompson	Methodist / transferred to Christian Connection	1822
Sarah Thornton	Freewill Baptist	1825
"Sister" Thurston	Freewill Baptist	1831
Juliann Jane Tilmann	African Methodist	1841
Nancy Towle (1796–1876)	nondenominational	1821
Sarah Wright Townsend (1719–80)	Separate Baptist	1759
Sojourner Truth (Isabella Van Wagenen) (1797?–1883)	nondenominational	1843
Molancy Wade / became Molancy Parker in 1834	Christian Connection	1832
Sally Waldren	Christian Connection	1821
R. Watkins	Primitive Methodist	1832
Mary D. Wellcome (1823–95)	Millerite	1845
Ellen Harmon White (1827–1915)	Millerite / founder of Seventh-Day Adventists	1844
Lydia Wiard	Freewill Baptist	1828
Jemima Wilkinson (1752–1819)	Universal Friends	1776

 # Notes

INTRODUCTION

1. See the accounts published in the *National Intelligencer*, January 9, 1827; *Newburyport Herald*, January 19, 1827; and *The New York Commercial Advertiser*, January 11, 1827. Livermore published an impressive number of books during her lifetime; for a full listing, see the Bibliography. Not included in the Bibliography are three rare works that I could not locate: *Millennial Tidings*, no. 2 (publisher and date unknown); *Millennial Tidings*, no. 3 (Philadelphia: published by Harriet Livermore, 1838); and *The Sparrow*, vol. 2, no. 1 (Philadelphia, 1848). With the exception of two letters in the Abraham H. Cassel Collection (MSS 60, Juniata College, Huntingdon, Pa.), virtually all of her manuscripts have disappeared. For a contemporary account of her, see "Harriet Livermore," *Southern Literary Messenger* 7, no. 2 (February 1841): 156. See also C. C. Chase, "Harriet Livermore," *Contributions of the Old Residents' Historical Association* (Lowell, Mass.) 4, no. 1 (August 1888): 17–23; Rebecca Davis, *Gleanings from Merrimac Valley* (Portland, Maine: Hoyt, Fogg, and Donham, 1881); Samuel T. Livermore, *Harriet Livermore, the "Pilgrim Stranger"* (Hartford: Case, Lockwood, and Brainard Company, 1884); Harvey L. Long, "Harriet Livermore: Guest of the Brethren," *Brethren Life and Thought* 24 (Autumn 1979): 220–24; John J. Currier, *History of Newburyport, Massachusetts, 1764–1909* (Newburyport, Mass.: n.p., 1909), 2:476–80; and Elizabeth F. Hoxie, "Harriet Livermore, 'Vixen and Devotee,'" *New England Quarterly* 18 (March 1945): 39–50. Livermore is also the subject of a fascinating doctoral dissertation by Cynthia Jürisson, "Federalist, Feminist, Revivalist: Harriet Livermore (1788–1868) and the Limits of Democratization in the Early Republic" (Princeton Theological Seminary, 1994).

2. Harriet Livermore, *A Narration of Religious Experience* (Concord, N.H.: Jacob B. Moore, 1826), p. 276. Samuel Livermore, *Harriet Livermore*, p. 85.

3. *National Intelligencer*, January 9, 1827; *Newburyport Herald*, January 19, 1827; *The New York Commercial Advertiser*, January 11, 1827; and Charles Francis Adams, ed., *Memoirs of John Quincy Adams, Comprising Portions of His Diary from 1795 to 1848* (Philadelphia: J. B. Lippincott, 1876), 10:7–8.

4. Livermore complained that she was called "a disorderly character," "that eccentric individual," and "that crazy thing." Harriet Livermore, *A Wreath from Jessamine Lawn; or, Free Grace, the Flower that Never Fades* (Philadelphia: printed for the authoress, 1831), 1:vi, and *The Counsel of God, Immutable and Everlasting* (Philadelphia: L. R. Bailey, 1844), p. 22.

5. One exception is an excellent article by Louis Billington, "Female Laborers in the Church: Women Preachers in the Northeastern United States, 1790–1840," *Journal of American Studies* (Great Britain) 19 (1985): 369–94. See also William T. Noll, "Women as Clergy and Laity in the

Nineteenth-Century Methodist Protestant Church," *Methodist History* 15 (January 1977): 107–21, and Leonard I. Sweet, *The Minister's Wife: Her Role in Nineteenth-Century American Evangelicalism* (Philadelphia: Temple University Press, 1983), chap. 5. Elizabeth Muir mentions several American women in her history of female preaching in Canada. See *Petticoats in the Pulpit: The Story of Early Nineteenth-Century Methodist Women Preachers in Upper Canada* (Toronto: United Church Publishing House, 1991). Recent scholarship on women and religion includes Ann Braude, *Radical Spirits: Spiritualism and Women's Rights in Nineteenth-Century America* (Boston: Beacon Press, 1989); Marjorie Procter-Smith, *Women in Shaker Community and Worship: A Feminist Analysis of the Uses of Religious Symbolism* (Lewiston, N.Y.: Edwin Mellen Press, 1985); Catherine Wessinger, ed., *Women's Leadership in Marginal Religions: Explorations Outside the Mainstream* (Chicago: University of Illinois Press, 1993); and Patricia R. Hill, *The World Their Household: The American Woman's Foreign Mission Movement and Cultural Transformation, 1870–1920* (Ann Arbor: University of Michigan Press, 1985).

6. Nancy Towle, *Vicissitudes Illustrated, in the Experience of Nancy Towle, in Europe and America*, 2d ed. (Portsmouth, N.H.: John Caldwell, 1833), pp. 24, 26.

7. The memoirs or diaries of Jarena Lee, Zilpha Elaw, Julia Foote, Rebecca Jackson, and Sojourner Truth have recently been reprinted in modern editions. See William L. Andrews, ed., *Sisters of the Spirit: Three Black Women's Autobiographies of the Nineteenth Century* (Bloomington: Indiana University Press, 1986); Sue E. Houchins, ed., *Spiritual Narratives* (New York: Oxford University Press, 1988); Jean McMahon Humez, ed., *Gifts of Power: The Writings of Rebecca Jackson, Black Visionary, Shaker Eldress* (Amherst: University of Massachusetts Press, 1981); and Olive Gilbert, *Narrative of Sojourner Truth; A Bondswoman of Olden Time, With a History of Her Labors and Correspondence Drawn from Her "Book of Life"* (Battle Creek, Mich., 1878; reprint, New York: Oxford University Press, 1991). On Truth, see Nell Irvin Painter, *Sojourner Truth: A Life, A Symbol* (New York: Norton, 1996). See also Jualynne Dodson, "Nineteenth-Century A.M.E. Preaching Women," in *Women in New Worlds: Historical Perspectives on the Wesleyan Tradition*, ed. Hilah F. Thomas, Rosemary Skinner Keller, and Louise L. Queen (Nashville: Abingdon Press, 1982), 1:276–89; and Jean M. Humez, "'My Spirit Eye': Some Functions of Spiritual and Visionary Experiences in the Lives of Five Black Women Preachers, 1810–1880," in *Women and the Structure of Society*, ed. Barbara Harris and JoAnn McNamara (Durham, N.C.: Duke University Press, 1984), pp. 129–43.

8. This is the interpretation offered by Paul E. Johnson, *A Shopkeeper's Millennium: Society and Revivals in Rochester, New York, 1815–1837* (New York: Hill and Wang, 1978); Anthony F. C. Wallace, *Rockdale: The Growth of an American Village in the Early Industrial Revolution* (New York: Knopf, 1978); and George M. Thomas, *Revivalism and Cultural Change: Christianity, Nation-Building, and the Market in the Nineteenth-Century United States* (Chicago: University of Chicago Press, 1989).

9. Harriet Livermore, *Narration*, p. 202, and Harriet Livermore, *Addresses to the Dispersed of Judah* (Philadelphia: L. R. Bailey, 1849), p. 113.

10. Harriet Livermore, *Scriptural Evidence in Favor of Female Testimony in Meetings for the Worship of God* (Portsmouth, N.H.: R. Foster, 1824), p. 120.

11. Elisabeth Anthony Dexter, *Career Women of America, 1776–1840* (Francestown, N.H.: Marshall Jones, 1950), p. 61.

12. See Elleanor Warner Knight, *A Narrative of the Christian Experience, Life and Adventures, Trials and Labours of Elleanor Knight, Written by Herself* (Providence: n.p., 1839), and Rebecca Miller, "Duty of Females," *Christian Palladium* 10, no. 2 (May 15, 1841): 21–22.

13. "Minutes of an Occasional Elders' Conference held in the Quarterly Meeting of New-durham [*sic*] at Gilmanton, August 21, 1801," in the New Durham, N.H., Freewill Baptist Church Quarterly Meeting Conference Records, 1792–1889, vol. 1, New Hampshire Historical Society, Concord, N.H.

14. William Smyth Babcock Papers, November 4, 1802, American Antiquarian Society, Worcester, Mass.

15. Gerda Lerner, "The Challenge of Women's History," in her *The Majority Finds Its Past: Placing Women in History* (Oxford: Oxford University Press, 1979), p. 177.

16. See Nathan O. Hatch, *The Democratization of American Christianity* (New Haven: Yale University Press, 1989), p. 9. See also William G. McLoughlin, *Revivals, Awakenings, and Reform: An Essay on Religion and Social Change in America, 1607–1977* (Chicago: University of Chicago Press, 1978).

17. Harriet Livermore, *Counsel of God*, p. v.

18. Michael Kammen, *People of Paradox: An Inquiry Concerning the Origins of American Civilization* (New York: Knopf, 1974).

19. See Carroll Smith-Rosenberg, "The Female World of Love and Ritual," in *Disorderly Conduct: Visions of Gender in Victorian America* (New York: Oxford University Press, 1985), pp. 53–76; and Mark C. Carnes, *Secret Ritual and Manhood in Victorian America* (New Haven: Yale University Press, 1989). The last quote is from Karen Halttunen, *Confidence Men and Painted Women: A Study of Middle-Class Culture in America, 1830–1870* (New Haven: Yale University Press, 1982), p. 59.

20. Linda K. Kerber, Nancy F. Cott, Robert Gross, Lynn Hunt, Carroll Smith-Rosenberg, and Christine Stansell, "Beyond Roles, Beyond Spheres: Thinking about Gender in the Early Republic," *William and Mary Quarterly* 46 (July 1989): 565–85. See also Karen V. Hansen, *A Very Social Time: Crafting Community in Antebellum New England* (Berkeley: University of California Press, 1994), p. 17; Nancy A. Hewitt, *Women's Activism and Social Change: Rochester, New York, 1722–1872* (Ithaca: Cornell University Press, 1984); Mary Beth Norton, *Founding Mothers and Fathers: Gendered Power and the Forming of American Society* (New York: Knopf, 1996); Mary P. Ryan, *Cradle of the Middle Class: The Family in Oneida County, New York, 1790–1865* (Cambridge: Cambridge University Press, 1981); and Mary P. Ryan, *Women in Public: Between Banners and Ballots, 1825–1880* (Baltimore: Johns Hopkins, 1990).

21. Because I argue that the definitions of "femininity" and "masculinity" have changed over time, I have usually put these terms in quotation marks in the text. In order to avoid distracting my readers, I have omitted the quotation marks wherever the context allows. On the transformation from a one-sex to two-sex model of gender, see Thomas Laquer, *Making Sex: Body and Gender from the Greeks to Freud* (Cambridge: Harvard University Press, 1990), and Kathleen M. Brown, "Brave New Worlds: Women's and Gender History," *William and Mary Quarterly* 50, no. 2 (April 1993): 314. On using gender as a category of analysis, see Joan W. Scott, "Gender: A Useful Category of Historical Analysis," *American Historical Review* 91 (December 1985): 1053–75; Caroline Walker Bynum, Stevan Harrell, and Paula Richman, eds., *Gender and Religion: On the Complexity of Symbols* (Boston: Beacon Press, 1986); and Susan Juster and Lisa MacFarlane, eds., *A Mighty Baptism: Race, Gender, and the Creation of American Protestantism* (Ithaca: Cornell University Press, 1996).

22. Both Thomas Laquer and Susan Juster have argued that the one-sex model allowed more fluid understandings of "femininity" and "masculinity." See Laquer, *Making Sex*, and Susan Juster, *Disorderly Women: Sexual Politics and Evangelicalism in Revolutionary New England* (Ithaca: Cornell University Press, 1994).

23. For recent discussions of the centrality of class in the Second Great Awakening, see Hatch, *Democratization*, and Jama Lazerow, *Religion and the Working Class in Antebellum America* (Washington: Smithsonian Institution Press, 1995). Both of these authors reject the social control interpretations offered by Johnson, *Shopkeeper's Millennium*, and Wallace, *Rockdale*. Laurie E. Maffly-Kipp points out the divisions among evangelicals in her *Religion and Society in Frontier California* (New Haven: Yale University Press, 1994), p. 183.

24. On the Livermore family, see Samuel Livermore, *Harriet Livermore*, and Everett S. Stackpole, *History of New Hampshire* (New York: American Historical Society, 1916), 2:285–87. For descriptions of Livermore's later appearances in front of Congress in 1832, 1838, and 1843, see William C. Richards, *Great in Goodness; A Memoir of George N. Briggs, Governor of the Commonwealth of Massachusetts, From 1844 to 1851* (Boston: Gould and Lincoln, 1867), p. 109; Adams, *Memoirs of John Quincy Adams*, 10:6; and Harriet Livermore, *Counsel of God*, p. v. Thomas Jefferson allowed Dorothy Ripley to preach in the Hall of Representatives in 1806. For more information on her, see Dorothy Ripley, *The Bank of Faith and Works United* (Philadelphia: J. H. Cunningham, 1819); Dorothy Ripley, *The Extraordinary Conversion and Religious Experience of Dorothy Ripley, With Her First Voyage and Travels in America* (New York: G. & R. Waite, 1810); and *Letters Addressed to Dorothy Ripley from Several Africans and Indians, on Subjects of Christian Experience* (Chester: J. Hemingway, 1807).

CHAPTER I

1. This and subsequent paragraphs summarize the "Advice to Mr. and Mrs. Kingsley," Jonathan Edwards Papers, Andover Newton Theological School, Newton Centre, Mass. See also "The Publick Records of the Church at Westfield," Westfield Atheneum, Westfield, Mass. I am greatly indebted to Kenneth Minkema for sharing his transcription of the Kingsley case and other information about Kingsley with me.

2. There are many excellent studies of the social and political dimensions of the revivals. For a small sampling, see Gary B. Nash, *The Urban Crucible: The Northern Seaports and the Origins of the American Revolution* (Cambridge: Harvard University Press, 1986); Richard L. Bushman, *From Puritan to Yankee: Character and the Social Order in Connecticut, 1690–1765* (Cambridge: Harvard University Press, 1967); and William G. McLoughlin, *New England Dissent, 1630–1833: The Baptists and the Separation of Church and State*, 2 vols. (Cambridge: Harvard University Press, 1971). For studies that link the Great Awakening to the American Revolution, see Harry S. Stout, "Religion, Communications, and the Ideological Origins of the American Revolution," *William and Mary Quarterly* 34 (1977): 519–41, and Alan Heimert, *Religion and the American Mind: From the Great Awakening to the Revolution* (Cambridge: Harvard University Press, 1966). For studies of women in the Great Awakening, see Barbara E. Lacey, "Women and the Great Awakening in Connecticut" (Ph.D. diss., Clark University, 1982); Susan Juster, *Disorderly Women: Sexual Politics and Evangelicalism in Revolutionary New England* (Ithaca: Cornell University Press, 1994); and Martha Tomhave Blauvelt and Rosemary Skinner Keller, "Women and Revivalism: The Puritan and Wesleyan Traditions," in *Women and Religion in America*, vol. 2, *The Colonial and Revolutionary Periods*, ed. Rosemary Radford Ruether and Rosemary Skinner Keller (San Francisco: Harper and Row, 1983), pp. 316–28.

3. This episode occurred in 1709. See Patricia U. Bonomi, *Under the Cope of Heaven: Religion, Society, and Politics in Colonial America* (New York: Oxford University Press, 1986), p. 107.

4. Mary Beth Norton, *Founding Mothers and Fathers: Gendered Power and the Forming of American*

Society (New York: Knopf, 1996), pp. 24, 10, 19–23. See also John Demos, *A Little Commonwealth* (New York: Oxford University Press, 1970.)

5. Laurel Thacher Ulrich, *Good Wives: Image and Reality in the Lives of Women in Northern New England, 1650–1750* (Oxford: Oxford University Press, 1980), pp. 35–50.

6. Harry S. Stout, *The New England Soul: Preaching and Religious Culture in Early New England* (New York: Oxford University Press, 1986), p. 20.

7. John Cotton, "Psalm Singing a Godly Exercise" (1650), in *A Library of American Literature, from the Earliest Settlement to the Present Time,* ed. Edmund Clarence Stedman and Ellen Mackay Hutchinson (New York: Charles L. Webster, 1891), 1:266.

8. On Gorton, see Lyle Koehler, *A Search for Power: The Weaker Sex in Seventeenth-Century New England* (Chicago: University of Chicago Press, 1980), pp. 308–10, and Philip Gura, *A Glimpse of Sion's Glory: Puritan Radicalism in New England, 1620–1660* (Middletown: Wesleyan University Press, 1984), pp. 276–303. On the Separates, see David S. Lovejoy, *Religious Enthusiasm in the New World: Heresy to Revolution* (Cambridge: Harvard University, 1985), p. 51. Roger Williams, *George Fox Digg'd Out of His Burrowes* (Boston: John Foster, 1676), p. 12, quoted in Koehler, *Search for Power,* p. 306. On the gendering of public speech in early New England, see Jane Kamensky, *Governing the Tongue: The Politics of Speech in Early New England* (New York: Oxford University Press, 1997).

9. On radical religious movements in seventeenth-century England, see Christopher Hill, *The World Turned Upside Down: Radical Ideas during the English Revolution* (New York: Viking Press, 1972; reprint, New York: Peregrine Books, 1984).

10. On Fox and Fell, see Richard Bauman, *Let Your Words Be Few: Symbolism of Speaking and Silence among Seventeenth-Century Quakers* (Cambridge: Cambridge University Press, 1983), p. 36, and Margaret Hope Bacon, *Mothers of Feminism: The Story of Quaker Women in America* (San Francisco: Harper and Row, 1986), pp. 7–17. On Fell and other Quaker women in seventeenth-century England, see Phyllis Mack, *Visionary Women: Ecstatic Prophecy in Seventeenth-Century England* (Berkeley: University of California Press, 1992).

11. See the letter from Mary Dyer to the General Court reprinted in Ruth Talbot Plimpton, *Mary Dyer: Biography of a Rebel Quaker* (Boston: Branden, 1994), p. 165.

12. Quakers were influenced by Isaiah 20:2–4. For a full discussion of "going naked as a sign," see Bauman, *Let Your Words Be Few,* pp. 84–94. Cotton, "Psalm Singing," p. 266. On Wilson, see Koehler, *Search for Power,* p. 251.

13. For works that take a negative view of Puritanism's impact on women's religious status, see Ben Barker-Benfield, "Anne Hutchinson and the Puritan Attitude toward Women," *Feminist Studies* 1, no. 2 (1972–73): 65–96; Lyle Koehler's *Search for Power* and his "The Case of the American Jezebels: Anne Hutchinson and Female Agitation during the Years of Antinomian Turmoil, 1636–1640," *William and Mary Quarterly* 31 (1974): 55–78; Mary Maples Dunn, "Saints and Sisters: Congregational and Quaker Women in the Early Colonial Period," *American Quarterly* 30 (1978): 582–601; and Carol Karlsen, *The Devil in the Shape of a Woman: Witchcraft in Colonial New England* (New York: Norton, 1987). Studies that take a more positive view include Laurel Thacher Ulrich, "Vertuous Women Found: New England Ministerial Literature, 1688–1735," in *A Heritage of Her Own,* ed. Nancy F. Cott and Elizabeth H. Pleck (New York: Simon and Schuster, 1979), pp. 58–80; Lonna M. Malmsheimer, "Daughters of Zion: New England Roots of American Feminism," *New England Quarterly* (September 1977): 484–504; and three works by Amanda Porterfield: *Female Piety in Colonial New England* (Oxford: Oxford University Press, 1992), *Feminine Spirituality in America: From Sarah Edwards to Martha Graham* (Philadelphia: Temple

University Press, 1980), and "Women's Attraction to Puritanism," *Church History* 60 (June 1991): 196–209.

14. James Hillhouse, *A Sermon Concerning the Life, Death, and Future State of Saints* (Boston, 1721), p. 117, quoted in Ulrich, "Vertuous Women Found," p. 62.

15. John Winthrop, "A Short Story," in *The Antinomian Controversy, 1636–1638: A Documentary History*, ed. David D. Hall (Durham, N.C.: Duke University Press, 1990), pp. 263–65, 215. "The Examination of Mrs. Anne Hutchinson at the Court at Newtown," in Hall, *Antinomian Controversy*, pp. 312, 337. The description of Rhode Island comes from John Woodbridge Jr. to Richard Baxter, in Raymond Phineas Stearns, ed., "Woodbridge-Baxter Correspondence," *New England Quarterly* 10 (1937), p. 573, quoted in Carla Pestana, *Quakers and Baptists in Colonial Massachusetts* (Cambridge: Cambridge University Press, 1991), p. 2. On Anne Hutchinson, see Barker-Benfield, "Anne Hutchinson"; Koehler, "The Case of the American Jezebels"; Emery Battis, *Saints and Sectaries: Anne Hutchinson and the Antinomian Controversy in the Massachusetts Bay Colony* (Chapel Hill: University of North Carolina Press, 1962); Edmund S. Morgan, *The Puritan Dilemma: The Story of John Winthrop* (Boston: Little, Brown, and Company, 1958), pp. 134–54; Amy Scrager Lang, *Prophetic Woman: Anne Hutchinson and the Problem of Dissent in the Literature of New England* (Berkeley: University of California Press, 1987); and Kamensky, *Governing the Tongue*, pp. 71–81.

16. In *Founding Mothers and Fathers*, Mary Beth Norton argues that "high-status women took precedence over low-status men, since their fathers' or husbands' rank was more important in determining their social rank than their gender" (p. 10). Yet even though elite women had limited access to power, they did not enjoy true equality. The "Filmerian" system, as Norton terms the colonial worldview, "offered certain women the short-term potential for wielding authority while at the same time in the long run depriving them of its reality" (p. 398).

17. On Moody, see Peter Ross, *A History of Long Island* (New York: Lewis, 1902), 1:357; Benjamin F. Thompson, *History of Long Island* (New York: Robert H. Dodd, 1918), 3:106–7, 111–13; David Benedict, *A General History of the Baptist Denomination in America and Other Parts of the World* (1813; New York: Lewis Colby and Company, 1850), p. 370; and Norton, *Founding Mothers and Fathers*, p. 166. The original transcript of Anne Eaton's trial is contained in the Records of the First Church of New Haven, 1:17–23, at Center Church Parish House, New Haven, Conn. The account is reprinted by Newman Smyth, ed., "Mrs. Eaton's Trial (in 1644; as it Appears upon the Records of the First Church of New Haven," in *Papers of the New Haven Historical Society* 5 (1869). See pp. 135, 143. For more on Anne Eaton, see Lillian Handlin, "Dissent in a Small Community," *New England Quarterly* 59 (1985): 193–220, and Norton, *Founding Mothers and Fathers*, pp. 165–74.

18. On Keayne, see *The Records of the First Church of Boston, 1630–1868*, ed. Richard Donald Pierce (Boston: Colonial Society of Massachusetts, 1961), 1:46, 49; Ulrich, *Good Wives*, pp. 111–13; and *Winthrop Papers, 1645–1649*, ed. Allyn B. Forbes (Boston: Merrymount Press, 1947), pp. 5, 144.

19. Dunn, "Saints and Sisters," p. 590.

20. For a discussion of the transatlantic connections among the revivals, see chapter 8 of Michael J. Crawford, *Seasons of Grace: Colonial New England's Revival Tradition in Its British Context* (New York: Oxford University Press, 1991); W. Reginald Ward, *The Protestant Evangelical Awakening* (Cambridge: Cambridge University Press, 1992); and Leigh Eric Schmidt, *Holy Fairs: Scottish Communions and American Revivals in the Early Modern Period* (Princeton: Princeton University Press, 1989). Jon Butler has pointed out that the term "Great Awakening" was not even coined

until 1842. In his view, the Great Awakening is an "interpretive fiction" that historians have created in order to explain how Puritans became Yankees. See Jon Butler, "Enthusiasm Described and Decried: The Great Awakening as Interpretive Fiction," *Journal of American History* 69 (1982): 305–25. Since I agree that the term "Great Awakening" obscures regional and denominational diversity, I often refer to "revivals" in the plural. For stylistic considerations, however, I have chosen not to put "the Great Awakening" in quotation marks throughout the text.

21. The best overview of the Awakening is Joseph Tracy, *The Great Awakening* (Boston: Tappan and Dennet, 1842). The scholarship on this topic is voluminous. On the Awakening in New England, see Edwin Scott Gaustad, *The Great Awakening in New England* (Gloucester, Mass.: Peter Smith, 1965); Crawford, *Seasons of Grace*; C. C. Goen, *Revivalism and Separatism in New England, 1740–1800: Strict Congregationalists and Separate Baptists in the Great Awakening* (New Haven: Yale University Press, 1962); and Bushman, *From Puritan to Yankee*. On the Middle Colonies, sources include Randall Balmer, *A Perfect Babel of Confusion: Dutch Religion and English Culture in the Colonies* (New York: Oxford University Press, 1989); Charles Hartshorn Maxson, *The Great Awakening in the Middle Colonies* (Chicago: University of Chicago Press, 1920); and Marilyn J. Westerkamp, *Triumph of the Laity: Scots-Irish Piety and the Great Awakening, 1625–1760* (New York: Oxford University Press, 1988). Good general sources on the revivals include Harry S. Stout, *The Divine Dramatist: George Whitefield and the Rise of Modern Evangelicalism* (Grand Rapids, Mich.: Eerdmans, 1991); Stout, "Religion, Communications, and the Ideological Origins of the American Revolution"; Butler, "Enthusiasm Described and Decried"; J. M. Bumsted and John E. Van de Wetering, *What Must I Do to Be Saved? The Great Awakening in Colonial America* (Hinsdale, Ill.: Dryden Press, 1976); and Jon Butler, *Awash in a Sea of Faith: Christianizing the American People* (Cambridge: Harvard University Press, 1990), pp. 164–93.

22. Ezra Stiles, *Discourse on the Christian Union* (Newport, 1761), quoted in David Harlan, *The Clergy and the Great Awakening in New England* (Ann Arbor, Mich.: UMI Research Press, 1980), p. 66. There are many parallels between the 1640s in England and the 1740s in America. In both decades, there were revolutionary experiments that did not last, but which pointed the way toward the future.

23. See the comprehensive overview of the background to the revivals in Bumsted and Van de Wetering, *What Must I Do*. Gilbert Tennent, *Solemn Warning to the Secure World from the God of Terrible Majesty* (Boston, 1735), reprinted in *The Great Awakening: Documents on the Revival of Religion, 1740–1745*, ed. Richard L. Bushman (New York: Atheneum, 1970; Chapel Hill: University of North Carolina Press, 1989), p. 17. For the classic statement of declension, see Perry Miller, *The New England Mind: The Seventeenth Century* (Cambridge: Harvard University Press, 1939), and Perry Miller, *The New England Mind: From Colony to Province* (Cambridge: Harvard University Press, 1953). Scholars who have questioned the model of declension include Stout, *New England Soul*; Robert G. Pope, *The Half-Way Covenant: Church Membership in Puritan New England* (Princeton: Princeton University Press, 1969); and Harry S. Stout and Catherine A. Brekus, "Declension, Gender, and the New Religious History," in *Belief and Behavior: Essays in the New Religious History*, ed. Philip R. VanderMeer and Robert P. Swierenga (New Brunswick, N.J.: Rutgers University Press, 1991), pp. 15–37.

24. Philip Greven, *Four Generations: Population, Land, and Family in Colonial Andover, Massachusetts* (Ithaca: Cornell University Press, 1970). As the market expanded, so did the number of legal cases involving prosecutions for debt. See Bushman, *From Puritan to Yankee*, pp. 135–36. For a different view of the relationship between the Awakening and market expansion, see

Christine Leigh Heyrman, *Commerce and Culture: The Maritime Communities of Colonial Massachusetts, 1690–1750* (New York: Norton, 1984), pp. 366–405.

25. George Whitefield, *The Marriage of Cana* (Philadelphia, 1742), reprinted in Bushman, *Great Awakening*, p. 33. For two discussions of Whitefield's relationship to the market, see Frank Lambert, *"Pedlar in Divinity": George Whitefield and the Transatlantic Revivals* (Princeton: Princeton University Press, 1994), and Stout, *Divine Dramatist*.

26. In "New Lights in New London: A Group Portrait of the Separatists," *William and Mary Quarterly* 37 (1980): 627–43, Peter S. Onuf argues that the Separates were not economically disadvantaged, although they tended to be "outsiders" in other ways. In contrast, Richard Bushman claims that Connecticut New Lights drew their membership from new merchants and entrepreneurs who were ambivalent about their new prosperity. See Bushman, *From Puritan to Yankee*, especially part 2. In opposition to both Onuf and Bushman, Gary B. Nash argues that lower-class Philadelphians were particularly attracted to the revivals. See Nash, *Urban Crucible*, pp. 126–32. C. C. Goen and Edwin Gaustad argue that the revivals crossed class lines. See Goen, *Revivalism and Separatism*, pp. 185–92; Gaustad, *Great Awakening*, p. 52; and Heimert, *Religion and the American Mind*, p. 10.

27. On Jonathan Edwards, see the introduction to John E. Smith, ed., *Religious Affections* (New Haven: Yale University Press, 1959). On Tennent and Frelinghuysen, see Milton J. Coalter Jr., *Gilbert Tennent, Son of Thunder: A Case Study of Continental Pietism's Impact on the First Great Awakening in the Middle Colonies* (New York: Greenwood Press, 1986), and James R. Tanis, *Dutch Calvinistic Pietism in the Middle Colonies: A Study in the Life and Theology of Theodorus Jacobus Frelinghuysen* (The Hague: Martinus Nijhoff, 1967). Both books are valuable as intellectual histories but neither offers insight into lay spirituality.

28. Edwards was quoting the famous seventeenth-century Puritan minister, Thomas Shepard. See Jonathan Edwards, *Some Thoughts Concerning the Present Revival*, in *The Great Awakening*, ed. C. C. Goen (New Haven: Yale University Press, 1972), p. 388; Jonathan Edwards, *A Treatise Concerning Religious Affections*, in Smith, *Religious Affections*, pp. 93–461.

29. Gilbert Tennent, *The Danger of an Unconverted Ministry* (Boston, 1742), reprinted in Bushman, *Great Awakening*, p. 91.

30. Quoted in Leigh Eric Schmidt, " 'A Second and Glorious Reformation': The New Light Extremism of Andrew Croswell," *William and Mary Quarterly* 43, no. 2 (April 1986): 227–28. Nathan Bowen's "Almanacs," quoted in Clarke Garrett, *Spirit Possession and Popular Religion: From the Camissards to the Shakers* (Baltimore: Johns Hopkins, 1987), p. 117. On the revivalists' use of sacred space, see Juster, *Disorderly Women*, pp. 21–26.

31. See *The Christian History*, September 3, 1743, p. 209. Eleazar Wheelock reported that in 1741 in Taunton, Massachusetts, "almost all the negroes in town [are] wounded; three or four converted." Tracy, *Great Awakening*, p. 202. George Whitefield, *Journals* (1740), reprinted in Bushman, *Great Awakening*, pp. 30–31. On the challenge the revivals posed to all forms of traditional boundaries, see Timothy D. Hall, *Contested Boundaries: Itinerancy and the Reshaping of the Colonial American Religious World* (Durham, N.C.: Duke University Press, 1994).

32. Several historians have also suggested that women's repeated labors in childbirth may have made them more aware of their mortality and hence more concerned with the state of their souls. See Gerald F. Moran, "Sisters in Christ: Women and the Church in Seventeenth-Century New England," in *Women in American Religion*, ed. Janet Wilson James (Philadelphia: University of Pennsylvania Press, 1980), p. 57. For statistics on membership by gender in a New Haven church, see Stout and Brekus, "Declension, Gender, and the New Religious History"; and also

Harry S. Stout and Catherine A. Brekus, "A New England Congregation: Center Church, New Haven, 1638–1989," in *American Congregations*, ed. James P. Wind and James W. Lewis (Chicago: University of Chicago Press, 1994), pp. 14–102. For membership statistics for Boston, see Richard D. Shiels, "The Feminization of American Congregationalism, 1730–1835," *American Quarterly* 33 (1981): 48. Women seem to have also predominated in German and Lutheran Reformed churches in Pennsylvania and in Dutch Reformed churches in New York, although the statistics for these churches are less conclusive. In Virginia, there were usually more women than men in attendance at Baptist meetings. See Bonomi, *Under the Cope of Heaven*, pp. 112–13.

33. *The Christian History*, May 6, 1744, p. 99. See Stout, *New England Soul*, p. 197. Jonathan Edwards also commented on the surprising number of male converts. See Jonathan Edwards, *A Faithful Narrative of the Surprising Work of God. . .* , in Goen, *Great Awakening*, p. 158. Statistical studies of church membership patterns have confirmed these ministers' impressions. See Cedric B. Cowing, "Sex and Preaching in the Great Awakening," *American Quarterly* 20 (Fall 1968); Maxson, *Great Awakening*, p. 63; and Bumsted and Van de Wetering, *What Must I Do*, pp. 131–34.

34. George Whitefield, *Marriage of Cana*, p. 33.

35. On men's use of bridal imagery, see Schmidt, *Holy Fairs*, pp. 164–65. Joseph Bean, Spiritual Diary, typescript at Bryn Mawr College Library, Bryn Mawr, Pa., quoted in Philip J. Greven, *The Protestant Temperament: Patterns of Child-Rearing, Religious Experience, and the Self in Early America* (New York: Knopf, 1977), p. 126. See *The Diary of Isaac Backus*, ed. William G. McLoughlin (Providence: Brown University Press, 1979), 1:382.

36. Michael Crawford, ed. "The Spiritual Travels of Nathan Cole," *William and Mary Quarterly* 33 (January 1976): 96–97.

37. "Testimonials of Persons Who Joined the Church at Chebacco, 1764," in the John Cleaveland Papers, 1742–1848, Essex Institute, Salem, Mass. John Cleaveland describes these revivals in his *A Short and Plain Narrative of the Late Work of God's Spirit at Chebacco in Ipswich, in the Years 1763 and 1764* (Boston: Fowle and Freeman, 1767). My analysis of these narratives largely agrees with the interpretations offered by Juster, *Disorderly Women*, pp. 46–74, and Barbara Leslie Epstein, *The Politics of Domesticity: Women, Evangelism, and Temperance in Nineteenth-Century America* (Middletown: Wesleyan University Press, 1981), pp. 11–44. As I argue below, however, I perceive women's greater emphasis on their bodily pollution as a particularly telling difference. In the next century, as "self-made" men would confidently celebrate their power to choose their own destinies, men's and women's religious language would become even more distinct. See Susan Juster, "'In a Different Voice': Male and Female Narratives of Religious Conversion in Post-Revolutionary America," *American Quarterly* 41 (March 1989): 34–62, and Epstein, *Politics*, pp. 45–66.

38. "Testimonials of Persons Who Joined the Church at Chebacco, 1764"; Bean, Spiritual Diary, quoted in Greven, *Protestant Temperament*, p. 69; Ebenezer Prime, *A Sermon Preached in Oyster Bay Feb. 27, 1743–4: At the Funeral of Mrs. Freelove Wilmot, Consort of the Rev. Mr. Walter Wilmot . . . To Which is Added an Appendix Containing Extracts from Her Private Papers* (New York: J. Parker, 1744), p. 62.

39. Prince was quoting from George Whitefield. Thomas Prince, *The Sovereign God Acknowledged and Blessed, both in Giving and Taking Away: A Sermon Occasioned by the Decease of Mrs. Deborah Prince . . . With a Brief Account of the Dealings of God Toward Her* (Boston: Rogers and Fowle, 1744), p. 39. Samuel Hopkins, ed., *The Life and Character of Miss Susanna Anthony* (Hartford: Hudson and Goodwin, 1799), pp. 63, 66–67, 28, 151.

40. Thomas Laquer, *Making Sex: Body and Gender from the Greeks to Freud* (Cambridge: Harvard University Press, 1990), p. 4.

41. Ibid., p. 108, and Roger Thompson, *Sex in Middlesex: Popular Mores in a Massachusetts County, 1649–1699* (Amherst: University of Massachusetts Press, 1986), p. 141. See also Karlsen, *Devil in the Shape of a Woman*, pp. 168–69; Koehler, *Search for Power*, pp. 74–80; Edmund S. Morgan, "The Puritans and Sex," *New England Quarterly* 15 (1942): 591–607; and John D'Emilio and Estelle B. Freedman, *Intimate Matters: A History of Sexuality in America* (New York: Harper and Row, 1988), pp. 15–38. On the nineteenth century, see Nancy F. Cott, "Passionlessness: An Interpretation of Victorian Sexual Ideology, 1790–1850," in *A Heritage of Her Own*, ed. Nancy F. Cott and Elizabeth H. Pleck (New York: Simon and Schuster, 1979), pp. 162–81.

42. Benjamin Colman, *The Duty and Honour of Aged Women* (Boston: B. Green, 1711), p. 5. Edwards, *Faithful Narrative*, p. 149. Ruth H. Bloch, "Women, Love, and Virtue in the Thought of Edwards and Franklin," in *Benjamin Franklin, Jonathan Edwards, and the Representation of American Culture*, ed. Barbara B. Oberg and Harry S. Stout (New York: Oxford, 1993), p. 141. On positive images of women in Puritan sermons, see Malmsheimer, "Daughters of Zion," and Ulrich, "Vertuous Women Found," pp. 58–80.

43. See Elizabeth Reis, "The Devil, the Body, and the Feminine Soul in Puritan New England," *Journal of American History* 82 (June 1995): 15–36. "Advice to Mr. and Mrs. Kingsley." Here I disagree with Susan Juster, who argues that eighteenth-century Baptists saw women as "archetypal saints." See Juster, *Disorderly Women*, p. 150.

44. Hopkins, *Life and Character*, p. 17; "The Religious Journal of Sarah Prince Gill, 1743–1764," ed. Rebecca Ann Husman, p. 9. Husman's transcript of Gill's journal (completed as a senior project at Bard College) can be found at the Kellogg Library, Bard College, Annandale-on-Hudson, N.Y. The original "Sarah Prince Gill Papers, 1743–64," are located at the Boston Public Library.

45. Hopkins, *Life and Character*, pp. 23–25.

46. Letter from Timothy Allen to Eleazar Wheelock, in the Papers of Eleazar Wheelock, Dartmouth College Library, Hanover, N.H., quoted in Richard Warch, "The Shepherd's Tent: Education and Enthusiasm in the Great Awakening," *American Quarterly* 30, no. 2 (Summer 1978): 188; and "Religious Journal of Sarah Prince Gill," p. 15.

47. Sarah's narrative is reprinted in *The Works of Jonathan Edwards*, ed. Sereno Dwight (London: William Ball, 1839), 1:civ–cxii. For the quotations cited above, see pp. civ–cv, cvii. Jonathan Edwards included his own version of Sarah's account in *Some Thoughts*, pp. 331–41. In many sections the language is almost identical, but he removed all references to her gender and eliminated the social context of her conversion, probably in order to make her story more universal. For an excellent analysis of Sarah's own narrative, see Julie Ellison, "The Sociology of 'Holy Indifference': Sarah Edwards' Narrative," *American Literature* 56, no. 4 (1984): 479–95. Another good discussion is Porterfield, *Feminine Spirituality*, chap. 2.

48. Martin E. Marty, *Religion, Awakening, and Revolution* ([Wilmington, N.C.]: Consortium, 1977), p. 81.

49. Sarah Edwards, "Narrative," 1:cvii–cviii.

50. Charles Chauncy, *Seasonable Thoughts on the State of Religion in New England* (1743; reprint, New York: Regina Press, 1975), pp. 104–5. See also Nathan Bowen, who complained about the "Giddy Mobb" and the "silly women" who attended New Light meetings. Nathan Bowen, "Extracts from Interleaved Almanacs of Nathan Bowen, 1742–1799," *The Essex Institute Historical Collections* 41 (1955): 164.

51. Chauncy, *Seasonable Thoughts*, p. ix. Chauncy was quoting directly from Thomas Weld's preface to John Winthrop's "A Short Story," reprinted in Hall, *Antinomian Controversy*, p. 206.

52. See [Charles Chauncy], *The Wonderful Narrative, or, a Faithful Account of the French Prophets, their Agitations, Extasies, and Inspirations* (Glasgow: Robert Foulis, 1742), and Butler, *Awash*, p. 178. On the French Prophets, see Garrett, *Spirit Possession*, especially chapter 2, and Hillel Schwartz, *The French Prophets: The History of a Millenarian Group in Eighteenth-Century England* (Berkeley: University of California Press, 1980).

53. Edwards, *Some Thoughts*, p. 312, and Joshua Hempstead, *The Diary of Joshua Hempstead of New London, Connecticut* (New London, n.p., 1901), pp. 402–3.

54. *Diary of Isaac Backus*, 1:98, 445.

55. Ross W. Beales Jr., ed., "Solomon Prentice's Narrative of the Great Awakening," *Proceedings of the Massachusetts Historical Society* 83 (1971): 141; and Tracy, *Great Awakening*, p. 138.

56. On the importance of the sermon as a "central ritual of social order and control," see Stout, *New England Soul*, p. 3.

57. Beales, "Solomon Prentice's Narrative," pp. 138, 136; and Francis G. Walett, ed. "The Diary of Ebenezer Parkman, 1739–1744," *Proceedings of the American Antiquarian Society* 72 (1962): 187. See also "The Diary of Nathaniel Gilman," ed. William Kidder (master's thesis, University of New Hampshire, 1972), p. 271; Tracy, *Great Awakening*, pp. 210, 177; *Diary of Isaac Backus*, 1:90, 36; "Religious Excitement One Hundred and Odd Years Ago" [Extract from the Diary of Samuel Chandler, 1746], *The New England Historical and Genealogical Register* 15 (1861): 23.

58. David Hall Diary, vol. 1, 1740–69, Massachusetts Historical Society, Boston.

59. For a New Light defense of "crying out," see Edwards, *Some Thoughts*, p. 312.

60. Ebenezer Parkman quoted in Tracy, *Great Awakening*, p. 210; George Whitefield, *George Whitefield's Journals* (Gainesville, Fla.: Scholars Facsimiles and Reprints, 1969), p. 419; and "Diary of Nathaniel Gilman," p. 222.

61. Edwards, *Faithful Narrative*, p. 194.

62. [Charles Chauncy], *A Letter from a Gentleman in Boston, to Mr. George Wishart, One of the Ministers of Edinburgh, Concerning the State of Religion in New England* (Edinburgh: n.p., 1742), reprinted in *Religious Enthusiasm and the Great Awakening*, ed. David S. Lovejoy (Englewood Cliffs, N.J.: Prentice-Hall, 1969), p. 46. In 1742 the Connecticut Assembly passed "An Act for regulating Abuses and correcting Disorders in Ecclesiastical Affairs" because of their alarm over "illiterate" men exhorting in public. See "An Act for regulating Abuses and correcting Disorders in Ecclesiastical Affairs" (1742), reprinted in Bushman, *Great Awakening*, p. 58. Many ministers complained about lay men's exhorting. For a few examples, see Jonathan Parsons, *A Needful Caution in a Critical Day* (New London: T. Green, 1742), pp. 48–50; Theophilus Pickering, *The Rev. Mr. Pickerings' Letters to the Rev. N. Rogers and Mr. D. Rogers of Ipswich* (Boston: Thomas Fleet, 1742), pp. 6, 11; and John Caldwell, *An Impartial Trial of the Spirit Operating in This Part of the World* (Boston: Thomas Fleet, 1742), p. 22. Both Andrew Croswell and Joseph Park allowed lay men to exhort. See Andrew Croswell, *A Letter from the Reverend Mr. Croswell to the Reverend Mr. Turell* (Boston: Rogers and Fowle, 1742), p. 5, and *The Christian History*, August 27, 1743.

63. McLoughlin, *New England Dissent*, 1:347n. Twenty-two more Separate churches were formed after 1754. For Separates' protests against Congregationalism, see the Scotland, Conn., Brunswick Separate Church Records, 1746–1846, Connecticut State Library, Hartford, Conn., and the "Articles of Faith and Church Covenant, 1746," in the North Stonington, Conn., Separate or Strict Congregationalist Church Records, 1746–1822, Connecticut State Library. For details on their theological disagreements with Congregationalists, see Goen, *Revivalism and*

Separatism, pp. 162–64, 75; Ebenezer Frothingham, *A Key to Unlock the Door, that Leads in, to Take a Fair View of the Religious Constitution, Established by Law, in the Colony of Connecticut* (New Haven: n.p., 1767), p. v; and Alan Heimert and Perry Miller, eds., *The Great Awakening: Documents Illustrating the Crisis and Its Consequences* (Indianapolis: Bobbs-Merrill, 1967), pp. 423–26. The best discussions of the Separate churches are McLoughlin, *New England Dissent*, and Goen, *Revivalism and Separatism*. Unfortunately, none of these books discuss women in the Separate movement.

64. For examples of Separates who complained about the restriction of their "gifts" in the established churches, see S. L. Blake, *The Separates or Strict Congregationalists of New England* (Boston: Pilgrim Press, 1902), pp. 59–60; Frederic Denison, *Notes of the Baptists, and their Principles, in Norwich, Connecticut from the Settlement of the Town to 1850* (Norwich: Manning, 1857), p. 27; Garrett, *Spirit Possession*, p. 128; Tracy, *Great Awakening*, p. 318; William G. McLoughlin, "Free Love, Immortalism, and Perfectionism in Cumberland, Rhode Island, 1748–1768," *Rhode Island History* 33, no. 3 (August 1974): 74; and Joseph Fish, *The Church of Christ a Firm and Durable House* (New London: Timothy Green, 1767), pp. 147–48.

65. Ebenezer Frothingham, *The Articles of Faith and Practice, with the Covenant, That is Confessed by the Separate Churches of Christ in General in This Land* (Newport: J. Franklin, 1750), pp. 361, 358. The emphasis is mine.

66. See the essays in Catherine Wessinger, ed., *Women's Leadership in Marginal Religions: Explorations Outside the Mainstream* (Chicago: University of Illinois Press, 1993). Frothingham, *Articles of Faith*, pp. 361–62.

67. Frothingham, *Articles of Faith*, pp. 358–62. The passage he refers to is from Luke 11:27–28. He also cited passages from Luke 3:47, John 4:28–29, 39, Canticles (Song of Solomon) 3–5, Matthew 28:10, Luke 24:10–11, Joel 2:28–29, 1 Corinthians 11:5, and Acts 2:16–18.

68. Peter S. Onuf speculates that Margaret Adams of Canterbury, aged seventeen, and Rebecca Church of Plainfield, aged twenty-three, may have studied with Timothy Allen at the Shepherd's Tent. See Onuf, "New Lights in New London," p. 633. For more on the Shepherd's Tent, see Warch, "The Shepherd's Tent," pp. 177–98. Frothingham, *A Key to Unlock the Door*, p. 199.

69. *Minutes of the Philadelphia Baptist Association, 1707 to 1807* (Philadelphia, 1851), p. 53, and Record Book, First Baptist Church of Lyme, January 25 and February 16, 1771, Connecticut State Library. Both sources are quoted in Juster, *Disorderly Women*, pp. 43, 86. On voting, see Juster, *Disorderly Women*, pp. 41–42. It is difficult to determine how many women spoke publicly in Baptist churches. Although Juster argues that the Baptists allowed women to exhort, the bulk of her evidence comes from the records of Separate churches. The Baptists and Separates eventually united in 1787, but they were not identical in the 1740s and 1750s.

70. *Diary of Isaac Backus*, 1:91.

71. Edwards, *Some Thoughts*, pp. 484–86, 312, 405.

72. Ebenezer Turell, *Mr. Turell's Dialogue Between a Minister and His Neighbour About the Times*, 2d ed. (Boston: Rogers and Fowle, 1742), pp. 10–11; Jonathan Ashley, *The Great Duty of Charity* (Boston: J. Draper for S. Eliot, 1742), p. 5; Chauncy, *Seasonable Thoughts*, p. 240; and Bowen, "Extracts from Interleaved Almanacs," p. 169. See also Chauncy, *Seasonable Thoughts*, p. 226; Ebenezer Turell, *Mr. Turell's Directions to his People with Relation to the Present Times* (Boston: Rogers and Fowle, 1742), p. 12; and Lovejoy, *Religious Enthusiasm and the Great Awakening*, pp. 65–66.

73. Perhaps their numbers were even higher, but because of the controversies swirling around

the revivals, it is difficult to tell how many women spoke only rarely and how many exhorted more frequently. I have tried to be conservative in my estimates.

74. Juster argues that Baptists embraced a "feminine" style of worship, although she admits that the Baptists themselves would never have used this word. According to her, "the very attempt to efface sexual boundaries placed one squarely in the feminine realm of flux and dissolution." Unfortunately, her historical rather than theoretical reasons for identifying the Baptists as "feminine" are unclear. Juster, *Disorderly Women*, p. 21.

75. 1 Corinthians 11:3–7. See Denise Lardner Carmody, *Biblical Woman: Contemporary Reflections on Scriptural Texts* (New York: Crossroad, 1988), p. 136; and Lone Fatum, "Image of God and Glory of Man: Women in the Pauline Congregations," in *Image of God and Gender Models in Judaeo-Christian Tradition*, ed. Kari Elisabeth Børresen (Oslo: Solum Forlag, 1991), p. 84.

76. The number of Old and New Light ministers who complained about visionary "enthusiasm" suggests that it was fairly widespread during the revivals. See Tracy, *Great Awakening*, p. 201; Isaac Stiles, *A Looking-glass for Changlings*, quoted in Heimert and Miller, *Great Awakening*, p. 312; Joseph Fish, *The Church of Christ A Firm and Durable House* (New London: Timothy Green, 1767), p. 139; Alexander Garden, *Regeneration, and the Testimony of the Spirit*, in Heimert and Miller, *Great Awakening*, p. 49; Croswell, *Letter*, p. 11; Joseph Seccombe, *Some Occasional Thoughts on the Influence of the Spirit* (Boston: Kneeland and Green, 1742), p. 8; Nathaniel Appleton, *Evangelical and Saving Repentance* (Boston: S. Kneeland and T. Green, 1741), p. 22; Parsons, *Needful Caution*, p. 31; Moses Bartlett, *False and Seducing Teachers to be Expected in the Gospel State, and Latter Days of the Church* (New London: John Green, 1757), p. 40; John Thomson, *The Government of the Church of Christ*, in Heimert and Miller, *Great Awakening*, pp. 123–24; and Jonathan Edwards, "The State of Religion at Northampton in the County of Hampshire, About a Hundred Miles Westward of Boston," in Goen, *Great Awakening*, p. 550.

77. Chauncy, *Seasonable Thoughts*, p. 129.

78. Ibid., pp. 128–29.

79. Manuscript letter from Samuel Buell to Eleazar Wheelock, April 20, 1742, Dartmouth College Archives, quoted in Bushman, *Great Awakening*, p. 44.

80. "Diary of Nathaniel Gilman," p. 301.

81. This episode is recounted in *Diary of Isaac Backus*, 2:821–22. For other accounts of women who were so "loud" and "fervent" that they could be heard from "far off," see Beales, "Solomon Prentice's Narrative," p. 136, and Walett, "Diary of Ebenezer Parkman, 1739–1744," p. 187.

82. Hempstead, *Diary*, pp. 402–3.

83. "Advice to Mr. and Mrs. Kingsley."

84. *South Carolina Gazette*, June 21, 1742, quoted in Hall, *Contested Boundaries*, p. 58.

85. Charles Chauncy, *Enthusiasm Described and Cautioned Against* (Boston, 1742), quoted in Heimert and Miller, *Great Awakening*, p. 241.

86. James Davenport, *The Reverend Mr. Davenport's Confessions and Retractions* (Boston: Kneeland and Green, 1744).

87. For "ridiculous," see Turell, *Dialogue*, p. 10. Lacey, "Women and the Great Awakening," p. 152.

88. Norton discusses the strength of "paternal power" in *Founding Mothers and Fathers*, pp. 96–137. On the breakdown of paternal authority, see Steven Mintz and Susan Kellogg, *Domestic Revolutions: A Social History of American Family Life* (New York: Free Press, 1988), pp. 17–21; and Daniel Scott Smith, "Parental Power and Marriage Patterns: An Analysis of Historical Trends in

Hingham, Massachusetts," in *The American Family in Social-Historical Perspective*, ed. Michael Gordon, 3d ed. (New York: St. Martin's Press, 1983), pp. 255–68.

89. Edwards, *Some Thoughts*, p. 444. Robert Ross, *A Plain Address to the Quakers, Moravians, Separatists. . .* (New Haven: Parker and Company, 1762), pp. 146–48, 151.

90. *American Weekly Mercury*, Postscript, July 31, 1740, quoted in Hall, *Contested Boundaries*, p. 58.

91. "Report of the Council held in Suffield, Connecticut, concerning the position of women in the churches," in Canterbury, Conn., Separate Church Papers, 1748–84, Connecticut State Library.

92. Nathaniel S. Prime, *A History of Long Island* (New York: n.p., 1845), pp. 267–68, and *The Diary of Mary Cooper: Life on a Long Island Farm*, ed. Field Horne (Oyster Bay, N.Y.: Oyster Bay Historical Society, 1981), p. 63.

93. Killingly Convention of Strict Congregational Churches, *An Historical Narrative and Declaration, Shewing the Cause and Rise of the Strict Congregationalist Churches in the State of Connecticut* (Providence: n.p., 1781), quoted in Goen, *Great Awakening*, pp. 174–75.

94. Elias Smith, *The Life, Conversion, Preaching, Travels, and Sufferings of Elias Smith* (Portsmouth, N.H., 1840; reprint, New York: Arno Press, 1980), p. 248. McLoughlin, *New England Dissent*; *The Sentiments and Plan of the Warren Association* (Germantown, Penn.: Christopher Sower, 1769), p. 3, quoted in Juster, *Disorderly Women*, p. 113. Juster writes that "the surest way for dissenters to engage the Standing Order on their own terrain was to reorganize their polity along the model of the patriarchal household"--a household in which women were explicitly subordinated to men. See Juster, *Disorderly Women*, pp. 108, 124–25.

95. Rhys Isaac, *The Transformation of Virginia, 1740–1790* (Chapel Hill: University of North Carolina Press, 1982), p. 173. For other useful sources on the Awakening in the South, see Wesley M. Gewehr, *The Great Awakening in Virginia, 1740–1790* (Durham, N.C.: Duke University Press, 1930), and Harvey H. Jackson, "Hugh Bryan and the Evangelical Movement in South Carolina," *William and Mary Quarterly* 43 (October 1986): 594–614. On southern women, see Joan R. Gundersen, "The Non-Institutional Church: The Religious Role of Women in Eighteenth-Century Virginia," *Historical Magazine of the Protestant Episcopal Church* 51 (December 1982): 347–57; William L. Lumpkin, "The Role of Women in Eighteenth-Century Virginia Baptist Life," *Baptist History and Heritage* 8 (1973): 158–67; Leon McBeth, *Women in Baptist Life* (Nashville: Broadman Press, 1979); and Alice Mathews, "The Religious Experience of Southern Women," in Ruether and Keller, *Women and Religion in America*, 2:193–232.

96. Robert B. Semple, *A History of the Rise and Progress of the Baptists in Virginia* (Richmond: John O'Lynch, 1810), p. 4, and Robert G. Gardiner, *Baptists of Early America: A Statistical History, 1639–1790* (Atlanta: Georgia Baptist Historical Society, 1983), p. 57. For biographical sketches of Shubal Stearns and Daniel Marshall, see James B. Taylor, *Lives of Virginia Baptist Ministers* (1837; New York: Sheldon and Company, 1860), 1:13–24. For other primary accounts of the early years of the Separate Baptists in the South, see John Taylor, *A History of Ten Baptist Churches* (1827; reprint, New York: Arno Press, 1980); Morgan Edwards, *Materials towards a History of the Baptists*, 2 vols. (Philadelphia: Joseph Crukshank and Isaac Collins, 1770; reprint, Danielsville, Ga.: Heritage Papers, 1984); Leon McBeth, ed., *A Sourcebook for Baptist Heritage* (Nashville: Broadman Press, 1990), pp. 142–69; and Benedict, *General History*. Useful secondary sources include Donald G. Mathews, *Religion in the Old South* (Chicago: University of Chicago Press, 1977); William L. Lumpkin, *Baptist Foundations in the South: Tracing through the Separates the Influence of the Great Awakening, 1754–1787* (Nashville, 1961), reprinted in his *Colonial Baptists and Southern Revivals*

(New York: Arno Press, 1980); Chas B. Williams, *A History of the Baptists in North Carolina* (Raleigh: Edwards and Broughton, 1901); Isaac, *Transformation*, pp. 161–77; Leon McBeth, *The Baptist Heritage: Four Centuries of Baptist Witness* (Nashville: Broadman Press, 1987); Garnett Ryland, *The Baptists of Virginia, 1699–1926* (Richmond: Virginia Baptist Board of Missions and Education, 1955); Leah Townsend, *South Carolina Baptists, 1670–1805* (Florence, S.C.: Florence Printing Company, 1935); Robert A. Baker, *The Southern Baptist Convention and Its People, 1607–1972* (Nashville: Broadman Press, 1974); and George W. Purefoy, *A History of the Sandy Creek Baptist Association in A.D. 1758, to A.D. 1858* (1859; reprint, New York: Arno Press, 1980).

97. Taylor, *History*, p. 27; Richard J. Hooker, ed., *The Carolina Backcountry on the Eve of the Revolution: The Journal and Other Writings of Charles Woodmason, Anglican Itinerant* (Chapel Hill: University of North Carolina Press, 1953), p. 104; and Morgan Edwards quoted in Lumpkin, *Baptist Foundations in the South*, p. 39.

98. Daniel Fristoe quoted in Ryland, *Baptists of Virginia*, pp. 35–36. Taylor, *History*, p. 106.

99. Semple, *History*, 374. Marshall is also described in Lumpkin, "Role of Women," p. 164, and Taylor, *Virginia Baptist Ministers*, p. 23.

100. On Margaret Meuse Clay, see Lumpkin, "Role of Women," pp. 164–65. According to Lumpkin, her family's account of this episode can be found in the Virginia Baptist Historical Library.

101. *Lay My Burden Down: A Folk History of Slavery*, ed. B. A. Botkin (Chicago: University of Chicago Press, 1945), p. 214. In *Southern Cross: The Beginnings of the Bible Belt* (New York: Knopf, 1997), Christine Leigh Heyrman argues that black female converts do not seem to have been given the same "gospel liberty" as white women in the late-eighteenth-century South (p. 165). Because of the scarcity of evidence, however, it is hard to draw a strong conclusion about slave women's participation in religious meetings. What *is* clear is that white clergymen rarely mentioned black women in their memoirs. In contrast, there are more nineteenth-century accounts of black women's religiosity because slaves (mostly men) began to tell their own stories in print.

102. Morgan Edwards, *Materials*. I have arrived at these numbers by compiling Edwards's information on each church. Morgan Edwards, *The Customs of Primitive Churches* (Philadelphia: n.p., 1768), p. 41.

103. Elizabeth Fox-Genovese and Eugene D. Genovese, "The Divine Sanction of Social Order: The Religious Foundations of the Southern Slaveholders' World View," *Journal of the American Academy of Religion* 55 (1987): 212, 219–20. On the hierarchical ordering of southern society before the revivals, see Isaac, *Transformation*, pp. 131–38.

104. Most historians agree that the Separate Baptists in the South drew their members from the lower classes, although not the desperately poor. See Isaac, *Transformation*, p. 166, and Mathews, *Religion in the Old South*, p. 37. Semple, *History*, p. 26. On the countercultural tendencies of the revivals, see Isaac, *Transformation*, pp. 163–72.

105. Hooker, *Carolina Backcountry*, p. 104. For a discussion of southern female evangelicals who were accused of sexual deviance, see Heyrman, *Southern Cross*, pp. 181–84.

106. Baker, *Southern Baptist Convention*, p. 49. The resolution of the Philadelphia Association is cited in Leon McBeth, "The Changing Role of Women in Baptist History," *Southwestern Journal of Theology* 22 (1979–80): 88; the Kehukee Baptist Association is quoted in Lemuel Burkitt and Jesse Read, *A Concise History of the Kehukee Baptist Association from its Original Rise Down to 1803* (1850; reprint, New York: Arno Press, 1980), p. 80. Semple, *History*, p. 5.

107. On the union of the Separate and Regular Baptists, see Semple, *History*, p. 74, and Albert Henry Newman, *A History of the Baptist Churches in the United States*, 6th ed. (Philadelphia:

American Baptist Publication Society, 1915), p. 302. Leon McBeth argues that the Separates' acceptance of female preaching helped delay the merger. See his *Baptist Heritage*, p. 233, and his "Changing Role of Women," p. 90.

108. Semple, *History*, p. 39. Benedict, *General History*, p. 940.

109. See "Advice to Mr. and Mrs. Kingsley" and "Publick Records of the Church at Westfield."

CHAPTER 2

1. Gordon S. Wood, *The Radicalism of the American Revolution* (New York: Knopf, 1992), pp. 3, 5. Historians disagree over how radical the Revolution was. For differing viewpoints, see Bernard Bailyn, *The Ideological Origins of the American Revolution* (Cambridge: Belknap Press of Harvard University Press, 1967); Pauline Maier, *From Resistance to Revolution: Colonial Radicals and the Development of American Opposition to Britain, 1765–1776* (New York: Knopf, 1972); and Gary Nash, *The Urban Crucible: The Northern Seaports and the Origins of the American Revolution* (Cambridge: Harvard University Press, 1986).

2. See Jean Bethke Elshtain, *Public Man, Private Woman: Women in Social and Political Thought*, 2d ed. (Princeton: Princeton University Press, 1993).

3. J. Hector St. John Crèvecoeur, *Letters from an American Farmer* (1782; reprint, New York: Fox Duffield and Co., 1904), p. 54. Carroll Smith-Rosenberg, "Dis-Covering the Subject of the 'Great Constitutional Discussion,' 1786–1789," *Journal of American History* 79 (December 1992): 843, 855–56. John Adams quoted in Sara M. Evans, *Born for Liberty: A History of Women in America* (New York: Free Press, 1989), p. 47. On the role of racism in the creation of the American republic, see Edmund S. Morgan, *American Slavery, American Freedom: The Ordeal of Colonial Virginia* (New York: Norton, 1975); Winthrop D. Jordan, *White over Black: American Attitudes toward the Negro, 1550–1812* (Chapel Hill: University of North Carolina Press, 1968; New York: Norton, 1977), pp. 269–311; and Barbara Jeanne Fields, "Slavery, Race, and Ideology in the United States of America," *New Left Review* 181 (May/June 1990): 95–118.

4. *Adams Family Correspondence*, ed. Lyman H. Butterfield (Cambridge: Harvard University Press, 1963), 1:370, quoted in Mary Beth Norton, *Liberty's Daughters: The Revolutionary Experience of American Women, 1750–1800* (Boston: Little, Brown, 1980), p. 226. On women in the Revolution, see Linda K. Kerber, *Women of the Republic: Intellect and Ideology in Revolutionary America* (Chapel Hill: University of North Carolina Press, 1980); Susan Juster, *Disorderly Women: Sexual Politics and Evangelicalism in Revolutionary New England* (Ithaca: Cornell University Press, 1994), pp. 135–44; Ronald Hoffman and Peter J. Albert, eds., *Women in the Age of the American Revolution* (Charlottesville: University Press of Virginia, 1989); Joan Hoff-Wilson, "The Illusion of Change: Women and the American Revolution," in *The American Revolution: Explorations in the History of American Radicalism*, ed. Alfred E. Young (Dekalb, Ill., 1976), pp. 383–445; Glenna Mathews, *The Rise of Public Woman: Woman's Power and Woman's Place in the United States, 1630–1970* (New York: Oxford University Press, 1992), pp. 52–71; and Joan R. Gundersen, *To Be Useful to the World: Women in Revolutionary America, 1740–1790* (New York: Twayne, 1996).

5. On boycotts, spinning bees, ritual processions, and other forms of female political activism, see Carol Berkin, *First Generations: Women in Colonial America* (New York: Hill and Wang, 1996), pp. 165–94; Laurel Thatcher Ulrich, " 'Daughters of Liberty': Religious Women in Revolutionary New England," in Hoffman and Albert, *Women in the Age of the American Revolution*, pp. 211–43; Linda K. Kerber, " 'History Can Do It No Justice': Women and the Reinterpretation of

the American Revolution," in Hoffman and Albert, *Women in the Age of the American Revolution*, pp. 18–26; Kerber, *Women of the Republic*, pp. 37–41; and Norton, *Liberty's Daughters*, pp. 155–94.

6. Kerber, *Women of the Republic*, p. 136. On the Revolutionary challenge to all forms of patriarchal authority, see Jay Fliegelman, *Prodigals and Pilgrims: The Revolution against Patriarchal Authority* (Cambridge: Cambridge University Press, 1982). On women's relationship to the ideology of individualism, see Linda K. Kerber, "Can a Woman Be an Individual? The Limits of Puritan Tradition in the Early Republic," *Texas Studies in Literature and Language* 25, no. 1 (Spring 1983): 165–77.

7. On the transformation from a Filmerian to a Lockean conception of government, see Mary Beth Norton, *Founding Mothers and Fathers: Gendered Power and the Forming of American Society* (New York: Knopf, 1996), pp. 4–12, 404–5.

8. Nancy F. Cott, *The Bonds of Womanhood: "Woman's Sphere" in New England, 1780–1835* (New Haven: Yale University Press, 1977).

9. On women's exclusion from citizenship, see Juster, *Disorderly Women*, p. 143. On similar developments during the French Revolution, see Joan B. Landes, *Women and the Public Sphere in the Age of the French Revolution* (Ithaca: Cornell University Press, 1988). For a more positive view of the American Revolution's effect on women's self-perceptions, see Norton, *Liberty's Daughters*, pp. 228–55.

10. Thomas Jefferson quoted in Mathews, *Rise of Public Woman*, p. 71. On the transformation from "virtu" to "virtue," see Ruth H. Bloch, "The Gendered Meanings of Virtue in Revolutionary America," *Signs* 13 (Autumn 1987): 37–58. On republican motherhood, see Kerber, *Women of the Republic*, pp. 269–88.

11. *Herald of Gospel Liberty* 5, no. 8 (December 11, 1812): 445–46. See also Thomas Andros, *Discourse on Several Important Theological Subjects* (Boston: Samuel T. Armstrong, 1817), p. 169.

12. For her weekly schedule, see Samuel Hopkins, ed., *Memoirs of the Life of Mrs. Sarah Osborne who Died at Newport*, 2d ed. (Catskill, N.Y.: N. Elliot, 1814), pp. 77–82. For more on Osborn, see Sarah Osborn, "Letters, 1743–1770; 1779," American Antiquarian Society, Worcester, Mass.; Mary Beth Norton, ed., "'My Resting Reaping Times': Sarah Osborn's Defense of Her 'Unfeminine Activities,'" *Signs* 2 (1976): 524; and Charles E. Hambrick-Stowe, "The Spiritual Pilgrimage of Sarah Osborn (1714–1796)," *Church History* 61 (December 1992): 408–21.

13. Norton, "'My Resting Reaping Times,'" pp. 522–26. For more on the relationship between Osborn and Fish, see Barbara E. Lacey, "The Bonds of Friendship: Sarah Osborn of Newport and the Reverend Joseph Fish of North Stonington, 1743–1779," *Rhode Island History* 45 (November 1986), pp. 126–36.

14. See Joseph A. Conforti, *Samuel Hopkins and the New Divinity Movement: Calvinism, the Congregational Ministry, and Reform in New England Between the Great Awakenings* (Grand Rapids, Mich.: Christian University Press, 1981), pp. 103, 105–6.

15. On eighteenth-century Quaker women, see Mary Maples Dunn, "Latest Light on Women of Light," in *Witnesses for Change: Quaker Women over Three Centuries*, ed. Elisabeth Potts Brown and Susan Mosher Stuard (New Brunswick: Rutgers University Press, 1989); and Margaret Hope Bacon, *Mothers of Feminism: The Story of Quaker Women in America* (San Francisco: Harper and Row, 1986), pp. 24–85. On Quaker women ministers, see Phebe A. Hanaford, *Daughters of America; or, Women of the Century* (Augusta, Maine: True and Company, 1883), chap. 12; Barry Levy, *Quakers and the American Family: British Settlement in the Delaware Valley* (New York: Oxford University Press, 1988), pp. 193–230; and Joan M. Jensen, *Loosening the Bonds: Mid-Atlantic Farm Women, 1750–1850* (New Haven: Yale University Press, 1986), pp. 145–66. The journals of Su-

sanna Morris (1682–1755), Elizabeth Hudson (1722–1783), and Ann Moore (1710–1783) are reprinted in *Wilt Thou Go on My Errand? Three Eighteenth-Century Journals of Quaker Women Ministers*, ed. Margaret Hope Bacon (Wallingford, Pa.: Pendle Hill Publications, 1994).

16. Jensen, *Loosening the Bonds*, p. 151.

17. Bacon, *Mothers*, p. 34. According to historian Joan M. Jensen, almost 40 percent of the American Quaker ministers who visited England were women. *Loosening the Bonds*, p. 150. On Cook, see Algie I. Newlin, *Charity Cook: A Liberated Woman* (Richmond, Ind.: Friends United Press, 1981), p. 63.

18. For more on women's meetings, see Jean R. Soderlund, "Women's Authority in Pennsylvania and New Jersey Quaker Meetings, 1680–1760," *William and Mary Quarterly* 44 (1987): 722–49.

19. See Frederick B. Tolles, *Meeting House and Counting House: The Quaker Merchants of Colonial Philadelphia, 1692–1763* (New York: Norton, 1948), pp. 87, 49, and Jack D. Marietta, *The Reformation of American Quakerism, 1748–1783* (Philadelphia: University of Pennsylvania Press, 1984). On the class background of the early Quakers, see Levy, *Quakers and the American Family*, chap. 1.

20. On Quaker women ministers' economic status, see Levy, *Quakers and the American Family*, p. 214. Newlin, *Charity Cook*, p. 127, and Patience Brayton, *A Short Account of the Life and Religious Labors of Patience Brayton* (New Bedford: n.p., 1801), p. 108.

21. On Quaker quietism, see Rufus M. Jones, *The Later Periods of Quakerism* (London, 1921; Westport, Conn.: Greenwood Press, 1970), 1:36.

22. See Stephen A. Marini, *Radical Sects of Revolutionary New England* (Cambridge: Harvard University Press, 1982); Louis Billington, "Northern New England Sectarianism in the Early Nineteenth Century," *Bulletin of the John Rylands University Library of Manchester* 70 (Autumn 1988): 123–34; G. A. Rawlyk, *The Canada Fire: Radical Evangelicalism in British North America, 1775–1812* (Kingston, Ont.: McGill-Queen's University Press, 1994), pp. 5–18; and Hugh D. McLellan, *History of Gorham, Maine* (Portland: Smith and Sale, 1903), pp. 200–221.

23. Sydney Ahlstrom has referred to the years between 1760 and 1800 as a time of "religious depression." See *A Religious History of the American People* (New Haven: Yale University Press, 1972), p. 365. For opposing views, see two studies of religion in Revolutionary New York: Patricia U. Bonomi, *Under the Cope of Heaven: Religion, Society, and Politics in Colonial America* (New York: Oxford University Press, 1986), and Richard W. Pointer, *Religious Pluralism and the New York Experience* (Bloomington: Indiana University Press, 1988).

24. Billington, "Northern New England Sectarianism," p. 124. One of the most popular revivalists in New England was Henry Alline, a pacifist. See Rawlyk, *Canada Fire*, pp. 5–18; G. A. Rawlyk, *Ravished by the Spirit: Religious Revivals, Baptists, and Henry Alline* (Kingston, Ont.: McGill-Queen's University Press, 1984); and J. M. Bumsted, *Henry Alline, 1748–1784* (Toronto: University of Toronto Press, 1971). On Revolutionary challenges to religious authority, see Nathan O. Hatch, *The Democratization of American Christianity* (New Haven: Yale University Press, 1989), and Alan Taylor, *Liberty Men and Great Proprietors: The Revolutionary Settlement on the Maine Frontier, 1760–1820* (Chapel Hill: University of North Carolina Press, 1990), chap. 5.

25. Thomas Brown, *An Account of the People called Shakers* (Troy, N.Y.: Parker and Bliss, 1812), p. 14. See also Daniel Rathbun, *A Letter from Daniel Rathbun* (Springfield, Mass.: n.p., 1785), p. 112.

26. Marini, *Radical Sects*, p. 53, and McLellan, *History*, p. 200. On Ireland, see Clarke Garrett, *Spirit Possession and Popular Religion: From the Camissards to the Shakers* (Baltimore: Johns Hopkins, 1987), pp. 137–38, and Stephen J. Stein, *The Shaker Experience in America: A History of the United*

Society of Believers (New Haven: Yale University Press, 1992), pp. 23–24. For a fascinating discussion of beliefs in immortalism, see John L. Brooke, *The Refiner's Fire: The Making of Mormon Cosmology, 1644–1844* (Cambridge: Cambridge University Press, 1994), pp. 56–57, 67–71.

27. McLellan, *History*, p. 200.

28. Clifford Shipton, *Sibley's Harvard Graduates: Biographical Sketches of Those Who Attended Harvard College* (Boston: Massachusetts Historical Society, 1951), 8:256–57. For more on Prentice, see *The Diary of Isaac Backus*, ed. William G. McLoughlin (Providence: Brown University Press, 1979), 1:294; Ezra Stiles, *Extracts from the Itineraries*, ed. Franklin Bowditch Dexter (New Haven: Yale University, 1916), p. 418; William G. McLoughlin, "Free Love, Immortalism, and Perfectionism in Cumberland, Rhode Island, 1748–1768," *Rhode Island History* 33, no. 3 (August 1974): 76; and Garrett, *Spirit Possession*, pp. 135–38. For a description of her conversion, see Ross W. Beales Jr., ed., "Solomon Prentice's Narrative of the Great Awakening," *Proceedings of the Massachusetts Historical Society* 83 (1971): 135–36. Shipton is the only one of these authors to claim that Prentice preached. Neither Backus nor Stiles describe her as a preacher.

29. Herbert A. Wisbey Jr., *Pioneer Prophetess: Jemima Wilkinson, the Publick Universal Friend* (Ithaca: Cornell University Press, 1964), p. 111.

30. Ezra Stiles, *The Literary Diary of Ezra Stiles*, ed. Franklin Bowditch Dexter, 3 vols. (New York: Charles Scribner's Sons, 1901), 3:243, and Priscilla J. Brewer, *Shaker Communities, Shaker Lives* (Hanover: University Press of New England, 1986), pp. 2–8. On Smith, see Abner Brownell, "Diary, 1779–1787," undated entry for the year 1781, American Antiquarian Society.

31. Elizabeth Drinker quoted in Wisbey, *Pioneer*, p. 84. There are a number of useful primary sources for studying Wilkinson. She published two tracts under the name of the "Universal Friend" during her life: *The Universal Friend's Advice to Those of the Same Religious Society* (Philadelphia, 1784), which is reprinted in Wisbey, *Pioneer*, pp. 197–204, and *Some Considerations, Propounded to the Several Sorts and Sects of Professors* (n.p., 1779). In addition, many manuscripts written by her and her followers still survive. See Jemima Wilkinson Papers, 1771–1849, Collection of Regional History, Cornell University Library, Ithaca, N.Y. The Papers are available on microfilm. One of Wilkinson's former followers, Abner Brownell, published a tract entitled *Enthusiastical Errors, Transcribed and Detected* (New London: n.p., 1783) and also left a diary. See Brownell, "Diary, 1779–1787."

32. The only full-scale modern biography of Jemima Wilkinson is Wisbey, *Pioneer*. See also Susan Juster, "To Slay the Beast: Visionary Women in the Early Republic," in *A Mighty Baptism: Race, Gender, and the Creation of American Protestantism*, ed. Susan Juster and Lisa MacFarlane (Ithaca: Cornell University Press, 1996), pp. 19–37. A nineteenth-century biography, David Hudson's *History of Jemima Wilkinson, A Preacheress of the Eighteenth Century* (Geneva, N.Y.: S. P. Hull, 1821), is filled with factual inaccuracies. Other secondary sources include Israel Wilkinson, *Memoirs of the Wilkinson Family in America* (Jacksonville, Ill.: Davis and Penniman, 1869); Charles Lowell Marlin, "Jemima Wilkinson: Errant Quaker Divine," *Quaker History* 52, no. 2 (Autumn 1963): 90–94; Robert P. St. John, "Jemima Wilkinson," *Proceedings of the New York State Historical Association* 28 (1930): 158–75; Mrs. Walter A. Hendricks and Arnold J. Potter, "The Universal Friend: Jemima Wilkinson," *New York History* 23 (January 1942): 159–65; O[rasmus] Turner, *History of the Pioneer Settlement of Phelps and Gorham's Purchase, and Morris' Reserve* (Rochester: William Alling, 1851), pp. 153–62, 477–78; Stafford C. Cleveland, *History and Directory of Yates County, Containing a Sketch of Its Original Settlement by the Public Universal Friends*, vol. 1 (Penn Yan, N.Y.: S. C. Cleveland, 1873); Clayton Mau, *The Development of Central and Western New York* (Rochester: DuBois Press, 1944), pp. 78–82, 168–71, 328–29; Wilkins Updike, *A History of the*

Episcopal Church in Narragansett, Rhode Island (Boston: Merrymount Press, 1907), 1:266–72, 574–77; and Mrs. William Hathaway, *A Narrative of Thomas Hathaway and His Family . . . with Incidents in the Life of Jemima Wilkinson* (New Bedford, Mass.: E. Anthony and Sons, 1869). Many of these repeat folklore about Wilkinson that is almost certainly untrue, such as the dubious claim that she publicly identified herself as Christ. Since Wisbey's account is the most scholarly and balanced, it should be used as a starting point.

33. François Jean de Chastellux, *Travels in North America* (London: n.p., 1787), 1:288–89; and Eugene Parker Chase, ed., *Our Revolutionary Forefathers: The Letters of François, Marquis de Barbe-Marbois* (New York: Duffield, 1929), pp. 165–66. See also Israel Wilkinson, *Memoirs*, p. 420, and Hudson, *History*, p. 39. For a helpful account of Wilkinson's evangelism in Pennsylvania, see Wisbey, *Pioneer*, pp. 77–96.

34. *American Museum* (Philadelphia) 1 (1787): 221. Chase, *Our Revolutionary Forefathers*, pp. 165–66; William Savery, *A Journal of the Life, Travels, and Religious Labors of William Savery*, comp. Jonathan Evans (Philadelphia: n.p., 1861), p. 95.

35. The first quote comes from the fragment of a manuscript dated 1783, and the other is from the "Journal of Sarah Richards," undated manuscripts, 1790–94. Both can be found in Wilkinson Papers.

36. "A Memorandum of the introduction of that fatal Fever, call'd in the Year 1776, The Columbus fever," in Wilkinson Papers.

37. Ibid.

38. On the Cumberland church, see McLoughlin, "Free Love," p. 75. On perfectionism, see Brooke, *Refiner's Fire*, pp. 38–58. Brooke briefly discusses Wilkinson's connection to perfectionism. See ibid., pp. 117–18.

39. "A Memorandum." The emphasis is mine. Wilkinson's follower quoted in Wisbey, *Pioneer*, p. 182. John Lincklaen, who visited her settlement in 1791, claimed that she saw herself as Christ's messenger, not his second incarnation: "She sets forth that she is sent by Jesus Christ, and enlightened by his spirit to convert mankind." John Lincklaen, *Journals of John Lincklaen* (New York: G. P. Putnam's Sons, 1897), p. 62. Israel Wilkinson interviewed two of her surviving followers in 1869, "the Misses Comstock," and they assured him that she had never claimed to be divine. See Israel Wilkinson, *Memoirs*, p. 420. Even David Hudson, who wrote a vicious biography of her, admitted that there was no proof that Wilkinson had ever claimed to be Christ. Hudson, *History*, p. 120. See also *National Intelligencer* (Washington, D.C.), September 11, 1819.

40. Brownell also accused Wilkinson of insinuating that she was Christ. *Enthusiastical Errors*, p. 21.

41. "Journal of Sarah Richards."

42. Stiles, *Extracts from the Itineraries*, p. 418, quoted in Brooke, *Refiner's Fire*, p. 56. Isaac Holden to Isaac Parker, copied by Parker in his letter to Isaac Backus, June 28, 1784, Backus Papers, Trask Library, Andover-Newton Seminary, Newton, Mass., quoted in Garrett, *Spirit Possession*, p. 179.

43. Hudson, *History*, p. 118. "Journal of Sarah Richards," and Brownell, "Diary." For another example of this neutered language, see the "Journal of James Hathaway," in Wilkinson Papers.

44. *Universal Friend's Advice,* reprinted in Wisbey, *Pioneer*, p. 200. Hudson made the unsubstantiated claim that she separated spouses in his *History*, pp. 131–33. Wisbey, *Pioneer*, p. 68.

45. See Edward Warwick, Henry C. Pitz, and Alexander Wyckoff, *Early American Dress: The Colonial and Revolutionary Periods* (New York: Benjamin Blom, 1965), especially pp. 220–21 ("pouter pigeon," "buffont") and p. 204 (Quakers), and also Elisabeth McClellan, *History of*

American Costume, 1607–1870 (New York: Tudor, 1937), pp. 191–206. Chase, *Our Revolutionary Forefathers*, p. 164.

46. In all of my research, I found only one writer who described her appearance as gender-neutral rather than masculine. One Philadelphia writer observed: "As she is not to be supposed of either sex, so this neutrality is manifest in her personal appearance." See Israel Wilkinson, *Memoirs*, p. 438, quoting from a description in a 1787 edition of *Connecticut Magazine*. For descriptions of her "masculinity," see Wisbey, *Pioneer*, p. 25; and *Extracts from the Diary of Jacob Hiltzheimer, of Philadelphia, 1765–1798*, ed. Jacob Cox Parsons (Philadelphia: William F. Fell, 1893), pp. 66, 145. Other descriptions include Brownell, *Enthusiastical Errors*, p. 5; "Lang Syne," account of Jemima Wilkinson, *Poulson's American Daily Advertiser*, July 24, 1828, reprinted in John F. Watson, *Annals of Philadelphia and Pennsylvania, in the Olden Time* (Philadelphia: J. B. Lippincott, 1870), 1:554; Savery, *Journal*, p. 96; Hudson, *History*, pp. 106–7; and T[homas] C[ooper], *A Ride to Niagara in 1809* (Rochester, 1915), reprinted in Mau, *Development*, p. 169. One critic claimed that her voice was "masculine" as well. See *The Freemen's Journal* (Philadelphia), February 14, 1787.

47. On the gendering of dress, see Joanne B. Eicher and Mary Ellen Roach-Higgins, "Definition and Classification of Dress: Implications for Analysis of Gender Roles," in *Dress and Gender: Making and Meaning*, ed. Ruth Barnes and Joanne Eicher (New York: Berg, 1992), pp. 8–28. Marina Warner, *Joan of Arc: The Image of Female Heroism* (New York: Knopf, 1981), pp. 139–58.

48. Rudolf M. Decker and Lotte C. Van de Pol, *The Tradition of Female Transvestism in Early Modern Europe* (New York: St. Martin's Press, 1989). See also Marjorie Garber, *Vested Interests: Cross-Dressing and Cultural Anxiety* (New York: Routledge, 1992), and Vern L. Bullough and Bonnie Bullough, *Cross Dressing, Sex, and Gender* (Philadelphia: University of Pennsylvania Press, 1993).

49. Hudson, *History*, pp. 131–33, 201. For the charge that she separated husbands and wives, see *Freeman's Journal* (Philadelphia), March 28, 1787.

50. Chastellux, *Travels*, 1:288–89. See the extracts from Thomas Morris's manuscripts reprinted in Turner, *History*, pp. 477–78; Israel Wilkinson, *Memoirs*, 424; Reuben Aldridge Guild, *Early History of Brown University, Including the Life, Times, and Correspondence of President Manning, 1756–1791* (Providence: Snow and Farnham, 1896), p. 363; and Savery, *Journal*, pp. 95–97.

51. Undated letter to Ruth Pritchard; letter from the Universal Friend to James Parker, September 2, 1788; unsigned letter to the Universal Friend, October 24, 1787; all in Wilkinson Papers.

52. Stiles, *Literary Diary*, 2:511. Garber, *Vested Interests*, p. 32. *Freeman's Journal* (Philadelphia), February 14, 1787.

53. Stiles, *Literary Diary*, 2:511. See the letter from the Universal Friend to James Parker. For contemporary critiques of her "deformity" and "fanaticism," see *Freeman's Journal* (Philadelphia), March 28, 1787, and February 14, 1787. One of the most persistent (and unsupported) stories swirling around Wilkinson was that one of her followers, Abigail Dayton, had tried to murder a nonbeliever. See *New Haven Gazette and Connecticut Magazine* 2 (1787): 57–59, and *Freeman's Journal*, August 22, 1787, and September 5, 1787.

54. Shakers, *Testimonies of the Life, Character, Revelations, and Doctrines of Our Ever Blessed Mother Ann Lee* (Hancock, Mass.: Tallcott and Deming, 1816), p. 197. Hereafter cited as *Testimonies* (1816). Benjamin West, *Scriptural Cautions Against Embracing a Religious Scheme, Taught by a Number of Europeans* (Hartford: Bavil Webster, 1783), p. 4.

55. For an alternative view, see Garber, who objects to this "progress narrative." *Vested Interests*, p. 10.

56. Wisbey, *Pioneer*, pp. 42–46, and Samuel Kriebel Brecht, *The Genealogical Record of the*

Schwenkfelder Families (New York: Rand McNally, 1923), 2:1442. See Morris reprinted in Turner, *History*, pp. 477–78. For a complete description of the families who associated with the Friends, see Israel Wilkinson, *Memoirs*, pp. 113–38.

57. Chase, *Our Revolutionary Forefathers*, p. 165; *The Christian Disciple* 5 (1817): 277–79, quoted in Wisbey, *Pioneer*, p. 132; and *Universal Friend's Advice*, reprinted in Wisbey, *Pioneer*, p. 198.

58. On her millennialism, see Brownell, *Enthusiastical Errors*, pp. 12–13. The books that she copied from were William Sewel, *The History of the Rise, Increase, and Progress of the Christian People Called Quakers* (London, 1722), and Isaac Pennington, *The Works of the Long-Mourning and Sorely Distressed Isaac Pennington* (London, 1681).

59. "Journal of Ruth Spence," in Wilkinson Papers.

60. Biblical scholars divide the book of Isaiah into three sections: First Isaiah (chapters 1–39), Deutero-Isaiah (chapters 40–55), and Third Isaiah (chapters 56–66). See John F. A. Sawyer, "The Book of Isaiah," in *The Oxford Companion to the Bible*, ed. Bruce M. Metzger and Michael D. Coogan (New York: Oxford University Press, 1993), pp. 325–29.

61. She preached on Jeremiah 17:9, "Oh the Heart is deceitful above all things, and desperately wicked, who can know it? I the Lord, I see the heart"; Ezekiel 33:32, "They Come before me as my People, and they sit before me as my People; and they hear my words, but they will not do them"; and Matthew 17:21–23. See "Journal of Ruth Spence."

62. Brownell, *Enthusiastical Errors*, p. 14.

63. Israel Wilkinson, *Memoirs*, p. 432. On controversies over land, see Wisbey, *Pioneer*, pp. 113–18. She based her sermon on Matthew 6:24. She also preached on Proverbs 28:6, "Better is the Poor that walketh in the integrity of his heart than he that is perverse in his way, tho' he be rich." These texts are not recorded in Ruth Spence's journal, but in other loose documents included in the Wilkinson Papers.

64. Brownell, *Enthusiastical Errors*, p. 6. Isaiah 13:9–11, as recorded in "Journal of Ruth Spence." By the 1790s, according to the records, Wilkinson rarely (if ever) preached on Revelation, but she still preached on texts (especially from Matthew and Isaiah) proclaiming the near approach of the kingdom of God. After she was disappointed in her prediction that the world would end in 1780, she may have given up trying to interpret Revelation's obscure and allegorical language.

65. Brownell, *Enthusiastical Errors*, pp. 8, 13. Luke 12:47. Not all of Wilkinson's sermons were so alarming, and she tried to balance her threats to sinners with promises of God's mercy. For example, she preached not only on texts from First Isaiah predicting the destruction of the world, but from Deutero-Isaiah, the "Book of Comfort." See "Journal of Ruth Spence."

66. This was the remembrance of Henry Barnes, one of Wilkinson's followers. See Israel Wilkinson, *Memoirs*, p. 100.

67. Cleveland, *History*, p. 89. Abner Brownell complained, "She seems to strangely affect many people, that they must all be ministers, both male and female, and bring in their witnesses for God." See *Enthusiastical Errors*, p. 16.

68. Israel Wilkinson claims that several of Wilkinson's followers were revered as "Mothers." See *Memoirs*, pp. 89, 92, 95. Description of Richardson quoted in Wisbey, *Pioneer*, p. 63. When Wilkinson visited Philadelphia in 1782, her two female companions were wearing dresses that were reportedly "singular or uncommon." See *American Museum* 1 (1787): 221.

69. Israel Wilkinson makes this claim in his *Memoirs*, p. 432. See also David Hudson, *History*, p. 129. Wisbey dismisses these stories as slander (*Pioneer*, p. 180), but given Wilkinson's denial of gender and her claims to prophetic inspiration, I think it is quite possible that they were true.

70. Thomas Laquer, *Making Sex: Body and Gender from the Greeks to Freud* (Cambridge: Harvard University Press, 1990), pp. 4, 62.

71. Letter from the Universal Friend to James Parker. For an obituary of her, see *National Intelligencer* (Washington, D.C.), July 21, 1819.

72. When Wilkinson moved to New Jerusalem, she asked Sarah Richards to serve as the trustee of her land because she refused to own any property in her own name. However, after Richards died, her daughter claimed the property as her own inheritance. The court battles were not settled until after Wilkinson was dead. The best account of this complicated story is Wisbey, *Pioneer*, pp. 142–54.

73. For scholarship on Ann Lee and the early Shakers, see Edwin Deming Andrews, "Ann Lee," in *Notable American Women, 1607–1950: A Biographical Dictionary*, ed. Edward T. James, Janet Wilson James, and Paul S. Boyer (Cambridge: Harvard University Press, 1971), 2:385–87; Edwin Deming Andrews, *The People Called Shakers: A Search for the Perfect Society* (New York: Oxford University Press, 1953); Priscilla J. Brewer, *Shaker Communities, Shaker Lives* (Hanover: University Press of New England, 1986); Lawrence Foster, *Religion and Sexuality: The Shakers, the Mormons, and the Oneida Community* (Oxford: Oxford University Press, 1981), pp. 21–71; Garrett, *Spirit Possession*, pp. 140–241; Jean M. Humez, " 'Ye Are My Epistles': The Construction of Ann Lee Imagery in Early Shaker Sacred Literature," *Journal of Feminist Studies in Religion* 8, no. 1 (Spring 1992): 83–104; Frederick W. Evans, *Ann Lee (The Founder of the Shakers), A Biography, with Memoirs*, 4th ed. (Mount Lebanon, N.Y.: F. W. Evans, 1869); Stephen A. Marini, "A New View of Mother Ann Lee and the Rise of American Shakerism," *The Shaker Quarterly* (Summer/Fall 1990): 47–62, 95–111; Marini, *Radical Sects*; Marjorie Procter-Smith, " 'Who Do You Say that I Am?' Mother Ann as Christ," in *Locating the Shakers: Cultural Origins and Legacies of an American Religious Movement*, ed. Mick Gidley with Kate Bowles (Exeter: University of Exeter Press, 1990), pp. 83–95; Marjorie Procter-Smith, *Women in Shaker Community and Worship: A Feminist Analysis of the Uses of Religious Symbolism* (Lewiston, N.Y.: Edwin Mellen Press, 1985); and Stephen J. Stein, *The Shaker Experience in America: A History of the United Society of Believers* (New Haven: Yale University Press, 1992), pp. 1–38. Jean Humez has collected and edited the published and unpublished testimonies of many of Ann Lee's early female followers in her book, *Mother's First-Born Daughters: Early Shaker Writings on Women and Religion* (Bloomington: Indiana University Press, 1993.)

74. Benjamin Seth Youngs, *Testimony of Christ's Second Appearing* (Lebanon, Ohio: John M'Clean, 1808), p. 438, and *Testimonies* (1816), p. vi. *Testimony* appeared under several different authorships: Youngs alone, Youngs and Calvin Green, and Youngs, David Darrow, and John Meacham. For an earlier, unpublished statement of Shaker theology that dates from 1806, see Stephen J. Stein, " 'A Candid State of Our Principles': Early Shaker Theology in the West," *Proceedings of the American Philosophical Society* 133 (1989): 503–19. For a later elaboration of the Shakers' conception of a dual-gender God, see Calvin Green and Seth Wells, *Summary View of the Millennial Church* (Albany: Packard and Van Benthuysen, 1823).

75. *Testimonies* (1816), p. 2.

76. Valentine Rathbun, *An Account of the Matter, Form, and Manner of a New and Strange Religion, Taught and Propagated by a Number of Europeans* (Providence: Bennett Wheeler, 1781), pp. 20, 12. Brown, *Account*; Amos Taylor, *A Narrative of the Strange Principles, Conduct and Character of the People Known by the Name of Shakers* (Worcester, Mass.: Isaiah Thomas, 1782); Daniel Rathbun, *A Letter from Daniel Rathbun* (Springfield, Mass.: n.p., 1785); Reuben Rathbun, *Reasons Offered for Leaving the Shakers* (Pittsfield, Mass.: Chester Smith, 1800); and West, *Scriptural Cautions*.

77. Daniel Rathbun, *Letter*, p. 45; Isaac Backus, *A History of New England* (1871; reprint, New York: Arno Press, 1969), 2:297; Jeremy Belknap to Ebenezer Harvard, February 27, 1784, "The Belknap Papers," *Collections of the Massachusetts Historical Society*, 5th. ser. (Boston: Massachusetts Historical Society, 1877), 2:307, quoted in Garrett, *Spirit Possession*, p. 205; and *Testimonies* (1816), p. 17.

78. For a detailed analysis of the form and content of the *Testimonies*, see Humez, "'Ye Are My Epistles.'"

79. *Testimonies* (1816), p. iv. Historians have argued over whether or not the *Testimonies* should be treated as a reliable source. Stephen Marini suggests that it should be treated as "an oral tradition, a compilation of stories long circulated in the Shaker community by the eyewitnesses themselves." In contrast, Stephen Stein argues that the book tells us more about the Shaker church in 1816 than in the 1780s and 1790s. See Marini, "New View," p. 51, and Stein, *Shaker Experience*, pp. 25–29, 79–85.

80. *Testimonies* (1816), pp. vi, 5.

81. Ibid., p. 18. On the multiple images of Ann Lee in the *Testimonies*, see Marini, "New View." Seth Y. Wells to Benjamin S. Youngs, February 22, 1819, Shaker Collection, IV A 77, Western Reserve Historical Society, Cleveland, Ohio, quoted in Stein, *Shaker Experience*, p. 84. See also Humez, "'Ye Are My Epistles,'" p. 88.

82. Valentine Rathbun, *Account*, p. 20. Ezra Stiles, the president of Yale University, lamented in his diary: "It is remarkable that there sh[oul]d be two Women deceiving the public at the same time with two such diff[erent] monstrous & sacrilegious Systems." Stiles, *Literary Diary*, 2:510–11. See also Guild, *Early History*, pp. 363–64. On Wilkinson's knowledge of Lee, see the letter from "M.T." reprinted in Wisbey, *Pioneer*, p. 72, and the letter from William Carter to the Universal Friend, dated March 14, 1799, in Wilkinson Papers.

83. Stein, *Shaker Experience*, p. 3. *Testimonies* (1816), p. 5. Stein found the death certificate of only one child in his search of British archives.

84. *Testimonies* (1816), p. 6; Valentine Rathbun, *Account*, p. 8.

85. Daniel Rathbun, *Letter*, pp. 21, 119. See also Reuben Rathbun, *Reasons*, p. 6. Valentine Rathbun accused the Shakers of "burning all the books of divinity and learning they come at." *Account*, p. 17.

86. Valentine Rathbun, *Account*, p. 7.

87. Garrett, *Spirit Possession*, pp. 195–213.

88. Valentine Rathbun, *Account*, pp. 6–7, 12. Marjorie Procter-Smith carefully analyzes all of these images in her article, "'Who Do You Say that I Am,'" pp. 87–91.

89. *Testimonies* (1816), pp. 205–7, 20, 45. Most scholars agree that Lee herself probably never claimed to be Christ. See Andrews, "Ann Lee," pp. 385–87, and Linda A. Mercadante, *Gender, Doctrine, and God: The Shakers and Contemporary Theology* (Nashville: Abingdon Press, 1990), pp. 44–45. Mercadante includes a helpful discussion of the Shakers' later elaboration of a dual-god imagery in chapter 3 of *Gender*.

90. Amos Taylor, *Narrative*, p. 9. *Testimonies* (1816), p. 226.

91. *Testimonies* (1816), pp. 211, 213. Significantly, Lee's male and female followers described her relationship to Christ with strikingly different images. Both rooted Lee's authority in her intimate connection to Christ, but while women tended to remember Lee walking with him "side by side" and speaking to him "face to face" as a lover and equal, men remembered her submitting to him as her "lord and head." Humez points out these gender differences in "'Ye Are My Epistles,'" p. 101.

92. See "Jemima Blanchard's Stories as Recalled by Roxalana Grosvenor," in Humez, *Mother's First-Born Daughters*, p. 57; and *Testimonies* (1816), pp. 349, 107.

93. "Jemima Blanchard's Stories," p. 57; Marini, "New View," p. 104; and *Testimonies* (1816), pp. 25–26.

94. Kerber, *Women of the Republic*, p. 269.

95. West, *Scriptural Cautions*, p. 7. Ezra Stiles suspected that the Shakers "have been sent over into America by Ministerial Connexions, to excite Confusion & religious Disturbance and propagate principles against fighting & resist[ing] G[reat] Britain; and also to cover themselves with this cloud of religious Dust while they are acting as Spies among us & faithfully transmitt[ing] political Intelligence to the Enemy." See *Literary Diary*, 2:510–11.

96. On colonial child-rearing styles, see Philip J. Greven, *The Protestant Temperament: Patterns of Child-Rearing, Religious Experience, and the Self in Early America* (New York: Knopf, 1977). *Testimonies* (1816), pp. 314, 226, 252–53, 32.

97. "Jemima Blanchard's Stories," p. 57. Daniel Rathbun claimed that what was true of Lee as an individual was true of the Shakers as a whole. They were kind to those who lived in obedience to the Shaker gospel, but fierce in their condemnation of sinners. See Rathbun, *Letter*, pp. 36, 12.

98. *Testimonies* (1816), p. 253, and Daniel Rathbun, *Letter*, pp. 27–28, 37.

99. *Testimonies* (1816), pp. 156, 54, 58.

100. *Testimonies* (1816), quoted in Kathleen Deignan, *Christ Spirit: The Eschatology of Shaker Christianity* (Metuchen, N.J.: American Theological Library Association and Scarecrow Press, 1992), p. 48. *Testimonies* (1816), pp. 43, 19, 231, 238.

101. *Testimonies* (1816), p. 31.

102. See Procter-Smith, "'Who Do You Say that I Am,'" p. 86. Stephen Marini argues that Lee's genius "was to remove the female roles of mother and housewife from their subordinate status in eighteenth-century social structure and to place them at the center of a new religious communitas." See his "New View," p. 101.[*]

103. *Testimonies* (1816), pp. 32, 226.

104. For a positive view of nineteenth-century Shaker women's celibacy, see Sally L. Kitch, *Chaste Liberation: Celibacy and Female Cultural Status* (Urbana: University of Illinois Press, 1989), especially pp. 126–41.

105. *Testimonies* (1816), p. 304. Daniel Rathbun, *Letter*, pp. 19, 29–30. In his diary, Isaac Backus recorded that three Shakers in Taunton, Massachusetts, including Abigail Pitts, had been fined "for strip[p]ing Pitts's mother naked." *Diary of Isaac Backus*, 2:1148.

106. *Testimonies* (1816), pp. 321, 15. I have borrowed the phrase "deputy husband" from Laurel Thacher Ulrich, *Good Wives: Image and Reality in the Lives of Women in Northern New England, 1650–1750* (Oxford: Oxford University Press, 1980).

107. On nineteenth-century conflicts about women's leadership among the Shakers, see Jean M. Humez, "Weary of Petticoat Government: The Specter of Female Rule in Early Shaker Politics," *Communal Societies* (Spring 1991): 1–17.

108. *Testimonies* (1816), pp. 39, 343, 92, 129, and Valentine Rathbun, *Account*, p. 5.

CHAPTER 3

1. Ephraim Stinchfield Papers, 1777–1830, box 1, folder 6, September 5, 1795, Maine Historical Society, Portland, Maine.

2. Pittsfield, N.H., Freewill Baptist Church Records, 1791–1838, July 11, 1796, New Hampshire Historical Society, Concord, N.H. For other references to Parsons, see Stinchfield Papers, box 1, folder 6, June 10, 1797, November 4, 1797, and June 8, 1798; Stinchfield Papers, box 1, folder 3, undated manuscripts from the 1790s; Pittsfield Freewill Baptist Church Records, September 1798; and *The Morning Star*, April 2, 1845. There is a brief biographical sketch of Parsons in Nancy A. Hardesty, *Great Women of Faith: The Strength and Influence of Christian Women* (Grand Rapids, Mich.: Baker Book House, 1980), pp 67–68.

3. *Journals of Bronson Alcott*, ed. Odell Shepard (Boston: Little, Brown, 1938), pp. 40–41, quoted in *Antebellum American Culture: An Interpretive Anthology*, ed. David Brion Davis (Lexington, Mass.: D. C. Heath, 1979), p. 456.

4. Historians have debated whether early America was characterized by economic subsistence or nascent capitalism. See James A. Henretta, "Families and Farms: Mentalité in Pre-Industrial America," *William and Mary Quarterly* 35 (1978): 3–32; Michael Merrill, "Cash Is Good to Eat: Self-Sufficiency and Exchange in the Rural Economy of the United States," *Radical History Review* 3 (1977): 42–71; Winifred B. Rothenberg, "The Market and Massachusetts Farmers, 1750–1855," *Journal of Economic History* 41 (1981): 283–314; Bettye Hobbs Pruitt, "Self-Sufficiency and the Agricultural Economy of Eighteenth-Century Massachusetts," *William and Mary Quarterly* 41 (1984): 333–64; Christopher Clark, "The Household Economy: Market Exchange and the Rise of Capitalism in the Connecticut Valley, 1800–1860," *Journal of Social History* 13 (1979): 169–89; and Louis Hartz, *The Liberal Tradition in America: An Interpretation of American Political Thought Since the Revolution* (New York: Harcourt, Brace and World, 1955).

5. Gregory Nobles, "The Rise of Merchants in Rural Market Towns: A Case Study of Eighteenth-Century Northampton, Massachusetts," *Journal of Social History* 24, no. 1 (Fall 1990): 10, 14; Jonathan Prude, "Town-Factory Conflicts in Antebellum Rural Massachusetts," in *The Countryside in the Age of Capitalist Transformation: Essays in the Social History of Rural America*, ed. Steven Hahn and Jonathan Prude (Chapel Hill: University of North Carolina Press, 1985), pp. 71–102; and Thomas Dublin, "Women and Outwork in a Nineteenth-Century New England Town: Fitzwilliam, New Hampshire, 1830–1850," in Hahn and Prude, *Countryside*, pp. 51–70. On the "anxious spirit of gain," see the documents reprinted in Davis, *Antebellum American Culture*, pp. 105–28.

6. Jedidiah Morse quoted in Jon Butler, *Awash in a Sea of Faith: Christianizing the American People* (Cambridge: Harvard University Press, 1990), p. 219.

7. Harry S. Stout and Catherine A. Brekus, "A New England Congregation: Center Church, New Haven, 1638–1989," in *American Congregations*, ed. James Lewis and James Wind (Chicago: University of Chicago Press, 1994), pp. 14–102.

8. For a sampling of the scholarship on the "Second Great Awakening," see Jon Butler, "Christian Power in the American Republic," chapter 9 of *Awash*, pp. 257–88; Timothy L. Smith, *Revivalism and Social Reform: American Protestantism on the Eve of the Civil War* (Baltimore: Johns Hopkins, 1980); William G. McLoughlin, *Revivals, Awakenings, and Reform: An Essay on Religion and Social Change in America, 1607–1977* (Chicago: University of Chicago Press, 1978), pp. 98–140; Donald G. Mathews, "The Second Great Awakening as an Organizing Process, 1780–1830," in *Religion in American History: Interpretive Essays*, ed. John M. Mulder and John F. Wilson (Englewood Cliffs, N.J.: Prentice-Hall, 1978), pp. 199–217; Paul E. Johnson, *A Shopkeeper's Millennium: Society and Revivals in Rochester, New York, 1815–1837* (New York: Hill and Wang, 1978); Charles Sellers, *The Market Revolution: Jacksonian America, 1815–1846* (New York: Oxford University Press, 1992), pp. 202–36; Mary P. Ryan, *Cradle of the Middle Class: The Family in Oneida*

County, New York, 1790–1865 (Cambridge: Cambridge University Press, 1981); Nathan O. Hatch, *The Democratization of American Christianity* (New Haven: Yale University Press, 1989); and George M. Thomas, *Revivalism and Cultural Change: Christianity, Nation-Building, and the Market in the Nineteenth-Century United States* (Chicago: University of Chicago Press, 1989). Because I believe that the Millerite movement represented the culmination of antebellum revivalism, I have chosen to date the revivals from 1790 to 1845.

9. Butler, *Awash*, p. 268.

10. Alexis de Tocqueville, *Democracy in America* (1840; reprint, New York: Knopf, 1945), 2:114.

11. See *The Autobiography of Lyman Beecher*, quoted in Edwin S. Gaustad, *A Documentary History of Religion in America to the Civil War* (Grand Rapids, Mich.: Eerdmans, 1982), p. 318; [Lyman Beecher], *An Address to the Charitable Society for the Education of Indigent Pious Young Men for the Ministry of the Gospel* (New Haven, 1814), pp. 5–8, quoted in Hatch, *Democratization*, p. 18; and George Keely, *The Nature and Order of a Gospel Church* (Haverhill, Mass.: P. N. Green, 1819).

12. There are exceptions to every generalization, and there were certainly individual Congregational ministers, especially on the frontier, who allowed the laity to exhort.

13. Matthew La Rue Perrine, *Women Have a Work to Do in the House of God* (New York: Edward W. Thompson, 1817), p. 10. See also Joseph Richardson, *A Sermon on the Duty and Dignity of Woman Delivered April 22, 1832* (Hingham, Mass.: Jedidiah Farmer, 1833).

14. Here I disagree with Donald Mathews, although I have been influenced by his work. Like Mathews, I believe that the revivals emerged in response to "grave social unrest," but I do not believe that they ultimately succeeded as an "organizing process." Mathews, "Second Great Awakening."

15. New Durham, N.H., Freewill Baptist Church Quarterly Meeting Conference Records, vol. 2, August 17 and 18, 1803, New Hampshire Historical Society. *Freewill Baptist Magazine* 1, no. 2 (August 1826): 63. Billy Hibbard, *The Life and Travels of B. Hibbard, Minister of the Gospel* (New York: J. C. Totten, 1825), pp. 237–38. For more on Schulyer, see George Coles, *Heroines of Methodism; or, Pen and Ink Sketches of the Mothers and Daughters of the Church* (New York: Carlton and Porter, 1857), p. 156. For a small sample of other examples, see *A Religious Magazine* 1, no. 2 (April 1811); 2, no. 1 (August 1820); and 2, no. 4 (August 1821). New Durham Freewill Baptist Quarterly Meeting Conference Records, 2:117, meeting held May 17, 1804. See also ibid., 3:64, meeting held August 18, 1813. Boscawen, Canterbury, and Concord, N.H., Christian Church Records, 1826–39, February 3, 1827, New Hampshire Historical Society. Pittsfield Freewill Baptist Church Records, October 25, 1805.

16. "Mourners" who were under "convictions" frequently asked pious women to pray aloud on their behalf. For three examples, see David Marks, *The Life of David Marks* (Limerick, Maine: Morning Star Office, 1831), p. 142; Eleazer Sherman, *The Narrative of Eleazer Sherman, Giving an Account of his Life, Experience, Call to the Ministry of the Gospel, and Travels* (Providence: H. H. Brown, 1832), 2:45; and the letter from Abel Thornton reprinted in *Freewill Baptist Magazine* 1, no. 4 (February 1827): 113.

17. I. C. Goff, *Autobiography and Memoirs of Rev. Joseph Blackmar with Miscellaneous Selections of His Writings* (Dayton, Ohio: Croy, McFarland, and Company, 1879), p. 20. Betsey Eaton, a Freewill Baptist, provides a less dramatic example of "testimony." She "Related the goodness of God to her Soul, and the Love and Peace that she Now Enjoyed." See Pittsfield Freewill Baptist Church Records, November 9, 1807.

18. Joseph Thomas, *The Life, Travels, and Gospel Labors of Elder Joseph Thomas, More Widely Known as the "White Pilgrim"* (New York: M. Cummings, 1861), p. 132. For a northern example, see

E[benezer] F[rancis] Newell, *Life and Observations of Rev. E. F. Newell . . . Who Has Been More than Forty Years an Itinerant Minister in the Methodist Episcopal Church* (Worcester, Mass.: C. W. Ainsworth, 1847), p. 100.

19. James Erwin, *Reminiscences of Early Circuit Life* (Toledo, Ohio: Spear, Johnson, & Company, 1884), p. 191. Marks, *Life*, p. 159. See also Henry Kendall, *Autobiography of Elder Henry Kendall* (Portland, Maine: published by the author, 1853), p. 71.

20. Erwin, *Reminiscences*, p. 16. For accounts of women speaking during love feasts, see Lucy Richards, *Memoirs of the Late Miss Lucy Richards, of Parris, Oneida County, N.Y.* (New York: G. Lane and P. P. Sanford for the M.E. Church, 1842), pp. 47, 73, and Ellen Stewart, *Life of Mrs. Ellen Stewart, Together with Biographical Sketches of Other Individuals. Also, A Discussion with Two Clergymen, and Arguments in Favor of Woman's Rights* (Akron, Ohio: Beebe and Elkins, 1858), p. 11.

21. William Winans, Journal, February 18, 1821, J. B. Cain Archives, Millsaps College, Jackson, Miss., quoted in Randy J. Sparks, *On Jordan's Stormy Banks: Evangelicalism in Missississi, 1773–1876* (Athens: University of Georgia Press, 1994), p. 31; John G. A. Jones, *A Complete History of Methodism in the Mississippi Conference* (Nashville, 1908), 2:205, quoted in Sparks, *On Jordan's Stormy Banks*, p. 45; and Isaac N. Jones, "The Reformation in Tennessee," cited in J. M. Grant, "A Sketch of the Reformation in Tennessee," manuscript in the Center for Restoration Studies, Abilene Christian University, Abilene, Tex., p. 55. I am grateful to Richard T. Hughes for this citation.

22. *The American Slave: A Composite Autobiography*, Supplement, ser. 2, vol. 3, *Texas Narratives*, pt. 8, ed. George P. Rawick (Westport, Conn.: Greenwood Press, 1979), p. 3666. See also ibid., pt. 2, ed. George P. Rawick (Westport, Conn.: Greenwood Press, 1979), p. 523. See also Elizabeth Fox-Genovese, "Religion in the Lives of Slaveholding Women in the Antebellum South," in *That Gentle Strength: Historical Perspectives on Women in Christianity*, ed. Lynda L. Coon, Katherine J. Haldane, and Elisabeth W. Sommer (Charlottesville: University Press of Virginia, 1990), pp. 223–24.

23. Clifton H. Johnson, *God Struck Me Dead: Voices of Ex-Slaves* (Cleveland: Pilgrim Press, 1969), pp. 69, 76, 67. *The American Slave: A Composite Autobiography*, Supplement, ser. 1, vol. 9, *Mississippi Narratives*, pt. 4, ed. George P. Rawick (Westport, Conn.: Greenwood Press, 1979), p. 1664.

24. Henry Holcombe, *The First Fruits, in a Series of Letters* (Philadelphia: Ann Cochran, 1812), pp. 59–60. I am grateful to Sylvia Frey for this citation.

25. On Miller, see Learner [Launer] Blackman, Journal, p. 19, J. B. Cain Archives, Millsaps College, Jackson, Miss., quoted in Sparks, *On Jordan's Stormy Banks*, p. 47. For more on Hosier, see Albert J. Raboteau, *Slave Religion: The "Invisible Institution" in the Antebellum South* (Oxford: Oxford University Press, 1978), p. 134, and Hatch, *Democratization*, p. 106. On southern attitudes toward women, see James L. Leloudis II, "Subversion of the Feminine Ideal," in *Women in New Worlds: Historical Perspectives on the Wesleyan Tradition*, ed. Hilah F. Thomas, Rosemary Skinner Keller, and Louise L. Queen, 2 vols. (Nashville: Abingdon Press, 1982), 2:60–75; Victoria E. Bynum, *Unruly Women: The Politics of Social and Sexual Control in the Old South* (Chapel Hill: University of North Carolina Press, 1992); and Elizabeth Fox-Genovese, *Within the Plantation Household: Black and White Women of the Old South* (Chapel Hill: University of North Carolina Press, 1988). On women's participation in southern revivals, see Christine Leigh Heyrman, *Southern Cross: The Beginnings of the Bible Belt* (New York: Knopf, 1997), pp. 161–205, and Stephanie McCurry, *Masters of Small Worlds: Yeoman Households, Gender Relations, and the Political Cul-*

ture of the Antebellum South Carolina Low Country (New York: Oxford University Press, 1995), pp. 181–91.

26. John I. Rogers, ed., *Autobiography of Elder Samuel Rogers*, 3d ed. (Cincinnati: Standard Publishing Company, 1881), pp. 145–46; and Prince Williams Primitive Baptist Church, Beaufort District, Record Book, February 16, 1834, South Caroliniana Library, University of South Carolina, cited in McCurry, *Masters of Small Worlds*, p. 181.

27. Nathan O. Hatch, "The Christian Movement and the Demand for a Theology of the People," *Journal of American History* 67 (1980): 545–67. On the Christian movement in the South, see Richard Hughes, "Christians in the Early South: The Perspective of Joseph Thomas, 'The White Pilgrim,'" *Discipliana* 46 (1986): 35–43.

28. On evangelical challenges to the southern social order, see Sparks, *On Jordan's Stormy Banks*; Rhys Isaac, *The Transformation of Virginia, 1740–1790* (Chapel Hill: University of North Carolina Press, 1982); Donald G. Mathews, *Religion in the Old South* (Chicago: University of Chicago Press, 1977); A. Gregory Schneider, *The Way of the Cross Leads Home: The Domestication of American Methodism* (Bloomington: Indiana University Press, 1993), pp. 111–21; and Russell E. Richey, *Early American Methodism* (Bloomington: Indiana University Press, 1991), pp. 47–64. On southern revivalism, see John B. Boles, *The Great Revival, 1787–1805* (Lexington: University Press of Kentucky, 1972).

29. On the image of the southern lady, see Anne Firor Scott, *The Southern Lady: From Pedestal to Politics, 1830–1930* (Chicago: University of Chicago Press, 1970), pp. 3–21. On the myth of the black "mammy," see Deborah Gray White, *Ar'n't I a Woman: Female Slaves in the Plantation South* (New York: Norton, 1985), pp. 58–59; and Cheryl Thurber, "The Development of the Mammy Image and Mythology," in *Southern Women: Histories and Identities*, ed. Virginia Bernhard, Betty Brandon, Elizabeth Fox-Genovese, and Theda Purdue (Columbia: University of Missouri Press, 1992), pp. 87–108.

30. On the evangelical distinction between exhorting and preaching, see Leonard I. Sweet, *The Minister's Wife: Her Role in Nineteenth-Century American Evangelicalism* (Philadelphia: Temple University Press, 1983), p. 128, and Earl Kent Brown, *Women of Mr. Wesley's Methodism* (New York: Edwin Mellen Press, 1983), p. 23.

31. On the differences between church and sect, see Ernst Troeltsch, *The Social Teaching of the Christian Churches*, trans. Olive Wyon, 2 vols. (London: Allen and Unwin, 1931; reprint, Chicago: University of Chicago Press, 1976), 1:331–42; H. Richard Niebuhr, *The Social Sources of Denominationalism* (New York: Henry Holt, 1929), pp. 17–21; and Benton Johnson, "On Church and Sect," *American Sociological Review* 28 (August 1963): 539–49. The Freewill Baptists and Christians never would have identified themselves as sects because of their own unique understanding of the word. In their usage, sectarians were people who were so committed to party creeds and party doctrines that they had destroyed the unity of the primitive Christian church. See Timothy Earl Fulop, "Elias Smith and the Quest for Gospel Liberty: Popular Religion and Democratic Radicalism in Early Nineteenth-Century New England" (Ph.D. diss., Princeton University, 1992), pp. 51–52.

32. I. D. Stewart, *The History of the Freewill Baptists* (Dover, N.H.: William Burr, 1862), 1:450; J. M. Brewster, *The Centennial Record of Freewill Baptists, 1780–1880* (Dover, N.H.: The Printing Establishment, 1881), p. 239; Ruth O. Bordin, "The Sect to Denomination Process in America: The Freewill Baptist Experience," *Church History* 34 (1964): 79; *Gospel Banner* 1, no. 2 (October 6, 1827); Daniel Alexander Payne, *History of the African Methodist Episcopal Church* (Nashville: Pub-

lishing House of the A.M.E. Sunday-school Union, 1891; reprint, New York: Arno Press, 1969), p. 38; and Hatch, *Democratization*, p. 3. David Millard estimated that the Christians numbered 100,000 in 1837, but he was probably exaggerating. See *Christian Journal* 3, no. 17 (November 16, 1837).

33. For scholarship on the Methodists, see Nathan O. Hatch, "The Puzzle of American Methodism," *Church History* 63 (June 1994): 175–89; John H. Wigger, "Taking Heaven by Storm: Enthusiasm and Early American Methodism, 1770–1820," *Journal of the Early Republic* 14, no. 2 (Summer 1994): 167–94; Russell E. Richey, Kenneth E. Rowe, and Jean Miller Schmidt, eds., *Perspectives on American Methodism: Interpretive Essays* (Nashville: Abingdon Press, 1993); Russell E. Richey and Kenneth E. Rowe, eds., *Rethinking Methodist History* (Nashville: United Methodist Publishing House, 1985); Doris Elizabett Andrews, "Popular Religion and the Revolution in the Middle Atlantic Ports: The Rise of the Methodists, 1770–1800" (Ph.D. diss., University of Pennsylvania, 1986); Richey, *Early American Methodism*; William H. Williams, *The Garden of American Methodism: The Delmarva Peninsula, 1769–1820* (Wilmington, Del.: Scholarly Resources, 1984); and Schneider, *Way of the Cross*.

34. Benjamin Abbott, *Experience and Gospel Labours of the Rev. Benjamin Abbott* (New York: J. Collord, 1832), p. 159.

35. See Wesley's letter to Mary Bosanquet, reprinted in Jacqueline Field-Bibb, *Women Towards Priesthood: Ministerial Politics and Feminist Praxis* (Cambridge: Cambridge University Press, 1991), p. 11; Paul Wesley Chilcote, *John Wesley and the Women Preachers of Early Methodism* (Metuchen, N.J.: Scarecrow Press, 1991), p. 143; and Deborah M. Valenze, *Prophetic Sons and Daughters: Female Preaching and Popular Religion in Industrial England* (Princeton: Princeton University Press, 1985). For more on women preachers in British Methodism, see Leslie F. Church, *More About the Early Methodist People* (London: Epworth Press, 1949), chap. 4; Brown, *Women of Mr. Wesley's Methodism*; D. Colin Dewes, "Ann Carr and the Female Revivalists of Leeds," in *Religion in the Lives of English Women, 1760–1930*, ed. Gail Malmgreen (London: Croom Helm, 1986), pp. 68–87; and F. W. Bourne, *The Bible Christians—Their Origin and History, 1815–1900* (N.p.: Bible Christian Book Room, 1905).

36. For recent scholarship on women in the early Methodist movement in America, see Schneider, *Way of the Cross*; Diane Helen Lobody, "Lost in the Ocean of Love: The Mystical Writings of Catherine Livingston Garretson" (Ph.D. diss., Drew University, 1990); Diane H. Lobody, " 'That Language Might Be Given Me': Women's Experiences in Early Methodism," in Richey, Rowe, and Schmidt, *Perspectives on American Methodism*, pp. 127–44; Joanna Bowen Gillespie, "*The Ladies Repository*, 1841–1861: The Emerging Voice of the Methodist Woman," in Richey and Rowe, *Rethinking Methodist History*, pp. 148–58; Andrews, "Popular Religion," pp. 164–217; Thomas, Keller, and Queen, *Women in New Worlds*; and Elizabeth Muir, *Petticoats in the Pulpit: The Story of Early Nineteenth-Century Methodist Women Preachers in Upper Canada* (Toronto: United Church Publishing House, 1991), pp. 139–64.

37. On Riker, see Richard Whatcoat, Journal, June 8, 1792, Library of Congress, Washington, D.C., cited in Andrews, "Popular Religion," p. 200. Ellen Stewart, *Life*, p. 75. Nancy Towle, *Vicissitudes Illustrated, in the Experience of Nancy Towle, in Europe and America*, 2d ed. (Portsmouth, N.H.: John Caldwell, 1833), p. 196. Elice Miller Smith is the "Miss Miller" that George Brown described in his *Recollections of Itinerant Life: Including Early Reminiscences* (Cincinnati: R. W. Carool, 1866), p. 183. Towle claims that Smith was from Connecticut, but an article in a Freewill Baptist periodical states that she was from Massachusetts. See *The Morning Star* 1, no. 15 (August 17,

1826). She eventually married a Methodist minister named William Smith in Virginia and became a class leader rather than a preacher.

38. On the A.M.E. Church, see Richard Allen, *The Life, Experience, and Gospel Labors of the Rt. Rev. Richard Allen* (1833; reprint, Nashville: Abingdon Press, 1960); Payne, *History*; Will B. Gravely, "African Methodisms and the Rise of Black Denominationalism," in Richey, Rowe, and Schmidt, *Perspectives on American Methodism*, pp. 108–26; and Gary B. Nash, *Forging Freedom: The Formation of Philadelphia's Black Community, 1720–1840* (Cambridge: Harvard University Press, 1988), pp. 100–133. See also David W. Wills, "Womanhood and Domesticity in the A.M.E. Tradition: The Influence of Daniel Alexander Payne," in *Black Apostles at Home and Abroad*, ed. David W. Wills and Richard Newman (Boston: G. K. Hall, 1982), pp. 133–46.

39. The 1836 edition of Jarena Lee's *The Life and Religious Experience of Mrs. Jarena Lee, A Coloured Lady, Giving an Account of her Call to Preach the Gospel* (Philadelphia: n.p.), is reprinted in *Sisters of the Spirit: Three Black Women's Autobiographies of the Nineteenth Century*, ed. William L. Andrews (Bloomington: University of Indiana, 1986). The 1849 edition, *Religious Experience and Journal of Mrs. Jarena Lee, Giving the Account of Her Call to Preach the Gospel* (Philadelphia: printed for the author), which contains much greater detail about her itinerancy, is reprinted in *Spiritual Narratives*, ed. Sue E. Houchins (New York: Oxford University Press, 1988). On Rachel Evans, see James A. Handy, *Scraps of African Methodist Episcopal History* (Philadelphia: A.M.E. Book Concern, 1901), p. 345, and L[ewellyn] L[ongfellow] Berry, *A Century of Missions of the African Methodist Episcopal Church* (New York: Gutenberg Printing Company, 1942), p. 39. For a brief biographical sketch of her husband, Robert Evans, who was a deacon in Bordertown, New Jersey, see Alexander W. Wayman, *Cyclopaedia of African Methodism* (Baltimore: Carroll, 1882), p. 57.

40. Zilpha Elaw, *Memoirs of the Life, Religious Experience, Ministerial Travels and Labours of Mrs. Zilpha Elaw, An American Female of Colour*, reprinted in Andrews, *Sisters of the Spirit*, pp. 81–82; *Elizabeth, A Colored Minister of the Gospel, Born in Slavery* (Philadelphia: Tract Association of Friends, 1889); Julia A. J. Foote, *A Brand Plucked From the Fire: An Autobiographical Sketch* (Cleveland: W. F. Schneider, 1879), reprinted in Andrews, *Sisters of the Spirit*; Olive Gilbert, *Narrative of Sojourner Truth; A Bondswoman of Olden Time, With a History of Her Labors and Correspondence Drawn from her "Book of Life"* (Battle Creek, Mich., 1878; reprint, New York: Oxford University Press, 1991); and Jean McMahon Humez, ed., *Gifts of Power: The Writings of Rebecca Jackson, Black Visionary, Shaker Eldress* (Amherst: University of Massachusetts Press, 1981). On Julia Pell, see Lydia Maria Child, *Letters from New York*, 3d ed. (New York: C. S. Francis, 1876), pp. 73–82. Jarena Lee mentions Juliann Tilmann, whom she calls "Tilgham" in *Religious Experience*, p. 93.

41. Lee preached with a "female speaker" in 1830 in Baltimore, Maryland; she left Philadelphia to travel in company with a "sister preacher" in 1831; she traveled with another "sister speaker" in New Jersey in 1837; and she enjoyed a cup of tea at the house of a "lady preacher" in Athens, New York, in 1841. See Lee, *Religious Experience*, pp. 61, 63, 94–95. Lewis V. Baldwin, "Black Women and African Union Methodism, 1813–1983," *Methodist History* 21, no. 4 (July 1983): 225–37.

42. The Wesleyan Methodists claimed 6,000 members in 1848. The Methodist Protestants were much larger, numbering 60,000 in 1843. See Wesley Bailey, "History of the Reformed Methodist Church," in *History of All the Religious Denominations in the United States*, ed. John Winebrenner (Harrisburg, Pa.: John Winebrenner, 1848), p. 388; James R. Williams, "History of the Methodist Protestant Church," in Winebrenner, *History*, p. 380; and Ira Ford McLeister,

History of the Wesleyan Methodist Church (Syracuse, N.Y.: Wesleyan Methodist Publishing Association, 1934), p. 38.

43. On "despotism," see the report of the Convention of Reformed Methodists in *Gospel Luminary* 2, no. 8 (August 1826). Reeves was invited to preach in front of the General Conference of the Methodist Protestants on two separate occasions. "Mrs. Hannah Reeves, Preacher of the Gospel," *Methodist Quarterly Review* 59 (July 1877): 440. See also Ellen Stewart, *Life*, pp. 61, 101.

44. Fulop, "Elias Smith," p. 41. On the Freewill Baptists, see Hosea Quinby, "History of the Freewill Baptists," *Freewill Baptist Quarterly Magazine* 2 (September 1840); *A Treatise on the Faith of the Freewill Baptists: With an Appendix, Containing a Summary of Their Usages in Church Government* (Dover, N.H.: n.p., 1834); Norman Allen Baxter, *History of the Freewill Baptists: A Study in New England Separatism* (Rochester, N.Y.: American Baptist Historical Society, 1957); Bordin, "Sect to Denomination Process"; Brewster, *Centennial Record*; I. D. Stewart, *History*; and Frederick Wiley, *The Life and Influence of the Rev. Benjamin Randel, Founder of the Freewill Baptist Denomination* (Philadelphia: American Baptist Publication Society, 1915). On the Christian Connection, see *The Christian Denomination* (Newburyport, Mass.: William H. Huse & Co., 1859); Hatch, "Christian Movement"; Milo True Morrill, *A History of the Christian Denomination in America, 1794–1811* (Dayton, Ohio: Christian Publishing Association, 1912); and Michael G. Kenny, *The Perfect Law of Liberty: Elias Smith and the Providential History of America* (Washington: Smithsonian Institution Press, 1994).

45. I. D. Stewart, *History*, 1:394.

46. *Christian Palladium* 2, no. 2 (June 1833): 71. New Durham Freewill Baptist Church Quarterly Meeting Conference Records, 3:92.

47. For a few examples, see Pittsfield Freewill Baptist Church Records, September 1, 1803, January 14, 1805, and October 22, 1832; New Sharon, Maine, First Freewill Baptist Church Records, 1824–45, April 3, 1830, Maine Historical Society; and William Smyth Babcock Papers, August 12, 1801, American Antiquarian Society, Worcester, Mass. Women also wrote letters that were read aloud at Quarterly Meetings. See Record of the Proceedings of Quarterly Meetings of the Freewill Baptist Churches Held in Maine and New Hampshire, 1783–1792 . . . and Yearly Meetings, 1792–1793, April 29, 1790, and September 5, 1793, New Hampshire Historical Society. The Methodist Protestants passed a resolution in favor of women voting on the admission of female members but eliminated it in their 1828 constitution. William T. Noll, "Women as Clergy and Laity in the Nineteenth-Century Methodist Protestant Church," *Methodist History* 15 (January 1977): 109. A group of dissenters led out of the Methodist church in 1820 by William Stilwell allowed women to vote on church business. This group, known as the Methodist Society in the City of New York, numbered 2,000 members in 1825. See William Robert Sutton, "'To Grind the Faces of the Poor': Journeyman for Jesus in Jacksonian Baltimore" (Ph.D. diss., University of Illinois at Urbana-Champaign, 1993), p. 1.

48. Stinchfield Papers, box 1, folder 3, undated manuscript.

49. Sherman, *Narrative*, 2:68–69. See also "The Commentator," *The Morning Star* 2, no. 14 (August 9, 1827).

50. P. R. Russell, "Female Preaching: A Short Sermon," *Christian Journal* 4, no. 5 (May 31, 1838). Russell was responding to Parsons Cooke, *Female Preaching, Unlawful and Inexpedient. A Sermon* (Lynn, Mass.: James R. Newhall, 1837).

51. Ryan, *Cradle of the Middle Class*; New Durham Freewill Baptist Church Quarterly Meeting Conference Records, vol. 1, October 19, 1798. Curtis D. Johnson, *Islands of Holiness: Rural*

Religion in Upstate New York, 1790–1860 (Cornell: Cornell University Press, 1989), p. 53. In 1844 the Freewill Baptist Church in Dover listed 73 male members and 232 female members. Records of the First Freewill Baptist Church, Dover, N.H., vol. 1, 1843–66, New Hampshire Historical Society. The Freewill Baptist Church in New Sharon, Maine, had sixteen male members and thirty female in 1825. New Sharon First Freewill Baptist Church Records.

52. Bordin, "Sect to Denomination Process," p. 79, 71. In 1822, 143 African Methodist clergymen were responsible for 9,888 members. See Payne, *History*, p. 38. Among the Methodists, there were 174,560 members in 1810 and 636 traveling preachers. See Nathan Bangs, "History of the Methodist Episcopal Church," in Winebrenner, *History*, pp. 378–79.

53. Ray Potter, *Memoirs of the Life and Religious Experience of Ray Potter, Minister of the Gospel, Pawtucket* (Providence: H. H. Brown, 1829), p. 46. *Christian Journal* 4, no. 6 (June 14, 1838).

54. Coles, *Heroines*, pp. 322–23.

55. *Christian Palladium* 2, no. 3 (July 1833): 83.

56. Francis Asbury, *The Journal of the Reverend Francis Asbury: Bishop of the Methodist Episcopal Church* (New York: N. Bangs and T. Mason, 1821), p. 164; Levi Hathaway, *The Narrative of Levi Hathaway* (Providence: Miller and Hutchens, 1820), p. 104; and De Tocqueville, *Democracy in America*, 2:142.

57. For an example of a Freewill Baptist protracted meeting, see Marks, *Life*, p. 47. Abbott, *Experience*, p. 140. For examples of children exhorting, see Mark Fernald, *Life of Elder Mark Fernald, Written by Himself* (Newburyport: G. M. Payne and D. P. Pike; Philadelphia: Christian General Book Concern, 1852), p. 51; I. D. Stewart, *History*, 1:219; Sherman, *Narrative*, 2:40; W. B. Strickland, *Autobiography of Rev. James B. Finley, or Pioneer Life in the West* (Cincinnati: Methodist Book Concern, 1853), p. 366; and *Rhode Island Baptist* (Providence) 1, no. 4 (January 1824): 96. These "new measures" are most commonly associated with Charles Finney, but they began earlier among the Methodists and other dissenting sects. See Richard Carwardine, "The Second Great Awakening in the Urban Centers: An Examination of Methodism and the 'New Measures,'" *Journal of American History* 59 (1972): 327–40.

58. John Stewart, *Highways and Hedges; or Fifty Years of Western Methodism* (Cincinnati: Hitchcock and Waldren, 1872), p. 79. A. H. Redford, *The History of Methodism in Kentucky* (Nashville, 1868), 1:266–70, quoted in Bernard A. Weisberger, *They Gathered at the River: The Story of the Great Revivalists and Their Impact upon Religion in America* (Chicago: Quadrangle Books, 1985), p. 25.

59. Robert Davidson, *History of the Presbyterian Church in the State of Kentucky; With a Preliminary Sketch of the Churches in the Valley of Virginia* (New York: Robert Carter, 1847), pp. 143–52. Davidson's book is particularly valuable because of its extensive excerpts from primary documents. Hiram Munger, *The Life and Religious Experience of Hiram Munger*, 3d ed. (Boston: Advent Christian Publication Society, 1885); Rogers, *Autobiography*, p. 42; and I. D. Stewart, *History*, 1:366.

60. *Christian Palladium* 8, no. 10 (September 16, 1839): 182. *Christian Palladium* 12, no. 23 (April 10, 1844): 374–75. For conference minutes that list Rebecca Miller, see *Christian Palladium* 3, no. 13 (December 1, 1834): 239; 4, no. 14 (November 16, 1835): 215; 6, no. 12 (October 16, 1837): 184; 7, no. 10 (September 15, 1838): 155; 8, no. 17 (January 1, 1840): 268; 9, no. 10 (September 15, 1840): 157; 10, no. 10 (September 15, 1841): 156; 11, no. 11 (October 1, 1842): 173; and 12, no. 11 (November 15, 1843): 172. See also Evans William Humphreys, *Memoirs of Deceased Christian Ministers; or, Brief Sketches of the Lives and Labors of 975 Ministers, Who Died Between 1793 and 1880* (Dayton, Ohio: Christian Publishing Association, 1880), p. 241.

61. *A Religious Magazine* 1, no. 4 (October 1811). Rebecca Miller, "Female Improvement," *Christian Palladium* 10 (1841): 36. See also I. D. Stewart, *History*, 1:176–78.

62. He was quoting from Galatians 1:12. *The Religious Informer* 2, no. 1 (January 1821).

63. Benjamin Putnam, *A Sketch of the Life of Elder Benjamin Putnam* (Woodstock, Vt.: David Watson, 1821), p. 25.

64. Ironically, Smith became a schoolmaster at the age of eighteen, even though "I could write but poorly, and did not understand the rules of reading; and, to save my life, could enumerate only three figures." See Elias Smith, *The Life, Conversion, Preaching, Travels, and Sufferings of Elias Smith* (Portsmouth, N.H., 1840; reprint, New York: Arno Press, 1980), pp. 46, 49–50, 90. *A Religious Magazine* 2, no. 8 (September 1822). In New Hampshire between 1748 and 1800, nine-tenths of the 199 ministers were college educated. See Baxter, *History*, p. 15.

65. Abraham Snethen, *Autobiography of Abraham Snethen, the Barefoot Preacher* (Dayton, Ohio: Christian Publishing Association, 1909), pp. 75–76. See also George M. Marsden, "Everyone's Own Interpreter? The Bible, Science, and Authority in Mid-Nineteenth-Century America," in *The Bible in America: Essays in Cultural History*, ed. Nathan O. Hatch and Mark A. Noll (New York: Oxford University Press, 1982).

66. Rebecca Miller, "Duty of Females," *Christian Palladium* 10, no. 2 (May 15, 1841): 21–22. See also Towle, *Vicissitudes*, p. 27.

67. Mary Bradley, *A Narrative of the Life and Christian Experience of Mrs. Mary Bradley* (Boston: Strong and Broadhead, 1849), p. 93. Snethen, *Autobiography*, p. 71. On magic and the occult, see Butler, *Awash*, chap. 3, and Jon Butler, "Magic, Astrology, and the Early American Religious Heritage, 1600–1760," *American Historical Review* 84 (1979): 317–46.

68. Abbott, *Experience*, p. 17.

69. Charles R. Harding, "Autobiography, 1807–1869," American Antiquarian Society, Worcester, Mass.

70. *Elizabeth*, pp. 10, 4. Zilpha Elaw resolved that "the one who would be a master in Israel should possess such an experimental knowledge of the Christian religion, as an university cannot bestow, but which is the exclusive endowment of the Holy Ghost." See Elaw, *Memoirs*, p. 115.

71. Stinchfield Papers, box 1, folder 6, manuscript dated June 10, 1797. Stinchfield Papers, box 1, folder 3, undated manuscript.

72. Ruth H. Bloch, "The Gendered Meanings of Virtue in Revolutionary America," *Signs* 13 (Autumn 1987): 37–58. Readers who are familiar with the work of Susan Juster will recognize that I disagree with her argument that nineteenth-century evangelicals "feminized" the concept of sin. Juster argues that even though *both* men and women were disciplined in Baptist churches, women were "charged with repeated acts of deviance which signalled a fundamentally disordered nature." After closely examining church disciplinary records, she concludes that evangelical Christians did not share the common middle-class faith in women's "passionlessness"; instead, they resurrected "the ancient model of women as seducing Eve."

Although I find Juster's conclusions provocative, I see several flaws in her argument. First, her statistics do not necessarily prove that Baptist women were more likely to face church discipline than men. Admittedly, if measured by sheer numbers, women made up the majority of those who were perceived as "disorderly": 688 men and 777 women were disciplined by their churches between 1771 and 1830. Unfortunately, however, Juster does not provide statistics on the percentages of men and women in the church population *as a whole*. If women were a significant majority in most Baptist churches, then it is not surprising that they should be the majority of those disciplined as well. Indeed, given the predominance of women in most evangelical churches, it is extraordinary that such large numbers of men also faced church discipline.

Juster's most striking finding is that Baptist women were far more likely to be accused of sexual misconduct than men. According to her interpretation, evangelicals believed that women were particularly lustful and licentious: they were "Eves" plotting to lead men into sexual transgression. Yet perhaps an alternate explanation for her findings—one that is equally negative—is possible as well. If evangelicals believed that women were "naturally" pure and virtuous, they may have been especially shocked by "ungodly" women and hence more likely to admonish or excommunicate them. See Susan Juster, *Disorderly Women: Sexual Politics and Evangelicalism in Revolutionary New England* (Ithaca: Cornell University Press, 1994), pp. 155, 175, 151.

73. Laurel Thacher Ulrich, *Good Wives: Image and Reality in the Lives of Women in Northern New England, 1650–1750* (Oxford: Oxford University Press, 1980), and Amanda Porterfield, *Female Piety in Colonial New England* (Oxford: Oxford University Press, 1992).

74. As Ruth Bloch has argued, Franklin regarded virtue as "a quality of autonomous males," and he restricted membership in his proposed "United Party of Virtue" to "young and single men only." Ruth H. Bloch, "Women, Love, and Virtue in the Thought of Edwards and Franklin," in *Benjamin Franklin, Jonathan Edwards, and the Representation of American Culture*, ed. Barbara B. Oberg and Harry S. Stout (New York: Oxford University Press, 1993), p. 146. Jefferson was quoting from Thomas Otway's *The Orphan*. See *Jefferson's Literary Commonplace Book*, ed. Douglas L. Wilson, in *Papers of Thomas Jefferson*, 2d ser. (Princeton: Princeton University Press, 1989), quoted in Kenneth A. Lockridge, *On the Sources of Patriarchal Rage: The Commonplace Books of William Byrd and Thomas Jefferson and the Gendering of Power in the Eighteenth Century* (New York: New York University Press, 1992), pp. 60, 79.

75. Amos Chase, *On Female Excellence* (Litchfield, Conn.: n.p., 1792); Nathan Strong, *The Character of a Virtuous and Good Woman; a Discourse Delivered by the Desire and in the Presence of the Female Beneficent Society, in Hartford, Oct. 4th, A.D. 1809* (Hartford: Hudson and Goodwin, 1809); Thomas Branagan, *The Excellency of the Female Character Vindicated* (New York: Samuel Wood, 1807); and Gardiner Spring, *The Excellence and Influence of the Female Character*, 2d ed. (New York: n.p., 1825). The quote is from "Comparison of the Sexes," *American Museum*, January 1789, p. 59, cited in Bloch, "Gendered Meanings," p. 51.

76. Ann Braude, "Women's History *Is* American Religious History," in *Retelling United States Religious History*, ed. Thomas A. Tweed (Berkeley: University of California Press, 1997), p. 100. Bloch, "Women, Love, and Virtue," p. 146.

77. Bloch, "Women, Love, and Virtue," p. 136. Bloch, "Gendered Meanings," pp. 49–53. On sentimental novels, see Cathy N. Davidson, *Revolution and the Word: The Rise of the Novel in America* (New York: Oxford University Press, 1986), pp. 110–50.

78. Linda K. Kerber, *Women of the Republic: Intellect and Ideology in Revolutionary America* (Chapel Hill: University of North Carolina Press, 1980), p. 269, and Sara M. Evans, *Born for Liberty: A History of Women in America* (New York: Free Press, 1989), p. 56. On changing cultural perceptions of motherhood, see Ruth H. Bloch, "American Feminine Ideals in Transition: The Rise of the Moral Mother, 1785–1815," *Feminist Studies* 4, no. 2 (June 1978): 101–26; and Jan Lewis, "Motherhood and the Construction of the Male Citizen in the United States, 1750–1850," in *Constructions of the Self*, ed. George Levine (New Brunswick: Rutgers University Press, 1992), pp. 143–64.

79. "Female Influence," *New York Magazine* (May 1795): 299–305, quoted in Bloch, "Gendered Meanings," p. 47.

80. *The Morning Star* 1 no. 12 (July 27, 1826). The classic description of the rise of "separate spheres" is Nancy F. Cott, *The Bonds of Womanhood: "Woman's Sphere" in New England, 1780–1835*

(New Haven: Yale University Press, 1977). See also Steven Mintz and Susan Kellogg, *Domestic Revolutions: A Social History of American Family Life* (New York: Free Press, 1988), pp. 49–60. On changing meanings of manhood, see Anthony E. Rotundo, *American Manhood: Transformations in Masculinity from the Revolution to the Modern Era* (New York: Basic Books, 1993), and John Demos, "The Changing Faces of Fatherhood," chapter 3 of *Past, Present, and Personal: The Family and the Life Course in American History* (New York: Oxford University Press, 1986).

81. Barbara Welter, "The Cult of True Womanhood, 1820–1860," *American Quarterly* 18 (1966): 151–74. Thomas Laquer, *Making Sex: Body and Gender from the Greeks to Freud* (Cambridge: Harvard University Press, 1990), p. 196; Horace Bushnell, *Woman's Suffrage; The Reform Against Nature* (New York: Charles Scribner and Company, 1869), p. 36. Christine Stansell, *City of Women: Sex and Class in New York, 1789–1860* (Urbana: University of Illinois Press, 1987), p. 36.

82. Nancy Cott argues that ministers' attitudes toward "separate spheres" became more restrictive after 1820. "Positive appeals to women to contribute to society with benevolent works, pious influence, and child nurture dominated ministers' attitudes from 1790 to 1820, but in the next decades their sermons more often sprang from negative tenets." See Cott, *Bonds of Womanhood*, p. 157. Lori D. Ginzberg, *Women and the Work of Benevolence: Morality, Politics, and Class in the Nineteenth-Century United States* (New Haven: Yale University Press, 1990). See also Nancy A. Hewitt, *Women's Activism and Social Change: Rochester, New York, 1822–1872* (Ithaca: Cornell University Press, 1984).

83. John Bangs, *Autobiography of Reverend John Bangs, of the New York Annual Conference* (New York: n.p., 1846), pp. 16–17. For two other examples of Methodist women who proved instrumental in converting family members, see Richards, *Memoirs*, pp. 78–82, and Philip Slaughter, *Memoir of Col. Joshua Fry . . . With an Autobiography of His Son, Rev. Henry Fry* (n.p., n.d), pp. 84–85. In her study of the awakening in Utica, New York, Mary Ryan argues that women were often instrumental in converting their husbands. See Mary P. Ryan, "A Women's Awakening: Evangelical Religion and the Families of Utica, New York, 1800–1840," *American Quarterly* 30 (Winter 1978): 604. A. Gregory Schneider has suggested that the Methodists played a central role in the creation of this domestic ideology. See *Way of the Cross*, especially pp. 122–35, and also his "Social Religion, the Christian Home, and Republican Spirituality in Antebellum Methodism," *Journal of the Early Republic* 10 (Summer 1990): 163–89. Barry Levy has made a similar claim for the Quakers. See Barry Levy, *Quakers and the American Family: British Settlement in the Delaware Valley* (New York: Oxford University Press, 1988).

84. Almond H. Davis, *The Female Preacher, or Memoir of Salome Lincoln* (Providence, 1843; reprint, New York: Arno Press, 1972), p. 41. *Christian Herald* 9, no. 6 (May 4, 1843).

85. *Mutual Rights and Methodist Protestant* 2, no. 37 (September 14, 1832): 295.

86. The Freewill Baptists were especially hostile to the Shakers. Led by their minister, Edward Lock, a small group of radical Freewill Baptists in New Hampshire had defected to the Shakers in early 1783.

87. Russell, "Female Preaching."

88. Susan Juster has suggested that the celebration of motherhood represented a decline in female spiritual authority. See Susan Juster, "To Slay the Beast": Visionary Women in the Early Republic," in *A Mighty Baptism: Race, Gender, and the Creation of American Protestantism*, ed. Susan Juster and Lisa MacFarlane (Ithaca: Cornell University Press, 1996), p. 34. On "Mothers in Israel," see Rachel Adler, "'A Mother in Israel': Aspects of the Mother-Role in Jewish Myth," in *Beyond Androcentrism: New Essays on Women and Religion*, ed. Rita M. Gross (Missoula, Mont.: Scholars Press, 1977); and Valenze, *Prophetic Sons and Daughters*, pp. 35–37. The biblical refer-

ences to "Mothers in Israel" are Judges 5:7 and 2 Samuel 20:19. The reference to Phebe is from Romans 16:1–2. "New Testament Worship," *Christian Herald* 9, no. 13 (June 22, 1843), and "Answer to Israel Seekers' Queries," *The Religious Enquirer* (1811), p. 9.

89. "Bold soldier" quoted in Schneider, *Way of the Cross*, p. 183. On Priscilla Baltimore, see Berry, *Century of Missions*, p. 37; Handy, *Scraps*, pp. 345–46; Wayman, *Cyclopaedia*, p. 18; and Susie I. Shorter, *Heroines of African Methodism* (Jacksonville, Fla.: Chew, 1891), p. 27. Shorter mistakenly refers to her as "Anna" Baltimore. On Roberts, see *Christian Palladium* 1, no. 5 (September 1832): 109. See also *Christian Palladium* 2, no. 3 (July 1833): 83.

90. Lyman Beecher quoted in Page Putnam Miller, *A Claim to New Roles* (Philadelphia: American Theological Library Association; Metuchen, N.J.: Scarecrow Press, 1985), p. 50. Harding, "Autobiography."

91. Pittsfield Freewill Baptist Church Records, March 9, 1801. Record of the Free Baptist Church, Greene, Maine, June 23, 1831, typescript by Samuel D. Rumery, Maine Historical Society. On the Methodist conception of the "family of God," see Schneider, *Way of the Cross*, pp. 123–24.

92. Elaw, *Memoirs*, p. 52. I have borrowed the phase "islands of holiness" from Johnson, *Islands of Holiness*. Donald Mathews has pointed out that in the South, evangelicals strove to create tightly ordered communities that would set "believers" apart from "worldlings." See Mathews, *Religion in the Old South*, p. 40.

93. *A Religious Magazine* 1, no. 3 (August 1811). Elaw, *Memoirs*, p. 52. In 1826 the Christian Church in Canterbury, New Hampshire, resolved to renounce "all creeds[,] articles of faith, disciplines[,] Church platforms and covenants written in addition to the Bible." Boscawen, Canterbury, and Concord Christian Church Records, 1826–39. On primitivism, see Richard T. Hughes and C. Leonard Allen, *Illusions of Innocence: Protestant Primitivism in America, 1630–1875* (Chicago: University of Chicago Press, 1988); Richard T. Hughes, ed., *The American Quest for the Primitive Church* (Urbana: University of Illinois Press, 1988); and Theodore Dwight Bozeman, *To Live Ancient Lives: The Primitivist Dimension in Puritanism* (Chapel Hill: University of North Carolina Press, 1988).

94. Harriet Livermore, *A Narration of Religious Experience* (Concord, N.H.: Jacob B. Moore, 1826), p. 139. On the ritual significance of baptism, see Mircea Eliade, *The Sacred and the Profane: The Nature of Religion* (New York: Harcourt Brace, 1959), p. 130. See also Paul S. Sanders, "The Sacraments in Early American Methodism," in Richey, Rowe, and Schmidt, *Perspectives on American Methodism*, pp. 77–92. On the early Christians, see Wayne A. Meeks, *The Origins of Christian Morality: The First Two Centuries* (New Haven: Yale University Press, 1993).

95. Leigh Eric Schmidt, *Holy Fairs: Scottish Communions and American Revivals in the Early Modern Period* (Princeton: Princeton University Press, 1989), pp. 69, 74, 101, 108.

96. Heman Bangs, *The Autobiography and Journal of Rev. Heman Bangs* (New York: N. Tibbals and Son, 1872), pp. 48, 14, 92. For a sampling of hymns, see Nancy Gove Cram, *A Collection of Hymns and Poems. Designed to Instruct the Inquirer; and Furnish the Public with a Small Variety* (Schenectady: n.p., 1815). For one example of foot washing, see Babcock Papers, February 15, 1801.

97. *The Christian Herald and Journal* 5 (September 12, 1839). *Christian Palladium* 1, no. 5 (September 1832): 116. For a discussion of evangelical resistance to fashionable dress, see Richard L. Bushman, *The Refinement of America: Persons, Houses, Cities* (New York: Knopf, 1992), pp. 314–19. For descriptions of women's fashions in the 1820s and 1830s, see Elisabeth McLellan, *History of American Costume, 1607–1870* (New York: Tudor, 1937), pp. 373–433.

98. Quoted in I. D. Stewart, *History*, 1:109–11.

99. Strickland, *Autobiography*, p. 183. On Crockett, see Schneider, *Way of the Cross*, p. 65; and Carroll Smith-Rosenberg, "Davy Crockett as Trickster: Pornography, Liminality, and Symbolic Inversion in Victorian America," in her *Disorderly Conduct: Visions of Gender in Victorian America* (New York: Oxford University Press, 1985), pp. 90–108. Several Methodist historians have commented on the "feminine" language and style of early evangelicals. See Williams, *Garden of American Methodism*, p. 110; Mathews, *Religion in the Old South*, p. 123; and Lobody, "'That Language Might Be Given Me,'" pp. 127–44.

100. Sociologist Jacqueline Field-Bibb argues that women become important symbolically whenever there is criticism of authority or an attempt to create a more egalitarian community. See her *Women Towards Priesthood*, pp. 201–2. On symbolic gender reversals, see Caroline Walker Bynum, *Holy Feast and Holy Fast: The Religious Significance of Food to Medieval Women* (Berkeley: University of California Press, 1987), p. 284.

101. David Edmund Millard, *Memoir of Rev. David Millard; with Selections from His Writings. By His Son* (Dayton, Ohio: Christian Publishing Association, 1874), p. 128. Martin Cheney, a Freewill Baptist elder, also opposed slavery. For a sermon he preached against it, see George T. Day, *The Life of Rev. Martin Cheney* (Providence: George H. Whitney, 1853), pp. 129–36.

102. Millard, *Memoir*, p. 71; Davis, *Female Preacher*, p. 104; Richard Allen, *Life*, p. 21; Lee, *Religious Experience*, pp. 27, 38, 41, 49, 54, 58, 80, 84. Richard Allen fondly referred to Benjamin Abbott (a white Methodist) as a "friend and father," while Abbott insisted that "God is no respecter of persons; but all of them who fear him and work righteousness, of every nation, are accepted of him." Richard Allen, *Life*, p. 19, and Abbott, *Experience*, p. 187. Ellen Stewart attended a Reformed Methodist prayer group which included several African Americans. As a result, other people derided them as "the black society." See Ellen Stewart, *Life*, p. 85.

103. In 1827 the Freewill Baptists officially resolved that "the color of a candidate for the ministry should have no influence on his ordination, provided he be otherwise qualified." Quoted in I. D. Stewart, *History*, 1:441.

104. John Lewis, *The Life, Labors, and Travels of Elder Charles Bowles* (Watertown, Mass.: Ingall's and Stowell's, 1852), pp. 30–31. There is no biography or autobiography of Clarissa Danforth, but accounts of her in the religious press make it clear that she was immensely popular. For a letter from her, see *The Religious Informer* 1, no. 16 (March 1820). For other references, see *The Religious Informer* 2, no. 3 (March 1821); 3, no. 8 (August 1822); and 1 (October 1820); and *Christian Journal* 1, no. 13 (September 17, 1835). She is also mentioned in the Babcock Papers. See also Hardesty, *Great Women of Faith*; I. D. Stewart, *History*, 1:300, 318, 366, 389, 391; and Gideon A. Burgess and John T. Ward, *Free Baptist Cyclopedia, Historical and Biographical* (n.p., 1889), pp. 148–49.

105. On Protestant clergymen's rejection of cultural values, see Mark Y. Hanley, *Beyond a Christian Commonwealth: The Protestant Quarrel with the American Republic, 1830–1860* (Chapel Hill: University of North Carolina Press, 1994).

106. Jon Butler has noted that the Revolution gave birth to a "bewildering variety" of millennialist predictions. See *Awash*, pp. 216–17. On millennialism during the Revolutionary period, see Ruth Bloch, *Visionary Republic: Millennial Themes in American Thought* (Cambridge: Cambridge University Press, 1985); Nathan O. Hatch, *The Sacred Cause of Liberty* (New Haven: Yale University Press, 1977); and James West Davidson, *The Logic of Millennial Thought: Eighteenth-Century New England* (New Haven: Yale University Press, 1977). Most historians have argued that post- rather than premillennialism characterized evangelicalism before the Millerite movement. See Michael Barkun, *Crucible of the Millennium: The Burned-over District of New York in the 1840s*

(Syracuse: Syracuse University Press, 1986), p. 25; and Jonathan M. Butler, "Adventism and the American Experience," in *The Rise of Adventism: Religion and Society in Mid-Nineteenth-Century America*, ed. Edwin S. Gaustad (New York: Harper and Row, 1974), p. 174. I agree that post-millennialism was more prevalent than premillennialism, but I believe that historians have overlooked a persistent strain of apocalypticism in the early nineteenth century. See James H. Moorhead, "Between Progress and Apocalypse: A Reassessment of Millennialism in American Religious Thought, 1800–1880," *Journal of American History* 71 (December 1984): 524–42.

107. Quoted in Baxter, *History*, p. 86.

108. Snethen, *Autobiography*, pp. 59–61. The woman was quoting from Mark 13:8 and Luke 21:11. For another example of the fear that the appearance of a comet could cause, see Rogers, *Autobiography*, p. 134. In New Hampshire, a Methodist woman thought the world was ending when she saw a red moon and "singular light . . . all over the heavens." Harding, "Autobiography."

109. Towle, *Vicissitudes*, p. 13. See also Sherman, *Narrative*, 2:68–69, and Elaw, *Memoirs*, p. 75.

110. Meeks, *Origins*, p. 36. Elleanor Warner Knight, *A Narrative of the Christian Experience, Life and Adventures, Trials and Labours of Elleanor Knight, Written by Herself* (Providence: n.p., 1839), p. iv. To use more theoretical language, these sects were "subaltern counterpublics": "parallel discursive arenas where members of subordinated social groups invent and circulate counter-discourses to formulate oppositional interpretations of their identities, interests, and needs." On one hand, Nancy Fraser explains, subaltern counterpublics "function as spaces of withdrawal and regroupment; on the other hand, they also function as bases and training grounds for agitational activities directed toward wider publics." See Nancy Fraser, "Rethinking the Public Sphere: A Contribution to the Critique of Actually Existing Democracy," in *Habermas and the Public Sphere*, ed. Craig Calhoun (Cambridge: Massachusetts Institute of Technology Press, 1992), pp. 123–24.

CHAPTER 4

1. Elleanor Warner Knight, *A Narrative of the Christian Experience, Life and Adventures, Trials and Labours of Elleanor Knight, Written by Herself* (Providence: n.p., 1839), pp. 21, 8–9, 11–12. Knight is often very vague about dates, so I have had to piece together the chronology of her life from clues in her narrative.

2. Ibid., pp. 32–33.

3. Ibid., pp. 33–34.

4. Ibid., pp. 34–35.

5. Ibid., pp. 35–36.

6. Ibid., p. 54.

7. Ibid., pp. 63–65, and *Christian Herald* 7, no. 15 (July 8, 1841).

8. Knight, *Narrative*, pp. iv, 47, 124.

9. The preachers' memoirs are Zilpha Elaw, *Memoirs of the Life, Religious Experience, Ministerial Travels and Labours of Mrs. Zilpha Elaw, An American Female of Colour* (London, 1846), reprinted in *Sisters of the Spirit: Three Black Women's Autobiographies of the Nineteenth Century*, ed. William L. Andrews (Bloomington: University of Indiana, 1986), pp. 149–60; Julia A. J. Foote, *A Brand Plucked From the Fire: An Autobiographical Sketch* (Cleveland: W. F. Schneider, 1879), reprinted in Andrews, *Sisters of the Spirit*, pp. 161–234: Laura Smith Haviland, *A Woman's Life-Work: Labors and Experiences of Laura S. Haviland*, 4th ed. (Chicago: Publishing Association of Friends,

1889); Knight, *Narrative*; Harriet Livermore, *A Narration of Religious Experience* (Concord, N.H.: Jacob B. Moore, 1826); Ellen Stewart, *Life of Mrs. Ellen Stewart, Together with Biographical Sketches of Other Individuals. Also, A Discussion with Two Clergymen, and Arguments in Favor of Woman's Rights* (Akron, Ohio: Beebe and Elkins, 1858); Nancy Towle, *Vicissitudes Illustrated, in the Experience of Nancy Towle, in Europe and America*, 2d ed. (Portsmouth, N.H.: John Caldwell, 1833); Lydia Sexton, *Autobiography of Lydia Sexton* (Dayton, Ohio: United Brethren Publishing House, 1882); and Jarena Lee, *The Life and Religious Experience of Mrs. Jarena Lee, A Coloured Lady, Giving an Account of her Call to Preach the Gospel* (Philadelphia, 1836), reprinted in Andrews, *Sisters of the Spirit*, pp. 25–48. Lee published a later edition of her memoir as *Religious Experience and Journal of Mrs. Jarena Lee, Giving the Account of Her Call to Preach the Gospel* (Philadelphia: printed for the author, 1849), reprinted in *Spiritual Narratives*, ed. Sue E. Houchins (New York: Oxford University Press, 1988). Deborah Peirce included a brief account of her conversion in *A Scriptural Vindication of Female Preaching* (Carmel, N.Y.: E. Burroughs, 1820). The exhorters' narratives are Mary Bradley, *A Narrative of the Life and Christian Experience of Mrs. Mary Bradley* (Boston: Strong and Broadhead, 1849); Nancy Caldwell, *Walking with God: Leaves from the Journal of Mrs. Nancy Caldwell*, ed. Rev. James O. Thompson (Keyser, W.Va.: n.p., 1886); E. J. Marden, *A Letter from Mrs. E. J. Marden, of Bangor, Maine. Containing her Experience in the Blessing of Entire Sanctification; Also an Account of Her Receiving, by Faith, the Doctrine of the Second Advent of Our Lord Jesus Christ in 1843* (Haverhill, Mass.: Essex Banner Office, 1842); Fanny Newell, *Memoirs of Fanny Newell; Written by Herself, and Published by the Desire and Request of Numerous Friends*, 3d ed. (Springfield and New York: n.p., 1833); and Cordelia Thomas, *The Sheaf; or, The Work of God in the Soul; As Illustrated in the Personal Experiences of Mrs. Cordelia Thomas* (Boston: H. V. Degen, 1852). For Cogswell, see *Christian Journal* 2 (April 21, 1836): 5. For Miller, see *Christian Palladium* 8 (September 16, 1839): 158–59. For Rice, see "The Labors of Olive Maria Rice," *The Midnight Cry* 4 (July 6, 1843).

10. *Elizabeth, A Colored Minister of the Gospel, Born in Slavery* (Philadelphia: Tract Association of Friends, 1889), and [Olive Gilbert], *Narrative of Sojourner Truth, A Northern Slave* (Boston: printed for the author, 1850).

11. George Brown, *The Lady Preacher; Or, the Life and Labors of Mrs. Hannah Reeves, Late the Wife of the Rev. William Reeves of the Methodist Church* (Philadelphia: Daughaday and Becker; Springfield, Ohio: Methodist Publishing House, 1870); Almond H. Davis, *The Female Preacher, or Memoir of Salome Lincoln* (Providence, 1843; reprint, New York: Arno Press, 1972); O. R. Fassett, *The Biography of Mrs. L. E. Fassett, a Devoted Christian, a Useful Life* (Boston: Advent Christian Publication Society, 1885); Philetus Roberts, *Memoir of Mrs. Abigail Roberts; An Account of Her Birth, Early Education, Call to the Ministry* (Irvington, N.J.: Moses Cummings, 1858). Fifteen other female preachers published religious articles, tracts, poems, and hymns or sent letters to religious periodicals describing their "labors in the harvest," but they did not give detailed accounts of their conversions or their calls to preach. (Female preachers' use of the publishing industry will be discussed further in Chapter 6.)

12. Juanita Brooks, ed., *Not by Bread Alone: The Journal of Martha Spence Heywood, 1850–56* (Salt Lake City: Utah State Historical Society, 1978); Jean McMahon Humez, ed., *Gifts of Power: The Writings of Rebecca Jackson, Black Visionary, Shaker Eldress* (Amherst: University of Massachusetts Press, 1981); and Davis, *Female Preacher*, p. 10.

13. Lee, *Religious Experience*, p. 97. In her memoir, Nancy Towle mentioned the many "valuable writings" that she wanted to someday "publish to the world." Towle, *Vicissitudes*, p. 121. Rebecca Miller's obituary revealed that she had "devoted considerable time to writing" during the last years of her life, but very few of her articles ever appeared in print. *Christian Palladium* 12,

no. 23 (April 10, 1844): 374–75. It is quite possible that some of these women's documents are tucked away in attics or in small, local historical societies.

14. See Joycelyn Moody, "Self-Effacement and Collective Identity in Five Black Women's Autobiographies, 1835–1879" (Ph.D. diss., University of Kansas, 1993), p. 114. For other studies of women's religious memoirs, see Ann Taves, "Early Memoirs of New England Women," in *American Women's Autobiography: Fea(s)ts of Memory*, ed. Margo Culley (Madison: University of Wisconsin Press, 1992), pp. 57–74; and Joanna Bowen Gillespie, " 'The Clear Leadings of Providence': Pious Memoirs and the Problems of Self-Realization for Women in the Early Nineteenth Century," *Journal of the Early Republic* 5 (Summer 1985): 197–221. For general studies of women's autobiography, see Joanne M. Braxton, *Black Women Writing Autobiography: A Tradition within a Tradition* (Philadelphia: Temple University Press, 1989), and Estelle C. Jelinek, ed., *Women's Autobiography: Essays in Criticism* (Bloomington: Indiana University Press, 1980).

15. Knight, *Narrative*.

16. For a fuller discussion of the traditional conversion accounts that most influenced nineteenth-century Protestants, see Virginia Lieson Brereton, *From Sin to Salvation: Stories of Women's Conversions, 1800 to the Present* (Bloomington: Indiana University Press, 1991), pp. 10–13.

17. Mary Clarke Lloyd, *Meditations on Divine Subjects* (New York: J. Parker, 1750), Elizabeth Lawrence Bury, *An Account of the Life and Death of Mrs. Elizabeth Bury . . . Chiefly Collected out of Her Own Diary* (Boston: D. Henchman, 1743), and Elizabeth White, *Experience of God's Gracious Dealing* (Boston: n.p., 1741). All of these books were published posthumously.

18. Elizabeth Singer Rowe, *Devout Exercises of the Heart in Meditation and Soliloquy, Prayer and Praise* (n.p., 1742). *The Morning Star* 7, no. 27 (November 2, 1832): 105.

19. Livermore, *Narration*, p. 18. Jeanne Marie (Bouvier de la Motte) Guyon was Roman Catholic, but she was persecuted by the ecclesiastical hierarchy in France, and after her death her popularity crossed denominational boundaries. See Thomas Digby Brooke, *The Exemplary Life of the Pious Lady Guion* (Philadelphia: Joseph Crukshank, 1804), and Jeanne Marie Guyon, *The Life and Religious Experience of the Celebrated Lady Guion* (New York: Hoyt and Bolmore, 1820), which was republished in Baltimore in 1821 and in New York in 1825. See also Jeanne Marie Guyon, *Poems, Translated from the French of Madame de la Mothe Guion* (Philadelphia: Kimber, Conrad, and Co., 1804), which was also published in Wilmington, Delaware, in 1806, in Philadelphia in 1808, and in Burlington, New Jersey, in 1815.

20. Caldwell, *Walking with God*, p. 27, and Stewart, *Life*, p. 41. See also Livermore, *Narration*, p. 18. Hester Ann Rogers, *A Short Account of the Experience of Mrs. Hester Ann Rogers* (New York: Daniel Hill, 1811), and Henry Moore, *The Life of Mrs. Mary Fletcher* (London: Methodist Book Room, 1817).

21. Elizabeth Ashbridge, *Some Account of the Early Part of the Life of Elizabeth Ashbridge* (Philadelphia: n.p., 1807); Patience Brayton, *A Short Account of the Life and Religious Labors of Patience Brayton* (New Bedford: n.p., 1801); and Jane Hoskens, *The Life and Spiritual Sufferings of That Faithful Servant of Christ* (Philadelphia: n.p., 1771). See also Elizabeth Collins, *Memoir of Elizabeth Collins* (Philadelphia: N. Kite, 1833), and William J. Allinson, comp., *Memorials of Rebecca Jones*, 2d ed. (Philadelphia: H. Longstreth, 1849).

22. Elaw, *Memoirs*, pp. 54–55, 73, and Livermore, *Narration*, p. 73. Abigail Roberts was raised as a Quaker, and Ellen Stewart lived with a Quaker family for ten months when she was twelve years old. Roberts, *Memoir*, p. 10, and Stewart, *Life*, p. 7. The expression "poor worm" was a standard one in spiritual autobiographies. It is based on a verse from Psalms 22:6, "But I am a worm, and no man; a reproach of men, and despised of the people." For Quaker examples, see

Collins, *Memoir*, p. 77, and Brayton, *Short Account*, p. 99. For evangelical examples, see Livermore, *Narration*, p. 183; Newell, *Memoirs*, p. 166; and Marden, *Letter*, p. 75.

23. Stewart, *Life*, p. 12. Gilbert McMaster linked Christian Connection female preachers, especially Nancy Cram, to Lee and Wilkinson in *An Essay in Defense of Some Fundamental Doctrines of Christianity; including a Review of the Writings of Elias Smith and the Claims of His Female Preachers* (Schenectady: Riggs and Stevens, 1815), p. 110.

24. Levi Hathaway, *The Narrative of Levi Hathaway* (Providence: Miller and Hutchens, 1820); John Colby, *The Life, Experiences, and Travels of Elder John Colby* (Portland, Maine: n.p., 1815; reprint, Newport, N.H.: French and Brown, 1831); and Billy Hibbard, *The Life and Travels of B. Hibbard, Minister of the Gospel* (New York: J. C. Totten, 1825).

25. When Elleanor Knight told Elder Martin Cheney that she had been called to preach, he responded by suggesting that she had been "deceived." Knight, *Narrative*, p. 70.

26. Lee, *Religious Experience*, p. 82.

27. In her fascinating dissertation, Elizabeth Elkin Grammer has suggested that female preachers were so "marginalized in their culture" and "uncertain of their identity" that "they lacked the self-knowledge that facilitates the mastery of narrative form, the transformation of the formless life into a 'purposeful,' patterned autobiography." Comparing women's narratives to those written by Peter Cartwright and Charles Finney, she claims that men's narratives were generally more linear. See Elizabeth Elkin Grammer, "'A Pen in His Hand': A Pen in Her Hand. Autobiographies by Female Itinerant Evangelists in Nineteenth-Century America" (Ph.D. diss., University of Virginia, 1995), p. 256. I agree that Cartwright's and Finney's narratives are more structured than women's, but these two men are not representative of evangelical male preachers as a whole. Narratives such as Abraham Snethen's *Autobiography of Abraham Snethen, the Barefoot Preacher* (Dayton, Ohio: Christian Publishing Association, 1909), Eleazer Sherman's *The Narrative of Eleazer Sherman, Giving an Account of his Life, Experience, Call to the Ministry of the Gospel, and Travels* (Providence: H. H. Brown, 1832), Benjamin Putnam's *A Sketch of the Life of Elder Benjamin Putnam* (Woodstock, Vt.: David Watson, 1821), and David Marks' *Life of David Marks* (Limerick, Maine: Morning Star Office, 1831), are all rather formless and fragmentary. Unlike Grammer, I find the *structures* of men's and women's memoirs to be quite similar, even though I argue below that there are subtle differences in content.

28. Lee, *Religious Experience*, p. 17. See also Towle, *Vicissitudes*, p. 22; Davis, *Female Preacher*, p. 37; and *Christian Journal* 2, no. 2 (April 21, 1836): 5. For a male example, see Elias Smith, *The Life, Conversion, Preaching, Travels, and Sufferings of Elias Smith* (Portsmouth, N.H., 1840; reprint, New York: Arno Press, 1980), p. 142.

29. Grammer, "'A Pen in His Hand,'" p. 200.

30. Towle, *Vicissitudes*, p. 22. She quoted from Mark 16:15, Psalms 102:9, Psalms 132:4, Jonah 4:3, Jeremiah 9:2, and Jeremiah 31:16. Towle often italicized her scriptural references.

31. Elaine J. Lawless, "Rescripting Their Lives and Narratives: Spiritual Life Stories of Pentecostal Women Preachers," *Journal of Feminist Studies in Religion* 7, no. 1 (Spring 1991): 53–72, and Elaine J. Lawless, *Handmaidens of the Lord: Pentecostal Women Preachers and Traditional Religion* (Philadelphia: University of Pennsylvania Press, 1988), pp. 57–88.

32. Lawless argues that Pentecostal women's life stories are "fictions," which she defines as created stories. Her point is important: these women make their narratives "say" what they want them to say. Yet because the word "fiction" is usually associated with novels, it obscures these women's commitment to telling the "truth" as they perceived it. See Lawless, "Rescripting," and Lawless, *Handmaidens*, pp. 57–88.

33. Jocelyn Moody argues that Jarena Lee portrayed herself as both "a self-effacing feminine apologist" and "a divinely-protected female apostle." Moody, "Self-Effacement and Collective Identity," p. 113.

34. Lee, *Religious Experience*, p. 5. The sermon text was from Acts 8:21.

35. For useful discussions of the common stages involved in conversion, see Jon Alexander, ed., *American Personal Religious Accounts, 1600–1980: Toward an Inner History of America's Faiths* (New York: Edwin Mellen Press, 1983); Daniel B. Shea Jr., *Spiritual Autobiography in Early America* (Princeton: Princeton University Press, 1968); and Brereton, *From Sin to Salvation*, p. 6.

36. Mark Fernald, *Life of Elder Mark Fernald, Written by Himself* (Newburyport: G. M. Payne and D. P. Pike; Philadelphia: Christian General Book Concern, 1852), pp. 23–24. Davis, *Female Preacher*, pp. 29–30. She was quoting Deuteronomy 28:23.

37. Towle mentions that Susan Humes lost her parents at the age of twelve. See *Vicissitudes*, pp. 37–38. Elaw, *Memoirs*, pp. 54, 56. Rebecca Cox Jackson lost her mother at the age of thirteen, and Harriet Livermore was only five when her mother died.

38. Roberts, *Memoir*, p. 37; Gideon A. Burgess and John T. Ward, *Free Baptist Cyclopedia, Historical and Biographical* (n.p., 1889), p. 551.

39. Both Green and Lambson claimed to have been cured by a faith healer named Jacob Pratt. See Knight, *Narrative*, p. 91, and *The Bethlehem Star* 1, no. 3 (May 1824): 83–88. D. M. Graham, *The Life of Clement Phinney* (Dover, N.H.: William Burr, 1851).

40. Sylvester Bliss, *Memoirs of William Miller: Generally Known as a Lecturer on the Prophecies, and the Second Coming of Christ* (Boston: J. V. Himes, 1853), p. 4. Charles Bowles fought in the Revolutionary War before becoming one of the few black Freewill Baptist ministers. See John Lewis, *The Life, Labors, and Travels of Elder Charles Bowles* (Watertown, Mass.: Ingall's and Stowell's, 1852).

41. Evans Williams Humphreys, *Memoirs of Deceased Christian Ministers; or, Brief Sketches of the Lives and Labors of 975 Ministers, Who Died Between 1793 and 1880* (Dayton, Ohio: Christian Publishing Association, 1880), p. 167; Roberts, *Memoir*, pp. 34–35; and Nell Irvin Painter, *Sojourner Truth: A Life, A Symbol* (New York: Norton, 1996), pp. 15–16.

42. For examples of these men and women expressing anger, see Lee, *Religious Experience*, p. 5, and Putnam, *Sketch*, p. 14. Several historians have noted that women's narratives tend to focus more on anger than men's. See Brereton, *From Sin to Salvation*, pp. 32–33; Barbara Leslie Epstein, *The Politics of Domesticity: Women, Evangelism, and Temperance in Nineteenth-Century America* (Middletown: Wesleyan University Press, 1981), pp. 45–65; and Susan Juster, *Disorderly Women: Sexual Politics and Evangelicalism in Revolutionary New England* (Ithaca: Cornell University Press, 1994), pp. 188–89.

43. Lee, *Religious Experience*, p. 6.

44. Brereton, *From Sin to Salvation*, p. 38. Fernald, *Life*, p. 24, and Lee, *Religious Experience*, p. 6. For another discussion of women's nineteenth-century conversion narratives, see Susan Juster, "'In a Different Voice': Male and Female Narratives of Religious Conversion in Post-Revolutionary America," *American Quarterly* 41 (March 1989): 34–62.

45. *Christian Herald* 9, no. 13 (June 22, 1843).

46. Joseph Richardson, *A Sermon on the Duty and Dignity of Woman Delivered April 22, 1832* (Hingham, Mass.: Jedidiah Farmer, 1833), p. 11. Catherine Reed Williams, *Fall River: An Authentic Narrative* (Providence: Marshall, Brown, and Company, 1834), p. 182. On the "cult of true womanhood," see Barbara Welter, "The Cult of True Womanhood, 1820–1860," *American Quarterly* 18 (1966): 151–74.

47. Lee, *Religious Experience*, pp. 23, 8, 14. Ann Braude argues that when Spiritualist women

spoke as "mediums," they were able to become religious leaders while also remaining "compliant with the complex of values of the period that have come to be known as the cult of true womanhood." See Ann Braude, *Radical Spirits: Spiritualism and Women's Rights in Nineteenth-Century America* (Boston: Beacon Press, 1989), p. 82.

48. Lee remembered that she had first been "convicted" by a verse from Psalms: "Lord I am vile, conceived in sin, Born unholy and unclean." Lee, *Religious Experience*, p. 3.

49. Livermore, *Narration*, pp. 155, 50, and David Edmund Millard, *Memoir of Rev. David Millard; with Selections from His Writings. By His Son* (Dayton Ohio: Christian Publishing Association, 1874), p. 30. Davis, *Female Preacher*, pp. 30–31.

50. Elaw, *Memoirs*, pp. 66–67. For a few other women's descriptions of sanctification, see Lee, *Religious Experience*, pp. 9–10; Marden, *Letter*, pp. 11, 14; Livermore, *Narration*, pp. 231–34, 248; and Humez, *Gifts of Power*, pp. 9–10. On sanctification, see Andrews, introduction to *Sisters of the Spirit*, p. 15; and Jean M. Humez, " 'My Spirit Eye': Some Functions of Spiritual and Visionary Experiences in the Lives of Five Black Women Preachers, 1810–1880," in *Women and the Structure of Society*, ed. Barbara Harris and JoAnn McNamara (Durham, N.C.: Duke University Press, 1984), pp. 133–36.

51. Brereton, *From Sin to Salvation*, pp. 28–29. Elaw, *Memoirs*, p. 51, quoting 2 Corinthians 12:9.

52. Marks, *Life*, p. 32. Foote, *Brand*, p. 200.

53. Abel Thornton, *The Life of Elder Abel Thornton* (Providence: J. B. Yerrinton, 1828), p. 24, and Helen Dunn Gates, *A Consecrated Life: A Sketch of the Life and Labors of Rev. Ransom Dunn* (Boston: Morning Star Publishing House, 1901), p. 29. See also Lorenzo Dow, *The Life, Travels, Labors, and Writings of Lorenzo Dow* (Philadelphia: John E. Potter, n.d.), p. 20.

54. Exodus 3:10. Bradley, *Narrative*, p. 58.

55. Millard, *Memoir*, p. 18. The emphasis is mine. Marks, *Life*, p. 32. The first emphasis is mine. James P. Horton, *A Narrative of the Early Life, Remarkable Conversion, and Spiritual Labors of James P. Horton* (n.p.: the author, 1839), p. 52. The emphases are mine. For other examples of this distancing language, see ibid., pp. 86, 135.

56. Towle, *Vicissitudes*, p. 21.

57. Foote, *Brand*, p. 200. Almost all the African American female preachers considered in this study recorded intense mystical encounters with the divine. Several possible exceptions are Rachel Evans, Julia Pell, and Sister Tilmann, about whom very little is known. For two excellent discussions of the visionary experience of black female preachers, see Humez, " 'My Spirit Eye,' " and her introduction to *Gifts of Power*. Several historians have also suggested that black women's intense visionary experiences represented a link to their African heritage. See Carla L. Peterson, *"Doers of the Word": African-American Women Speakers and Writers in the North* (New York: Oxford University Press, 1995), p. 84, and Candis A. LaPrade, "Pens in the Hand of God: The Spiritual Autobiographies of Jarena Lee, Zilpha Elaw, and Rebecca Cox Jackson" (Ph.D. diss., University of North Carolina at Chapel Hill, 1994), pp. 31–33.

58. I. M. Lewis has noted that women in male-dominated societies who behave as if they are possessed by the spirit are often able to "exert mystical pressures on their superiors." See I. M. Lewis, *Religion in Context: Cults and Charisma* (Cambridge: Cambridge University Press, 1986), p. 39.

59. Foote, *Brand*, pp. 201, 204.

60. Elaw, *Memoirs*, pp. 82, 51.

61. Humez, *Gifts of Power*, p. 149. Humez has noted that the main theme of Jackson's diary is

"the necessity of learning to act in ways that will earn and invite divine protection from the constant, debilitating threat of sudden violence, both natural and human."

62. Ibid., pp. 100, 15, 95–96.

63. Elaw, *Memoirs*, pp. 85, 51, 135. Elaw also quoted from Acts 17:26, "God hath made of one blood all the nations of men that dwell upon the face of the earth," and Psalms 68:31, "Ethiopia shall soon stretch out her hands unto God." Ibid., pp. 85–86.

64. Lee, *Religious Experience*, p. 18.

65. Elaw, *Memoirs*, pp. 82, 136. See also *Elizabeth*, pp. 3–4.

66. Elaw, *Memoirs*, p. 87.

67. Elihu Holland, *Memoir of Rev. Joseph Badger*, 3d ed. (New York: C. S. Francis and Co.; Boston, B. H. Greene, 1854), p. 65; and Davis, *Female Preacher*, pp. 37–38. See also *Elizabeth*, p. 8.

68. Putnam, *Sketch*, pp. 25–26.

69. Fernald, *Life*, p. 30.

70. Horton, *Narrative*, p. 63.

71. Kenneth Cmiel, *Democratic Eloquence: The Fight over Popular Speech in Nineteenth-Century America* (Berkeley: University of California Press, 1990), pp. 78, 83. Heman Bangs, *The Autobiography and Journal of Rev. Heman Bangs* (New York: N. Tibbals and Son, 1872), pp. 16–17.

72. Doris G. Yoakam, "Women's Introduction to the American Platform," in *A History and Criticism of American Public Address*, ed. William Norwood Brigance (New York: McGraw-Hill, 1943), 1:159. See also Cmiel, *Democratic Eloquence*, pp. 70–71, and Celia Morris Eckhardt, *Fanny Wright: Rebel in America* (Cambridge: Harvard University Press, 1984).

73. Caldwell, *Walking with God*, p. 47, and Bradley, *Narrative*, p. 76. On Rachel Baker, see *An Account of the Singular Case of Rachel Becker, the Celebrated Somniloquist, or Sleeping Preacher* (New York: J. W. Butler, 1815), and Wealtha Brown, "Letters about Rachel Baker," in the Hooker Collection, Folder 22:2, Schlesinger Library, Radcliffe College.

74. Stewart, *Life*, p. 16.

75. Ibid., pp. 49, 72, 120.

76. Ibid., pp. 103, 11–12.

77. Thornton, *Life*, p. 27; *Christian Herald* 9, no. 6 (May 4, 1843); Stewart, *Life*, p. 63; Lee, *Religious Experience*, p. 45; Bradley, *Narrative*, p. 187; and Livermore, *Narration*, pp. 7–8, 33–34, 150, 126. In her *Thoughts on Important Subjects* (Philadelphia: Crissy and Markley, 1864), Livermore continually referred to herself as "poor Harriet." See pp. 17, 85, 117, 124.

78. Livermore, *Narration*, pp. 9–10, 15, 196. Livermore echoed the language of Hebrews 10:33, "Ye were made a gazing-stock both by reproaches and afflictions."

79. Caldwell, *Walking with God*, p. 50.

80. Elaw, *Memoirs*, p. 78.

81. Livermore, *Narration*, p. 13.

82. Humez, *Gifts of Power*, pp. 107, 90, and Lee, *Religious Experience*, p. 62.

83. Lee, *Religious Experience*, p. 45. Psalms 81:10.

84. Livermore, *Narration*, pp. 8–9, 210. *Christian Herald* 9, no. 6 (May 4, 1843).

85. In her study of Quaker prophetesses in seventeenth-century England, Phyllis Mack argues that the language of women as "instruments" of God reinforced negative stereotypes. See Phyllis Mack, "Women as Prophets during the English Civil War," *Feminist Studies* 8, no. 1 (Spring 1982): 19–45.

86. Caldwell, *Walking with God*, pp. 38–39; Stewart, *Life*, p. 63; and Livermore, *Narration*, p. 7.

87. Towle, *Vicissitudes*, pp. 252–53.

88. Knight, *Narrative*, p. 125.

CHAPTER 5

1. Philetus Roberts, *Memoir of Mrs. Abigail Roberts; An Account of Her Birth, Early Education, Call to the Ministry* (Irvington, N.J.: Moses Cummings, 1858), p. 103.

2. Ibid., pp. 90–91.

3. Ibid., pp. 46, 80, 36.

4. Ibid., pp. 72, 66, 98, 104.

5. See Maria Stewart, *Productions of Mrs. Maria W. Stewart, Presented to the First African Baptist Church and Society of the City of Boston* (Boston, 1835), reprinted in *Spiritual Narratives*, ed. Sue E. Houchins (New York: Oxford University Press, 1988), and Dorothy Sterling, *Ahead of Her Time: Abby Kelley and the Politics of Antislavery* (New York: Norton, 1991), p. 47n.

6. See the description of Elaw in Henry Gardiner Adams, *God's Image in Ebony* (London: Partridge and Oakey, 1854), p. 154. On Truth's clothing, see Nell Irvin Painter, *Sojourner Truth: A Life, A Symbol* (New York: Norton, 1996), pp. 42–43.

7. Richard Bauman, *Let Your Words Be Few: Symbolism of Speaking and Silence among Seventeenth-Century Quakers* (Cambridge: Cambridge University Press, 1983), pp. 21–25, 124–27.

8. Richard J. Stockham, "The Misunderstood Lorenzo Dow," *Alabama Review* 16 (1963): 32, quoted in Nathan O. Hatch, *The Democratization of American Christianity* (New Haven: Yale University Press, 1989), p. 130; and Samuel Goodrich, *Recollections of a Lifetime* (1856), quoted in Hatch, *Democratization*, p. 125. The estimate of audience size comes from David Marks, who attended Dow's meetings in New York in 1823. See David Marks, *The Life of David Marks* (Limerick, Maine: Morning Star Office, 1831), pp. 153–54.

9. *Christian Journal* 2, no. 4 (May 19, 1836): 14. This article had been reprinted from *The Morning Star*, a Freewill Baptist journal. For a description of "uncouth" preachers, see Catherine Reed Williams, *Fall River: An Authentic Narrative* (Providence: Marshall, Brown, and Company, 1834), p. 173. On "the triumph of vernacular preaching," see Hatch, *Democratization*, pp. 133–41.

10. Jarena Lee recorded speaking on this text from Isaiah in *Religious Experience and Journal of Mrs. Jarena Lee, Giving the Account of Her Call to Preach the Gospel* (Philadelphia: printed for the author, 1849), reprinted in *Spiritual Narratives*, ed. Sue E. Houchins (New York: Oxford University Press, 1988), p. 83.

11. Almond H. Davis, *The Female Preacher, or Memoir of Salome Lincoln* (Providence, 1843; reprint, New York: Arno Press, 1972), p. 45. Jarena Lee spoke from the same passage in Hebrews on at least four separate occasions, twice in 1821, and twice in 1823, and Elleanor Knight preached on the same text from Isaiah a minimum of three times. Lee's text was Hebrews 2:3, and Knight's was Isaiah 55:1. See Lee, *Religious Experience*, pp. 21–22, 25–26, and Elleanor Warner Knight, *A Narrative of the Christian Experience, Life and Adventures, Trials and Labours of Elleanor Knight, Written by Herself* (Providence: n.p., 1839), pp. 83, 85, 90.

12. William C. Richards, *Great in Goodness; A Memoir of George N. Briggs, Governor of the Commonwealth of Massachusetts, From 1844 to 1851* (Boston: Gould and Lincoln, 1867), p. 109. For another description of Livermore's singing, see *Newburyport Herald*, January 19, 1827. On the importance of music to the revivals, see Hatch, *Democratization*, pp. 146–60.

13. *Freewill Baptist Magazine* 1, no. 6 (August 1827): 191–92; Marks, *Life*, pp. 238, 177–78, 182–85, 250; and Nancy Towle, *Vicissitudes Illustrated, in the Experience of Nancy Towle, in Europe and*

America, 2d ed. (Portsmouth, N.H.: John Caldwell, 1833), pp. 33, 37–38, 45–46. For more on Humes, see Abel Thornton, *The Life of Elder Abel Thornton* (Providence: J. B. Yerrinton, 1828), pp. 48–49, 53, 113–14, 118–19, 121, and *Freewill Baptist Magazine* 1, no. 4 (February 1827): 113.

14. Knight, *Narrative*, p. 90. She was speaking from Psalms 46:7. Hannah Reeves also "related some part of her experience" during her meetings. See George Brown, *The Lady Preacher; Or, the Life and Labors of Mrs. Hannah Reeves, Late the Wife of the Rev. William Reeves of the Methodist Church* (Philadelphia: Daughaday and Becker; Springfield, Ohio: Methodist Publishing House, 1870), p. 51.

15. Roberts, *Memoir*, pp. 26–27, and Towle, *Vicissitudes*, p. 109.

16. For Burritt's account of this episode, see Charles D. Burritt, *Methodism in Ithaca* (Ithaca: Andrus, Gauntlett, and Co., 1852), pp. 101–4. For Towle's account, see *Vicissitudes*, p. 166.

17. See Harriet Livermore, *A Narration of Religious Experience* (Concord, N.H.: Jacob B. Moore, 1826), pp. 174, 217–18. Elizabeth often "caused offence" because of her "outspeaking way." *Elizabeth, A Colored Minister of the Gospel, Born in Slavery* (Philadelphia: Tract Association of Friends, 1889), pp. 12–13. When Abigail Roberts preached in Milford, New Jersey, she deliberately tried to draw a visiting Presbyterian minister into an argument. Roberts, *Memoir*, pp. 105–6.

18. Roberts, *Memoir*, pp. 15, 81. Towle, *Vicissitudes*, pp. 42, 13.

19. John Carroll, *Case and his Contemporaries or, The Canadian Itinerants' Memorial* (Toronto: Methodist Conference Office, 1867–77), 3:184; Roberts, *Memoir*, p. 152; J. F. Burnett, *Early Women of the Christian Church* (Dayton: Christian Publishing Association, 1921), p. 27; and Olive Gilbert, *Narrative of Sojourner Truth; A Bondswoman of Olden Time, With a History of Her Labors and Correspondence Drawn from Her "Book of Life"* (Battle Creek, Mich., 1878; reprint, New York: Oxford University Press, 1991), pp. 119, 138.

20. Davis, *Female Preacher*, p. 53; *Christian Palladium* 12, no. 23 (April 10, 1844): 374–75. For other accounts that stress women's intelligence, see the description of Ann Rexford in Elihu Holland, *Memoir of Rev. Joseph Badger*, 3d ed. (New York: C. S. Francis and Co.; Boston, B. H. Greene, 1854), p. 227, and the description of Sally Barns Dunn in E. R. Hanson, *Our Woman Workers. Biographical Sketches of Women Eminent in the Universalist Church for Literary, Philanthropic, and Christian Work* (Chicago: Starr and Covenant Office, 1882), p. 21.

21. Livermore, *Narration*, pp. 267, 269. Nancy Cram arranged a "silk net-work" over her hair when she preached, and Rachel Thompson commonly wore "a white cap on her head." See Burnett, *Early Women*, p. 11, and *Christian Herald* 7, no. 28 (October 7, 1841).

22. Parsons Cooke, *Female Preaching, Unlawful and Inexpedient. A Sermon* (Lynn, Mass.: James R. Newhall, 1837), p. 17.

23. Roberts, *Memoir*, p. 63, and Burnett, *Early Women*, p. 11. "Harriet Livermore: 'The Pilgrim Stranger,'" *Essex Antiquarian* (Salem, Mass.) 5 (1901): 7; *The Letters of John Greenleaf Whittier*, ed. John B. Pickard, vol. 3, 1861–1892 (Cambridge: Harvard University Press, 1975), pp. 412, 431; and John Greenleaf Whittier, *Snow-Bound: A Winter Idyl* (Boston: Ticknor and Fields, 1867), p. 38. Ann Braude has made the same argument about the appeal of female Spiritualists in the 1850s and 1860s. See her *Radical Spirits: Spiritualism and Women's Rights in Nineteenth-Century America* (Boston: Beacon Press, 1989), p. 108.

24. Lydia Maria Child, *Letters from New York*, 3d ed. (New York: C. S. Francis and Co., 1846), p. 81. Dorothy Ripley, *The Extraordinary Conversion and Religious Experience of Dorothy Ripley, With Her First Voyage and Travels in America* (New York: G. & R. Waite, 1810), pp. 64, 77, 68.

25. Louis Billington makes this point about fluid class lines in "Female Laborers in the Church: Women Preachers in the Northeastern United States, 1790–1840," *Journal of American*

Studies (Great Britain) 19 (1985): 372–73. Zilpha Elaw, *Memoirs of the Life, Religious Experience, Ministerial Travels and Labours of Mrs. Zilpha Elaw, An American Female of Colour* (London, 1846), reprinted in *Sisters of the Spirit: Three Black Women's Autobiographies of the Nineteenth Century*, ed. William L. Andrews (Bloomington: University of Indiana, 1986), pp. 96, 99. Ephraim Stinchfield Papers, box 1, folder 5, p. 9, Maine Historical Society, Portland, Maine.

26. Williams, *Fall River*, pp. 188, 182. Williams does not give the name of this female preacher, but Nancy Towle, Martha Spaulding, Susan Humes, and Sally Thompson all attended this meeting. See Towle, *Vicissitudes*, pp. 36–37.

27. Williams, *Fall River*, p. 188.

28. There have been several excellent studies of nineteenth-century British female preachers, but they have rarely discussed what these women actually said in the pulpit. For example, see Paul Wesley Chilcote, *John Wesley and the Women Preachers of Early Methodism* (Metuchen, N.J.: Scarecrow Press, 1991), and Deborah M. Valenze, *Prophetic Sons and Daughters: Female Preaching and Popular Religion in Industrial England* (Princeton: Princeton University Press, 1985).

29. Knight, *Narrative*. *Christian Herald* 7, no. 28 (October 7, 1841).

30. Roberts, *Memoir*, p. 55. Holland, *Memoir of Rev. Joseph Badger*, p. 155. See also Abraham Snethen, *Autobiography of Abraham Snethen, the Barefoot Preacher* (Dayton, Ohio: Christian Publishing Association, 1909), pp. 192–93; Nancy Gove Cram, *A Collection of Hymns and Poems. Designed to Instruct the Inquirer; and Furnish the Public with a Small Variety* (Schenectady: n.p., 1815), p. 30; and Abner Jones, *Memoir of Elder Abner Jones* (Boston: William Crosby, 1842), pp. 34–36.

31. Towle, *Vicissitudes*, pp. 175, 178, 42–43, 52–53, 180, 243, 234.

32. Davis, *Female Preacher*, p. 54, and Thornton, *Life*, p. 51. Lee, *Religious Experience*, p. 83, and John Lewis, *The Life, Labors, and Travels of Elder Charles Bowles* (Watertown, Mass.: Ingall's and Stowell's, 1852), p. 76.

33. Jarena Lee preached on Matthew 3:12, "He will burn up the chaff with unquenchable fire." Lee, *Religious Experience*, p. 75. Livermore, *Narration*, p. 219.

34. George T. Day, *The Life of Rev. Martin Cheney* (Providence: George H. Whitney, 1853), p. 206; Davis, *Female Preacher*, p. 86. Lincoln was preaching on Isaiah 35:8. *Christian Palladium* 9, no. 5 (July 1, 1840): 77.

35. Knight, *Narrative*, pp. 83, 85, 88. She preached from Isaiah 55:1 and 7. See also the description of Martin Cheney's sermon "Am I not free?" in Day, *Life of Rev. Martin Cheney*, p. 204.

36. Livermore, *Narration*, pp. 237, 247, and Lee, *Religious Experience*, p. 6. On the "death of Satan" in the nineteenth century, see Andrew Delbanco, *The Death of Satan: How Americans Have Lost the Sense of Evil* (New York: Farrar, Straus, and Giroux, 1995), pp. 91–121.

37. Elaw, *Memoirs*, p. 87. On the Augustinian (and Edwardsian) conception of evil as estrangement from God, see Delbanco, *Death of Satan*, pp. 46–51, 87–88.

38. Laura Smith Haviland, *A Woman's Life-Work: Labors and Experiences of Laura S. Haviland*, 4th ed. (Chicago: Publishing Association of Friends, 1889), p. 201 ("only foundation"); Elaw, *Memoirs*, p. 105 ("crucified redeemer"); and Livermore, *Narration*, p. 192 ("Divine Savior"). Haviland was preaching from 1 Corinthians 3, and Elaw from John 3:15. Harriet Livermore, *The Counsel of God, Immutable and Everlasting* (Philadelphia: L. R. Bailey, 1844), p. 228. Day, *Life of Rev. Martin Cheney*, p. 212. Lee, *Religious Experience*, p. 70. She was preaching on Isaiah 59:1.

39. Knight, *Narrative*. The remainder of her sermons were drawn from Proverbs, Psalms, and Habakkuk. Harriet Livermore, *Thoughts on Important Subjects* (Philadelphia: Crissy and Markley, 1864), p. 129. Of the fifteen sermons recorded in Martin Cheney's memoir, nine were from the

New Testament, three were from Psalms, and the others were drawn from Isaiah, Proverbs, and Daniel. See Day, *Life of Rev. Martin Cheney*, pp. 200–252.

40. Elaw, *Memoirs*, p. 99, and Davis, *Female Preacher*, p. 47. Benjamin Abbott, *Experience and Gospel Labours of the Rev. Benjamin Abbott* (New York: J. Collord, 1832), p. 64. For a study of a male minister who described Christ as a lover who "ravished" his believers, see George A. Rawlyk, *Ravished by the Spirit: Religious Revivals, Baptists, and Henry Alline* (Kingston, Ont.: McGill-Queen's University Press, 1984).

41. Knight, *Narrative*, p. 97, and Elaw, *Memoirs*, p. 116. For other examples, see Lee, *Religious Experience*, p. 30, and Davis, *Female Preacher*, p. 81. On feminine imagery in the Bible, see John H. Otwell, *And Sarah Laughed: The Status of Woman in the Old Testament* (Philadelphia: Westminster Press, 1977), pp. 180–85.

42. Both Danforth and Towle preached on Revelation 12:1. See *A Religious Magazine* 2, no. 4 (August 1821): 113; and Burritt, *Methodism in Ithaca*, p. 104.

43. Davis, *Female Preacher*, p. 65. Lincoln was preaching on Deuteronomy 32:11–12. For two discussions of maternal images of God in the Old Testament, see Leonard Swidler, *Biblical Affirmations of Woman* (Philadelphia: Westminster Press, 1979), pp. 30–35, and Barbara J. MacHaffie, *Her Story: Women in Christian Tradition* (Philadelphia: Fortress Press, 1986), pp. 10–11.

44. Livermore, *Counsel of God*, pp. 137–38. She was quoting from Isaiah 49:14–15, "But Zion said, The Lord hath forsaken me, and my Lord hath forgotten me. Can a woman forget her sucking child, that she should not have compassion on the son of her womb? yea, they may forget, yet will I not forget thee," and Isaiah 66:12–13, "As one whom his mother comforteth, so will I comfort you, and ye shall be comforted in Jerusalem."

45. Lincoln was preaching on Psalms 11:3, "If the foundations be destroyed, what can the righteous do." The quote describing the punishment of the wicked comes from the passage that follows. See Davis, *Female Preacher*, p. 55. Towle's text was from Ezekiel 9:5–6. (She mistakenly identified it in her memoir as Ezekiel 9:6–7.) See Towle, *Vicissitudes*, pp. 186, 225.

46. Ann Douglas, *The Feminization of American Culture* (New York: Knopf, 1977), pp. 11, 13, 124. See also Richard D. Shiels, "The Feminization of American Congregationalism, 1730–1835," *American Quarterly* 33 (1981): 46–62. For a challenge to Douglas, see David S. Reynolds, "The Feminization Controversy: Sexual Stereotypes and the Paradoxes of Piety in Nineteenth-Century America," *New England Quarterly* 53 (March 1980): 96–106.

47. *Christian Herald* 4, no. 4 (November 8, 1821). Her text was Isaiah 3:10–11.

48. Daniel P. Buchanan, "Identifying the Image of God: A Theology of Nonviolent Power in the Antebellum United States" (Ph.D. diss., University of Chicago, 1998).

49. Lee, *Religious Experience*, pp. 63, 75. The second quote comes from a sermon she preached on Matthew 3:12.

50. Ibid., pp. 36–37, and Elaw, *Memoirs*, p. 128. See also Elias Smith, who claimed that "awful judgments were sent on several of those who opposed me and the work of God. Several were taken out of the world in a sudden and awful manner." Elias Smith, *The Life, Conversion, Preaching, Travels, and Sufferings of Elias Smith* (Portsmouth, N.H., 1840; reprint, New York: Arno Press, 1980), pp. 137–38.

51. Elleanor Knight preached on Luke 10:16, "He that heareth you heareth me; and he that despiseth you despiseth me; and he that despiseth me despiseth him that sent me." Knight, *Narrative*, p. 76. Towle, *Vicissitudes*, pp. 300, 123.

52. Miller was preaching on Isaiah 25:7–8. See A. L. McKinney, *Memoir of Eld. Isaac N. Wal-*

ter (Cincinnati: Rickey, Mallory, and Webb, 1857), p. 119. Nancy Towle was reassured by a verse from Psalms: "Though I pass through the dark valley of the shadow of death, I will fear no evil: for even there, also, thy rod, and thy staff,—they shall comfort me." Towle, *Vicissitudes*, pp. 118–19.

53. *Christian Herald* 3, no. 3 (October 27, 1820): 64. For a discussion of how nineteenth-century women variously interpreted the Bible, see Carolyn De Swarte Gifford, "American Women and the Bible: The Nature of Woman as a Hermeneutical Issue," in *Feminist Perspectives on Biblical Scholarship*, ed. Adela Yarbro Collins (Chico, Calif.: Scholar's Press, 1985), pp. 11–29.

54. S. A., "The Rights of Females," *Christian Palladium* 9 (1841): 306; Rebecca Miller, "Duty of Females," *Christian Palladium* 10, no. 2 (May 15, 1841): 21; and Towle, *Vicissitudes*, p. 28. Towle preached one of her first sermons on the book of Esther. See *Vicissitudes*, p. 42.

55. For a few examples of references to Joel, see Towle, *Vicissitudes*, pp. 26–27; Rebecca L. Miller, "Female Improvement," *Christian Palladium* 10, no. 3 (June 1, 1841): 35–36; Ellen Stewart, *Life of Mrs. Ellen Stewart, Together with Biographical Sketches of Other Individuals. Also, A Discussion with Two Clergymen, and Arguments in Favor of Woman's Rights* (Akron, Ohio: Beebe and Elkins, 1858), pp. 18, 168; Miller, "Duty of Females," p. 22; Elaw, *Memoirs*, p. 124; Lee, *Religious Experience*, p. 3; Davis, *Female Preacher*, p. 16; and Sarah Righter Major, "Pamphlet" (1835), reprinted in Donald F. Durnbaugh, ed., "She Kept on Preaching," *Messenger* (Church of the Brethren) 124 (April 1975): 21. In 1835 Major wrote a letter defending female preaching to Jacob Sala, a Brethren printer in Canton, Ohio, which he subsequently published. Durnbaugh's article is the only place where it is reprinted. Only one copy is known to exist, and it is privately owned.

56. Miller, "Female Improvement," pp. 35–36.

57. This was the typical explanation of the Pauline injunction, but one daring woman offered a more radical refutation. Ellen Stewart accused Paul of committing blasphemy by ordering women to "keep silence." She asked, "If the same Holy Ghost teaches the same gospel to females, and teaches them that they must preach it, who is Paul, or any other man, that they shall say they shall not?" See Ellen Stewart, *Life*, pp. 168, 19.

58. Miller, "Duty of Females," pp. 21–22. See also Deborah Peirce, *A Scriptural Vindication of Female Preaching* (Carmel, N.Y.: E. Burroughs, 1820), p. 13. For scriptural references to these women, see Romans 16 and Acts 21:9. For a few examples of female preachers who mentioned them, see Elaw, *Memoirs*, p. 124; Ellen Stewart, *Life*, p. 168; Knight, *Narrative*, p. 124; and Miller, "Female Improvement," p. 35.

59. Phebe is mentioned in Romans 16:1–2. Miller, "Female Improvement," p. 36. Lee, *Religious Experience*, p. 76. As an example, Miller cited Paul's words, "We preach not ourselves; but Jesus Christ, the Lord, and we, your servants for Jesus' sake." Her interpretation has been echoed by contemporary biblical scholars. Relying on a more precise translation from the Greek, they argue that Phebe was actually a church "ruler" or "leader." See Swidler, *Biblical Affirmations*, pp. 295, 310, and MacHaffie, *Her Story*, pp. 23–24. See also Constance F. Parvey, "The Theology and Leadership of Women in the New Testament," in *Religion and Sexism: Images of Woman in the Jewish and Christian Traditions*, ed. Rosemary Radford Ruether (New York: Simon and Schuster, 1974), pp. 117–49. For other examples of female preachers who discuss Phebe, see Elaw, *Memoirs*, p. 124; Ellen Stewart, *Life*, p. 168; Peirce, *Scriptural Vindication*, p. 13; and Miller, "Female Improvement," p. 36.

60. On these "certain women," see Livermore, *Narration*, p. 12. On the woman of Samaria, see Ellen Stewart, *Life*, p. 175. On Mary Magdalene, see Lee, *Religious Experience*, p. 11. Towle,

Vicissitudes, 12–13. For modern-day biblical commentaries on these women, see MacHaffie, *Her Story*, pp. 16–18, and Swidler, *Biblical Affirmations*, pp. 189–95.

61. Lee, *Religious Experience*, pp. 12–13; Miller, "Female Improvement," p. 36.

62. See Gerda Lerner, "One Thousand Years of Feminist Bible Criticism," in *The Creation of Feminist Consciousness: From the Middle Ages to Eighteen-seventy* (New York: Oxford University Press, 1993), pp. 138–66.

63. Mrs. A. J. Graves, *Woman in America: Being an Examination into the Moral and Intellectual Condition of American Female Society* (New York: Harper and Bros., 1841), excerpts quoted in *Root of Bitterness: Documents of the Social History of American Women*, ed. Nancy F. Cott (Boston: Northeastern University Press, 1986), p. 144. See also Joseph Richardson, *A Sermon on the Duty and Dignity of Woman Delivered April 22, 1832* (Hingham, Mass.: Jedidiah Farmer, 1833), pp. 10–11. Livermore, *Narration*, p. 186.

64. Towle, *Vicissitudes*, pp. 37–38, 49; I. D. Stewart, *The History of the Freewill Baptists* (Dover, N.H.: William Burr, 1862), 1:191–92; Elaw, *Memoirs*, p. 84; and Humez, *Gifts of Power*, p. 87.

65. Lee also took her son with her on at least one preaching trip. Lee, *Religious Experience*, pp. 18, 20. For examples of women who brought their children with them while they preached, see Brown, *Lady Preacher*, p. 201, and Ellen Stewart, *Life*, p. 54.

66. Harriet Livermore, *Addresses to the Dispersed of Judah* (Philadelphia: L. R. Bailey, 1849), p. 24.

67. The husbands of Mary Stevens Curry and Sally Thompson were also lay men who escorted their wives on their tours. For Thompson, see *Christian Palladium* 11, no. 3 (June 1, 1842): 42. After helping his wife in her "labors" for two years, Ezekiel Curry decided to become a minister himself. See Evans Williams Humphreys, *Memoirs of Deceased Christian Ministers; or, Brief Sketches of the Lives and Labors of 975 Ministers, Who Died Between 1793 and 1880* (Dayton, Ohio: Christian Publishing Association, 1880), pp. 102–3.

68. Durnbaugh, "She Kept on Preaching," p. 19. "Mrs. Hannah Reeves, Preacher of the Gospel," *Methodist Quarterly Review* 59 (July 1877): 440. Brown, *Lady Preacher*, pp. 102, 122.

69. Durnbaugh, "She Kept on Preaching," pp. 20–21, and Elaw, *Memoirs*, pp. 61–62.

70. On Clemens, see A. W. Drury, *History of the Church of the United Brethren in Christ* (Dayton, Ohio: United Brethren Publishing House, 1924), p. 425. Miller, "Female Improvement," p. 36. Peirce, *Scriptural Vindication*, p. 13. See also Ellen Stewart, *Life*, p. 174; S. A., "Rights of Females," p. 307; Knight, *Narrative*, p. 124; and Brown, *Lady Preacher*, p. 12.

71. Stewart included a quote from the feminist Margaret Fuller: "We would have all unnecessary and arbitrary barriers thrown down; we would have every faith laid open to woman as freely as to man. Were this done, and a slight fermentation allowed to subside, we should see crystallizations more pure, and of varied beauty." See Ellen Stewart, *Life*, pp. 140, 127.

72. Towle, *Vicissitudes*, p. 252. For "impudent hussey," see the correspondence of Alice Izard to Margaret Manigault, May 29, 1801, Manigault Papers, South Caroliniana Library, University of South Carolina, quoted in Mary Beth Norton, *Liberty's Daughters: The Revolutionary Experience of American Women, 1750–1800* (Boston: Little, Brown, 1980), p. 251. See Mary Wollstonecraft, *A Vindication of the Rights of Woman* (London: n.p., 1792).

73. Haviland, *A Woman's Life-Work*. This description of Truth was written by Marius Robinson, who saw her speak at the Ohio Woman's Rights Convention in 1851. Salem *Anti-Slavery Bugle*, June 7, 1851, quoted in Painter, *Sojourner Truth*, p. 125. Painter, *Sojourner Truth*, p. 221.

74. Lee, *Religious Experience*, pp. 90, 78. She was speaking from Isaiah 61:1. See also *Elizabeth*,

p. 11. Zilpha Elaw also attended a meeting of the American Anti-Slavery Society. See Elaw, *Memoirs*, pp. 98, 138.

75. Elaw, *Memoirs*, pp. 138, 98.

76. For one example of this line of thinking, see Livermore, *Narration*, p. 15, and Livermore, *Counsel of God*, p. 37.

77. Towle, *Vicissitudes*, p. 96; *Christian Herald* 3, no. 3 (October 27, 1820): 64; and Holland, *Memoir of Rev. Joseph Badger*, pp. 226–27. On Parker, see Charles W. Kern, *God, Grace, and Granite: The History of Methodism in New Hampshire, 1768–1988* (Canaan, N.H.: Phoenix Publishing, 1988), p. 131. For a sampling of other descriptions, see the account of Nancy Shepard's meeting in Mark Fernald, *Life of Elder Mark Fernald, Written by Himself* (Newburyport: G. M. Payne and D. P. Pike; Philadelphia: Christian General Book Concern, 1852), p. 110; Brother J. D. Richmond's account of Mrs. Peavey's visit in *Christian Palladium* 6, no. 23 (April 2, 1838): 367; Warren Hathaway, *A Faithful Pastor: Biographical Sketches of John Ross* (Newburgh, N.Y.: Journal Publishing House, 1880), pp. 26–27; I. D. Stewart, *History*, 1:377; and *Religious Informer* 1, no. 18 (May 1820): 71.

78. Lee, *Religious Experience*, p. 87. See also Richard Eddy, *Universalism in America*, 2:137–44, quoted in Elisabeth Anthony Dexter, *Career Women of America, 1776–1840* (Francestown, N.H.: Marshall Jones, 1950), p. 62.

79. *The Midnight Cry* 7, no. 3 (August 1, 1844).

80. Karin Erdevig Gedge, " 'Without Benefit of Clergy': Women in the Pastoral Relationship in Victorian American Culture" (Ph.D. diss., Yale University, 1994). O. R. Fassett, *The Biography of Mrs. L. E. Fassett, a Devoted Christian, a Useful Life* (Boston: Advent Christian Publication Society, 1885), p. 16.

81. Ellen Stewart, *Life*, pp. 54, 83.

82. Elaw, *Memoirs*, p. 85; Lee, *Religious Experience*, p. 17; and Davis, *Female Preacher*, p. 38.

83. See Humphreys, *Memoirs*, pp. 96–97; Hathaway, *A Faithful Pastor*, pp. 26–27; Roberts, *Memoir*, p. 35; and David Edmund Millard, *Memoir of Rev. David Millard; with Selections from His Writings. By His Son* (Dayton, Ohio: Christian Publishing Association, 1874), pp. 26–27, 31. Similarly, Clarissa Danforth "convicted" Ahab Read, who later became an elder in the Christian Connection. See *Religious Informer* 4, no. 6 (June 1823): 85–86.

84. *Christian Palladium* 4, no. 16 (December 15, 1835): 253.

85. P. R. Russell, "Female Preaching: A Short Sermon," in *Christian Journal* 4, no. 5 (May 31, 1838). Part 2 of the article appears in vol. 4, no. 6 (June 14, 1838). For other clerical defenses of female preaching, see *Christian Herald* 6, no. 3 (July 31, 1823): 72; "Why Gag Them?" *Christian Herald* 9, no. 8 (May 18, 1843); "New Testament Worship," *Christian Herald* 9, no. 13 (June 22, 1843); and "Female Rights and Influence," *Christian Herald* 8, no. 45 (February 2, 1843).

86. On Richards, see *Christian Palladium* 11, no. 6 (July 15, 1842): 93–94. For other references to Richards, see *Christian Palladium* 9, no. 11 (October 1, 1840): 171, and 1, no. 9 (January 1833): 214–15. At least two male ministers, Daniel Quimby and James Spencer, became followers of Niles before returning to the Christians. See Humphreys, *Memoirs*, pp. 289, 338. Niles is mentioned briefly in *Christian Palladium* 13, no. 4 (July 3, 1844): 30.

87. *Christian Palladium* 10, no. 9 (September 1, 1841): 144.

CHAPTER 6

1. See Harriet Livermore, *The Counsel of God, Immutable and Everlasting* (Philadelphia: L. R. Bailey, 1844), p. 278. She was quoting from Mark 10:24–25.

2. Harriet Livermore, *The Harp of Israel, to Meet the Loud Echo in the Wilds of America* (Philadelphia: J. Rakestraw, 1835), p. 3.

3. *Christian Herald* 7, no. 4 (August 12, 1824): 97.

4. George Whitefield had first seen the potential of using promotional techniques to foster revivals in the 1740s. Through newspaper advertising, serial publication of his works, and testimonials and endorsements, he publicized his religious beliefs in both Great Britain and America. See Frank Lambert, *"Pedlar in Divinity": George Whitefield and the Transatlantic Revivals* (Princeton: Princeton University Press, 1994), and Harry S. Stout, *The Divine Dramatist: George Whitefield and the Rise of Modern Evangelicalism* (Grand Rapids, Mich.: Eerdmans, 1991), especially pp. xvii–xviii, 34–48.

5. T. H. Breen, " 'Baubles of Britain': The American and Consumer Revolutions of the Eighteenth Century," *Past and Present* 119 (May 1988): 78. Lorena S. Walsh, "Urban Amenities and Rural Sufficiency: Living Standards and Consumer Behavior in the Colonial Chesapeake, 1643–1777," *Journal of Economic History* 43 (March 1983): 111. Neal W. Allen Jr., ed., *Province and Court Records of Maine* (Portland, Maine, 1975), 6:72–76, quoted in David Jaffee, "Peddlers of Progress and the Transformation of the Rural North, 1760–1860," *Journal of American History* 78, no. 2 (September 1991): 514.

6. Jonathan Prude, *The Coming of Industrial Order: Town and Factory Life in Rural Massachusetts, 1810–1860* (Cambridge: Cambridge University Press, 1983), pp. xiii–xiv, and Allan Kulikoff, "The Transition to Capitalism in Rural America," *William and Mary Quarterly* 46, no. 1 (January 1989): 125, 141. See also Christopher Clark, *The Roots of Rural Capitalism: Western Massachusetts, 1780–1860* (Ithaca: Cornell University Press, 1990), and Steven Hahn and Jonathan Prude, eds., *The Countryside in the Age of Capitalist Transformation: Essays in the Social History of Rural America* (Chapel Hill: University of North Carolina Press, 1985).

7. On new access to household goods, see Richard L. Bushman, *The Refinement of America: Persons, Houses, Cities* (New York: Knopf, 1992). Christopher Clark argues that in rural New England, the sources of economic change were internal as well as external. See Clark, *Roots of Rural Capitalism*, p. 323. In *The Market Revolution: Jacksonian America, 1815–1846* (New York: Oxford University Press, 1992), Charles Sellers argues that the majority of early-nineteenth-century Americans preferred a subsistence culture over capitalism. Alan Taylor offers the best summary of rural Americans' attitude toward the market. As he explains, most were "capitalists" in the sense that they wanted to improve their economic circumstances through market exchange, but they also resisted capitalism "as a system of social relations of production in which most people must sell their labor for monetary wages to capitalists who own the means of production." See Alan Taylor, *Liberty Men and Great Proprietors: The Revolutionary Settlement on the Maine Frontier, 1760–1820* (Chapel Hill: University of North Carolina Press, 1990), p. 8.

8. Sellers, *Market Revolution*, pp. 131–71. Sellers quotes the New Jersey farmer on p. 138.

9. Jama Lazerow, *Religion and the Working Class in Antebellum America* (Washington: Smithsonian Institution Press, 1995), p. 27. On the effects of the 1837–43 depression on New York workers, see Sean Wilentz, *Chants Democratic: New York City and the Rise of the American Working Class, 1780–1850* (New York: Oxford University Press, 1984), pp. 294–96.

10. Nancy Osterud, *Bonds of Community: The Lives of Farm Women in Nineteenth-Century New York* (Ithaca: Cornell University Press, 1991), pp. 202–30. On the value of antebellum women's housework, see Jeanne Boydston, "To Earn Her Daily Bread: Housework and Antebellum Working-Class Subsistence," *Radical History Review* 35 (April 1986): 7–25.

11. *Lowell Offering*, new ser., vol. 5, no. 1 (January 1845), quoted in Lise Vogel, "Hearts to Feel

and Tongues to Speak: New England Mill Women in the Early Nineteenth Century," in *Class, Sex, and the Woman Worker*, ed. Milton Cantor and Bruce Laurie (Westport, Conn.: Greenwood Press, 1977), p. 76. Osterud, *Bonds of Community*, p. 202.

12. On Cram, see William Little, *The History of Weare, New Hampshire, 1735–1888* (Lowell, Mass.: S. W. Huse and Co., 1888), p. 880; Nathan Franklin Carter, *The Native Ministry of New Hampshire* (Concord, N.H.: Rumford Printing Company, 1906), p. 795; Philetus Roberts, *Memoir of Mrs. Abigail Roberts; An Account of Her Birth, Early Education, Call to the Ministry* (Irvington, N.J.: Moses Cummings, 1858), pp. 34–35; Warren Hathaway, *A Faithful Pastor: Biographical Sketches of John Ross* (Newburgh, N.Y.: Journal Publishing House, 1880), pp. 26–27; and Levi Hathaway, *The Narrative of Levi Hathaway* (Providence: Miller and Hutchens, 1820), pp. 88–89. For a different view, see the discussion of class in Louis Billington, "Female Laborers in the Church: Women Preachers in the Northeastern United States, 1790–1840," *Journal of American Studies* (Great Britain) 19 (1985): 372. See also his "Northern New England Sectarianism in the Early Nineteenth Century," *Bulletin of the John Rylands University Library of Manchester* 70 (Autumn 1988): 123–34.

13. Jarena Lee, *Religious Experience and Journal of Mrs. Jarena Lee, Giving the Account of Her Call to Preach the Gospel* (Philadelphia: printed for the author, 1849), reprinted in *Spiritual Narratives*, ed. Sue E. Houchins (New York: Oxford University Press, 1988), p. 3.

14. By the middle of the century, Mary Ryan argues, local newspapers were filled with advertisements for "bake ovens, plate stoves, flatirons, parlor furnaces, washing machines, sewing machines, and numerous smaller home implements." Mary P. Ryan, *Cradle of the Middle Class: The Family in Oneida County, New York, 1790–1865* (Cambridge: Cambridge University Press, 1981), p. 201.

15. Lee, *Religious Experience*, p. 22. "Poverty a Blessing," *The Morning Star* 1, no. 45 (March 15, 1827). This article was reprinted from the Methodist periodical, *Christian Advocate*. Historian Deborah Valenze has argued that female preaching in England developed as a protest against the new industrial order. When women such as Ann Carr became itinerants, they dramatically demonstrated their lack of domestic security; they stood as stark symbols of the social and economic dislocations caused by the Industrial Revolution. Because they were single and had not yet moved into their own homes, they epitomized the plight of male laborers who were facing unemployment, emigration, and deferred marriage. See Deborah M. Valenze, *Prophetic Sons and Daughters: Female Preaching and Popular Religion in Industrial England* (Princeton: Princeton University Press, 1985). For more on British female preachers, see D. Colin Dewes, "Ann Carr and the Female Revivalists of Leeds," in *Religion in the Lives of English Women, 1760–1930*, ed. Gail Malmgreen (London: Croom Helm, 1986), pp. 68–87.

16. Livermore, *Counsel of God*, p. 278.

17. *Christian Palladium* 12, no. 25 (May 1, 1844): 398. *Christian Palladium* 1, no. 5 (September 1832): 116. Her "rules" were also reprinted in the *Christian Luminary* 2, no. 3 (October 4, 1832): 12. On Protestant attitudes toward American culture, see Mark Y. Hanley, *Beyond a Christian Commonwealth: The Protestant Quarrel with the American Republic, 1830–1860* (Chapel Hill: University of North Carolina Press, 1994).

18. Thomas L. Haskell, "Capitalism and the Origins of the Humanitarian Sensibility," part 1, *American Historical Review* 90 (April 1985): 339–61, and part 2, *American Historical Review* 90 (June 1985): 547–66. For alternate views, see David Brion Davis, "Reflections on Abolitionism and Ideological Hegemony," *American Historical Review* 92 (October 1987): 797–812, and Sellers, *Market Revolution*. For the connections between the growth of republican and capitalist ideology,

see Joyce Oldham Appleby, *Capitalism and a New Social Order: The Republican Vision of the 1790s* (New York: New York University Press, 1984). In "Popular Religion and the Revolution in the Middle Atlantic Ports: The Rise of the Methodists, 1770–1800" (Ph.D. diss., University of Pennsylvania, 1986), Doris Elizabett Andrews argues that Methodism began as a religion to counteract commercial mores. George M. Thomas argues that revivalism and capitalism were integrally connected. See *Revivalism and Cultural Change: Christianity, Nation-Building, and the Market in the Nineteenth-Century United States* (Chicago: University of Chicago Press, 1989).

19. Elleanor Warner Knight, *A Narrative of the Christian Experience, Life and Adventures, Trials and Labours of Elleanor Knight, Written by Herself* (Providence: n.p., 1839), p. 107. On outworkers, see Mary H. Blewett, "The Sexual Division of Labor and the Artisan Tradition in Early Industrial Capitalism: The Case of New England Shoemaking, 1780–1860," in *"To Toil the Livelong Day": America's Women at Work, 1780–1980,* ed. Carol Groneman and Mary Beth Norton (Ithaca: Cornell University Press, 1987), pp. 35–46; and Clark, *Roots of Rural Capitalism,* pp. 179–89.

20. *The Morning Star* 1, no. 29 (November 23, 1826), and 4, no. 29 (November 18, 1829). On the Fall River revival, see Jama Lazerow, *Religion and the Working Class in Antebellum America* (Washington: Smithsonian Institution Press, 1995), p. 77. For examples of revivals in factory towns, see *Freewill Baptist Magazine* 1, no. 3 (November 1826): 89; *The Morning Star* 2, no. 1 (May 10, 1827); and Eleazer Sherman, *The Narrative of Eleazer Sherman, Giving an Account of his Life, Experience, Call to the Ministry of the Gospel, and Travels* (Providence: H. H. Brown, 1832), 2:33, 39. On revivals that disrupted factory discipline, see Teresa Anne Murphy, *Ten Hours' Labor: Religion, Reform, and Gender in Early New England* (Ithaca: Cornell University Press, 1992), p. 79. "Character and Fortune," *The Morning Star* 1, no. 39 (February 1, 1827).

21. Almond H Davis, *The Female Preacher, or Memoir of Salome Lincoln* (Providence, 1843; reprint, New York: Arno Press, 1972), p. 51. On women mill workers, see Thomas Dublin, *Women at Work: The Transformation of Work and Community in Lowell, Massachusetts, 1826–1860* (New York: Columbia University Press, 1979); Alice Kessler-Harris, *Out to Work: A History of Wage Earning Women in America* (New York: Oxford University Press, 1982); Christine Stansell, *City of Women: Sex and Class in New York, 1789–1860* (Urbana: University of Illinois Press, 1987), pp. 105–29; and Vogel, "Hearts to Feel," pp. 64–82. Dublin and Kessler-Harris emphasize the independence working women gained from living in boardinghouses away from home.

22. Lazerow, *Religion and the Working Class,* pp. 127, 146–47.

23. Knight's text was Romans 8:15–16. The quote comes from Romans 8:18. Knight, *Narrative,* p. 78. *Christian Palladium* 7, no. 18 (January 15, 1839): 285. See also Taylor, *Liberty Men,* p. 141.

24. Bruce Laurie, *Working People of Philadelphia, 1800–1850* (Philadelphia: Temple University Press, 1980), p. 178; Paul E. Johnson, *A Shopkeeper's Millennium: Society and Revivals in Rochester, New York, 1815–1837* (New York: Hill and Wang, 1978), pp. 120, 138; and Anthony F. C. Wallace, *Rockdale: The Growth of an American Village in the Early Industrial Revolution* (New York: Knopf, 1978), pp. 296–397. In an early, influential article, David Montgomery claimed that evangelicalism splintered the working class in Philadelphia and made them ineffective politically. See "The Shuttle and the Cross: Weavers and Artisans in the Kensington Riots of 1844," *Journal of Social History* 5 (Summer 1972): 411–46. Johnson argues that evangelical theology absolved businessmen and master workmen from responsibility for workers' actions by "teaching that virtue and order were not products of external authority but of choices made by morally responsible individuals" (p. 111).

25. *Mechanic* (Fall River, Mass.) 18 (January 25, 1845), quoted in Lazerow, *Religion and the*

Working Class, p. 144; and Michael Zuckerman, "Holy Wars, Civil Wars: Religion and Economics in Nineteenth-Century America," in *Prospects: An Annual of American Cultural Studies*, ed. Jack Salzman (Cambridge: Cambridge University Press, 1991), 16:212. For critiques of the social control thesis, see Lazerow, *Religion and the Working Class*, pp. 1–14; Nathan O. Hatch, *The Democratization of American Christianity* (New Haven: Yale University Press, 1989), pp. 222–25; and William Robert Sutton, "'To Grind the Faces of the Poor': Journeyman for Jesus in Jacksonian Baltimore" (Ph.D. diss., University of Illinois at Urbana-Champaign, 1993), pp. 50–74. Other historians have also noted the importance of evangelicalism to the labor movement. See Ronald Schultz, "God and Workingmen: Popular Religion and the Formation of Phila-delphia's Working Class, 1790–1830," in *Religion in a Revolutionary Age*, ed. Ronald Hoffman and Peter J. Albert (Charlottesville: University Press of Virginia, 1994), pp. 125–55; and Murphy, *Ten Hours' Labor*. On evangelical clergy's support for the labor movement, see Jama Lazerow, "Spokesmen for the Working Class: Protestant Clergy and the Labor Movement in Antebellum New England," *Journal of the Early Republic* 13 (Fall 1993): 323–54.

26. Stout, *Divine Dramatist*, p. xvii, and R. Laurence Moore, *Selling God: American Religion in the Marketplace of Culture* (New York: Oxford University Press, 1994), p. 7.

27. Richardson Wright, *Hawkers and Walkers in Early America* (Philadelphia: J. B. Lippincott Company, 1927), p. 18; J. R. Dolan, *The Yankee Peddlers of Early America* (New York: Clarkson N. Potter, 1964), pp. 113–89; Priscilla Carrington Kline, "New Light on the Yankee Peddler," *New England Quarterly* 12 (March 1939): 93; Jaffee, "Peddlers," pp. 531–33; and James Guild, "From Tunbridge, Vermont, to London, England—The Journal of James Guild, Peddler, Tinker, Schoolmaster, Portrait Painter, from 1818 to 1824," in *Proceedings of the Vermont Historical Society* 5, no. 3 (1937): 259.

28. On all these itinerants, see Peter Benes, ed., *Itinerancy in New England and New York* (Boston: Boston University Press, 1986). See also Guild, "From Tunbridge, Vermont"; and Donald M. Scott, "Itinerant Lecturers and Lecturing in New England, 1800–1850," in Benes, *Itinerancy*, p. 65.

29. General Conference of the Freewill Baptist Connection, *Minutes of the General Conference of the Freewill Baptist Connection* (Dover, N.H.: William Burr, 1859), p. 179. Sometimes women could not even count on their sex to attract audiences; they faced competition from other female itinerants who worked as artists. At least eleven women, including Susanna Paine and Ruth Henshaw Bascom, supported themselves by traveling as portraitists in the late eighteenth and early nineteenth centuries. See Joyce Hill, "New England Itinerant Portraitists," in Benes, *Itinerancy*, p. 156n; and Eileen Fouratt, "Ruth Henshaw Bascom, Itinerant Portraitist," in Benes, *Itinerancy*, pp. 190–205.

30. Scott, "Itinerant Lecturers," p. 69. David Jaffee has argued that peddlers "promoted the transformative power of commodities" and "encouraged social emulation by the purchase of their goods." Jaffee, "Peddlers," p. 524.

31. Davis, *Female Preacher*, p. 148. Lincoln was preaching from 2 Corinthians 5:17. For exam-ples of people who converted because of the example of a friend or relative, see John Peacock, *A Sketch of the Christian Experience, Call to the Ministry, and Ministerial Labors of the Rev. John Peacock, Domestic Missionary* (Concord, N.H.: Tripp and Osgood, 1851), pp. 29–30; *The Bethlehem Star* 1, no. 1 (January, 1824): 5; and Lucy Richards, *Memoirs of the Late Miss Lucy Richards, of Parris, Oneida County, N.Y.* (New York: G. Lane and P. P. Sanford for the M.E. Church, 1842), pp. 78–82.

32. *Christian Palladium* 11, no. 18 (January 16, 1843): 287.

33. Lee, *Religious Experience*, pp. 51, 75, 77, 79. On female preachers' "feverish restlessness" in

the "marketplace of salvation," see Elizabeth Elkin Grammer, " 'A Pen in His Hand": A Pen in Her Hand. Autobiographies by Female Itinerant Evangelists in 19th-Century America (Ph.D. diss., University of Virginia, 1995), chap. 2.

34. See Grammer, " 'A Pen in His Hand,' " pp. 127–28, 133.

35. Stevens lived in Corinth in Saratoga County (in eastern New York), but she attended a General Meeting in Steuben County in western New York. See *Christian Palladium* 3, no. 5 (July 1, 1834): 77, and 1, no. 8 (December 1832): 201.

36. On the influence of religious denominations in settling frontier areas, see William Warren Sweet, *Religion in the Development of American Culture, 1765–1840* (New York: Charles Scribner's Sons, 1953). On Hannah Cogswell, see *Christian Herald* 7, no. 6 (May 6, 1841), and *Christian Journal* 2, no. 2 (April 21, 1836): 5; 2, no. 14 (October 6, 1836): 55; 2, no. 18 (December 1, 1836): 70; 4, no. 6 (June 14, 1838): 22; 4, no. 16 (November 1, 1838): 63; and 4, no. 23 (February 7, 1839): 91. For more information on Cogswell's family, see the obituary of her mother, Elizabeth Peavey, in *Christian Palladium* 14, no. 18 (January 7, 1846): 283. Two of Hannah's brothers and her sister-in-law, known only as Mrs. Peavey, also served as Christian Connection preachers. Her sister Mary Peavey married Joseph Badger, an influential Christian elder.

37. Hatch, *Democratization*, p. 87.

38. Wealthy Monroe married Roberts Edmunds one or two years after she moved to Michigan; in 1843 she began to appear in denominational publications as Wealthy Edmunds. For information on Wealthy Monroe Edmunds, see *Christian Herald and Journal* 6, no. 15 (July 9, 1840). See also *Christian Palladium* 2, no. 2 (June 1833): 71; 2, no. 8 (December 1833): 262–63; 9, no. 5 (July 1, 1840): 71; 9, no. 7 (August 1, 1840): 108; 10, no. 1 (May 1, 1841): 11; 10, no. 3 (June 1, 1841): 42; 10, no. 7 (August 2, 1841): 111; 11, no. 2 (May 16, 1842): 27; 11, no. 5 (July 1, 1842): 75; 11, no. 7 (August 1, 1842): 108; and 13, no. 2 (June 12, 1844): 30. For Michigan conference minutes that list Stiles, Stone, and Edmunds, see *Christian Palladium* 14, no. 8 (August 20, 1845): 125; 15, no. 16 (December 2, 1846): 252; and 16, no. 11 (July 10, 1847): 164. For Michigan conference minutes that list only Stiles and Edmunds, see *Christian Palladium* 13, no. 7 (August 14, 1844): 108. For a biographical sketch of Stiles, see Evans Williams Humphreys, *Memoirs of Deceased Christian Ministers; or, Brief Sketches of the Lives and Labors of 975 Ministers, Who Died Between 1793 and 1880* (Dayton, Ohio: Christian Publishing Association, 1880), pp. 342–43.

39. Nancy Towle, *Vicissitudes Illustrated, in the Experience of Nancy Towle, in Europe and America*, 2d ed. (Portsmouth, N.H.: John Caldwell, 1833), pp. 245–46.

40. Zilpha Elaw, *Memoirs of the Life, Religious Experience, Ministerial Travels and Labours of Mrs. Zilpha Elaw, An American Female of Colour*, reprinted in *Sisters of the Spirit: Three Black Women's Autobiographies of the Nineteenth Century*, ed. William L. Andrews (Bloomington: University of Indiana, 1986), p. 91. On the legal risks that free black preachers faced in the South, see Andrews, *Sisters in the Spirit*, p. 241n.

41. For a sampling of books that discuss revivalism in western New York, see Whitney R. Cross, *The Burned-over District: The Social and Intellectual History of Enthusiastic Religion in Western New York, 1800–1850* (New York: Harper, 1965); Ryan, *Cradle of the Middle Class*; Michael Barkun, *Crucible of the Millennium: The Burned-over District of New York in the 1840s* (Syracuse: Syracuse University Press, 1986); and Johnson, *Shopkeeper's Millennium*.

42. For Hedges, see *Christian Palladium* 3, no. 5 (July 1, 1834): 77, and *Gospel Luminary* 2, no. 8 (August 1826). For Mary Stratton, see *Christian Herald* 5, no. 3 (August 29, 1822), and 6, no. 3 (July 31, 1823). On Rachel Thompson, see *Christian Herald* 7, no. 26 (September 23, 1841), and Humphreys, *Memoirs*, p. 173. On Sabrina Lambson, see Humphreys, *Memoirs*, p. 199. On Dan-

forth, see *The Religious Informer* 4, no. 6 (June, 1823): 85–86. For a discussion of revivals in Vermont, see David M. Ludlum, *Social Ferment in Vermont, 1791–1850* (New York: Columbia University Press, 1939).

43. For examples of female preachers who preached in Cranberry Creek, New York, see *Christian Palladium* 7, no. 7 (August 1, 1838): 105; *Christian Palladium* 15, no. 25 (March 24, 1847): 398; *Christian Journal* 1, no. 23 (February 4, 1836): 91; and *Christian Herald* 6, no. 3 (July 31, 1823): 73. On Humes, see David Marks, *The Life of David Marks* (Limerick, Maine: Morning Star Office, 1831), p. 183. On Vienna, see Daniel E. Wager, ed., *Our Country and Its People: A Descriptive Work on Oneida County in New York* (Boston History Company: n.p., 1896), pp. 588, 590, and Pomroy Jones, *Annals and Recollections of Oneida County* (Rome, N.Y.: A. J. Rowley, 1851), p. 695. For references to Roberts and Cram preaching in Ballston, see Roberts, *Memoir*, pp. 27–29. Rexford spoke at a Christian Connection General Meeting there in 1822. See *Christian Herald* 4, no. 6 (January 31, 1822): 131. On Ballston, see Edward F. Grose, *Centennial History of the Village of Ballston Spa, Including the Towns of Ballston and Milton* (Ballston: Ballston Journal, 1907), pp. 137–38.

44. For a discussion of urban revivalism, see Terry D. Bilhartz, *Urban Religion and the Second Great Awakening: Church and Society in Early National Baltimore* (Rutherford, N.J.: Associated University Presses, 1986), especially chapter 6.

45. Towle, *Vicissitudes*, pp. 58–59, 94. See also Davis, *Female Preacher*, p. 41. George Whitefield had used testimonials during the eighteenth century. See Lambert, " 'Pedlar in Divinity,' " p. 827.

46. Roberts, *Memoir*, pp. 98, 49. George Brown, *The Lady Preacher; Or, the Life and Labors of Mrs. Hannah Reeves, Late the Wife of the Rev. William Reeves of the Methodist Church* (Philadelphia: Daughaday and Becker; Springfield, Ohio: Methodist Publishing House, 1870), p. 278.

47. Elaw, *Memoirs*, p. 100.

48. Davis, *Female Preacher*, p. 50, and Towle, *Vicissitudes*, p. 242. On Riker, see Richard Whatcoat, Journal, June 8, 1792, Library of Congress, Washington, D.C., quoted in Andrews, "Popular Religion and the Revolution," p. 200.

49. Roberts, *Memoir*, p. 61; *Christian Palladium* 2, no. 8 (December 1833): 262–63; and Knight, *Narrative*, pp. 105, 82.

50. Elaw, *Memoirs*, p. 89. Richard Eddy, *Universalism in America*, 2:137–44, quoted in Elizabeth Anthony Dexter, *Career Women of America, 1776–1840* (Francestown, N.H.: Marshall Jones, 1950), p. 62. Knight, *Narrative*, p. 90.

51. On Rexford, see *Christian Palladium* 1, no. 7 (November 1832): 167. Clarissa Danforth Richmond did continue holding meetings immediately after her marriage in 1822. See *The Religious Informer* 3, no. 8 (August 1822): 116. But according to an early Freewill Baptist historian, she preached only occasionally after that. See I. D. Stewart, *The History of the Freewill Baptists* (Dover, N.H.: William Burr, 1862), 1:391. She disappeared from religious periodicals until 1834, when she held several meetings with Philetus Roberts, the son of the female preacher Abigail Roberts. See *Christian Palladium* 3, no. 12 (October 15, 1834): 191.

52. Olive Gilbert, *Narrative of Sojourner Truth; A Bondswoman of Olden Time, With a History of Her Labors and Correspondence Drawn from Her "Book of Life"* (Battle Creek, Mich., 1878; reprint, New York: Oxford University Press, 1991), pp. 164, 100–101. For the full story of Isabella's transformation into Sojourner Truth, see Nell Irvin Painter, *Sojourner Truth: A Life, A Symbol* (New York: Norton, 1996). For her success at marketing herself, see Nell Irvin Painter, "Representing Truth: Sojourner Truth's Knowing and Becoming Known," *Journal of American History* 81, no. 2 (1994): 461–92. On Matthias, whose real name was Robert Matthews, see Paul E. Johnson and

Sean Wilentz, *The Kingdom of Matthias: A Story of Sex and Salvation in Nineteenth-Century America* (New York: Oxford University Press, 1994).

53. Harriet Livermore, *A Narration of Religious Experience* (Concord, N.H.: Jacob B. Moore, 1826), p. 149 ("much worn down"). Towle, *Vicissitudes*, p. 24.

54. Lee, *Religious Experience*, p. 93. Nancy Towle also traveled on the Erie Canal. See *Vicissitudes*, pp. 148, 106. Seymour Dunbar, *A History of Travel in America* (New York: Tudor Publishing House, 1973), pp. 743, 750.

55. Ellen Stewart, *Life of Mrs. Ellen Stewart, Together with Biographical Sketches of Other Individuals. Also, A Discussion with Two Clergymen, and Arguments in Favor of Woman's Rights* (Akron, Ohio: Beebe and Elkins, 1858), p. 114. See also Patricia Cline Cohen, "Safety and Danger: Women on American Public Transport, 1750–1850," in *Gendered Domains: Rethinking Public and Private in Women's History*, ed. Dorothy O. Helly and Susan M. Reverby (Ithaca: Cornell University Press, 1992), pp. 109–23.

56. On this episode, see Painter, *Sojourner Truth*, p. 210. Elaw, *Memoirs*, p. 133.

57. Robert Boyd, *Personal Memoirs: Together With a Discussion Upon The Hardships and Sufferings of Itinerant Life* (Cincinnati: Methodist Book Concern, 1860), pp. 184–85.

58. Towle, *Vicissitudes*, pp. 239, 46; Davis, *Female Preacher*, p. 161; *The Bethlehem Star* 1, no. 1 (January 1824): 30–32; Humphreys, *Memoirs*, p. 199. For reports of Rebecca Miller's illness, see *Christian Palladium* 9, no. 23 (April 1, 1841), and 11, no. 7 (August 1, 1842): 109. For her obituary, see *Christian Palladium* 12, no. 23 (April 10, 1844): 374–75. For the obituary of Susan Humes, see *Freewill Baptist Magazine* 1, no. 6 (August 1827): 191–92. See also the obituary of Sarah Hedges in *Christian Palladium* 12, no. 1 (July 5, 1843): 16.

59. Hatch, *Democratization*, p. 88.

60. On Rexford, see Towle, *Vicissitudes*, p. 93. Abigail Roberts spoke for several months in two Christian churches that she had organized in New Jersey, and Zilpha Elaw preached in the same meetinghouse on Nantucket for two years. After Nancy Cram established a church in Ballston Spa, New York, she became its unofficial minister for over a year. See Roberts, *Memoir*, pp. 83, 86–88, 110, and Elaw, *Memoirs*, pp. 130, 134. On Nancy Gove Cram, see David Edmund Millard, *Memoir of Rev. David Millard; with Selections from His Writings. By His Son* (Dayton, Ohio: Christian Publishing Association, 1874), p. 27; Roberts, *Memoir*, pp. 20–21, 34–35; Humphreys, *Memoirs*, pp. 96–97; J. F. Burnett, *Early Women of the Christian Church* (Dayton: Christian Publishing Association, 1921), pp. 9–12; Caroline Dall, *The College, the Market, and the Court; or, Women's Relation to Education, Labor, and Law* (Boston: Lee and Shepard, 1867; reprint, New York: Arno Press, 1972), p. 437; and Hatch, *Democratization*, p. 78.

61. James D. Hart, *The Popular Book: A History of America's Literary Taste* (Westport, Conn.: Greenwood Press, 1950), p. 67. On other technological advances that influenced reading, such as better illumination and less expensive spectacles, see Ronald J. Zboray, "Antebellum Reading and the Ironies of Technological Innovation," in *Reading in America: Literature and Social History*, ed. Cathy N. Davidson (Baltimore: Johns Hopkins University Press, 1989), p. 196.

62. David Paul Nord, "The Evangelical Origins of Mass Media in America, 1815–1835," *Journalism Monographs* 88 (1984): 1–30. Hatch, *Democratization*, pp. 70, 141–46; Elias Smith, *The Life, Conversion, Preaching, Travels, and Sufferings of Elias Smith* (Portsmouth, N.H., 1840; reprint, New York: Arno Press, 1980), p. 383. By 1839, the Christian General Book Association, the Genessee Christian Association, the Eastern Christian Publishing Association, the Ohio Christian Book Association, and the Southern Christian Publishing Committee had all been created.

See Milo True Morrill, *A History of the Christian Denomination in America, 1794–1811* (Dayton, Ohio: Christian Publishing Association, 1912), chap. 6. For Freewill Baptists' use of the press, see J. M. Brewster, *The Centennial Record of Freewill Baptists, 1780–1880* (Dover, N.H.: The Printing Establishment, 1881). For an excellent overview of how religious groups have taken advantage of the "communications revolution," see the essays in Leonard I. Sweet, ed., *Communication and Change in American Religious History* (Grand Rapids, Mich.: Eerdmans, 1993).

63. Ephraim Stinchfield, *Some Memoirs of the Life, Experience and Travels of Elder Ephraim Stinchfield* (Portland, Maine: F. Douglas, 1819); Elias Smith, *Life*; and Marks, *Life*.

64. Hatch, *Democratization*, p. 36. Jon Butler, *Awash in a Sea of Faith: Christianizing the American People* (Cambridge: Harvard University Press, 1990), p. 241. For more on Dow, see Charles Coleman Sellers, *Lorenzo Dow: The Bearer of the Word* (New York: Minton, Balch, and Company, 1928).

65. Harriet Livermore, *Addresses to the Dispersed of Judah* (Philadelphia: L. R. Bailey, 1849), p. 21.

66. Livermore, *Narration*, p. 189; Painter, *Sojourner Truth*, pp. 111, 185–99; and Lee, *Religious Experience*, p. 77. Lee managed to sell sixty dollars worth of copies of her *Life and Religious Experience* in just four months in 1836, and the response was so favorable that she issued a more detailed, expanded version in 1849.

67. *Christian Palladium* 7, no. 18 (January 15, 1839): 285. For letters from Stevens, see *Christian Palladium* 8, no. 9 (September 2, 1839): 182; 15, no. 10 (September 9, 1846): 156–57; and 12, no. 25 (May 1, 1844). See also *Christian Palladium* 1, no. 3 (July 1832): 63; 1, no. 5 (September 1832): 116; 1, no. 8 (December 1832), 201; 3, no. 3 (June 2, 1834): 49; 3, no. 5 (July 1, 1834): 77; 3, no. 13 (November 1, 1834): 210; 4, no. 2 (May 15, 1835): 91; 4, no. 5 (July 1, 1835): 75; 5, no. 5 (July 1, 1836): 77; and 9, no. 5 (July 1, 1840): 71. See also *Gospel Luminary* 4, no. 10 (July 1831), and 5, no. 12 (September 1832). For a brief biographical sketch of Stevens, see Humphreys, *Memoirs*, pp. 102–3.

68. Lee, *Religious Experience*, pp. 9–10, and Jarena Lee, *The Life and Religious Experience of Mrs. Jarena Lee, A Coloured Lady, Giving an Account of her Call to Preach the Gospel* (Philadelphia, 1836), reprinted in Andrews, *Sisters of the Spirit*, pp. 33–34. See Rebecca Miller, "Immortality of the Soul," *Christian Palladium* 11, no. 4 (June 15, 1842): 54–55.

69. *Christian Palladium* 11, no. 3 (June 1, 1842): 42. *Christian Herald* 7, no. 15 (July 8, 1841). See also the letter from Sarah Thornton in *The Morning Star and City Watchman* 1, no. 10 (March 1828). On platform speakers, see Scott, "Itinerant Lecturers," p. 74.

70. See the discussion of this picture in Candis A. LaPrade, "Pens in the Hand of God: The Spiritual Autobiographies of Jarena Lee, Zilpha Elaw, and Rebecca Cox Jackson" (Ph.D. diss., University of North Carolina at Chapel Hill, 1994), pp. 78–80.

71. Painter, *Sojourner Truth*, p. 196. On the tensions between Truth's voice and Gilbert's voice, see ibid., pp. 106–10. See also Gilbert, *Narrative of Sojourner Truth*.

72. Grammer, "'A Pen in His Hand,'" p. 37. Towle, *Vicissitudes*, p. 241.

73. Sarah R. Ingraham, comp., *Walks of Usefulness, or Reminiscences of Mrs. Margaret Prior* (New York: American Female Moral Reform Society, 1843; reprint, New York: Garland Publishing, 1987), pp. 56, 116, 18–19, 60.

74. Mrs. A. J. Graves, *Woman in America: Being an Examination into the Moral and Intellectual Condition of American Female Society* (New York: Harper and Brothers, 1841), excerpts quoted in *Root of Bitterness: Documents of the Social History of American Women*, ed. Nancy F. Cott (Boston: Northeastern University Press, 1986), p. 144. *Ladies Magazine* 4 (1831): 3–4, quoted in Ann Douglas, *The Feminization of American Culture* (New York: Knopf, 1977), p. 93. Alfred Lee, ed., *A Life Hid with Christ in God* (Philadelphia: J. B. Lippincott, 1856). On women's pious memoirs, see

Douglas, *Feminization*, pp. 188–99, and Joanna Bowen Gillespie, " 'The Clear Leadings of Providence': Pious Memoirs and the Problems of Self-Realization for Women in the Early Nineteenth Century," *Journal of the Early Republic* 5 (Summer 1985): 197–221.

75. Towle, *Vicissitudes*, p. 9. Livermore, *Narration*, pp. 6–7. For other examples of women's apologies, see the letter from Rebecca Miller reprinted in *Christian Palladium* 8, no. 10 (September 16, 1839): 158–59, and the letter from Hannah Cogswell in *Christian Journal* 2, no. 2 (April 21, 1836): 5. Even Nancy Cram, who merely edited a collection of Christian Connection hymns, apologized for her "feeble endeavors." See Nancy Gove Cram, *A Collection of Hymns and Poems. Designed to Instruct the Inquirer; and Furnish the Public with a Small Variety* (Schenectady: n.p., 1815), page entitled "Apology" after the title page.

76. Livermore, *Counsel of God*, p. iv. Livermore, *Narration*, pp. 6–7. Mary Kelley, *Private Woman, Public Stage: Literary Domesticity in Nineteenth-Century America* (New York: Oxford University Press, 1984), pp. xii, 181, 146, 28, 125–26. Although Kelley may exaggerate these women's ambivalence, there is no doubt that they were more timid than female preachers. For more on female novelists, see Douglas, *Feminization*, pp. 71–76.

77. Mary Stevens criticized aspirations for "worldly honor, riches, and a vain show." See *Christian Palladium* 7, no. 18 (January 15, 1839): 285. Towle, *Vicissitudes*, p. 11.

78. Stewart, *Life*, p. 127.

79. On Cram's influence, see Humphreys, *Memoirs*, pp. 96–97, and Roberts, *Memoir*, p. 35. On Danforth, see Towle, *Vicissitudes*, p. 19. On Livermore and Major, see Livermore, *Narration*, p. 161; Samuel T. Livermore, *Harriet Livermore, the "Pilgrim Stranger"* (Hartford: Case, Lockwood, and Brainard Company, 1884), p. 95; and Donald F. Durnbaugh, ed., "She Kept on Preaching," *Messenger* (Church of the Brethren) 124 (April 1975): 18–21.

80. Livermore had given her power of attorney to a lawyer, Thomas Havens, who apparently considered her too "imbecile" to manage the money. Despite her threats of legal action, she never received a single cent of her brother's bequest. See the letter from Harriet Livermore to Thomas Haven, December 1866, MSS 60, Abraham H. Cassel Collection, Juniata College, Huntingdon, Pa. On her peddling, see Livermore, *Addresses*, p. 235. Charles Francis Adams, ed., *Memoirs of John Quincy Adams, Comprising Portions of His Diary from 1795 to 1848* (Philadelphia: J. B. Lippincott, 1877), 12:9–10. For her descriptions of herself as "poor Harriet," see *Thoughts on Important Subjects* (Philadelphia: Crissy and Markley, 1864), pp. 17, 85, 117, 124.

CHAPTER 7

1. Williams never referred to Thompson by name, but only as "Mrs. T." However, it is clear from other records that Thompson, who was married, was present at the Smithfield camp meeting. Nancy Towle (who was single), Martha Spaulding, and Susan Humes were also present. Towle records the meeting in her *Vicissitudes Illustrated, in the Experience of Nancy Towle, in Europe and America*, 2d ed. (Portsmouth, N.H.: John Caldwell, 1833), pp. 36–37. For more on Thompson, see Philetus Roberts, *Memoir of Mrs. Abigail Roberts; An Account of Her Birth, Early Education, Call to the Ministry* (Irvington, N.J.: Moses Cummings, 1858), pp. 145–47, and *Christian Herald* 8, no. 48 (February 23, 1843). See also *Christian Palladium* 5, no. 6 (July 15, 1836): 95; 4, no. 21 (March 1, 1836): 332–33; 5, no. 22 (March 15, 1837): 350; 7, no. 7 (August 1, 1838): 105; 11, no. 3 (June 1, 1842): 42; 14, no. 21 (February 18, 1846): 332; and 15, no. 25 (March 24, 1847): 398.

2. Catherine Reed Williams, *Fall River: An Authentic Narrative* (Providence: Marshall, Brown, and Company, 1834), pp. 181–82, 188.

3. Sally Thompson, *Trial and Defence of Mrs. Sally Thompson, On a Complaint of Insubordination to the Rules of the Methodist Episcopal Church, Evil Speaking and Immorality* (West Troy, N.Y.: W. Hollands, 1837), pp. 5, 11.

4. Ibid., pp. 2, 4.

5. Ibid., pp. 4–5.

6. Elias Smith, *The Life, Conversion, Preaching, Travels, and Sufferings of Elias Smith* (Portsmouth, N.H., 1840; reprint, New York: Arno Press, 1980), p. 317. See Abraham Snethen, *Autobiography of Abraham Snethen, the Barefoot Preacher* (Dayton, Ohio: Christian Publishing Association, 1909), p. 134. James Finley, a Methodist, tangled with a man who pushed him violently and "cursed" him, calling him a "Methodist dog." W. B. Strickland, *Autobiography of Rev. James B. Finley, or Pioneer Life in the West* (Cincinnati: Methodist Book Concern, 1853), p. 187. See also Benjamin Abbott, who was threatened with being tarred and feathered. Benjamin Abbott, *Experience and Gospel Labours of the Rev. Benjamin Abbott* (New York: J. Collord, 1832), p. 64. J. F. Burnett, *Early Women of the Christian Church* (Dayton: Christian Publishing Association, 1921), p. 19.

7. *Christian Herald* 1, no. 3 (September 1818): 59; Roberts, *Memoir*, p. 97; Burnett, *Early Women*, p. 19; and Ellen Stewart, *Life of Mrs. Ellen Stewart, Together with Biographical Sketches of Other Individuals. Also, A Discussion with Two Clergymen, and Arguments in Favor of Woman's Rights* (Akron, Ohio: Beebe and Elkins, 1858), p. 80.

8. George Keely, *The Nature and Order of a Gospel Church* (Haverhill, Mass.: P. N. Green, 1819), p. 24.

9. Zilpha Elaw, *Memoirs of the Life, Religious Experience, Ministerial Travels and Labours of Mrs. Zilpha Elaw, An American Female of Colour* (London, 1846), reprinted in *Sisters of the Spirit: Three Black Women's Autobiographies of the Nineteenth Century*, ed. William L. Andrews (Bloomington: University of Indiana, 1986), pp. 100, 133, 128.

10. For examples of women being locked out of the buildings where they were supposed to preach, see Roberts, *Memoir*, pp. 31, 95; Abel Thornton, *The Life of Elder Abel Thornton* (Providence: J. B. Yerrinton, 1828), p. 115; and Almond H. Davis, *The Female Preacher, or Memoir of Salome Lincoln* (Providence, 1843; reprint, New York: Arno Press, 1972), p. 66. See also Elleanor Warner Knight, *A Narrative of the Christian Experience, Life and Adventures, Trials and Labours of Elleanor Knight, Written by Herself* (Providence: n.p., 1839), p. 81, and Towle, *Vicissitudes*, p. 74. Towle was arrested for "obstructing the way and making a disturbance" while she was traveling through England, but she was acquitted.

11. J[onathan] F[rench] Stearns, *Female Influence and the True Christian Mode of Its Exercise. A Discourse Delivered in the First Presbyterian Church of Newburyport, July 30, 1847* (Newburyport, Mass.: John G. Tilton, 1837), p. 20, and Towle, *Vicissitudes*, p. 227.

12. Historians generally agree that an evangelical "mainline" existed in nineteenth-century America, but depending on their time frame, they include different groups in their definition of it. For example, Paul Conkin and Laurie E. Maffly-Kipp both include the Methodists as part of the "mainline." Laurie E. Maffly-Kipp, *Religion and Society in Frontier California* (New Haven: Yale University Press, 1994), and Paul K. Conkin, *The Uneasy Center: Reformed Christianity in Antebellum America* (Chapel Hill: University of North Carolina Press, 1995). Since my focus here is on the 1830s and 1840s, I define this word more narrowly. Indeed, one of the arguments of this book is that the Methodists, Christians, and Freewill Baptists stood apart from the "mainline" during their early histories but eventually became absorbed by it.

13. E. F. Newell, *Life and Observations of Rev. E. F. Newell . . . Who Has Been More than Forty Years an Itinerant Minister in the Methodist Episcopal Church* (Worcester, Mass.: C. W. Ainsworth, 1847),

p. 184. Edward E. Bourne, *History of Wells and Kennebunk* (Portland, Maine: B. Thurston, 1875), p. 633. See also W. B. Strickland, *Autobiography of Rev. James B. Finley, or Pioneer Life in the West* (Cincinnati: Methodist Book Concern, 1853), p. 257.

14. See Joseph Richardson, *A Sermon on the Duty and Dignity of Woman Delivered April 22, 1832* (Hingham, Mass.: Jedidiah Farmer, 1833), p. 11. Albert Barnes, *Notes Explanatory and Practical on the Epistles of Paul to the Corinthians* (London, 1837), quoted in *Presbyterian Women in America: Two Centuries of a Quest for Status*, ed. Lois A. Boyd and R. Douglas Brackenridge (Westport, Conn.: Greenwood Press, 1983), p. 91.

15. Towle, *Vicissitudes*, pp. 182, 227.

16. See Ann Douglas, *The Feminization of American Culture* (New York: Knopf, 1977), pp. 17–43.

17. Theodore Ledyard Cuyler, D.D., LL.D, *Recollections of a Long Life: An Autobiography* (New York, 1902), pp. 4, 120–21, quoted in Douglas, *Feminization*, p. 99. Douglas discusses clergymen's dependence on women in chapter 3, "Ministers and Mothers," pp. 80–117.

18. See Boyd and Brackenridge, *Presbyterian Women*, p. 6, and Douglas, *Feminization*, pp. 109–15. Walter Harris, *A Discourse to the Members of the Female Cent Society in Bedford, New Hampshire, July 18, 1814* (Concord, N.H.: George Hough, 1814), pp. 10–11. I have borrowed the phrase "pulpit envy" from Douglas, *Feminization*, p. 103.

19. Arethusa Hall, *Life and Character of the Reverend Sylvester Judd* (Boston, 1854), p. 148, quoted in Douglas, *Feminization*, p. 102. This paragraph follows the argument of Nancy F. Cott, *The Bonds of Womanhood: "Woman's Sphere" in New England, 1780–1835* (New Haven: Yale University Press, 1977), pp. 64–74.

20. Richard Carwardine, "The Second Great Awakening in the Urban Centers: An Examination of Methodism and the 'New Measures,'" *Journal of American History* 59 (1972): 327–40. Letter from Asahel Nettleton to S. C. Aiken, January 13, 1827, quoted in Charles C. Cole Jr., "The New Lebanon Convention," *New York History* 31 (1950): 388; Boyd and Brackenridge, *Presbyterian Women*, pp. 93–94; and Page Putnam Miller, *A Claim to New Roles* (Philadelphia: American Theological Library Association; Metuchen, N.J.: Scarecrow Press, 1985), pp. 48–49. See also Paul E. Johnson, *A Shopkeeper's Millennium: Society and Revivals in Rochester, New York, 1815–1837* (New York: Hill and Wang, 1978).

21. *Letters of Theodore Dwight Weld, Angelina Grimké Weld and Sarah Grimké*, ed. Gilbert H. Marvelled and Dwight L. Drummond (New York, 1934), p. 433, quoted in Miller, *Claim to New Roles*, pp. 47–48; and Stewart, *Life*, p. 118.

22. "The Woman Question," *The Presbyterian*, April 21, 1877, p. 1, quoted in Boyd and Brackenridge, *Presbyterian Women*, pp. 93–94.

23. On Cook, see Steven Rensselaer Smith, *Historical Sketches and Incidents Illustrative of the Establishment and Progress of Universalism in the State of New York* (Buffalo: Steele's Press, 1843), 1:31; Elisabeth Anthony Dexter, *Career Women of America, 1776–1840* (Francestown, N.H.: Marshall Jones, 1950), p. 62; and E. R. Hanson, *Our Woman Workers. Biographical Sketches of Women Eminent in the Universalist Church for Literary, Philanthropic, and Christian Work* (Chicago: Starr and Covenant Office, 1882), pp. 424–26. On Dunn, see Hanson, *Our Woman Workers*, pp. 21–24.

24. Hanson, *Our Woman Workers*, pp. 424–26, and A. W. Drury, *History of the Church of the United Brethren in Christ* (Dayton, Ohio: United Brethren Publishing House, 1924), p. 425.

25. Towle, *Vicissitudes*, p. 53, and David Marks, *The Life of David Marks* (Limerick, Maine: Morning Star Office, 1831), p. 347. Elizabeth Cazden, *Antoinette Brown Blackwell: A Biography* (Old Westbury, N.Y.: Feminist Press, 1983).

26. Sarah M. Grimké, *Letters on the Equality of the Sexes and the Condition of Woman* (New York: Burt Franklin, 1837), p. 100. On female platform speakers, see Doris G. Yoakam, "Women's Introduction to the American Platform," in *A History and Criticism of American Public Address*, ed. William Norwood Brigance (New York: McGraw-Hill, 1943), 1:153–92. The quote is from 1 Corinthians 11:3.

27. Celia Morris Eckhardt, *Fanny Wright: Rebel in America* (Cambridge: Harvard University Press, 1984), pp. 123, 3, 184. See also Yoakam, "Women's Introduction," 1:157–60.

28. Grimké, *Letters*, pp. 102, 100.

29. *New York Commercial Advertiser*, January 12, 1829, quoted in Eckhardt, *Fanny Wright*, p. 186.

30. "Few thought his outburst ludicrous," writes Dorothy Sterling. See Dorothy Sterling, *Ahead of Her Time: Abby Kelley and the Politics of Antislavery* (New York: Norton, 1991), p. 108.

31. Quoted in Eckhardt, *Fanny Wright*, p. 157.

32. Grimké, *Letters*, p. 4, and Sterling, *Ahead of Her Time*, pp. 60–81. Maria Stewart, *Productions of Mrs. Maria W. Stewart, Presented to the First African Baptist Church and Society of the City of Boston* (Boston, 1835), reprinted in *Spiritual Narratives*, ed. Sue E. Houchins (New York: Oxford University Press, 1988), pp. 7, 3; and Maria W. Stewart, "Mrs. Stewart's Farewell Address to Her Friends in the City of Boston," reprinted in *Maria W. Stewart: America's First Black Woman Political Writer: Essays and Speeches*, ed. Marilyn Richardson (Bloomington: Indiana University Press, 1987), p. 68.

33. On Kent, see *The Bethlehem Star* 1, no. 1 (January 1824): 30–32. For a brief biographical sketch of Stewart, see Richardson, *Maria W. Stewart*, pp. 4–27.

34. Grimké, *Letters*, p. 98.

35. Quoted in Eckhardt, *Fanny Wright*, p. 135.

36. Parsons Cooke, *Female Preaching, Unlawful and Inexpedient. A Sermon* (Lynn, Mass.: James R. Newhall, 1837), p. 9. For a response to Cooke's "unmanly, unchristian attack" on "mothers and sisters in Israel," see P. R. Russell, "Female Preaching: A Short Sermon," in *Christian Journal* 4, no. 5 (May 31, 1838).

37. Russell, "Female Preaching."

38. In 1842 the Ohio Synod of the Dutch Reformed Church reiterated their disapproval of "women praying aloud in promiscuous assemblies or prayer meetings." *The Presbyterian*, November 16, 1872, and "Woman Preaching Viewed in the Light of God's Work and Church History," *Reformed Quarterly Review* 29 (January 1882): 124, both quoted in Boyd and Brackenridge, *Presbyterian Women*, p. 259n. See also the *Minutes of the General Assembly of the Presbyterian Church in the United States of America* (1832), p. 378, and *The Presbyterian*, June 18, 1832, and June 20, 1832, both quoted in Boyd and Brackenridge, *Presbyterian Women*, p. 94. The Yearly Meeting of the Church of the Brethren condemned female preaching in 1834. See Donald F. Durnbaugh, ed., "She Kept on Preaching," *Messenger* (Church of the Brethren) 124 (April 1975): 18.

39. "The General Association of Massachusetts (Orthodox) to the Churches Under their Care," reprinted in *The Feminist Papers: From Adams to de Beauvoir*, ed. Alice S. Rossi (Toronto: Bantam Books, 1973), pp. 305–6. Keely, *Nature and Order of a Gospel Church*, p. 23.

40. On women's "appropriate retirement," see Catharine Beecher, *Essay on Slavery and Abolitionism with Reference to the Duty of American Females* (Philadelphia: H. Perkins, 1837), reprinted in *Women, the Family, and Freedom: The Debate in Documents*, ed. Susan Groag Bell and Karen M. Offen (Stanford: Stanford University Press, 1983), 1:182. Harriet Livermore, *A Narration of Religious Experience* (Concord, N.H.: Jacob B. Moore, 1826), p. 15; Richard Eddy, *Universalism in America: A History*, 2 vols. (Boston: Universalist Publishing House, 1884), quoted in Dexter, *Career Women*

of America, pp. 62–63; Smith, *Historical Sketches and Incidents*, 1:31–32; and Roberts, *Memoir*, p. 80. Zilpha Elaw met a woman in New York who objected that "it was unbecoming in a woman to preach; and also, that God never commissioned women to preach." Elaw, *Memoirs*, p. 131.

41. Kathryn Kish Sklar, *Catharine Beecher: A Study in American Domesticity* (New Haven: Yale University Press, 1973), pp. 155–63. On the "cult of domesticity," see Barbara Welter, "The Cult of True Womanhood, 1820–1860," *American Quarterly* 18 (1966): 151–74.

42. Beecher, *Essay on Slavery and Abolitionism*, 1:182. Men also read the speeches of Emma Willard and Dorothea Dix. See Ann Braude, *Radical Spirits: Spiritualism and Women's Rights in Nineteenth-Century America* (Boston: Beacon Press, 1989), p. 91.

43. On Wiard, see David Marks, *Life*, p. 296. On Cram, see Levi Hathaway, *The Narrative of Levi Hathaway* (Providence: Miller and Hutchens, 1820), p. 88; Evans Williams Humphreys, *Memoirs of Deceased Christian Ministers; or, Brief Sketches of the Lives and Labors of 975 Ministers, Who Died Between 1793 and 1880* (Dayton, Ohio: Christian Publishing Association, 1880), pp. 96–97; David Edmund Millard, *Memoir of Rev. David Millard; with Selections from His Writings. By His Son* (Dayton, Ohio: Christian Publishing Association, 1874), p. 27; Roberts, *Memoir*, pp. 34–35; Burnett, *Early Women*, pp. 9–12; and Caroline Dall, *The College, the Market, and the Court; or, Women's Relation to Education, Labor, and Law* (Boston: Lee and Shepard, 1867; reprint, New York: Arno Press, 1972), p. 437. Dall mistakenly refers to Cram's maiden name as "Gore" instead of "Gove." On Roberts, see Roberts, *Memoir*, and Burnett, *Early Women*. Sarah Barns Dunn, a Universalist from Maine, was supposedly as influential within her denomination as any of her male colleagues. Hanson, *Our Woman Workers*, p. 21.

44. On the "allure of respectability," see Nathan O. Hatch, *The Democratization of American Christianity* (New Haven: Yale University Press, 1989), pp. 201–6.

45. Two clergymen, Daniel Quimby and James Spencer, became followers of Niles in the early 1820s, but both eventually returned to the Christian Connection. See Humphreys, *Memoirs*, pp. 289, 338. I could find very little information about Niles, but she may have been associated with Fanny Martin, another female radical. They were mentioned together in an article in the *Christian Palladium* 13, no. 4 (July 3, 1844): 30.

46. For one example, see the statistics reprinted in J. M. Brewster, *The Centennial Record of Freewill Baptists, 1780–1880* (Dover, N.H.: The Printing Establishment, 1881), p. 239. In 1810 there was one Freewill Baptist minister for every thirty-five congregants (1:35). By 1832, the ratio had widened to 1:69.

47. Stewart, *Life*, p. 75. Charles R. Harding, "Autobiography, 1807–1869," American Antiquarian Society, Worcester, Mass. On changing standards of refinement in the nineteenth century, see Richard L. Bushman, *The Refinement of America: Persons, Houses, Cities* (New York: Knopf, 1992), pp. 74–78. Nathan Hatch has noted that "Methodism resonated with the logic of capitalism and liberal individualism." Nathan O. Hatch, "The Puzzle of American Methodism," *Church History* 63 (June 1994): 187.

48. Stewart, *Life*, p. 7; Gideon A. Burgess and John T. Ward, *Free Baptist Cyclopedia, Historical and Biographical* (n.p., 1889), p. 551. Many sociologists have noted the connection between Protestantism and economic progress. For the classic statement, see Max Weber, *The Protestant Ethic and the Spirit of Capitalism*, trans. Talcott Parsons (London: George Allen and Unwin, 1930).

49. There were 1,167 separate Freewill Baptist congregations in 1844, and they had almost as many ministers as the Episcopalians. See Brewster, *Centennial Record*, p. 239, and Hatch, *Democratization*, p. 4. On the Christians, see Robert Baird, *Religion in the United States of America* (Glasgow: Blackie and Son, 1844), p. 639. The Christians may have inflated their membership figures. On

the growth of the Methodists, see William H. Williams, *The Garden of American Methodism: The Delmarva Peninsula, 1769–1820* (Wilmington, Del.: Scholarly Resources, 1984), p. 49, and Sydney E. Ahlstrom, *A Religious History of the American People* (New Haven: Yale University Press, 1972), p. 437. For other statistics, see Nathan Bangs, "History of the Methodist Episcopal Church," in *History of All the Religious Denominations in the United States*, ed. John Winebrenner (Harrisburg, Pa.: John Winebrenner, 1848), pp. 378–79.

50. *Christian Palladium* 4, no. 12 (October 15, 1835): 196. Norman Allen Baxter, *History of the Freewill Baptists: A Study in New England Separatism* (Rochester, N.Y.: American Baptist Historical Society, 1957), p. 87; *Christian Palladium* 16, no. 7 (June 12, 1847): 98. See the statistics in Ruth O. Bordin, "The Sect to Denomination Process in America: The Freewill Baptist Experience," *Church History* 34 (1964): 82.

51. Records of the Quarterly Meeting of the First Methodist Episcopal Church, Concord, N.H., vol. 2, March 8, 1845, New Hampshire Historical Society, Concord, N.H. Daniel Alexander Payne, *History of the African Methodist Episcopal Church* (Nashville: Publishing House of the A.M.E. Sunday-school Union, 1891), p. 141.

52. In 1818, for example, a Methodist minister in Maine lost his preaching license after bragging that he had seduced a woman. Journal of the Quarterly Conference, Scarborough Circuit of the Methodist Episcopal Church, 1808–73, Scarborough, Maine, December 19–20, 1818, Maine Historical Society, Portland, Maine.

53. For criticisms of relying on visions or dreams, see *Christian Herald* 8, no. 46 (February 9, 1846), and 9, no. 1 (March 30, 1843).

54. *Christian Palladium* 2, no. 5 (September 1833): 144–45. For two letters defending people's right to "shout" or "make noise" in meetings, see *Christian Palladium* 2, no. 9 (January 1834): 277–78, and 2, no. 3 (June 2, 1834): 46.

55. Mark Fernald, *Life of Elder Mark Fernald, Written by Himself* (Newburyport: G. M. Payne and D. P. Pike; Philadelphia: Christian General Book Concern, 1852), p. 307; Abner Jones, *Memoir of Elder Abner Jones* (Boston: William Crosby, 1842), p. 77; and *Christian Palladium* 2, no. 3 (July 1833): 75.

56. Elder J. Chadwick, "An Exposition of I. Cor. XIV 34, 35," *Christian Palladium* 10, no. 2 (May 15, 1841): 24.

57. *Christian Journal* 2, no. 20 (December 29, 1836): 77. General Conference of the Freewill Baptist Connection, *Minutes of the General Conference of the Freewill Baptist Connection* (Dover, N.H.: William Burr, 1859), p. 237. This document includes all the minutes from the General Conference between 1827 and 1856.

58. Records of the Freewill Baptist Church, Northwood, N.H., 1844. For other examples of resolutions in favor of reform and benevolent organizations, see the New Durham, N.H., Freewill Baptist Church Quarterly Meeting Conference Records, 1792–1889, vol. 4, October 23, 1838, p. 112; and Records of the First Free Will Baptist Church of Christ, New Market, N.H., 1834–1912, December 30, 1843, p. 72. All of these records can be found at the New Hampshire Historical Society. See also "The Prospect of our Denomination," *The Morning Star* 7, no. 44 (February 26, 1833): 174.

59. Ernst Troeltsch, *The Social Teaching of the Christian Churches*, trans. Olive Wyon, 2 vols. (London: Allen and Unwin, 1931; reprint, Chicago: University of Chicago Press, 1976), 1:334.

60. See H. Richard Niebuhr, *The Social Sources of Denominationalism* (New York: Henry Holt, 1929), pp. 17–21, and Troeltsch, *Social Teaching*, 1:131, 331–43.

61. Niebuhr, *Social Sources*, p. 25; Bryan R. Wilson, "An Analysis of Sect Development,"

American Sociological Review 24 (February 1959): 4–5; Benton Johnson, "On Church and Sect," *American Sociological Review* 28 (August 1963): 539–49; Rodney Stark and William Sims Bainbridge, *The Future of Religion: Secularization, Revival, and Cult Formation* (Berkeley: University of California Press, 1985), pp. 19–37; John Wilson, *Religion in American Society: The Effective Presence* (Englewood Cliffs, N.J.: Prentice-Hall, 1978), pp. 139–46.

62. Donald G. Mathews, *Slavery and Methodism: A Chapter in American Morality, 1780–1845* (Princeton: Princeton University Press, 1965).

63. Thompson, *Trial and Defence*, p. 11. Using milder language, Zilpha Elaw complained that "the life and power of religion is not identified with, nor in proportion to, the polish of the minister, the respectability of the congregation, or the regularity and method of its services." Elaw, *Memoirs*, p. 107.

64. Milton J. Yinger, *Religion in the Struggle for Power: A Study in the Sociology of Religion* (Durham, N.C.: Duke University Press, 1946; reprint, New York: Russell and Russell, 1961), p. 226.

65. General Conference of the Freewill Baptist Connection, *Minutes*, pp. 179, 246.

66. *The Morning Star* 5, no. 10 (July 7, 1830).

67. "Female Virtues," *Christian Palladium* 3, no. 11 (October 1, 1834): 175.

68. Quoted in Elizabeth Muir, "The Bark School House: Methodist Episcopal Missionary Women in Upper Canada, 1827–1833," in *Canadian Protestant and Catholic Missions, 1820s–1960s*, ed. John S. Moir and C. T. McIntire (New York: Peter Lang Publishing, 1988), p. 32.

69. See John Higham, *From Boundlessness to Consolidation: The Transformation of American Culture, 1848–1860* (Ann Arbor, Mich.: Clements Library, 1969), p. 15. Although Higham does not discuss gender in his essay, he provides a broad framework for interpreting the dramatic changes in nineteenth-century American society. See also Robert H. Wiebe, *The Opening of American Society: From the Adoption of the Constitution to the Eve of Disunion* (New York: Knopf, 1984).

70. Abel Stevens, *Life and Times of Nathan Bangs* (New York: Carlton and Porter, 1863), p. 183. On Gatchell, see John Carroll, *Case and his Contemporaries or, The Canadian Itinerants' Memorial* (Toronto: Methodist Conference Office, 1867), 1:224. *Christian Guardian* quoted in Muir, "Bark School House," p. 32. On Riker and Mills, see Doris Elizabett Andrews, "Popular Religion and the Revolution in the Middle Atlantic Ports: The Rise of the Methodists, 1770–1800" (Ph.D. diss., University of Pennsylvania, 1986), p. 200. Elice Miller Smith was the "Miss Miller" mentioned in George Brown, *Recollections of Itinerant Life: Including Early Reminiscences* (Cincinnati: R. W. Carool, 1866), p. 183. For more on her, see Towle, *Vicissitudes*, p. 196.

71. See the obituary of Sarah Hedges in the *Christian Palladium* 12, no. 1 (July 5, 1843): 16.

72. See Wesley Bailey, "History of the Reformed Methodist Church," in Winebrenner, *History*, p. 388; and James R. Williams, "History of the Methodist Protestant Church," in Winebrenner, *History*, p. 380. See also William T. Noll, "Women as Clergy and Laity in the Nineteenth-Century Methodist Protestant Church," *Methodist History* 15 (January 1977): 107–21; Angel H. Bassett, *A Concise History of the Methodist Protestant Church, From Its Origin*, 3d ed. (Pittsburgh: William McCracken, 1882); and Edward J. Drinkhouse, *History of Methodist Reform Synoptical of General Methodism, 1703–1898*, 2 vols. (Baltimore: Board of Publication of the Methodist Protestant Church, 1899).

73. See Laura Smith Haviland, *A Woman's Life-Work: Labors and Experiences of Laura S. Haviland*, 4th ed. (Chicago: Publishing Association of Friends, 1889), p. 201. On the Wesleyan Methodists, see Ira Ford McLeister, *History of the Wesleyan Methodist Church of America* (Syracuse, N.Y.: Wesleyan Methodist Publishing Association, 1934).

74. Payne, *History*, quoted in Jean M. Humez, " 'My Spirit Eye': Some Functions of Spiritual

and Visionary Experiences in the Lives of Five Black Women Preachers, 1810–1880," in *Women and the Structure of Society*, ed. Barbara Harris and JoAnn McNamara (Durham, N.C.: Duke University Press, 1984), p. 279n. David W. Wills, "Womanhood and Domesticity in the A.M.E. Tradition: The Influence of Daniel Alexander Payne," in *Black Apostles at Home and Abroad*, ed. David W. Wills and Richard Newman (Boston: G. K. Hall, 1982), pp. 140–42. Payne's child-rearing book, entitled *A Treatise on Domestic Education*, appeared in 1885 after he had studied the topic for almost fifty years. On maternal associations, see Richard A. Meckel, "Educating a Ministry of Mothers: Evangelical Maternal Associations, 1815–1860," *Journal of the Early Republic* 2 (Winter 1982): 403–23.

75. Payne, *History*, p. 190.

76. Julia A. J. Foote, *A Brand Plucked From the Fire: An Autobiographical Sketch* (Cleveland: W. F. Schneider, 1879), reprinted in Andrews, *Sisters of the Spirit*, p. 216. Payne, *History*, pp. 237, 273.

77. See David Marks, *Life*, pp. 177–78, 182–85, 238, 291, 296. For more on Quinby, see Towle, *Vicissitudes*, p. 33.

78. Compare David Marks, *Life*, p. 291, to Marilla Marks, *Memoirs of the Life of David Marks, Minister of the Gospel* (Dover, N.H.: William Burr, 1846), p. 202.

79. For references to Humes, see David Marks, *Life*, pp. 177–78, 182–85, 238, 250.

80. David wrote, "I retired from the scene with a heart full of feeling, and proceeding to Ashford I held a meeting, and tarried the night with Mr. Richmond, a merchant, who married Clarissa H. Danforth, the female preacher." In contrast, the edited version of his memoir states, "I retired from the scene with a heart full of feeling, and returned to Rhode Island, preaching by the way." Compare David Marks, *Life*, p. 177, to Marilla Marks, *Memoirs*, p. 126. See also A. D. Williams, *The Rhode Island Freewill Baptist Pulpit* (Boston: Gould and Lincoln, 1852), which ignores Danforth even though she preached extensively in Rhode Island.

81. On Cram, see David Millard's account of the revival in Charleston, reprinted in Roberts, *Memoirs*, pp. 18–21. "Extract of a letter from Elder Jabez King," *Christian Herald* 1, no. 3 (September 1818): 59. Jabez King's memoir is reprinted in *Christian Palladium* 13, no. 19 (February 5, 1845): 271.

82. Hathaway, *Narrative*, p. 88.

83. "Mrs. Hannah Reeves, Preacher of the Gospel," *Methodist Quarterly Review* 59 (July 1877): 446.

84. See *Christian Palladium* 3, no. 13 (November 1, 1834): 210, and Burgess and Ward, *Free Baptist Cyclopedia*. The *Christian Herald* published a front-page article urging women to "lend a helping hand in the triumph of the gospel" in "the dark lands of heathenism." See "She Hath Done What She Could," *Christian Herald* 6, no. 37 (December 10, 1840). For secondary sources, see Barbara Welter, "She Hath Done What She Could: Protestant Women's Missionary Careers in Nineteenth-Century America," *American Quarterly* 30 (Winter 1978): 625–38, and Anne M. Boylan, "Evangelical Womanhood in the Nineteenth Century: The Role of Women in Sunday Schools," *Feminist Studies* 4, no. 3 (October 1978): 62–80.

85. *Christian Advocate*, April 1, 1831, p. 122, quoted in Muir, "Bark School House," p. 32. He was lecturing to the Dorcas Society in New York City.

86. "Why Gag Them?" *Christian Herald* 9, no. 8 (May 18, 1843). "New Testament Worship," *Christian Herald* 9, no. 13 (June 22, 1843). See also "Female Rights and Influence," *Christian Herald* 8, no. 45 (February 2, 1843), and *Christian Palladium* 4, no. 5 (July 1, 1835): 67.

87. See the letter from Thornton to Elias Smith reprinted in *The Morning Star and City Watchman* 1, no. 10 (March 1828).

88. On Eliza Barnes, see Elizabeth Muir, *Petticoats in the Pulpit: The Story of Early Nineteenth-Century Methodist Women Preachers in Upper Canada* (Toronto: United Church Publishing House, 1991), pp. 108–16. Nancy Towle met Barnes on a preaching tour of New Hampshire in 1825. See Towle, *Vicissitudes*, pp. 43–44. The Sally Waldren who led a revival in 1821 is probably the "Mrs. Waldron" (notice the different spelling) who preached to Canadian Indians in 1828, although the evidence is not conclusive. On Waldren, see John Carroll, *Case and his Contemporaries or, The Canadian Itinerants' Memorial* (Toronto: Methodist Conference Office, 1867–77), 3:171, and *Religious Intelligencer*, January 1821.

89. Towle, *Vicissitudes*, p. 196. For a description of a meeting that Elice Miller held in Baltimore, see *The Morning Star* 1, no. 15 (August 17, 1826).

90. Harding, "Autobiography." On Taylor, see Leonard I. Sweet, *The Minister's Wife: Her Role in Nineteenth-Century American Evangelicalism* (Philadelphia: Temple University Press, 1983), p. 119, and Gilbert Haven and Thomas Russell, *Father Taylor, the Sailor Preacher* (Boston: B. B. Russell, 1872).

91. On Macomber, see Dana L. Robert, *American Women in Mission: A Social History of Their Thought and Practice* (Macon, Ga.: Mercer University Press, 1996), p. 55. The American Board of Commissioners for Foreign Missions was so troubled by Colton's seeming desire to "preach" that they decided to "proceed with caution" before appointing her as a missionary. See E. P. Rogers to D. Greene, October 16, 1845, American Board of Commissioners for Foreign Missions Testimonials, 18:92, Houghton Library, Harvard University, quoted in Lydia Huffman Hoyle, "Missionary Women among the American Indians, 1815–1865" (Ph.D. diss., University of North Carolina at Chapel Hill, 1992), pp. 32, 9–10.

92. Towle, *Vicissitudes*, p. 97. See the description of Ann Judson in Joan Jacobs Brumberg, *Mission for Life: The Judson Family and American Evangelical Culture* (New York: Free Press, 1980), p. 103.

93. *Christian Palladium* 2, no. 2 (June 1833): 71.

94. *Christian Palladium* 10, no. 3 (June 1, 1841): 42. See also the letter from her in *Christian Palladium* 11, no. 5 (July 1, 1842): 75. I have not been able to find any evidence of what happened to Monroe after 1846.

95. For information on Spaulding's "labors" in Canada, see *The Morning Star* 3, no. 12 (July 23, 1828); 3, no. 26 (October 29, 1828); 4, no. 14 (August 7, 1829); 4, no. 19 (September 11, 1829); and 4, no. 26 (October 30, 1829). On Stiles and Stone, see *Christian Palladium* 14, no. 8 (August 20, 1845): 125; 15, no. 16 (December 2, 1846): 252; and 16, no. 11 (July 10, 1847): 164. For more on Stiles, see John Presley Barrett, *The Centennial of Religious Journalism* (Dayton, Ohio: Christian Publishing Association, 1908): 504; Humphreys, *Memoirs*, pp. 342–43; and *Christian Palladium* 9, no. 7 (August 1, 1840): 107; 12, no. 6 (September 6, 1843): 16; and 13, no. 7 (August 14, 1844): 108.

96. Foote, *Brand*, pp. 207, 201.

97. Lydia Sexton, *Autobiography of Lydia Sexton* (Dayton, Ohio: United Brethren Publishing House, 1882), p. 401.

98. Jarena Lee, *Religious Experience and Journal of Mrs. Jarena Lee, Giving the Account of Her Call to Preach the Gospel* (Philadelphia: printed for the author, 1849), reprinted in *Spiritual Narratives*, ed. Sue E. Houchins (New York: Oxford University Press, 1988), p. 97.

99. Elaw, *Memoirs*, p. 62.

100. Thompson, *Trial and Defence*, p. 12. See also *Christian Palladium* 4, no. 21 (March 1, 1836): 332–33; *Zion's Herald* 7, no. 12 (March 23, 1836); and Roberts, *Memoir*, pp. 145–47. Her travels

during the 1830s and 1840s were reported in *Christian Palladium* 5, no. 6 (July 15, 1836): 95; 5, no. 22 (March 15, 1837): 350; 7, no. 7 (August 1, 1838): 105; 11, no. 3 (June 1, 1842): 42; 14, no. 21 (February 18, 1846): 332; and 15, no. 25 (March 24, 1847): 398.

CHAPTER 8

1. Olive Maria Rice, "The Labors of Olive Maria Rice," *The Midnight Cry* 4, no. 19 (July 6, 1843).

2. Ibid. For more on Rice, see *Signs of the Times* 4, no. 21 (February 8, 1843), and *The Midnight Cry* 5, no. 1 (August 24, 1843); 5, no. 10 (October 19, 1843); 5, no. 12 (November 2, 1843); 6, no. 1 (January 25, 1844); and 6, no. 23 (June 20, 1844).

3. Rice, "Labors of Olive Maria Rice."

4. Ibid.

5. For recent scholarship on the Millerites, see Ronald L. Numbers and Jonathan M. Butler, eds., *The Disappointed: Millerism and Millenarianism in the Nineteenth Century* (Bloomington: Indiana University Press, 1987); David L. Rowe, *Thunder and Trumpets: Millerites and Dissenting Religion in Upstate New York, 1800–1850* (Chico, Calif.: Scholar's Press, 1985); Gary Land, ed., *Adventism in America: A History* (Grand Rapids, Mich.: Eerdmans, 1986); Edwin S. Gaustad, ed., *The Rise of Adventism: Religion and Society in Mid-Nineteenth-Century America* (New York: Harper and Row, 1974); Ruth Alden Doan, *The Miller Heresy, Millennialism, and American Culture* (Philadelphia: Temple University Press, 1987); Michael Barkun, *Crucible of the Millennium: The Burned-over District of New York in the 1840s* (Syracuse: Syracuse University Press, 1986); and Stephen D. O'Leary, *Arguing the Apocalypse: A Theory of Millennial Rhetoric* (New York: Oxford University Press, 1994).

6. For Miller's account of his early life, see "Memoir of William Miller," *The Midnight Cry* 1, no. 1 (November 17, 1842). See also Sylvester Bliss, *Memoirs of William Miller: Generally Known as a Lecturer on the Prophecies, and the Second Coming of Christ* (Boston: J. V. Himes, 1853), and Joshua Himes, *Views of the Prophecies and Prophetic Chronology, Selected from Manuscripts of William Miller, with a Memoir of His Life* (Boston: Moses A. Dow, 1841).

7. William Miller, *Apology and Defence* (Boston: Joshua V. Himes, 1845), p. 4. Bliss, *Memoirs of William Miller*, p. 4.

8. Himes, *Views of the Prophecies*, pp. 20, 11. In a lecture that he delivered in 1843, Miller explained, "I had Cruden's Concordance, which I think is the best in the world, so I took that and my Bible, and sat down to my desk, and read nothing else except the newspapers a little, for I was determined to know what my Bible meant. I began at Genesis and read on slowly; and when I came to a text I could not understand, I searched through the Bible to find out what it meant." See *The Advent Shield* 1, no. 1 (May 1844). For a discussion of Miller's "woodenly literal" interpretation, see Ernest R. Sandeen, "Millennialism," in Gaustad, *Rise of Adventism*, pp. 113–14.

9. Revelation 8:7–8, 9:8, 12:3, 17:6. For a useful commentary that outlines John's visions, see Adela Yarbo Collins, "The Apocalypse (Revelation)," in *The New Jerome Biblical Commentary*, ed. Raymond E. Brown, Joseph A. Fitzmyer, and Roland E. Murphy (Englewood Cliffs, N.J.: Prentice-Hall, 1990), pp. 996–1016.

10. In 1776 the Reverend Ebenezer Baldwin, a Congregational minister from Connecticut, exulted that America would be "the principal Seat of that glorious kingdom, which Christ shall erect upon earth in the latter Days." Ebenezer Baldwin, *The Duty of Rejoycing Under Calamities and Afflictions* (New York, 1776), p. 38, quoted in Harry S. Stout, *The New England Soul: Preaching and Religious Culture in Early New England* (New York: Oxford University Press, 1986), p. 308.

11. Ray Potter, *Memoirs of the Life and Religious Experience of Ray Potter, Minister of the Gospel, Pawtucket* (Providence: H. H. Brown, 1829), pp. 282–83. Harriet Livermore, *The Harp of Israel, to Meet the Loud Echo in the Wilds of America* (Philadelphia: J. Rakestraw, 1835), p. 180. On Sinda, see Frances Anne Kemble, *Journal of a Residence on a Georgian Plantation in 1838–1839*, ed. John A. Scott (New York: Alfred A. Knopf, 1961), pp. 118–19.

12. Himes, *Views of the Prophecies*, p. 12.

13. William Miller, "Explanation of Prophetic Figures," in Himes, *Views of the Prophecies*, p. 27. Historian Ruth Alden Doan points out that Miller "found a remarkable consistency among the prophetic numbers. The 1,335 days (Dan. 12:12) began with the establishment of papal supremacy—about 508 A.D. Add 1,335 to 508 and the end is slated for 1843. Miller later claimed that papal Rome rose in 538. Undeterred, he then added 538 to the 1,260 days of the woman in the wilderness (Rev. 12:14) to reach 1798, the fall of the papacy before the power of Napoleon. The last days, then, comprised the 45 years from 1798 to 1843. Or Miller would subtract the 70 weeks of Daniel 9:24—representing 490 years—from the 2,300 days, add the life of Christ (33 years), and come to the same conclusion—1843." Doan, *Miller Heresy*, pp. 32–33. See also William Miller, "A Dissertation on Prophetic Chronology," in Himes, *Views of the Prophecies*, pp. 40–53.

14. William Miller, *Evidence from Scripture and History of the Second Coming of Christ, About the Year 1843* (Troy, N.Y.: Elias Gates, 1838). See David T. Arthur, "Joshua V. Himes and the Cause of Adventism," in Numbers and Butler, *The Disappointed*, pp. 36–58.

15. For numerical estimates of the Millerites, see Barkun, *Crucible*, p. 33. Charles R. Harding, "Autobiography, 1807–1869." American Antiquarian Society, Worcester, Mass.

16. Josiah Litch, "History of the Adventists," in *History of All the Religious Denominations in the United States*, ed. John Winebrenner (Harrisburg, Pa.: John Winebrenner, 1848), p. 37.

17. See Anthony F. C. Wallace, *The Death and Rebirth of the Seneca* (New York: Random House, 1969), pp. 303–37; Sandeen, "Millennialism," p. 106; and Anthony F. C. Wallace, "Revitalization Movements," *American Anthropologist* 58 (1956): 264–81. For a discussion of the classic interpretations of millennialism, see Rowe, *Thunder and Trumpets*, pp. 161–63.

18. See *The Midnight Cry*, November 6, 1843, quoted in David L. Rowe, "Millerites: A Shadow Portrait," in Numbers and Butler, *The Disappointed*, p. 7. Introduction to Gaustad, *Rise of Adventism*, p. xviii. On the Millerites' relative economic standing, see Rowe, *Thunder and Trumpets*, p. 106; Sandeen, "Millennialism," p. 111; and Barkun, *Crucible*, p. 43.

19. William Ellery Channing quoted in John Higham, *From Boundlessness to Consolidation: The Transformation of American Culture, 1848–1860* (Ann Arbor, Mich.: Clements Library, 1969), p. 6.

20. Barkun notes that the Millerites barely mentioned the depression in their periodicals, and as a group they tended to be financially secure. Nevertheless, he argues that the "pervasiveness of stress and suffering raised fundamental questions concerning the nature of good and evil." Barkun, *Crucible*, p. 119. On the pessimism that characterized these years, see Lewis O. Saum, *The Popular Mood of Pre–Civil War America* (Westport, Conn.: Greenwood Press, 1980).

21. Edwin Scott Gaustad, *Historical Atlas of Religion in America* (New York: Harper and Row, 1962), pp. 4, 43. On nativism, see Barbara Welter, "From Maria Monk to Paul Blanshard: A Century of Protestant Anti-Catholicism," in *Uncivil Religion: Interreligious Hostility in America*, ed. Robert N. Bellah and Frederic E. Greenspahn (New York: Crossroad Press, 1987), pp. 43–71; and Jenny Franchot, *Roads to Rome: The Antebellum Protestant Encounter with Catholicism* (Berkeley: University of California Press, 1994).

22. See the detailed discussion of "Natural Disasters and the Millennium" in Barkun, *Crucible*, pp. 103–12. The climactic disturbance was caused by a volcanic eruption in Indonesia in 1815.

23. See ibid., p. 58, and Doan, *Miller Heresy*, pp. 74–75.

24. E[mily] C. C[lemons], "Love for the World," *The Voice of Truth* 2, no. 4 (June 1, 1844).

25. Everett N. Dick, "The Millerite Movement, 1830–1845," in Land, *Adventism in America*, p. 34; and Rowe, "Millerites," p. 9. Harding remembered, "The church was the Babylon of the Apocalips [*sic*], and all who would be saved must come out of her." See Harding, "Autobiography."

26. See *The Midnight Cry* 7, no. 1 (July 18, 1844).

27. For more on Marsh, see Jane Marsh Parker, "A Little Millerite," *Century Magazine* 11 (November 1886–April 1887): 312–17. On Himes, see Arthur, "Joshua V. Himes," pp. 36–58. On Storrs, see Albert C. Johnson, *Advent Christian History: A Concise Narrative of the Origin and Progress, Doctrine and Work of This Body of Believers* (Boston: Advent Christian Publication Society, 1918), pp. 169–71.

28. Cordelia Thomas, *The Sheaf; or, The Work of God in the Soul; As Illustrated in the Personal Experiences of Mrs. Cordelia Thomas* (Boston: H. V. Degen, 1852), pp. 43–44, 55, 19. 76.

29. In 1842 a correspondent to the *Christian Palladium* reported that Richards and her followers were "looking for the speedy appearing of our Lord and Savior." See *Christian Palladium* 11, no. 18 (January 16, 1843), p. 287. For more on Richards, see the letter from "Brother Rhodes" reprinted in *The Midnight Cry* 5, no. 1 (August 24, 1843). On Seymour, see the preface to Mary A. Seymour, *The Excellency of the Lord's Anointed or Christ the Promised Messiah* (Hillsdale, Mich.: H. B. Rowlson, 1855).

30. Women were listed as conference members in many Millerite periodicals. For one example, see *Signs of the Times* 2, no. 17 (December 1, 1841). For an example of female exhorting, see *The Midnight Cry* 4, nos. 20–21 (July 13, 1843).

31. See *The Voice of Truth* 8, no. 12 (December 18, 1845), and 9, no. 2 (January 7, 1845). See also the letters from C. Stowe in *The Advent Herald* 8, no. 9 (October 2, 1844), and *The Voice of Truth* 3, no. 12 (October 10, 1844), and from E. S. Bryant in *The Voice of Truth* 8, no. 11 (December 19, 1845), and 9, no. 11 (March 11, 1846). The editor of *The Voice of Truth*, Joseph Marsh, explicitly invited women to submit contributions. For example, after receiving a brief letter from the preacher Clorinda Minor, he responded, "Will sister M[inor] write for our humble pages occasionally?" *The Voice of Truth* 5, no. 5 (February 26, 1845).

32. See *The Advent Message to the Daughters of Zion* 1, no. 1 (May 1844): 1–2, and 1, no. 2 (September 1844).

33. According to Joshua Himes, there were approximately 300 or 400 Millerite preachers in 1842. See *Signs of the Times*, January 15, 1842, quoted in Arthur, "Joshua V. Himes," p. 46.

34. Eight believers in Watertown, Massachusetts, issued a "Statement and Protest" against these two women in 1843. They accused them of practicing "strange, disgusting, and indecent 'exercises,' which they ascribed to the 'power of God,' while all who could not approve them were denounced as *blind*, spiritually *dead*, and exposed to hell." *The Advent Herald* 7, no. 24 (July 17, 1844).

35. See the letter from J. D. Pickands reprinted in *The Voice of Truth* 5, no. 3 (February 12, 1845). *The Midnight Cry* 5, no. 10 (October 19, 1843), and the letter from L. C. Collins in *Signs of the Times* 4, no. 21 (February 8, 1843). For more on Higgins, see *The Midnight Cry* 7, no. 13 (October 3, 1844); 7, no. 15 (October 11, 1844); 7, no. 16 (October 12, 1844); 7, no. 17 (October 19, 1844); and 7, no. 22 (November 28, 1844). See also *The Morning Watch* 8, no. 3 (January 16, 1845), and *The Voice of Truth* 10, no. 7 (May 13, 1846).

36. See *The Midnight Cry* 7, no. 13 (October 3, 1844), and 7, no. 3 (August 1, 1844). For other

favorable accounts of female preachers, see the descriptions of "Sister" Higgins in *The Midnight Cry* 7, no. 15 (October 11, 1844), "Sister" Stoddard in *The Advent Herald* 10, no. 25 (January 28, 1846), H. A. Parks in *The Voice of Truth* 13, no. 6 (February 3, 1847), and "Sister" Plumb in *The Voice of Truth* 6, no. 11 (June 11, 1845).

37. *The Midnight Cry* 4, no. 19 (July 6, 1843), and 7, no. 3 (August 1, 1844). According to a correspondent to *The Voice of Truth*, H. A. Parks had "more calls to lecture than she can possibly fill." *The Voice of Truth* 13, no. 6 (February 3, 1847). Lucy Hersey reported that when she and Parks preached together in Collins, New York, in 1843, "the interest was such that notwith-standing the storms, and very unfavorable travelling, loads of people would come from three to five miles to hear an evening lecture." See *The Midnight Cry* 5, no. 12 (November 2, 1843).

38. *The Midnight Cry* 7, no. 19 (September 12, 1844). Emily C. Clemons described "The Last Day" in *The Advent Message to the Daughters of Zion* 1, no. 1 (May 1844): 11–12.

39. O. R. Fassett, *The Biography of Mrs. L. E. Fassett, a Devoted Christian, a Useful Life* (Boston: Advent Christian Publication Society, 1885), p. 27.

40. E. J. Marden, *A Letter from Mrs. E. J. Marden, of Bangor, Maine. Containing Her Experience in the Blessing of Entire Sanctification; Also an Account of Her Receiving, by Faith, the Doctrine of the Second Advent of Our Lord Jesus Christ in 1843* (Haverhill, Mass.: Essex Banner Office, 1842), p. 31. *The Midnight Cry* 7, no. 16 (October 12, 1844).

41. *The Midnight Cry* 7, no. 1 (July 18, 1844), and 7, no. 7 (August 22, 1844). For a similar account, see the story of Mrs. Baker in *The Midnight Cry* 7, no. 17 (October 19, 1844). Another woman named Mrs. Carlson claimed that as a child, she had been sent a dream from God revealing that the world would end in 1843. See *Signs of the Times* 3, no. 14 (July 6, 1842).

42. *The Midnight Cry* 4, no. 19 (July 6, 1843). Marden, *Letter*, p. 24. After seeing Lucy Maria Hersey preach at a camp meeting, Martha Spence wrote: "In her weakness, the Lord, by his spirit, makes her very strong." See *The Midnight Cry* 7, no. 3 (August 1, 1844).

43. *The Midnight Cry* 7, no. 15 (October 11, 1844). For other accounts of Higgins preaching in New York City, see *The Midnight Cry* 7, no. 17 (October 19, 1844), and *The Morning Watch* 8, no. 3 (January 16, 1845). On Hersey, see *The Midnight Cry* 6, no. 24 (June 27, 1844).

44. See Dick, "Millerite Movement," p. 18; and "The Rise and Progress of Adventism," *The Advent Shield* 1, no. 1 (May, 1844). On Brewer, see *The Midnight Cry* 7, no. 17 (October 19, 1844). For a description of an emotional meeting held in the Great Tent in Salem, Massachusetts, see *Signs of the Times* 4, no. 6 (October 26, 1842).

45. See Neil Harris, *Humbug: The Art of P. T. Barnum* (Boston: Little, Brown, 1973), p. 259.

46. Rice mentioned using the chart in her letter to *The Midnight Cry* 4, no. 19 (July 6, 1843). For an excellent discussion of the promotional value of these charts, see Dick, "Millerite Movement," p. 15. *New Hampshire Patriot* (Concord, N.H.), November 9, 1843, quoted in Dick, "Millerite Movement," p. 20.

47. These statistics are from Dick, "Millerite Movement," pp. 13–14. In 1840 alone, when the movement was still fairly small, the Millerites gave away 8,000 issues of the *Signs of the Times* in Boston. See *Signs of the Times*, January 15, 1841, quoted in Arthur, "Joshua V. Himes," p. 42.

48. See Dick, "Millerite Movement," p. 16. E[benezer] F[rancis] Newell, *Life and Observations of Rev. E. F. Newell . . . Who Has Been More Than Forty Years an Itinerant Minister in the Methodist Episcopal Church* (Worcester, Mass.: C. W. Ainsworth, 1847), p. 264. The statistic appears in Barkun, *Crucible*, p. 132. Luther Boutelle, a Millerite lecturer, remembered that "The *Advent Herald*, the *Midnight Cry*, and other Advent papers, periodicals, pamphlets, tracts, leaflets, voic-ing the coming glory, were scattered broadcast and everywhere, like autumn leaves in the forest.

Every house was visited by them." Luther Boutelle, *Sketch of the Life and Religious Experience of Eld. Luther Boutelle* (Boston: Advent Christian Publication Society, 1891), reprinted in the appendix to Numbers and Butler, *The Disappointed*, p. 210.

49. For letters from Seymour, see *The Voice of Truth* 10, no. 10, (June 3, 1846); 10, no. 12 (June 17, 1846); 13, no. 2 (January 6, 1847); and 14, no. 13 (June 23, 1847). Seymour also wrote three articles—"Millerites and Ascension Robes," "Charity! Charity!!" and "The Bridegroom"— which were reprinted in *The Voice of Truth* 5, no. 1 (January 29, 1845), and 8, no. 9 (November 26, 1845). In 1855 she published a book entitled *The Excellency of the Lord's Anointed or Christ the Promised Messiah* (Hillsdale, Mich.: H. B. Rowlson, 1855). For other articles or letters that mention her, see *The Advent Herald* 11, no. 21 (July 1, 1846), and *The Midnight Cry* 7, no. 3 (August 1, 1844); 7, no. 4 (August 8, 1844); 7, no. 12 (September 26, 1844); and 7, no. 16 (October 12, 1844). Seymour was married to a Millerite minister named A. N. Seymour. For letters from him that mention her, see *The Advent Herald* 13, no. 4 (March 3, 1847), and *The Voice of Truth* 9, no. 12 (March 18, 1846), and 12, no. 3 (October 14, 1846).

50. For letters from Parks, see *The Voice of Truth* 6, no. 7 (May 14, 1845); 7, no. 7 (August 13, 1845); 9, no. 1 (December 31, 1845); 9, no. 7 (February 11, 1846); 12, no. 2 (October 7, 1846); 12, no. 13 (December 23, 1846); and 14, no. 1 (March 31, 1847). See also *The Morning Watch* 8, no. 15 (April 10, 1845). For more information on Parks, see *The Midnight Cry* 5, no. 12 (November 2, 1843); *The Advent Herald* 11, no. 21 (July 1, 1846); and *The Voice of Truth* 10, no. 12 (June 17, 1846); 13, no. 6 (February 3, 1847); and 14, no. 13 (June 23, 1847).

51. *The Midnight Cry* 4, no. 19 (July 6, 1843). According to a letter from a Millerite named David Plum, "more than two hundred" had been converted in Utica, New York, "through the instrumentality of one sister." See *The Midnight Cry* 3, nos. 3 and 4 (March 3, 1843).

52. See E[mily] C. Clemons, "Redemption Nigh," *The Advent Herald* 7, nos. 1 and 2 (February 14, 1844). For these two poems, see *The Voice of Truth* 5, nos. 10 and 11 (March 19, 1845), and *The Advent Herald* 11, no. 3 (February 25, 1846). For a partial list of Clemons's articles, see the Bibliography. Her output was so prodigious that a full listing is impossible. Her poems and articles appear in virtually every Millerite periodical, often identified only by her initials, "E.C.C." A manuscript letter from her to William Miller is reprinted in Francis D. Nichol, *The Midnight Cry* (Takoma Park, Md.: Review and Herald Publishing Association, 1944), pp. 478–80.

53. I was unable to locate a single extant copy of *Hope Within the Veil*. The American Antiquarian Society owns one issue of *The Hope of Israel* (Portland, Maine) and several of *The Bible Advocate* (Hartford, Conn.). *The Bible Advocate* is also available on microfilm as part of the sixty-reel microfilm series on "The Millerites and Early Adventists" available from University Microfilms International, Ann Arbor, Michigan. Clemons was praised for writing "clearly and powerfully" by a correspondent to *The Voice of Truth* 11, no. 4 (July 22, 1846). For letters from Clemons, see *The Midnight Cry* 7, no. 17 (October 19, 1844); *The Advent Herald* 10, no. 21 (December 31, 1845); and *The Voice of Truth* 3, no. 4 (August 28, 1844); 4, no. 8 (December 18, 1844); 5, nos. 8 and 9 (March 12, 1845); and 5, nos. 10 and 11 (March 19, 1845). For letters or articles that mention her, see *The Midnight Cry* 7, no. 4 (August 8, 1844); 7, no. 3 (August 1, 1844); and 7, no. 16 (October 12, 1844). See also *The Voice of Truth* 5, no. 3 (February 12, 1845), and 7, no. 11 (September 10, 1845).

54. The phrase comes from *Jane Marsh* Parker, *The Midnight Cry: A Novel* (New York: Dodd, Mead, and Co., 1886), p. 118.

55. *The Midnight Cry* 4, no. 19 (July 6, 1843).

56. On Ongley and her husband, see *The Voice of Truth* 11, no. 11 (September 9, 1846); 12, no. 5 (October 28, 1846); 13, no. 13 (March 24, 1847); and 8, no. 12 (December 18, 1845).

57. The emphasis is mine. For more information on the Brewers, see *The Midnight Cry* 7, no. 12 (September 26, 1844); 7, no. 9 (September 5, 1844); 7, no. 10 (September 12, 1844); and 7, no. 17 (October 19, 1844). See also *The Advent Herald* 10, no. 7 (September 24, 1845). I have included "Sister" Brewer on my list of female preachers in the Appendix because of several references to her and her husband "laboring" together.

58. E[mily] C. C[lemons], "A Voice from Slave Land," *The Advent Message to the Daughters of Zion* 1, no 2 (September 1844): 35. The emphasis is mine.

59. Truth became a "great favorite" at Millerite camp meetings. A riveting preacher, Truth was renowned for her "remarkable gift in prayer, and still more remarkable talent for singing." Olive Gilbert, *Narrative of Sojourner Truth; A Bondswoman of Olden Time, With a History of Her Labors and Correspondence Drawn from Her "Book of Life"* (Battle Creek, Mich., 1878; reprint, New York: Oxford University Press, 1991), pp. 110–14. For more on Truth's association with the Millerites, see Nell Irvin Painter, *Sojourner Truth: A Life, a Symbol* (New York: Norton, 1996), pp. 79–87. On Grimké, see Gerda Lerner, *The Grimké Sisters from South Carolina: Rebels against Slavery* (Boston: Houghton Mifflin, 1967).

60. *Signs of the Times*, June 28, 1843, quoted in Doan, *Miller Heresy*, p. 269n. "Perfectionism and Millerism United," *Baptist Register*, April 16, 1844, quoted in Rowe, *Thunder and Trumpets*, p. 128.

61. Parker, *Midnight Cry*, pp. 182, 164.

62. *The Advent Herald* 8, no. 12 (October 30, 1844). In October of 1844, just a few weeks before the expected return of Christ, Martha Spence reported that Millerites in Toronto, Canada, were holding meetings all day because they did not believe it was "consistent to follow their daily occupations, as time is short." *The Midnight Cry* 7, no. 16 (October 12, 1844).

63. *Christian Reflector*, January 18, 1843, quoted in Doan, *Miller Heresy*, p. 153. Doan provides a useful discussion of nineteenth-century attitudes toward work, pp. 151–58.

64. Boutelle, *Sketch*, p. 209; Parker, "A Little Millerite," pp. 315–16; Dick, "Millerite Movement," p. 29; and Boutelle, *Sketch*, p. 211.

65. *The Advent Herald* 8, no. 11 (October 16, 1844). The description of the "rapture" comes from Clemons, "The Last Day," p. 12.

66. See the letter from George Grigg in *The Midnight Cry* 7, no. 18 (October 31, 1844), and the letter from C. S. Minor in *The Voice of Truth* 5, nos. 10 and 11 (March 19, 1845). See also the account of their "fanaticism" in *The Voice of Truth* 6, no. 1 (April 2, 1845).

67. Parker, "A Little Millerite," p. 316. Hiram Edson, undated manuscript, Heritage Room, Andrews University Library, reprinted in the appendix to Numbers and Butler, *The Disappointed*, p. 215. The preacher Sarah Higgins wrote, "I confess I have been disappointed. I did believe with all my soul that I should see the 'King in his beauty' on the tenth day of the seventh month [October 22, 1844], and when the day had passed, I felt like sitting alone and weeping." *Midnight Cry* 7, no. 22 (November 28, 1844). See also Parker, *Midnight Cry*, p. 141.

68. *Sketches of the Christian Life and Public Labors of William Miller*, ed. James White (Battle Creek, Mich.: Seventh-Day Adventist Publishing Association, 1875), p. 310, quoted in Dick, "Millerite Movement," p. 30; and Boutelle, *Sketch*, p. 211.

69. *The Voice of Truth* 10, no. 7 (May 13, 1846). For contemporary descriptions of the "door-shutters," see *The Morning Watch* 8, no. 24 (June 12, 1845); *The Advent Herald* 10, no. 9 (October 8, 1845); and *The Advent Herald* 10, no. 21 (December 31, 1845). For a fuller discussion of the

competing sects which emerged out of the Millerite movement, see Godfrey T. Anderson, "Sectarianism and Organization, 1846–1864," in Land, *Adventism in America*, pp. 36–65; and Rowe, *Thunder and Trumpets*, pp. 141–60. On Ellen White and the Seventh-Day Adventists, see Ronald L. Numbers, *Prophetess of Health: Ellen G. White and the Origins of Seventh-Day Adventist Health Reform* (Knoxville: University of Tennessee Press, 1992); and Jonathan M. Butler, "The Making of a New Order: Millerism and the Origins of Seventh-Day Adventism," in Numbers and Butler, *The Disappointed*, pp. 189–208. On Spence, see Juanita Brooks, ed., *Not by Bread Alone: The Journal of Martha Spence Heywood, 1850–56* (Salt Lake City: Utah State Historical Society, 1978). On the Shakers, see Lawrence Foster, "Had Prophecy Failed? Contrasting Perspectives of the Millerites and Shakers," in Numbers and Butler, *The Disappointed*, pp. 173–88. For a personal account of one man's conversion from Millerism to Shakerism, see Henry B. Bear, *Henry B. Bear's Advent Experiences* (Whitewater, Ohio: n.p., n.d.), reprinted in the appendix to Numbers and Butler, *The Disappointed*, pp. 217–26.

70. See "Warning to Adventists," *The Morning Watch* 8, no. 14 (April 3, 1845).

71. Josiah Litch, "History of the Adventists," in Winebrenner, *History*, pp. 37–41; and *Proceedings of the Mutual Conference of Adventists Held in the City of Albany* (New York: n.p., 1845).

72. Isaiah 55:13. Clorinda Minor, *Meshullam! or, Tidings from Jerusalem. From the Journal of a Believer Recently Returned from the Holy Land*, 2d ed. (Philadelphia: John C. Robb, 1851), pp. 71, x–xi. See also Clorinda S. Minor, *The New Earth: A Poem* (Philadelphia: Barrett and Jones, 1842). For other information about her, see Lester I. Vogel, *To See a Promised Land: Americans and the Holy Land in the Nineteenth Century* (University Park, Pa.: Pennsylvania State University Press, 1993), pp. 128–32; V. D. Lipman, ed., *Americans and the Holy Land through British Eyes, 1820–1917: A Documentary History* (London: V. D. Lipman, in association with the Self Pub. Association, 1989), pp. 119–25, 127–31; Ruth Kark, "Millenarism and Agricultural Settlement in the Holy Land in the Nineteenth Century," *Journal of Historical Geography* 9 (1983): 47–62; and Moshe Davis, ed., *With Eyes toward Zion*, vol. 4 of *America and the Holy Land* (New York: Arno Press, 1977), pp. 183–86.

73. See Mary D. Wellcome, *A Sketch Being a Vindication of the Writer's Course in Regard to Her Public Works in the Cause of God; and Final Separation from Her Family* (Augusta, Maine: Farmers Office, 1856), and Abigail Mussey, *Life Sketches and Experiences* (Cambridge, Mass.: Dakin and Metcalf, 1866). On White, see Numbers, *Prophetess of Health*, pp. 26, 201, and Jonathan M. Butler, "Prophecy, Gender, and Culture: Ellen Gould Harmon [White] and the Roots of Seventh-Day Adventism," *Religion and American Culture* 1 (Winter 1991): 3–29.

74. Henry Grew, "On Women Speaking in the Church," *Advent Harbinger and Bible Advocate* (Rochester, N.Y.) 2 (December 14, 1850): 208. Z. G. Bliss quoted in Craig R. Dunham, *Women Ministers?! Women in Paul and Advent Christendom* (Lenox, Mass.: Henceforth Publications, 1986), p. 20.

75. "Declaration of Sentiments," in *History of Woman Suffrage*, ed. Elizabeth Cady Stanton, Susan B. Anthony, and Matilda Joslyn Gage (New York: Fowler and Wells, 1881; reprint, New York: Arno Press, 1969), 1:70–73.

76. On the religious roots of the nineteenth-century women's rights movement, see Nancy Gale Isenberg, " 'Coequality of the Sexes': The Feminist Discourse of the Antebellum Women's Rights Movement in America" (Ph.D. diss., University of Wisconsin–Madison, 1990), and Catherine A. Brekus, " 'Restoring the Divine Order to the World': Religion and the Family in the Antebellum Woman's Rights Movement," in *Religion, Feminism, and the Family*, ed. Anne Carr and Mary Stewart Van Leeuwen (Louisville, Ky.: Westminster John Knox Press, 1995), pp. 166–82.

77. Beulah Matthewson, *Woman from a Bible Stand-point; or Do the Scriptures Forbid the Public Labor of Woman* (Boston: Advent Christian Publication Society, 1873), p. 7. See also Beulah Matthewson, "Female Preaching," *Advent Harbinger and Bible Advocate* 4 (June 26, 1852): 10.

EPILOGUE

1. *The Morning Watch* 8, no. 15 (April 10, 1845), and *The Voice of Truth* 7, no. 7 (August 13, 1845). *The Voice of Truth* 11, no. 10 (September 2, 1846).

2. Harriet Livermore, *A Narration of Religious Experience* (Concord, N.H.: Jacob B. Moore, 1826), pp. 15, 202.

3. Nancy Towle, *Vicissitudes Illustrated, in the Experience of Nancy Towle, in Europe and America*, 2d ed. (Portsmouth, N.H.: John Caldwell, 1833), pp. 10–11, 121.

4. For Bangs's defense of Phoebe Palmer, see Abel Stevens, *Life and Times of Nathan Bangs* (New York: Carlton and Porter, 1863), p. 351. Richard Wheately, *The Life and Letters of Phoebe Palmer* (1881; reprint, New York: Garland Publishing, 1984), p. 614. See also Harold E. Raser, *Phoebe Palmer: Her Life and Thought* (Lewiston, N.Y.: Edwin Mellen Press, 1987), pp. 76–79.

5. See Russell E. Richey, *Early American Methodism* (Bloomington: Indiana University Press, 1991), p. xii.

6. See Janette Hassey, *No Time for Silence: Evangelical Women in Public Ministry around the Turn of the Century* (Grand Rapids, Mich.: Academie Books, 1986), pp. 81–94; David G. Roebuck, "Pentecostal Women in Ministry: A Review of Selected Documents," *Perspectives in Religious Studies* 16 (Spring 1989): 29–44; Edith L. Blumhofer, *Aimee Semple McPherson: Everybody's Sister* (Grand Rapids, Mich.: Eerdmans, 1993); and John R. Rice, *Bobbed Hair, Bossy Wives, and Women Preachers: Significant Questions for Honest Christian Women Settled by the Word of God* (Wheaton, Ill.: Sword of the Lord Publishers, 1941). On women in the fundamentalist movement, see Betty A. DeBerg, *Ungodly Women: Gender and the First Wave of American Fundamentalism* (Minneapolis: Fortress Press, 1990), and Margaret Lamberts Bendroth, *Fundamentalism and Gender, 1875 to the Present* (New Haven: Yale University Press, 1993).

7. Anna Oliver, "Test Case on the Ordination of Women" (New York: W. N. Jennings, 1880), reprinted in *Sourcebook of American Methodism*, ed. Frederick A. Norwood (Nashville: Abingdon Press, 1982), p. 450. On Oliver, see Kenneth E. Rowe, ed., "The Ordination of Women: Round One; Anna Oliver and the General Conference of 1880," in *Perspectives on American Methodism: Interpretive Essays*, ed. Russell E. Richey, Kenneth E. Rowe, and Jean Miller Schmidt (Nashville: Kingswood Books, 1993), pp. 298–308.

8. On women's ordination, see Barbara Brown Zikmund, "Winning Ordination for Women in Mainstream Protestant Churches," in *Women and Religion in America*, ed. Rosemary Radford Ruether and Rosemary Skinner Keller (San Francisco: Harper and Row, 1986), 3:339–48; Virginia Lieson Brereton and Christa Ressmeyer Klein, "American Women in Ministry: A History of Protestant Beginning Points," in *Women in American Religion*, ed. Janet Wilson James (Philadelphia: University of Pennsylvania Press, 1980), pp. 171–90; and Mark Chaves, *Ordaining Women: Culture and Conflict in Religious Organizations* (Cambridge: Harvard University Press, 1997). See also Nancy A. Hardesty, *Your Daughters Shall Prophesy: Revivalism and Feminism in the Age of Finney* (Brooklyn, N.Y.: Carlson Publishing, 1991), and Cynthia Grant Tucker, *Prophetic Sisterhood: Liberal Women Ministers of the Frontier, 1880–1930* (Boston: Beacon Press, 1990).

9. For an extended discussion of this theme, see Gerda Lerner, *The Creation of Feminist Consciousness: From the Middle Ages to Eighteen-seventy* (New York: Oxford University Press, 1993).

Bibliography

PRIMARY SOURCES

Memoirs, Tracts, and Articles Written by Female Preachers and Exhorters

Bradley, Mary. *A Narrative of the Life and Christian Experience of Mrs. Mary Bradley*. Boston: Strong and Broadhead, 1849.

Brooks, Juanita, ed. *Not by Bread Alone: The Journal of Martha Spence Heywood, 1850–56*. Salt Lake City: Utah State Historical Society, 1978.

Caldwell, Nancy. *Walking with God: Leaves from the Journal of Mrs. Nancy Caldwell*. Edited by Rev. James O. Thompson. Keyser, W.Va.: n.p., 1886.

Clemons, E[mily] C. "All Things Made New." *The Advent Herald* 8, no. 9 (October 2, 1844).

——. "And at Midnight There Was a Cry Made." *The Voice of Truth* 6, no. 1 (April 2, 1845).

——. " 'Because They Have No Changes, They Fear Not God.' " *The Advent Herald* 8, no. 5 (September 4, 1844).

——. "Death at Hand Instead of Judgement." *The Voice of Truth* 2, no. 1 (May 11, 1844).

——. "Extracts from Old Writers." *The Advent Herald* 8, no. 6 (September 11, 1844).

——. "Faith." *The Voice of Truth* 1, no. 6 (March 23, 1844).

——. "The Final Adieu Versus Resurrection." *The Voice of Truth* 2, no. 8 (June 29, 1844).

——. "The General Resurrection." *The Advent Herald* 10, no. 5 (April 29, 1846).

——. "The Good Old Way." *The Advent Herald* 8, no. 5 (September 4, 1844).

——. "He that Winneth Souls is Wise." *The Bible Advocate* 1, no. 1 (July 11, 1846).

——. "The Hope of the Gospel." *The Voice of Truth* 2, no. 5 (June 8, 1844).

——. "If Any Man Worship the Beast." *The Voice of Truth* 5, nos. 12 and 13 (March 26, 1845).

——. "The Jonahs." *The Voice of Truth* 2, no. 6 (June 15, 1844).

——. "The Just Shall Live by Faith." *The Voice of Truth* 6, no. 1 (April 2, 1845).

——. Letter to William Miller. Reprinted in Francis D. Nichol, *The Midnight Cry*, pp. 478–80. Takoma Park, Md.: Review and Herald Publishing Association, 1944.

——. "Lord, Teach Us to Pray." *The Voice of Truth* 4, no. 9 (December 25, 1844).

——. "Love for the World." *The Voice of Truth* 2, no. 4 (June 1, 1844).

——. "The Martyrs." *The Advent Herald* 8, no. 20 (December 25, 1844).

——. "Of Life, Death, and Resurrection." *The Voice of Truth* 9, no. 13 (March 25, 1846); 10, nos. 1 and 2 (April 1, 1846).

——. "Of the Coming Destruction." *The Voice of Truth* 2, no. 8 (June 29, 1844).

——. "Pilate and Herod Made Friends. Part I." *The Advent Herald* 7, no. 11, (April 17, 1844).

——. "Pilate and Herod Made Friends. Part II." *The Advent Herald* 7, no. 12 (April 24, 1844); no. 13 (May 1, 1844).

——. "The Reaping Time." *The Advent Herald* 8, no. 23 (January 15, 1845).

——. "Redemption Nigh." *The Advent Herald* 7, nos. 1 and 2 (February 14, 1844).

——. "Two Disciples Going to Emmaus." *The Voice of Truth* 2, no. 12 (July 27, 1844).

——. "A Voice from Slave Land." *The Advent Message to the Daughters of Zion* 1, no. 2 (September 1844): 35.

Cram, Nancy Gove. *A Collection of Hymns and Poems. Designed to Instruct the Inquirer; and Furnish the Public with a Small Variety*. Schenectady: n.p., 1815.

Elaw, Zilpha. *Memoirs of the Life, Religious Experience, Ministerial Travels and Labours of Mrs. Zilpha Elaw, An American Female of Colour*. London, 1846. Reprinted in *Sisters of the Spirit: Three Black Women's Autobiographies of the Nineteenth Century*, edited by William L. Andrews. Bloomington: University of Indiana, 1986.

Elizabeth, A Colored Minister of the Gospel, Born in Slavery. Philadelphia: Tract Association of Friends, 1889.

Foote, Julia A. J. *A Brand Plucked From the Fire: An Autobiographical Sketch*. Cleveland: W. F. Schneider, 1879. Reprinted in *Sisters of the Spirit: Three Black Women's Autobiographies of the Nineteenth Century*, edited by William L. Andrews. Bloomington: University of Indiana, 1986.

Haviland, Laura Smith. *A Woman's Life-Work: Labors and Experiences of Laura S. Haviland*. 4th ed. Chicago: Publishing Association of Friends, 1889.

Higgins, Sarah J. "The Power of Faith." *The Midnight Cry* 7, no. 16 (October 12, 1844).

——. "The Secret of the Lord is With Them that Fear Him." *The Midnight Cry* 7, no. 16 (October 12, 1844).

Humez, Jean McMahon, ed. *Gifts of Power: The Writings of Rebecca Jackson, Black Visionary, Shaker Eldress*. Amherst: University of Massachusetts Press, 1981.

Knight, Elleanor Warner. *A Narrative of the Christian Experience, Life and Adventures, Trials and Labours of Elleanor Knight, Written by Herself*. Providence: n.p., 1839.

Lee, Jarena. *The Life and Religious Experience of Mrs. Jarena Lee, A Coloured Lady, Giving an Account of her Call to Preach the Gospel*. Philadelphia, 1836. Reprinted in *Sisters of the Spirit: Three Black Women's Autobiographies of the Nineteenth Century*, edited by William L. Andrews. Bloomington: University of Indiana, 1986.

——. *Religious Experience and Journal of Mrs. Jarena Lee, Giving the Account of Her Call to Preach the Gospel*. Philadelphia: printed for the author, 1849. Reprinted in *Spiritual Narratives*, edited by Sue E. Houchins. New York: Oxford University Press, 1988.

Livermore, Harriet. *Addresses to the Dispersed of Judah*. Philadelphia: L. R. Bailey, 1849.

——. *The Anointed Shepherd at the War Camp of Israel*. Philadelphia: the authoress, 1856.

——. *The Counsel of God, Immutable and Everlasting*. Philadelphia: L. R. Bailey, 1844.

——. *An Epistle of Love*. Philadelphia: J. Rakestraw, 1826.

——. *The Glory of the Lord in the Land of the Living, By Redemption of the Purchased Possession, To the Praise of His Glory*. New York: J. D. Bedford, 1842.

——. *The Harp of Israel, to Meet the Loud Echo in the Wilds of America*. Philadelphia: J. Rakestraw, 1835.

——. *A Letter to John Ross, the Principal Chief of the Cherokee Nation*. Philadelphia: published by Harriet Livermore, 1838.

——. *Millennial Tidings*, no. 1. Philadelphia: Harriet Livermore, 1831.

——. *Millennial Tidings*, no. 4. Philadelphia: Harriet Livermore, 1839.

——. *A Narration of Religious Experience*. Concord, N.H.: Jacob B. Moore, 1826.

——. *Scriptural Evidence in Favor of Female Testimony in Meetings for the Worship of God*. Portsmouth, N.H.: R. Foster, 1824.

——. *A Testimony for the Times*. New York: Piercy and Reed, 1843.

——. *Thoughts on Important Subjects*. Philadelphia: Crissy and Markley, 1864.

——. *A Wreath from Jessamine Lawn; or, Free Grace, the Flower that Never Fades*. Philadelphia: printed for the authoress, 1831.

Major, Sarah Righter. "Pamphlet." 1835. Reprinted in Donald F. Durnbaugh, ed., "She Kept on Preaching." *Messenger* (Church of the Brethren) 124 (April 1975): 18–21.

Marden, E. J. *A Letter from Mrs. E. J. Marden, of Bangor, Maine. Containing her Experience in the Blessing of Entire Sanctification; Also an Account of Her Receiving, by Faith, the Doctrine of the Second Advent of Our Lord Jesus Christ in 1843*. Haverhill, Mass.: Essex Banner Office, 1842.

Matthewson, Beulah. "Female Preaching." *Advent Harbinger and Bible Advocate* 4 (June 26, 1852): 10.

——. *God's Plan of Giving and Sacrifice*. Boston: Advent Christian Publication Society, 1892.

——. *Woman from a Bible Stand-point; or Do the Scriptures Forbid the Public Labor of Woman*. Boston: Advent Christian Publication Society, 1873.

Miller, Rebecca. "Duty of Females." *Christian Palladium* 10, no. 2 (May 15, 1841): 21–22.

——. "Female Improvement." *Christian Palladium* 10, no. 3 (June 1, 1841): 35–36.

——. "Immortality of the Soul." *Christian Palladium* 11, no. 4 (June 15, 1842): 54–55.

——. "Incentives to Duty." *Christian Palladium* 9, no. 3 (June 1, 1840): 37–38.

Minor, Clorinda. *Meshullam! or, Tidings from Jerusalem. From the Journal of a Believer Recently Returned from the Holy Land*. 2d ed. Philadelphia: John C. Robb, 1851.

——. *The New Earth: A Poem*. Philadelphia: Barrett and Jones, 1842.

Newell, Fanny. *Memoirs of Fanny Newell; Written by Herself, and Published by the Desire and Request of Numerous Friends*. 3d ed. Springfield and New York: n.p., 1833.

Peirce, Deborah. *A Scriptural Vindication of Female Preaching*. Carmel, N.Y.: E. Burroughs, 1820.

Rice, Olive Maria. "The Labors of Olive Maria Rice." *The Midnight Cry* 4, no. 19 (July 6, 1843).

S. A. "The Rights of Females." *Christian Palladium* 9, no. 20 (February 15, 1841): 306–7.

Sexton, Lydia. *Autobiography of Lydia Sexton*. Dayton, Ohio: United Brethren Publishing House, 1882.

Seymour, Mary A. "The Bridegroom." *Voice of Truth* 8, no. 9 (November 26, 1845).

——. "Charity! Charity!!" *Voice of Truth* 5, no. 1 (January 29, 1845).

——. *The Excellency of the Lord's Anointed or Christ the Promised Messiah*. Hillsdale, Mich.: H. B. Rowlson, 1855.

——. "Millerites and Ascension Robes." *Voice of Truth* 5, no. 1 (January 29, 1845).

——. "Women May Preach." *Advent Harbinger and Bible Advocate* 2 (December 14, 1850): 108; 2 (March 26, 1851): 354; 2 (June 14, 1851): 410; and 3 (July 19, 1951): 35.

Stevens, Polly. "A Defence." Reprinted in Philetus Roberts, *Memoir of Mrs. Abigail Roberts; An Account of Her Birth, Early Education, Call to the Ministry*, p. 197. Irvington, N.J.: Moses Cummings, 1858.

Stewart, Ellen. *Life of Mrs. Ellen Stewart, Together with Biographical Sketches of Other Individuals. Also, A Discussion with Two Clergymen, and Arguments in Favor of Woman's Rights*. Akron, Ohio: Beebe and Elkins, 1858.

Thomas, Cordelia. *The Sheaf; or, The Work of God in the Soul; As Illustrated in the Personal Experiences of Mrs. Cordelia Thomas*. Boston: H. V. Degen, 1852.

Towle, Nancy. *Some of the Writings, and Last Sentences, of Adolphus Dewey, Executed at Montreal, Aug. 30, 1833*. Montreal: J. A. Hoisington, 1833.

——. *Vicissitudes Illustrated, in the Experience of Nancy Towle, in Europe and America*. 2d ed. Portsmouth, N.H.: John Caldwell, 1833.

Wellcome, Mary D. "Faith and Obedience." Part 1, *World's Crisis* 2 (April 26, 1854): 2–3; Part 2, *World's Crisis* 2 (May 3, 1854): 3; Part 3, *World's Crisis* 2 (May 10, 1854): 4; Part 4, *World's Crisis* 2 (May 31, 1854): 3; Part 5, *World's Crisis* 2 (June 17, 1854): 2; Part 6, *World's Crisis* 2 (July 12, 1854): 1.

——. *A Sketch Being a Vindication of the Writer's Course in Regard to Her Public Works in the Cause of God; and Final Separation from Her Family*. Augusta, Maine: Farmers Office, 1856.

Nineteenth-Century Biographies of Female Preachers

An Account of the Singular Case of Rachel Becker, the Celebrated Somniloquist, or Sleeping Preacher. New York: J. W. Butler, 1815.

Brown, George. *The Lady Preacher; Or, the Life and Labors of Mrs. Hannah Reeves, Late the Wife of the Rev. William Reeves of the Methodist Church*. Philadelphia: Daughaday and Becker; Springfield, Ohio: Methodist Publishing House, 1870.

"A Colored Teacher." *National Anti-Slavery Standard*, April 7, 1842, p. 174.

Davis, Almond H. *The Female Preacher, or Memoir of Salome Lincoln*. Providence, 1843. Reprint, New York: Arno Press, 1972.

Fassett, O. R. *The Biography of Mrs. L. E. Fassett, a Devoted Christian, a Useful Life*. Boston: Advent Christian Publication Society, 1885.

Gilbert, Olive. *Narrative of Sojourner Truth; A Bondswoman of Olden Time, With a History of Her Labors and Correspondence Drawn from Her "Book of Life."* Battle Creek, Mich., 1878. Reprint, New York: Oxford University Press, 1991.

[——]. *Narrative of Sojourner Truth, A Northern Slave*. Boston: printed for the author, 1850.

"Harriet Livermore." *Southern Literary Messenger* (Richmond, Va.) 7, no. 2 (February 1841): 156.

"Mrs. Hannah Reeves, Preacher of the Gospel." *Methodist Quarterly Review* 59 (July 1877): 430–47.

Roberts, Philetus. *Memoir of Mrs. Abigail Roberts; An Account of Her Birth, Early Education, Call to the Ministry*. Irvington, N.J.: Moses Cummings, 1858.

Lay Women's Religious Writings

Andrews, C. W. *Memoir of Mrs. Ann R. Page*. 2d ed. New York: Protestant Episcopal Society for the Promotion of Evangelical Knowledge, 1856. Reprint, New York: Garland Publishing, 1987.

The Diary of Mary Cooper: Life on a Long Island Farm. Edited by Field Horne. Oyster Bay, N.Y.: Oyster Bay Historical Society, 1981.

Edwards, Sarah. "Narrative." In *The Works of Jonathan Edwards*, edited by Sereno Dwight, 1:civ–cxii. London: William Ball, 1839.

Grimké, Sarah M. *Letters on the Equality of the Sexes and the Condition of Woman*. New York: Burt Franklin, 1837.

Hopkins, Samuel, ed. *Memoirs of the Life of Mrs. Sarah Osborne who Died at Newport*. 2d ed. Catskill, N.Y.: N. Elliot, 1814.

Ingraham, Sarah R., comp. *Walks of Usefulness, or Reminiscences of Mrs. Margaret Prior*. New York: American Female Moral Reform Society, 1843. Reprint, New York: Garland Publishing, 1987.

Letters Addressed to Dorothy Ripley from Several Africans and Indians, on Subjects of Christian Experience. Chester: J. Hemingway, 1807.

Parker, Jane Marsh. "A Little Millerite." *Century Magazine* 11 (November 1886–April 1887): 312–17.

Ripley, Dorothy. *The Bank of Faith and Works United*. Philadelphia: J. H. Cunningham, 1819.

——. *The Extraordinary Conversion and Religious Experience of Dorothy Ripley, With Her First Voyage and Travels in America*. New York: G. & R. Waite, 1810.

Stewart, Maria. *Productions of Mrs. Maria W. Stewart, Presented to the First African Baptist Church and Society of the City of Boston*. Boston, 1835. Reprinted in *Spiritual Narratives*, edited by Sue E. Houchins. New York: Oxford University Press, 1988.

——. *Religion and the Pure Principles of Morality*. Boston, 1831. Reprinted in *Early Negro Writing, 1760–1837*, edited by Dorothy Porter. Boston: Beacon Press, 1971.

Williams, Catherine Reed. *Fall River: An Authentic Narrative*. Providence: Marshall, Brown, and Company, 1834.

The Shakers and the Universal Friends

Brown, Thomas. *An Account of the People called Shakers*. Troy, N.Y.: Parker and Bliss, 1812.

Evans, Frederick W. *Ann Lee (The Founder of the Shakers), A Biography, with Memoirs*. 4th ed. Mount Lebanon, N.Y.: F. W. Evans, 1869.

Rathbun, Daniel. *A Letter from Daniel Rathbun*. Springfield, Mass.: n.p., 1785.

Rathbun, Reuben. *Reasons Offered for Leaving the Shakers*. Pittsfield, Mass.: Chester Smith, 1800.

Rathbun, Valentine. *An Account of the Matter, Form, and Manner of a New and Strange Religion, Taught and Propagated by a Number of Europeans*. Providence: Bennett Wheeler, 1781.

Shakers. *Testimonies of the Life, Character, Revelations, and Doctrines of Our Ever Blessed Mother Ann Lee*. Hancock, Mass.: Tallcott and Deming, 1816.

Taylor, Amos. *A Narrative of the Strange Principles, Conduct and Character of the People Known by the Name of Shakers*. Worcester, Mass.: Isaiah Thomas, 1782.

West, Benjamin. *Scriptural Cautions Against Embracing a Religious Scheme, Taught by a Number of Europeans*. Hartford: Bavil Webster, 1783.

[Wilkinson, Jemima]. *The Universal Friend's Advice to Those of the Same Religious Society*. 1784. Reprinted in Herbert A. Wisbey Jr., *Pioneer Prophetess: Jemima Wilkinson, the Publick Universal Friend*, pp. 197–204. Ithaca: Cornell University Press, 1964.

Youngs, Benjamin Seth. *Testimony of Christ's Second Appearing*. Lebanon, Ohio: John M'Clean, 1808.

Writings by Eighteenth-Century Clergymen

Bartlett, Moses. *False and Seducing Teachers to be Expected in the Gospel State, and Latter Days of the Church*. New London: John Green, 1757.

Beales, Ross W., Jr., ed. "Solomon Prentice's Narrative of the Great Awakening." *Proceedings of the Massachusetts Historical Society* 83 (1971): 130–47.

Bellamy, Joseph. *True Religion Delineated; or, Experimental Religion, as Distinguished from Formality on the One Hand, and Enthusiasm on the Other, Set in a Spiritual and Rational Light*. Boston: Kneeland, 1750.

Bowen, Nathan. "Extracts from Interleaved Almanacs of Nathan Bowen, 1742–1799." *The Essex Institute Historical Collections* 41 (1955).

Buell, Samuel. *A Faithful Narrative of the Remarkable Revival of Religion, in the Congregation of East-Hampton, on Long Island, in the Year of Our Lord 1764*. New York: Samuel Brown, 1766.

Burkitt, Lemuel, and Jesse Read. *A Concise History of the Kehukee Baptist Association from its Original Rise Down to 1803*. 1850. Reprint, New York: Arno Press, 1980.

Caldwell, John. *An Impartial Trial of the Spirit Operating in This Part of the World*. Boston: Thomas Fleet, 1742.

Chauncy, Charles. *Enthusiasm Described and Cautioned Against*. Boston, 1742. Reprinted in *The Great Awakening: Documents Illustrating the Crisis and Its Consequences*, edited by Alan Heimert and Perry Miller. Indianapolis: Bobbs-Merrill, 1967.

[———]. *A Letter from a Gentleman in Boston, to Mr. George Wishart, One of the Ministers of Edinburgh, Concerning the State of Religion in New England*. Edinburgh: n.p., 1742. Reprinted in *Religious Enthusiasm and the Great Awakening*, edited by David S. Lovejoy. Englewood Cliffs, N.J.: Prentice-Hall, 1969.

———. *Seasonable Thoughts on the State of Religion in New England*. 1743. Reprint, New York: Regina Press, 1975.

[———]. *The Wonderful Narrative, or, a Faithful Account of the French Prophets, Their Agitations, Extasies, and Inspirations*. Glasgow: Robert Foulis, 1742.

Cleaveland, John. *A Short and Plain Narrative of the Late Work of God's Spirit at Chebacco in Ipswich, in the Years 1763 and 1764*. Boston: Fowle and Freeman, 1767.

Croswell, Andrew. *A Letter from the Reverend Mr. Croswell to the Reverend Mr. Turell*. Boston: Rogers and Fowle, 1742.

Davenport, James. *The Reverend Mr. Davenport's Confessions and Retractions*. Boston: Kneeland and Green, 1744.

Devotion, Ebenezer. *An Answer to the Pastor and Brethren of the Third Church in Windham to Twelve Articles Exhibited by Several of its Separating Members*. New London: T. Green, 1747.

The Diary of Isaac Backus. Edited by William G. McLoughlin. 3 vols. Providence: Brown University Press, 1979.

The Diary of Joshua Hempstead of New London, Connecticut. In *Collections of the New London County Historical Society*. Vol. 1. New London: New London County Historical Society, 1901.

Dickinson, Jonathan. *A Display of God's Special Grace*. Boston: Rogers and Fowle, 1742.

———. *Familiar Letters to a Gentleman*. Boston: Rogers & Fowle and Blanchard, 1745.

Edwards, Jonathan. *An Account of the Life of the Late Reverend David Brainerd*. In *The Life of David Brainerd*, edited by Norman Pettit. New Haven: Yale University Press, 1985.

———. *The Distinguishing Marks of a Work of God*. In *The Great Awakening*, edited by C. C. Goen, pp. 226–88. New Haven: Yale University Press, 1972.

———. *A Faithful Narrative of the Surprising Work of God*. . . . In *The Great Awakening*, edited by C. C. Goen, pp. 144–211. New Haven: Yale University Press, 1972.

———. *Personal Narrative*. In *Jonathan Edwards: Representative Selections*, edited by Clarence H. Faust and Thomas H. Johnson, pp. 57–72. New York: Hill and Wang, 1962.

———. *Some Thoughts Concerning the Present Revival*. In *The Great Awakening*, edited by C. C. Goen, pp. 291–530. New Haven: Yale University Press, 1972.

———. *The State of Religion at Northampton in the County of Hampshire, About a Hundred Miles West-*

ward of Boston. In *The Great Awakening*, edited by C. C. Goen, pp. 544–57. New Haven: Yale University Press, 1972.

——. *A Treatise Concerning Religious Affections.* In *Religious Affections*, edited by John E. Smith, pp. 93–461. New Haven: Yale University Press, 1959.

Edwards, Morgan. *The Customs of Primitive Churches.* Philadelphia: n.p., 1768.

——. *Materials Towards a History of the Baptists.* 2 vols. Philadelphia: Joseph Crukshank and Isaac Collins, 1770. Reprint, Danielsville, Ga.: Heritage Papers, 1984.

Fish, Joseph. *The Church of Christ A Firm and Durable House.* New London: Timothy Green, 1767.

Frothingham, Ebenezer. *The Articles of Faith and Practice, with the Covenant, That is Confessed by the Separate Churches of Christ in General in This Land.* Newport: J. Franklin, 1750.

——. *A Key to Unlock the Door, that Leads in, to Take a Fair View of the Religious Constitution, Established by Law, in the Colony of Connecticut.* New Haven: n.p., 1767.

Hancock, John. *The Danger of an Unqualified Ministry. . . .* Boston: Rogers and Fowle, 1743.

Hooker, Richard J., ed. *The Carolina Backcountry on the Eve of the Revolution: The Journal and Other Writings of Charles Woodmason, Anglican Itinerant.* Chapel Hill: University of North Carolina Press, 1953.

Killingly Convention of Strict Congregational Churches. *An Historical Narrative and Declaration, Shewing the Cause and Rise of the Strict Congregationalist Churches in the State of Connecticut.* Providence: n.p., 1781.

Parsons, Jonathan. *A Needful Caution in a Critical Day.* New London: T. Green, 1742.

Pickering, Theophilus. *The Rev. Mr. Pickerings' Letters to the Rev. N. Rogers and Mr. D. Rogers of Ipswich.* Boston: Thomas Fleet, 1742.

"Religious Excitement One Hundred and Odd Years Ago" [Extract from the Diary of Samuel Chandler, 1746]. *The New England Historical and Genealogical Register* 15 (1861): 23–24.

Ross, Robert. *A Plain Address to the Quakers, Moravians, Separatists. . . .* New Haven: Parker and Company, 1762.

Seccombe, Joseph. *Some Occasional Thoughts on the Influence of the Spirit.* Boston: Kneeland and Green, 1742.

Semple, Robert B. *A History of the Rise and Progress of the Baptists in Virginia.* Richmond: John O'Lynch, 1810.

Tennent, Gilbert. *The Danger of an Unconverted Ministry.* Boston, 1742. Reprinted in *The Great Awakening: Documents on the Revival of Religion, 1740–1745*, edited by Richard L. Bushman. New York: Atheneum, 1970; Chapel Hill: University of North Carolina Press, 1989.

Turell, Ebenezer. *Mr. Turell's Dialogue Between a Minister and His Neighbour About the Times.* 2d ed. Boston: Rogers and Fowle, 1742.

——. *Mr. Turell's Directions to his People with Relation to the Present Times.* Boston: Rogers and Fowle, 1742.

Whitefield, George. *George Whitefield's Journals.* Gainesville, Fla.: Scholars Facsimiles and Reprints, 1969.

Writings by Nineteenth-Century Clergymen

Abbott, Benjamin. *Experience and Gospel Labours of the Rev. Benjamin Abbott.* New York: J. Collord, 1832.

Adams, Henry Gardiner. *God's Image in Ebony.* London: Partridge and Oakey, 1854.

Allen, Richard. *The Life, Experience, and Gospel Labors of the Rt. Rev. Richard Allen.* 1833. Reprint, Nashville: Abingdon Press, 1960.

Allen, Stephen, and W. H. Pilsbury. *History of Methodism in Maine.* Augusta, Maine: C. E. Nash, 1887.

Andros, Thomas. *Discourse on Several Important Theological Subjects.* Boston: Samuel T. Armstrong, 1817.

Asbury, Francis. *The Journal of the Reverend Francis Asbury: Bishop of the Methodist Episcopal Church.* New York: N. Bangs and T. Mason, 1821.

Bailey, Wesley. "History of the Reformed Methodist Church." In *History of All the Religious Denominations in the United States*, edited by John Winebrenner, pp. 383–90. Harrisburg, Pa.: John Winebrenner, 1848.

Bangs, Heman. *The Autobiography and Journal of Rev. Heman Bangs.* New York: N. Tibbals and Son, 1872.

Bangs, John. *Autobiography of Reverend John Bangs, of the New York Annual Conference.* New York: n.p., 1846.

Batchelder, George W. *A Narrative of the Life, Travels, and Religious Experience, of George W. Batchelder.* Philadelphia: Barrett and Jones, 1843.

Bates, Joseph. *The Autobiography of Elder Joseph Bates: Embracing A Long Life on Shipboard . . . and a Brief Account of the Advent Movement of 1840–1844.* Battle Creek, Mich.: Seventh-Day Adventist Publishing Association, 1868.

Benedict, David. *A General History of the Baptist Denomination in America and Other Parts of the World.* 1813. New York: Lewis Colby and Company, 1850.

Bliss, Sylvester. *Memoirs of William Miller: Generally Known as a Lecturer on the Prophecies, and the Second Coming of Christ.* Boston: J. V. Himes, 1853.

Bolles, Lucius. *A Discourse Delivered Before the Members of the Salem Female Charitable Society.* Salem, Mass.: Thomas C. Cushing, 1810.

Boyd, Robert. *Personal Memoirs: Together With a Discussion Upon The Hardships and Sufferings of Itinerant Life.* Cincinnati: Methodist Book Concern, 1860.

Bradley, Joshua. *Accounts of Religious Revivals in Many Parts of the United States from 1815 to 1818.* Albany: G. J. Loomis & Co., 1819. Reprint, Wheaton, Ill.: Richard Owen Roberts, 1980.

Brown, George. *Recollections of Itinerant Life: Including Early Reminiscences.* Cincinnati: R. W. Carool, 1866.

Burritt, Charles D. *Methodism in Ithaca.* Ithaca: Andrus, Gauntlett, and Co., 1852.

Buzzell, John. *The Life of Elder Benjamin Randel.* Limerick, Maine: Hobbs, Woodman and Co., 1827.

Colby, John. *The Life, Experiences, and Travels of Elder John Colby.* Portland, Maine: n.p., 1815. Reprint, Newport, N.H.: French and Brown, 1831.

Coles, George. *Heroines of Methodism; or, Pen and Ink Sketches of the Mothers and Daughters of the Church.* New York: Carlton and Porter, 1857.

Constitution and Discipline of the Methodist Protestant Church. Baltimore: John J. Harrod, 1830.

Cooke, Parsons. *Female Preaching, Unlawful and Inexpedient. A Sermon.* Lynn, Mass.: James R. Newhall, 1837.

Day, George T. *The Life of Rev. Martin Cheney.* Providence: George H. Whitney, 1853.

Dow, Lorenzo. *The Dealings of God, Man, and the Devil, as Exemplified in the Life, Experience, and Travels of Lorenzo Dow, in a Period of More than Half a Century.* 4th ed. Norwich: William Faulkner, 1833.

———. *The Life, Travels, Labors, and Writings of Lorenzo Dow*. Philadelphia: John E. Potter, n.d.

Edmunds, E. *Memoir of Elder Benjamin Taylor, A Minister of the Christian Connexion, and Pastor of the Bethel Church in Providence, R.I*. Boston: George White, 1850.

Erwin, James. *Reminiscences of Early Circuit Life*. Toledo, Ohio: Spear, Johnson, & Company, 1884.

Fernald, Mark. *Life of Elder Mark Fernald, Written by Himself*. Newburyport: G. M. Payne and D. P. Pike; Philadelphia: Christian General Book Concern, 1852.

Finley, James B. *Sketches of Western Methodism, Biographical, Historical, and Miscellaneous*. Cincinnati: Methodist Book Concern, 1854.

Gates, Helen Dunn. *A Consecrated Life: A Sketch of the Life and Labors of Rev. Ransom Dunn*. Boston: Morning Star Publishing House, 1901.

General Conference of the Freewill Baptist Connection. *Minutes of the General Conference of the Freewill Baptist Connection*. Dover, N.H.: William Burr, 1859.

Goff, I. C. *Autobiography and Memoirs of Rev. Joseph Blackmar with Miscellaneous Selections of His Writings*. Dayton, Ohio: Croy, McFarland, and Company, 1879.

Graham, D. M. *The Life of Clement Phinney*. Dover, N.H.: William Burr, 1851.

Harris, Walter. *A Discourse to the Members of the Female Cent Society in Bedford, New Hampshire, July 18, 1814*. Concord, N.H.: George Hough, 1814.

Hathaway, Levi. *The Narrative of Levi Hathaway*. Providence: Miller and Hutchens, 1820.

Hathaway, Warren. *A Faithful Pastor: Biographical Sketches of John Ross*. Newburgh, N.Y.: Journal Publishing House, 1880.

Hibbard, Billy. *The Life and Travels of B. Hibbard, Minister of the Gospel*. New York: J. C. Totten, 1825.

Himes, Joshua. *Views of the Prophecies and Prophetic Chronology, Selected from Manuscripts of William Miller, with a Memoir of His Life*. Boston: Moses A. Dow, 1841.

Holland, Elihu. *Memoir of Rev. Joseph Badger*. 3d ed. New York: C. S. Francis and Co.; Boston, B. H. Greene, 1854.

Horton, James P. *A Narrative of the Early Life, Remarkable Conversion, and Spiritual Labors of James P. Horton*. N.p.: the author, 1839.

Jarratt, Devereux. *The Life of the Reverend Devereux Jarratt, Rector of Bath Parish, Dinwiddie County, Virginia*. Baltimore: Warner and Hanna, 1806.

Jones, Abner. *Memoir of Elder Abner Jones*. Boston: William Crosby, 1842.

Keely, George. *The Nature and Order of a Gospel Church*. Haverhill, Mass.: P. N. Green, 1819.

Kendall, Henry. *Autobiography of Elder Henry Kendall*. Portland, Maine: published by the author, 1853.

Kendrick, Elder Ariel. *Sketches of the Life and Times of Elder Ariel Kendrick. Written By Himself*. Ludlow, Vt.: Barton and Tower, 1847.

Lednum, John. *A History of the Rise of Methodism in America: Containing Sketches of Methodist Itinerant Preachers, from 1736 to 1780 . . . Also a Short Account of Lay Members*. Philadelphia: the author, 1859.

Leland, John. *The Writings of the Late Elder John Leland, Including Some Events in His Life, Written By Himself*. New York: G. W. Wood, 1845.

Lewis, John. *The Life, Labors, and Travels of Elder Charles Bowles*. Watertown, Mass.: Ingall's and Stowell's, 1852.

Litch, Josiah. *The Probability of the Second Coming of Christ about A.D. 1843*. Boston: David H. Ela, 1838.

McFarland, Asa. *Signs of the Last Times. A Discourse Delivered at Concord, New Hampshire*. Concord: George Hough, 1808.

McKinney, A. L. *Memoir of Eld. Isaac N. Walter*. Cincinnati: Rickey, Mallory, and Webb, 1857.

McMaster, Gilbert. *An Essay in Defense of Some Fundamental Doctrines of Christianity; including a Review of the Writings of Elias Smith and the Claims of His Female Preachers*. Schenectady: Riggs and Stevens, 1815.

Marks, David. *The Life of David Marks*. Limerick, Maine: Morning Star Office, 1831.

Marks, Marilla. *Memoirs of the Life of David Marks, Minister of the Gospel*. Dover, N.H.: William Burr, 1846.

Mathes, James. *Life of Elijah Goodwin, the Pioneer Preacher*. St. Louis: John Burns, 1880.

Maynard, Sampson. *The Experience of Sampson Maynard, Local Preacher of the Methodist Episcopal Church*. New York: William C. Taylor, 1828.

Meacham, Albert Gallatin. *A Compendious History of the Rise and Progress of the Methodist Church*. Hallowell, Canada: Joseph Wilson, 1832.

Millard, David Edmund. *Memoir of Rev. David Millard; with Selections from His Writings. By His Son*. Dayton, Ohio: Christian Publishing Association, 1874.

Miller, William. *Apology and Defence*. Boston: Joshua V. Himes, 1845.

——. *Evidence from Scripture and History of the Second Coming of Christ, About the Year 1843*. Troy, N.Y.: Elias Gates, 1838.

Munger, Hiram. *The Life and Religious Experience of Hiram Munger*. 3d ed. Boston: Advent Christian Publication Society, 1885.

Newell, E[benezer] F[rancis]. *Life and Observations of Rev. E. F. Newell . . . Who Has Been More than Forty Years an Itinerant Minister in the Methodist Episcopal Church*. Worcester, Mass.: C. W. Ainsworth, 1847.

Osborn, Elbert. *Passages in the Life and Ministry of Elbert Osborn, An Itinerant Minister of the Methodist Episcopal Church*. New York: Joseph Longking, 1853.

Payne, Daniel Alexander. *History of the African Methodist Episcopal Church*. Nashville: Publishing House of the A.M.E. Sunday-school Union, 1891. Reprint, New York: Arno Press, 1969.

Peacock, John. *A Sketch of the Christian Experience, Call to the Ministry, and Ministerial Labors of the Rev. John Peacock, Domestic Missionary*. Concord, N.H.: Tripp and Osgood, 1851.

Perrine, Matthew La Rue. *Women Have a Work to Do in the House of God*. New York: Edward W. Thompson, 1817.

Porter, Stephen. *A Discourse, in Two Parts, Addressed to the Presbyterian Congregation in Ballston*. Ballston Spa, N.Y.: James Comstock, 1814.

Potter, Ray. *Memoirs of the Life and Religious Experience of Ray Potter, Minister of the Gospel, Pawtucket*. Providence: H. H. Brown, 1829.

Prescott, Jedediah B. *Memoir of Jedediah B. Prescott, Late Pastor of the Christian Church in Monmouth*. Monmouth, Maine: n.p., 1861.

Purefoy, George W. *A History of the Sandy Creek Baptist Association in A.D. 1758, to A.D. 1858*. 1859. Reprint, New York: Arno Press, 1980.

Putnam, Benjamin. *A Sketch of the Life of Elder Benjamin Putnam*. Woodstock, Vt.: David Watson, 1821.

Raybold, George A. *Annals of Methodism or Sketches of the Origin and Progress of Methodism in Various Portions of West Jersey*. Philadelphia: T. Stokes, 1847.

Richardson, Joseph. *A Sermon on the Duty and Dignity of Woman Delivered April 22, 1832*. Hingham, Mass.: Jedidiah Farmer, 1833.

Rogers, John I., ed. *Autobiography of Elder Samuel Rogers*. 3d ed. Cincinnati: Standard Publishing Company, 1881.

Shaw, Elijah. *Memoir of Elder Elijah Shaw. By his Daughter*. Boston: L. J. Shaw; Philadelphia: Christian General Book Concern, 1852.

Sherman, Eleazer. *The Narrative of Eleazer Sherman, Giving an Account of his Life, Experience, Call to the Ministry of the Gospel, and Travels*. Vols. 2 and 3 (bound together). Providence: H. H. Brown, 1832.

Smith, Steven Rensselaer. *Historical Sketches and Incidents Illustrative of the Establishment and Progress of Universalism in the State of New York*. 2 vols. Buffalo: Steele's Press, 1843, 1848.

Snell, Thomas. *Women Ministering to Christ. A Discourse Delivered in the West Parish of Brookfield, Before the Female Bible Cent Society*. Brookfield, Mass.: E. Merriam, 1815.

Snethen, Abraham. *Autobiography of Abraham Snethen, the Barefoot Preacher*. Dayton, Ohio: Christian Publishing Association, 1909.

Stacy, Nathaniel. *Memoirs of the Life of Nathaniel Stacy*. Columbus, Pa.: Abner Vedder, 1849.

Stearns, J[onathan] F[rench]. *Female Influence and the True Christian Mode of Its Exercise. A Discourse Delivered in the First Presbyterian Church of Newburyport, July 30, 1847*. Newburyport, Mass.: John G. Tilton, 1837.

Stevens, Abel. *A Compendious History of American Methodism*. New York: Carlton and Porter, 1867.

——. *Life and Times of Nathan Bangs*. New York: Carlton and Porter, 1863.

——. *Memorials of the Early Progress of Methodism in the Eastern States*. Boston: C. H. Peirce, 1852.

——. *The Women of Methodism: Its Three Foundresses, Susanna Wesley, the Countess of Huntingdon and Barbara Heck*. New York: Carlton and Lanahan, 1869. Reprint, New York: Garland Press, 1987.

Stewart, John. *Highways and Hedges; or Fifty Years of Western Methodism*. Cincinnati: Hitchcock and Waldren, 1872.

Stinchfield, Ephraim. *Some Memoirs of the Life, Experience and Travels of Elder Ephraim Stinchfield*. Portland, Maine: F. Douglas, 1819.

Strickland, W. B. *Autobiography of Rev. James B. Finley, or Pioneer Life in the West*. Cincinnati: Methodist Book Concern, 1853.

Strong, Nathan. *The Character of a Virtuous and Good Woman; a Discourse Delivered by the Desire and in the Presence of the Female Beneficent Society, in Hartford, Oct. 4th, A.D. 1809*. Hartford: Hudson and Goodwin, 1809.

Summerbell, Nicholas, ed. *The Autobiography of Elder Matthew Gardner, a Minister in the Christian Church*. Dayton, Ohio: Christian Publishing Association, 1874.

Taylor, James B. *Lives of Virginia Baptist Ministers*. 1837. New York: Sheldon and Co., 1860.

Taylor, John. *A History of Ten Baptist Churches*. 1827. Reprint, New York: Arno Press, 1980.

Thomas, Joseph. *The Life, Travels, and Gospel Labors of Elder Joseph Thomas, More Widely Known as the "White Pilgrim."* New York: M. Cummings, 1861.

Thornton, Abel. *The Life of Elder Abel Thornton*. Providence: J. B. Yerrinton, 1828.

A Treatise on the Faith of the Freewill Baptists: With an Appendix, Containing a Summary of Their Usages in Church Government. Dover, N.H.: n.p., 1834.

Watkins, N. *Female Preaching Defended. To Which Is Added, A Sermon: By Miss R. Watkins*. Albany: printed for the subscribers, 1832.

Williams, A. D. *The Rhode Island Freewill Baptist Pulpit*. Boston: Gould and Lincoln, 1852.

Winebrenner, John. *History of All the Religious Denominations in the United States*. Harrisburg, Pa.: John Winebrenner, 1848.

Young, Jacob. *Autobiography of a Pioneer: or, The Nativity, Experience, Travels, and Ministerial Labors of Rev. Jacob Young, with Incidents, Observations, and Reflections*. Cincinnati: L. Swormstedt and A. Poe, 1859.

Manuscripts

American Antiquarian Society, Worcester, Mass.
    Babcock, William Smyth. Papers.
    Harding, Charles R. "Autobiography, 1807–1869."
Connecticut State Library, Hartford, Conn.
    Canterbury, Conn. Separate Church Papers, 1748–84.
    North Stonington, Conn. Separate or Strict Congregationalist Church Records, 1746–1822.
    Scotland, Conn. Brunswick Separate Church Records, 1746–1846.
Cornell University Library, Ithaca, N.Y.
    Wilkinson, Jemima. Papers, 1771–1849. The Collection of Regional History.
Juniata College, Huntingdon, Pa.
    Abraham H. Cassel Collection, MSS 60.
Maine Historical Society, Portland, Maine
    Fullonton, Joseph. "Historical Sketches of Freewill Baptist Churches." Typescript. All accounts taken from *The Morning Star*.
    Greene, Maine. The Record of the Free Baptist Church. Typescript by Samuel D. Rumery.
    New Sharon, Maine. First Freewill Baptist Church Records, 1824–45.
    Pierce, Marshall, comp. "Miscellaneous Papers, 1784–1849, relating to the Freewill Baptist Church in Maine and New Hampshire, including the correspondence of Elder John Buzzell."
    Poland, Maine. Minutes of the Quarterly Conference of the Poland Circuit of the Methodist Episcopal Church, 1808–72.
    Portland, Maine. Free Baptist Church Records, 1810–30.
    Scarborough, Maine. Journal of the Quarterly Conference, Scarborough Circuit of the Methodist Episcopal Church, 1808–73.
    Stinchfield, Ephraim. Papers, 1777–1830.
Massachusetts Historical Society, Boston, Mass.
    Cotton, Josiah. "Memoirs Containing Some Account of the Predecessors Relations, Posterity & Alliances (with some remarkable occurrences in the Life of and Circumstances) of Josiah Cotton of Plymouth in New England, Esq."
    Hall, David. Diary. Vol. 1, 1740–69.
    Skinner, Thomas. "Letter to Ebenezer Turell about New Lights in New London," March 12, 1743.
New Hampshire Historical Society, Concord, N.H.
    Albany, N.H. The Record Book of the Freewill Baptist Society of Albany, New Hampshire, August 8, 1811 to May 24, 1851.
    Barnstead, N.H. Records of the First Free Baptist Church of Christ, 1803–46.
    Barnstead, N.H. Records of the First Free Baptist Society, 1832–75.
    Barrington, N.H. Records of the First [Free] Baptist Church, 1816–73.
    Boscawen, N.H. Records of the Second Christian Society, 1842–50.
    Boscawen, Canterbury, and Concord, N.H. Christian Church Records, 1826–39.

Bridgewater, N.H. Second Freewill Baptist Church Records, 1819–91.

Concord, N.H. Records of the Quarterly Meeting of the First Methodist Episcopal Church, 1831–64. 2 vols.

Dover, N.H. Records of the First Freewill Baptist Church. Vol. 1, 1843–66.

New Durham, N.H. Elders' Conference Records, 1801–13, 1841–48. 2 vols.

New Durham, N.H. Freewill Baptist Church Quarterly Meeting Conference Records, 1792–1889. 5 vols.

New Durham, N.H. Records of the Ministers' Conference of the [Freewill] Baptist Church. Vol. 1, 1843–65.

Newmarket, N.H. Records of the First Christian Church, 1840.

Newmarket, N.H. Records of the First Free Will Baptist Church of Christ, 1834–1912.

Newmarket, N.H. Records of the First Freewill Baptist Society, 1840–1912.

Northwood, N.H. Records of the Freewill Baptist Church, 1832–65. Vols. 1, 2, and 4.

Pittsfield, N.H. Freewill Baptist Church Records, 1791–1838.

Record of the Proceedings of Quarterly Meetings of the Freewill Baptist Churches Held in Maine and New Hampshire, 1783–1792 . . . and Yearly Meetings, 1792–1793.

Wentworth, James J. Diary, 1803–30, 1829–32. 2 vols.

Wolfeborough, N.H. Records of the Second Freewill Baptist Church, 1833–85.

Old Sturbridge Village Library, Sturbridge, Mass.

Sturbridge, Mass. Separates' Letters.

Schlesinger Library, Radcliffe College, Cambridge, Mass.

Brown, Wealtha. Letters about Rachel Baker. In the Hooker Collection, Folder 22: 2.

Yale Divinity School Library, New Haven, Conn.

Saxton, Noah C. Papers, 1816–34. Includes Diaries, 1827–30.

Religious Periodicals

The Advent Herald and Signs of the Times Reporter (New York). 1844–46.

The Advent Message to the Daughters of Zion (Boston). 1844.

The Advent Shield and Review (Boston). 1844–45.

The Bethlehem Star (Woodstock, Vt.). 1824.

The Bible Advocate (Hartford, Conn.). 1846–48.

The Christian (Boston, Mass.; Portland, Maine; and Concord, N.H.).

Christian Herald (Portsmouth, N.H.). 1818–35.

The Christian History, Containing Accounts of the Revival and Propagation of Religion in Great Britain and America For the Year. . . . (Boston). 1743–45.

Christian Journal (Exeter, N.H.). 1835–39.

Christian Luminary (Danville, Vt.). 1832.

Christian Luminary (Stowe, Vt.). 1832.

Christian Palladium (Union Mills, N.Y.). 1832–49.

Christian Repository (New York). 1829.

The Christian's Magazine, Reviewer, and Religious Intelligencer (Portsmouth, N.H.). 1805–8.

Freewill Baptist Magazine (Providence, R.I.). 1826–30.

Freewill Baptist Quarterly Magazine (Dover, N.H.). 1839–41.

Gospel Banner (Woodstock, Vt.). 1827.

Gospel Luminary (West Bloomfield and Rochester, N.Y.). 1825–33.

Gospel Palladium (Boston, Mass., and Warren, R.I.). 1823–24.

Halcyon Itinerary and True Millennium Messenger (Marietta, Ohio). 1807–8.

Herald of Gospel Liberty (Portsmouth, N.H.). 1808–18.

The Hope of Israel (Portland, Maine). 1845.

Maine Baptist Herald (Brunswick, Maine). 1825–27.

Maine Free-Will Baptist Repository (Saco, Maine). 1843.

Methodist Protestant and Family Visitor (Baltimore). 1840–76.

The Midnight Cry (New York). 1842–44.

The Morning Star (Limerick, Maine). 1826–33.

The Morning Star and City Watchman (Boston). 1827–29.

The Morning Watch (New York). 1845.

Mutual Rights and Methodist Protestant (Baltimore). 1831.

Mutual Rights of the Ministers and Members of the Methodist Episcopal Church (Baltimore). 1824–25.

Olive Branch and Christian Inquirer (New York). 1828.

The Primitive Christian (Auburn, N.Y.). 1835–36.

The Primitive Christian and Investigator (Auburn, N.Y.). 1836–37.

Religious Enquirer (Cooperstown, N.Y.). 1811.

The Religious Informer, Being a Selection of Numbers from a Periodical Work, Bearing the Above Title, Containing Accounts of Revivals of Religion Among Different Denominations of Christians, A General Statement of the People called Freewill Baptists in the United States, etc. (Enfield, N.H.). 1819–25.

A Religious Magazine: Containing a Short History of the Church of Christ, Gathered at New Durham, New Hampshire, in the Year 1780 (Portland, Maine). 1811–12, 1820–21.

Signs of the Times (Boston). 1840–43.

Star of Bethlehem (Taunton, Mass.). 1827.

The Voice of Elijah (Montreal and Quebec). 1843–44.

The Voice of Truth, and Glad Tidings of the Kingdom at Hand (Rochester, N.Y.). 1844–47.

Wesleyan Repository (Philadelphia). 1822–24.

Wesleyan Repository and Religious Intelligencer (Trenton, N.J.). 1821–22.

The Western Midnight Cry (Cincinnati, Ohio). 1842.

Zion's Banner (Lowell and Boston, Mass.). 1839–42.

SELECTED SECONDARY SOURCES

Ahlstrom, Sydney E. *A Religious History of the American People*. New Haven: Yale University Press, 1972.

Albaugh, Gaylord P. "History and Annotated Bibliography of American Religious Periodicals and Newspapers, 1730–1830, with Library Locations and Microform Sources." Worcester, Mass.: American Antiquarian Society, 1994.

Alexander, Jon, ed. *American Personal Religious Accounts, 1600–1980: Toward an Inner History of America's Faiths*. New York: Edwin Mellen Press, 1983.

Allen, Stephen, and W. H. Pilsbury. *History of Methodism in Maine*. Augusta, Maine: Charles E. Nash, 1887.

Andrews, Doris Elizabeth. "Popular Religion and the Revolution in the Middle Atlantic Ports: The Rise of the Methodists, 1770–1800." Ph.D. diss., University of Pennsylvania, 1986.

Andrews, Edwin Deming. *The People Called Shakers: A Search for the Perfect Society*. New York: Oxford University Press, 1953.

Andrews, William L. *To Tell a Free Story: The First Century of Afro-American Autobiography, 1760–1865*. Urbana: University of Illinois Press, 1986.

Bacon, Margaret Hope. *Mothers of Feminism: The Story of Quaker Women in America*. San Francisco: Harper and Row, 1986.

———, ed. *Wilt Thou Go on My Errand? Three Eighteenth-Century Journals of Quaker Women Ministers*. Wallingford, Pa.: Pendle Hill Publications, 1994.

Baker, Robert A. *The Southern Baptist Convention and Its People, 1607–1972*. Nashville: Broadman Press, 1974.

Baldwin, Lewis V. *"Invisible" Strands in African Methodism: A History of the African Union Methodist Protestant and Union American Methodist Episcopal Churches, 1805–1980*. Metuchen, N.J.: Scarecrow Press, 1983.

Barbour, Hugh. "Quaker Prophetesses and Mothers in Israel." In *Seeking the Light: Essays in Quaker History in Honor of Edwin B. Bronner*, edited by J. Frost and J. Moore, pp. 41–60. Wallingford, Pa.: Pendle Hill, 1986.

Barkun, Michael. *Crucible of the Millennium: The Burned-over District of New York in the 1840s*. Syracuse: Syracuse University Press, 1986.

Bass, Dorothy C., and Sandra Hughes Boyd. *Women in American Religious History: An Annotated Bibliography and Guide to Sources*. Boston: G. K. Hall, 1986.

Bassard, Katherine Clay. "Spiritual Interrogations: Conversion, Community, and Authorship in the Writings of Phyllis Wheatley, Ann Plato, Jarena Lee, and Rebecca Cox Jackson." Ph.D. diss., Rutgers University, 1992.

Bassett, Angel H. *A Concise History of the Methodist Protestant Church, From Its Origin*. 3d ed. Pittsburgh: William McCracken, 1882.

Baxter, Norman Allen. *History of the Freewill Baptists: A Study in New England Separatism*. Rochester, N.Y.: American Baptist Historical Society, 1957.

Beale, G. B. *Semple's A History of the Rise and Progress of the Baptists of Virginia*. Richmond: Pitt and Dickinson, 1894.

Bednarowski, Mary Farrell. "Outside the Mainstream: Women's Religion and Women Religious Leaders in Nineteenth-Century America." *Journal of the American Academy of Religion* 48 (June 1980): 207–31.

Bendroth, Margaret Lamberts. *Fundamentalism and Gender, 1875 to the Present*. New Haven: Yale University Press, 1993.

Benes, Peter, ed. *Itinerancy in New England and New York*. Boston: Boston University Press, 1986.

Benson, Mary Sumner. *Women in Eighteenth Century America*. New York: Columbia University Press, 1935.

Bernard, Jacqueline. *Journey toward Freedom: The Story of Sojourner Truth*. New York: Norton, 1967. Reprint, New York: Feminist Press, 1980.

Bilhartz, Terry D. *Urban Religion and the Second Great Awakening: Church and Society in Early National Baltimore*. Rutherford, N.J.: Associated University Presses, 1986.

Billington, Louis. "Female Laborers in the Church: Women Preachers in the Northeastern United States, 1790–1840." *Journal of American Studies* (Great Britain) 19 (1985): 369–94.

———. "Northern New England Sectarianism in the Early Nineteenth Century." *Bulletin of the John Rylands University Library of Manchester* 70 (Autumn 1988): 123–34.

Blake, S. L. *The Separates or Strict Congregationalists of New England*. Boston: Pilgrim Press, 1902.

Blauvelt, Martha Tomhave. "Society, Religion, and Revivalism: The Second Great Awakening in New Jersey, 1780–1830." Ph.D. diss., Princeton University, 1975.

Bloch, Ruth. "The Gendered Meanings of Virtue in Revolutionary America." *Signs* 13 (Autumn 1987): 37–58.

———. *Visionary Republic: Millennial Themes in American Thought*. Cambridge: Cambridge University Press, 1985.

Blumhofer, Edith L. *Aimee Semple McPherson: Everybody's Sister*. Grand Rapids, Mich.: Eerdmans, 1993.

Boles, John B. *The Great Revival, 1787–1805*. Lexington: University Press of Kentucky, 1972.

Bonomi, Patricia U. *Under the Cope of Heaven: Religion, Society, and Politics in Colonial America*. New York: Oxford University Press, 1986.

Bordin, Ruth O. "The Sect to Denomination Process in America: The Freewill Baptist Experience." *Church History* 34 (1964): 77–94.

Boyd, Lois A., and R. Douglas Brackenridge. *Presbyterian Women in America: Two Centuries of a Quest for Status*. Westport, Conn.: Greenwood Press, 1983.

Brackney, William H. *The Baptists*. New York: Greenwood Press, 1988.

Braude, Ann. *Radical Spirits: Spiritualism and Women's Rights in Nineteenth-Century America*. Boston: Beacon Press, 1989.

Braxton, Joanne M. *Black Women Writing Autobiography: A Tradition within a Tradition*. Philadelphia: Temple University Press, 1989.

Breen, T. H. " 'Baubles of Britain': The American and Consumer Revolutions of the Eighteenth Century." *Past and Present* 119 (May 1988): 73–104.

———. "An Empire of Goods: The Anglicization of Colonial America, 1690–1776." *Journal of British Studies* 25 (October 1986): 467–99.

Brereton, Virginia Lieson. *From Sin to Salvation: Stories of Women's Conversions, 1800 to the Present*. Bloomington: Indiana University Press, 1991.

Brewer, Priscilla J. *Shaker Communities, Shaker Lives*. Hanover: University Press of New England, 1986.

Brewster, J. M. *The Centennial Record of Freewill Baptists, 1780–1880*. Dover, N.H.: The Printing Establishment, 1881.

Brooke, John L. *The Refiner's Fire: The Making of Mormon Cosmology, 1644–1844*. Cambridge: Cambridge University Press, 1994.

Brown, Earl Kent. *Women of Mr. Wesley's Methodism*. New York: Edwin Mellen Press, 1983.

Brown, Kathleen M. "Brave New Worlds: Women's and Gender History." *William and Mary Quarterly* 50, no. 2 (April 1993): 311–27.

Brumberg, Joan Jacobs. *Mission for Life: The Judson Family and American Evangelical Culture*. New York: Free Press, 1980.

Bullough, Vern L., and Bonnie Bullough. *Cross Dressing, Sex, and Gender*. Philadelphia: University of Pennsylvania Press, 1993.

Bumsted, J. M., and John E. Van de Wetering. *What Must I Do to Be Saved? The Great Awakening in Colonial America*. Hinsdale, Ill.: Dryden Press, 1976.

Burgess, Gideon A., and John T. Ward. *Free Baptist Cyclopedia, Historical and Biographical*. N.p., 1889.

Burnett, J. F. *Early Women of the Christian Church*. Dayton: Christian Publishing Association, 1921.

Bushman, Richard L. *From Puritan to Yankee: Character and the Social Order in Connecticut, 1690–1765*. Cambridge: Harvard University Press, 1967.

———, ed. *The Great Awakening: Documents on the Revival of Religion, 1740–1745*. New York: Atheneum, 1970; Chapel Hill: University of North Carolina Press, 1989.

Butler, Jon. *Awash in a Sea of Faith: Christianizing the American People*. Cambridge: Harvard University Press, 1990.

——. "Enthusiasm Described and Decried: The Great Awakening as Interpretive Fiction." *Journal of American History* 69 (1982): 305–25.

Bynum, Caroline Walker. *Holy Feast and Holy Fast: The Religious Significance of Food to Medieval Women*. Berkeley: University of California Press, 1987.

Bynum, Caroline Walker, Stevan Harrell, and Paula Richman, eds. *Gender and Religion: On the Complexity of Symbols*. Boston: Beacon Press, 1986.

Bynum, Victoria E. *Unruly Women: The Politics of Social and Sexual Control in the Old South*. Chapel Hill: University of North Carolina Press, 1992.

Carter, Nathan Franklin. *The Native Ministry of New Hampshire*. Concord, N.H.: Rumford Printing Company, 1906.

Carwardine, Richard. "The Second Great Awakening in the Urban Centers: An Examination of Methodism and the 'New Measures.'" *Journal of American History* 59 (1972): 327–40.

——. *Transatlantic Revivalism: Popular Evangelicalism in Britain and America, 1790–1865*. Westport, Conn.: Greenwood Press, 1978.

Chase, C. C. "Harriet Livermore." In *Contributions of the Old Residents' Historical Association* (Lowell, Mass.) 4, no. 1 (August 1888): 17–23.

The Christian Denomination. Newburyport, Mass.: William H. Huse & Co., 1859.

Clark, Christopher. *The Roots of Rural Capitalism: Western Massachusetts, 1780–1860*. Ithaca: Cornell University Press, 1990.

Clark, Elizabeth B. "Women and Religion in America, 1780–1870." In *Church and State in America: A Bibliographical Guide*, edited by John F. Wilson, 1:365–413. New York: Greenwood Press, 1986.

Cleveland, Stafford C. *History and Directory of Yates County, Containing a Sketch of Its Original Settlement by the Public Universal Friends*. Vol. 1. Penn Yan, N.Y.: S. C. Cleveland: 1873.

Coalter, Milton J., Jr. *Gilbert Tennent, Son of Thunder: A Case Study of Continental Pietism's Impact on the First Great Awakening in the Middle Colonies*. New York: Greenwood Press, 1986.

Conkin, Paul K. *The Uneasy Center: Reformed Christianity in Antebellum America*. Chapel Hill: University of North Carolina Press, 1995.

Conway, Jill. *The Female Experience in Eighteenth- and Nineteenth-Century America*. Princeton: Princeton University Press, 1982.

Cott, Nancy F. *The Bonds of Womanhood: "Woman's Sphere" in New England, 1780–1835*. New Haven: Yale University Press, 1977.

——. "Passionlessness: An Interpretation of Victorian Sexual Ideology, 1790–1850." In *A Heritage of Her Own*, edited by Nancy F. Cott and Elizabeth H. Pleck, pp. 162–81. New York: Simon and Schuster, 1979.

——. "Young Women in the Second Great Awakening." *Feminist Studies* 3 (Fall 1975): 15–29.

Crawford, Michael J. *Seasons of Grace: Colonial New England's Revival Tradition in Its British Context*. New York: Oxford University Press, 1991.

——, ed. "The Spiritual Travels of Nathan Cole." *William and Mary Quarterly* 33 (January 1976): 89–126.

Cross, Whitney R. *The Burned-over District: The Social and Intellectual History of Enthusiastic Religion in Western New York, 1800–1850*. New York: Harper, 1965.

Dall, Caroline. *The College, the Market, and the Court; or, Women's Relation to Education, Labor, and Law*. Boston: Lee and Shepard, 1867. Reprint, New York: Arno Press, 1972.

Davis, Gwenn, and Beverly A. Joyce, comps. *Personal Writings by Women to 1900: A Bibliography of American and British Writers*. London: Mansell Publishing, 1989.

Davis, Rebecca. *Gleanings from Merrimac Valley*. Portland, Maine: Hoyt, Fogg, and Donham, 1881.

DeBerg, Betty A. *Ungodly Women: Gender and the First Wave of American Fundamentalism*. Minneapolis: Fortress Press, 1990.

Deignan, Kathleen. *Christ Spirit: The Eschatology of Shaker Christianity*. Metuchen, N.J.: American Theological Library Association and Scarecrow Press, 1992.

Delbanco, Andrew. *The Death of Satan: How Americans Have Lost the Sense of Evil*. New York: Farrar, Straus, and Giroux, 1995.

Demos, John. *Past, Present, and Personal: The Family and the Life Course in American History*. New York: Oxford University Press, 1986.

Dexter, Elisabeth Anthony. *Career Women of America, 1776–1840*. Francestown, N.H.: Marshall Jones, 1950.

Doan, Ruth Alden. *The Miller Heresy, Millennialism, and American Culture*. Philadelphia: Temple University Press, 1987.

Dodson, Jualynne. "Nineteenth-Century A.M.E. Preaching Women." In *Women in New Worlds: Historical Perspectives on the Wesleyan Tradition*, edited by Hilah F. Thomas, Rosemary Skinner Keller, and Louise L. Queen, 1:276–89. 2 vols. Nashville: Abingdon Press, 1982.

Dolan, J. R. *The Yankee Peddlers of Early America*. New York: Clarkson N. Potter, 1964.

Douglas, Ann. *The Feminization of American Culture*. New York: Knopf, 1977.

Drinkhouse, Edward J. *History of Methodist Reform Synoptical of General Methodism, 1703–1898*. 2 vols. Baltimore: Board of Publication of the Methodist Protestant Church, 1899.

Drury, A. W. *History of the Church of the United Brethren in Christ*. Dayton, Ohio: United Brethren Publishing House, 1924.

Dunbar, Seymour. *A History of Travel in America*. New York: Tudor Publishing House, 1973.

Dunn, Mary Maples. "Latest Light on Women of Light." In *Witnesses for Change: Quaker Women over Three Centuries*, edited by Elisabeth Potts Brown and Susan Mosher Stuard, pp. 71–84. New Brunswick: Rutgers University Press, 1989.

——. "Saints and Sisters: Congregational and Quaker Women in the Early Colonial Period." *American Quarterly* 30 (1978): 582–601.

Eckhardt, Celia Morris. *Fanny Wright: Rebel in America*. Cambridge: Harvard University Press, 1984.

Edkins, Carol. "Quest for Community: Spiritual Autobiographies of Eighteenth-Century Quaker and Puritan Women in America." In *Women's Autobiography: Essays in Criticism*, edited by Estelle C. Jelinek, pp. 39–53. Bloomington: Indiana University Press, 1980.

Epstein, Barbara Leslie. *The Politics of Domesticity: Women, Evangelism, and Temperance in Nineteenth-Century America*. Middletown: Wesleyan University Press, 1981.

Field-Bibb, Jacqueline. *Women Towards Priesthood: Ministerial Politics and Feminist Praxis*. Cambridge: Cambridge University Press, 1991.

Foster, Frances Smith. "Adding Color and Contour to Early American Self-Portraitures: Autobiographical Writings of Afro-American Women." In *Conjuring: Black Women, Fiction, and Literary Tradition*, edited by Marjorie Pryse and Hortense J. Spillers, pp. 25–38. Bloomington: Indiana University Press, 1985.

——. "Neither Auction Block nor Pedestal: The Life and Religious Experience of Jarena Lee, a Coloured Lady." In *The Female Autograph*, edited by Domna C. Stanton. New York: New York Literary Forum, 1984.

——. *Written by Herself: Literary Production by African-American Women, 1746–1892*. Bloomington: Indiana University Press, 1993.

Foster, Lawrence. *Religion and Sexuality: The Shakers, the Mormons, and the Oneida Community*. Oxford: Oxford University Press, 1981.

Fox-Genovese, Elizabeth. "Two Steps Forward, One Step Back: New Questions and Old Models in the Religious History of American Women." *Journal of the American Academy of Religion* 53 (September 1985): 465–71.

Fox-Genovese, Elizabeth, and Eugene D. Genovese. "The Divine Sanction of Social Order: The Religious Foundations of the Southern Slaveholders' World View." *Journal of the American Academy of Religion* 55 (1987): 211–33.

Friedman, Jean E. *The Enclosed Garden: Women and Community in the Evangelical South, 1830–1900*. Chapel Hill: University of North Carolina Press, 1985.

Garber, Marjorie. *Vested Interests: Cross-Dressing and Cultural Anxiety*. New York: Routledge, 1992.

Garrett, Clarke. *Spirit Possession and Popular Religion: From the Camissards to the Shakers*. Baltimore: Johns Hopkins, 1987.

Gaustad, Edwin Scott. *The Great Awakening in New England*. Gloucester, Mass.: Peter Smith, 1965.

——, ed. *The Rise of Adventism: Religion and Society in Mid-Nineteenth-Century America*. New York: Harper and Row, 1974.

Gewehr, Wesley M. *The Great Awakening in Virginia, 1740–1790*. Durham, N.C.: Duke University Press, 1930.

Gillespie, Joanna Bowen. " 'The Clear Leadings of Providence': Pious Memoirs and the Problems of Self-Realization for Women in the Early Nineteenth Century." *Journal of the Early Republic* 5 (Summer 1985): 197–221.

Ginzberg, Lori D. *Women and the Work of Benevolence: Morality, Politics, and Class in the Nineteenth-Century United States*. New Haven: Yale University Press, 1990.

Goen, C. C. *Revivalism and Separatism in New England, 1740–1800: Strict Congregationalists and Separate Baptists in the Great Awakening*. New Haven: Yale University Press, 1962.

Goode, Gloria Davis. "Preachers of the Word and Singers of the Gospel: The Ministry of Women among Nineteenth-Century African-Americans." Ph.D. diss., University of Pennsylvania, 1990.

Grammer, Elizabeth Elkin. " 'A Pen in His Hand': A Pen in Her Hand. Autobiographies by Female Itinerant Evangelists in Nineteenth-Century America." Ph.D. diss., University of Virginia, 1995.

Greaves, Richard L., ed. *Triumph over Silence: Women in Protestant History*. Westport, Conn.: Greenwood Press, 1985.

Gundersen, Joan R. "The Non-Institutional Church: The Religious Role of Women in Eighteenth-Century Virginia." *Historical Magazine of the Protestant Episcopal Church* 51 (December 1982): 347–57.

Hackett, David G. *The Rude Hand of Innovation: Religion and Social Order in Albany, New York, 1652–1836*. New York: Oxford University Press, 1991.

Hahn, Steven, and Jonathan Prude, eds. *The Countryside in the Age of Capitalist Transformation:*

Essays in the Social History of Rural America. Chapel Hill: University of North Carolina Press, 1985.

Hall, David D. *Worlds of Wonder, Days of Judgment: Popular Religious Belief in Early New England*. New York: Knopf, 1989.

Hall, Timothy D. *Contested Boundaries: Itinerancy and the Reshaping of the Colonial American Religious World*. Durham, N.C.: Duke University Press, 1994.

Hambrick-Stowe, Charles E. "The Spiritual Pilgrimage of Sarah Osborn (1714–1796)." *Church History* 61 (December 1992): 408–21.

Hanaford, Phebe A. *Daughters of America; or, Women of the Century*. Augusta, Maine: True and Company, 1883.

Handy, James A. *Scraps of African Methodist Episcopal History*. Philadelphia: A.M.E. Book Concern, 1901.

Hansen, Karen V. *A Very Social Time: Crafting Community in Antebellum New England*. Berkeley: University of California Press, 1994.

Hanson, E. R. *Our Woman Workers. Biographical Sketches of Women Eminent in the Universalist Church for Literary, Philanthropic, and Christian Work*. Chicago: Starr and Covenant Office, 1882.

Hardesty, Nancy A. *Women Called to Witness: Evangelical Feminism in the Nineteenth Century*. Nashville: Abingdon Press, 1984.

——. *Your Daughters Shall Prophesy: Revivalism and Feminism in the Age of Finney*. Brooklyn, N.Y.: Carlson Publishing, 1991.

Harlan, David. *The Clergy and the Great Awakening in New England*. Ann Arbor, Mich.: UMI Research Press, 1980.

Hassey, Janette. *No Time for Silence: Evangelical Women in Public Ministry around the Turn of the Century*. Grand Rapids, Mich.: Academie Books, 1986.

Hatch, Nathan O. "The Christian Movement and the Demand for a Theology of the People." *Journal of American History* 67 (1980): 545–67.

——. *The Democratization of American Christianity*. New Haven: Yale University Press, 1989.

——. *The Sacred Cause of Liberty*. New Haven: Yale University Press, 1977.

Heimert, Alan. *Religion and the American Mind: From the Great Awakening to the Revolution*. Cambridge: Harvard University Press, 1966.

Heimert, Alan, and Perry Miller, eds. *The Great Awakening: Documents Illustrating the Crisis and Its Consequences*. Indianapolis: Bobbs-Merrill, 1967.

Helly, Dorothy O., and Susan M. Reverby. *Gendered Domains: Rethinking Public and Private in Women's History*. Ithaca: Cornell University Press, 1992.

Hewitt, Nancy A. *Women's Activism and Social Change: Rochester, New York, 1722–1872*. Ithaca: Cornell University Press, 1984.

Heyrman, Christine Leigh. *Commerce and Culture: The Maritime Communities of Colonial Massachusetts, 1690–1750*. New York: Norton, 1984.

——. *Southern Cross: The Beginnings of the Bible Belt*. New York: Knopf, 1997.

Higham, John. *From Boundlessness to Consolidation: The Transformation of American Culture, 1848–1860*. Ann Arbor, Mich.: Clements Library, 1969.

Hine, Darlene Clark, Wilma King, and Linda Reed, eds. *"We Specialize in the Wholly Impossible": A Reader in Black Women's History*. Brooklyn, N.Y.: Carlson Publishing, 1995.

Hoffman, Ronald, and Peter J. Albert, eds. *Religion in a Revolutionary Age*. Charlottesville: University Press of Virginia, 1994.

——. *Women in the Age of the American Revolution*. Charlottesville: University Press of Virginia, 1989.

Hoxie, Elizabeth F. "Harriet Livermore, 'Vixen and Devotee.'" *New England Quarterly* 18 (March 1945): 39–50.

Hoyle, Lydia Huffman. "Missionary Women among the American Indians, 1815–1865." Ph.D. diss., University of North Carolina at Chapel Hill, 1992.

Humez, Jean M. "'My Spirit Eye': Some Functions of Spiritual and Visionary Experiences in the Lives of Five Black Women Preachers, 1810–1880." In *Women and the Structure of Society*, edited by Barbara Harris and JoAnn McNamara, pp. 129–43. Durham, N.C.: Duke University Press, 1984.

——. "'Ye Are My Epistles': The Construction of Ann Lee Imagery in Early Shaker Sacred Literature." *Journal of Feminist Studies in Religion* 8, no. 1 (Spring 1992): 83–104.

——, ed. *Mother's First-Born Daughters: Early Shaker Writings on Women and Religion*. Bloomington: Indiana University Press, 1993.

Humphreys, Evans Williams. *Memoirs of Deceased Christian Ministers; or, Brief Sketches of the Lives and Labors of 975 Ministers, Who Died Between 1793 and 1880*. Dayton, Ohio: Christian Publishing Association, 1880.

Isaac, Rhys. *The Transformation of Virginia, 1740–1790*. Chapel Hill: University of North Carolina Press, 1982.

Jaffee, David. "Peddlers of Progress and the Transformation of the Rural North, 1760–1860." *Journal of American History* 78, no. 2 (September 1991): 511–35.

James, Janet Wilson, ed. *Women in American Religion*. Philadelphia: University of Pennsylvania Press, 1980.

Jelinek, Estelle C., ed. *Women's Autobiography: Essays in Criticism*. Bloomington: Indiana University Press, 1980.

Jensen, Joan M. *Loosening the Bonds: Mid-Atlantic Farm Women, 1750–1850*. New Haven: Yale University Press, 1986.

Johnson, Albert C. *Advent Christian History: A Concise Narrative of the Origin and Progress, Doctrine and Work of This Body of Believers*. Boston: Advent Christian Publication Society, 1918.

Johnson, Benton. "On Church and Sect." *American Sociological Review* 28 (August 1963): 539–49.

Johnson, Curtis D. *Islands of Holiness: Rural Religion in Upstate New York, 1790–1860*. Ithaca: Cornell University Press, 1989.

Johnson, Paul E. *A Shopkeeper's Millennium: Society and Revivals in Rochester, New York, 1815–1837*. New York: Hill and Wang, 1978.

Johnson, Paul E., and Sean Wilentz. *The Kingdom of Matthias: A Story of Sex and Salvation in Nineteenth-Century America*. New York: Oxford University Press, 1994.

Jürisson, Cynthia. "Federalist, Feminist, Revivalist: Harriet Livermore (1788–1868) and the Limits of Democratization in the Early Republic." Ph.D. diss., Princeton Theological Seminary, 1994.

Juster, Susan. *Disorderly Women: Sexual Politics and Evangelicalism in Revolutionary New England*. Ithaca: Cornell University Press, 1994.

——. "'In a Different Voice': Male and Female Narratives of Religious Conversion in Post-Revolutionary America." *American Quarterly* 41 (March 1989): 34–62.

Juster, Susan, and Lisa MacFarlane, eds. *A Mighty Baptism: Race, Gender, and the Creation of American Protestantism*. Ithaca: Cornell University Press, 1996.

Keller, Rosemary Skinner. "Women and the Nature of Ministry in the United Methodist Tradition." *Methodist History* 22 (January 1984): 99–114.

Kelley, Mary. *Private Woman, Public Stage: Literary Domesticity in Nineteenth-Century America*. New York: Oxford University Press, 1984.

Kerber, Linda K. "Can a Woman Be an Individual? The Limits of Puritan Tradition in the Early Republic." *Texas Studies in Literature and Language* 25, no. 1 (Spring 1983), pp. 165–77.

———. *Women of the Republic: Intellect and Ideology in Revolutionary America*. Chapel Hill: University of North Carolina Press, 1980.

Kerber, Linda K., Nancy F. Cott, Robert Gross, Lynn Hunt, Carroll Smith-Rosenberg, and Christine Stansell. "Beyond Roles, Beyond Spheres: Thinking about Gender in the Early Republic." *William and Mary Quarterly* 46 (July 1989): 565–85.

Kulikoff, Allan. "The Transition to Capitalism in Rural America." *William and Mary Quarterly* 46, no. 1 (January 1989): 120–44.

Lacey, Barbara E. "Women and the Great Awakening in Connecticut." Ph.D. diss., Clark University, 1982.

———. "The World of Hannah Heaton: The Autobiography of an Eighteenth-Century Connecticut Farm Woman." *William and Mary Quarterly* 45 (April 1988): 280–304.

Lambert, Frank. *"Pedlar in Divinity": George Whitefield and the Transatlantic Revivals*. Princeton: Princeton University Press, 1994.

Land, Gary, ed. *Adventism in America: A History*. Grand Rapids, Mich.: Eerdmans, 1986.

Lang, Amy Scrager. *Prophetic Woman: Anne Hutchinson and the Problem of Dissent in the Literature of New England*. Berkeley: University of California Press, 1987.

LaPrade, Candis A. "Pens in the Hand of God: The Spiritual Autobiographies of Jarena Lee, Zilpha Elaw, and Rebecca Cox Jackson." Ph.D. diss., University of North Carolina at Chapel Hill, 1994.

Laquer, Thomas. *Making Sex: Body and Gender from the Greeks to Freud*. Cambridge: Harvard University Press, 1990.

Laurie, Bruce. *Working People of Philadelphia, 1800–1850*. Philadelphia: Temple University Press, 1980.

Lawless, Elaine J. *Handmaidens of the Lord: Pentecostal Women Preachers and Traditional Religion*. Philadelphia: University of Pennsylvania Press, 1988.

Lazerow, Jama. *Religion and the Working Class in Antebellum America*. Washington: Smithsonian Institution Press, 1995.

———. "Spokesmen for the Working Class: Protestant Clergy and the Labor Movement in Antebellum New England." *Journal of the Early Republic* 13 (Fall 1993): 323–54.

Lerner, Gerda. *The Creation of Feminist Consciousness: From the Middle Ages to Eighteen-seventy*. New York: Oxford University Press, 1993.

———. *The Majority Finds Its Past: Placing Women in History*. Oxford: Oxford University Press, 1979.

Lewis, I. M. *Religion in Context: Cults and Charisma*. Cambridge: Cambridge University Press, 1986.

Lindley, Susan Hill. *"You Have Stept Out of Your Place": A History of Women and Religion in America*. Louisville, Ky.: Westminster John Knox Press, 1996.

Livermore, Samuel T. *Harriet Livermore, the "Pilgrim Stranger"*. Hartford: Case, Lockwood, and Brainard Company, 1884.

Ludlum, David M. *Social Ferment in Vermont, 1791–1850*. New York: Columbia University Press, 1939.

Lumpkin, William L. *Baptist Foundations in the South: Tracing through the Separates the Influence of the Great Awakening, 1754–1787*. Nashville: Broadman Press, 1961. Reprinted in his *Colonial Baptists and Southern Revivals*. New York: Arno Press, 1980.

——. "The Role of Women in Eighteenth-Century Virginia Baptist Life." *Baptist History and Heritage* 8 (1973): 158–67.

Mabee, Carleton. *Sojourner Truth: Slave, Prophet, Legend*. New York: New York University Press, 1993.

McBeth, Leon. *The Baptist Heritage: Four Centuries of Baptist Witness*. Nashville: Broadman Press, 1987.

——. "The Changing Role of Women in Baptist History." *Southwestern Journal of Theology* 22 (1979–80): 84–96.

——. *Women in Baptist Life*. Nashville: Broadman Press, 1979.

——, ed. *A Sourcebook for Baptist Heritage*. Nashville: Broadman Press, 1990.

McCurry, Stephanie. *Masters of Small Worlds: Yeoman Households, Gender Relations, and the Political Culture of the Antebellum South Carolina Low Country*. New York: Oxford University Press, 1995.

MacHaffie, Barbara J. *Her Story: Women in Christian Tradition*. Philadelphia: Fortress Press, 1986.

Mack, Phyllis. *Visionary Women: Ecstatic Prophecy in Seventeenth-Century England*. Berkeley: University of California Press, 1992.

McLoughlin, William G. *New England Dissent, 1630–1833: The Baptists and the Separation of Church and State*. 2 vols. Cambridge: Harvard University Press, 1971.

——. *Revivals, Awakenings, and Reform: An Essay on Religion and Social Change in America, 1607–1977*. Chicago: University of Chicago Press, 1978.

Marietta, Jack D. *The Reformation of American Quakerism, 1748–1783*. Philadelphia: University of Pennsylvania Press, 1984.

Marini, Stephen A. "A New View of Mother Ann Lee and the Rise of American Shakerism." *The Shaker Quarterly* (Summer/Fall 1990): 47–62, 95–111.

——. *Radical Sects of Revolutionary New England*. Cambridge: Harvard University Press, 1982.

Marsden, George M. "Everyone's Own Interpreter? The Bible, Science, and Authority in Mid-Nineteenth-Century America." In *The Bible in America: Essays in Cultural History*, edited by Nathan O. Hatch and Mark A. Noll. New York: Oxford University Press, 1982.

Marty, Martin E. *Pilgrims in Their Own Land: Five Hundred Years of American Religion*. Boston: Little, Brown, 1984.

——. *Protestantism in the United States: Righteous Empire*. 2d ed. New York: Scribner's, 1986.

——. *Religion and Republic: The American Circumstance*. Boston: Beacon Press, 1987.

——. *Religion, Awakening and Revolution*. [Wilmington, N.C.]: Consortium, 1977.

Masson, Margaret W. "The Typology of the Female as a Model for the Regenerate: Puritan Preaching, 1690–1730." *Signs* 2, no. 2 (Winter 1976): 304–15.

Mathews, Donald G. *Religion in the Old South*. Chicago: University of Chicago Press, 1977.

——. "The Second Great Awakening as an Organizing Process, 1780–1830." In *Religion in American History: Interpretive Essays*, edited by John M. Mulder and John F. Wilson, pp. 199–217. Englewood Cliffs, N.J.: Prentice-Hall, 1978.

——. *Slavery and Methodism: A Chapter in American Morality, 1780–1845*. Princeton: Princeton University Press, 1965.

Mathews, Glenna. *The Rise of Public Woman: Woman's Power and Woman's Place in the United States, 1630–1970*. New York: Oxford University Press, 1992.

Maxson, Charles Hartshorn. *The Great Awakening in the Middle Colonies*. Chicago: University of Chicago Press, 1920.

Mercadante, Linda A. *Gender, Doctrine, and God: The Shakers and Contemporary Theology*. Nashville: Abingdon Press, 1990.

Miller, Page Putnam. *A Claim to New Roles*. Philadelphia: American Theological Library Association; Metuchen, N.J.: Scarecrow Press, 1985.

Miller, Russell E. *The Larger Hope: The First Century of the Universalist Church in America, 1770– 1870*. Boston: Unitarian Universalist Association, 1979.

Moody, Joycelyn. "Self-Effacement and Collective Identity in Five Black Women's Autobiographies, 1835–1879." Ph.D. diss., University of Kansas, 1993.

Moore, R. Laurence. *Religious Outsiders and the Making of Americans*. New York: Oxford University Press, 1986.

——. *Selling God: American Religion in the Marketplace of Culture*. New York: Oxford University Press, 1994.

Morrill, Milo True. *A History of the Christian Denomination in America, 1794–1811*. Dayton, Ohio: Christian Publishing Association, 1912.

Muir, Elizabeth. *Petticoats in the Pulpit: The Story of Early Nineteenth-Century Methodist Women Preachers in Upper Canada*. Toronto: United Church Publishing House, 1991.

Murphy, Teresa Anne. *Ten Hours' Labor: Religion, Reform, and Gender in Early New England*. Ithaca: Cornell University Press, 1992.

Nash, Gary B. *Forging Freedom: The Formation of Philadelphia's Black Community, 1720–1840*. Cambridge: Harvard University Press, 1988.

——. *The Urban Crucible: The Northern Seaports and the Origins of the American Revolution*. Cambridge: Harvard University Press, 1986.

Niebuhr, H. Richard. *The Social Sources of Denominationalism*. New York: Henry Holt, 1929.

Noll, William T. "Women as Clergy and Laity in the Nineteenth-Century Methodist Protestant Church." *Methodist History* 15 (January 1977): 107–21.

Nord, David Paul. "The Evangelical Origins of Mass Media in America, 1815–1835." *Journalism Monographs* 88 (1984): 1–30.

Norton, Mary Beth. *Founding Mothers and Fathers: Gendered Power and the Forming of American Society*. New York: Knopf, 1996.

——. *Liberty's Daughters: The Revolutionary Experience of American Women, 1750–1800*. Boston: Little, Brown, 1980.

——, ed. " 'My Resting Reaping Times': Sarah Osborn's Defense of Her 'Unfeminine Activities.' " *Signs* 2 (1976): 515–29.

Numbers, Ronald L. *Prophetess of Health: Ellen G. White and the Origins of Seventh-Day Adventist Health Reform*. Knoxville: University of Tennessee Press, 1992.

Numbers, Ronald L., and Jonathan M. Butler, eds. *The Disappointed: Millerism and Millenarianism in the Nineteenth Century*. Bloomington: Indiana University Press, 1987.

Osterud, Nancy. *Bonds of Community: The Lives of Farm Women in Nineteenth-Century New York*. Ithaca: Cornell University Press, 1991.

Painter, Nell Irvin. "Representing Truth: Sojourner Truth's Knowing and Becoming Known." *Journal of American History* 81, no. 2 (1994): 461–92.

——. *Sojourner Truth: A Life, A Symbol*. New York: Norton, 1996.

Peterson, Carla L. *"Doers of the Word": African-American Women Speakers and Writers in the North*. New York: Oxford University Press, 1995.

Porterfield, Amanda. *Female Piety in Colonial New England*. Oxford: Oxford University Press, 1992.

——. *Feminine Spirituality in America: From Sarah Edwards to Martha Graham*. Philadelphia: Temple University Press, 1980.

——. "Women's Attraction to Puritanism." *Church History* 60 (June 1991): 196–209.

Procter-Smith, Marjorie. "'Who Do You Say that I Am?' Mother Ann as Christ." In *Locating the Shakers: Cultural Origins and Legacies of an American Religious Movement*, edited by Mick Gidley with Kate Bowles, pp. 83–95. Exeter: University of Exeter Press, 1990.

——. *Women in Shaker Community and Worship: A Feminist Analysis of the Uses of Religious Symbolism*. Lewiston, N.Y.: Edwin Mellen Press, 1985.

Prude, Jonathan. *The Coming of Industrial Order: Town and Factory Life in Rural Massachusetts, 1810–1860*. Cambridge: Cambridge University Press, 1983.

Raboteau, Albert J. *Slave Religion: The "Invisible Institution" in the Antebellum South*. Oxford: Oxford University Press, 1978.

Rawlyk, G. A. *The Canada Fire: Radical Evangelicalism in British North America, 1775–1812*. Kingston, Ont.: McGill-Queen's University Press, 1994.

——. *Ravished by the Spirit: Religious Revivals, Baptists, and Henry Alline*. Kingston, Ont.: McGill-Queen's University Press, 1984.

Richardson, Marilyn, ed. *Black Women and Religion: A Bibliography*. Boston: G. K. Hall, 1980.

——. *Maria W. Stewart, America's First Black Woman Political Writer: Essays and Speeches*. Bloomington: Indiana University Press, 1987.

Richey, Russell E. *Early American Methodism*. Bloomington: Indiana University Press, 1991.

Richey, Russell E., and Kenneth E. Rowe, eds. *Rethinking Methodist History*. Nashville: United Methodist Publishing House, 1985.

Robert, Dana L. *American Women in Mission: A Social History of Their Thought and Practice*. Macon, Ga.: Mercer University Press, 1996.

Roebuck, David G. "Pentecostal Women in Ministry: A Review of Selected Documents." *Perspectives in Religious Studies* 16 (Spring 1989): 29–44.

Rowe, David L. *Thunder and Trumpets: Millerites and Dissenting Religion in Upstate New York, 1800–1850*. Chico, Calif.: Scholar's Press, 1985.

Ruether, Rosemary Radford, and Rosemary Skinner Keller, eds. *In Our Own Voices: Four Centuries of American Women's Religious Writing*. San Francisco: Harper San Francisco, 1994.

——. *Women and Religion in America*. 3 vols. San Francisco: Harper and Row, 1981–86.

Russell, Daniel James. *History of the African Union Methodist Protestant Church*. Philadelphia: Union Star Book and Job Printing, 1920.

Ryan, Mary P. *Cradle of the Middle Class: The Family in Oneida County, New York, 1790–1865*. Cambridge: Cambridge University Press, 1981.

——. *Women in Public: Between Banners and Ballots, 1825–1880*. Baltimore: Johns Hopkins, 1990.

——. "A Women's Awakening: Evangelical Religion and the Families of Utica, New York, 1800–1840." *American Quarterly* 30 (Winter 1978): 602–23.

Schmidt, Leigh Eric. *Holy Fairs: Scottish Communions and American Revivals in the Early Modern Period*. Princeton: Princeton University Press, 1989.

Schneider, A. Gregory. *The Way of the Cross Leads Home: The Domestication of American Methodism*. Bloomington: Indiana University Press, 1993.

Scott, Joan W. "Gender: A Useful Category of Historical Analysis." *American Historical Review* 91 (December 1985): 1053–75.

Sellers, Charles. *The Market Revolution: Jacksonian America, 1815–1846*. New York: Oxford University Press, 1992.

Sellers, Charles Coleman. *Lorenzo Dow: The Bearer of the Word*. New York: Minton, Balch, and Company, 1928.

Shea, Daniel B., Jr. *Spiritual Autobiography in Early America*. Princeton: Princeton University Press, 1968.

Shiels, Richard D. "The Feminization of American Congregationalism, 1730–1835." *American Quarterly* 33 (1981): 46–62.

Simpson, Matthew, ed. *Cyclopaedia of Methodism*. 5th ed. 2 vols. Philadelphia: Louis H. Everts, 1882.

Sklar, Kathryn Kish. *Catharine Beecher: A Study in American Domesticity*. New Haven: Yale University Press, 1973.

Smith-Rosenberg, Carroll. *Disorderly Conduct: Visions of Gender in Victorian America*. New York: Oxford University Press, 1985.

Sparks, Randy J. *On Jordan's Stormy Banks: Evangelicalism in Mississippi, 1773–1876*. Athens: University of Georgia Press, 1994.

Stein, Stephen J. *The Shaker Experience in America: A History of the United Society of Believers*. New Haven: Yale University Press, 1992.

Sterling, Dorothy. *Ahead of Her Time: Abby Kelley and the Politics of Antislavery*. New York: Norton, 1991.

Stewart, I. D. *The History of the Freewill Baptists*. Vol. 1. Dover, N.H.: William Burr, 1862.

Stout, Harry S. *The Divine Dramatist: George Whitefield and the Rise of Modern Evangelicalism*. Grand Rapids, Mich.: Eerdmans, 1991.

——. *The New England Soul: Preaching and Religious Culture in Early New England*. New York: Oxford University Press, 1986.

——. "Religion, Communications, and the Ideological Origins of the American Revolution." *William and Mary Quarterly* 34 (1977): 519–41.

Sutton, William Robert. " 'To Grind the Faces of the Poor': Journeyman for Jesus in Jacksonian Baltimore." Ph.D. diss., University of Illinois at Urbana-Champaign, 1993.

Sweet, Leonard I. *The Evangelical Tradition in America*. Macon, Ga.: Mercer University Press, 1984.

——. *The Minister's Wife: Her Role in Nineteenth-Century American Evangelicalism*. Philadelphia: Temple University Press, 1983.

——, ed. *Communciation and Change in American Religious History*. Grand Rapids, Mich.: Eerdmans, 1993.

Sweet, William Warren. *Religion in the Development of American Culture, 1765–1840*. New York: Charles Scribner's Sons, 1953.

——, ed. *Circuit-Rider Days along the Ohio, Being the Journals of the Ohio Conference from Its Organization in 1812 to 1826*. New York: Methodist Book Concern, 1923.

——, ed. *The Rise of Methodism in the West, Being a Journal of the Western Conference, 1800–1811*. New York: Methodist Book Concern, 1920.

Taylor, Alan. *Liberty Men and Great Proprietors: The Revolutionary Settlement on the Maine Frontier, 1760–1820*. Chapel Hill: University of North Carolina Press, 1990.

Taylor, James B. *Virginia Baptist Ministers*. 2 vols. New York: Sheldon and Company, 1860.

Thomas, George M. *Revivalism and Cultural Change: Christianity, Nation-Building, and the Market in the Nineteenth-Century United States*. Chicago: University of Chicago Press, 1989.

Thomas, Hilah F., Rosemary Skinner Keller, and Louise L. Queen, eds. *Women in New Worlds: Historical Perspectives on the Wesleyan Tradition.* 2 vols. Nashville: Abingdon Press, 1982.

Tolles, Frederick B. *Meeting House and Counting House: The Quaker Merchants of Colonial Philadelphia, 1692–1763.* New York: Norton, 1948.

Townsend, Leah. *South Carolina Baptists, 1670–1805.* Florence, S.C.: Florence Printing Company, 1935.

Tracy, Joseph. *The Great Awakening.* Boston: Tappan and Dennet, 1842.

Troeltsch, Ernst. *The Social Teaching of the Christian Churches.* Translated by Olive Wyon. 2 vols. London: Allen and Unwin, 1931. Reprint, Chicago: University of Chicago Press, 1976.

Tucker, Cynthia Grant. *Prophetic Sisterhood: Liberal Women Ministers of the Frontier, 1880–1930.* Boston: Beacon Press, 1990.

Ulrich, Laurel Thacher. *Good Wives: Image and Reality in the Lives of Women in Northern New England, 1650–1750.* Oxford: Oxford University Press, 1980.

Valenze, Deborah M. *Prophetic Sons and Daughters: Female Preaching and Popular Religion in Industrial England.* Princeton: Princeton University Press, 1985.

Walett, Francis G., ed. *The Diary of Ebenezer Parkman, 1703–1782.* Worcester, Mass.: American Antiquarian Society, 1974.

———. "The Diary of Ebenezer Parkman, 1739–1744." *Proceedings of the American Antiquarian Society* 72 (1962): 31–233.

Wallace, Anthony F. C. *Rockdale: The Growth of an American Village in the Early Industrial Revolution.* New York: Knopf, 1978.

Ward, W. Reginald. *The Protestant Evangelical Awakening.* Cambridge: Cambridge University Press, 1992.

Wayman, Alexander W. *Cyclopaedia of African Methodism.* Baltimore: Carroll, 1882.

Weber, Max. *From Max Weber: Essays in Sociology.* Translated and edited by Hans Gerth and C. Wright Mills. New York: Oxford University Press, 1946.

———. *The Protestant Ethic and the Spirit of Capitalism.* Translated by Talcott Parsons. London: George Allen and Unwin, 1930.

Wellcome, Isaac C. *The History of the Second Advent Message and Mission, Doctrine and People.* Boston: Advent Christian Publication Society, 1874.

Welter, Barbara. "The Cult of True Womanhood, 1820–1860." *American Quarterly* 18 (1966): 151–74.

———. *Dimity Convictions: The American Woman in the Nineteenth Century.* Athens: Ohio University Press, 1976.

———. "She Hath Done What She Could: Protestant Women's Missionary Careers in Nineteenth-Century America." *American Quarterly* 30 (Winter 1978): 625–38.

Wessinger, Catherine, ed. *Religious Institutions and Women's Leadership: New Roles Inside the Mainstream.* Columbia: University of South Carolina Press, 1996.

———. *Women's Leadership in Marginal Religions: Explorations Outside the Mainstream.* Chicago: University of Illinois Press, 1993.

Westerkamp, Marilyn J. *Triumph of the Laity: Scots-Irish Piety and the Great Awakening, 1625–1760.* New York: Oxford University Press, 1988.

Williams, William H. *The Garden of American Methodism: The Delmarva Peninsula, 1769–1820.* Wilmington, Del.: Scholarly Resources, 1984.

Wills, David W., and Richard Newman, eds. *Black Apostles at Home and Abroad.* Boston: G. K. Hall, 1982.

Wilson, H. Fisher. *The Hill Country of Northern New England*. New York: Columbia University Press, 1936.

Wisbey, Herbert A., Jr. *Pioneer Prophetess: Jemima Wilkinson, the Publick Universal Friend*. Ithaca: Cornell University Press, 1964.

Wright, Richardson. *Hawkers and Walkers in Early America*. Philadelphia: J. B. Lippincott Company, 1927.

Yoakam, Doris G. "Women's Introduction to the American Platform." In *A History and Criticism of American Public Address*, edited by William Norwood Brigance, 1:153–92. New York: McGraw-Hill, 1943.

Zuckerman, Michael. "Holy Wars, Civil Wars: Religion and Economics in Nineteenth-Century America." In *Prospects: An Annual of American Cultural Studies*, edited by Jack Salzman, 16:205–40. Cambridge: Cambridge University Press, 1991.

 # Acknowledgments

Many friends and colleagues have helped me along the pilgrimage that became this book. As a graduate student at Yale University, I had the good fortune to work with a superb group of scholars who guided me through the difficulties of dissertation research. My first thanks must go to Jon Butler, who introduced me to Nancy Towle and encouraged me to write about her. Without exaggeration, I can say that this book never would have been written without him. I am also grateful to Nancy Cott, who generously shared her encyclopedic knowledge of women's history with me, and John Demos, who nurtured my fledgling interest in colonial America. To Harry Stout, my advisor, I owe nothing less than my calling as an American religious historian. Before taking my first course with Skip, I had never imagined that I would someday write a book about religion. Ever since that course, however, I haven't been able to imagine writing about anything else. Over the years I have deeply appreciated his criticism, his advice, and his friendship.

While turning my dissertation into a book, I learned a lesson that nineteenth-century female preachers knew by heart. Although individual hard work is important, nothing is possible without the support of a larger community. I am grateful to several scholars, including Sylvia Frey, Richard T. Hughes, Edwin Gaustad, Vern Carter, Carol Sheriff, Christopher Grasso, Stephen Bullock, Stephen Nissenbaum, Liam Riordan, Kenneth Minkema, Jane Kamensky, Blair Pogue, David Wills, and Jill Mulvey Derr, for sharing citations or helping me track down elusive books, photographs, and manuscripts. Virginia Taylor very kindly sent me a photograph of Nancy Towle, one of the more colorful members of her family tree. I will never forget my excitement when I finally saw the face of the woman whose memoir originally inspired this book.

I delivered many conference papers as I worked on this book, and several scholars—Randall Balmer, Ann Braude, Nathan Hatch, Rosemary Skinner Keller, Gregory Schneider, and Leslie Tentler—offered incisive criticisms of my ideas. I owe a special thanks to Stephen Marini, whose energy and enthusiasm managed to make even a sweltering session at a meeting of the Society for Historians of the Early American Republic seem like fun. His perceptive comments made me rethink my chapter on Millerite women.

Several colleagues read chapters of the manuscript either in dissertation or book form. I am grateful to Elizabeth Abrams, Daniel Buchanan, Kathleen Cannon, Scott Caspar, Monica Cawvey, Ellen Curtis Boiselle, Christina Devlin, Kathleen Flake, David Hackett, Benjamin Leff, Sarah Sadowski, the History of Christianity Working Group at the University of Chicago, and the members of the American Religious History Seminar at Notre Dame. On the kind invitation of Edith Blumhofer, the former head of the Institute for the Study of American Evangelicals, I spent several summer days in 1994 discussing my work with a marvelous group of scholars. Their enthusiasm for this project greatly encouraged me at a time when I needed encouragement. George Rawlyk, who was unfailingly generous with his time and ideas, helped me to clarify my thoughts about eighteenth-century conversion narratives. One of my great regrets is that he did not live to see this book completed.

I am very grateful to the friends and scholars who read and critiqued the whole manuscript. Thanks to Margaret Lamberts Bendroth, Jerald Brauer, Virginia Lieson Brereton, Karin Gedge, W. Clark Gilpin, R. Marie Griffith, Martin Marty, Mark Noll, Leigh Eric Schmidt, Alan Taylor, Thomas Tweed, and John Wigger for their suggestions. As one of my readers for the University of North Carolina Press, Jean Humez offered such lengthy, helpful comments on my first draft that I kept them within reach during years of revision. I could not have asked for a more insightful reader. I also owe a great debt to Nell Painter, who took the time to read the book *twice*, and Kate Douglas Torrey, who has been an exceptionally patient and reassuring editor. In the final stages of copyediting, when I thought I couldn't bear to read my prose one more time, Ron Maner and Mary Reid saved me from many embarrassing mistakes.

For financial assistance, I gratefully acknowledge the support of a Charlotte W. Newcombe Doctoral Dissertation Fellowship from the Woodrow Wilson National Fellowship Foundation and a John F. Enders Research Grant from Yale University. As a Frances Hiatt Fellow at the American Antiquarian Society, I was privileged to use a truly outstanding collection of books, manuscripts, and newspapers. I will always remember the staff there with fondness, particularly Joanne Chaison and Dennis Laurie. I finished this book with the help of a grant from the Pew Program in Religion and American History.

A portion of the Introduction originally appeared as "Harriet Livermore, the 'Pilgrim Stranger': Female Preaching and Biblical Feminism in Early-Nineteenth-Century America" in *Church History* 65 (September 1996): 389–404. I acknowledge the American Society of Church History for giving me permission to reprint it.

I am thankful to all of my colleagues at the University of Chicago Divinity School, especially W. Clark Gilpin, Martin E. Marty, Jerald Brauer, Susan Schreiner, Stephanie Paulsell, and Elena Vassallo, for making it such a wonderful intellectual home for me. They, like many of my students, will hear echoes of our conversations in the pages of this book. I owe a special debt to my research assistants—Sarah Sadowski, Monica Cawvey, and Paula Gallito—for tracking down elusive sources, making stylistic suggestions on the manuscript, and sharing their love of American religious history with me.

I owe a different kind of debt to Anna Zampona, Shari Auerbach, and Stacey Landsly, who have helped care for my daughter during my hours in the library and the classroom. They have been good friends.

My deepest thanks go to the people who have never let me forget that life is about more than writing books. Richard Rosengarten, the Dean of Students at the University of Chicago Divinity School, has been an exceptionally kind and generous friend. Tom Tweed has been my favorite e-mail correspondent, encouraging me (and making me laugh) across the distance. Three friends from graduate school, Karin Gedge, Elizabeth Abrams, and Ellen Curtis Boiselle, have been to me what "Sister Mack" was to Ellen Stewart.

My family, both the Brekus and Sontheimer clans, have never let me lose faith that someday this book *would* be finished. My godmother, Liliana Lawrynowicz, has always supported me in whatever I have done. Through her courage under suffering, she has taught me many lessons about the power of faith and the importance of historical memory. Without intending it, my mother, Trudy Brennan Brekus, raised me to be a historian by filling my childhood with stories about my family's past. No matter how many times she told me the story of my Irish great-grandmother, Catherine, I never tired of hearing it. Thanks to my mother, I understood the importance of women's history long before I ever began writing it. My father, Gordon Brekus, has embraced my career with his characteristic energy and drive, searching catalogues and bookstores for rare history books. One of his best finds, a nineteenth-century exposé of Jemima Wilkinson, sits on my bookshelf as a reminder of his thoughtfulness.

The two most important people in my life are the two who are the most difficult to thank. Approaching the end of a long book, I find that words are simply not enough. My daughter, Claire Brennan Sontheimer, who was born in the middle of this project, has brought inexpressible joy to my life. So has my husband, Erik Sontheimer. With love, I dedicate this book to him.

Index